Family Law

'That something named as "family law" is a veritable minefield. Here remains in constant collision the endless desire for domination of women confronted by the aspirations for accelerated social change for securing equality and justice for all women as human beings and as citizens. With a characteristically lucid combination of scholarly analysis and activist insight, Flavia Agnes brings to us a fuller understanding of these contending politics of desire juxtaposing coequally the diverse elements in religious traditions and customary social/cultural practices with some progressive accidents of legislative and judicial decisions. But 'more' is also needed in the hyperglobalizing Indian conjuncture. Agnes suggests the imperatives of retooling and recrafting activist critique in the service of a better future of women's rights as human rights.'

Upendra Baxi
Emeritus Professor, Universities of Warwick and Delhi

'This book is an outstanding contribution to the understanding of the jurisprudential foundations and constitutional underpinnings of family law. This work fulfills an important gap in the existing literature by providing an interdisciplinary and critical analysis of family law relating to a number of religions in contemporary India.'

C. Raj Kumar
Vice Chancellor, O.P. Jindal Global University and
Dean, Jindal Global Law School

'Flavia's book is a very timely one and one that will be welcomed by law schools and more importantly law students. This work is an invaluable resource to law students, legal researchers and those engaged in feminist legal advocacy.'

Ratna Kapur
Director, Centre for Feminist Legal Research, New Delhi

'This work is thorough and exhaustive and has the potential of becoming a source book on women's rights and law for jurists, teachers, students and activists.'

Kalpana Kannabiran
Senior Fellow and Director, Chityala Ailamma Centre for Interdisciplinary Research,
Secunderabad

'The much needed analysis of family law in India based on the practical experience of lawyers and women litigants is finally here. The two volumes instead of focussing on what the law is or even what it ought to be have rather focussed on "the impact of varied legal processes upon the lives of women". Flavia Agnes has not shied away from using the tools of feminist legal theory to examine the law and the legal system and challenge its basic concepts and theoretical footing. The volumes thus fill the huge gap in the research and writing on family law, and will be a much valued possession for students and teachers of family law and provide a useful perspective for practitioners as well.'

Elizabeth V.S.
Additional Professor, NLSUI Bangalore

Family Law

Volume 2
Marriage, Divorce, and Matrimonial Litigation

Flavia Agnes

OXFORD
UNIVERSITY PRESS

OXFORD
UNIVERSITY PRESS

Oxford University Press is a department of the University of Oxford.
It furthers the University's objective of excellence in research, scholarship,
and education by publishing worldwide. Oxford is a registered trademark of
Oxford University Press in the UK and in certain other countries

Published in India by
Oxford University Press
22 Workspace, 2nd Floor, 1/22 Asaf Ali Road, New Delhi 110002, India

© Oxford University Press 2011

The moral rights of the authors have been asserted

First published 2011
Second impression 2011
Digitally Printed in 2024

ISBN-13 (print edition): 978-0-19-807220-1
ISBN-10 (print edition): 0-19-807220-1

ISBN-13 (eBook): 978-0-19-908848-5
ISBN-10 (eBook): 0-19-908848-9

Typeset in Arno Pro 11/13
by BeSpoke Integrated Solutions, Puducherry, India 605 008
Printed at Manipal Technologies Limited, Manipal

To the women from whom I learnt the interface between life and law

Contents

Section B

Tables and Boxes

Tables

Boxes

Abbreviations

AC	Appeal Cases	Crl	Criminal
AIMPLB	All India Muslim Personal Law Board	CSI	Church of South India
		DA	Divorce Act
AIR	All India Reporter	Decd.	Deceased
ALD	Andhra Legal Decisions	Del	Delhi High Court
All	Allahabad High Court	DLT	Delhi Law Times
All.ER	All England Reporter	DMC	Divorce and Matrimonial Cases
AP	Andhra Pradesh High Court	DNA	Deoxy Ribonucleic Acid
Art.	Article	FB	Full Bench
BHCR	Bombay High Court Reporter	FLR	Family Law Reporter
BLR	Bombay Law Reporter	Gau	Gauhati High Court
Bom	Bombay High Court	Guj	Gujarat High Court
Bom.CR	Bombay Case Reporter	HAMA	Hindu Adoption and Maintenance Act of 1956
Bom.LR	Bombay Law Reporter		
Cal	Calcutta High Court	HIV	Human Immuno Deficiency Virus
Cal.LT	Calcutta Law Times	HMA	Hindu Marriage Act
CPC	Civil Procedure Code	HP	Himachal Pradesh
CEDAW	Convention on the Elimination of All Forms of Discrimination against Women	HSA	Hindu Succession Act, 1956
		HUF	Hindu Undivided family
		IA	Indian Appeals
		IA	Interim Application
CMRA	Child Marriage Restraint Act	ICMA	Indian Christian marriage Act
CNI	Church of North India	ICR	Indian Case Reporter
Cr.PC	Criminal Procedure Code	IDA	Indian Divorce Act
CRA	Criminal Appeal	IEA	Indian Evidence Act
Cri.LJ	Criminal Law Journal		

ILR	Indian Law Reporter		P&H	Punjab and Haryana High Court
IPC	Indian Penal Code		Pat	Patna High Court
J&K	Jammu and Kashmir High Court		PC	Privy Council
Jha	Jharkand High Court		PMDA	Parsi Marriage and Divorce Act
Kar	Karnataka High Court		POC	Perry's Oriental Cases
Ker	Kerala High Court		Punj	Punjab High Court
L.R.	Legal Representatives		PWDVA	The Protection of Women from
Lah	Lahore High Court		(DVA)	Domestic Violence Act
LSD	Lok Sabha Debates		Raj	Rajastan High Court
Lt.Col	Lieutenant Colonel		RCR	Restitution of Conjugal Rights
Mad	Madras High Court		Rep.	Represented
Mad.LJ	Madras Law Journal		RNA	Ribonucleic Acid
Mat.LR	Matrimonial Law Reporter		SB	Special Bench
MBBS	Bachelor of Medicine and Bachelor		SC	Supreme Court
	of Surgery		SCC	Supreme Court Cases
MIA	Moore's Indian Appeals		SCW	Supreme Court Weekly
MLJ	Madras Law Journal		SDA	Sadar Diwani Adalat
MLJ	Maharashtra Law Journal		SLR	Singapore Law Reporter
MLJ	Malayan Law Journal		SMA	Special Marriage Act
MLR	Matrimonial Law Reporter		UCC	Union Civil Code
MP	Matrimonial Petition		UP	Uttar Pradesh High Court
MP	Madhya Pradesh High Court		Utt	Uttaranchal High Court
MWPA	Married Women's Property Act		WP	Writ Petition
Nag	Nagpur High Court		WR	Weekly Reporter
NCT	National Capital Territory		WRAG	Women's Research and Action
Ori	Orissa High Court			Group

Foreword

It is indeed a matter of great privilege for me to have been entrusted with the task of writing the Foreword to the two volumes of *Family Law*. Despite the size of the volumes, when taken together, there is an unwavering clarity of thought in both the volumes. The author stays true to her image of a person whose primary aim behind writing the present book (as also the ones previously written by her) is to bring a number of problems in the society to the fore, and not merely to enter into an academic exercise of compilation of information.

There is no gainsaying that India has undergone an unprecedented transformation in last few decades. However, other than the changes in the economic and political spheres, the Indian society has also changed exponentially, leading to an upheaval in human relations. Since India is being observed and scrutinized at the world stage more than ever before, there is an impending duty upon the legislature to do away with some of the draconian and exceedingly conservative personal laws that are considered to be unequal and biased against women and, thereby, present a more liberal face before the world. In the march towards becoming an economic superpower, an equally important need to create a balanced society can certainly not be underplayed.

Personal laws have witnessed rapid advances due to the constantly changing nature of human relations. Therefore, to keep pace with such changes is a great challenge for both, the legislature and the judiciary. However, the courts have shown a positive and a fair amount of proactiveness, combined with judicial creativity in meeting with the demands of a dynamic society. At the same time, in keeping pace with the changing trends in the society, the courts have taken utmost care to preserve the social fabric.

These volumes greatly emphasize the idea that 'justice' in its true sense, can never be achieved without bringing about a sense of fairness and parity in the society. It is in this light that the author delves into the real idea of a truly participative democracy and the need to accord an equal place to women in the society. The uniqueness of these books lies in the fact that they have tried to view the idea of fairness and justice from the point of view of women, particularly those who have hitherto been marginalized as to what is their idea of a fair social order. The books cover vast contours of the society, thereby making it a multi-dimensional work.

In volume 1, chapter 1 elaborately examines the various personal laws of the Hindus, Muslims, Christians, Parsis, and Jews and states that the personal laws of each religious community is a cumulative result of the social, economic, and political factors prevalent in the society. Therefore, the concept of justice differs in each religion depending upon such factors. However, the common thread running through all these religions is the underlying and impending need for a change in the personal laws and to increasingly bring it in conformity with the modern advances in the society.

Chapter 2 of the same volume studies the constitutional provisions which have a bearing on the field of personal laws and the role of the judiciary in reconciling the personal laws of each community with the supreme constitutional provisions. The author also intellectually enters into areas which are currently mired in political debates, such as the comparison of personal laws of the minority communities with that of the majority, Uniform Civil Code and so on.

In volume 2, chapter 1 scrutinizes the institution of marriage and its evolution from olden times to its swiftly changing nature in today's society owing to various social, moral, and economic factors. The author further examines the legislative changes brought about to maintain harmony and preservation of this institution, such as the Protection of Women from Domestic Violence Act. This chapter also highlights several problems that have perennially plagued the society, such as child marriage, registration of marriages, and traditional notions of heterosexual marriages.

In volume 2, chapter 2 provides a broad perspective on the rights and duties of spouses, not only towards each other, but also in relation to other family members, especially children. In addition, the author has also discussed the various legal mechanisms in place for enforcement of these rights and duties.

Chapter 3 in volume 2 is a detailed study of the procedural aspects of matrimonial laws and whether such procedural mechanisms are in consonance with the idea of justice. However, inspite of the present legal mechanisms, the author has also given due importance to conciliatory measures as an alternative means to avoid litigation.

Personal laws occupy a unique position in today's age and play a pivotal role in keeping the society within the moral and civil bounds. It is trite to say that every person is covered under the ambit of such personal laws, and is greatly affected by changes that are brought about in this field. Therefore, there is an indispensable need to educate, not only the lawyers, but also the citizenry about the importance and impact of personal laws. It is informative books such as these that help in positively shaping the public opinion.

The legislative and judicial decisions mentioned on every subject are a result of extensive collection from a number of sources and have been carefully edited to cover each realm of the subject. Legal principles have been succinctly extracted from these decisions and lucidly interpreted. The books are, therefore, an exhaustive amalgamation of legal principles, decisions, and opinions. However, apart from reliance on legal texts and case laws, the author has not lost sight of the ground realities and the practicalities that exist in the society as well as the operation of law. Further, an extensive subject index has been provided for an uncomplicated search of the point under reference, keeping in mind the wide nature of the laws that these books cover.

It would not be incorrect to say that going through the entire two volumes has been a highly enriching experience for me. I am of the sincere belief that this educative work is highly useful and will be well received by the members of the Bench, Bar, students of law, and academics.

NEW DELHI   Justice Ajit Prakash Shah
10 November 2010   (Former Chief Justice of
                                 the High Court of Delhi)

Acknowledgements

Two volumes of Family Law that have spanned over five years gather a lot of debt. They have evolved through innumerable contributions from friends and colleagues involved with the women's movement and from the legal fraternity to whom I remain indebted. My ideology of legal feminism and feminist lawyering is grounded within two seemingly diverse disciplines—the domain of formal law and litigation with its own grammar and set of rules, and a counter perspective of women's rights which challenges the notions of 'neutrality' and 'formal equality' within law, while bringing isolated experiences of individual women who venture out to claim their rights, into the precincts of formal courts. These volumes are an attempt to bridge the gap between the two.

There are many, who have constructively contributed to these works. At the top of this list are students, too numerous to list, from various law universities and colleges, who have interned with *Majlis* in Mumbai over the past few years. Their enthusiasm and reassurance that both the books would be extremely useful to students of family law helped boost my confidence and sustain my interest in this project. Thanks are also due to Prof. Vijay Ghormade, Principal, G.J. Advani Law College, Mumbai, who urged me to embark on this journey. Without his assurance, I could not have ventured into the project.

I deeply appreciate the invaluable contribution of Aparna Ray who assisted me during the initial phase of this project and scanned through reams of unruly material that I sent her and reworked it into a comprehensive framework of a textbook. I am grateful to my colleague Nausheen Yousuf for pointing out the gaps in the sections on Muslim law and for her assistance in filling these gaps. I am also grateful to Persis Sidhva, a fifth year student of Government Law College, Mumbai, for her unstinting support and help in sourcing material and checking references.

The entire team of lawyers and researchers at *Majlis* has patiently stood by me through these years and shared my concerns. My special thanks to Pooja Kute, Audrey D'Mello, Dolly Mendonca, and Anisha Gopi as well as my ex-colleagues, Veena Gowda, Sumangala Biradar, and Apurva Parsekar. The insights gained while strategizing for women's rights and litigating on their behalf have helped me grasp the complex interface between life, law, and litigation and have enriched these works.

My friends, Vasudha Nagaraj, Monica Sakhrani, Mitra Sharafi, Chaitanya Lakkimsetti, and Shoba Ghosh read some of the chapters as they evolved and made valuable suggestions. Madhusree Dutta has been an integral part of this project and has shared my anxieties, frustrations, and fatigue. The books evolved while responding to her critical comments and to probing questions from someone who stands outside the realm of formal law and litigation but who has a great impulse for the culture of rights. I sincerely appreciate her valuable contribution to the books.

I thank Justice, A.P. Shah, former Chief Justice of the Delhi High Court for writing the Foreword which has added value to both the volumes. I would also like to mention the contributions of Prof. Upendra Baxi, whose legal engagements have been a constant source of inspiration.

I also owe a debt to Prof. Werner Mensky and Prof. Marc Galantar whose engagements with legal pluralism and people's law have influenced my own writings.

Special thanks are also due to Justice A.K. Ganguly of the Supreme Court with whom I have shared a platform on a number of occasions on issues of gender sensitization for the judiciary. I also thank Justice D. Y. Chandrachud of the Bombay High Court and Director, Maharashtra Judicial Academy, for providing me with an opportunity to interact with the lower judiciary in Maharashtra on concerns of women's rights. Special thanks are also due to Prof. Mohan Gopal, Director, National Judicial Academy, for involving me in various programmes of the Academy as a visiting faculty. These interactions have helped me frame women's rights within a formal legal discourse and to contribute, in a modest way, to the evolution of feminist jurisprudence in the Indian context.

I gratefully acknowledge the initial grant from Christian Aid which helped me take up this project.

I wish to extend my sincere appreciation to the editors at Oxford University Press for goading me on and for constantly setting new deadlines as I kept lapsing. The comments from the anonymous reviewer and the queries raised by editors at OUP have helped in sharpening some of the arguments and removing some of the inconsistencies and ambivalence.

My family, particularly my daughters, Audrey and Odile, has patiently awaited the completion of these books. However, they now share with me the joy of completion of both the works.

Flavia Agnes
November 2010

Law, Justice, and Gender

THE THEORY AND PRACTICE OF LAW

The primary concern while setting out to write this book (brought to you in two volumes), *Family Law*, has been to weave women's rights into legal theory. Law, justice, and gender have been its three major concerns. The book examines the interface between life and law, between meta-narratives of justice and the lived experiences of women, and provides in-depth exposé of the complex realm of family laws while exploring the overlaps and contradictions within them.

The vibrancy of law, as it evolves through litigation, is examined in this context. It is within this dynamic space that judges, lawyers, and litigants interact to challenge or validate the lived-in practices or people's law against the grain of formal law, which leads to multiple interpretations and varied negotiations. Hence the book does not confine itself to a discussion on formal law enshrined within statutes, codes, sections, and articles.

Writing this book has provided me with an opportunity to test legal premises and skills of litigation against the rigour of academic discourse. The thread that binds the five chapters in the two volumes is the concern about the impact of varied legal processes upon the lives of women. This is a question lawyers defending women's rights are constantly confronted with. The book reflects this concern and places these contestations beyond the immediacy of legal practice, in an attempt to translate them into legal academics and legal pedagogy. While negotiating the boundaries of formal law, the book contextualizes social realities, legal campaigns, and judicial discretions. Hence, from the formal terrain of law, the discussion often spills on to historical and sociological processes as well contemporary concerns. The title, *Family Law* is located within this wider framework.

The term '*Law*' is not reflective of legal positivism[1] but conceptualizes law as a social mediator of relationships between people within the broader spectrum of legal realism. The theory of legal realism asserts that law should

---

[1] Legal theorists Jeremy Bentham, John Austin and later Hans Kelsen and H.L.A. Hart, among others, subscribed to the philosophy of legal positivism or 'law's autonomy' and viewed law as 'natural law and natural rights', a sovereign command or a 'set of rules usually enforced by a set of institutions'.

be understood and determined by the actual practices of courts, law offices, and police stations, rather than as rules and doctrines set forth in statutes or learned treatises.[2] This premise contested the autonomy of law by affirming that judges made law through discretionary acts of interpretation. It served to usher in a series of 'critical movements' in law, such as law and society, the critical legal studies, legal anthropology, legal pluralism, and feminist legal theory, to name a few. However despite these multiple and innovative interventions, it is widely accepted that inter-disciplinarity, as a pedagogic approach to law, continues to remain at the margins.

It is imperative that legal theory is embedded within sociological, historical, and economic contexts, in what Roger Cotterrell (1989) refers to as 'politics of jurisprudence'. Cotterrell argues that there is a need to study both the doctrine and the social, economic, and political contexts of the doctrine in order to be able to explain how legal change takes place. An understanding of social effects of laws and of the sociological factors that shape it, requires a theory which attempts to systematically explain the nature of law. Cotterrell argues that since all theories are partial and contextual, theories generated in the North American or European contexts may not achieve universality, despite their claims.

Reflecting similar concerns, this book is an attempt to fill the void within the rubric of a contemporary and evolving discipline, 'gender and law', which, by its very formulation, is inter-disciplinary in its approach. In this context, this book attempts to bridge the gap between the theory and practice of law, between the 'doctrinal' and 'non-doctrinal', between the 'ideal' and the 'technical' and hopes to blur these

binaries through a comprehensive and inclusive approach.

Within these trajectories in the realm of legal theory, the book explores a wide range of topics. The history and development of personal laws and their textual sources, the impact of statutory codes, evolution of the institution of marriage and its dissolution, rights and obligations which accrue through the contract of marriage, state recognition of informal sexual relationships and polygamous practices—these are some of the issues which are explored from the perspective of both legal theory and legal practice. Extraneous influences of other socio-political and historical developments, such as Anglo-Saxon legal traditions and their impact upon pre-colonial non-state adjudication, women's entry into the political domain and their role in framing the Indian Constitution, the manner in which assurances of equality and freedom allude women, the notion of honour in the context of citizenship, the determination of morality in the context of women's economic rights, tribunalization of formal court structures and its impact upon women—these diverse strands become important scripts in this exploration. Contestations, negotiations, and subversions by women with their families, communities and state structures through which a women oriented legal theory is evolved is the recurring theme of the book.

THE '*JUSTICE*' CLAIMS OF WOMEN

Moving away from grand theories and master narratives of law, the notion of '*justice*' is explored in the context of legal interpretations of women's claims. While tracking diverse strands, the challenge has been to examine what constitutes 'justice' for women within the normative patriarchal social structures of both formal and informal laws. Law is always presumed to 'do justice' and it is believed that if case law is unjust today, it can be reformed to do

---

[2]   The theory of legal realism had a great impact in the United States. Oliver Wendell Holmes, Jr. J., Roscoe Pound, Benjamin Cardozo J., and Karl Llewellyn were some of the renowned proponents of this theory.

justice. However, a consensus on what exactly 'justice' and 'equity' mean is hard to attain. As a consequence, it is always the notion of justice held by dominant groups that is reflected in the laws of the region, which invariably causes injustice to the weaker and marginalized sections of society.

'Justice' is the key concern of law or in other words, law is centrally implicated in the project of justice. Philosophers and social thinkers down the ages have called law to account in the name of justice and demanded that law provide a language for justice. But Sarat and Kearns (1998) argue that running through the history of jurisprudence and legal theory is a recurring concern about the ways in which law is implicated in injustice. Theories of law and theories of justice often work in tandem.

Interpreting justice as fairness and equality, John Rawls (1971) advanced a distributive model of justice which has been critiqued by several later theorists.[3] Iris Young (1990) argues that Rawls distributive model based on impartiality, formal equality and the unitary model of subjectivity, fails to consider institutional arrangements of exclusions of people of other cultural traditions such as non-western and non-white. She urges social theorists to define and assess the distributive paradigm and emphasizes the need for affirmation rather than suppression of social group differences, concluding that the concept of justice coincides with the concept of the political.

Several feminist theorists have argued that the instrumental characterization of law as a tool for the potential transformation of society is far too simplistic. They hold that law is a crude and limited device and is circumscribed by the dominant ideologies of the society in which it is produced. Existing beliefs and assumptions shape the context of a legal provision. Even when changes are successfully made on a doctrinal level, they can and will fail if judges or others charged with the application of new laws revert to interpretations that merely replicate old results. The impact of dominant ideologies on the shape and content of law and the legal process makes the idea of 'progress' through legal reforms problematic (MacKinnon 1989; Fineman 1995; Sunder Rajan 2003; Menon 2004). Since legal, moral, and social codes are determined by hegemonic claims of patriarchy, an exploration into the notion of justice and fairness to women can be embarked upon only after piercing the veil of 'neutrality', 'impartiality' and 'formal equality' within law.

The core which runs through this volume is women's rights, hence it becomes imperative for me to address the doctrinal concern—whether a woman-centric legal doctrine can be termed 'biased' and lacking a 'neutral' perspective?[4] Can the lens of feminism or concern for women's rights be labeled as 'biased'? Further, is there a framework of neutrality that prevails beyond it, which a legal scholar must adhere to? These questions have been addressed by several feminist legal scholars, too numerous to list here, both Western and non-Western. I have merely followed their footsteps and have contextualized this premise within the context of concerns raised in this book.

While challenging the premise of 'neutrality of law', I ground my arguments within feminist legal theory, posited as 'perspective scholarship',

---

[3]   See also Amartya Sen's critique of this theory in *The Idea of Justice* (2009), where he argues that justice as relational and a process of challenging injustice.

[4]   This is usually formulated as '*the woman question*' a phrase first used by Simone De Beauvoir, in her path breaking treatise, *The Second Sex* in 1949 (English translation Penguin: 1972). Since then, several feminists have explored this theme in various disciplines such as philosophy, political theory, literature, etc. See Bartlett 1990: 829–888.

which challenges the traditional notion that law is a neutral, objective, relational set of rules, unaffected in content and form by the passions and perspectives of those who possess and wield the power inherent in law and legal institutions. Perspective scholarship adds the explicit consideration of diverse perspectives to the realist, law-in-society tradition and is based on the premise that certain groups historically have been unrepresented (or under-represented) in law and that their exclusion has led to biases and an incompleteness or deficit in contemporary legal analysis and legal institutions. Perspective scholars argue the corresponding contention that historically excluded groups have different, perhaps unique, views and experiences that are relevant to the issues and circumstances regulated and controlled by law. This scholarship adds nuance to the traditional and rather monotone canvas of law. It makes more complete and more complex our consideration of the questions, 'what is law?' and 'what are the roles and function of law in our society?' (Fineman 1995: 24-25) Within the realm of perspective scholarship, feminist legal theory has helped to redefine the prevailing notions of justice within both the private domain of the family and the public domain of the civil society.

Within this perspective, the concern of this book is to assess how women perceive justice, how they pursue and access it, and what are the measures of determining the success of these pursuits. These complex questions need to be addressed in order to evolve a women-centric theory of justice, based on the experiences of women who seek it. The book attempts to capture these contests and provides new critical frames to engage with justice. It documents the narratives of women's successes and failures in challenging injustice in their lives, through an exploration of legal precedents, relying extensively on the 'case law' methodology.

While theorizing about women's rights, 'gender' becomes a useful term to signify a deeply entrenched institutionalization of sexual difference which permeates our society. It has now become evident that much of what has traditionally been thought of as inherent sexual differences are socially produced. Many injustices are experienced by women by virtue of the fact that they are women. This is primarily due to the gendered nature of the family and society, which adversely affects women. Susan Okin (1989) terms this as a major 'justice crisis' in contemporary Western societies arising from concerns of gender. The term 'gender' and 'justice' is used in a similar context, to examine the 'justice crisis' within family laws in India.

Substantive law is enmeshed within procedural technicalities and hinders the process of accessing justice. As Katharine Bartlett (1990: 829–88) has argued there has not been sufficient theorization about methodological aspects of what 'doing' of law should entail and what true status should be given to contesting legal claims. Procedures and methodological aspects are important because the claims of law's legitimacy are based on what constitutes 'truth' and mould our views about the possibilities of legal practice and reform. The process of determining 'truth' is critical while examining the procedures under criminal law, but it also has a bearing on civil law while examining issues such as validity of marriage, sexual conduct of women, determination of paternity, etc. These aspects which affect women's rights, depend on the legal appreciation of 'truth' (and credibility), legal 'presumptions' and popular notions of legality.

Within the rights discourse, the domain of the law is entwined within the domain of the courts. The space within which the rights claims are located become important symbols of 'justice' in popular perceptions. It is within this 'sacrosanct' space that the magisterial power of law is experienced, claims are secured and rights are protected. The family courts are the terrain where law, justice and gender interlock within a contested frame. The conceptual framework of these courts, their functioning, the sensitivity of the judges and court officials, and the infrastructure provided to women litigants from vulnerable and marginalized groups are important yardsticks for measuring the notions of procedural justice.

In the interface between life and law, the isolated experiences of individual women who venture out to claim their rights become central to the enquiry. In this interface, the mundane and the ordinariness of life gets intermingled with lofty jurisprudential concepts and gets transformed into a 'legal narrative'. The manner in which women negotiate their claims and entitlements within the realm of law is an important indicator for testing out our notions of 'law', 'justice' and 'legality'. Marc Galanter (1989) has pointed out, a case law centered methodology, though popular among legal scholars, is extremely constraining. To get a more rounded perspective, the exploration must extend beyond legal texts to the workings of the lawyers' chambers and proceedings in trial courts. Here the pre-litigation legal strategies, interim orders and timely negotiations play a more vital role in securing rights than alluring legal principles and theories of justice. In an attempt to bring these negotiations into the realm of formal legal pedagogy, the interface of life and law is examined through legal narratives from a lawyer's perspective.

EXAMINING THE CONTOURS OF FEMINIST LEGAL THEORY

Within the broad canvas of 'gender and law', the two volumes of this book on family law problematize three specific themes in contemporary feminist legal theory in India:

i. The notion of 'equality' or 'sameness' between men and women within marriage and

implications of using a gender neutral term 'spouse';

ii. The use of a generic term 'women', devoid of its specific socio-cultural context and location and its implications for women from minority communities, in the context of the demand for a uniform civil code; and

iii. The notion of 'universal' human rights values as evolved in the West and the desirability of applying them within specific local contexts of the non-West.

The following is a further elaboration of these three themes.

i. *The notion of 'equality' or 'sameness' between men and women within marriage and implications of using a gender neutral term 'spouse'.*

Principles of 'equality' and 'sameness' can be applied only to those situated equally. Applying the standard of equality to those who are situated unequally serves only to widen the gulf of inequality. Marriage and family are inherently gendered institutions with clearly defined gender roles. I argue that since women are judged as 'women' according to gendered expectations, gender-specific terms such as 'husband' and 'wife' help us to grasp the implications of these terms within matrimonial relationships. The gender neutral term 'spouse' tends to gloss over the inequality inherent within the institution of marriage where gender roles are clearly defined.

To elaborate further, though 'adultery' is a ground for divorce for both men and women, the social and legal implications for the husband and the wife differ widely. Historically, Hindu husbands had sanctions of polygamy and institutions such as concubinage and prostitution served to cater to men's polygamous and extramarital sexual desires. Hence as per popular perceptions of legality, adultery by men tends to be condoned, by community, law and even by wives themselves as their own social status and economic rights depend upon their marriage. But in the context of the high premium awarded to women's chastity, any lapse on the part of women seem to be viewed far more stringently, leading to denial of maintenance and may even hamper rights to custody of children.[5]

Even innocuous terms such as 'cruelty' or 'desertion' which may superficially appear to be devoid of a gendered context, when used as grounds for divorce acquire a specific gendered meaning. The problem gets exaggerated in proceedings for maintenance, where economic claims are pitted against women's sexual morality. Chapters 1 and 2 of this volume address this concern.

To draw out the way in which the meaning of 'men' and 'women' has served to structure major social institutions is not to fall back on purely 'natural' categories. Women are disadvantaged not only by the fact of gender differences but also by rules that ignore the difference.

While campaigning for rights in the public domain, such as the right to vote, the right to hold public office, and for the right to equal remuneration, liberal feminists in the West evolved the equality paradigm, emphasizing sameness of treatment. Hesitant to accommodate differences, they demanded that gender-neutral terms (e.g., person) should replace gender specific terms (e.g., men). There was a fear among some feminist scholars that a reference to 'men' and 'women' may reinforce the patriarchal claim that 'woman' is a natural and timeless category defined by certain innate, biological characteristics (Pateman 1988: 17).

The 'sameness' model feminists emphasize that the way for women to achieve legal recognition of their equal status to men is to deny the legal relevance of their differences and insist

that women should be recognized as gender-neutral legal persons. But Fineman (1991) counters this with the argument that while there are powerful symbolic reasons for applying the sameness model, symbolism cannot be a primary concern if application of formal equality (or rule equality) standards perpetuates status inequality. Feminist legal theory must take the unequal position of women as a present given and must incorporate gendered differences as an explicit part of its analysis of family law.

ii. *The use of a generic term 'women', devoid of its specific socio-cultural context and locations and its implications for women from minority communities, in the context of the demand for a uniform civil code (UCC).*

While examining the demand for a uniform set of family laws applicable to all communities, a question that needs to be interrogated is whether the term 'women' is a universal category, devoid of specific socio-cultural contexts and locations and whether personal laws can be examined *ahistorically*, stripped of their colonial and post-colonial groundings?

The demand for a UCC places gender as a neutral terrain, distanced from contemporary political processes. The demand projects minority women as lacking a voice and an agency either in their own communities or through the process of litigation, to claim their rights within existing structures. It projects legislative intervention in the form of an enactment of a uniform code as the only option to attain gender justice for minority women.

The claims of women from minority communities cannot be formulated merely within the narrow context of a progression from community control to state control and needs to be contextualized within the multiple hierarchies and complex negotiations between community, nation-state and the female subject, and the dynamics of contemporary majority-minority

[5]　*Dwarakabai v. Prof. Mainam Mathews*, AIR 1953 Mad 792

politics. In the wake of increasing hostilities to-wards minority communities, 'personal laws' have become important markers of community/religious identity for minority groups. Women are an integral part of this identity and get marked as prime targets during communal riots and are subjected to gruesome sexual violence, as was evident during the communal violence which took place in Gujarat in 2002 (Agnes forthcoming).

Faced with this painful reality, I have argued that a process of reform within personal laws is better suited to protect women from these communities against their own internal patriarchies, rather than endorsing a majoritarian Hindu agenda of enforcing a uniform civil code as a feminist project. Such a project, which would inadvertently situate minority women in an antagonist relationship against their own communities, and hence may not receive the support of women from these communities, who have been subjected to extreme violence and humiliation, as Muslims, during communal violence. The solution to the problem cannot lie within separate registers of 'gender' and 'minority identity' and feminism needs to develop an intersectional approach which would factor in the multiple layers of discriminations which Muslim women are subjected to. This issue is discussed in Chapter 2 of the previous volume.

While using the generic term 'women', it cannot be denied that there are many important differences amongst women. Since all women are not similarly situated, there is a need to contextualize the specificities of women belonging to marginalized communities. Since women's oppression is not homogenous in content and since it is not determined by one root, underlying cause, there cannot be one 'feminist method', or 'feminist epistemology' (Fraser and Nicholson 1988).

While examining the rights of minority women in the Indian context, the formulations of critical race theorists in the United States, specifically the term 'intersectionality of race and gender', coined by Kimberlé Crenshaw (1989: 139–67) to contextualize black women's situation, is an important analytical tool.[6] Crenshaw argues that the experiences of black women cannot be subsumed within the traditional boundaries of either race or gender discrimination and the intersection of racism and sexism factors into black women's lives in ways that cannot be captured wholly by looking at the race or gender dimensions of those experiences separately.

iii. *The notion of 'universal' human rights values as evolved in the West and the desirability of applying them within specific local contexts of the non-West.*

The legitimacy of pluralistic and non-state customary laws has been subjected to criticism within the international human rights discourse under the coinage, 'women's rights are human rights'. Issues such as violence against women and trafficking of women for sex work have also been prominent concerns in this discourse. But alongside, there have been other issues such as polygamous marriages, child marriages, etc. I argue against the demand for universal application of human rights as articulated by international women's groups from the West (and endorsed by some women's groups and feminist scholars in India) in favour of a more nuanced and culture specific theory of women's rights.

Here I find Chandra Mohanty's (2003) critique of euro-centrism within Western developmental discourses of modernity through the lens of racial, sexual, and class-based assumptions useful. Mohanty points out that gender essentialism, i.e., over generalized claims about

---

[6]   The term was first coined in the context of 'feminist thought and critical race theory' and refers to the manner in which various socially and culturally constructed categories of discrimination interact on multiple and often simultaneous levels, contributing to systematic social inequality. Also see Crenshaw (1991: 1241–1299).

women, assumes that women have a coherent group identity within different cultures prior to their entry into social relations. Such generalizations are hegemonic in that they represent the problems of privileged women who are often (though not exclusively) white, western, and middle class. These generalizations, based on some abstract notion of strategic sisterhood, efface the problems, perspective, and political concerns of women, marginalized because of class, race, religion, ethnicity, and/or sexual orientation.

The demand for compulsory registration of marriage and for declaring all unregistered marriages as well as all child marriages as void needs to be examined in the context of increasing state control and raises a concern whether such control will be beneficial to women or, on the contrary, serve to defeat their existing rights. Law-making cannot be a narrow and short-sighted venture at the instance of some pressure groups, acting upon certain international mandates of human rights. It carries very deep implications for a vast majority of people.

The question of Muslim polygamy also needs to be examined in the context of Hindu polygamy and the implications of imposing monogamy through the enactment of the Hindu Marriage Act, 1955. Women in culturally accepted polygamous or marriage-like relationships were denied their right to maintenance due to these hegemonic claims.

These concerns become critical while we examine the issues of child marriages and registration of marriages and maintenance to women in polygamous marriages which are discussed in Chapters 1 and 2 of this volume. I have argued that the contemporary feminist discourse needs to be far more nuanced while addressing these issues. Rather than blindly advocating a 'universally' accepted position framed by a First world feminist discourse, women's rights groups need to advance a position which is rooted within Third world realities. A feminist voice must lend credence to the claims of the weaker against the might of the *status quo*-ists institutional authorities.

Fine tuning this delicate balance is a challenging task, but this precisely has been the aspiration while setting out to write this book. Often, the positions taken here may seem contrary to the well-trodden feminist path or even ambiguous and contradictory to the positions advocated elsewhere within this book itself. I have tried to examine each issue within its own contours to provide the reader a diverse and complex view of the manner in which legal dictums unfold upon the lives of women. The overall attempt has been to address the debates within the contemporary women's movement in India and bring them within the domain of legal pedagogy.

OVERVIEW OF CHAPTERS

The first volume of this book traced the history of diverse personal laws in India and women's claims within them as well as women's rights located within the Constitution of India and gendered notions of citizenship claims.

This volume addresses three distinct concerns—women's rights within the law of marriage and divorce, matrimonial rights and obligations, and the procedural aspect of the functioning of family courts in India.

Chapter 1 addresses the contemporary concerns of family law and contains the 'lawyer's law'. In its introduction, the chapter examines the material and historical basis of 'marriage' as an indissoluble and sacrosanct unit and its gradual progression towards divorce—first on fault grounds, later to consent divorce, moving gradually towards 'no fault' divorce or the 'breakdown theory of divorce'. This chapter establishes the link between economic developments and the changing nature of marriage. The concern here is how 'gender' or 'women's rights' are contextualized within these developments.

The focus of this chapter is contemporary litigation around the validity of marriage and procedures of dissolving it. The extensive case law provides a glimpse of contemporary trends in matrimonial litigation and unfolds the manner in which fault grounds such as cruelty, desertion, and adultery assume a gendered interpretation in the context of women's subordinate role within marriage. The attempt at introducing gender neutral terms such as 'spouse' within the domain of matrimonial law and the impact such reforms have had upon women's rights in other countries have been examined. I have strongly urged that while introducing newer grounds into matrimonial statutes, such as the breakdown theory of marriage, a gendered analysis of its impact upon women is needed so that the historical mistakes made while enacting the Hindu Marriage Act are not repeated.

In addition to the core issues of marriage and divorce, the chapter also addresses other contemporary concerns around marriage, such as child marriage, marriages involving non-resident Indians (popularly referred to as NRI marriages), and registration of marriages. The section on child marriage revisits the nineteenth century debate and juxtaposes it with the contemporary. The patriarchal control exercised by parents and the manner in which seemingly pro-women statutory provisions become susceptible to manipulations to serve the interest of a dominant feudal, patriarchal order is foregrounded in this discourse. It makes an argument that feminist theorizing should examine an issue from the perspective of its impact upon vulnerable girls and not align with patriarchal collusions between parents and state authorities. The concern here is also about universal standards of human rights and their application to local situations, without contextualizing local realities and the problems it creates. The rights and values have to be internalized

by communities and cannot merely be enforced by an oppressive legal regime.

The section on registration of marriages also makes out a case for viewing the issue of marriages and sexual relationships from the perspective of women's rights rather than mere state control. The demand for increasing state control by way of compulsory registration is contradictory to the current trend of viewing sexual relationships as private partnerships with minimal state interference. At one level, the Protection of Women from Domestic Violence Act, 2005 (PWDVA) has awarded statutory recognition for informal relationships. The historical Delhi High Court judgment reading down section 377, IPC which criminalized adult, consensual homosexuality (*Naz Foundation* v. *Government of NCT*) and curtailed state intervention into the private lives of citizens is another important landmark. Both these have dealt a blow to traditional notions of monogamous and heterosexual marriages and have served to broaden the discourse on sexual morality and curtailed state control over sexual choices and sexual relationships. The glaring contradictions between these developments and the demand by some women's groups for compulsory registration of marriages and for declaring non-registered marriages as void need to be juxtaposed in order to be reconciled.

The section on NRI marriages explores the concerns of women who are trapped in violent marriages, where rights lie beyond national legal domains and flow into transnational realms of conflicting laws and rights. At times, these rights get entangled between issues of nationalities, domicile, and citizenship and women lose out. Judicial interventions in the realm of private international law which governs this sphere of law, provide a cultural context for determination of rights and protection of women.

Chapter 2 helps us gauge the movement within family laws from the sacramental premises of 'love and honour', 'obedience and subservience', and 'duties and obligations', to modern frames of 'rights and entitlements' and to examine gender concerns within unequal contractual partnerships. The primary focus is the financial obligation which accrues as an incident of marriage, which is termed as 'maintenance' and 'matrimonial residence'. The third concern here is women's right to custody and guardianship of their children.

Under the law of maintenance, the historical basis for the right of maintenance, the issues and processes involved in maintenance litigation, and the difficulties which women endure to enforce maintenance orders are discussed in detail. Since the issue of maintenance concerns a large number of women and is embedded in legal technicalities, this section also contains a discussion on procedural law. These technicalities often hinder the substantive rights of women and serve to delay the process of justice. Hence it was felt important to provide an overview of the procedural aspects of maintenance law. Going beyond the rights of women as wives, the chapter also examines the claims of other dependents, such as parents and children.

Within the gendered institutions of marriage and family, it is not surprising that financial claims of maintenance are judged against the code of sexual purity. Women's moral character gets foregrounded in legal arguments and issues such as dispute over legitimacy and paternity are invoked to deny maintenance to women. Of even greater concern is the manner in which men's sexual transgressions and violations of the norm of monogamy are invoked with ease to defeat women's claims. A concern of this section is the gap between the norm of monogamy introduced by the Hindu Marriage Act in 1955 and the ground reality where sexual relationships continue in informal and bigamous cohabitations. While people live in their cultures, they litigate in law. When there is a disjunct between accepted cultural practices and legal rules, women become the worst sufferers. But occasionally, an activist judiciary, in an attempt to 'do justice', has circumvented the problem while providing some solace to women trapped into these complex relationships.

Shelter is of grave concern to women in conflict marriages. Since divorce deprives women of this crucial right, many women continue in violent marriages to avail of this right. Marriage laws do not specifically spell out this right though there is an implicit acknowledgement of it. Here the judiciary stepped in and affirmed the claims of women and secured their rights. The provisions of the PWDVA which provide a statutory right of matrimonial residence and the manner in which these have been interpreted by the judiciary have also been dealt with. Of special concern here is the norm of joint family residence, where the ownership of the matrimonial residence does not lie with the husband, but usually with his parents.

While acknowledging that marriage is an economic partnership, our matrimonial laws do not provide for division of assets at the time of divorce. This is a growing concern, since women who are not entitled to maintenance are deprived of their contribution to the domestic partnership. To provide an overview and to chart out a course for legal reform in this realm, development of this law in other countries is traced. But admittedly, they would have to be fine-tuned to deal with Indian realities such as the joint family households.

In the context of custody and guardianship of children, the last section of this chapter traces its historical basis and subsequent developments from a highly patriarchal premise of prescribing the father as the natural guardian to women as 'natural' care takers of children of 'tender age'. The notion of a sexually pure and 'good' woman has been invoked often to deny women the right of custody. In contemporary times, the legal maxim has moved away from parental 'rights' to parental 'obligations' and the principle 'welfare of the minor is paramount' has been introduced while determining parental claims of custody. The manner in which women are implicated within this new legal doctrine is a concern that needs to be addressed. Conflicting court orders beyond national boundaries in cases concerning NRI marriages, is an emerging concern for both women's rights and children's rights.

Chapter 3 addresses the procedural aspects of matrimonial law. Since most matrimonial litigation in metropolitan cities originates within family courts, this subject has gained relevance in academic discourse on family laws. The chapter focuses on the various aspects of the norm of informality which was introduced into matrimonial litigation through the enactment of the Family Courts Act and the implications of the mandate of 'reconciliation and speedy settlements' mandated by the Act. With this in view the powers of a judge were enhanced and judges were not bound by strict procedural and evidentiary rules in order to provide justice to women litigants. The Act envisaged a diminished role of lawyers and it introduced the institution of marriage counseling to aid the process of reconciliation and settlements.

The concern of the chapter is to examine whether these procedural changes are being used within the framework of gender justice and the extent to which family courts have brought in changes within the established norm of adversarial litigation in family laws. Since there is very little material available on this subject, as a methodological device, I have relied upon a study of family courts conducted by me in four states, Maharashtra, Karnataka, Andhra Pradesh, and West Bengal, and my own experience of legal practice in the family court at Mumbai, in addition to judicial interpretations.

In the concluding chapter, I have attempted to explore the interface between life and law. The life experiences do not neatly correspond to formal institutional locations. There is a constant shift from the formal to the informal, from the civil to the criminal, from contests to negotiations, from the legal to the extra legal. The chapter attemps to trace these journeys and probes into the transitions when mundane and ordinary lives are transposed into the legal domain. I argue that it is through these lived in experiences that the law gets constituted in a 'bottom up' manner as opposed to the top down process of law making by legislators and judges.

Law is a dynamic and evolving process and one is inundated with material generated through reported cases. The book contains only a glimpse of legal trends and selective leading cases. But hopefully, it will prove to be a comprehensive resource for teaching family law in India.

A word of caution: There is no certainty in judicial verdicts and through a stroke of pen a judgment can undo several earlier rulings which had laboriously carved out a space for women's rights. The recent ruling of Markandey Katju and T.S. Thakur JJ in *D. Velusamy* v. *D. Patchaiammal* is a case in point. This judgment has constrained the scope of the Domestic Violence Act, which had provided a safety net for women trapped in informal and bigamous marriages. Several rulings of various high courts and the Supreme Court had also attempted to expand the scope of maintenance under Section 125 of Cr.PC to secure the rights of women in this category. A reference made in *Chanmuniya* v. *Virendra Kumar Sing Kushwaha* by G.S. Singhvi and A.K. Ganguly JJ (also of the Supreme Court), on 7 October 2010 to a larger bench, which is pending, will hopefully undo the harm caused by this ruling and place the rights of women in informal relationships on a firmer footing.

1

Marriage and its Dissolution

Section A

MARRIAGE AND MATRIMONIAL RELIEFS

This chapter deals with the institution of marriage, as defined by legal codes and statutes and as determined within formal court structures through contentious litigation. It traces the transition of marriage from a sacrament to a contract and, within this framework of a contractual union, the ingredients of a valid marriage and various matrimonial relief such as annulment, judicial separation, restitution of conjugal rights, and dissolution of marriage are examined. Further, the progression from 'contest' to 'consent', and 'fault' to 'no fault' are also discussed. The chapter provides insight into the contemporary trends in family law. Structured around reported cases, the chapter examines the theories of (doctrinal) law in the context of their impact in practical situations wherein individual women stake their claims for justice. The legal provisions are assessed through the prism of women's rights. The application of a theory of 'gender neutrality' in family law located within a gendered society which stipulates clearly defined gender roles within the family is also a concern of this chapter.

MARRIAGE: A SOCIAL INSTITUTION

Evolution of the Institution of Marriage

The existence of the institution of marriage, irrespective of the form it may take, has been a universal constant of human society after the primitive stage. The most common form of marriage in contemporary society is monogamy (albeit serial monogamy in many societies) between individual members of opposite sexes.[1] However, anthropological studies indicate that group pairings pre-date the system of monogamous marriages and even today, a range of marriage practices prevail among various tribes, sects, social groupings, and religious denominations, such as polygamy among some Hindu and Muslim communities, polyandry among

---

[1] Recently some Scandinavian countries, the United Kingdom, and some states in the United States of America have awarded legal recognition to marriages between persons of the same sex. Despite this, heterosexual marriages continue to be the norm in most societies.

the Todas of Nilgiri Hills and some Himalayan tribes, fraternal polyandry among the Tibetan groups, levirate unions[2] among the Jats of Haryana and informal alliances (*sambandham*) among Nair women and upper caste men, etc. These diverse forms of marriage evolved to meet the needs of a particular society or geographical region and indicate that marriage is not merely a bond between two (or more individuals), but has wider social ramifications because it affects issues fundamental to the survival of a society, such as the legitimacy and nurturing of children and inheritance of private property. Thus marriage is connected not merely to the way in which a society views relations between the sexes, but more fundamentally to how it views itself and the norms and mores it uses to perpetuate itself.

In an agricultural, feudal economy society like India, the primary social need was the protection and preservation of agricultural land. Large joint family households and male progeny were important to continue the family/clan lineage and fulfil the social needs of this agrarian economy. Within this social and economic structure, while male polygamy was accepted, there was strict control on women's sexuality in order to maintain caste purity. But there were several non-agrarian communities—food gathering and nomadic tribes as well as tribes practicing shifting agriculture—which evolved other forms of social organization where there were fewer restrictions on women and marriages did not have the same rigidity or sanctimony as marriages among the upper caste Hindus of feudal India (Karve 1953; Srinivas 1998; Uberoi 1993; Gough: 1989). While acknowledging these social organizations, the scope of this chapter does not permit elaboration of this theme, which is the subject of social anthropology and sociology.

Material Basis for the Notion of Sacramental Indissolubility

Since European/English legal principles have a bearing upon our legal system, this section provides a brief sketch of the institution of marriage under the Judeo-Christian legal regimes of Europe (continental) and England (common law) and attempts to draw comparisons with the Indian legal system of the corresponding period.

Historically, within most feudal societies, marriage was viewed as an essential social institution and its stability as a desirable social objective which could be ensured by prohibiting its dissolution. This was done by prescribing marriage as an indissoluble sacrament and by merging women's identities with their husbands. Under Judaic and medieval European legal systems, women were considered as the property (chattel) of their husbands. The church had the power to restore to the husband an estranged wife who escaped from his custody. The right of exclusive sexual union was so highly regarded that any man who had sexual relations with the wife of another could be punished under the criminal law of adultery.[3] The husband could even seek compensation from the adulterer for violating his property rights. Remnants of this concept can be found in the Christian matrimonial law, the Indian Divorce Act, until it was amended in 2001.[4] In addition, the property of an adulterous wife could be

---

[2] The term refers to the Jewish custom of a younger brother marrying the elder brother's childless widow. Several communities in India also practice this custom.

[3] This archaic feudal remedy is still retained under Section 497 of the Indian Penal Code.

[4] Sections 34 and 35 of the Indian Divorce Act which has now been deleted.

settled in favour of her children.[5] A similar stipulation is found in the Parsi Marriage and
Divorce Act, 1936 even after the amendment
in 1988.[6]

Since inheritance depended upon the legitimacy of the male child, a very high premium
was placed on a woman's virginity at the time
of marriage and her chastity thereafter. Only
through strict sexual control of women could
the legitimacy of children be ensured. Under
Christian law, the principle of monogamy
applied to both men and women but under
Muslim and Hindu law, it applied only to
women. In addition, under Hindu law, other
sexual relations with women of the lower caste
were also awarded legitimacy under the institution of concubinage. But for upper caste Hindu
women, the sacred bond of marriage could not
be dissolved even after the death of the husband.
Institutions such as child marriage, restraint
upon widow remarriage, and the practice of *sati*
evolved to ensure the chastity of women not
only during the subsistence of marriage but even
after the death of the husband.[7]

Yet another way to ensure the stability of marriage was by denying women property rights.[8]
Under Roman, Continental (European), and
English common law, upon marriage, a woman
lost all rights over her individual property, which
became the property of her husband. The Roman
law of marriage and property, which derived its

roots from Judaic law, was based on the notion
of a patriarchal family consisting of wives, sons,
and slaves. Hence, the suppression of women's
rights after marriage was effected to a greater
extent under Roman jurisprudence. Under the
concept of *paterfamilias* and *patrias potestas*,[9] the
head of the family acquired total control over the
person, property, and labour of all members of
his household. The wife was treated as the ward
of the husband and she had no independent
identity.[10]

Divorce was not recognised in Europe
(including England) till the advent of the industrial era. In pre-industrial Europe, economic
wealth and power were regulated through concepts of status. Marriage became a crucial link
in determining the status of both the spouses
and their children. This system facilitated the
accumulation of property and power within
recognized groups and enabled the landed
families of England, Europe, and colonial
America to retain and increase their posses-
sions. The Christian concept of a holy union
bestowed a sacramental character on these
unions. Divorce would have disrupted production, undermined security of land tenure,
brought families into conflict and created acute
problems over the succession of land (Sachs
and Wilson 1978). Merging the husband and
wife into a single legal identity was appropriate
for a feudal society in which the home and the

---

[5]   Section 39 of the Indian Divorce Act which has
also been deleted.

[6]   Section 50 of the Parsi Marriage and Divorce
Act, 1936.

[7]   See *19th Century Social Reform Movements* in
Chapter 1 *Personal Laws and Women's Rights* of the first
volume of this book for a detailed discussion.

[8]   The matrilineal inheritance patterns followed in
some parts of Africa, North-East India, and the Malabar
Coast are an exception to this norm. But many of these
customary practices were eroded with the advent of
colonization.

[9]   The term '*paterfamilias*' refers to the father of a
patriarchal family, under Roman Law. The term '*Patrias
potestas*' denotes the aggregate of those peculiar powers
and rights which belong to the head of a family in
respect to his wife, children. and lineal descendents.
The power of the father was extensive, including the
power of life and death. But gradually, this power was
curtailed and finally it amounted to little more than a
right in the *paterfamilias* to hold as his own any property or acquisition of one under his power (Black's
Law, 1990, 6[th]edn. pp.1126–7).

[10]   For a detailed discussion see Agnes 2000: 106–37.

land around it formed the centre of production. This principle was first enunciated by the Roman Catholic Church in the twelfth century. In 1769, the English jurist William Blackstone explained the concept as follows:

By marriage, the husband and wife are one person in law, that is, the very being or legal existence of the woman is suspended during the marriage or at least is incorporated and consolidated into that of the husband under whose wing, protection and cover she performs everything. Her husband is her baron or lord. (Bromley 1976: 107)

Under the principle laid down by Blackstone, the woman lost her legal existence upon marriage, which signified legal death. The woman could not contract, sue, or be sued. All her individual property belonged to her husband and he could not only use it but even alienate it without her consent. Upon the death of her husband, the property devolved upon the husband's heirs and she lost all access to it. Only the woman's clothing (apparel) and jewellery reverted to her, but if the husband was insolvent, his creditors could claim even this (Bromley 1976: 425–35).

From seventeenth century onwards, the demands of emerging capitalism rendered it necessary to redeem the land of its inalienable characteristics. So, a gradual change in the nature of land tenures is discernible, culminating in the enactment of several legislations in nineteenth century. The object of these legislations was to facilitate the alienation of feudal manors and agricultural land tenures for the construction of factories, mines, and townships. It is only during this period that women in England could wage a sustained struggle for their right of divorce and for the right to own separate property.

The status of women under Muslim law was slightly better as women did not lose their identity upon marriage and the legal system offered some economic safeguards to married women through the system of *mehr*. It also acknowledged the inheritance rights of women. But even here, women's rights were not equal to that of men. Ironically, in the early stages of colonial administration, the British jurists looked down on the Islamic notion of contractual marriage, viewing it as a loose sexual alliance which could easily be dissolved on the whim of the husband.[11] Through such interpretations, the protection awarded to women under Islamic law was eroded. With the onset of modernity, European, later the British, and finally the Hindu legal system adopted the principle of contractual and dissoluble marriages, consent divorces, and even the concept of irretrievable breakdown of marriage as acceptable principles of matrimonial law. But since both sacramental and contractual marriages were based on patriarchal premises, the position of women was subordinate to that of men under all legal systems (Diwan and Diwan 1997: x).

The Journey from Sacrament to Contract
The decree of the Council of Trent (1563) rejected the opinion propounded by Martin Luther and other reformers that marriage should be brought under the jurisdiction of civil courts.[12] But the Reformation and the emerging ideology of Protestantism, which challenged the supremacy of the Roman Catholic Church, resulted in bringing about significant changes in public life. Important among them were the separation of church and state and a transformation of marriage from a status to a contract. In respect of the right to

[11]   Krishna Iyer J., *Islamic Law in Modern India* at p. 23 as cited by Diwan & Diwan (1997) p. 22, fn 8
[12]   Instead it was laid down that the presence of a priest and three witnesses is essential for solemnization of a marriage.

dissolve marriages, there was a sharp divide within the Christian world. The struggle was to wrest temporal issues, such as the regulation of marriage, divorce, and property, out of the authority and control of the church. Protestant-dominated countries introduced the notion that marriages are dissolvable contracts and awarded the power of dissolving the marriages to civil courts (Diwan and Diwan 1997: 24).

Protestant ideology was rooted in a new economic order of capitalism and industrialization that was sweeping through Europe. As mentioned earlier, a feudal system based on agrarian land holdings considered land inalienable and marriage indissoluble.

The dissolubility of marriage is also the manifestation of an individualistic philosophy. Industrial revolution's claims of liberty, equality, and pursuit of happiness gave impetus to the liberation of marriage from the fetters of the church. A new dogma now began gaining acceptance—one who has the liberty to enter matrimony should also have the liberty to opt out of it. Once marriage was accepted as a contract, the next logical step was to consider it a dissoluble union. Marriage came to be recognized as a human institution, based on the free volition of men and women who were not infallible and hence, should be awarded the right and liberty to dissolve a marriage that had become burdensome.

The proponents of this philosophy advocated that though marriage is a bond and a civil contract, it is not bondage or slavery in the garb of a super-imposed sacramentality and indissolubility. While the Catholics continued to uphold and follow the ecclesiastical doctrinaire view of sacramentality and indissolubility of marriage, Protestants adopted the notion of a contractual and dissolvable marriage. Since the colonial rulers were Protestants belonging to the Anglican Church, these concepts entered the Indian legal system and influenced the Indian matrimonial statutes.

The term 'divorce' owes its origins to the French term, '*diverter*' and the Latin term '*divortium*', which mean 'to divert'. The French Civil Code of 1800 (also called the Napoleonic Code) was the first to recognize marriage as a civil contract. Marriages thus ceased to be controlled by church dictates and became dissolvable civil contracts. Later, in 1857, the Matrimonial Causes Act provided similar remedies to English women. In 1865, the Parsi Marriage and Divorce Act and in 1869, the Indian Divorce Act also recognized the right of a judicial divorce. In comparison, the Hindu women did not get the right of divorce until 1955.

Under Muslim law, since its origin, marriages have been recognized as contractual and dissoluble and the right to dissolve the marriage is a Quranic right. The word *talaq* derives its origins from the root word '*talaqqa*', which means to release, and signifies the repudiation of the marriage by the husband alone (Fyzee 1974: 150). While talaq denotes the husband's right to divorce the wife, the term *khul* (or *khoola*) denotes divorce by consent. The literal meaning of the word *khul* is to 'untie' or 'disrobe' and in the context of marriage, the word denotes 'to lay down one's authority over one's wife' (Fyzee 1974:163). Though under the uncodified Muslim law women could dissolve their marriages under certain conditions, in 1939, the Dissolution of Muslim Marriages Act (DMMA) granted Muslim women the right to judicial divorce.

Hindu Women and Right to Divorce

A common misconception prevails that marriage amongst all castes and sections of Hindus is an indissoluble institution. However, within a pluralistic society, there were many castes and tribes which awarded a customary right of divorce to women, as well as the right of remarriage. But these were regarded as the customs of the sub-stratum of society by colonial rulers and were not acknowledged as the custom of Hindu society. The legal machinery introduced by the British was contextualized within the concerns of the upper castes and relied upon scriptures while adjudicating over disputes between native Hindus. Though the scriptures also recognized the right of divorce in certain situations, the philosophy of marriage as a holy union was paramount and this notion coincided with the notion then prevailing in England of a sacramental bond.

Over time, many practices of the upper castes, including the notion of an indissoluble and sacramental marital union spread to the lower castes through Sanskritization and a woman's right to divorce and remarriage was curtailed (Srinivas: 1998). Even after the death of the husband, a widow could not marry. It was only during the mid-nineteenth century, after a sustained struggle, that a statute was enacted granting widows the right to remarry.[13]

The problem of indissolubility of marriage did not affect the husband since he had the option to discard an earlier wife and remarry. There were many cases of elderly men marrying child brides. Hindu husbands did not suffer from any restraint regarding the number of times they could remarry. But the rights of women were severely constrained due to the denial of divorce and remarriage. Social reformers had to wage a sustained struggle during the first half of the twentieth century to secure Hindu women's right to divorce. The campaign met with resistance as there was an overwhelming fear that awarding women the right to divorce would loosen the grip of strict sexual control enforced upon them through the notion of indissoluble sacramental marriages.

But towards the mid-twentieth century, changes that were taking place in England influenced some nationalist leaders and social reformers who campaigned for introducing similar changes in Hindu matrimonial law. At the forefront of this struggle for change was Dr G.V. Deshmukh, who had also campaigned for the Hindu woman's right to property.[14] He drafted a bill, which was introduced on 20 September 1938 in the legislative assembly and was later circulated to gauge public opinion.[15] During discussions on the bill which commenced on 11 April 1939, Deshmukh argued that the Bill was not meant to offer an avenue by which women could manipulate the system. It was merely a mechanism through which they would be empowered. He submitted that the Bill took into account the essence of Hinduism and had the approval of stalwarts like C. Rajagopalachari and V. D. Savarkar, whose opinion carried weight among the orthodox section of the Hindu community.

However the Bill faced strong opposition from conservative elements who perceived it as a measure by the colonial government to interfere with the Hindu philosophy and way of life. It was also suggested that it was futile to introduce these provisions since proving some of these grounds in a court of law would be an impossible task. For instance, it would be impossible for a wife to prove her husband's bigamy if the husband projected the second wife as a mere concubine. Impotency, which is an intimate matter between a husband and wife, could not be determined by a court of law. Bhulabhai

---

[13]   See section titled 'Social Reform Movements and Legislative Reforms' of Chapter 1 *Personal Laws and Women's Rights* of the first volume of this book where this issue is discussed in detail.

[14]   This has been discussed in detail in section titled 'Codified Law and Illusory Inheritance Rights' of Chapter 1 *Personal Laws and Women's Rights* of the first volume of this book.

[15]   Legislative Assembly Debates Vol.VII Session 20 September 1938 p. 2830.

Desai, a nationalist leader and member of the Assembly, felt that the scope of the Bill was too wide and hence it did not serve the purpose. He strongly objected to the phrase 'right to divorce', suggesting that such an interpretation would prove fatal to the sacred relationship between a man and woman (Basu 2001: 102).

Bhai Parmanand of the Congress party criticized the provision of the Bill concerning divorce on the ground that it was an attempt to bring into India, a system that had already wreaked havoc in the families of the Western world. Ironically, some leaders felt that it was far too one sided, favouring women alone. These men conveniently overlooked the advantages a Hindu husband enjoyed under the prevailing marriage system of the upper castes. The greatest opposition came from orthodox Hindus, who tried to establish the sacramental nature of the Hindu marriage. On the other hand, the Bill was also opposed by some women who believed that it would create unnecessary hardships in their marital lives as they would have to live under the constant threat of divorce from their husbands. The Bill received support from some social thinkers who were ready to adopt an alternative view to the problem. Sir Yamin Khan of the Muslim League supported the Bill and pointed out that this principle was accepted by Islam several generations ago (Basu 2001: 104).

Overall, there was strong opposition to changing the status of a Hindu marriage from a holy and indissoluble union to a dissoluble contract. On 15 September 1939, the Legislative Assembly rejected the Bill stating that the country was not ready to accept such a radical change in its beliefs and practices. But Deshmukh remained undaunted and pursued his campaign by re-introducing the Bill again in December 1940 (Basu 2001: 104). The reformulated bill explicitly offered remedies along the lines of English matrimonial statutes and suggested separate residence and maintenance for wives, in addition to remedies such as annulment of marriage, judicial separation, and divorce. It was supported by Akhil Chandra Datta, Deputy President of the Assembly, and was adopted in the legislature. The Government of India appointed a committee on 25 January 1941, under the Chairmanship of Sir B.N. Rau, a judge of the Calcutta High Court.[16] The committee aimed to codify all laws related to Hindu marriage and succession. In June 1941, a report was published by the committee which recommended the preparation of a complete code of Hindu law on marriage and property.[17]

Following this, a second Hindu Law Committee was constituted in 1944. After soliciting the opinions of jurists and the public, the committee submitted its report to the Federal Parliament in April 1947. The recommendations were debated in the Provincial Parliament between 1948 and 1951 and again from 1951 to 1954. On 20 December 1952, a motion was adopted in the Council of States to introduce the Hindu Marriage and Divorce Bill of 1952. This was again circulated to solicit public opinion. Finally, the right to divorce was granted to Hindu women by the enactment of the Hindu Marriage Act on 18 May 1955.

The Act severed the sacred tie of Hindu conjugality by rendering Hindu marriages contractual. But though the contractual element was introduced, the sacramental and ritualistic features were retained. Hence in judicial discourse, Hindu marriage is deemed both as a sacrament and as a contract. Looking back, one can find several faults in this enactment and question its claim of protecting the rights of Hindu women. But its passing is considered a major milestone in

[16]   Later, he was also appointed as India's permanent member to the United Nations.
[17]   Report of the Hindu Law Committee 1941: 23

Table 1.1   Matrimonial Remedies Under Various Personal Laws

Matrimonial Remedies	HMA	SMA	ML	DA	PMDA
Annulment	Section 11/12	Section 24/25	Uncodified	Section 18/19	Section 30
Restitution of Conjugal Rights	Section 9	Section 22	Uncodified	Section 32	Section 36
Judicial Separation	Section 10	Section 23	No remedy*	Section 22	Section 34
Divorce	Section 13	Section 27	Uncodified & DMMA	Section 10	Section 32

Note: *Muslim law provides for a separation agreement

the history of the Indian women's struggle for empowerment and legal equality.[18]

MATRIMONIAL REMEDIES

Statutory law or codified law revolves around four basic arenas of matrimonial relief—annulment of marriage, restitution of conjugal rights, judicial separation, and divorce. The first three were well established principals of matrimonial law even prior to the introduction of the right to divorce. Initially, these concepts were introduced to the Indian legal system through judge decreed laws. After codification, these became stipulated rights under personal law.

In the following and subsequent tables which appear in this chapter, the various legal provisions under five different matrimonial statutes/legal systems, i.e., the Hindu Marriage Act, 1955 (HMA), the Special Marriage Act, 1954 (SMA), uncodified Muslim law (ML), the Dissolution of Muslim Marriages Act, 1939 (DMMA), the Indian Divorce Act, 1869 (DA), and the Parsi Marriage and Divorce Act, 1939 (PMDA) are tabulated for easy reference (see Table 1.1).

These remedies are discussed in detail later in this chapter, but following is a concise meaning of these legal terms.

The term 'annulment' refers to the process of declaring a marriage which suffers from a legal defect as 'null and void'. The legal defects are of two categories—void and voidable. A void marriage does not confer any status, rights, or obligations upon the spouses. While a marriage can be declared 'null and void' through a judicial decree, even without such a declaration, the marriage is deemed to be void and the parties cannot claim any rights against each other. It is in this context that the validity of marriage becomes a highly contested issue while claiming maintenance. A voidable marriage remains valid until it is declared as null and void through a judicial decree.

Restitution of conjugal rights refers to the right of one spouse to the sexual companionship of the other. Initially only husbands could avail of this remedy. Though this was not an accepted remedy under Hindu and Muslim law, it was introduced into Indian family law through the intervention of the courts.[19] Later, it was incorporated into various personal laws and both the husband and the wife were awarded the right to enforce conjugality upon the other.

A decree of judicial separation awards the spouse claiming relief the right to live separately from the other spouse, while keeping the marital bond intact. When the provisions for obtaining a divorce were stringent, a decree of judicial

---

[18]   For a detailed discussion on this act including its loopholes, see section titled 'Law of Marriage and Divorce' in Chapter 1 *Personal Laws and Women's Rights* of the first volume of this book.

[19]   See the judgment in *Rukhmabai case* discussed in detail in Chapter 1 *Personal Laws and Women's Rights* of the first volume of this book.

separation entitled spouses to live separately without the fear of facing litigation for restitution of conjugal rights. This was more relevant for women as they could leave their husband's home and live separately and also claim maintenance from their husbands. But the decree did not give them the right to remarry.

A decree of divorce dissolves the matrimonial tie and the spouses cease to be husband and wife and hence can not claim conjugality from each other. Since the bond of marriage is severed, the divorced spouses are entitled to remarry. After divorce, the parties do not have the right to succeed to each other's property.

Ancillary reliefs such as alimony, maintenance, and custody of children can be claimed along with any of the four matrimonial remedies mentioned above. Under the scheme of current matrimonial litigation, filing a suit for restitution of conjugal rights as well as judicial separation enables wives who do not wish to obtain a decree of divorce, gain an entry into the litigation arena for claiming ancillary and interim reliefs.

Nullity of Marriage

Marriage confers the status of 'husband' and 'wife' upon a man and woman, thereby providing legitimacy to the sexual relationship (in legal terms, conjugality) between them. As a consequence of this relationship, certain mutual rights and obligations accrue. However, the creation of these rights presupposes the capacity of the parties to enter into a valid marriage. The concept of the nullity is linked to the capacity of an individual to enter a valid marriage. If the person lacks the capacity to contract marriage, the marriage is void or voidable.

Essential Conditions of a Valid Marriage

Every community/legal system lays down certain requirements or conditions for a valid marriage. A marriage solemnized or contracted in violation of any of these conditions is deemed to be an invalid marriage. The stipulated conditions for the performance of a valid marriage and the consequences of a marriage contracted in violation of these conditions, differs under various personal laws. Some conditions are treated as absolute, while others are less so. The violation of absolute conditions renders the marriage void, while the violation of other renders the marriage voidable.

Section 5 of the Hindu Marriage Act, 1955 addresses the essential conditions of a valid Hindu marriage and states that a marriage may be solemnized between 'any two Hindus', if the stipulated conditions are fulfilled. These wordings indicate that a Hindu marriage can be solemnized only between two Hindus. Essential conditions include that neither party has a spouse living at the time of marriage, that the marriage was solemnized with the free consent of the parties, that they are not suffering from a serious mental disorder, they are not below the stipulated minimum age of marriage, and they are not within prohibited degrees of relationship. The prohibited degrees of relationship are enumerated in Section 2 of the Act. Section 7 of the Act stipulates the necessary ceremonies for a valid Hindu marriage.

The Special Marriage Act, 1954 permits marriages in keeping with the conditions enumerated in Section 4 of the Act. Monogamy, free consent, mental capacity, stipulated minimum age, and prohibited degrees of relationship are its important features. Since it is a secular civil law, religion of the parties is not a significant factor and a marriage between persons of different religions is valid.

The manner of solemnizing a Muslim marriage is simple. Religious ceremonies are not mandatory for a Muslim marriage. The marriage (or *nikah*) constitutes a declaration or offer (*ijab*) from one side and acceptance (*qabul*) by the other (or by the guardians, as the case may be) (Fyzee 1974: 91). The conditions for a Muslim marriage include restraint on marriage on the grounds of consanguinity, affinity, fosterage, unlawful conjugation, bar against inter-religious marriages, and free consent.

Section 60 of the Indian Christian Marriage Act, 1872 lays down the conditions of marriage, stating that the parties must be above the minimum stipulated age, that neither party should have a living spouse at the time of marriage, that consent should be free, and they should not be suffering from any mental disorder of a serious kind. An inter-religious marriage is not invalid under this law.

The conditions of marriage with reference to Parsi law are enumerated in Section 3 of the Parsi Marriage and Divorce Act, 1936. The parties must not be among the prohibited degrees of relationship, a ceremony called 'Ashirvad' must be performed and the parties must be above the prescribed minimum age, there

should be free consent and the parties should not be suffering from a serious mental disorder.

The following table provides a comparative listing of essential conditions of a valid marriage under the five statutes/codes.

Customary law also prescribes certain customs of the community as necessary conditions for entering marriage. They may vary from one community to the other or from one tribe to the next, but they are binding upon the community governed by the particular customary law.[20]

A marriage contracted in violation of essential conditions and valid ceremonies may be rendered void or voidable. The main difference

[20] For a custom to be valid it must be ancient, continuous, and not against public policy. See section titled 'Constitutional Challenges' of Chapter 1 *Personal Laws and Women's Rights* of the first volume where customary laws of marriage are discussed.

Table 1.2   Essential Ingredients of a Valid Marriage

Essential Ingredients	HMA	SMA	ML	PMDA	ICMA
Bar on inter-religious marriage	Yes	No	Yes	Yes	No
Stipulation of prohibited degrees of relationship	Yes# SECTION 5(iv)	Yes# SECTION 4(d)	No	Yes SECTION 3 (a)	Yes SECTION 19 (2)
Ceremonies of marriage	Yes SECTION 7	No	Yes – Nikah	Yes SECTION 3(b)*	Yes**
Parties to be majors	Yes SECTION 5(iii)	Yes SECTION 4(c)	No	Yes SECTION 3 (c)	Yes
Bigamous marriages prohibited	Yes SECTION 5(i)	Yes SECTION 4(a)	Bigamy permitted for men	Yes	Yes SECTION 19 (4)
consent of the parties mandatory	Yes SECTION 5(ii)- implies	Yes SECTION 4(b)- implies	Yes	Yes	Yes SECTION 19-in case of minor
The spouses should not be of unsound mind or suffering from mental disorder	Yes SECTION 5(ii)(a), (b), (c)	Yes SECTION 4(b) (i) (ii) (iii)	Yes	Yes	Yes SECTION 19(3)
Marriage should not be solemnized during Iddat period			Yes		

Notes: *In the Parsi ceremony, this includes the ceremony of Ashirvad, and the presence of two Parsi witnesses.

** For Christians the essential ceremony is either church nuptials or a civil ceremony before the Registrar of Marriages.

Except where custom permits.

between void and voidable marriages is that of legal status. A void marriage does not confer the status of husband and wife on the parties and hence it does not give rise to mutual obligations and rights.

Void and Voidable Marriages

A void marriage, in the eyes of the law, is one which is deemed to have never taken place. Its very existence is negated and hence the term used for describing such marriages is void *ab initio*. Even when the parties have not obtained a court decree invalidating the marriage, the marriage cannot be deemed as valid. A formal decree permits the court to make a judicial declaration of the fact that the marriage is void. The premise most often used for the plea of declaring the marriage void is bigamy. The issue of validity

HMA	SMA	ML	DA	PMDA
S.11/12	S.23/24	Uncodified	S.18/19	S.30

Table 1.3   Grounds for Annulment of Marriage

Grounds	HMA	SMA	ML	DA	PMDA
Bigamy	S.5 (i) / S.11	S.4 (a) / S.24 (i)		S.19 (4)	S.5
Marriage with married woman			Uncodified		
Prohibited degrees of relationship / Sapinda	S.5 (iv)/S.11	S.4 (d) /S.24 (i)	Uncodified	Yes S.19 (2)	S.3 (1) (a)
Force / coercion / fraud misrepresentation	Yes S.12(1) (c)	Yes S.25 (iii)	Yes Uncodified		
Impotency	S.12 (1) (a)	S.24 (ii)		S.19 (1)	S.30
Refusal to consummate marriage		Yes S.25 (i)			Yes S.30
Unsoundness of mind / Mental disorder / Insanity	Yes S.5(ii)(a-b-c) / S.12 (1) (b)	Yes S.4 (b) / S.24 (i)		Yes S.19(3)	
minors	**	Yes S.4 (c) / S.24 (i)			S.3 (1) (c)***
Pre-marital pregnancy	Yes S.12 (1) (d)	Yes S.25 (ii)			
Repudiation of marriage	S.13 (2) (iv)****		Yes Uncodified		

*Notes: * Unless permitted by custom.

** Though not a ground for annulment under HMA, a minor girl who is married before the age of 15 can repudiate the marriage (whether it was consummated or not) between the age of 15 to 18 and obtain divorce on this ground.

*** PMDA stipulates a minimum age of marriage (18 for the bride and 21 for the bridegroom) but does not specifically provide for annulment of marriage on this ground.

**** The scope of this provision has been expanded under the recently enacted Prevention of Child Marriage Act, 2006. Under its provisions, both boys and girls are permitted to annul the marriage contracted when they were minors. The petition has to be filed within two years of attaining the age of marriage i.e. 18 for girls and 21 for boys.

of marriage surfaces most often when women claim their right to maintenance.[21]

A voidable marriage is one which will be considered valid until a decree annulling it has been pronounced by a court of competent jurisdiction. The invalidation is only at the instance of one of the parties. Until such a declaration, the marriage is deemed valid and the parties are bound by mutual rights and obligations.

Muslim law does not recognize any distinction between void and voidable marriages. Marriages may be either classified as valid (*sahih*), void (*batil*), and irregular (*fasid*). A void marriage is one which is performed in violation of any of the rules laid down by the respective laws governing Sunni and Shia sects. No legal action is necessary. However, it is possible to file a declaratory suit under the Specific Relief Act, 1963. A *fasid* marriage is a term specific to Muslim law. Here the irregularity can be remedied by removing the impediment.

Grounds of Annulment of Marriage

In England, until the introduction of the *Matrimonial Causes Act*, the power to annul a marriage vested with the ecclesiastical court.

Under the scriptural law, marriage was deemed a sacrament and once performed, it could not be invalidated. Consent of the parties or even the incapacity to perform marital or sexual obligations were not considered as grounds on which a marriage could be annulled or dissolved. But after the enactment of the Hindu Marriage Act in 1955, the position changed substantially and lack of consent and capacity became grounds of annulment as Table 1.3 indicates.

Under HMA and SMA, not every violation of the essential condition listed above renders the marriage void. Violation of some conditions makes the marriage void where as violation of other conditions makes the marriage merely voidable. For instance, while bigamous marriages are void *ab initio*, a marriage of a minor is merely voidable. Similarly, impotency and pre-marriage pregnancy render the marriage voidable and hence such marriages are legal and valid until they are dissolved through a judicial decree.

Grounds of void marriage under the personal laws vary a great deal. For instance, many of the grounds which are stipulated for annulment of marriage under other statutes, such as non consummation of marriage, insanity and pre-marriage pregnancy are grounds for divorce under the Parsi Law.

The grounds for the annulment of marriage are elaborated below.

Bigamy

The codification of Hindu law of marriage in 1955 rendered Hindu marriages monogamous. But this legislative change did not reflect in the community practices and Hindu marriages have continued to be bigamous/polygamous. But these marriages are void under the law and the second wife acquires no rights. Since Muslim law permits polygamy, bigamous marriages are not void and women in such marriages have legal rights. Under the Christian, Parsi, and civil marriage under the Special Marriage Act, bigamous marriages are void and hence the women in such relationships acquire no legal rights. However, children from void marriages are deemed legitimate and are entitled to maintenance and succession.[22]

Since bigamous marriages are void *ab initio*, the woman is not awarded the status of a wife.

---

[21]   See sections titled 'Rights of Women in Bigamous Marriages' and 'Rights of Women in Informal Relationships' of Chapter 2 *Matrimonial Rights and Obligations* for further discussion on this issue.

[22]   The issue is discussed later under the sub section, '*Children of void and voidable marriages*'.

Since these marriages are not valid, there is no requirement to obtain a judicial decree of annulment. But the innocent party may approach the court and obtain a decree of annulment or a declaration that the marriage is void.

Scriptural law mandated taking a second wife if the first wife was childless, in order to fulfil the religious obligation of begetting children. Hence, an erroneous notion still prevails that a childless person can take a second wife with the consent of his first wife. But such a marriage is bigamous and hence void. However, this erroneous notion led a district court in Himachal Pradesh to grant a declaration on the suit filed by the wife that on account of her frail health she was not in a position to beget children and hence her husband be allowed to take a second wife. But the high court of Himachal Pradesh held such declaration to be illegal and against public policy.[23]

While the Hindu Marriage Act prohibits bigamous marriages, it awards no remedy for the first wife to obtain an injunction against her husband to prevent his second marriage. Her only option under the Act is to obtain a divorce on the ground of bigamy. However, it is possible to obtain a civil injunction restraining the husband from contracting a second marriage, under order xxxix of the Code of Civil Procedure read with Section 39 of the Specific Relief Act, 1963.[24]

Upon the husband's second marriage, the first wife can prosecute him for bigamy under Section 494 of the IPC. But the second marriage has to be strictly proved in order to obtain a conviction. Proof of mere adultery or cohabitation is not sufficient. Even proof of birth of a child from the bigamous relationship is not sufficient to prove bigamy.[25]

If a spouse files for annulment of the marriage on the ground of the other spouse's bigamy and is able to prove that the previous marriage was valid and subsisting at the time when his/her own marriage was performed, the court has no discretion in the matter and is bound to annul the marriage.[26] But the allegation of bigamy must be strictly proved.

In *Santosh Kumari v. Harish Kumar,*[27] the husband filed a petition for annulment marriage on the ground that the wife was married to one Subhash prior to her marriage with him. The trial court upheld this contention and annulled the marriage. But on appeal, the high court set aside the decree and held that there is no proof that the wife was married to anyone else on the date when she married the petitioner. The documents which the husband had produced for proving bigamy were concocted and the same could not be relied upon. The man posing to be her husband had committed a fraud on her by falsely declaring that he was married to her. But the woman herself was unaware of this fraud at the time of her marriage. The court also commented that at the relevant time, the woman was just a minor and a student and there was no evidence of any marriage having taken place or of her cohabiting with anyone else prior to her marriage with her husband. In her defense, the wife had alleged that when she was pregnant, she was harassed for dowry and was driven out of the house. Subsequently she gave birth to a child but her husband refused to accept her back and that he had filed these proceedings only in order to get rid of her by making false allegations against her.

[23] *Santosh Kumari v. Surjit Singh,* AIR 1990 HP 70.

[24] *Shankarappa v. Basamura,* AIR1964 Mys 247.

[25] *Bhaurao Shanker Lokhande v. State of Maharashtra,* AIR 1965 SC 1564; *Kanwal Ram v. The*

H.P. Administration, AIR 1966 SC 614; and *Priya Bala Ghosh v. Suresh Chandra Ghosh,* AIR 1971 SC 1153.

[26] *Annu Thomas v. Mathew Thomas,* II (2001) DMC 586 Ker.

[27] I (2005) DMC 453 P&H

An interesting issue regarding annulment of bigamous marriage was decided by the Punjab and Haryana High Court in *Balwinder Kaur* v. *Gurumukh Singh*.[28] The husband obtained a decree of annulment of marriage on the ground of wife's bigamy. While the appeal against this decree was pending, the wife died. The daughter sought permission to continue the appeal on behalf of her mother. She contended that even though she was not a direct party, the outcome of the matrimonial petition would vitally affect her status. If the marriage was held to be valid she would be a legitimate child and her inheritance and coparcenary rights would be protected. But if the marriage was declared void, she would lose her rights.[29] The court upheld her contentions and permitted her to be a party and continue the litigation.

The issue of bigamy gets foregrounded frequently when women claim maintenance. The plea of bigamy is advanced by husbands to deny women their right of maintenance. Within the judicial discourse, there are two parallel streams—while some courts have upheld the second wife's right to maintenance, others have denied her maintenance on the ground that the marriage is void *ab initio* and hence no rights accrue out of such relationships.[30]

Force/Coercion,...Fraud/Misrepresentation

Free consent of the parties was an important ingredient under ecclesiastical law. But in the Indian context, marriages were performed with the consent of the elders of the family. Hence, though under codified Hindu law as well as Muslim law the consent of the parties is essential for contracting a marriage, consent given by the parents to the marriage is deemed as valid. At times, the consent is implied. The husband cannot annul the marriage on the ground that he had not personally consented to the marriage if his father had given his consent to the marriage. Courts have also held that the absence of consent will not render a Hindu marriage invalid if such a marriage was performed in accordance with Section 5 of the HMA and the same cannot be used to deny the wife maintenance.[31]

But where women are concerned, the courts have upheld their right to annul the marriage for lack of consent. If the consent of the bride was obtained by force by her parents the marriage can be annulled. For instance, in *Rajni Thomas* v. *Annie Thomas*,[32] the parties lived together for barely one week and there was no response from the wife to the husband's sexual advances. The Delhi High Court, while holding the marriage as null and void, commented that the girl had succumbed under filial force and obedience and that her consent was not free from force or duress. Hence it was not voluntary.[33]

If the consent is vitiated on the ground that it was obtained through force, coercion, fraud, or misrepresentation, it is not a valid consent. If a girl is abducted by force and marriage is performed against her wish, it amounts to force or coercion. But the courts have held that mere pressure, strong advice, or persuasion is not force. In fraud, there is an element of deceit. The deceit can be regarding the nature of the ceremony or any material fact or circumstance concerning the respondent. But not every

---

[28]   AIR 2007 P&H 74

[29]   See the discussion on 'the Rights of Children of Void and Voidable Marriages' later in this section.

[30]   See section titled 'Maintenance Rights of Women' of Chapter 2 *Matrimonial Rights and Obligations*.

[31]   *Basanti Mohanti* v. *Parikhit Rout*, I (2003) DMC 214 Ori

[32]   II (2001) DMC 419 Del

[33]   The right of women to maintenance in cases where the husband advances the defense of non-consent is discussed in Chapter 2 *Matrimonial Rights and Obligations* at section titled 'Violation of Essential Conditions of Marriage'.

misrepresentation or concealment amounts to fraud under matrimonial law. Courts are in tune with the social norm of arranged marriages where exaggerated claims regarding physical attributes, qualifications, and virtue are routinely advanced on behalf of the bride as well as the groom. But such claims do not amount to fraud or misrepresentation.

The petition for annulment of marriage on the ground of fraud within one year of the fraud being discovered or coercion has ceased operate and it becomes time barred thereafter. After the force has ceased or fraud has been detected, no sexual intercourse should take place between the parties.

The Supreme Court, in *Gullipilli Sowria Raj* v. *Bandaru Pavani*,[34] has held that since the Hindu Marriage Act applies only to Hindus, a marriage between a Christian and a Hindu performed under as per the Hindu rites by exchanging *'thali'* in a temple is void as per Section 12 (1) (c) of the Hindu Marriage Act. This was at the instance of the wife as she had alleged fraud and misrepresentation and pleaded that her husband had misrepresented his social status and his religion and projected himself as a Hindu. It appears that this was construed to be a ground of voidable marriage. There are several other judgments which have validated such marriages while granting women the right of maintenance.[35]

At times, the ground for fraud is used casually and frivolously by husbands who wish to escape from marital obligations. But the courts have held that mere general statements as to fraud in the pleadings are not sufficient to prove the offence of fraud. The husband is required to prove every item of fraud and how it was practiced upon him. It is also necessary to prove that

he was influenced by this fraud or misrepresentation. In *Naba Kumar Mondal* v. *Lilabati Mondal*,[36] the husband alleged that fraud was committed upon him regarding the age, complexion, and educational qualifications of the bride. The petition was filed after three years of cohabitation. The Calcutta High Court held that the husband miserably failed to prove that any misrepresentation or fraud was practiced upon him. The court also held that the petition was also barred by limitation since a petition for annulment of marriage on the ground of fraud had to be filed within one year of marriage. In addition, the husband could not cohabit with his wife after the fraud had come to light. The Madhya Pradesh High Court, in *Prakash Singh Thakur* v. *Bharati*,[37] held that statements regarding the earlier marriage or divorce of the wife are untrustworthy and that it is inconceivable that the husband would not know about the earlier marriage or divorce of the wife and that he came to know of it on the very next day of their marriage. The court held that the husband's statements were untrustworthy. In *Perminder Charan Singh* v. *Harjit Kaur*,[38] the matrimonial advertisement given by the wife's father prior to marriage mentioned her status as 'legally divorced'. Later, the husband filed for annulment on grounds of fraud and misrepresentation that she was married earlier or alternatively, for a decree of divorce on the ground of cruelty and desertion. The trial court rejected the contentions and dismissed the petition. In appeal, the Punjab and Haryana High Court and the Supreme Court upheld the dismissal and held that there was no fraud or misrepresentation on the part of the wife. The courts also held that the allegations of cruelty

---

[34] I (2009) DMC 164 SC

[35] See section titled 'Inter-Religious Marriages' of Chapter 2 *Matrimonial Rights and Obligations*.

[36] I (2000) DMC 709 Cal

[37] II (2000) DMC 368 MP

[38] I (2003) DMC 742 SC

and desertion were untrue. It was held that the evidence disclosed that the wife had to take shelter in an orphanage along with her child, which proved that she was driven out of house by her husband. In *Amritpal Singh* v. *Satwinder Kaur*,[39] it was alleged that the wife was suffering from cancer prior to her marriage and this fact was concealed by her. But the court rejected the husband's application for the wife to be examined by the Cancer Institute. In appeal, the high court held that it is for the husband to prove his case and the wife cannot be compelled to submit herself for medical examination, especially when evidence led by the husband was not credible. In *Anju Kundu* v. *Shyamal Kumar Kundu*[40] where the husband alleged that wife had a tumour in her breast which was not disclosed to him prior to the marriage and there she had falsely staged that she is a graduate while she had yet to clear one subject, does not amount to fraud. The husband had filed a petition after the tumour was removed and one year after the alleged fraud was discovered. Setting aside the decree of annulment granted to the husband, the Calcutta High Court held that the same does not amount to fraud. The tumour in the breast also does not render the wife impotent.

Concealment of certain illnesses amounts to fraud. However, concealment of every disease cannot be construed as fraud which would entitle the other party to obtain a decree of annulment. In *Tiveni Singh* v. *State of UP*,[41] the father-in-law had filed a petition before the family court at Agra for a declaration that the marriage between his son and daughter-in-law should be declared void. The husband and wife were both HIV positive and the husband had

died. But it was not recorded that he had died of AIDS. The contention of the father-in-law was that the wife was HIV positive before marriage and she had concealed this fact and had communicated the disease to his son. In the proceedings for quashing these proceedings, the high court held that there is nothing in Section 5 of the HMA which would empower the courts to annul a marriage on the ground of HIV infection or any other disease. The court commented that a marriage cannot be declared null and void on the ground of any disease, except mental illness as provided under Section 5 read with Section 12 of the HMA. The court also held that there was no evidence to indicate that the wife was HIV positive before marriage and hence there is no question of concealment of an illness. The proceedings filed by the father-in-law were held to be abuse of process of law and were quashed.

Impotency

Historically, exclusive sexual access for the purpose of procreation was the primary objective of marriage. The physical and mental capacity to consummate the marriage therefore became an essential condition for a valid marriage. If one of the spouses lacks this capacity, the marriage can be annulled. Impotency may arise on account of a physical defect or mental condition, such as total repugnance to the sexual act. The legal requirement of this medical condition is that it should be incurable.

The exact wordings of the legal provision under Section 12 (1) (a) of the Hindu Marriage Act are—'that the marriage has not been consummated owing to the impotency of the respondent'. Under Section 24 (1) (ii) of the Special Marriage Act the wordings are—'that the respondent was impotent at the time of the marriage and at the time of the institution of the suit'. The wordings under Section 19 (1) of

39   I (2008) DMC 233 P&H
40   I (2010) DMC 667
41   I (2008) DMC 731 All

the (Indian) Divorce Act. These wordings make it clear that only the non-impotent spouse is entitled to file the petition (or suit, as the case may be). But under the Parsi Marriage and Divorce Act, 1936 the impotent spouse can file for nullity, as the relevant provision under Section 30 of the Act says *at the instance of either party*. Allegations of impotency have to be strictly proved. The courts are cautious while entertaining a husband's petition for annulment of marriage on the ground of the wife's impotency, as the following cases reveal.

In *Sunil Mirchandani v. Reena Mirchandani*,[42] the Bombay High Court held that it is the duty of the party pleading impotency to lead corroborative evidence and the evidence should be trustworthy. In this case, the husband had written a letter five months after marriage indicating satisfactory sexual relations with his wife. Hence his plea of non-consummation could not be proved. In *Ajay Kumar Samal v. Jotsnamayee Samal*,[43] the husband did not examine any doctor to prove impotency and hence it was held that he failed to prove the allegations and discharge the burden of proof. In *Uppu Lakshmi v. Uppu Narayan*,[44] the Andhra Pradesh High Court set aside the *ex parte* decree granted by the trial court and held that there is no evidence to believe the case of the husband that the wife persisted in her attitude of exhibiting repulsion to the sexual act. The court further held that the trial court had committed legal infirmities in passing a decree which cannot be sustained in law. In *E.G. Ravi v. Jayshree*,[45] the husband, in his cross-examination, had admitted that he had not informed anybody about the sexual aversion of his wife. The wife categorically stated that the marriage was consummated on the day of marriage itself. The medical certificate indicated that she was used to sexual intercourse. The psychiatrist testified that she was fit for married life. Hence the Madras High Court held that the husband could not prove his case.

Impotency does not signify sterility but incapacity to have normal sexual intercourse. In *Beena v. Varghese*,[46] the Kerala High Court rejected the husband's plea of the wife's impotency and explained that incapacity to conceive is not impotency and is not a ground for annulment of marriage. Similarly, in *P Devraj v. V. Geetha*,[47] it was held that removal of the uterus does not render the wife unfit for sexual intercourse. Hence it cannot be a ground for annulling the marriage.

The courts will not easily concede to the husband's demand for the wife to undergo a virginity test to prove his case of non-consummation of marriage. In *Zahida Begum v. Mushtaque Ahmed*,[48] the wife had made out a case that the marriage could not be consummated as the husband was impotent and he was unable to perform his matrimonial obligation. The husband alleged that the wife is impotent and sought a direction for her to undergo a virginity test. While setting aside this direction, the Karnataka High Court held that the question whether the wife is a virgin is irrelevant and that the trial court could not have directed her to undergo a virginity test. But the order directing the husband to undergo a medical test regarding his impotency was sustained.

A petition for annulment of marriage on the ground of impotency can be filed even after several years of marriage and the one year bar which operates for cases under force, fraud,

---

[42] I (2000) DMC 79 Bom
[43] II (2005) DMC 408 Ori
[44] I (2006) DMC 622 AP
[45] I (2007) DMC 878 Mad

[46] I (2000) DMC 704 Ker FB
[47] AIR 2007 (NOC) 145 Mad
[48] I (2006) DMC 110 Kar

coercion and misrepresentation does not operate for the ground of impotency.[49]

Insanity/Mental Disorder

Under Section 5 (ii) of the HMA, an essential condition of marriage is a sane mind. Hence, if at the time of marriage either party is incapable of giving a valid consent due to unsoundness of mind, or has been suffering from a mental disorder of such a kind or to such an extent as to be unfit for marriage and procreation of children, or has been suffering from recurrent attacks of insanity, it becomes a ground for annulment of marriage under Section 12 (1) (b). Since the marriage is voidable, it remains valid until it is annulled through a court decree and the parties are bound by mutual rights and obligations.

Under the Special Marriage Act, violation of the condition of sound mind renders the marriage void under Section 24 (i). Under S.19 (3) of the Indian Divorce Act, the ground is narrow and the marriage is voidable if it can be proved that the spouse was a lunatic or an idiot at the time of marriage. Under Section 32 (b) and (bb) of the Parsi Marriage and Divorce Act unsoundness of mind and mental disorder are grounds for divorce.

For obtaining a decree of nullity, it should be proved that due to the mental disorder, the respondent was unable to know the nature and consequences of his/her act at the time of contracting the marriage and was incapable of understanding the normal responsibilities of marriage.[50] The essential condition of 'free consent' gets vitiated if the mental illness of one of the parties was concealed at the time of the marriage. This would amount to consent obtained by misrepresentation or fraud and due

to the lack of valid consent and the marriage may be annulled.[51]

In *Ajitrai Shivprasad Mehta* v. *Bai Vasumati*,[52] the Gujarat High Court differentiated between mental illness and insanity and observed:

A person whose mental defect does not reach the state of insanity known as idiocy or lunacy can enter into a valid marriage tie and it would be absurd to nullify the marriage based on a wide interpretation of 'unsoundness of mind'. Feeble-minded persons or persons of dull intellect where mental infirmity is not serious enough to make them incapable of knowing the nature and consequences of marriage cannot be considered as a person of 'unsound mind' in the legal sense.

In *Pramatha Kumar Maity* v. *Ashima Maity*,[53] where the husband had alleged unsoundness of the mind of his wife, the Calcutta High Court commented:

The legislature has not made unsoundness of mind or a mental disorder in itself, a matrimonial fault. Unless the unsoundness is incurable and the disorder disables the person from becoming a reasonably tolerable matrimonial partner, it cannot be a ground for annulment of marriage.

It was also held that in such cases the court would keep in mind the needs of the wife who is the weaker party.

The courts have maintained that not every case of mental illness or every type of schizophrenia entitles the other spouse to obtain a decree of annulment. The illness has to be of a serious nature and incurable. A medical report and the doctor's evidence will be considered in determining the extent of mental illness. In *Vidyadhar Chodankar* v. *Malini Chodankar*,[54] the wife was suffering from schizophrenia, but from the evidence of the doctor it was not

---

[49]   D. Balakrishnan v. Pavalamani, I (2001) DMC 640 Mad.

[50]   Usha v. Abraham, AIR 1988 Ker 96.

[51]   Kiran Bala Asthana v. Bhaire Prasad Srivastava, AIR 1982 All 242.

[52]   AIR 1969 Guj 48

[53]   AIR 1991 Cal 123

[54]   II (2006) DMC 609 Bom

found to be incurable. Hence the husband's plea of annulment was rejected. The Bombay High Court clarified that not every type of mental illness or schizophrenia is covered by the expression 'incurable disease'. In *Nandakishore Agarwala* v. *Meena Agrawal*,[55] the husband's plea for annulment of marriage on the ground that the wife is suffering from a mental disorder of such a kind that makes her unfit for protection of children was rejected. The Chhattisgarh High Court held that this plea carries with it a heavy burden which must be effectively discharged. Merely stating that the wife was undergoing treatment of some kind from a doctor for some mental disorder is not sufficient. This is more so in the absence of any judicial notice of an indication of any serious mental disorder of the wife.

In cases of this nature, the opinion of a medical expert is usually sought. Where the mental condition of a spouse is a controversial issue, the court has the authority to issue directions for a medical examination. The question whether the right to privacy is invaded in a matrimonial case where the parties are subjected to a medical test has been authoritatively decided by the Supreme Court in *Sharada* v. *Dharampal*,[56] where it was held that privacy is not an absolute right. Hence in matrimonial litigation, directing a spouse to undergo a medical test does not violate the provision of Article 21 of the Constitution (right to life and liberty). But the court cautioned that this power has to be exercised only if a strong *prima facie* case is made out by the party seeking such a direction.

The court will also examine other circumstances while examining the issue of insanity. If the individual has been cured of a previous illness or does not suffer from a mental disorder which is harmful to one's own self or to others, the court may not annul the marriage. When allegations are made against the wife, the court may adopt a sympathetic approach towards her, as she is the weaker party, and take measures for her protection by granting permanent alimony in certain special circumstances. Rather than attributing guilt to a wife suffering from an incurable mental illness, the approach of the courts ought to be one of compassion. In *Hirdaya Narain* v. *Ratanjay Pradhan*,[57] the plea of mental illness was upheld and the marriage was annulled. But the court commented sympathetically that due to her condition, the wife deserves proper alimony. But since the husband was not in a position to pay more, the court awarded her Rs 50,000. On a compassionate note, the court commented that if some government funds were available, the same should be made available for treatment of women in this condition.

The husband cannot take advantage of the illness and continue to cohabit with the wife after he has come to know about her illness. In *Prakash Kumar Bachlaus* v. *Chanchal*,[58] despite the allegation that the wife was suffering from paranoid schizophrenia, the husband continued to cohabit with her. Hence, it was held that he was not entitled to a decree of annulment.

Pre-marriage Pregnancy

This ground is often used, either to end a conflict marriage or to deny the wife and the child maintenance. But it cannot be used lightly or frivolously. This ground, contained in Section 12 (1)(d) of the HMA and Section 25 (ii) of the SMA, has certain stringent riders. The stipulation is with reference to pre-marriage pregnancy

[55] AIR 2007 Chh 110
[56] I (2003) DMC 627 : AIR 2003 SC 3450
[57] II (2008) DMC 171 All
[58] AIR 2007 NOC 1032 Raj

and not pre-marriage promiscuity.[59] Thus the delivery of an illegitimate child or an abortion prior to marriage does not come under the scope of these provisions. It applies only to specific instances in which the wife has attempted to conceal the pre-marriage pregnancy from another man by falsely projecting it as the offspring of her husband. The burden of proof lies upon the petitioner-husband and proof beyond reasonable doubt is required.[60] The essential requirements of this ground of voidable marriage are:

- The respondent was pregnant at the time of the marriage
- She was pregnant from a person other than the petitioner
- The petitioner was unaware of the respondent's pregnancy at the time of the marriage
- The petitioner did not have marital intercourse with his pregnant wife after the discovery of her pregnancy. If the petitioner has had intercourse with his pregnant wife after he had knowledge of her pregnancy, then his petition would not succeed as it would amount to condonation of the offence.
- The petition must be presented within one year of the marriage

The Supreme Court ruling, delivered by M.B. Shah J. and Arun Kumar J., in *Amina* v. *Hassn Koya*[61] provides an elaborate discussion on the issue. When the wife filed for maintenance under Section 125, Cr.PC, the husband pleaded for annulment on the ground of the wife's pre-marriage pregnancy. Rejecting this contention, the magistrate's court awarded maintenance of Rs 150 per month for the wife and Rs 125 per month for the daughter. But in appeal, the sessions court as well as the Kerala High Court upheld the husband's plea and denied the wife maintenance. Against this ruling, the wife approached the Supreme Court. While considering the husband's plea that he was not aware of the fact that the wife was pregnant at the time of marriage, as this fact was concealed by her, the Supreme Court held that such reasoning could not be accepted. It was very difficult to believe that a woman who is five months pregnant would be able to conceal the pregnancy from her husband. If he was aware of this fact and thereafter cohabited with her, the marriage can not be held void. The husband was present at the time of the delivery of the child and gave his name as the father of the child for official records. Even thereafter, for nearly four years he continued with the marriage and brought up the child. Only when the wife claimed maintenance did he challenge the validity of the marriage. The court ruled that a reasonable person would have immediately turned the wife out of the house on learning about the pregnancy. After considering the facts of the case, the Apex Court held that the husband was aware of the pregnancy at the time of the marriage and, therefore, he could not later plead that it was invalid on that ground. The judgments of the sessions court and the high court were set aside, and the judicial magistrate's ruling awarding the wife maintenance was restored.

In *Devendra Sharma* v. *Sandhya*,[62] the husband sought annulment alleging that the wife was pregnant by a person other than him at the time of marriage, without his knowledge. It was held that the husband is required to prove not only such pregnancy but also that he refrained from cohabitation since its discovery. His failure to prove either would disentitle him to a remedy. Though the husband succeeded in

---

59   *Surjeet* v. *Raj Kumari*, AIR 1967 Pun 172.
60   *Nandkishore* v. *Munibai*, AIR 1979 MP 45.
61   (2003) 6 SCC 93: I (2003) DMC 728 SC

62   AIR 2007 MP 103

proving pre-marital pregnancy, he was not awarded a decree as he failed to establish that he had not voluntarily lived with her after the discovery of this fraud. But in *Maya Ram* v. *Kamla Devi*,[63] a child was born within six months of marriage. The Himachal Pradesh High Court held that the husband led cogent, reliable, and convincing evidence to prove beyond reasonable doubt that he had no access to the wife at the time when the child was begotten. In *B. Vandana Kumari* v. *P. Praveen Kumar*,[64] the high court upheld the order of the trial court for conducting a DNA test to prove paternity in a case filed by the husband on the ground of pre-marriage pregnancy.

Marriage of Minors

Though Section 5 (iii) of the Hindu Marriage Act, 1955, prescribes a minimum statutory age of 21 for boys and 18 for girls, a marriage performed between a couple where either or both parties are below the statutory age does not render the marriage void. The marriage is deemed valid until one of the parties obtains a judicial decree of annulment of the marriage. But the spouses performing such a marriage may be liable to be sentenced to a term of simple imprisonment which may extend to 15 days or with a fine which may extend to Rs 1,000, or with both.[65] A husband cannot use this provision to wriggle out of the obligation to pay maintenance to the wife merely on the ground that the wife was a minor at the time of marriage. Courts are extremely cautious while declaring a minor's marriage as void and have refrained from invalidating such marriages as it would cause untold misery to young girls who were married before the stipulated age of

marriage and also deprive them of their legal rights.[66]

Legitimacy of Children of Void and Voidable Marriages

A significant difference between void and voidable marriages is the effect it has upon the legitimacy of children. Initially, English law deemed children of void marriages illegitimate and conferred no legal rights on them. Most legal systems distinguished between children born into a legally recognized marriage and those born outside it, i.e., within a void marriage or through illicit or casual unions. In common law, an illegitimate child had no legal relationship with its father. But as a result of successive Acts of the Parliament, the harshness of this position was significantly mitigated and certain rights were awarded to illegitimate children. As a result of these developments, the question whether a child is legitimate or illegitimate has lost its significance in legal discourse regarding the right of the child to maintenance.

When the Indian Divorce Act was enacted in 1869, the statute did not render the children illegitimate only in two instances of void marriages: (i) if the person had contracted a bigamous marriage in good faith that the former spouse was dead and (ii) when the marriage was annulled on the ground of insanity. This was based on the then prevailing philosophy of English law. Similarly, the Special Marriage Act and the Hindu Marriage Act enacted in the 1950s did not bestow legitimacy upon children born of marriages which were void *ab initio*, but children of voidable marriages were deemed legitimate.

Subsequently, under English law, the distinction between legitimate and illegitimate

---

[63] I (2008) DMC 249 HP
[64] I (2007) DMC 246 AP
[65] Section 18 (a) of HMA

[66] The issue of child marriage is discussed in detail later in this chapter.

children was extinguished and illegitimate children have been conferred rights similar to those of legitimate children. This development, in turn, influenced the Indian legal system and the children of both void and voidable marriages were deemed legitimate children and the right of maintenance and succession were bestowed upon them (Diwan and Diwan 1997: 295). Incorporating these changes, initially the children of void marriages were granted rights only if the marriage was declared void by a judicial decree. However, after the Marriage Law (Amendment) Act of 1976, and under Section 16 of the Hindu Marriage Act and Section 26 of the Special Marriage Act, children of both void and voidable marriages are deemed legitimate and the requirement of obtaining a judicial declaration of annulment has been dispensed with. Some discrepancy with respect to children of valid marriages and those of void marriages prevail—the latter can inherit the property of their own parents but not of other relatives of their parents.[67]

The right to maintenance and inheritance extends not only to children of void marriages but even to illegitimate children, i.e., children whose parents have never been married.[68]

Restitution of Conjugal Rights

HMA	SMA	ML	DA	PMDA
S.9	S.22	Uncodified	S.32	S.36

This remedy emerged in an extremely anti-woman context in medieval Europe where the Roman Catholic Church had the power to physically restore to the husband, wives who had escaped from their custody. Later, it was incorporated into English law. Though neither Hindu nor Muslim law recognized this concept, it was used by English lawyers who were practicing in the newly set up courts both in Presidency and moffusil towns. Two important cases within the newly set up anglicised judicial system where this remedy was contested and awarded are *Moonshee Buzloor Ruheem* v. *Shumsoonnissa Begum*[69] and *Dadaji Bhikaji* v. *Rukhmabai*.[70] In the first case, the Privy Council, in 1876, applied the principle to Mohammedan law and held:

On authority as well as principle, there is no doubt that a Mussalman husband may institute a suit in the Civil Court of India for a declaration of his right to the possession of his wife and for a sentence that she return to cohabitation.

In the second case, a single judge, Pinhey J., who had initially heard the case in 1885 had refused to grant the husband the remedy based on the following two grounds: Firstly, the remedy can only be applied to situations when a couple has cohabited. It would be barbarous, cruel, and revolting thing to compel a young lady to go to a man whom she dislikes, in order that he may cohabit with her against her will. Secondly, that the remedy was transplanted from England and it has no foundation in Hindu law.[71] This historical judgment succeeded in drawing attention to the vexed question of the relationship between morality and law and in embedding the case within a broader legal-humanitarian framework. The verdict made the case inseparable from the women's cause. But within six months, in

---

[67] Section 16 (3) of HMA and Section 26 (3) of SMA. But in *Sarojamma* v. *Neelamma*, II (2005) DMC 567 Kar, the court awarded illegitimate children rights in ancestral property. See Chapter 2 *Matrimonial Rights and Obligations*.

[68] The right of maintenance of illegitimate children is discussed later in Chapter 2 *Matrimonial Rights and Obligations*.

[69] (1867) 11 MIA 551

[70] (1886) 10 Bom 301

[71] *Dadaji Bhikaji* v. *Rukhmabai*, (1885) ILR 9 Bom 529.

appeal, a Division Bench of the Bombay High Court, comprising two senior most judges, Sargent C.J. and Sir Bayley J., set it aside and awarded the husband a decree of restitution of conjugal rights. This case, of historical significance, has been discussed in detail in Chapter 1 of the first volume of this book.[72]

This remedy, often viewed as anachronistic, has been at the centre of several controversies regarding its constitutionality. It has also surfaced in reference to the husbands' authority and control over their wives who had refused to give up their jobs.[73]

Though initially only husbands availed of this remedy, later it was also used by deserted wives to restore their marriages. It has been incorporated into all matrimonial statutes. It has also been introduced into the Muslim law through judge-made laws. However, since the Muslim law recognizes the husband's right to unilateral talaq, a wife's claim is usually defeated by pronouncement of talaq. Hence this remedy tends to be used more by husbands than wives.[74]

The most important legal requisite for seeking the remedy of restitution of conjugal rights is to prove the withdrawal of one spouse from the society of the other. As has already been mentioned, there are certain rights and obligations which arise as a consequence of the contract of marriage. The phrase 'withdrawal from society' has been taken to mean the refusal of one spouse to continue with these obligations. There is a great deal of confusion surrounding the accurate interpretation of what constitutes withdrawal from one's society. Whether 'cohabitation' implies only sexual intercourse has also been the subject matter of debate within this controversy. It has been held that prior consummation of marriage is not a precondition for enforcing this remedy. Further, 'withdrawal from society' may take place even when the parties are living under the same roof. When the husband himself is instrumental in driving the wife out of her matrimonial home, it cannot be construed that the wife has 'withdrawn' from the society of her husband.

The defence available to the remedy of restitution is one reasonable excuse or reasonable cause. If the cause or excuse for withdrawal is reasonable, courts will not award a decree of restitution of conjugal rights to the petitioner. A 'reasonable excuse' may often seem to be under the ambit of subjectivity; however there has been a consistent opinion held by the courts, that the following constitutes a 'reasonable cause':

- An act on the part of the petitioner which can constitute a ground for relief to the respondent for obtaining any other matrimonial relief
- A matrimonial misconduct that is grave, but cannot be considered a ground for matrimonial relief
- An act, an omission, or conduct, which makes it impossible for the respondent to live with the petitioner

An act which can be construed as a ground for divorce, judicial separation, or nullity of marriage is a complete defense to the respondent in a petition for restitution of conjugal rights. A reasonable cause or excuse has been considered to include behaviour such as the

---

[72] See section titled 'A Moment of Defiance: The Rukhmabai Case' of Chapter 1 *Personal Laws and Women's Rights* of the first volume.

[73] For judicial decisions on this issue as well as constitutional challenges to this remedy see section titled 'The Legal Loopholes and Constitutional Challenges' of Chapter 1 *Personal Laws and Women's Rights* of the first volume.

[74] But more recently, it has been held that once litigation commences, the husband cannot pronounce divorce upon his wife. See cases discussed under section titled 'validity of triple talaq', in Chapter 1 *Personal Laws and Women's Rights* of the first volume.

husband's insistence that the wife live with his parents, wife's apprehension that it is unsafe to continue living with her husband, the husband having another wife or bringing another woman into the house, false accusation of adultery or immorality against the wife, etc. In case the husband himself is responsible for the wife's desertion or in other words, if he is guilty of constructive desertion, he is not entitled to a decree of restitution of conjugal rights. On the contrary, a wife who has been deserted is entitled to such a decree.

Though technically both husband and wife are able to use this remedy, studies reveal that far more husbands file for this remedy than wives.[75] When a wife files for maintenance, as a retaliatory measure, husbands are advised to file a petition for restitution of conjugal rights. Very often, this remedy is used as a legal ploy to defeat the wife's claim, rather than a genuine intention of reconciliation.

In *Dalbir Singh* v. *Simar Kaur*,[76] the husband filed a petition for restitution of conjugal rights on the ground that the wife had withdrawn from his company without reasonable cause. In reply, the wife contested the petition stating that the husband had filed this petition to avoid maintenance proceedings. She pleaded that she was thrown out of the matrimonial home by her husband, who used to beat her. She also pleaded that the children from the previous marriage of the husband were adults and they terrorised her to such an extent that she apprehended that it would not be safe for her to return to the matrimonial home. The trial court found that the wife's apprehension was genuine. Hence the petition filed by the husband for restitution of conjugal rights was dismissed. In appeal, the high court confirmed that the wife's apprehension of being unsafe in the husband's house was not ill-founded and that in such circumstances a decree of restitution of conjugal rights could not be granted to the husband.

In *Vijaykumar Bhate* v. *Neela Bhate*,[77] the wife had filed for divorce on the ground of cruelty. In his written statement, the husband made baseless and derogatory allegations of sexual immorality against the wife, which were ordered to be deleted by way of an amendment. The wife's petition was decreed and she was awarded a decree of divorce on the ground of mental cruelty. In retaliation, the husband filed a petition for restitution of conjugal rights, which was dismissed. The Bombay High Court dismissed the appeal filed by the husband, so he approached the Supreme Court. The Supreme Court held that the fact that the husband treated the wife with cruelty was established the day the allegations were made in his written statement, which caused indelible impact upon her and which cannot be said to have been dissolved by carrying out the amendments which were ordered. Allegations and counter allegations exchanged are indicative of strong hatred and rancour between the parties. Once the decree of divorce is granted, the relief sought for by the husband for restitution of conjugal rights, merely out of despair and not with any genuine purpose, must inevitably fail. The court held:

The question that requires to be answered first is as to whether the averments, accusations and character assassination of the wife in the written statement constitutes mental cruelty for sustaining the claim for divorce. Such aspersions of perfidiousness attributed to the wife, viewed in the context of an educated Indian wife and judged by Indian conditions and standards would amount to worst form of insult and cruelty, warranting the claim of the wife being allowed. Such allegations made in the written statement or in cross-examination,

---

[75]   See Chapter 1 *Personal Laws and Women's Rights* of the first volume.

[76]   II (2002) DMC 371 P&H

[77]   I (2003) DMC 685 SC : AIR 2003 SC 2462

satisfy the requirement of law. On going through the relevant portions of such allegations, we find that no exception could be taken to the findings recorded by the family court as well as the high court. We find that they are of such quality, magnitude and consequence as to cause mental pain, agony and suffering, amounting to the reformulated concept of cruelty in matrimonial law causing profound and lasting disruption of matrimonial life. The wife's apprehension that it would be dangerous for her to live with a husband who was taunting her in this manner is reasonable.

In *Puspa Kumari v. Parichhit Pandey*,[78] the wife had filed criminal cases against the husband and in-laws on grounds of cruelty and demand of dowry. In retaliation, the husband filed for restitution of conjugal rights. The trial court passed a decree in his favour. While setting aside the decree awarded by the trial court, the high court held:

In the present society, it is very difficult to force any person to live according to the desire of the other and, therefore, the S. 9 of the Hindu Marriage Act for restitution of conjugal rights is losing its force because even if the prayer for restitution of conjugal rights is allowed, this decree cannot be enforced against the desire of the wife who does not want to live with her husband. The cases filed by the wife under Section 498(A) of IPC and the Dowry Prohibition Act are pending against husband and in-laws. In these circumstances if the prayer for restitution of conjugal rights is allowed, it would amount to demolishing the cases filed by her. When this fact had come on record, prayer for restitution of conjugal rights cannot be allowed at all because there is always the danger that the wife may be put to further trouble in some other form.

In a petition filed by the husband for divorce on the ground of cruelty or desertion, the wife can plead restitution of conjugal rights. In *C.R. Chenthilkumar v. K. Sutha*,[79] it was held that there is no hard and fast rule that to express the intention to resume cohabitation, there should be an application for restitution of conjugal rights.

Restitution of conjugal rights is a mere paper decree as it cannot be enforced. But it helps to secure ancillary relief such as maintenance, custody of children, etc., in case the wife is not willing to file for divorce and wants retain her marital tie or is hoping for reconciliation with her husband. While moving the court on this ground, one needs to be cautious that the decree serves as a backdoor entry towards divorce on the ground of irretrievable breakdown of marriage.

In *Ram Niwas Singh Rathore v. Sumitra Singh Rathore*,[80] the Madhya Pradesh High Court upheld the decree of restitution of conjugal rights granted to the wife by the trial court on the ground that the husband denied the wife her right to lead marital life without any reasonable cause. The husband was held guilty of matrimonial misconduct for making reckless and unfounded allegations against the wife that she was leading an unchaste life and had an illegitimate daughter. He also ill-treated her and turned her out of the matrimonial home. Hence, it was held that he was not entitled to a decree of divorce on the ground of desertion. His plea was that the wife is living away from him since 1991 and had not cohabited with him even after a decree of restitution of conjugal rights. The court held that the husband cannot take advantage of his own wrong. Since the husband, without any reasonable cause or excuse, had denied the wife marital company, it was held that the decree of restitution of conjugal rights was rightly passed against the husband by the trial court.

The Supreme Court, in *Saroj Rani v. Sudarshan Kumar Chhadha*,[81] held contrary to the above ruling. In this case, the wife filed a petition for restitution of conjugal rights. On 28

[78] 2005 MLR 551

[79] II (2008) DMC 278 Mad

[80] I (2004) DMC 442 MP

[81] AIR 1984 SC 1562

March 1978, the husband appeared and made a statement that the wife may be granted a decree in her favour. A year later, on 19 April 1979, the husband filed for divorce under Section 13 (1-A) on the ground that one year had passed since the passing of the decree and no actual cohabitation had taken place between the parties. The wife alleged that when she had gone to the husband's house to enforce the decree, she was turned out within two days. The wife also alleged that she had approached the lower court for enforcement of the decree. The trial court dismissed the husband's petition for divorce. In an appeal, the husband was granted a decree of divorce. The wife approached the Supreme Court for setting aside the high court decree on the ground that the husband cannot be permitted to take advantage of his own wrong. It was argued in her favour that Indian wives should not be made to suffer at the hands of cunning and dishonest husbands. But the Supreme Court ruled that non compliance of the decree of restitution of conjugal rights does not amount to 'taking advantage of his or her own wrong' as stipulated under Section 23(1) of the Hindu Marriage Act. The court held that whatever be the reasons, the marriage had broken down irretrievably and the parties could no longer live together as husband and wife and in such a situation it was better to close the chapter. If such conduct of the husband is intended to be treated as wrong, then it required legislation to that effect. The court commented:

We cannot rule out the possibility of a party obtaining a decree of restitution of conjugal rights and in not enforcing the same with the sole purpose of getting a divorce after the lapse of statutory period, but such abuse can be prevented only by bringing necessary legislation to plug the loophole. It is certainly a matter which requires the serious consideration of the Parliament. But as the law stands now, the court is helpless in the matter and can only grant relief as one naturally flowing from compliance of statutory requirement.

In the same ruling, the Apex Court also upheld the constitutional validity of this provision on the ground that it is a benevolent provision which would facilitate reconciliation and save the marriage.

When the husband himself obstructs the execution of the decree of restitution of conjugal rights, the wife is entitled to claim divorce. In *Prabhat Kumar Chakraborty* v. *Papiya Chakraborty*,[82] it was held that a husband cannot be allowed to take advantage of his own wrong. Since the husband himself had obstructed the compliance of the decree, it was held that it can not be construed as the wife was 'taking advantage of her own wrong'. Hence the wife was granted a decree of divorce. The Calcutta High Court held:

Mere non-compliance with the decree for restitution of conjugal rights cannot be taken as a 'wrong' within the meaning of S.23(1)(a)[83] of the Act as to deny the right of the wife to seek a divorce under S. 13(1A) (ii)[84] of the Act. But the situation may be different where the party consciously by force prevents the decree to be complied with and in such cases the party should not be allowed to take advantage of his/her own wrong. From the evidence on record we find that there was no sincere attempt by the husband to take back his wife. In his cross-examination the husband stated that he never wrote any letter to his wife after the disposal of the earlier suit for restitution of conjugal rights, expressing his intention to accept her back. On the contrary, he initiated different proceedings, both civil and criminal, against his wife, her parents and her brother. These incidents clearly suggest that there was no attempt by the husband to take back his wife.

In the context of the judgments discussed above, it appears that the more recent trend is a clear departure from the position adopted by

[82] 2004 MLR 576 (Cal)
[83] Section 23(1) (a), which deals with taking advantage of one's own wrong. This concept is discussed later.
[84] Non compliance of the decree of restitution of conjugal rights for one year.

the Supreme Court in *Saroj Rani* v. *Sudarshan Kumar Chhadha* (discussed earlier). Courts have refused to award a decree to a husband who is guilty of taking advantage of his own wrong. But if either of the parties, through their conduct prevent the decree from being executed, the aggrieved spouse would be entitled to a decree of divorce on the ground of non-compliance of the decree of restitution of conjugal rights.

Judicial Separation

HMA	SMA	ML	DA	PMDA
S.10	S.23	Uncodified	S.22	S.32/S.34

The relief of judicial separation flows in the reverse direction from the remedy of restitution of conjugal rights. While the latter is intended to enjoin the estranged couple, the former entitles one spouse to sever conjugal relations with the other, without breaking the matrimonial tie. The remedy was widely used when the stipulation for obtaining divorce were stringent. While adultery had to be proved to obtain divorce, judicial separation could be obtained on the grounds of desertion or cruelty. So for women who were subjected to cruelty, the right to judicial separation became an important remedy to obtain the right of separate residence, maintenance, and custody of children.

Later, this remedy was viewed as an intermediary measure for spouses who were facing matrimonial conflict but were not yet ready for a divorce and still harboured hopes of reconciliation. Since the parties continued to be husband and wife in law, they are not entitled to remarry after obtaining a decree of judicial separation. In the event of one party's death, the other will succeed to his or her property. Matters related to alimony and custody may be agitated even after a decree of judicial separation has been obtained.

In 1946, when Hindu women had not yet been granted the right to statutory divorce, the Hindu Married Women's Separate Residence and Maintenance Act came to their rescue. The Act recognized the right of Hindu wives to live separately and secure orders of maintenance for themselves under certain situations such as cruelty, desertion, bigamy, apostasy, contagious disease, etc. Later, the same remedy was incorporated into the Hindu Marriage Act, 1955 as 'judicial separation'.[85] After the enactment of the HMA, both the husband and the wife were granted the right to approach the courts for a decree of judicial separation on any one of the fault grounds specified in Section 13(1). The husband and wife are also entitled to file for judicial separation on failure of compliance with an order of restitution of conjugal rights.

With the exception of Muslim law, all other Indian matrimonial statutes contain a provision for judicial separation. Unlike in the remedy of restitution of conjugal rights, provisions relating to judicial separation are not identical across statutes.

Section 23 of the Special Marriage Act and Section 34 of the Parsi Marriage and Divorce Act provide for the remedy of judicial separation. Sections 22 and 23 of the Indian Divorce Act stipulates that a decree of judicial separation may be obtained on grounds of adultery, cruelty, and desertion of more than two years.

The court has the power to grant a decree for judicial separation in cases where the petitioner has not been able to establish a ground of divorce or has opted for judicial separation, instead of divorce. While the parties can reconcile after obtaining a decree of judicial separation and resume cohabitation, this is not mandatory. After one year of judicial separation, if the parties have not resumed cohabitation, either party becomes eligible for a decree of divorce merely on the

---

[85]   Section 10 of HMA

ground that they have not been able to resume cohabitation. They need not prove any other fault ground. This, in effect, becomes a ground of 'irretrievable breakdown of marriage.'[86]

At times when the parties are old and have been married for many years, the court may decline to dissolve the marriage and instead award a decree of judicial separation. In *Leeladevi* v. *Hari Rao*,[87] the Karnataka High Court held that the spouses had already entered the evening of their lives and it would be unlikely that either of them would find another life partner. Since they had been living separately for 15 years, it was held that continued separation sanctioned by a court decree would meet the ends of justice. The court awarded the wife Rs 7,500 per month as maintenance during the period of judicial separation.

Separation Agreements: These agreements are not part of matrimonial law but form part of the law of contract. This was viewed as an alternative to the remedy of judicial separation. Through private agreements, parties can free themselves from the duties and obligations of matrimonial cohabitation. Such agreements were prevalent in England. They came into vogue at a time when obtaining a decree of divorce or even judicial separation was extremely difficult. Parties began to enter into private agreements of separation so they could not be faulted for abdicating from their matrimonial responsibilities. Once entered into, neither party could accuse the other of desertion. Initially, when marriages were sacramental and indissoluble, such agreements were deemed to be against public policy under English law. After many conflicting opinions, a consensus was reached in the nineteenth century, whereby it was declared that such agreements were not against public policy (Diwan and Diwan, 1997: 393). But it was stipulated that such agreements should be entered into only when separation was inevitable or had already taken place.

While separation agreements may stipulate some consideration, the wife's claim of maintenance is not forfeited. Since the general law of contracts regulates the separation agreement, the general principles of a contract, such as consent, apply. An agreement may become voidable on the grounds of fraud, misrepresentation, coercion, and undue influence. Stipulations regarding maintenance, custody, and education of the children are enforceable. Hence in case of default, the aggrieved party can approach the courts for specific performance of the terms of agreement. The covenant granting maintenance must be payable under all circumstances even when the wife becomes unchaste, gets a divorce, judicial separation or annulment.

Muslim law provides for an agreement to live separately and the wife can exercise her right to separate residence and maintenance.[88]

The right of a spouse to sue for divorce, judicial separation, or nullity is not lost even if there is such a clause in the agreement to this effect. These are statutory rights which cannot be defeated by private agreements between the parties. Similarly, a clause in the agreement which bars the wife or children from claiming future maintenance is not binding as this is a statutory obligation of a husband/father.

The most important requisite of a separation agreement is the occurrence of actual separation or *de facto* separation. But primarily, separation under an agreement or a court decree is a separation from bed and board, which entitles the parties not to cohabit with each other. The woman is released from the covenant of a sexual contract with her husband

---

[86]   Section 13 (1-A) of HMA and Section 27 (2) of SMA.
[87]   I (2003) DMC 375 Kar

[88]   *Nizammul Haque* v. *Begum Noorjahan*, AIR (1966) Cal 465.

which she had entered into at the time of her marriage. So even if the parties live under the same roof, the wife (or the husband, as the case may be) will be entitled to exercise the freedom to refuse sexual intimacy. This principle was laid out by English courts in 1965 in *Montgomery* v. *Montgomery*.[89]

Section B

DIVORCE

DIVORCE ON FAULT GROUNDS

Fault Theory of Divorce

The central concern while transforming marriages from a status to contracts was to obtain the right to dissolve the marriage through a judicial decree, which would entitle the spouses to enter into a subsequent marriage. Once the sacred tie of marriage was severed, the bondage of marital servitude ended. This was a significant step for both Christians and Hindus.[90]

While today there are several ways through which a marriage can be dissolved, the 'fault theory' was the first step in this direction. Fault divorce forms the core of matrimonial litigation.

[89] (1964) 2 All ER 22
[90] As mentioned earlier, this concept was already incorporated within the Muslim law.

When the right to divorce or the right to dissolve the marital bond was first introduced into matrimonial law, it was based on the 'guilt' theory. Only if a spouse was guilty of a matrimonial misconduct or, in other words, had violated the terms or conditions of the marriage contract, did the other spouse have the right to dissolve the marriage. It was assumed that the purpose of the right to dissolve the marriage and set free the innocent spouse was to punish the party that had committed a matrimonial offence by depriving him or her of conjugal access of the other. Hence a marriage could not be dissolved on the ground of mutual incompatibility.

The basic ingredients of a fault ground divorce are:

i) There must exist a guilty party or a party who is responsible for having committed one of the specified matrimonial offences.

ii) There must also exist an innocent party who has suffered due to the misconduct of the guilty party.

iii) The innocent party should have no role in the cause of the misconduct i.e. there must be no collusion.

Initially, under English law as it evolved through the Matrimonial Causes Act of 1857,

HMA	SMA	DMMA	DA	PMDA
S.13	S.27	S.2	S.10	S.31/32

Table 1.4   Some Common Grounds of Divorce Under Various Personal Laws

Grounds	HMA	SMA	DMMA	DA	PMDA
Adultery/Living Immoral Life	S.13 (i)	S.27 (1) (a)	S.2 (viii) (b)	S.10 (1) (i)	S.32 (d)
Cruelty–physical or mental	S.13 (i) (i-a)	S.27 (1) (d)	S.2 (viii) (a)	S.10 (x)	S.32 (dd)
Desertion–actual or constructive	S.13 (i) (i-b)	S.27 (1) (b)	S.2 (ii)	S.10 (ix)	S.32 (g)
Unsoundness of Mind	S.13 (iii)	S.27 (i) (e)	S.2 (vi)	S.10 (1) (iii)	S.32 (b)
Suffering from Venereal Disease	S.13 (v)	S.27 (1) (f)	S.2 (vi)	S.10 (1) (v)	S.32 (e)
Unheard of for 7/4 years	S.13 (vii)	S.27 (1) (h)	S.2 (i)	S.10 (1) (vi)	S.31

adultery alone was a ground for divorce. Since Christian marriages were monogamous, a violation of the principle of monogamy through an act of adultery was deemed sufficient cause to dissolve the marriage. For women, it was made even more stringent as they had to prove incest, bigamy, cruelty, or desertion in addition to adultery. In 1923, the grounds for divorce for men and women were made equal and women could obtain a divorce on the ground of adultery simpliciter. In 1937, cruelty and desertion were included as grounds for divorce, along with incurable insanity.

Subsequently, the scope was widened to include certain physical inadequacies or diseases like impotency, mental disorder, epilepsy, contagious venereal diseases, and contagious diseases like leprosy. At this stage, the 'guilt' theory was replaced with a 'fault' theory since impotency, insanity, leprosy, epilepsy, etc., could not be termed as 'matrimonial misconduct'. They were more in the nature of an illness than a wilful misconduct. These were included as grounds of divorce since it was considered that healthy bodies are a necessary pre-condition for procreation and a disease in itself construed a matrimonial fault. Since marriage was deemed a sacrament, change of religion (apostasy) or relinquishing his or her religion (taking *sanyasa* under Hindu law) was also included as a matrimonial fault. By the time the Hindu Marriage Act was enacted in 1955, most of these had already been included as matrimonial faults under English family law. Hence, they were incorporated as grounds for divorce under the Hindu Marriage Act

As can be seen from the above table, there are six common grounds of divorce which are common to all personal laws. Apart from this, there are a range of other grounds which are stipulated under various personal laws. Some stipulations which appear as grounds for divorce under one personal law may be a ground for annulling the marriage under another law. For instance, pre-marriage pregnancy is accepted as a ground of divorce under Parsi law, but it is a ground for the annulment of marriage under the HMA and the SMA. Similarly, non-consummation of marriage is a ground for divorce under the Indian Divorce Act after the 2001 amendment. But it is a ground for annulment under Section 25 of the SMA. Under Muslim law, the wording is slightly different as non-fulfilment of matrimonial obligation which can easily be construed as the obligation to provide sexual access to the spouse. The HMA does not recognize this ground either for divorce or for annulment. But recently, the Supreme Court has ruled that refusal to have sexual intercourse amounts to mental cruelty.[91]

The Table 1.5 provides a listing of the grounds of divorce which are available under different personal laws.

The wording of a particular enactment reflects societal or community concern at the time the statute was enacted or the code was evolved. Any of these grounds can be relied upon to obtain a divorce depending upon the facts and circumstances of a particular case or the needs of the parties. Usually a lawyer will guide a litigant through the options which are available and choose the best one which can be applied. While only one ground will suffice, some lawyers prefer to opt for two or three grounds if the situation so warrants.

Some Commonly Used Fault Grounds

Regarding the substantive law of divorce, Lowe and Douglas (1998: 225) comment in the context of English law that the history of divorce law and its reform is marked by two features. First, there has always been a gap between the letter of law and the means by which spouses and their legal advisers use or sidestep its terms

---

[91]   *Samar Ghosh v. Jaya Ghosh*, I (2007) DMC 597 SC. The case is discussed in detail later.

to achieve their objective of ending the marriage tie. The second and related feature of divorce law is the extent to which it is the procedures, rather than the substance of the law which determine the grant of the divorce.[92] This comment brings to the fore the role of legal advise and litigation strategies which play an important role in divorce litigation. Though substantive law does play an important role in our matrimonial litigation, procedures and strategies also play an important role. Hence it would be useful to keep this in view as we go through this section.

The range of grounds stipulated under various personal laws is more a matter of academic interest and has very little bearing on legal practice. This is because litigation under matrimonial law revolves primarily around three grounds, adultery, cruelty, and desertion, which are of common application under various personal laws. Hence, they are discussed at length in this section. The wide scope awarded to cruelty through various judicial pronouncements renders even desertion and adultery redundant as these can also be construed as causing mental cruelty and can be brought under the rubric of cruelty. When multiple grounds such as adultery, cruelty, and desertion overlap in a judgment, it is difficult to segregate the decisions under the different subheads. So at times, a decree on the ground of cruelty may also have a reference to either adultery or desertion. But an attempt is made to categorize the judgments based on their primary focus.

Adultery

As previously mentioned, adultery was the first matrimonial fault introduced as a ground

for divorce. All matrimonial statutes have incorporated this ground, but under Muslim law, which awards men the right to polygamous marriages, the wording by which a wife can dissolve her marriage is slightly different. Instead of 'adultery' in general, Section 2 (viii)(b) of the Dissolution of Muslim Marriages Act stipulates 'association of women with ill-repute or leading infamous (immoral) life.

Adultery is both a matrimonial as well as a criminal offence (Section 497, IPC). In both instances, it is essential to prove a wilful act of sexual intercourse outside wedlock. It is not necessary to prove that the adulterer had the knowledge or reason to believe that the person concerned was the wife (or husband, as the case may be) of the petitioner. Though the words used in both the provisions is the same, there is a difference between the criminal and matrimonial law regarding 'adultery'. While under matrimonial law, both husband and wife can avail of this provision against the spouse who has committed an act of sexual intercourse outside marriage, in criminal law, the provision can be used only by the husband against the adulterer who has committed adultery with his wife. This is an archaic provision which views the wife as the property of the husband and an act of adultery as a violation of the proprietary rights. Under matrimonial law, the action is aimed at the erring spouse. The adulterer or the adulteress is merely a co-respondent.

Since 'sexual intercourse' contemplated by the matrimonial offence of adultery refers to consensual intercourse outside the wedlock, intercourse with the former or later wife of a polygamous marriage is not adultery. The mere attempt at sexual intercourse does not qualify for adultery. Further, the courts are emphatic on the point that rape is not adultery. A husband cannot obtain divorce on the ground of adultery merely because the wife was a victim of rape as the following case reveals:

[92] They further comment that after the reform in English law, the Family Law Act, 1996 has now replaced all pretence that substantive law is involved, by overtly introducing a purely procedural set of hurdles which must be jumped in order to achieve the desired divorce order.

In *Rajesh Kumar Singh* v. *Rekha Singh*,[93] the petition filed by the husband for divorce on the ground of the wife's adultery was dismissed by the trial court. In appeal, while affirming the order of the trial court, the Allahabad High Court held that the allegations against the wife were frivolous. The court clarified that the wife did not have any illicit relationship and that on the contrary, she was gang raped.

There is a fundamental difference between the two: one is with consent and the other is without consent", the court clarified. Regarding her refusal to disclose this fact to the husband, the court further commented: "Rape leaves physical as well as emotional scars on the victim. Her physical wounds may have healed but the emotional scars, though less visible, are more difficult to treat. The wife was not disclosing the entire picture, as it was natural for any woman to be hesitant to talk about such a gruesome crime against her.

The primary requirement of the ground for adultery is that the erring spouse should have consented to the act of adultery. Without consent, sexual relations outside wedlock do not constitute adultery. Similarly, if the party lacks the mental capacity to give consent on account of being a minor or a person of unsound mind, the presumption is that intercourse was not voluntary. Hence, the act cannot be used as a ground for divorce.

While even a single act of adultery, if proven, is sufficient ground to dissolve the marriage, courts are more inclined to grant divorce on an act of 'living in adultery' or a long-term adulterous relationship or cohabitation. The difference between 'living in adultery' and 'adultery' is that the former denotes a situation where there is a continuous adulterous relationship while the latter phrase refers to isolated acts of adultery.

In a petition for adultery, it is mandatory to add the adulterer as a co-respondent. In *Soya* v.

A.K. Mohanan,[94] the husband made allegations of adultery against his wife with his own brother but did not implead him as a co-respondent. In an appeal filed by the wife against the order of the trial court, the Kerala High Court set aside the decree of divorce on the ground that exemption granted to the husband against impleading his own brother as co-respondent in the proceedings was incorrect and hence the allegation of adultery was not proven. But if the allegations are that the spouse has had multiple sexual relationships or where the husband is specifically accused of visiting brothels, the requirement is dispensed with. Making the adulterer a party to the litigation makes the process cumbersome and time consuming. At times, there is collusion between the person named as adulterer and the husband which further complicates matters for the wife against whom the allegation of adultery is made. If the husband is able to obtain an affidavit from the adulterer, admitting the relationship, the courts will grant the husband a decree of divorce on the ground of adultery.

To be relied upon as a ground for divorce, the act of adultery should essentially be after the marriage has been solemnized. Pre-marital sexual intercourse or even pre-marriage pregnancy does not constitute 'adultery' under the provisions of matrimonial statutes and cannot be invoked as a ground for divorce. However, as discussed earlier, pre-marriage pregnancy is a ground of annulment of marriage. But this ground has to be strictly proved as per the stipulation under Section 12 (1) (d) of the Hindu Marriage Act.

In *Santoshi Devi @ Madhuri Devi* v. *Sadanand Das Goswami*,[95] the husband filed a petition on the ground of adultery and alleged that the wife was pregnant at the time of marriage and gave

93   AIR 2005 All 16

94   II (2006) DMC 298 Ker
95   II (2004) DMC 301 Jha

birth to a female child within six months of marriage. But there was no averment that after the said discovery, the husband had no marital intercourse with his wife. Hence it was held that he was not entitled to any relief under Section 12 (1) (d) of HMA (pre-marriage pregnancy). He also did not specify any incident of adultery after marriage. It was held that in order to avail of the ground of adultery under Section 13 (1) (i), it is mandatory that the act of sexual intercourse with a person other than the spouse should occur after the solemnization of marriage and during the subsistence of marriage. Despite the fact that the wife had delivered a child within six months of her marriage, this incident by itself could not be brought within the ambit of Section 13 (1) (i) of HMA.[96]

If the husband is able to prove that he had no access to the wife at the time when the child was conceived, it will be conclusive proof of adultery. Though there is a presumption of paternity under Section 112 of the Indian Evidence Act, it is a rebuttable and if the husband is able to make out a prima facie case of non access, the courts may grant permission for DNA testing to disprove paternity.[97] In *Jyothi Ammal* v. *K. Anjan*,[98] the husband's plea of adultery was upheld on the basis of the report of DNA test excluded the husband as the father of the child and he was awarded a decree of divorce on the ground of adultery.

The courts need to exercise great caution while deciding cases which contain flippant allegations against the moral character of women by their husbands. In *Meera* v. *Vijay Shankar*

Talchidia,[99] the trial court had awarded a decree of divorce to the husband on the ground of adultery and cruelty. In appeal, the Rajasthan High Court set aside the decree and commented:

The statement of the husband that he saw his wife sitting with a young boy who was indulging in undesirable and unjustified activities did not establish that the wife had any sexual relationship with that boy. It was also held that consuming three to four Crocin tablets, in an attempt to commit suicide, did not amount to cruelty to the husband for granting him a decree of divorce.

In *Rekhabai* v. *Gangaram*,[100] the trial court had granted a decree of divorce to the husband on the ground of the wife's adultery. The Madhya Pradesh High Court set aside the decree on the ground that the parties had lived happily together for about 8–10 years of marriage and had four children. The court commented:

There was no examination of witnesses of the locality and no clinching evidence. It is a case of oath against oath. From the statement of the wife it is clear that charges of adultery against her have not been proved. The trial court erred in awarding a decree of divorce to the husband.

In *Madhu* v. *Mukesh Naiyar*,[101] while setting aside the decree of divorce awarded by the family court at Jaipur, the Rajasthan High Court held that the evidence led by the husband was unworthy of credence. The court commented that it is highly unlikely that a woman, who sacrificed her youthful 24 years and lived as a '*pativrata*', would suddenly turn towards infidelity. The charge of adultery was levelled against a respectable woman, a mother of three children, implicating her maternal uncle and brother-in-law. The court commented that petty quibbles, trifling differences and quarrels that happen in day-to-day married life of spouses, do not amount to cruelty. Despite the quarrelsome conduct of the wife, the husband tolerated her

---

[96] See also *Arokia Rah Morias* v. *Mabai Bibai Rani Morias*, II (2007) DMC 209 Mad, where it was held that incident of adultery prior to marriage is not a ground of divorce.

[97] See the discussion on DNA testing in section titled 'Presumption of Paternity and DNA Testing' of Chapter 2 *Matrimonial Rights and Obligations*.

[98] I (2007) DMC 756 Mad

[99] II (1994) DMC 15 Raj

[100] II (2004) DMC 503 MP

[101] II (2007) DMC 762 Raj

and both led a normal sexual life, as a result of which the wife gave birth to three children. The husband failed to explain circumstances in which he came to lead a normal sexual life with his wife even after acts of alleged adultery and cruelty. The court further commented:

Despite all odds, the wife did not file even a single criminal complaint against the husband. On the contrary she devoted her life to serve her deaf, dumb and handicapped daughter. She still wants to live with her husband. The attention of the husband towards his invalid daughter is also required. In view of this, the marital ties cannot be snapped.

The high court also commented that the approach of the family court was too technical and hyper sensitive.

Since it is difficult to prove adultery through direct evidence of sexual intercourse in matrimonial cases, the courts usually rely on circumstantial evidence based on the theory of preponderance of possibilities. The court would rely upon trustworthy evidence which is coherent, consistent, and credible.[102] If the evidence is untrustworthy, the same will be disbelieved by the court. For instance, in *Gurbalwinder Singh v. Baljit Kaur*,[103] the husband alleged that he had witnessed his wife indulging in adultery but was not able to produce any evidence to corroborate it. Hence his petition was dismissed. But in *Rashmi v. Vijay Singh Negi*[104] the two sons deposed regarding their mother's adultery, including the son who was living with the mother. Hence it was held that the husband was successful in proving adultery.

In a rare case, *Swapna Ghosh v. Sadanand Ghosh*,[105] the wife found her husband in bed with the adulteress. Hence she was able to obtain divorce on the ground of adultery though the requirement for proving adultery was as stringent under the Indian Divorce Act as under the criminal law.[106] However, this is an extremely rare incident. Evidence of cohabitation, evidence of nights spent in hotels through hotel registers, photographs of physical intimacy, evidence of visits to brothels, contracting venereal diseases, confessions by concerned parties, the birth of a child when the husband had no access to the wife at the time of conception, reports of DNA tests in cases of disputed paternity, etc., have been used as evidence to prove adultery.

Adultery by the wife is also a relevant issue while claiming maintenance under Section 125, Cr.PC. Under Section 125 (4), a woman living in adultery is not entitled to maintenance. Hence, in order to wriggle out of the obligation of paying maintenance, husbands routinely make the allegation of adultery. If proven, this becomes a complete defence against the claim of maintenance by the wife. So women have to endure a great deal of humiliation during litigation while claiming maintenance. The proximity in law between sexual morality and right to maintenance has been discussed in detail later in the following chapter under the sub-title, *Right to Maintenance*.[107]

Cruelty

The notion of 'cruelty' as a ground of divorce has gone through substantial expansion over the last four decades. In contemporary legal discourse, a wide range of issues of matrimonial

---

[102] *Nidhi Dalela v. Deepak Dalela*, II (2002) DMC 182 Raj; *P.V. Joseph Christian v. Deenamma Christian* II, (2004) DMC 592 Guj.

[103] I (2005) DMC 595 P&H

[104] II (2007) DMC 559 Utt

[105] AIR 1989 Cal 1

[106] But the situation has been changed after the amendment of 2001 to the Indian Divorce Act of 1869 and courts are now mandated to apply the principle of 'preponderance of probability' rather than strict proof as per the maxim 'beyond reasonable doubt' as applicable under other matrimonial statutes.

[107] See Chapter 2 *Matrimonial Rights and Obligations*.

conflict can be brought within its purview. This has led to cruelty being the most widely used ground of matrimonial misconduct. Prior to the 1976 amendment to HMA and SMA, cruelty was defined within the narrow confines of conduct which would be harmful or injurious to the petitioner. Hence it was necessary to base the allegation of cruelty upon acts of physical violence.

In 1975, in the leading case *Dastane* v. *Dastane*,[108] the Supreme Court held that the standard of proving cruelty is not 'beyond reasonable doubt' as per the principles of English law. It was held that behaviour which would cause a reasonable apprehension in the mind of the petitioner that it will be harmful or injurious for him or her to live with the respondent would constitute 'cruelty'. The Supreme Court warned that the courts are not dealing with 'ideal' couples but with a particular man and a particular woman before it. Their social context is a relevant factor while determining the extent of cruelty that is inflicted by one spouse upon the other. In the following year, the Marriage Laws (Amendment) Act, 1976 widened the scope of the statutory provision to include conduct due to which it would be impossible for the petitioner to live with the respondent without agony, torture, or distress.[109]

From 'proof beyond reasonable doubt', to behaviour which would be 'harmful or injurious', the legal concept of cruelty has been diluted to 'behaviour which would cause agony, torture or distress'.

In the leading case, *V. Bhagat* v. *D. Bhagat*,[110] the Supreme Court explained the concept of mental cruelty as conduct which inflicts upon the other party such mental pain and suffering as would make it impossible for that party to live with the other. It must be of such a nature that the parties cannot reasonably be expected to live together. It is not necessary to prove that the mental cruelty is such as to cause injury to the health of the petitioner. Expanding further the guidelines laid down in *Dastane*, the court held that while deciding the issue of cruelty, regard must be had to the social status and educational level of the parties, the society they move in, the possibility or otherwise of the parties ever living together. What is cruelty in one case may not amount to cruelty in another. It is a matter to be determined on the basis of the facts and circumstances of each case.

Over the years, the term 'mental cruelty' was expanded further and incidents such as abusive behaviour, denial of access to sexual intercourse, non-payment of maintenance, denying access to children, denial of food and shelter, taunting and insulting comments about the spouse or family members, refusal to have a child, forced abortion or abortion without consent, false allegations of adultery, filing false criminal complaints, false allegations of sexual intimacy of the spouse with parents, siblings, or close relatives, etc., came to be construed as mental cruelty. The scope of this provision is so vast that even acts of adultery and desertion can be construed as cruelty. But normal wear and tear of married life cannot be construed as cruelty. This Section attempts to trace the changing notion of cruelty in judicial discourse.

The Madras High Court, in *A. Vishwanathan* v. *G. Lakshmi*,[111] explained that the concept of cruelty is deeply influenced by socio-cultural values and stereotypes regarding the roles of husband and wife in a marriage. As the perception of the parties, their standing in the eyes of the society

---

[108] AIR 1975 SC 1534

[109] *Meera* v. *Vijay Shankar Talchidia*, II (1994) DMC 15 Raj.

[110] (1994) 1 SCC 337: AIR 1994 SC 710

[111] AIR 207 Mad 462 (NOC)

and the emerging compulsions of modern life change, the definition of cruelty also would change. For example, in 1985, the Allahabad High Court, in *Kalpana Srivastava v. S. N. Srivastava*,[112] held that refusal to serve tea to visitors and husband's friend amounts to cruelty. But in 2007, the Delhi High Court, in *Narinder Singh v. Rekha*,[113] ruled that refusal to serve tea to the visitors does not amount to cruelty.

Since it is not possible to explore the vast case law on this subject within the limited scope of this book, an attempt is made to list out some broad categories of recurring themes. This will hopefully provide a glimpse of the nature of contests which occur within the broad realm of 'cruelty' in our matrimonial courts.

Filing Criminal Complaints Against the Husband and his Family

A recurring theme within the ambit of 'cruelty' is whether filing a criminal complaint against the husband and his family amounts to cruelty. There are two aspects to this issue. The first is, whether acquittal of the accused would entitle him to file for divorce on this ground and second, whether the complaint was false and the husband and his family were subjected to undue harassment and mental trauma on account of it.

In the leading case, *Shobha Rani v. Madhukar Reddi*,[114] the Supreme Court laid out that acquittal in a criminal case filed by the wife in itself cannot be construed as cruelty to the husband. The court explained the difference between cruelty under criminal law and matrimonial law and held that the degree of proving the offence is not the same under them. While in a criminal case, cruelty has to be proved 'beyond reasonable doubt', in matrimonial litigation, allegations have to be proved by 'preponderance of probabilities'. In this case, the wife had filed for divorce on the ground of cruelty. The trial court and the high court dismissed her plea on the ground that she could not prove the allegations. But the Supreme Court granted her a divorce on the ground that demands for dowry constitutes cruelty.

In *Chiranjeevi v. Lavanya*,[115] the Andhra Pradesh High Court held that mere acquittal in a criminal case filed by the wife against her husband and in-laws cannot be treated as an incident in favour of the husband, entitling him to seek divorce on grounds of cruelty. The court explained that cruelty has to be such as to cause reasonable apprehension in the petitioner's mind that it will be harmful or injurious for him/her to live with the other spouse. It was stated by the wife that harassment meted out at the hands of her husband and his parents became intolerable that it drove her to attempt suicide by pouring kerosene on herself. The court saw no merit in the contention of the husband that it is not safe to continue the marital relationship with a wife who has the tendency to commit suicide. The conduct of the husband in disputing paternity of the child goes against him and he cannot be allowed to take advantage of his own misconduct. The high court upheld the trial court's order of dismissal of the husband's petition and held that the husband failed to make out a case of cruelty against his wife.

In *Usha Rani v. Sham Lal*,[116] it was held that the criminal complaint filed by the wife under Sections 498A and 406 of the IPC that she was subjected to cruelty due to the demand for dowry by the husband and his family members

---

[112] AIR 1985 All 253
[113] AIR 2007 Del 118
[114] (1988) 1 SCC 105

[115] II (2006) DMC 553 AP
[116] II (2008) DMC 202 P&H

was true. On the other hand, the husband's allegations of cruelty were not proved and the incidents of cruelty mentioned in the petition were minor and could be construed as part of normal 'wear and tear' of married life. Hence, the Punjab and Haryana High Court set aside the decree of the trial court granting the husband divorce on the ground of cruelty.

If the criminal complaint filed by the wife against her husband is found to be false, it would amount to cruelty. For instance in *P. Mohan Rao* v. *Vijayalakshmi*,[117] where the wife in her criminal complaint implicated not only her husband but also his parents, brothers, and sister due to which they had to suffer imprisonment for a considerable time, the Andhra Pradesh High Court held that she was guilty of cruelty. In *Alka Dadhich* v. *Ajay Dadhich*,[118] it was held that mere filing of a criminal complaint on the ground of cruelty and demand for dowry would not amount to cruelty unless the complaint is found to be false. However, where the wife not only filed criminal cases against the husband and his family members, as a result of which they were detained in police custody, but she was also guilty of several other acts which amounted to cruelty, the husband's plea was upheld. The other acts of which she was accused of are—wandering around bare headed in the presence of her in-laws; sitting in the *verandah* only in her petticoat, refusing to serve tea and snacks to husband's friends when they visited him, defying his directions, etc.

Evidently, the question as to which acts construe cruelty is a matter of interpretations of cultural norms. The stereotypical roles assigned to women within a society and judicial notions regarding women's position are important factors for determining cruelty.

Wife's Refusal to Reside in the Joint Family

Since the joint family system still prevails among many rural and even urban communities, a woman's desire to set up a separate nuclear family often leads to matrimonial conflicts leading to divorce. Within a traditional set up, this demand may be construed as cruelty. But there are several judgements which have acknowledged the changing social scenario and the needs of a modern, educated woman to break away from the traditional joint family set up.

In *Rakesh Goyal* v. *Deepika Goyal*,[119] it was held that repeated demands of the wife for a separate residence do not amount to cruelty. The high court commented that the courts cannot be oblivious to present-day trends in society wherein most newly-wed women want their privacy and want to live separately from their in-laws. In *Ratna Banerjee* v. *Chandra Madhab Banerjee*[120] it was held that if the husband is in a transferable job and stays at different places away from the parental house, the demand of the wife to stay with him would not amount to cruelty. In *Arun Chettri* v. *Madhu Chettri*,[121] it was held that reluctance of the wife to live with her husband's mother and sister does not amount to cruelty.

In *Ramesh Jangid* v. *Sunita*,[122] the Rajasthan High Court took a contrary view and held that the Indian society expects a son to look after his aged parents and casts a duty upon him not only to provide for them financially but also to maintain a joint habitation with them so that he can accord them proper care. In such cases, if the wife insists that he should maintain a separate residence, it amounts to cruelty. Since the husband was the sole earning member, it was

---

[117] AIR 2007 NOC 2494 AP
[118] AIR 2007 NOC 158 Raj

[119] I (2007) DMC 457 P&H
[120] I (2007) DMC 566 Cal
[121] AIR 2007 NOC 563 MP
[122] AIR 2007 Raj 160

not possible for him to abandon his aged parents. At this point, the wife became abusive and refused to have physical relations with him. There was also a separation of fourteen years. In this context, the husband was awarded a decree of divorce on the ground of wife's cruelty and desertion.

Wife's Refusal to Perform Marital Obligations

Another recurring concern revolves around 'marital obligations' or, in other words, sexual access. The contract of marriage encompasses within it the right of mutual conjugality. Hence denial of sexual relationship to the spouse is construed as cruelty. Non-consummation of marriage, denying sexual access, and incapacity to perform sexual acts are matrimonial offences which will entitle the other spouse to either dissolve or annul the marriage. While the obligation is mutual, more often than not, it is the women who are called upon to fulfil this obligation. Hence withdrawal from sexual contact becomes a ground for divorce. In *Samar Ghosh* v. *Jaya Ghosh*,[123] while examining allegations of mental cruelty on the ground of the wife's refusal to cohabit with her husband, the Supreme Court ruled that it amounts to mental cruelty and commented as follows:

Once the wife had accepted the marriage, she had to respect the marital bond and discharge obligations of marital life, which includes cohabitation. The refusal to do so would amount to mental cruelty.

But the court issued a note of caution that mental cruelty cannot be given a comprehensive definition since cruelty in one case might not amount to cruelty in another. There can never be any straightjacket formula or fixed parameters for determining mental cruelty in matrimonial matters. Mental cruelty needs to be evaluated on the basis of facts and circumstances of each case and has to be decided on a case to case basis. Therefore, one can construe that not every case of refusal to fulfil marital obligations of sexual intercourse amounts to cruelty. If non-consummation is not entirely due to the fault of the wife, it cannot be construed as cruelty, as held in *Lakshmi Priya* v. *K.V. Krishnamurthy*.[124]

Normal Wear and Tear of Married Life is not Cruelty

A term which is used frequently while determining the extent of cruelty is 'normal wear and tear of married life'. Courts have held that the normal wear and tear of married life and minor quarrels do not constitute cruelty. To constitute cruelty under matrimonial statutes, the conduct of the other spouse has to be such that the affected spouse cannot reasonably be expected to live with him or her. Allegations of cruelty have to be weighty and not frivolous.

In *Asha Gupta alias Anju Gupta* v. *Rajiv Kumar Gupta*,[125] while setting aside the decree of divorce granted to the husband by the trial court, the high court held minor quarrels cannot be construed as cruelty. The court also commented that irretrievable breakdown of marriage cannot be invoked for dissolving the marriage. In *Nitin Tidke* v. *Sujata*,[126] it was held that a mismatch of personalities and friction caused thereof is not cruelty. The husband could not prove that he had suffered mental agony to such an extent that it could no longer be possible to continue co-habitation. In *Pran Nath* v. *Pushpa Devi*[127] and *Sukhwinder Kaur* v. *Jatinderbir Singh*,[128] it was held that the wife staying away from the matrimonial home for a few days cannot be construed as cruelty. It was

---

[123] (2007) 4 SCC 511: I (2007) DMC SC 597

[124] AIR 2007 NOC 800 Mad
[125] AIR 2005 P&H 134
[126] I (2007) DMC 446 Bom
[127] I (2007) DMC 211 Del
[128] I (2007) DMC 492 P&H

held that divorce cannot be granted based on general pleadings without citing specific incidents. In *C.R. Chenthilkumar* v. *K. Sutha*,[129] the husband's allegations that the wife refused to cook food and to have sexual intercourse, that she was mentally abnormal and she deserted the matrimonial home were not supported by appropriate evidence. The court commented that the allegations amount to ordinary wear and tear of matrimonial life and cannot be construed as cruelty. In *Jitender Singh* v. *Yeshwanti*,[130] the parties stayed together as husband and wife even after filing of divorce petition. Hence it was held that the alleged cruelty was condoned and the matrimonial bond was not ruptured beyond repair. The court also commented that a solitary incident of cruelty cannot be a ground for dissolution of marriage. Further, it was held that the ground of irretrievable breakdown of marriage cannot be invoked when one of the spouses is genuinely interested in living with other, forgiving and forgetting existing bitterness.

Wife's Demands for a Better Quality of Life
The desire to continue one's education or even for a better quality of cosmetics cannot be construed as cruelty. In *Padam Singh* v. *Anita Bai*,[131] it was held that the wife's demands for a better quality of face powder and to go shopping or not behaving properly with her husband or mother-in-law are not acts which amount to cruelty. The husband failed to produce reliable evidence that the behaviour of his wife was so cruel as to cause reasonable apprehension that it is not possible to continue married life. The court commented: 'It is clear that the wife has not deserted the husband but the wife was

living separately because the husband refused to keep her in the matrimonial house.'

In *Binapani Bhattacharjee* v. *Pratap Bhattacharjee*,[132] the wife came to her parents' house for the delivery of her child and stayed back to appear in her M.A. examination. Later, when she returned along with her brother to the matrimonial home, the husband misbehaved with her. Subsequently, he filed for divorce using this incident to prove cruelty. Dismissing the allegations of cruelty, the court held that the husband cannot take objection to his wife's decision to study further. The court commented that appearance in an exam cannot be termed as cruelty under any circumstances.

Filing criminal complaints for return of *stridhana* under Sections 406 and 498A of the IPC or initiating proceedings for maintenance can not be construed as cruelty which would entitle the husband to a decree of divorce. These are statutory rights which the wife is entitled to enforce against her husband.

When the Husband is Guilty of Misconduct
If the husband himself is guilty of a matrimonial misconduct, he cannot take advantage of his own wrong and obtain a decree of divorce.

In *S.K. Karg* v. *Chanchal Kumari*,[133] the Punjab and Haryana High Court held that baseless allegations of cruelty constitute mental cruelty of the gravest kind. Merely a claim that the wife used to beat the children cannot be construed as cruelty against the husband. On the other hand, it was proved that the husband caused injuries to the wife, resulting in a fracture of her arm for which she had to be operated upon. The court commented that it was the husband who had treated the wife with cruelty. In *Vinod Kumar*

---

[129] II (2008) DMC 278 Mad
[130] II (2008) DMC 482 Del
[131] I (2004) DMC 112 MP

[132] I (2007) DMC 460 Gau
[133] I (2005) DMC 96 P&H

Gupta v. *Santosh Gupta*,[134] it was held that if the wife is unable to receive proper treatment for mental stress caused by the husband and this aggravated her mental strain, it cannot be construed as cruel behaviour towards him.

Allegations of Cruelty by Wife Upheld

In order to obtain a decree of divorce, the allegations have to be grave and weighty and the husband should be able to prove them. The following instances were held to be sufficiently grave to award the husband a decree of divorce.

In *Susarla Subrahmanya Sastry* v. *S. Padmakshi*,[135] the allegations made by the wife against the husband that he was unable to perform sexual intercourse could not be proved. Hence it was held that these allegations amount to cruelty. It was further held that because of non co-operation and hostile attitude of the wife, the husband was subjected to serious traumatic experience which can be termed as 'cruelty'. Further, the court commented that when a marriage has irretrievably broken down, the question whether it was consummated or not loses it importance.

In *Mayadevi* v. *Jagadish Prasad*[136] it was proved that the wife used to demand money from the husband for her father and would quarrel with him if it was not paid. She would often not provide food to her husband, threaten to kill the children and implicate him in a false dowry case, mercilessly beat up the children and often tie them with ropes. While she was pregnant with the fourth child, she pushed her three children into a well and jumped in after them. She was rescued, but the three children died. A case of murder registered against her was pending. The Supreme Court held that the

wife's conduct amounted to cruelty and confirmed the decree of divorce granted by the lower courts.

In *Suman Kapur* v. *Sudhir Kapur*[137] it was held that the wife was interested in her career and neglected her matrimonial obligation. She terminated her pregnancy without the consent or knowledge of her husband. She also made allegations against the husband that he was married to another lady and referred to her in-laws as 'ghosts'. It was held that this behaviour amounts to mental cruelty. But while awarding the husband the decree of divorce, the court directed him to pay Rs 5,00,000 as alimony to the wife.

In *Harish Chandra Singh Chilwal* v. *Pushpa*,[138] the wife insulting the husband in the presence of others and taunting him that she was earning more than her husband was construed as cruelty. In *Indu Mishra* v. *Kavid Kumar Gaur*[139] it was held that baseless allegations of illicit relationship between the husband and his sister-in-law constitute cruelty. In *Neena Malhotra* v. *Ashok Malhotra*[140] it was held that allegations regarding illicit relationship of the husband with his mother amounts to cruelty of the highest degree as it casts aspersions on the pious relationship of mother and son.

Allegations of Cruelty by Husband Upheld

In the following cases, the wife's allegations of cruelty against the husband were upheld and she was granted a decree of divorce.

In *Binod Biswal* v. *Tikli @ Padmini Biswal*,[141] the wife alleged cruelty on the part of her husband. She also alleged sexual misbehaviour on the part of her father-in-law but the same could

---

[134] I (2007) DMC 871 Del
[135] II (2005) DMC 707 AP
[136] I (2007) DMC 325 SC: AIR 2007 SC 1426

[137] II (2008) DMC 774 SC
[138] II (2008) DMC 454 Utt
[139] I (2007) DMC 427 Raj
[140] II (2008) DMC 94 P&H
[141] II (2002) DMC 446 Ori

not be proved. The family court upheld her plea and granted her divorce. The court also ordered maintenance of Rs 400 per month and return of her stridhan. In an appeal against the order filed by the husband, the high court upheld the decree of divorce.

In *Puran Singh* v. *Shanty Devi*,[142] it was held that false charges of adultery levelled against the wife by the husband amounts to cruelty. The decree of divorce granted by the family court and maintenance of Rs 400 per month awarded to her was upheld by the high court. In *Man Mohan Vaid* v. *Meena Kumari*,[143] the marriage was inter-caste, contracted by the couple against the wishes of their parents. Thereafter the husband failed to not only protect the wife against humiliation and mental torture caused by his father and sister, but was himself guilty of beating and humiliating her and demanding dowry. It was held that the trial court was justified in holding the husband guilty of cruelty.

In a recent case, *Rayala M Bhuvaneswari* v. *Nagaphanender Rayala*,[144] the husband had taped the telephone conversations which the wife had with her parents and her friends while she was residing with him in the USA. In proceedings before the family court at Hyderabad, the wife denied part of the conversation and the husband filed an application for the wife to undergo a voice test. The same was granted by the court. In an appeal filed by the wife against this, it was held that tape recording telephone conversations is violative of the right to privacy under Article 21 of the Constitution and the same is not admissible as evidence in proceedings before the court. It was held that the tapes, even if true, cannot be used as evidence against the wife and hence there was no question of forcing the wife to undergo a voice test and then asking experts to compare portions denied by her with her admitted voice.

Desertion

Desertion implies the permanent abandoning of one spouse by the other. It is necessary that desertion should be accompanied without a reasonable cause, and without the consent of the other party. The statutory period for desertion to become a ground for divorce is two years in which there should be complete withdrawal by one spouse from carrying out his or her marital obligations. The essential elements of desertion are:

i) separation or *factum deserdendi*

ii) the intention to desert or *animus deserdendi*

The intention to desert does not have to precede the fact of separation. The moment, however, desertion is contemplated, the individual becomes a deserter. Supervening desertion thus refers to a situation where the factual separation already existed, but the intention to desert followed much later.

Desertion may be either actual or constructive. Hence, the spouse who leaves the matrimonial home may not always be the deserter. The spouse who is residing in the matrimonial home and has made it intolerable for the other spouse to continue living under the same roof can be construed as the deserter under the notion of 'constructive desertion'. This legal premise is particularly relevant to women who are compelled to leave their matrimonial home due to domestic violence or dowry harassment. As per Indian tradition, the bride usually has to leave her natal family and enter the matrimonial home, which is often a joint family. This family may not accept the young bride or subject her to humiliation and ill treatment. When the

---

[142] II (2002) DMC 279 Raj
[143] II (2003) DMC 723 Del
[144] II (2008) DMC 327 AP

situation becomes unbearable, the wife will be compelled to leave the matrimonial home. This act of leaving the matrimonial home cannot give rise to a petition for divorce on the ground of her desertion. The Supreme Court and several high courts have explained the notion of constructive desertion and held that the husband, who had caused the wife to leave, is guilty of constructive desertion. Further, he cannot take advantage of his own wrong. *Bipinchandra* v. *Prabhavati* and *Lachman* v. *Meena* are two landmark rulings of the Supreme Court which extended the scope of constructive desertion. Both these cases were filed by husbands. The trial court awarded them the decree of divorce on the ground of their wives' desertion. In appeal, the Bombay High Court set aside the decree of divorce, which the Supreme Court upheld.

Bipinchandra v. *Prabhavati*,[145] was a case where the wife left the matrimonial home due to allegations of adultery against her. When she wanted to return home, the husband sent her a telegram: 'Must not send Prabha'. Thereafter, he filed a petition for divorce on the ground of desertion. The trial court upheld his plea and awarded him a decree of divorce. But in an appeal, the Bombay High Court reversed the trial court decree and held that since the husband had prevented the wife from returning, it was he who was guilty of constructive desertion. The court explained the ingredients of desertion as follows:

Where the wife is forcibly turned out of her marital home by the husband, he is guilty of "constructive desertion" because the test is not who left the matrimonial home. If one spouse by his words and conduct compels the other spouse to leave the marital home, the former would be guilty of desertion, though it is the latter who has physically separated from the other and has been made to leave the marital home. ...The fact that the wife leaves her husband's place in shame

not having the courage to face the husband after the discovery of her reprehensible conduct does not render her in the eyes of the law a deserter.

In *Lachman* v. *Meena*,[146] the husband petitioned for judicial separation on the ground of the wife's desertion. In her reply, the wife stated that she was ill treated and constantly taunted by her mother-in-law. The trial court upheld the husband's plea and awarded a decree in his favour, but the Bombay High Court set aside the decree of divorce. The husband approached the Supreme Court which discussed the issue of desertion in detail and concluded that 'desertion in its essence means the intentional permanent forsaking and abandonment of one spouse by the other without that other's consent, and without reasonable cause'. The Court pointed out that there could not be a standard criterion of desertion. The nature of the act is such that it must be seen in the context of specific circumstances and motives.

The next two decades witnessed further expansion of the notion of constructive desertion. Discussed below are some judgments of 1980s and 1990s where high courts have rejected the husband's plea of desertion and pinned the blame on him for constructive desertion.

In *Om Wati* v. *Kishan Chand*,[147] the Delhi High Court set aside the trial court decree of divorce awarded to the husband on the ground of wife's desertion. It was held that the husband's refusal to attend the funeral of their child amounted to a conscious disregard of his marital duties. The husband had forsaken his family and the wife had no alternative but to separate as she could not continue living with her irate husband. Despite the parties living separately,

---

[145] AIR 1957 SC 176

[146] AIR 1964 SC 40
[147] AIR 1985 Del 43

the court observed that there was no *animus deserdendi* on the part of the wife and that it was the husband who was the deserter and it was a case of constructive desertion.

In *Kamal Kumar* v. *Kalyani*,[148] the Calcutta High Court observed that physical act of departure by the wife does not make her the deserter. If the husband created a situation in which it was impossible for her to live and she left her matrimonial home as a result of such a situation, it is the husband who is the deserter. The wife is entitled to insist that she should not be exposed to unpleasant situations and that suitable provisions should be made for her to live with her husband in privacy. If the husband fails to provide this and the wife leaves the matrimonial home, indicating that she is willing to join her husband as and when he is able to provide her such a home, it cannot be held as desertion by the wife entitling the husband for a decree of divorce. In *Renganayaki* v. *Arunagiri*,[149] the husband had an illicit relationship with the maid servant and he beat up the wife when she complained about it. The Madras High Court held that the wife was compelled by these circumstances to leave the home but this does not amount to desertion. In *Teerth Ram* v. *Parvati Devi*,[150] the wife insisted on a separate home away from husband's family and left the matrimonial home. The Rajasthan High Court held that the wife was not guilty of desertion as the mere fact of physical separation does not constitute desertion.

This concept was expanded further in the rulings of various high courts after 2000. The courts have clearly and emphatically ruled that if a husband is guilty of a matrimonial misconduct due to which the wife was compelled to leave the matrimonial home, he is not entitled to obtain a decree of divorce on the ground of his wife's desertion. In *Lovely Thomas* v. *Tomy Alexander*,[151] it was held that it is not relevant who left the matrimonial home. If the husband's words and conduct compel the wife to leave the marital home, he is guilty of desertion, even though it may be the wife who physically separated from the marital home. It is case of constructive desertion. In *Kamala Sharma* v. *Suresh Kumar Sharma*,[152] the woman's elder sister-in-law (the wife of her husband's eldest brother) was burnt to death by her in-laws. Hence the petitioner left the matrimonial home. It was held that the desertion was not without reasonable cause. In *Bishwanath Panday* v. *Anjana Devi*,[153] where the wife was living separately in a room, provided by the husband under compromise in proceedings for maintenance and the husband had another woman living with him, it was held that the separation does not amount to desertion by the wife. In *Bhupinder Kaur* v. *Budh Singh*,[154] the husband obtained divorce on the ground that his wife deserted him twenty two years ago. This was decreed in his favour. In appeal, the high court held that the husband had made no effort to take custody of the children, send them money, or resume cohabitation with his wife. The fact that the wife did not attend the cremation of the husband's parents or the fact that she did not file for restitution of conjugal rights cannot give rise to cruelty or desertion on her part.

In *Kishan Chand* v. *Smt. Munni Devi*,[155] the husband had an extra marital affair and had driven his wife out of the matrimonial home. After nine and a half years, he filed for divorce

---

[148] AIR 1988 Cal 111
[149] AIR 1993 Mad 174
[150] AIR 1995 Raj 86

[151] I (2000) DMC 609 Ker
[152] II (2001) DMC 680 Raj
[153] II (2002) DMC 397 Jha
[154] I (2002) DMC 735 P&H
[155] II (2003) DMC 472 Del

on the ground of cruelty and desertion. Denying him the decree the high court held:

The conduct of the husband compelled the wife to leave the matrimonial home and prompted her not to withdraw criminal proceedings and to back out from the compromise. The main facts considered by the district judge to conclude that the wife did not desert her husband was the refusal of the husband to transfer one room in his house to his wife's name, which made her feel insecure. The wife was justified in staying away from her husband as she had reasonable apprehension that she would continue to be ill treated and beaten up.

In *Pradip Kumar Kalita* v. *Hiran Kalita*,[156] the husband refused to admit the wife into his official residence and compelled her to live in his home in the village, along with his elder brother. It was held that she had justifiable reason to reside with her parents. It was held that the conduct of the husband in leaving his newly married wife with a minor child in the house of his elder brother would in itself amount to cruelty on his part. In *Damayanti Dei* v. *Pabitra Mohan Srichandan*,[157] after fourteen years of marriage, the husband filed for annulment of marriage before the family court at Cuttack on the ground of his wife's epilepsy and also that she was a minor at the time of marriage. After four years of marriage, the husband had remarried. Though the ground of annulment was not proved, the family court upheld his plea of desertion and awarded him a decree of divorce. The high court set it aside and held as follows:

When the second wife is living in the house, the first wife could not have volunteered to join him. Hence her staying separately from her husband cannot be termed as a desertion on her part. Under such circumstances, the family court, Cuttack was wrong in interpreting separation of 14 years as desertion by the wife.

The decree of divorce was set aside and the wife was awarded costs.

In *Chandra Mohan Khurana* v. *Neeta Khurana*,[158] in his cross-examination, the husband had admitted that his wife used to come to meet him from Lucknow, availing of medical leave. He also admitted that twins were born out of the wedlock, but he never visited them for seven years. It was held that with this evidence, the backbone of his case of cruelty and desertion is demolished. On other hand, the wife stated that even when she got a transfer, the husband did not permit her to cohabit with him. Hence it was held that it was the husband who had deserted his wife.

In *Rajesh Kumar Chaudhary* v. *Sunita Chaudhary*,[159] decided by the Himachal Pradesh High Court in 2008, it was held that there was no evidence on record to show that the wife did not make any attempt to join her husband. The husband himself admitted that he was willing to accept the wife but his parents were opposed to it. Being a newly married lady, the husband's family ought to have been more sensitive to her and ought not to have taunted her as a bad omen in the family and humiliated her by addressing her as *kalo mai*. In these circumstances, even if the wife lived apart from her husband, she would be justified in doing so and it would not amount to desertion.

If the wife is not able to prove that she has a reasonable ground for staying away from the matrimonial home, the courts will uphold the husband's plea of wife's desertion and award him the decree of divorce. Some recent rulings where the husbands' plea of desertion was upheld are discussed below:

In *Adhyatma Bhattar Alwar* v. *Adhyatma Bhattar Sri Devi*,[160] the husband's plea of desertion was upheld by the trial court. In appeal, the

---

[156] II (2003) DMC 316 Gau
[157] II (2005) DMC 83 Ori
[158] I (2006) DMC 780 Utt
[159] II (2008) DMC 670 HP
[160] (2002) 1 SCC 308

high court reversed the decree. But the Supreme Court upheld the trial court decree and held that the wife had failed to substantiate a serious allegation of molestation by the father-in-law. She also did not demonstrate her willingness to return to the matrimonial home and fulfil her matrimonial obligations. In *Raj Kumar* v. *Madhu*,[161] the Rajasthan High Court upheld the husband's plea of desertion by the wife and held that the wife had failed to prove that her husband made it impossible for her to live with him. The court also set aside the order of maintenance awarded to her. However, the maintenance of Rs 3,000 per month awarded to the daughter was upheld and in addition the husband was directed to pay Rs 1,000 per month towards her college expenses.

In *Ramesh Kumar Sharma* v. *Akash Sharma*,[162] decided by the Himachal Pradesh High Court in 2008, the parties were living separately since 1982 and admittedly, there was no cohabitation between them since that time. The wife had alleged that the husband was in an illicit relationship with his sister-in-law (*bhabhi*). The trial court dismissed the petition filed by the husband on the ground that a previous petition filed by him on the same ground had been dismissed by the high court. While setting aside the decree and granting divorce to the husband, the high court commented that the approach of the trial court was not judicious. In *Prakash* v. *Kavita*,[163] when the husband filed for divorce on the ground of desertion, as a counterblast the wife filed a false criminal complaint against the husband and in-laws under Section 498A of IPC (cruelty and dowry harassment) and tried her best to get them arrested. Thereafter she also

filed an application for restitution of conjugal rights. The Rajasthan High Court held that the application cannot be termed as *bona fide* and the husband was entitled to a decree of divorce on the ground of wife's desertion.

In the following cases filed by the wife on the ground of the husband's desertion, it was held that the wife could not prove desertion on the part of her husband. In *Darshan Kaur* v. *Kashmir Singh*,[164] the husband had gone abroad nine years ago. After about three years he stopped sending money to maintain the family. Apart from this no other evidence was brought on record which could establish that he permanently brought an end to cohabitation. It was held that the criteria for establishing desertion was conspicuously absent from the pleadings and desertion was not proved. In *Conceicao Fernandes* v. *Milagres Fernandes*,[165] the residence of the wife, under Portuguese law which was applicable to the parties, is the place where the husband resides. The matrimonial domicile or matrimonial home is a place where husband and wife, as a married couple, have established their home. The wife's mother's home cannot be accepted as their matrimonial home even if parties resided there after marriage. That place was not the permanent abode of the parties. The fact that the husband left that house can not help the wife's case that he abandoned the matrimonial home.

If the petition for divorce is based on cruelty, the ground of desertion cannot be added as an after thought at the appeal stage. For instance in *Suram Pal Singh* v. *Savita*,[166] the husband's petition for divorce was based on the ground of cruelty. Since he was not successful in obtaining

---

[161] II (2008) DMC 759 Raj
[162] II (2008) DMC 315 HP
[163] II (2008) DMC 390 Raj

[164] I (2004) DMC 257 P&H
[165] I (2006) DMC 765 Bom
[166] I (2007) DMC 833 Del

a divorce on this ground, at the appeal stage, he sought to include desertion. The Delhi High Court held that the ground of desertion was argued for the first time in the proceedings before the high court whereas the focus of the petition in the trial court was on the ground of cruelty and hence, it cannot be allowed.

Though desertion is not explicitly stated as a ground under Muslim law, the failure to perform one's marital obligations for a period of three years amounts to constructive desertion under the Dissolution of Muslim Marriages Act. Section 2(ii) of the Act stipulates that the wife can sue her husband for divorce on the ground that he has neglected to maintain her. There is nothing in the wording of Section 2(ii) of the Act to suggest that the failure to maintain wife must be wilful.

In *Najiman Nissa Begum* v. *Serajuddin Ahmed Khan*,[167] the husband's failure to pay the dower even after several pleas by the wife was construed by the courts as indicative of the husband's neglect to maintain her. In *Kochu Mohannad Kunju Ismail* v. *Mohammad Kadeja Umma*,[168] the Kerala High Court held that the Muslim wife could obtain divorce from her husband if he had failed to maintain her for a period of two years or more, irrespective of whether his failure arose out of wilful neglect or the inability to provide maintenance. In *A. Dastagir Sab* v. *N. Shariffunnissa*,[169] the wife refused to live with her husband due to non-payment of dower and non-fulfilment of the condition of protection. It was held that the husband could not refuse maintenance to her. His refusal would amount to default on his part and would provide her a ground to dissolve her

marriage under Section 2(ii) of DMMA. In *Yousuf* v. *Sowramma*,[170] it was held that it is absolutely immaterial whether the failure to maintain the wife is due to poverty, failing health, loss of work, imprisonment, or to any other cause. In *Mehaboz Alam Dastagirsab Killedar* v. *Shagufta*,[171] a divorce petition was filed by the wife on the ground of desertion. It was held that the trial judge was justified in granting relief to her, awarding her a decree of dissolution of marriage under Section 2(ii) of DMMA.

Desertion remains an inchoate offence until an action is brought. The offence may be terminated with the resumption of cohabitation, sexual intercourse, the offer of reconciliation, or a supervening agreement to separate or supervening marital misconduct. Every offer of reconciliation or resumption of cohabitation must contain certain essential features in order to be valid. The offer must be genuine, accompanied by reasonable conditions and the person must not be guilty of any other matrimonial misconduct. In *Priyamvada Limaye* v. *Sharad Limaye*,[172] it was held that if the documents brought on record by the wife on the date of filing the petition express her willingness to cohabit with her husband, desertion will come to an end.

Additional Fault Grounds

Other grounds for divorce include conversion or apostasy, insanity or mental disorder, venereal diseases, leprosy, renunciation of the world, presumption of death, conviction and imprisonment for a criminal offence, non-resumption of cohabitation for two years after a decree

---

[167] AIR 1946 Pat 467
[168] AIR 1959 Ker 151
[169] AIR 1953 Mys 145

[170] AIR 1971 Ker 261
[171] AIR 2003 Kar 373
[172] I (2000) DMC 134 Bom

restitution of conjugal rights or judicial separation, non-compliance of an order of maintenance, rape and unnatural offences like homosexuality, sodomy, and bestiality, marriage performed when a person was a minor, etc. Epilepsy also used to be a ground of divorce, but through efforts of health activists this ground has been deleted by the Marriage Laws (Amendment) Act of 1999.

Mental Illness

Mental illness is a ground for annulment for marriage as well as for divorce. For annulment, unsoundness of mind vitiates consent for a valid marriage and the other spouse can file for annulment on this ground.[173] To qualify as a ground for divorce, the person must be unfit to carry on the normal responsibilities of married life. Section 13 (1) (iii) stipulates that to be a ground for divorce, the respondent must be of incurably unsound mind or suffering from mental disorder of such kind and to such an extent that the petitioner cannot be reasonably expected to live with the respondent. Explanation to this section defines mental disorder as a state of arrested or incomplete development of the mind, a psychopathic disorder, or any other disorder or disability of the mind, including schizophrenia. Mental disorder as a ground for divorce has two requirements: (i) the respondent should be suffering from a mental disorder of an incurable nature and (ii) as a result of such a disorder it would be impossible to live with the person.

In a recent case, *Vinita Saxena* v. *Pankaj Pandit*,[174] the Supreme Court upheld the wife's plea that her husband was suffering from schizophrenia. After an elaborate discussion on this mental disorder, the court ruled that the wife had provided ample medical evidence to prove the ground and is required to prove no other ground. The marriage had lasted only five months and was not consummated because the husband was incapable of performing his matrimonial obligations due to his mental disorder. The lower courts disbelieved the wife's contentions. But the Supreme Court held that due to the mental disorder of her husband, the wife had suffered cruelty by and at the behest of her husband. The court commented:

Facts and circumstances as well as aspects pertaining to humanity and life give sufficient cogent reasons to allow the appeal and relieve the wife from the shackles and chains of her husband to live her own life.

In all cases of this nature, courts scrutinise evidence and documents before passing judgment. Arguments that are based only on unfounded and reckless allegations which are not supported and substantiated by documentary proof or expert opinion are rejected. For instance, merely alleging that an individual is suffering from a mental disorder by proving some erratic or irrational behaviour is not sufficient evidence to prove a mental disorder. Hence, substantial proof regarding the degree and nature of the mental disorder is required. Prognosis of the disorder, i.e., whether it is curable and controllable is an important aspect which is examined during trial.

Venereal Diseases

Venereal diseases and sexually transmitted diseases like HIV/AIDS, syphilis, and gonorrhea are also grounds for divorce. Venereal disease as a ground is rarely used to file for divorce and hence, there are hardly any reported cases in recent times concerning divorce under this particular ground.

---

[173] See the discussion under section titled 'Grounds for Annulment of Marriage'.

[174] AIR 2006 SC 1662

Table 1.5   Additional Grounds of Divorce Under Various Personal Laws

Grounds	HMA	SMA	DMMA	DA	PMDA
Conversion	S.13 (ii)		S.2 (ix)	S.10 (1)(ii)	S.32 (i)
Leprosy	S.13 (iv)	S.27 (1) (g)	S.2 (vi)	S.10 (1)(iv)	
Renouncing the World	S.13 (vi)				
Rape/Sodomy/Bestiality	S.13 (2) (ii)	S.27 (1-A) (i)		S.10 (2)	S.32 (d)
Non-consummation of Marriage			S.2 (iv)	S.10 (vii)	S.32(a)
Impotency			S.2 (v)		
Forcing into prostitution/immorality			S.2 (viii) (c)		S.32 (e)
Imprisonment		S.27 (1) (c)	S.2 (iii)		S.32 (f)
Disposes Wife's Property			S.2 (viii) (d)		
Obstructs perf of rel. Obligations			S.2 (viii) (e)		
Unequal Treatment between Wives			S.2 (viii) (f)		
Pre-marriage Pregnancy					S.32 (c)
Minor girl - Option of Puberty	S.13 (2) (iv)		S.2 (vii)		
Non-payment of Maintenance	S.13 (2) (iii)	S.27 (1-A) (ii)	S.2 (ii)		S.32 (h)
No cohabitation after JS decree	S.13 1-A (i)	S.27 (2) (i)			S.32A (i)
No cohabitation after RCR decree	S.13 1-A (ii)	S.27 (2) (ii)		S.10 (1) (viii)	S.32A (i)

Conviction

When a person is convicted of a crime and sentenced to four or seven or more years of imprisonment, the spouse of the convicted person can use this as a ground for divorce.

Conversion/apostasy

The ground of conversion/apostasy was used by Muslim women to dissolve their marriage prior to the enactment of Dissolution of Muslim Marriages Act in 1939. The act of conversion to another religion automatically dissolved the marriage. But after the enactment of DMMA, the conversion of the wife does not in itself dissolve the marriage and it would be necessary to obtain a judicial decree.

The Kerala High Court, in *Suresh Babu* v. *V. P. Leela*,[175] was called upon to decide whether a wife who had consented to the husband's

conversion is entitled to a decree of divorce on the ground of conversion. The husband who had converted to Islam pleaded that since the wife had given her consent to the conversion, she was prevented from seeking divorce on that ground. But the Kerala High Court rejected his argument and held that despite the fact that the wife may have given her consent, conversion in itself is a matrimonial misconduct and a ground on which the non-converting spouse is entitled to a decree of divorce. The right of the non-converting spouse is indefeasible. Since the statute does not provide for conversion with consent of the other spouse, it was held that the same cannot be pleaded as a defence against the allegation of conversion.

Minority

A marriage performed when a girl was minor can be repudiated when the girl attains majority. This is termed as 'option of puberty' under

[175] AIR 2007 NOC 285 Ker

Muslim law, which is available to a girl who was married before the age of 15 years and whose marriage is not consummated.[176] Under the Hindu Marriage Act, marriage of a minor girl can be dissolved if she was married when she was under 15 years of marriage and she repudiates the marriage between the age of 15 and 18 years, irrespective of whether the marriage was consummated or not.[177] But more recently, under the Prevention of Child Marriage Act, 2006, a minor married prior to the age of 18 can annul the marriage within two years of attaining majority. The option is available to both girls and boys irrespective of the laws under which they were married.[178]

Grounds such as conversion, apostasy, renunciation of the world, and presumption of death, as also rape, unnatural offences like homosexuality, sodomy, and bestiality are very rarely used in contemporary matrimonial litigation. Hence there are hardly any reported cases on these issues to assess judicial trends. As already mentioned, bulk of the matrimonial litigation revolves around the three main grounds, i.e., adultery, cruelty, and desertion, with cruelty gaining prominence even over the other two. Rather than resorting to quaint and obscure grounds of matrimonial 'guilt' or 'fault', the current trend is to progress towards a 'no fault' divorce on the ground of 'mutual incompatibility'.

CONSENT THEORY OF DIVORCE

Doctrine of 'No Fault' Divorce

The 'no fault' theory of divorce is based on the fact that marriages very often fail not because of the fault or guilt of one of the spouses but

---

[176] Section 2 (vii) of the Dissolution of Muslim Marriages Act, 1939

[177] Section 13 (2) (iv) of the HMA

[178] The issue of child marriage is discussed in detail later in this chapter in section titled 'Marriage of Minors'.

---

because the spouses are not compatible in their temperament. Despite their best efforts, they are unable to live together as husband and wife. But the fault theory requires that one of them (and only one of them) should be guilty of some matrimonial offence in order to dissolve the marriage. Before the introduction of the theory of 'no fault divorce', the only avenue open to such a couple was to fabricate a fault ground where one spouse accuses the other of a matrimonial fault and the other does not contests it. This is termed as a 'collusive' decree and is specifically prohibited under the matrimonial statutes. However, left with no other option, the couple would be forced to collude to secure their release from the matrimonial bondage. To remedy the problem faced by such couples, the notion of a 'consent divorce' came to be included in matrimonial laws. The purpose was to enable couples to adopt honest rather than fraudulent or collusive means to achieve legitimate ends.

The consent theory is a sharp departure from the sacramental notion of marriage and brings marriage to the level of a purely consensual contractual partnership. 'If spouses are free to enter a matrimonial contract, they are equally free to withdraw from the contract of marriage' is the premise which governs the notion of 'consent divorce'. Some legal scholars believe that this spelled the virtual death of traditional Hindu law which viewed marriage as a sacrament (Derrett 1978).

Within Muslim law, since its inception in the 7th century, was based on the premise of contractual and dissoluble marriages, there was no difficulty in accepting the notion of a consent divorce. The two forms of divorce by mutual consent accepted under Islamic law are *khula* and *mubaraa*. In khula, the desire for divorce comes from the wife while mubaraa is mutual. Since these provisions are under uncodified Muslim law, it is not mandatory to obtain a judicial decree. It can be done through a divorce agreement, signed by witnesses and the parties concerned. An agreement endorsed by a *qazi* is helpful but not mandatory.

Several centuries later, other legal systems adopted this approach. Soon after the Bolshevik Revolution in 1917, the Soviet Union introduced this theory in family law. The parties were allowed to dissolve their marriage by a private act, without recourse to a court of law. But because of the problems this experiment created, in 1944, marriages could be dissolved only with the intervention of the courts. In 1920, in New Zealand, Section 4 of the Divorce and Matrimonial Causes Amendment Act, 1920 gave the court the discretion to grant a decree of divorce to the parties when they had separated for three years under a decree of judicial separation or separation order by the magistrate or under a deed of separation or even by 'mutual consent'. Till such amendment, divorce after separation by parties on 'mutual consent' was unknown under the common law tradition.[179] Thereafter, this notion spread to several other countries like the People's Republic of China, Eastern European countries, Belgium, Norway, Sweden, Japan, Portugal, and Latin America (Diwan 1988: 36). This ground was accepted under the English law in 1963 through an amendment to the Matrimonial Causes Act, 1950 by removing the absolute bar on collusion.

In 1954, the Special Marriage Act (SMA) incorporated this ground, but the Hindu Marriage Act, enacted a year later, did not provide for it. This is because the SMA which provided for a civil marriage between persons belonging to any community, religion, nationality, or domicile was perceived to be for the benefit of the educated, sophisticated, and enlightened urban-based elites, whereas the HMA was meant for the vast Hindu masses who might not accept this form of divorce (Diwan and Diwan 1997:10).

Urging the government to incorporate this provision in Hindu law, Khanna CJ. speaking for the full bench in *Ram Kali* v. *Gopal Dass*[180] commented on the inadequacy of the existing divorce law in the following words: "It would be unreasonable and inhuman, to compel the parties to keep up the facade of marriage even though the rift between them is complete and there are no prospects of their ever living together as husband and wife." Accordingly, in 1976, the Hindu Marriage Act was amended and the provision of divorce by mutual consent was included as a ground under Section 13B of the Act. This ground is now incorporated into most marriage laws as a progressive step to end incompatible or acrimonious relationships, without the necessity of having to 'wash dirty linen in public' through exaggerated allegations of sexual infidelity, cruelty, or desertion.

Since the Roman Catholic Church was opposed to the notion of divorce, and accepted the sacramental notion of a marriage, there was opposition from the church to introducing this ground into the laws applicable to Christians. But finally, after sustained struggle, this ground was included in the Indian Divorce Act, 1869 through an amendment in 2001.[181]

Even after litigation has been initiated on a fault ground and the parties are entangled in a prolonged court battle, it is possible to withdraw allegations and convert the earlier petition into a petition for a mutual consent divorce. Trial court judges, marriage counsellors in family courts, and even high court judges in appeal cases prevail upon litigants to adopt this strategy. This is a

---

[179] See *Smruti Pahariya* v. *Sanjay Pahariya*, AIR 2009 SC 2840.

[180] 1971 RLR 10

[181] Section 10A of the Divorce Act, 1869.

modern trend which one witnesses in contemporary family law litigation.

Necessary Ingredients

HMA	SMA	ML	DA	PMDA
S.13B	S.28	Uncodified	S.10A	S.32B

The petition for obtaining a divorce by mutual consent has to be presented jointly by the husband and wife, adopting a standard format. Apart from the date of marriage and a few basic personal details of the parties, the petition should include the following standard averments:

i. That the husband and wife are living separately for a period of more than one year and they are not be able to live together any longer.[182] The Supreme Court has now defined 'living separately' as 'not living as husband and wife', or in other words not having a conjugal (sexual) relationship. Hence, a couple residing under the same roof is not prevented from filing for divorce by mutual consent if they affirm that they have ceased to have a conjugal relationship for a period of one year.[183]

ii. A clear declaration that all efforts at reconciliation have failed and there is no possibility of resuming matrimonial cohabitation.

iii. That the spouses are desirous of obtaining a decree of divorce by mutual consent.

In *Leela Mahadeo Joshi* v. *Mahadeo Sitaram Joshi*,[184] the Bombay High Court held that if the necessary ingredients are proved, courts do not have the jurisdiction to deny the decree of divorce. In this case, an elderly couple had approached the family court at Mumbai for a decree of divorce by mutual consent, which rejected their petition on the ground that the parties had not proved that they were unable to live together. The trial court concluded that the dissolution of marriage was sought with some ulterior motive such as saving the property from prospective actions of the creditors and that the divorce appeared to be an eye-wash. The high court commented:

It appears to us that the learned trial judge was disinclined to grant divorce to parties who had lived together in matrimony for long years. However, we do not think that personal predilections should be allowed to influence the provisions of a statue. If the necessary ingredients have been proved, there is no other course left open to a trial judge but to comply with the law.

The Bombay High Court, in *Miten* v. *Union of India*,[185] has held that the period of one year of 'living separately' is necessary for filing of petition under Section 13B. The court held that its waiver is not permissible as per any settled cannons of interpretation.

Usually, consent terms are filed along with the petition regarding property division, lump sum settlements and alimony to the wife or monthly maintenance, custody of children and terms of access to the non-custodial parent, as well as maintenance to children. The consent terms, which are mutually agreed upon, are binding on the parties and can be enforced by the court. These consent terms are in the nature of a private agreement between the parties, which, after obtaining the official seal of the court, become part of the consent decree. The terms and conditions cannot violate the rights of minors and should not be against public policy.

To prevent avoidable hardships to the parties, the high court or the Supreme Court may quash any pending criminal proceedings under Section 498A of the IPC, which under normal

---

[182] For Christians the period of separation is two years.

[183] *Sureshta Devi* v. *Omprakash*, AIR 1992 SC 1904: I (1991) DMC 313 SC.

[184] AIR 1991 Bom 105

[185] I (2009) DMC 93 Bom

circumstances are not compoundable. This is done in the interest of justice and in order to finally settle all disputes between the parties. Some criminal courts act on the consent terms filed before a family court or a civil court and bring to an end the criminal prosecution pending before them.

In *Harpit Singh Anand* v. *State of West Bengal*,[186] a compromise deed was signed by both parties in which they agreed to withdraw all the complaints pending before various courts. Relying upon its inherent power under Article 142 of the Constitution, the Supreme Court dissolved the marriage as per Section 13B of the HMA, on the ground of mutual consent, and issued directions to subordinate courts to allow the parties to withdraw proceedings pending before them.

In *Swati Verma* v. *Rajan Verma*,[187] the wife had initiated proceedings under Sections 498A and 406 of the IPC and Sections 3 and 4 of the Dowry Prohibition Act. A compromise deed was filed before the Supreme Court in which the husband agreed to return the wife's stridhan and also agreed to pay Rs 6,00,000 to her as settlement. Exercising its inherent jurisdiction under Article 142 of the Constitution, the Supreme Court dissolved the marriage under Section 13B on the ground that the marriage between parties has broken down irretrievably and the parties were allowed to withdraw proceedings pending before the lower courts.

In the following cases, high courts have granted permission to withdraw criminal proceedings pending before trial courts after the parties had reached a settlement. The Orissa High Court, in *Basanta Samal* v. *State of Orissa*,[188] held that since the parties have settled all their disputes by opting for a divorce by mutual consent, they should not be dragged to court to face criminal trial. The Punjab and Haryana High Court, in *Dharmender Singh* v. *Raj Bala*,[189] held that the parties had settled their disputes through the intervention of the panchayat and the wife had received a settlement of Rs 4,30,000 as permanent alimony. Hence the wife was permitted to withdraw the complaint filed by her under Section 498A of the IPC, prior to the settlement.

If there is no plea of mutual consent, courts cannot award a decree on this ground. For instance, in *Hina Singh* v. *Satya Kumar Singh*,[190] the husband had filed a petition for a decree for restitution of conjugal rights. The wife appeared before the court and sought time to file her reply, which was granted. But she failed to do so by the specified date. On the same date, the court passed a decree of divorce by mutual consent. In the appeal filed by the wife, the question before the court was: where the only relief sought was for a decree of restitution of conjugal rights, was the trial court within its power to pass a decree of divorce instead, that too on the ground of mutual consent? The question was answered in the negative and the case was remitted for deciding the issue in accordance with the law.

The law provides for a statutory period of six months after the petition is filed (which can be extended to a maximum of 18 months), for the couple to reconcile their differences and resume cohabitation. This is provided as a last chance to make the marriage work and to prevent hasty and capricious divorce. During this period, spouses can withdraw the petition and resume cohabitation through a joint application. This is provided with the hope that tempers may cool

---

[186] II (2003) DMC 741 SC
[187] II (2003) DMC 795 SC
[188] II (2005) DMC 105 Ori

[189] II (2005) DMC 214 P&H
[190] AIR 2007 Jha 34

sufficiently to save the marriage. This provision is reflective of the cautious approach of the courts and legislature towards hasty dissolution of marriages. After the expiry of six months, parties have to file an affidavit in court reaffirming their consent to obtain a divorce by mutual consent. Courts also insist on personal attendance of the parties to ascertain this fact and to ensure that the consent was not obtained by force, fraud, undue influence, or misrepresentation. At this stage, the court will also verify whether the woman has been compelled to relinquish her right to maintenance, child custody, etc.

This need has arisen due to several instances of husbands committing fraud while obtaining divorce by mutual consent. At times, the ploy adopted is to take some other woman and project her as the wife. In some cases the wife is taken to court under the false premise of filing an affidavit and is instead made to sign on the petition for divorce, without understanding the document and feels shattered that she has in fact been tricked into giving her consent for the dissolution of her marriage. Recently, matrimonial courts have become extremely cautious and have started insisting that the parties furnish along with a marriage photograph, a recent photograph and identification to ensure that there is no fraud.

Withdrawal of Consent

It is mandatory for the court to ascertain the consent of the parties at the expiry of the six months statutory waiting period and prior to passing the decree of divorce. Within this period, either party can withdraw the consent to the divorce, by filing an application before the court stating that he or she does not wish to give consent for a divorce. When such a declaration is made, the court is bound by it and will not grant a decree of divorce. In such an

eventuality, the option open to the other spouse is to file for a contested divorce by relying upon a fault ground such as adultery, desertion, cruelty, or any other ground as stipulated under the relevant matrimonial statute. The legal position regarding withdrawal of consent is reflected in the following judgments:

In *Sureshata Devi* v. *Omprakash*,[191] the court held that the significant aspect of this provision is that there should be mutual consent when the parties move the court with a request to pass a decree of divorce. The court should be satisfied about the bona fides and the consent of the parties. Otherwise, the court should make an enquiry. If there is no mutual consent at the time of the enquiry, the court has no jurisdiction to pass a decree of divorce. A decree which is passed at the instance of one of the parties and without the consent of the other can not be regarded as a decree by mutual consent.

In *Pralay Kumar Bose* v. *Shyama Bose*,[192] while setting aside the decree of divorce passed by the trial court, the Calcutta High Court held: The law requires that consent given by either spouse at the time of filing a joint petition on mutual agreement must continue till the decree of divorce is passed. Checks and balances provided under Section 13B, HMA do not permit the parties to act in haste. There was a legal requirement of both spouses to make motion after the statutory period of waiting from the date of filing of the petition so as to ultimately obtain a decree of divorce.

In *Manju Kohli* v. *Desh Deepak Kohli*,[193] the Madhya Pradesh High Court held that the waiting period of 6 to 18 months after a petition for divorce by mutual consent is filed, has to be

---

[191] AIR 1992 SC 1904: I (1991) DMC 313 SC
[192] II (1998) DMC 19 Cal
[193] I (1998) DMC 724 MP

compulsorily undergone by the parties. When parties file for a mutual consent divorce they are aware that this petition in itself does not snap their marital ties and that they will be given more time to conclusively decide. Hence, they should also be given the option to withdraw their consent in this transitional phase.

In *Rekharani* v. *Prabhu*,[194] the Kerala High Court held that the trial court should satisfy that consent of both the parties persisted during the entire period. If one party has a change of heart or second thoughts in the intervening period, the court has no jurisdiction to grant a decree of divorce. The trial court should be satisfied about the bona fides and consent of both the parties to the petition. If the court is held to have power to make a decree based solely on the initial petition, it negates the entire notion of mutuality.

The Supreme Court in *Smruti Pahariya* v. *Sanjay Pahariya*[195] reaffirmed this position and held as follows: "We are of the view that it is only on the continued mutual consent of the parties that decree for divorce under Section 13B of the said Act (HMA) can be passed by the Court. If petition for divorce is not formally withdrawn and is kept pending then on the date when the Court grants the decree, the Court has a statutory obligation to hear the parties to ascertain their consent. From the absence of one of the parties for two to three days, the Court cannot presume his/her consent as has been done by the learned family court Judge…" In this case when the husband did not appear before the family court at Mumbai, the presiding judge adjourned the matter to the next date, but upon the request of the wife, the case was preponed prior to the date and passed a decree of divorce on the ground of mutual consent. The husband successfully challenged this decree in the high court. Against this judgment the wife had approached the Supreme Court, which remanded the matter back to the family court for a fresh hearing.

One can discern a cautious approach on the part of the judiciary. The court does not accept the withdrawal of consent at its face value in every case. The party wishing to withdraw consent has to file a declaration regarding the withdrawal in order to prevent the divorce.

In *Suman* v. *Surendra Kumar*,[196] the Rajasthan High Court commented that the total silence of the husband at the time of filing the mandatory second affidavit on the expiry of the statutory waiting period of six months does not amount to a withdrawal of consent. The high court ruled that the consent of the husband for divorce was available and that the family court at Jodhpur ought to have granted a decree of divorce.

The possibility of withdrawal of consent within the statutory period can give rise to a situation where the husband can manipulate circumstances to his advantage. A situation may arise where a wife will withdraw a complaint of dowry harassment[197] or any other criminal complaint, or agree to a less than advantageous maintenance agreement in return for a speedy divorce by mutual consent. After this compromise, if the husband is allowed to withdraw his consent to the divorce, the woman is left without any recourse. The courts have clearly stated that the procedure for withdrawal of consent cannot be resorted to as a means to defeat justice, as the following case decided by the Delhi High Court indicates.

---

[194] I (2008) DMC 235 Ker
[195] AIR 2009 SC 2840

[196] I (2003) DMC (DB) 805 Raj
[197] Section 498(A) IPC

In *Rachna Jain* v. *Neeraj Jain*,[198] the husband and wife filed for a mutual consent divorce after the husband had already contracted a second marriage, thereby being guilty of bigamy. The wife agreed to withdraw her criminal complaint against the husband and agreed not to sue for maintenance. During the six-month waiting period between the initial application for divorce and the secondary application, the husband withdrew his consent. The court held that the husband was withdrawing his consent for absolutely no reason other than to cause distress to the wife. 'It is evident that the withdrawal of consent by the husband is tainted with mala fide, is baseless and unjust, and hence could not be allowed, the court commented further it was observed that the court cannot be a spectator to the duplicity of the husband who not only induced the hapless wife to forgo her maintenance claims for herself and her daughter, but also duped her into agreeing to withdraw the criminal complaints in the hope of starting her life afresh. Thus, the court established that the withdrawal of consent during the six month waiting period could not be arbitrary. It can only be allowed if it is clearly shown by one party that consent was achieved by force, fraud, or undue influence or when there is a possibility of reconciliation.

The ruling of the Andhra Pradesh High Court, in *Anita* v. *R. Rambilas*,[199] has negative implications for women's rights in the context that at times women are fraudulently induced into signing a joint petition for divorce. The judgment held that the wife had filed for withdrawal of consent on the ground of fraud and alleged that she was made to sign a joint petition for divorce under threat. Her plea was rejected by the family court, Secunderabad. In appeal against this order, the high court disbelieved her contentions and held that it was a concocted story and that the wife had failed to prove her husband's fraud. Curiously, the court ruled that the wife had given up custody of her child and right to maintenance *for reasons best known to her* (emphasis added).

In a social setting where women are deceived into giving up their claims and coerced into signing joint petitions for divorce, the court cannot brush aside contentions merely by commenting that the woman has given up her claim for 'reasons best known to her'. Courts, more specifically, family courts are mandated to refer the couple for counselling, where these allegations can be addressed and the root of the problem can be investigated. It is mandatory for the court to explore the reason why a woman has given up her claim to the custody of her children and maintenance as she is the weaker party in the proceedings. Unfortunately, in this case, the family courts in Andhra Pradesh did not have the support of marriage counsellors and even rules for appointment of counsellors had not been framed.[200]

Waiver of the Statutory Period

While the statutory period of six months waiting from the date of filing till the decree of divorce is pronounced is mandatory, in some instances, where it would cause extreme hardship to the parties, it has been waived by the trial court. This will be done only if the court is convinced that the provisions of the said section have been complied with and that there is no force, undue influence, or coercion exercised by one spouse against the other. But the waiver is on a case to case basis. The courts waive the period of waiting if the parties have been separated for a long

---

[198] II (2006) DMC 410 Del
[199] I (2003) DMC 95 AP

[200] They were framed subsequently in 2005. See the discussion on this issue in Chapter 3 *Family Courts and Gender Justice*.

period and have been engaged in prolonged litigation. During the litigation, if the parties are able to resolve their differences and arrive at a settlement, the courts waive the period of separation and grant a decree of divorce by mutual consent. A joint affidavit needs to be produced before the court, withdrawing all the allegations made against the other and stating their consent for obtaining a divorce by mutual consent. This helps bring to an end long drawn litigation and saves the time of the court. This also saves the parties further hardship of facing contentious trial to prove their case.

Gracy v. *Cleetus*[201] provides an example of how Christian women are able to use this provision after the amendment to Christian law. The wife filed a petition to declare her marriage null and void or alternatively for a decree of divorce on the grounds of cruelty, adultery, and fraud. After ascertaining that there was no possibility of reconciliation and that the parties have been residing separately for a period exceeding two years, the court granted a decree for divorce by mutual consent, waiving the statutory period of six months.

In *Anjana Kishore and Puneet Kishore*[202] a three judge bench of the Supreme Court invoking its extraordinary power under Article 142 of the Constitution directed the courts to do away with the statutory period of six months. In light of the aforesaid judgment a number of high courts and civil courts began to waive trial the six months period under the Act.

The Delhi High Court, in 2005, in *Abhay Chauhan* v. *Rachna Singh*,[203] laid out the following guidelines for waiving the statutory period of six months:

i) There was no possibility of reconciliation between the parties;

ii) The decision of the parties was not influenced by any external factors like coercion, intimidation, or undue influence by any person, including the parents;

iii) Both parities are educated and mature and fully comprehend the contemplated parting of ways;

iv) The parties are firm in their resolve to dissolve the marriage and their decision is not made in haste but is well considered.

One concern of the courts has been that young people should not be made to suffer further for the mistake they might have made at an earlier point in life and they should be permitted to move on in life. For instance, in 2008, the Punjab and Haryana High Court, in *Vijay Kumar* v. *Surinder Kaur @ Sunita*,[204] where the parties have been residing separately for six years, waived the statutory period of six months on the following reasoning:

The parties are young. There is no chance of reconciliation, the marriage has broken down irretrievably. They are also involved in criminal litigation. Hence no purpose is likely to be served, if they are forced to retain the bond of marriage for another six months. Statutory period of six months is dispensed with.

In 2008, the Delhi High Court, in *Purohotam Lal* v. *Surjeet*[205] and *Subhasree Datta* v. *Nil*,[206] reaffirmed that the six months period is not a mandatory requirement but is merely directory in nature and could be easily waived. The court commented that the very purpose of the liberalized concept of divorce by mutual consent would be frustrated if the six months waiting period is considered to be mandatory, especially when parties live separately and there is no chance of re-union.

---

[201] I (2002) DMC 401 Ker
[202] (2002) 10 SCC 194
[203] I (2005) DMC 801 Del

[204] I (2008) DMC 605 P&H
[205] II (2008) DMC 253 Del
[206] II (2008) DMC 582 Del

The Bombay High Court in *Rakesh Harsukhbhai Parekh* v. *State of Maharashtra*[207] while upholding the judgment of the family court which allowed the parties to obtain a divorce soon after they had converted their pending petition filed on fault ground into a petition for mutual consent divorce, held as follows: The parties, who settle their dispute, are not required to be penalised for settling their disputes. They have gone through the process of divorce in the court for more than six months when the petition remained pending. They have only modified their views upon settlement of the dispute. Hence such a petition has already lived through six months period in the family court. Consequently, the mandatory period of six months, which the law requires the parties to undergo is undergone. Only the acrimonious allegations are withdrawn so that the divorce can be granted amicably to both rather than to one of the spouses.

But the views on this issue are not uniform and a great deal of confusion prevails. For instance, in a reference made by the family court at Nagpur, Swatantra Kumar CJ. and Kanade J. of the Bombay High Court expressed a contrary view. In *Principal Judge, family court, Civil Lines, Nagpur* v. *Nil*,[208] it was held that the waiting period of six months is mandatory and cannot be waived. It is not merely directory as the statute does not even impliedly indicate such an intent of the legislature. The rule of plain interpretation is squarely attracted to provisions of Section 13B (2). The court further commented that just because the parties have to wait for a period of six months from the date of presentation of the petition, it cannot be termed as hardship, much less undue hardship, justifying the avoidance of the rule of plain interpretation. In *Anil Kumar Jain* v. *Maya Jain*[209] held contrary to *Anjana Kishore* (discussed earlier) and ruled that only the Supreme Court has the power to waive the six months statutory period invoking its extraordinary powers under Article 142 of the Constitution. Such power cannot be exercised by the high courts or trial courts. Subsequently, in *Manish Goel* v. *Rohini Goel*,[210] the Apex Court ruled that even the Supreme Court cannot waive the six months of statutory period. The court opined that in exercise of its extraordinary power under Article 142 the Supreme Court cannot ignore substantive provisions of a statue. In view of these conflicting rulings, the matter has been referred to a larger bench.[211]

Varied Customary Practices of Obtaining Consent Divorce

While the above rulings form one extreme end of the continuum, Lok Adalats can be placed at the other. Here it is possible to file for a mutual consent divorce and obtain a decree on the same day. Lawyers practising in family courts prefer to move the case from a regular court to a Lok Adalat, rather than the couple having to wait for six more months to obtain the decree.

In Mumbai, the marriage bureaus also issues 'quick divorce' by invoking custom. An affidavit is prepared by lawyers that the parties are willing for divorce and the terms of divorce are mentioned and this document is notarised. The parties believe that the divorce is valid. After the case of a woman who was deprived of her right to custody of children and maintenance was brought to light by the media and an NGO initiated proceedings, the Bombay High Court

---

[207] MANU/MH/0191/2010
[208] II (2008) DMC 402 Bom
[209] II (2009) DMC 449 : (2009) 10 SCC 415
[210] I (2010) DMC 601
[211] *Neeti Malviya* v. *Rakesh Malviya*, MANU/SC/0404/2010.

issued directions that such divorces are not valid and a court decree is essential.[212] But this created problems for Muslim women contracting a subsequent civil marriage under the Special Marriage Act as they could not produce a court decree of divorce since they were divorced through oral talaq. In a particular case the woman herself had accepted the talaq and there was a written document to prove the talaq. She was constrained to move the high court in the above proceedings pending before the high court and obtain directions to the Registrar of Marriages to register the marriage.[213]

Various police stations and the Crime Branch at Mumbai which conduct mediation between couples in conflict marriages also 'dissolve' the marriage and issue a document to this effect, invoking custom. This practice has been discontinued after the high court's directions in the case of fraudulent marriages, discussed earlier.

Several caste-based panchayats operating in urban areas also issue decrees of divorce to the parties after mediation has failed. Similarly, the Muslim *jamats* and individual *muftis* also dissolve the marriages by invoking the Muslim principle of khula or mubaraa. Most Muslim women approach these forums rather than formal courts. Generally there is a fear among the general public regarding courts and lawyers and hence people prefer to explore alternate dispute resolution fora for a quick resolution of the dispute.

These divorces do not usually come for scrutiny before the courts as both parties and their witnesses sign the document. The problem arises only at the time of registering the next marriage under civil law. Alternatively, when marital disputes arise in the subsequent marriage and when the wife approaches formal courts for her rights, the husband (supported by a lawyer) may invent the ground of invalidity of marriage, which causes immense problems to the wife. There is a chance of the second marriage getting invalidated since the first divorce was not valid in the eyes of law. If it is declared that the first marriage was subsisting, it will render the subsequent marriage bigamous and invalid. Problems also may arise when obtaining travel documents, such as passport and visa, where the parties may be required to produce a decree issued by a formal court. But if the parties do not have to interact with state agencies and approach community organizations like panchayats for rights, they will not face any problems and most rural people live by these community norms.

The Roman Catholic Church also has its own tribunals and here too a decree of annulment is issued and subsequently the parties remarry. The parties are not made aware of the fact that a civil decree is essential. When dispute arises and the courts declare the second marriage as void the women lose their rights.[214]

As discussed in the concluding section of Chapter 1 *Personal Laws and Women's Rights* of the first volume, while formal and enacted law with its rigid rules functions at one level, there is an entire substratum that functions from the basis of community practices. People find these fora

---

[212] Order passed by the Division Bench of Bombay High Court on 20 October 2004 in *Majlis Manch* v. *State of Maharashtra*, WP 2425/2004 (Unreported).

[213] A similar problem also arose in *Alungaprambil Abdual Khader Suhud* v. *State of Kerala*, I (2007) DMC 38. This case is discussed subsequently in the section on 'Registration of Marriages'.

[214] *Molly Joseph* v. *George Sebastian*, 1996 AIR SCW 4267. The issue is discussed in section titled 'Christian Law of Marriage and Succession' of Chapter 1 *Personal Laws and Women's Rights* of the first volume.

more approachable and affordable. As discussed earlier, there are also state organs too which participate and follow these informal practices.

Unless there is some meeting ground between the formal and informal legal norms, there is a possibility that the practices of entire sections of people would be declared as invalid through litigation process. Formal law must meet the requirements of a cross section of people and only then will it be acceptable and followed. Or else, customs evolved by people at the ground level will persist and will be accepted until individual cases are held up for scrutiny by formal courts and declared invalid.

The concern of formal structures should not only be of state control and strict adherence to legal principles. The governing principle for assessing the validity of a particular divorce should be whether the rights of the weaker parties were protected through the document of divorce or were they trampled upon. In some instances customary divorces or divorces conducted by Lok Adalats, marriage bureaus, and the police could lead to loss of rights of women. But in other instances, invalidating the divorce merely to enforce the rigidity of law will also lead to a loss of rights of the vulnerable sections.[215] It is crucial that state law meets people's law in this justice venture.

IRRETRIEVABLE BREAKDOWN OF MARRIAGE

Breakdown Theory of Divorce

Having progressed from fault to the consent theory of divorce, arriving at the breakdown theory was a logical step ahead. Gradually, courts began to ponder over whether it is prudent and convenient to grant a divorce when even one of the parties has concluded that the marriage has broken down irretrievably and that it would not

---

[215] The case of Molly Joseph cited earlier is an example.

be possible to continue with the relationship. The breakdown theory is based on the fact that irrespective of the fault of either or both parties, a marriage can be terminated if it is shown that nothing survives in the relationship. Borrowing the phrase used by some judges, a marriage which is reduced to 'dead wood' can be dissolved. This premise completes the process initiated in English matrimonial law in the nineteenth century that marriages are based on contracts. Hence if a person has the power to enter into a contract voluntarily, a person must also have the power to terminate the contract voluntarily.

The basic premise of the breakdown theory is that if a marriage has broken down without any possibility of repair (or irretrievably), it should be dissolved without ascertaining the 'fault' of either party. Where a marriage has for all intents and purposes ceased to exist, except for the legal tie, either party can apply to the court for a decree of divorce. This application can be made notwithstanding that the party applying for a divorce is unable to prove any of the grounds for dissolution/invalidity of the marriage as provided in matrimonial laws and without even obtaining the consent of the other spouse. However, the court must be satisfied that the breakdown of marriage is irretrievable and there is no possibility of saving it.

Irretrievable breakdown of marriage as a basis for divorce has always been recognized under Muslim law. The husband's unilateral right to divorce is based on this legal premise. The concept has also been extended to a woman's right to dissolve the marriage. In 1950, the Sind Chief Court held that 'there was no merit in preserving a marriage, parties to which were not able to live 'within the limits of Allah'. In a later judgment, Krishna Iyer J. observed that

While Islam recognized the sanctity of family life, there was also a corresponding recognition that incompatibility between spouses is a valid ground for dissolving the marriage, for it is intolerable to imprison the couple in a quarrelsome wedlock.[216]

In another ruling, the learned jurist traced the modern trend of the principle of breakdown of marriage in countries following the common law traditions to the Muslim law.[217]

The breakdown theory found acceptance in the Soviet family law of 1944. It was left to the discretion of the court to ascertain whether a marriage has broken down irretrievably. In English law, irretrievable breakdown of marriage was introduced by the Divorce Law Reform Act, 1969 after a national debate of more than two decades (Diwan 1988: ix). 'No fault' divorce was introduced in the state of California in the USA in 1969, which triggered off a 'divorce revolution' in the country.[218] By 1977, nine states had enacted provisions for 'no fault' divorce and by 1985 almost all the states in the USA had incorporated similar provisions. Many countries have introduced the breakdown principle in the following three forms:

i. If a petition is presented on the ground that the marriage has broken down irretrievably and the petitioner is able to prove it, then the petitioner would be entitled to a decree of divorce.

ii. If the petitioner is able to prove separation for a stipulated period, the petitioner will be entitled to a decree of divorce.

iii. Non-resumption of cohabitation for a certain period after a decree for judicial separation or non-compliance of a decree of restitution

of conjugal rights for a certain period entitles either party to seek divorce.

The breakdown theory and simplified procedures brought in a radical change in the notion regarding the sacramental character of Christian marriages. As opposed to the notion of permanency of marriages, marriages are now viewed as contractual and temporary which can easily be dissolved. The earlier notion of Christian monogamy was transformed into a newer concept of serial monogamy. With 'fault' theory receding into the background, the laws acquired a new gender neutral language. Under this, the 'spouses' are perceived to have equal or similar roles and responsibilities within the marriage. The need to prove allegations was taken out of the purview of matrimonial litigation. It became irrelevant as to who was responsible for the breakdown. The focus shifted from past behaviour to future entitlements. Financial settlements and provisions for welfare of children became the central focus of divorce proceedings. Only if a spouse (more specifically the wife) could establish that the divorce would cause great hardships to her, the divorce could be stalled. If this was not the case, a decree of divorce would be imminent within the framework of 'no fault' divorce. Interestingly, the term 'no fault' was borrowed from insurance companies who used it in the context of 'no-fault' car insurance. Since divorces could be obtained easily, the rate of divorce in these countries spiralled, with one report claiming around one million divorces in USA every year, which works out to be around 3000 divorces per day (Parejko 2009).

The 'no fault' theory of divorce led to the introduction of principles of division of property upon divorce in several common law countries.[219] The two principles—divorce without

---

[216] *A. Yousuf Rawther* v. *Sowramma*, AIR 1971 Ker 261

[217] *Aboobacker Haji* v. *Mamu Koya*, 1971 KLT 663

[218] Though California is given the credit of first introducing this provision, it was first introduced in 1953 in Oklahoma. But that did not trigger off a 'divorce revolution'. The term 'divorce revolution' is borrowed from the title of Lenore Weitman's book, *The Divorce Revolution*, published in 1985, where she assessed the impact of this provision upon the lives of women.

[219] The issue of division of property upon divorce is discussed at section titled 'Notion of Matrimonial Property and Rules for its Divisions' of Chapter 2 *Matrimonial Rights and Obligations*.

establishing fault and equal division of matrimonial property—became the pillars of the new divorce doctrine. Various guidelines for distribution of property were introduced into family laws, to take into account the non-financial contribution made by the wife during marriage which contributed to the accumulation of family assets.

Introduction of the Concept Through Judge-made Laws

In a convoluted manner, this theory found a place in the matrimonial statutes through an amendment in 1976. Section 13 (I-A) of the Hindu Marriage Act and Section 27(2) of the the Special Marriages Act provided that if there is no cohabitation between the couple for a period of one year after obtaining the decree of restitution of conjugal rights or judicial separation, either of the spouses, including the guilty spouse, is empowered to move the court for a decree of divorce merely on this ground, without the necessity of proving a matrimonial fault against the other spouse.[220]

The Law Commission, in its 71st report, had considered this issue and recommended the adoption of this ground into family law in India. Based on the recommendations of the Law Commission, a bill was introduced in Parliament, but it was withdrawn as it met with a great deal of opposition by several women's organizations (Diwan and Diwan 1997: xix).

Later, the notion of 'breakdown of marriage' came to be introduced in matrimonial litigation through judicial pronouncements, on a case to case basis. The Supreme Court and various high courts have awarded legal recognition to this concept and have granted divorce, usually as a last resort as the following cases illustrate.

In 1993, in *Chandralekha Trivedi* v. *S. P. Trivedi*,[221] the Supreme Court did not use the term 'irretrievable breakdown of marriage' but stated that the marriage is 'dead'. In this case, the husband had initiated divorce proceedings on the ground of cruelty and wife's intimacy with young boys. The wife made similar allegations against the husband. Their only daughter was already married when the high court granted a decree of divorce. In appeal, the Supreme Court upheld the decree of divorce granted by the high court on the ground that it would be futile to decide the allegations and counter-allegations as the marriage was 'dead'.

The landmark ruling on this issue was delivered by the Supreme Court in the following year, i.e. 1994, in *V. Bhagat* v. *D. Bhagat*.[222] The petition for divorce had been filed by the husband on the ground of adultery against the wife. The wife contested and made counter allegations against the husband and his family members of insanity. The husband retaliated by amending his petition and adding mental cruelty as a ground based on the allegations of insanity made by the wife against him. The spouses were highly educated and were well established professionals. The husband was a lawyer practising in the Delhi High Court. After several rounds of contentious litigation from the high court to the Supreme Court and back where allegations and counter allegations were hurled by the parties against each other, finally the Supreme Court dissolved the marriage. It was held that it would be a fit case for invoking the principle of 'irretrievable breakdown of marriage' though it is not a ground for divorce under the Hindu Marriage Act. But the Supreme Court issued a note of caution that this ruling could not be construed as a 'legal precedent' to be used in a routine manner in trial courts.

---

[220] Section 32A of Parsi Marriage and Divorce Act also provides a similar relief.

[221] (1993) 4 SCC 232
[222] (1994) 1 SCC 337 : AIR 1994 SC 710

In *Romesh Chander* v. *Savitri*,[223] in a divorce petition filed by the wife, the allegations made by her about her husband's cruelty and adultery could not be proved and hence, the trial court dismissed her petition. But the high court upheld the plea and granted her the divorce. The husband challenged the judgment in the Supreme Court and also expressed remorse for his conduct of neglecting his wife. But the wife was not willing to reconcile and the Supreme Court concluded that the marriage had broken down emotionally and practically. The court held: 'Where the marriage has broken down irretrievably, the apex court has the inherent power under Article 142 of the Constitution, to grant appropriate orders in the interest of justice'.

Later, several high courts also adopted the practice of dissolving marriages invoking the ground of irretrievable breakdown of marriage. In *Sanghamitra Singh* v. *Kailash Singh*,[224] the wife who was opposing the husband's petition for divorce informed the court that the husband had already clandestinely remarried and a criminal case had been filed against him. The Orissa High Court, while upholding the decree of divorce granted by the trial court, commented: 'Whether the husband has married for a second time or not, it is clear that the marriage has irretrievably broken down and both the parties do not want restoration of marital ties'. Accordingly, by applying the doctrine of irretrievable breakdown, the court granted a decree of divorce to the parties after obtaining the consent of both the parties.

More recently, the Calcutta High Court, in *Rajendra Kumar Jajodia* v. *Puja Jajodia*,[225] and the Allahabad High Court, in *Brajesh Kumar* v. *Anjali*,[226] declined to grant divorce on this ground to the husbands stating that high courts do not have such power and the power rests exclusively with the Supreme Court. In *Vishnu Dutt Sharma* v. *Manju Sharma*,[227] the Supreme Court held that even this Court (i.e. the Supreme Court) does not have the power to grant this remedy. Markandey Katju J. and V.S. Sirpurkar J. held that irretrievable breakdown of marriage is not a ground for dissolution of marriage under the Hindu Marriage Act. Since the legislature has not provided for it, courts cannot add this ground as it would amount to amending the Act, which is a function of the legislature. It was for the Parliament and not the courts to enact or amend the law and that the earlier rulings have not taken into account the correct legal position and cannot be held to be precedents. The court commented that a mere direction of the court without considering the legal position is not a precedent.

Law Commission in its 217th report in March, 2009, has once again recommended that irretrievable breakdown of marriage should be introduced as a ground for divorce. Accordingly, the government introduced a bill in the Rajya Sabha in August 2010 to incorporate this provisions in the Hindu Marriage Act and the Special Marriage Act.

Taking Advantage of One's Own Wrong

The breakdown theory contradicts with an earlier prevailing theory that a guilty party should not be allowed to take advantage of one's own wrong. This principle was incorporated into matrimonial law when divorce was based on the fault theory. As per this principle, only an innocent party was deemed eligible for matrimonial relief. The party committing a matrimonial

---

[223] I (1995) DMC 231 SC : 1995 (2) SCC 7
[224] AIR 2001 Ori.151
[225] I (2009) DMC 332 Cal

[226] I (2009) DMC 579 All
[227] I (2009) DMC 515 SC

fault was not entitled to any relief and was not permitted to 'take advantage of one's own wrong'. This earlier maxim clashes with the newer theory of 'irretrievable breakdown of marriage' whereby courts are not bound to ascertain the fault of the party seeking matrimonial relief. Courts have pointed out the dichotomy of these two theories. The Supreme Court, in *Saroj Rani* v. *Sudarshan Kumar Chhadha*,[228] where the guilty spouse was awarded a decree of divorce has met with a great deal of criticism. Whether a guilty spouse can take advantage of one's own wrong, prevent execution of the decree passed against himself/herself, and obtain a decree merely on the ground of non-compliance, has been a matter of much debate. In order to protect the interest of an innocent wife, some high courts have declined to invoke the breakdown theory in the event that the husband is a guilty partner.

The courts have adopted a cautious approach and have attempted to apply the stipulation under Section 23 of Hindu Marriage Act that a person should not be allowed to take advantage of one's own wrong, while examining the breakdown theory of marriage. There are many instances where the judges have attempted to harmoniously reconcile two contradictory legal mandates in the interest of justice to women despite the premise of formal equality written into the matrimonial laws.

In *Chetan Dass* v. *Kamla Devi*,[229] the husband filed for divorce. The trial court and the Rajasthan High Court rejected his petition. In appeal, the Supreme Court held:

The husband's adulterous conduct is proved. The defence of the wife that there was justified reason for her to live away from her husband is found to be correct. Hence it cannot be held that there is desertion on her part without reasonable cause. The behaviour of the husband falls in the category of misconduct and he cannot be allowed to take advantage of his own wrong. The wife is still willing to live with him provided he snaps his relationship with the other woman. But the husband prefers to snap the relationship with his wife rather than with the other woman. The decree of divorce on ground that the marriage has irretrievably broken cannot be granted.

This judgment advances a pro-women view as compared to the Orissa High Court ruling in *Sanghamitra Singh* v. *Kailash Singh*,[230] (discussed earlier) where despite a criminal case for bigamy filed by the wife against her husband was pending, the court granted divorce to the husband on the ground that marriage had irretrievably broken down.

There are several cases where in the trial court, the husband had obtained a divorce on the ground of the wife's cruelty but in appeal it was set aside by the concerned high court on the ground that the husband was taking advantage of his own wrong. Some of these cases are summarized below[231]:

In *Swapan Kumar Ganguly* v. *Smritikana Ganguly*,[232] the Calcutta High Court held that the husband had approached the court for a decree of divorce with unclean hands and that he had been torturing his wife mentally and physically. Further, there was no evidence that the wife tortured the husband mentally or physically. The court observed that under the Hindu Marriage Act, the legislature had, in its wisdom, not provided that a decree for divorce can be granted if the court finds that there has been an irretrievable breaking down of marriage between parties. Divorce can only be given on any of the grounds provided under Section 13.

---

[228] AIR 1984 SC 1562. This case is discussed under section titled 'Restitution of Conjugal Rights' earlier in this chapter.

[229] I (2001) DMC 714 SC

[230] AIR 2001 Ori.151

[231] See also the decision in *Chiranjeevi* v. *Lavanya*, II (2006) DMC 553 AP. discussed under sub-section 'Cruelty'.

[232] AIR 2002 Cal.6

Allowing divorce on any other ground is not permissible as it would amount to an act without the sanction of law.

In *Kamla Devi v. Shivakumarswamy*,[233] the trial court awarded a decree of divorce on the ground of cruelty to the husband. In her appeal against this decree, the wife pleaded that it was her husband who treated her with cruelty. She had been beaten, threatened with death, and dragged out of the house. The wife's family members tried to persuade the husband to take her back, but he flatly refused. Since then, she had been living in a rented room in the same town and the husband had refused to provide for her. The court upheld her plea and set aside the decree of divorce on the premise that the husband was taking advantage of circumstances he himself had caused.

In *Mst. Butti v. Gulab Chand Pandey*,[234] the husband filed a petition for divorce on the ground of the wife's cruelty and desertion. The trial court rejected both these grounds. The husband's second marriage was also proved. Despite this, the court granted the husband divorce on the ground that the marriage had irretrievably broken down. The Madhya Pradesh High Court, while setting aside the decree, observed that the legislature had intentionally not included irretrievable breakdown of marriage as a ground for divorce and therefore the trial court was not justified in granting divorce on that ground.

In *Arunima Bhattacharjee v. Shyama Prosad Bhattacharjee*,[235] while setting aside the decree of divorce awarded to the husband on the ground of the wife's alleged cruelty, the Calcutta High Court held that it was the husband who was at fault and that he had deliberately chosen to live separately from his wife and daughter. While the wife was maintaining the house, the

husband was merrily leading his own life without bearing any responsibility. Hence the plea of irretrievable break down of marriage advanced by the husband and upheld by the District Judge was more 'a make-believe than a reality'. It was held that trial courts must be cautious that the husband was not taking advantage of his own wrong in breaking the marriage irretrievably to obtain a divorce.

The judgments cited above are only a sample of a long list of cases which were wrongly decided by trial courts, invoking the 'breakdown theory' for awarding divorce to guilty husbands. But the high courts have been extremely cautious that the decree of divorce awarded to the husband does not contribute further to the injustice already caused to a destitute wife. This is indicative of a nuanced gender-based approach in matrimonial litigation.

Economic Settlements to the Wife and Children

Even when a decree of divorce is awarded to the husband, it is necessary to ensure that due economic settlements are made to the wife to secure her future. Some examples of such economic settlements are discussed below.

In *Laxmi Dora v. Narasingha Dora*,[236] the Orissa High Court rejected the reasons given by the family court for awarding a decree of divorce to the husband. But due to the bitterness in the relationship, the court invoked the doctrine of irretrievable breakdown of marriage and granted divorce, but ordered the husband to pay the wife a sum of Rs 2,00,000 by way of a lump sum settlement to the wife. In *Susmita Acharya v. Dr Rabindra Mishra*,[237] where the couple had been residing separately for nine years, the court granted divorce on the ground

---

[233] II (2002) DMC 738 Kar
[234] II (2002) DMC 177 MP
[235] II (2004) DMC 146 Cal

[236] II (2002) DMC 630 Ori
[237] I (2003) DMC 421 Ori

of irretrievable breakdown of marriage. But the wife was awarded Rs 5,00,000 towards her maintenance and the educational and marriage expenses of their daughter. In *Sadana Kolvankar v. Sachidanand Kolvankar*,[238] the Bombay High Court dissolved the marriage as there was no possibility of reconciliation. But the husband was ordered to pay the wife Rs 1,500 per month as maintenance in addition to Rs 1.5 lakh as permanent alimony to ensure her financial security. In *Naresh Kumar Gupta* v. *Jyoti*,[239] where the parties had been living separately for 12 years, the court held that there was no possibility of reconciliation. A decree of divorce on the ground of irretrievable breakdown of marriage was awarded and the husband was ordered to pay Rs 1.5 lakh to the wife as permanent alimony. In *Ajay Kumar* v. *Sunita*,[240] there was a separation of about 17 years, which rendered the possibility of the parties resuming normal married life remote. The husband underwent mental agony due to absence of normal sexual relation, which was also one of the reasons for the failure of the marriage. While dissolving the marriage, in the interest of justice, the Delhi High Court awarded Rs 2,00,000 as permanent alimony to the wife.

In *Satish Sitole* v. *Ganga*,[241] out of 16 years of marriage, the parties lived separately for 14 years. It was held that the marriage between the parties is dead for all practical purposes and there was no chance of it being retrieved. The wife had filed a criminal complaint against the husband for cruelty and dowry harassment. The court commented that continuation of such a marriage would itself amount to cruelty. But while upholding the decree of divorce awarded by the district court, the Supreme Court directed the husband to pay permanent alimony of Rs 2,00,000. The court also directed the husband to pay costs of appeal to the wife, assessed at Rs 25,000.

While lump sum settlements have been awarded in some cases by way of compensation to the deserted and destitute wife, the amount awarded is often paltry and can barely ensure the security of the woman and her children. So the question that arises is whether the introduction of irretrievable breakdown as a ground for divorce works against the interests of women, given the gender disparities and the large number of women deserted by their husbands. In the context of stark gender inequality and the absence of matrimonial property rights, this principle may prove to be extremely harmful to women's interests.

Granting the husband a divorce even when he has not proved a fault ground may not be the best option for women. The following ruling of the Bombay High Court, which declined to uphold the premise of long estrangement and breakdown theory, is an example of the way a court can go beyond the 'breakdown theory' in order to protect women's rights.

In *D. Santan Pretto* v. *Natalina Gomes*,[242] the husband sued for divorce on the basis of desertion, stating that his wife had taken their three children and established a separate residence over three years ago. The wife however stated that she had been compelled to reside separately so that her children could attend school near the hospital where she worked as a night nurse since the husband had not provided any maintenance for her and the three children. She further alleged that, in fact, it was the husband who had deserted her. The husband admitted the allegations, but claimed that divorce proceedings had been initiated eleven years ago and that the marriage had irretrievably broken down. The court

---

[238] II (2004) DMC 738 Bom
[239] II (2005) DMC 66 Jha
[240] II (2007) DMC 684 Del
[241] II (2008) DMC 167 SC

[242] I (2002) DMC 78 Bom

found that the distance between the couple had been caused entirely by the husband and that since the marriage had deteriorated due to his actions, he could not sue for divorce based on the premise that his marriage had irretrievably broken down. When a plea for the breakdown of marriage is advanced, it is pertinent for the trial court to enquire as to who is the cause of the breakdown. As per Section 23 (1) (a) of the HMA, before passing a decree in any matrimonial proceeding, it must be ensured that the petitioner is not in anyway taking advantage of his or her own disability for the purpose of acquiring relief.

In *Romesh Chander* v. *Savitri*,[243] (discussed earlier) where the Supreme Court invoked its inherent powers under Article 142 to apply the principle of irretrievable breakdown of marriage at the instance of the wife is an interesting ruling. Here the husband had filed an appeal in the Supreme Court against the decree of divorce granted to the wife. The Supreme Court not only upheld the decree of divorce granted by the high court but also directed the husband to transfer the house owned by him in the wife's name within four months of the decree.

The caution given by the Supreme Court in *V. Bhagat* v. *D.V. Bhagat*[244] (discussed earlier) is also needs to be taken note of:

Let the things be not misunderstood nor any permissiveness under the law be inferred, allowing an erring party who has been found to be so by recording of a finding of fact in judicial proceedings, that it would be quite easy to push and drive the spouse to a corner and then brazenly take a plea of desertion on the part of the party suffering so long at the hands of the wrongdoer, and walk away out of the matrimonial alliance on the ground that the marriage has broken down. Lest the institution of marriage and the matrimonial bonds get fragile, easily to be broken which may serve the purpose most welcome to the wrongdoer who, by hear, wished such an outcome by passing on the burden of

---

[243] I (1995) DMC 231 SC : 1995 (2) SCC 7
[244] AIR 1994 SC 710

his wrongdoing to the other party alleging her to be the deserter leading to the breaking point.

Trial courts, which are burdened with backlogs, may find it appealing to uphold a plea under the breakdown theory and bring an end to the litigation process. But the question which needs to be asked each time is, at whose cost? Is it at the cost of women and children who form the vulnerable section of society? Would such hasty divorces be a reward to a guilty husband who has deprived his wife and children of their basic right to shelter, education, and survival? If the answer is 'yes', then the plea of breakdown of marriage cannot be upheld in the interest of justice, unless the wife has been duly compensated for the injury suffered by her.

Section C

INCIDENTAL ISSUES CONCERNING MARRIAGE

MARRIAGE OF MINORS

The marriage of minors becomes a crucial question in a discourse on women's rights within marriage since girls far outnumber boys in respect of child marriages. This is due to the fact that both customary practices and legal dictates sanction that brides should be younger than the bridegrooms. The issue of child marriage impacts both matrimonial and criminal law.

Under matrimonial law, the issue relates to validity of marriages where either one or both spouses were minors at the time of solemnization. This question is often raised in the context of rights and obligations arising out of the marital relationship. More specifically, for deserted women it gets translated into their right to maintenance.

Under the criminal law, the issue is linked to the age of consent to sexual intercourse under rape law (Section 375, IPC), which is set at 16 years. Consensual sex with a girl less than 16 years amounts to rape. Where the husband is concerned, the bar is lowered to 15 years and warrants a lesser punishment. The issue also surfaces in cases of elopement and voluntary sexual intercourse between a young couple, where either one or both are minors. Within the general societal norm of arranged marriages, the elopement of the girl with a boy/man of her choice is deemed as a challenge to parental authority. In order to pressurize the girl to return (and then marry her off to a boy/man of their choice), the parents of the minor girl resort to filing criminal complaints of kidnap and rape against her lover and charges are pressed based on the minority of the girl since consensual sex with a minor girl below the age of 16 years is deemed as technical rape or statutory rape.

This section addresses these diverse concerns from the perspective of the minor girl and examines statutory provisions as well as the feminist legal discourse around the issue.

Campaigns by Social Reformers during Colonial Period

Law regarding child marriage has developed through sustained public campaigns initiated during the colonial period and carried out into the post-Independence period.

The law givers, such as Manu, Yagnavalkya, Narada, etc., did not mandate child marriage and adult marriages were the norm during the Vedic period. But later, during the post-*smriti* period, child marriages became the norm for the bride and girls were married between the ages of 8 and 12 among the upper castes (Kuppuswami 1993: 122). But among the lower castes (which followed the custom of bride price, sanctioned divorce, and remarriage for women), consensual marriages between adults were accepted as the norm.[245] Abolition of child marriages was a

primary focus of nineteenth century social reform movements, which has already been discussed in Chapter 1, *Personal Laws and Women's Rights* of the first volume. Following is a gist of the discussion, in order to contextualize the issue for the contemporary campaign.

During the nineteenth century reform movements, one of the major concerns for the reformers was to statutorily raise the age for marriage of girls. After the power of administration shifted from the East India Company to the British Crown in 1858, one of the earliest reforms introduced was the Age of Consent Act of 1860, which stipulated a minimum age of 10 years for sexual intercourse. Sexual intercourse with a girl below this age could be construed as rape. But the inadequacy of this legislation was highlighted in the Phulmonee case[246] where a child of 11 years had died due to the injuries caused to her during forcible sexual intercourse by her husband. But the husband could not be convicted for rape since he had a legal right to intercourse with his wife, who was above the age of 10. This incident became the focal point for galvanizing public opinion for the demand of raising the age of consent from 10 to 12 years. The conservative segments, known as *sanathanis*, opposed this demand on the ground that it would violate the religious dictate of pre-puberty marriage, through which the chastity of the bride could be guaranteed. But the public uproar against the verdict in Phulmonee's case finally led to the enactment of the Age of Consent Act of 1891,[247] which increased the minimum age of consent from 10 to 12 years.

But even this enactment did not resolve the issue of child marriage and the debate

---

[245] See Chapter 1 *Personal Laws and Women's Rights* of the first volume where this issue is discussed in detail.

[246] *Queens Empress* v. *Huree Mohan Mythee*, XVIII ILR (Cal) 49 (1891)

[247] See Chapter 1 *Personal Laws and Women's Rights* of the first volume for a further discussion on this issue.

continued well into the twentieth century with social reformers like Rai Saheb Harbilas Gour Sarda spearheading a campaign for the enactment of a legislation restraining child marriages. Several women's organizations, with their focus on women's education and health, also campaigned for this enactment as they felt that marriage and child birth at a very young age is detrimental for women's physical and intellectual development. Finally, after sustained campaign through the 1920s, the Child Marriage Restraint Act (CMRA) was enacted in 1929. The Act imposed a punishment on parents and husbands above the age of 18 years for arranging, contracting, performing, celebrating, and participating in child marriages. A maximum of three months imprisonment and a fine could be imposed on a male above the age of 21. If the male was above 18 and below 21, then the maximum punishment was imprisonment for 15 days or a fine of Rs 1,000, or both. Women and minor children could not be punished under the Act. District courts had the power to issue an injunction to prevent a child marriage from being performed, after giving notice to the parties involved to argue against the injunction.

The age of consent debate also has a resonance in the criminal provisions dealing with rape (Section 375, IPC). As discussed earlier,

under the statute, the age of consent for sexual intercourse for girls is laid down as 16 and hence voluntary sexual intercourse with a girl below that age amounts to rape. This is referred to more as 'statutory rape' or 'technical rape'. Under the provisions of rape law, forced sexual intercourse by a man with his wife is not an offence. However, non-consensual sex by a man with his wife who is less than 15 years amounts to rape. So it can be construed that the age of consent to sexual intercourse within marriage is set at 15. Further, Section 376 makes another distinction—if the wife is below 12 years of age, the punishment is severe,[248] while it is milder if she is between 12–15 years.

The law on statutory rape of married female minors by their husbands is anchored in the colonial legal history of the prevention of child marriage and continues to be viewed as a deterrent to child marriage rather than as entailing the protection of married minors from sexual abuse in marriage (Baxi 2009). The law treats the husband with greater laxity. Since marital rape is not an offence under Indian law, forcible

---

[248] Imprisonment of either description for a term which shall not be less than seven years but which may be for life or for a term which may extend to ten years and fine.

Table 1.6   Age of Consent and Minimum Age of Marriage

Year	Age of Consent under Section 375(5) IPC	Age mentioned in the Marital Rape - Exception to Section 375, IPC	Minimum Age of Marriage under the CMRA, 1929
1860	10 years	10 years	
1891 (amendment of IPC)	12 years	12 years	
1925 (after the amendment of IPC)	14 years	13 years	
1929 (after the passing of the CMRA)	14 years	13 years	14 years
1949 (after the amendment of the Penal Code and the CMRA)	16 years	15 years	15 years
1978	16 years	15 years	18 years

sexual intercourse by a husband amounts to rape only when the bride is less than 15 years of age. The control over the sexuality of underage girls is clearly gendered, for while the age of consent for girls is 16, there are no such legal standards set for boys. There is a further distinction between married and unmarried minors. A married female minor is not allowed to withhold consent to sexual relations within marriage when she turns 15, despite the law which prohibits women from marrying until they are legal adults at the age of 18.

The gradual increase in the age of consent for sexual intercourse and for marriage is reflected in the Table 1.6.

Validity of Child Marriages under Personal Law

The Child Marriage Restraint Act did not focus on the status of a child marriage and the rights and obligation which accrue from such a marriage. While child marriages under the Act were illegal and punishable, they were not void. The legal validity of a child marriage has to be ascertained by examining the provisions of matrimonial law.

Section 4 (c) of the Special Marriage Act stipulates that at the time of marriage the male must have completed the age of 21 years and the female, the age of 18 years. A marriage solemnized in contravention of this clause is deemed void and can be so declared under Section 24 of the Act. Section 3 (1) (c) of the Parsi Marriage and Divorce Act declares that a minor's marriage is invalid but does not specifically provide for its annulment. The Indian Christian Marriage Act of 1869, while defining 'minor' as a person below the age of 21 years, does not clearly invalidate a minor's marriage. Instead, under Section 19, it is mandatory to obtain the consent of the parent/guardian for the marriage of a minor. This provision renders

it possible to argue that marriage of a minor is valid.

Under Muslim law, girls can be married after they attain puberty. They can be married even before this age with the consent of the parent/guardian. But the law provides an option of puberty through which the girl can opt for dissolution of her marriage on the ground that the marriage was performed when she was below 15 years of age, that she had repudiated the marriage before she attained the age of 18, and the marriage has not been consummated.[249]

The Hindu Marriage Act does not render the marriage of a minor void; hence such a marriage is valid. But under Section 18 (a) of the Act, the spouses performing such a marriage may be sentenced to a term of simple imprisonment, which may extend to two years, or with fine, which may extend to Rs 10,000, or with both. In 1955, the Act stipulated a minimum age of 15 years for girls and 18 for boys. In 1976, the age of marriage was increased to 18 for girls and 21 for boys. At this stage, the Islamic concept of option of puberty was incorporated into the statute. A marriage performed when a girl was below 15 years of age, whether consummated or not, can be dissolved when she attains 18 years, provided that she has repudiated the marriage between the age of 15 and 18 years.[250]

In *Savitri Bai* v. *Sitaram*,[251] the wife petitioned for dissolution of her marriage on the ground that she was married when she was below 15 years of age and she repudiated her marriage before she turned eighteen. The high court relied upon the testimony of the girl's father and the horoscope to conclude that the wife was a minor below 15 years of age at the

[249] Section 2 (vii), Dissolution of Muslim Marriages Act, 1939.
[250] Section 13 (2) (iv), HMA.
[251] AIR 1986 MP 218

time of her marriage and dissolved the marriage.

While the option of puberty is a ground available only to women, in some instances even the husbands have been able to rely on the ground of non-age marriage to annul the marriage. In *Ram Gopal Choudhary* v. *Shanti Choudhary*,[252] both the husband and the wife were minors at the time of marriage. The husband filed a petition for dissolution of his marriage on this ground and pleaded that the subsequent *'gauna'* ceremony, which entitles the husband and wife to consummate their marriage, had not been performed and hence the marriage was not consummated. The trial court rejected his plea, but the high court found it a fit case for granting the relief to the husband and dissolved the marriage.

Rights of Married Minors to Maintenance

Since child marriage *per se* is not void, a husband cannot wriggle out of the obligation to pay maintenance to the wife merely on the ground that the wife was a minor at the time of marriage. Courts have refrained from invalidating such marriages as there would be grave repercussions if marriages of minors are declared as void.[253]

In *Gajara Naran Bhura* v. *Kanbi Kunverbai Parbat*,[254] when the wife filed for maintenance, the husband pleaded that the marriage was void since the wife was only 15 years old at the time of the marriage in 1967. The Gujarat High Court held that a marriage solemnized between two Hindus who are of the age which makes one of them punishable under the Child Marriage

Restraint Act does not render the marriage itself invalid or void. Therefore, rights and obligations arising from such valid marriage cannot be avoided by not recognizing the marriage at all.

In *V. Mallikarjunaiah* v. *H.C. Gowramma*,[255] the husband sought a declaration that his marriage was void on the ground that he was under 21 years of age at the time of the marriage. The trial court rejected his contention and dismissed the petition. In an appeal, the high court upheld the validity of marriage and commented that the purpose of the legislation is to prevent social consequences and the serious harm and damage that could occur to the parties if the marriage is declared null and void due to certain legal infirmities. M.F. Saldanhana J. who delivered the judgment held as follows:

In the particular social set up of the country, where misguided parents or relations may bind a young couple through a marriage, if at a subsequent point of time, merely on the basis of under-age, the marriage is to be declared as void, the consequences particularly to the girl or the young woman are absolutely irreversible. The legislature was conscious of the fact that such a provision should not have the result of rendering a large number of girls or young women virtually unmarried and destitute for life. The only security that a girl or a woman in such a situation was entitled to is within the framework of the marriage and if that marriage can be loosely undone or if it is not recognised by the law, it would result in disastrous social consequences which is the only reason why this section was specifically excluded from Ss. 11 & 12. If children were born it would not only be harsh, but absolutely brutal if a court were to technically void the marriage merely because the parties were under-age. Obviously, then the grave consequences of such a court order could be visited upon the parties virtually for no fault of theirs.

More recently, the Punjab and Haryana High Court, in *Mangat Ram* v. *Anju Bala*,[256] relied upon this principle to uphold the wife's

---

[252] II (2006) DMC 427 Raj

[253] *Lila Gupta* v. *Laxmi Narain*, AIR 1978 SC 1351; *Shankerappa* v. *Sushilabai*, AIR 1984 Kar 112; *Rabindra Prasad* v. *Sita Dass*, AIR 1986 Pat 128; *William Rebello* v. *Angelo Vaz*, II (1996) DMC 339 : AIR 1996 Bom 204.

[254] AIR 1997 Guj 185

[255] AIR 1997 Kar 77

[256] 2003 MLR 631 P&H

right to maintenance in a divorce proceeding filed by the husband.

In *Dnyanoba Kamble* v. *Mukta Kamble*,[257] when the wife filed for maintenance, the husband denied the marriage. But the wife pleaded that they were married twelve years ago when they were both minors and that in her community, child marriage is an accepted custom. While upholding the woman's claim of maintenance, the high court held that the fact that the respective parents had recognized the parties as a married couple and that the husband himself had accepted the woman as his wife, was sufficient to consider the marriage valid.

There have been some reported cases where the wife had approached the courts for declaring her marriage void on the ground of minority.[258] Women have also used this plea as a defense against their husbands' petition of restitution of conjugal rights.[259] Even in these cases, courts have held that such marriages are valid. This is because a clear framework of women's rights or gender justice is absent in our matrimonial statutes. In a gender-neutral manner, the judges merely endorsed the traditional and conservative notion regarding the sacramental aspect of Hindu marriage, as prescribed by the Smritis, even after the codification which has rendered Hindu marriages contractual.

These cases were decided before the amendment to Hindu Marriage Act in 1978. After the 1978 amendment, Hindu women have been granted a gender-specific option under Section 13 (2) (iv) to repudiate their marriage, which has mitigated the hurdles faced by young girls who were married in their childhood. Hence, in more recent times, one can observe that the plea of minority is raised more by husbands to defeat

the women's claim of maintenance. The concern of the courts in these cases has been towards protecting the rights of vulnerable women and children, as the consequences of declaring a marriage invalid would be disastrous for them.

Roop Narayan Verma v. *Union of India*[260] raised an interesting issue. As per the customs of the community, the marriage had taken place when the bride was only four and the groom just seven. Later, when the wife filed for maintenance, the husband challenged the constitutional validity of Section 13 (2) (iv) which grants a gender-specific remedy to women who were married when they were minors, of repudiating their marriage. A corresponding right is not awarded to men who were married when they were minors. It was argued that the provision discriminates against men and is violative of the constitutional guarantee of equality under Article 14 of the Constitution. He also pleaded that since the state had failed in its responsibility of preventing child marriage, it should be made responsible to provide maintenance to the child bride. The high court upheld the constitutional validity of the provision on the ground that it was within the scope of Article 15 (3) of the Constitution.

After the enactment of Prohibition of Child Marriages Act, 2006, the grievance raised by the husband in the above case has been rectified and men have been given the option of repudiating a marriage contracted when they were minors. But no respite has been given to men regarding the basic concern raised in this writ petition and a man cannot avoid the responsibility of paying compensation/maintenance to the wife even though the marriage was performed when he was a minor.[261]

---

[257] II (2002) DMC 791 Bom
[258] *Naumi* v. *Narotam*, AIR 1963 HP 15.
[259] *Premi* v. *Daya Ram*, AIR 1965 HP 15.

[260] AIR 2007 Chh 64
[261] See the discussion further

'Elopement' Marriages and Judicial Pronouncements

The issue of validity of child marriage has also surfaced in the context of 'love marriage' or marriages of choice contracted by a young couple against parental wishes. Usually the couple elopes and is subsequently brought back, under parental pressure and with the aid of the police. In several cases where parents have filed criminal cases against the minor girl and her husband, the courts have upheld the wishes of the minor and have permitted her to accompany her husband, even against the parents' wishes as the following cases reveal:

In *Jiten Bouri* v. *State of West Bengal*,[262] the Calcutta High Court, while permitting the minor girl to join her husband, declared as follows:

Although the victim girl has not attained majority yet she has reached age of discretion to understand her own welfare which is paramount consideration for grant of her custody. She may not have attained marriageable age as per the provision of S.5(3) of the *Hindu Marriage Act* yet marriage in contravention of age limits can neither be void nor voidable though it is punishable under S. 18 of the *Hindu Marriage Act*. The girl has insisted that she wants to go to her husband's place and not to her father's place.

In *Makemalla Sailoo* v. *Superintendent of Police Nalgonda Dist.*,[263] the Andhra Pradesh High Court held that although child marriage is an offence under the Child Marriage Restraint Act, such marriages are not void as per the provisions of both the relevant statutes—the Child Marriage Restraint Act and the Hindu Marriage Act.

In *Manish Singh* v. *State (NCT Delhi)*,[264] the Delhi High Court reiterated that marriages solemnized in contravention of the age prescribed under Section 5 (iii) of the HMA are neither void nor voidable. The court held that the judgment was based on public policy and the legislature was conscious of the fact that if such marriages are made void or voidable, it could lead to serious consequences and exploitation of women. This ruling was given in a *habeas corpus* writ petition filed by the husband of a minor girl and the statement given by another minor girl that she had married on her own will and wanted to live with her husband and not with her parents. The Division Bench, comprising Manmohan Sarin J. and Manju Goel J., ruled that once a girl or a boy attains the age of discretion and chooses a life partner on her or his own will their marriage cannot be nullified on the ground of being minor. They further held that 'it is not an offence if a girl of that age elopes with her boyfriend and then marries him against the wishes of her parents.'

In *Sunil Kumar* v. *State (NCT Delhi)*,[265] Manmohan Sarin J. and S.L. Bhayana J. pronounced the judgment on a habeas corpus petition filed by a minor girl's brother-in-law alleging and held that her father had confined her illegally and was not allowing her to meet her husband. The court held that

If a girl of around 17 years runs away from her parents' house to save herself from their onslaught and joins her lover or runs away with him, it is no offence either on the part of the girl or on the part of the boy.

The girl was not willing to go to her parents, who were not amenable to any reconciliation and wished to sever all relationship with her. The husband was gainfully employed and his family had accepted the girl without making any demand for dowry. The minor girl was permitted to live with her husband.

---

[262] II (2003) DMC 774 Cal
[263] II (2006) DMC 4 AP
[264] I (2006) DMC 1 : AIR 2006 Del 37

[265] I (2007) DMC 786 Del

Prohibition of Child Marriage Act, 2006

These judicial pronouncements were criticized by various women's organizations and the National Commission for Women on the ground that such a lax attitude towards child marriage on the part of the judiciary would be instrumental in increasing the incidents of child marriage in the country. There was a renewed demand to render child marriages void and for compulsory registration of marriages to curb the practice of child marriage.[266]

In response to the demands raised by various women's organizations and the National Commission for Women, the Central Government introduced the Prevention of Child Marriage Bill, 2004, which was referred to the Parliamentary Standing Committee which proposed a common marriageable age for both the sexes, i.e., 18 years. The Committee recommended that child marriage should be void *ab initio* and not voidable at the option of either contracting party, keeping in view the inhibitions that parties have against court proceedings. The Committee also recommended initiating social measures such as creation of rehabilitation fund for providing shelter, food, education, health, and security for the victims of child marriages and also recommended active support and coordination of officials of Panchayat, *taluka*, District, and State levels, NGOs, and social groups and agencies.

However, the Prohibition of Child Marriage Act, which was enacted in 2006, differed from these suggestions in various material respects. The main provisions in the present statute are discussed below.

The Act stipulates that a child marriage is voidable at the option of a contracting party who was a child at the time of marriage. Such a petition must be filed within two years of attaining majority which is 21 for boys and 18 for girls.[267] If the petitioner is a minor, the petition can be filed through the guardian or next friend with the Child Marriage Prevention Officer (CMPO).

Section 4 of the Act makes a provision for maintenance and residence of minor girls and makes the boy and, in case he is a minor, his parents liable for it. Section 5 also makes provision for custody and maintenance of children born of such unions. Section 6 of this Act declares that every child begotten or conceived of such marriage before the decree is made, whether born before or after the commencement of this Act, shall be deemed to be legitimate for all purposes.

Section 12 further lays down the few cases in which the marriage of a minor child is to be void, i.e., where the child is taken or enticed out of the keeping of the lawful guardian, or is by force compelled, or by any deceitful means induced, to go from any place, or is sold for the purpose of marriage and made to go through a form of marriage, or if the minor is married after which the minor is sold or trafficked or used for immoral purposes.

The punishment for a male adult marrying a child is rigorous imprisonment up to two years or fine up to rupees one lakh or both. Any person who permits such a marriage or fails to prevent such a marriage, or even attends or participates in such a marriage is also punishable.[268]

---

[266] See this chapter further for a detailed discussion on 'Registration of Marriages.'

[267] The minority of a child is defined under Section 2 (a) of the Act as a male below the age of 21 years and a female below the age of 18 years as that is the permissible age of marriage under various personal laws. This contravenes the definition of minority under all other provisions of law where it is defined as 18 years, including for voting rights.

[268] The Act makes an exception in case of women and provides that no woman shall be punishable with imprisonment.

Section 13 gives the courts the power to issue injunctions prohibiting child marriages. The Act provides for the appointment of CMPOs across the country, whose role is to prevent child marriages, investigate complaints, and gather evidence to prosecute any violation of the law. The CMPO is in charge of creating awareness on the issue, furnishing statistics on child marriage to the State government, and petitioning the court for orders related to maintenance, custody and injunctions. The State government can ask any person who is an officer of a *gram panchayat*, a municipality or a public sector undertaking, or an employee of an NGO to assist the CMPO.

Interrogating the Contemporary Feminist Discourse

The social movement against child marriage and the demand for state intervention to curb this malaise was first articulated in the nineteenth century and engagement with this issue continues even in the twenty-first century. But despite the fact that this was one of the earliest legal campaigns which originated in nineteenth century, there is very little incisive analyses as to why legal reform has failed to address the problem. While child marriage continues to be a concern, the solution to a problem rooted within socioeconomic structures is sought within the domain of the law. This, despite the ground reality that legal enactments have proved to be highly inadequate in making meaningful interventions in the realm of marriage and family relationships.

The contemporary discourse needs to be located within continuous structural shifts in the economic, cultural, and social frameworks. The concerns of nineteenth century reformers were located within the structure of the new colonial legal order designed to usher in modernity and state control. It posed a challenge to Brahminical patriarchy within which a high premium was placed upon the virginity of

brides. The opposition to this movement came from the revivalists who questioned the authority of colonial rulers to interfere in local customs, practices, and religious beliefs.

During the early twentieth century, when women's organizations entered the political arena, the focus shifted to women's health, protection from early pregnancies, and concern over women's education and general well being. To coincide with the reproductive cycle of women, the Child Marriage Restraint Act raised the age of marriage under for girls to 14 years, when biologically the female body would be more receptive to sexual intercourse and pregnancy. In 1949, the age was raised further to 15 years.

This became the basis while enacting the Hindu Marriage Act in the 1950s, which laid down a minimum age of 15 for girls and 18 for boys. But the enactment did not render underage marriages void. This was due to the continued ideology of Hindu marriages being sacramental (despite the codification) and due to the grave social implication such a move would have upon innocent children born out of such unions. Within this context, the CMRA came to be viewed more as rhetoric or an aspiration than a moral code or a legal mandate. Socially sanctioned community norms and customs prevailed over the legal dictate. Hence, despite the prolonged and highly visible campaign prior to the enactment, the Act was a non-starter with scholars commenting that there were hardly a hundred odd prosecutions under the Act during the first forty years of its enactment, as compared to the millions of child marriages taking place in the country. It was also noted that where the parties have been prosecuted, the motivations have come from family feuds and factional fights rather than from the diligence of the provisions of the Act (Sampath 1969). So even the rare prosecutions under the Act were confined within the patriarchal paradigm and used as community controls over the female body rather than as a safeguard against it as is popularly perceived.

In the 1970s, the minimum age of marriage was raised to 18 for girls and 21 for boys, as per the recommendations of the Committee on the Status of Women. But another contributory factor around this time was the belief that it would also serve as a measure of population control.[269] Several social factors such as urbanization, increased avenues of education of girls, and loosening of the grip of conservative religious leadership over communities, Westernization among the urban middle class, etc., have contributed to a gradual increase in the mean age of marriage of girls as Table 1.7 indicates:

This steady increase in the minimum age of marriage has served to bring an increased number of marriages within the ambit of 'child marriage' and has resulted in a skewed statistical profile. Currently the age of marriage in India is set at a higher level than in U.K., where the minimum age of marriage is 16 for girls and 18 for boys. Therefore, while a marriage between a 17-year-old girl and a 20-year-old boy would be valid and legal in the U.K., it would be termed as 'child marriage' under the Indian law (Mensky 2003: 371). The raising of the age has resulted in criminalizing a large number of marriages of choice and in greater family, community, and state control over them.

While child marriages still prevail in India, the concerns raised during the nineteenth century reformist movement is no longer valid. Rather than dictates of brahmincal patriarchy, the contemporary concern over child marriage needs to be located within socio-economic factors such as extreme poverty among the urban and rural poor, lack of resources and access to education of girl children, and fear of rape and

Table 1.7   Mean Age of Women at Marriage 1901–71[270]

Time Frame	Age of Consent/ Marriage	Mean Age at Marriage	Literacy Rate Women (General)
1901–11	12	13.2	-
1911–21	12	13.6	-
1921–31	12	12.6	-
1931–41	14	15.0	-
1941–51	14	15.4	8.86%
1951–61	15	16.1	13%
1961–71	15	17.2	18.04%
1981–91	15/18	19.3	39.2%
1998–99	15/18	19.7	

sexual abuse of young unmarried girls. More than the elite and middle class segments of upper castes, it is the backward castes, the Dalits, and Muslims who are burdened with these concerns. Ironically, these communities were not the focus of attention at the time when the debate was first initiated. Among many lower castes, adult marriages of women were the norm.[271]

Though there has been a consistent demand from urban, middle class, upper caste legal scholars and social activists to declare child marriages as void, there is a legislative reluctance to give-in to these demands even after the recent enactment of 2006. This has been done keeping in view the plurality of cultures and diverse

[269] The Medical Termination of Pregnancy Act, 1971 (MTP Act), which gave women the right of legal abortion, was also enacted in this context.

[270] For statistics of the Mean Age of Marriage 1901–1971, see *Towards Equality*, Report of the Committee on the Status of Women in India, 1974, p. 23, Table 14; for 1991–1999, source: National Family Health Survey. For Literacy Rates, source: Census Reports.

[271] Due to the process of sanskritization and Hinduization in the intervening years, many communities have started adopting upper caste Hindu practices. (Srinivas 1962). See Chapter 1 *Personal Laws and Women's Rights* of the first volume where this issue is discussed in detail.

Table 1.8A   Literacy Rates for Women

Year	Literacy Rate Women (General)	Literacy Rate S.C. Women
1961	13%	3.3%
1971	18.04%	6.4%
1981	24.8%	10.9%
1991	39.2%	23.8%

Table 1.8B   Mean Age of Marriage 1961–71: Difference in Urban/Rural Profile[271]

Rural	16.7
Urban	19.2
Total	17.2

socio-economic background of the Indian population. Some rural based social activists have, in the context of Rajasthan, highlighted the class and caste biases of the contemporary campaign against child marriage (Singh et al. 1994: 1377–9). They have also comment that within communities where child marriages are performed, the marriage itself is not a license for sexual intercourse. A further ceremony has to be performed after the girl attains puberty and is fit for sexual intercourse. This ceremony is referred to by various terms such as *gauna, gona, gohna, muklava, ana*, etc., in different regions. Only after the performance of this ceremony is the girl sent to the marital home for consumption of marriage. The facts of the *Rukhmabai case*[273] who, though married in childhood, was never sent to her husband's house for consumption of her marriage since the second ceremony had not been performed, validates this point. Many

reported cases also contain a reference to this custom.[274] Hence the official statistics on child marriage may not accurately reflect the instances of minors who cohabit or have cohabited with their husbands.[275]

Within the realm of matrimonial law, linked to the issue of validity of marriage, is the concern of maintenance to minor wives and legitimacy of children born of this union. Hence there has been a great hesitancy on the part of the judiciary to declare minor marriages as void. Judges have consistently upheld the legal validity of child marriages by strictly interpreting the provisions of Sections 11 and 12 of the HMA. In fact, the authoritative Supreme Court ruling on this issue, which discussed various high court rulings to validate child marriages, *Lila Gupta* v. *Lakshmi Narain*,[276] was concerned with the rights of a widow to inherit her deceased husband's property against the claims of her brother-in-law and nephew who had challenged the validity of her marriage. In this case, the Supreme Court laid down that though Section 5 (iii) of the Act prescribes a minimum age of marriage, a breach of this condition does not render the marriage void. The Bench comprising Y. V. Chandrachud C. I., D.A. Desai J., and R.S. Pathak J. commented that it would be hazardous for marriage laws to treat a marriage in breach of a certain condition as void even though the law does not expressly provide for it.[277]

---

[272]   Report of the Committee on the Status of Women in India, *Towards Equality*, 1974, Table 15, p. 23.

[273]   *Dadaji Bhikaji* v. *Rukhmabai*, (1885) ILR 9 Bom 529. See section titled 'A Moment of Defiance: The Rukhmabai Case' of Chapter 1 *Personal Laws and Women's Rights* of the first volume where this case is discussed in detail.

[274]   See for instance *Pushpabai* v. *Pratap Singh*, I (2001) DMC 110 MP (discussed in Chapter 2) *Matrimonial Rights and Obligations* in section titled 'Maintenance Rights of Second Wives' and *Roop Narayan Verma* v. *Union of India*, AIR 2007 Chh 64 discussed earlier in this section.

[275]   In any case, since most marriages are not registered, official statistics on child marriage may not accurately reflect the ground reality.

[276]   AIR 1978 SC 1351

[277]   p. 1354, para 8 of the judgment

Rather ironically, some of these judgments invoked criticism from various women's rights groups despite the fact that the judges were upholding the rights of women through these pronouncements. These groups urged the government to amend relevant statutes in order to declare child marriages void. The demand itself has a long history and the view adopted by these groups was extremely shortsighted.

In 1994, the draft bill prepared by the National Commission for Women, the Indian Marriage Bill,[278] had also proposed compulsory registration of marriages, stipulating that a declaration of marriage must be sent to the Registrar of Marriages within three days of its performance. It was recommended that a fine of Rs 100 per day should be levied for default for a period of one month and thereafter, the marriage should be deemed void.[279] Twenty years prior to this, the Report of the Status of Women Committee, *Towards Equality*, had also suggested as follows:

We recommend legislation prohibiting courts from granting any relief in respect of a marriage solemnized in violation of the age requirements prescribed by law unless both the parties have completed the age of 18 years. (1974: 114)

Another proponent of this position, Jaya Sagade, in her book, *Child Marriage in India* (2005), has examined the issue from the perspective of International Human Rights principles, using, according to her, a 'feminist legal framework'. Advocating that child marriages should be declared void, she argues that though this approach may seem drastic, nothing else is likely to be effective for the protection of young girls against the harsh physical, education, social, and economic consequences of

child marriage. She substantiates her argument by stating that the institution of patriarchy operates in the name of culture for justifying child marriage of young girls and one cannot continue to raise twentieth century arguments[280] in the twenty first century for not declaring child marriages void (Sagade 2005 : 54).

In direct contrast to this position, Prof Mensky comments,

… an analysis of case law on child marriages clearly shows that the judges had taken up the challenge of developing the legislative foundations into a socially meaningful system of regulation. Their major concern, to prevent certain individuals, who tend to be men, from taking duplicitous advantage of the argument that child marriages are against public policy, and thus should be void. Unlike many social reformers and text-book writers, some judges realize the extent of their social responsibility. (Mensky 2003 : 367)

Those advocating the declaration of child marriages as void base their arguments on the premise that some women may have to pay a price in order to bring in the necessary social transformation for the greater good of all women. There seems to be hardly any concern among those who advocate this position in the name of 'women's rights' that the women who are called to pay the price are poor, illiterate, teenaged girls on whom marriage may have been thrust upon. As we can see in the next chapter which deals with women's right to maintenance, the validity of marriage is often contested only when women claim their rights of maintenance. These deserted young girls and their children would be deprived of their basic right of survival if judges adopt the position of declaring these child marriages as void.

It is within this ground reality, even while bringing in the recent amendment to the Child Marriage Restraint Act, the state administration

---

[278] See Chapter 2 *Constitutional Law and Citizenship Claims* of the first volume for further discussion on this issue.

[279] Provision to Section 17 of the draft Bill

[280] Such as 'preventive measures should be adopted rather than invalidating the marriage'

found it extremely difficult to give in to the demand of social activists for declaring child marriages as void. Further, even while declaring the marriage void at the instance of the husband, the state was compelled to ensure that the rights of women to maintenance, custody of children, and rights of children to legitimacy and maintenance are not defeated. This position is contrary to the recommendation of the Committee on the Status of Women as well as the provision in the draft bill of the National Commission for Women, discussed earlier, and has been criticized by some of women's organizations.

It appears that the only new provision that the statute enacted, following the campaign by women's groups and recommendations by the National Commission for Women, has been to provide an easy option for husbands to wriggle out of the marriage contracted when they were minors by declaring such marriages as void without having to prove any other fault ground. Such option provided to husbands may not be in the best interest of the young girls for whom marriage still provides social status and legitimacy, economic security and shelter.

As far as the advantage to women is concerned, there was an 'option of puberty' for marriages performed before they were 15 years of age. This option now extends to marriages performed before they had reached the age of 18 years. This could easily have been effected by amending section 13 (2)(iv) of the Hindu Marriage Act and the corresponding provisions in other matrimonial statutes. In any case, if a woman wishes to dissolve her marriage, there are several other grounds which are available to her. As a lawyer concerned primarily with family law and women's rights, I can safely surmise that rarely does a teenaged girl dissolve her marriage only on the ground of minority. Usually there are other reasons, such as cruelty, dowry harassment, adultery, or desertion,

which prompt her to opt for the dissolution of her marriage.

Regarding declaration of marriage as void if the girl was enticed out of the custody of her lawful guardian or compelled, or induced into marriage by deceitful means, this can be construed as lack of valid consent or vitiated consent, which has always been a ground for annulment of marriage under all matrimonial laws.

Articulation of Agency and Feminist Locations

Sagade's argument that 'the institution of patriarchy operates in the name of culture for justifying child marriage of young girls' gets further problematised when we examine the elopement cases. As against the socio-economic constraints of child marriage due to poverty discussed earlier, these cases concern marriages of choice by young girls. Here the legal provision becomes a weapon to control the expression of sexuality and curb voluntary marriages, and is used to augment the patriarchal parental power. Even though the criminal provisions regarding kidnapping and statutory rape appear to be protecting minor girls, these provisions are concerned primarily with securing the rights of parents or guardians over the minor girl against her lover or husband. The young couple who has exercised the choice often gets trapped within family feuds or caste and community hostilities. There are no exceptions in the laws on abduction and kidnapping that allow a minor to opt out of guardianship or to leave her parental home on grounds of domestic abuse and neglect (Baxi 2009). The use (and abuse) of police power at the instance of parents with regard to marriages of choice, is in direct contrast to women's autonomy, agency, and free will.

The situation becomes precarious when an upper caste girl elopes with a lower caste boy or when a Hindu girl falls in love with a Muslim boy, crossing boundaries of Hindu upper caste dictates of purity and pollution. In a society ridden with prejudices against lower castes and communal strife, a young couple who dares to cross community dictates is severely punished. At times the price for choosing a partner would be a gruesome murder or public humiliation of the couple or their relatives (Chowdhry 2004; Welchman et al. 2005). The notion of women as sexual property of their communities is deeply internalized, leading to violence not merely by the girls' families but also the community.

In order to criminalize the choice of marriage by young girls, at times the fathers file complaints of kidnap and rape against the boy or man by falsely projecting even major girls as minors who are devoid of the legal authority to give their consent to marriage or sexual intercourse. Despite being aware of the fact that it is a marriage of choice and voluntary elopement, the police collude with the fathers to protect patriarchal interests and 'community honour'. Only if the girl is able to provide clear and unequivocal proof of her majority is she allowed to accompany her husband and cohabit with him. Otherwise the father's word regarding her age is accepted and she is reverted back to his custody, and criminal charges are pressed against the boy.

In rare cases where the girls vehemently refuse to return to the custody of their fathers, they are sent to state protection homes until they are majors. Even thereafter the girls are often not automatically released and the husband would have to initiate legal proceedings for the release of the girl. Judges have commented that many of the habeas corpus petitions filed by either the young husbands or fathers of the girls, for production of the girl in court are in fact cases concerning elopement marriages. This is a serious concern for the courts as the following recent judgments indicate.

In *Ajit Ranjan* v. *State*,[281] the Delhi High Court advised the state administration to view these types of cases more as a social problem than a criminal offence. In this case, the husband had filed a writ petition under habeas corpus seeking custody of his wife who had been confined by her parents and was not permitted to return to him. The court commented that the changing social scenario in the country was leading to a situation where there were more inter-caste and inter-religion marriages, which meet with societal and familial resistance. The court noted that what was required was not action under criminal law, but counseling of the parties in order to arrive at an amicable understanding. In *Kokkula Suresh* v. *State of Andhra Pradesh*,[282] the Andhra Pradesh High Court reaffirmed that the marriage of a minor girl below 18 years is not a nullity. The court further held that the husband is the natural guardian in respect of a married minor's person and property and he is entitled to her custody. Further, the father of the girl cannot claim the custody of the minor girl. In *Ashok Kumar* v. *State*,[283] the Punjab and Haryana High Court commented that couples performing love marriage are chased by police and relatives, often accompanied by musclemen. Often cases of rape and abduction are registered against the boy. At times the couple faces the threat of being killed and such killings are termed as 'honour killings'. Often the state is only a mute spectator. The court directed the state to speedily evolve a compassionate mechanism to redress grievances of young couples and their parents.

These judgments serve as a benchmark for the liberal interpretation of constitutional law on equality and individual freedom and also restrain the police and magisterial administration

---

[281] II (2007) DMC 136
[282] I (2009) DMC 646 AP
[283] I (2009) DMC 120 P&H

from performing arbitrary actions such as forcing women into 'protective custody' of the state. For instance, in *Payal Sharma alias Kamla Sharma* v. *Superintendent, Nari Niketan, Agra,*[284] the Allahabad High Court rejected the father's contention that the girl was a minor and instead accepted the woman's own contention that she was a major and declared that she has a right to go anywhere and live with anyone. The court commented:

In our opinion a man and a woman, even without getting married can live together, if they wish. This can be regarded as immoral by society but it is not illegal. There is a difference between law and morality.'

Since the girl had stated that her life was in danger, the court also ordered the police to ensure her security.

Some women's organizations such as Association for Advocacy and Legal Initiatives (AALI) have worked consistently over the issue of elopement marriages and have extended support to young girls in their struggle against parental authority. They have also appreciated the role courts have played in strengthening the rights of young women against parental authority.[285]

While determining whether the choices made by young girls are valid, courts have to counter allegations not just of minority but also of unsoundness of mind. To augment their claim, natal families base their arguments on phrases such as 'hormonal imbalances' and 'flush of youth', all of which are presumably indicators of her immaturity and inability to make a prudent choice regarding her life partner (Chakravarthy 2005).

The violent manner in which families and the caste panchayats (also known as *khap* panchayats), exercise their power over a young girl and her lover/husband has already been discussed in the conclusions to Chapter 1 of the first volume. There have been instances where the girl and her lover have been humiliated, ostracized or even killed for defying the community norms.

Right-wing Hindu mobilization in recent years has led to both ideological and organizational moves to counter inter-community marriages of choice. The following incident serves to highlight this point further. On 24 January 2009, members of Ram Sena, a Hindu fundamentalist organization, unleashed violence on girls, in broad day light, in a pub in Mangalore, Karnataka, in the name of protecting Indian culture. This attempt at moral policing attracted the attention of the national and international media. Following this, there were several other incidents where Hindu young girls were dragged out of busses and were humiliated for befriending Muslim boys. The groups also spread terror among the youth in several cities and warned them against celebrating Valentine's Day on the ground that it is an immoral 'Christian' festival and was against Indian tradition and culture. On 10 February 2009, a 17-year-old girl was dragged out of a bus and taken to the police station. Her parents were informed and the boy was arrested on charges of rape and kidnapping. Unable to bear the humiliation, the girl committed suicide.[286] Right-wing forces in Gujarat and Maharashtra have also kept a strict vigil over Hindu-Muslim unions by monitoring the notices displayed outside the office of the Registrar of Marriages and then threatening the Hindu girls with dire consequences if they refused to break off the relationship.

The inadequacy of the recent legislation prohibiting child marriage[287] was emphasized by

---

[284] AIR 2001 All 254

[285] AALI, *Choosing a Life… Crimes of Honor in India The right to, if, when and whom to Marry* Lucknow: AALI 2004 (Informal Publication of the NGO).

[286] *Indian Express*, Bombay Edition, 12 February 2009.

[287] Prohibition of Child Marriage Act, 2006

another incident reported in the media—a 17-year-old, pregnant girl was confined to a state-run institution while awaiting the outcome of a complaint filed by her parents. The question, whether after the amendment, custody of the girl could be handed over to the husband when the parents of the girl have alleged rape and kidnapping, were also raised. While the court, burdened with backlogs and delays, took a long time to decide the issue, the girl was compelled to languish in the protective home and deliver her child in these adverse surroundings.[288]

While looking at these recent incidents, one needs to address a complex legal question—since the girls were minors, were they juridical persons invested with the power to exercise free choice and would the consent given by them to the marriage be deemed as 'legally valid'? At times, judges, with a concern for social justice, have resolved the issue by resorting to basic principles of human rights in order to save the minor girls from the wrath of their parents and from institutionalization in state-run 'protective homes'. The only way they could do so was by holding these marriages as valid and by allowing the girls to cohabit with the husbands of their choice.

Examining these judgments through the prism of women's rights, could these judicial interventions in aid of minor girls be termed as regressive and the demand by women's groups to declare these marriages as 'null and void' be termed progressive? Could the curbing of the freedom of these minor girls to express their sexual choices, by their natal families with the aid of the mighty power of the state in a sexually repressive society be termed as a 'progressive intervention' and a 'challenge to patriarchy'? Even more disturbing is the realization that the

parents, who were determined to break the sexual alliances that girls had contracted of their own choice, were using the provisions of an apparently progressive legislation only to marry off the girls (while they were still minors) to a boy of their own choice within the confines of rigid caste and class hierarchies. It appears that choice, or desire, as expressed by a woman is somehow intrinsically illicit when it is against parental diktat and caste or community norms, and therefore needs to be disrupted (Chakravarthy 2005: 311). The provisions of the Act appear to be invoked more often to prevent voluntary marriages and augment patriarchal power than to pose a challenge to it.

Minor girls are not given a choice and marriages are thrust upon them, most often resulting in marital rape on the nuptial night. The fortified terrain of family, along with the interface of caste and community structures, works in tandem against them to strengthen traditional institutions and conservative notions. In a rare instance, as part of a governmental programme, when a community worker, Bhanwari Devi, intervened to stop a child marriage in an upper caste family, she was gang raped by upper caste men (Singh et al. 1994 : 1377–9). Worse, the District and sessions court, Jaipur acquitted all the five upper caste men accused of raping her. The court commented:

'Indian culture has not fallen to such low depths that someone who is brought up in it, an innocent, rustic man, will turn into a man of evil conduct who disregards caste and age differences—and becomes animal enough to assault a woman. How can persons of 40 and 60 years of age commit rape while someone who is seventy years old watches by...'[289]

[288] *Times of India*, Bombay Edition, 20 February 2009.

[289] The judgment was delivered on 15 November 1995 by Jagpal Singh J. For a brief comment see, Dandavate, Madhu (1996) 'Rape of Justice in Bhanwari Case', *Times of India*, Mumbai: 7 February 1996.

It is not my aim here to encourage marriages of minors. The point one is trying to advance is simply that the law has not helped in interventions at the community-level to curb child marriages arranged by natal families. Even public interest litigations filed by concerned individuals and groups have not yielded positive results.[290] There is a need for community-level sensitisation, greater security for girls in public spaces, and better resources for education of girls in poverty stricken villages and urban slums. But the point which is being underlined is that the campaign by reformers for stringent laws has only strengthened patriarchal power and weakened the negotiating power of young girls contracting marriages of choice. We need to differentiate between marriages of choice by the girls themselves and marriages contracted at the instance of parents. It is very difficult for women's rights groups to enter the bastion of caste-based patriarchal strongholds. Law comes into effect only when the parents or the community wishes to act against the interest of the girls. Here the collusion of the state with local patriarchal powers is clearly visible.

The collusion of the police with criminal elements is another factor that has caused insecurity among the poor, particularly, single mothers and has led to an increase in the rate of child marriages. Madhu Kishwar, a feminist scholar, has argued that increasing violence and insecurity is making the lives of women more vulnerable and, therefore, making families feel that bringing up daughters is a high-risk job. This is in large part due to the increasing lawlessness of the police and other arms of the government, as well as the large-scale criminalization of politics. In this context, it is difficult for a community to exercise restraint over anti-social elements because of the police patronage to criminals. Even in villages, families with one or more sons in politics or government jobs, especially in the police, come to acquire tyrannical hold over the lives of others. This power is often reflected in increased sexual assaults against women. Kishwar argues that concern over safety of girl children is pushing families into marrying their minor daughters. Once married, the girl ceases to be the responsibility of her parents and they are no longer burdened with the fear of the girl getting violated and losing her chastity, which would mar her chances of marriage (Kishwar 2008: 19).

Studies conducted in urban centres by the National Institute for Research in Reproductive Health, Mumbai also endorse this view. A report published in a local tabloid mentioned that one in every five slum dwellers practices child marriage. One of the reasons attributed to this phenomenon is the lack of safety for girls in the slums.[291]

Despite the fact that the law has not worked, some women's groups and legal scholars constantly demand stricter laws which will make minor girls even more vulnerable to state and family dictates. There is a tendency to impose ideologically determined formulas upon people's lives, without assesing the implication of such imposition on the people whose interest is sought to be served.

At another level, there is an increasing discomfort among certain feminist legal scholars about whether an authoritarian state intervention in a top-down manner is the only way through which social transformation can be brought about. For instance, Nandita Haksar comments that continual recourse to law is 'a substitute for the other harder option of building a movement for an alternative vision' (Haksar 1999).

---

[290] *Sushila Gothala v. State of Rajasthan*, AIR 1995 SC 90.

[291] '1 in 5 Slum Dwellers Practice Child Marriage', *Midday*, Mumbai: 14 March 2009.

A contradiction is generated by the interaction of the language of rights and the law. It arises from the belief of social movements that they are articulating universal values required by legal discourse when they use the language of rights, when in fact rights are constituted differently by the moral perspectives of different discourses. This opposition between the universality and uniformity required by the law on the one hand and the multi-layered formulations of rights on the other, becomes particularly problematic when feminist politics attempts to use the law, through the language of rights, to liberate women's bodies from the oppression of patriarchal structures and institutions (Menon 2004: 16–7). There is a further problem in treating human rights as universal norms that are to be globally institutionalized by international intervention. We can no longer be innocent of the implications of 'international consensus and pressure', in the context of the prevailing global balance of power (Menon 2004).

It is important that contemporary feminist discourse is far more nuanced than what one can observe in the recent campaigns against child marriages. Rather than blindly advocating a 'universally' accepted position framed by a First-world feminist discourse, women's rights groups need to advance a position which is rooted within Third-world realities, is contextualized within the urban-rural divide, and is etched by other social realities such as caste prejudices and communal conflicts. In final analysis, a feminist voice must lend credence to the claims of the weak against the might of *status quo*-ist institutional authorities. The agency exercised by a young teenaged girl and her voice of protest against the dictates of patriarchy would need articulation and support. It is within this complex tapestry that the claims of feminist jurisprudence must essentially lie.

MARRIAGES WITH EXPATRIATE INDIANS

Jurisdictional Concerns

An emerging concern on the horizon of Indian matrimonial law is regarding jurisdiction. It has arisen in the context of Indians who migrate to other countries but continue to retain dynamic ties with the country of their origin. While migrating they carry with them their tradition, culture, value system, and personal laws.[292] Some NRIs seek Indian brides from their own communities in India. These marriages are celebrated in traditional, customary manner but some also register their marriages under the civil law. After marriage, despite the fact that either one or both the parties to the marriage are residing in a foreign country, Indian courts have the authority to adjudicate over disputes which arise between the couple. The nomenclature commonly used to describe such marriages is 'NRI marriages'. The term 'Non-Resident Indian' (NRI) is often used as an omnibus phrase to include any Indian citizen or person of Indian origin who ordinarily resides outside the territory of India. For taxation and other official purposes, the Government of India has defined NRI as an Indian national who resides away from India for more than 183 days in a calendar year. But under matrimonial law, the term is often used in a wider sense and includes persons of Indian origin (PIO), overseas citizens of India (OCI), and other expatriate Indians. The question of jurisdiction of Indian courts with respect to NRI marriage will arise only when at least one of the parties to the marriage is an Indian citizen. Thus, matrimonial courts will have jurisdiction in any marriage of an NRI, as defined by the Government of India,

[292] For a detailed study of the cultural and legal pluralism among the South Asian migrant communities, see Prakash Shah, *Legal Pluralism in Conflict* (2005).

and in any marriage of an Indian citizen, whether with an overseas citizen of India, person of Indian origin, or expatriate Indian.

Conflict of Laws

In India, the Foreign Marriages Act of 1969 is a specific legislation which is applicable to a marriage of an Indian citizen to a non-Indian, solemnized abroad. This Act stipulates that marriages, where one of the parties is an Indian citizen and the other is a non-Indian, would be governed by the provisions of the Special Marriage Act, 1954. However, this Act is highly inadequate while addressing the wide range of issues which arise during matrimonial litigation. There is a great deal of uncertainty about the manner in which jurisdictional issues have to be resolved in marriages involving NRIs, which are solemnized or dissolved in a foreign country.

The laws of a country are generally based on its religious, social, economic, and political beliefs, ideologies, and traditions. These would essentially vary from one society to another as well as from one country to another. This usually gives rise to conflict of laws as the laws of one country may not be in consonance with the laws of another. This conflict between different legal regimes is generally resolved through rules and regulations of 'Private International Law' which provide certain guidelines which determine when the jurisdiction of a foreign court must be recognized and such decrees must be enforced by domestic courts.

In *Vishwanath* v. *Abdul Wajid*,[293] the Supreme Court explained the notion of Private Interational Law in the following words:

What is called Private International Law is not law governing relationship between two independent States. Private International Law, or as it is sometimes called, 'Conflict of Laws' is simply a branch of the civil law evolved to do justice between two litigating parties in respect of transactions or personal status involving a foreign element. The rules of Private International Law must therefore, in the very nature of things, differ, but by the comity of nations certain rules are recognized as common to civilized jurisdictions. Through part of the judicial system of each State, these common rules have been adopted to adjudicate upon disputes involving foreign element and to effectuate judgments of foreign courts in certain matters, or as a result of International Conventions.

In India, the rules of private international law are not codified and are scattered in different enactments such as the Civil Procedure Code, the Contract Act, the Indian Succession Act, the Indian Divorce Act, the Special Marriage Act, etc. Section 13 of the Civil Procedure Code (CPC) contains the underlying principles for awarding recognition to a judgment of a foreign court and provides that where reciprocity exists between India and a foreign country, judgments of such foreign country may be enforced through execution proceedings initiated in India. Foreign judgments are conclusive in Indian courts regarding any matter directly adjudicated between the same parties. It must also be noted that a decree of divorce obtained from a foreign country is not required to be confirmed by the courts in India.[294]

In this context, in *Vishwanath* v. *Abdul Wajid*,[295] the Supreme Court held that the courts in India will not inquire whether the conclusions recorded in the foreign judgment are supported by evidence or are otherwise correct, because the binding character of such a judgment may be displaced only by establishing that the case falls within one or more of the six clauses of Section 13 and not otherwise.

---

[293] AIR 1963 SC 1

[294] *Sharmishtha* v. *Sujoy Mitra*, II (2008) DMC 633.
[295] AIR 1963 SC 1.

Section 13 of CPC contains certain exceptions to the general rule that foreign judgment is conclusive and binding, by providing certain safeguards and mandates. Following are the six situations in which the judgments of a foreign court will not be recognized by Indian courts:

1. Where the foreign judgment has not been pronounced by a court of competent jurisdiction.

2. Where the foreign judgment has not been given on the merits of the case.

3. Where it appears on the face of the proceedings that the foreign judgment has been founded on an incorrect view of international law or refused to recognize the applicable law of India.

4. Where proceedings in the foreign court on which the foreign judgment is based were contrary to natural justice.

5. Where the foreign judgment was obtained by fraud.

6. Where the foreign judgment sustains claims founded on the breach of any law enforced in India.

Protection of Women through Judicial Pronouncements

Women who are married to men residing in a foreign country are placed in a vulnerable situation as marriages registered in India can be dissolved by a court in the country where the husband resides without the wife ever having submitted herself to the jurisdiction of the court in that country. An outdated, patriarchal legal premise that the domicile of the wife follows that of her husband is often used to deny women their rights. This is rather ironic since the dependent visa to enter the foreign country is issued only upon an application made by the husband on behalf of his wife and the wife does not have an independent right to enter or reside in the country despite the legal premise that the domicile of the wife follows that of her husband. This places women at a disadvantage as they are unable to contest divorce proceedings in a foreign country, even when the petition is served upon them. In their absence, such cases are decided *ex parte*.

In this context, it should be noted that Article 10 of the Hague Convention of 1968 on the Recognition of Divorce and Legal Separations[296] expressly provides that the contracting states may refuse to recognise a decree of that country, if such recognition is manifestly incompatible with the public policy of the host country.

Several landmark decisions of our Supreme Court have attempted to provide certain safeguards to women who are placed in this precarious situation for no fault of theirs. Some of these leading cases are discussed in detail here.

A leading case, *Satya* v. *Teja Singh*,[297] was decided by the Supreme Court in 1975. The facts of the case are as follows: The couple, both Indian citizens, married each other in 1955 and had two children. In 1959 the husband left for USA for higher studies and thereafter secured a job in Utah, USA. The wife continued to reside in India and when the husband refused to support her, she filed for maintenance of Rs 1000. While these proceedings were pending, the

[296] The Hague Convention is an international legislation, the purpose of which is to specify the heads of jurisdiction which would secure international recognition of the decrees of divorce or legal separation. The Hague Convention of 1902 (on marriage) and 1905 (on the effects of marriage) represented the first attempts to codify the conflict of law rules relating to marriage and its effects. The Hague Convention deals only with the recognition of foreign decrees of divorce and of legal separation and is not concerned with the assumptions of jurisdiction and questions of choice of law.

[297] AIR 1975 SC 105

husband obtained a decree of divorce from the Nevada State Court in USA by making a false representation that he was a bona fide resident and was domiciled in Nevada. The court in USA dissolved the marriage despite the fact that the wife had not submitted to the jurisdiction of the court. Thereafter, in proceedings for maintenance initiated by the wife, the husband pleaded that he is not bound to maintain his divorced wife. The trial court rejected the contentions of the husband on the ground that the court in the state of Nevada had no jurisdiction to grant the decree of divorce and granted Rs 300 as maintenance to the wife and an additional Rs 100 for each of the minor children. This order was confirmed by sessions court. But the high court set aside the order on the ground that since the domicile of the wife follows that of her husband, the court in Nevada where the husband resided had jurisdiction. Though the appeal before the Supreme Court was in the context of the wife's right to maintenance, the court held that the appeal raises issues far beyond the normal ambit of a summary maintenance proceeding and addressed the core of the controversy—whether Indian courts are bound by divorce decrees granted by foreign courts. While upholding the wife's right to maintenance, and setting aside the high court order, the Supreme Court provided a framework regarding principles governing private international law as applicable to Indian courts and held as follows:

It is a well recognized principle that Private International Law is not the same in all countries. There is no system of Private International Law which can claim universal recognition. Hence, the question whether a decree of divorce passed by a foreign court (in this case Nevada State Court in USA) is entitled to recognition in India must depend principally on the rules of Private International Law as recognized in India. It is no doubt true that whether it is a problem of municipal law or of Conflict of Laws, every case which

comes before an Indian court must be decided in accordance with Indian law. It is another matter that the Indian conflict of laws may require that the law of a foreign country ought to be applied in a given situation for deciding a case which contains a foreign element. Such a recognition is accorded not as an act of courtesy but on considerations of justice. It is implicit in that process that the foreign law must not offend against our public policy.

Principles of Private International Law governing matters within the divorce jurisdiction are so conflicting in the different countries that not often a man and a woman are husband and wife in one jurisdiction but treated as divorced in another jurisdiction.

The principles of the American or English conflict of law are not to be adopted blindly by Indian Courts. Our notion of a genuine divorce and substantial rights and our distinctive principles of our public policy must determine the rules of our private international law. But an awareness of foreign law in a parallel jurisdiction would be a useful guideline in determining these rules.

A foreign decree of divorce obtained by the husband from the Nevada State Court in USA *in absentum* of the wife without her submitting to its jurisdiction will not be valid and binding on a criminal court in proceedings for maintenance, when it is found from the facts on record that the decree of divorce was obtained by fraud or by making a false representation as to a jurisdictional fact that the husband was a bona fide resident and was domiciled in Nevada. The decree being open to collateral attack on the jurisdictional fact, the recital in the judgment of the Nevada court that the respondent was a bona fide resident of and was domiciled in Nevada is not conclusive and can be contracted by satisfactory proof.

Until the enactment of a suitable legislation in accordance with the Hague Convention of 1970, the courts shall have to exercise a residual discretion to avoid flagrant injustice, for, no rule of Private International Law could compel a wife to submit to a decree procured by the husband by trickery. Such decrees offend against our notions of substantial justice.

Another landmark ruling, *Y. Narasimha Rao v. Y. Venkata Lakshmi,*[298] dealt with recognition by an Indian court of a divorce decree granted by a USA court, in respect of a marriage solemnized

[298] 1991 3 SCC 451

by two Hindus in India. The husband had married in India and obtained a divorce in USA and subsequently contracted another marriage. The first wife filed a criminal case under Section 494 of IPC for bigamy. The divorce decree was granted on the ground that marriage had broken down irretrievably and that the husband had been a resident of the State of Missouri for 90 days, immediately prior to the filing of the petition for divorce. The Supreme Court, while relying upon *Satya* v. *Teja Singh* (discussed earlier), laid down the following rule for awarding recognition to judgments of foreign courts in matrimonial matters in our country.

The jurisdiction assumed by the foreign court as well as the ground on which the relief is granted must be in accordance with the matrimonial law under which the parties are married. The exceptions to this rule may be as follows: (i) where the matrimonial action is filed in the forum where the respondent is domiciled habitually and permanently resides and the relief is granted on a ground available in the matrimonial law under which the parties are married; (ii) where the respondent voluntarily and effectively submits to the jurisdiction of the forum and contests the claim which is based on a ground available under the matrimonial law under which the parties are married; (iii) where the respondent consents to the grant of the relief although the jurisdiction of the forum is not in accordance with the provisions of the matrimonial law of the parties.

The aforesaid rule with its stated exceptions has the merit of being just and equitable. It does no injustice to any of the parties. The parties do and ought to know their rights and obligations when they marry under a particular law. They cannot be heard to make a grievance about it later or allowed to bypass it by subterfuges as in the present case. The rule also has an advantage of rescuing the institution of marriage from the uncertain maze of the rules of the Private International Law of the different countries with regard to jurisdiction and merits based variously on domicile, nationality, residence - permanent or temporary or ad hoc forum, proper law etc., and ensuring certainly in the most vital field of national life and conformity with public policy. The rule further takes account of the needs of modern life and makes due allowance to accommodate them.

Above all, it gives protection to women, the most vulnerable section of our society, whatever the strata to which they may belong. In particular it frees them from the bondage of the tyrannical and servile rule that wife's domicile follows that of her husband and that it is the husband's domicilliary law which determines the jurisdiction and judges the merits of the case.

In *Shiv Mirchandani* v. *Natasha Advani*,[299] this concept was expanded further. While discussing in detail the relevance of foreign decrees, the judgment laid down the following principles:

i. Where in a matrimonial dispute judgment is passed by a foreign court, its jurisdictional competency is ordinarily dependent upon the domicile of the parties;

ii. the domicile of the wife follows the domicile of her husband. Therefore, ordinarily it is the court of that country where the husband has his domicile, which has the jurisdiction to pass a judgment in the matrimonial dispute;

iii. the above rule of common law operates very harshly against the wife who has for one reason or the other, to reside habitually or permanently in a country other than the county of her husband's domicile. The stringency of this rule is done away with by the modern theory, which acknowledges the right of a wife to file a matrimonial proceeding in that country to which she has real and substantial connection by her habitual or permanent residence. This theory now finds place in the statutory law of England and has also been acknowledged by the Hague Convention on Private International Law, 1970. In the absence of any legislation to the contrary, the rules of International Convention can be followed in India. The said theory is accepted and followed by the Supreme Court in Narasimha Rao's case[300] (discussed earlier);

iv. the question of grant or rejection or matrimonial relief must however, be decided with reference to the law under which the parties got married;

v. the present case falls under the third exception of the rule laid down in Narasimha Rao's case[301], since

---

[299] 2003 MLR 21 Bom

[300] *Y. Narasimha Rao* v. *Y. Venkata Lakshmi*, 1991 3 SCC 451.

[301] Where the respondent consents to the grant of the relief although the jurisdiction of the forum is not

the husband and the wife had voluntarily submitted to the jurisdiction of the Swedish court and consented to the relief of divorce. Hence, the judgment of the Swedish court has to be regarded as a judgment of the court of competent jurisdiction within the meaning of S.13 (a) of the CPC;

vi. the said judgment does not violate the other conditions stated in S.13 of CPC. Hence, for all purposes it has to be regarded as a conclusive judgment.

Anubha v. *Vikas Aggarwal*[302] is yet another highly contested case where the husband had challenged the decree of maintenance on the ground that he had obtained a divorce from a court in the USA on the ground of wife's desertion. Refuting this allegation, the Delhi High Court held as follows:

The marriage was solemnized in India according to Hindu rites. Hence the matrimonial dispute is governable by provisions of the *Hindu Marriage Act*. Since the wife did not submit to jurisdiction of USA Court nor did she consent for grant of divorce in a US Court, decree obtained by the husband from Connecticut Court of USA is neither recognisable nor enforceable in India.

Dismissing the allegation that the wife had deserted the husband, the court further commented:

The wife was subjected to not only physical but mental cruelty of an intimate nature. The wife had every reason to leave her matrimonial home. The spouse who physically leaves home is not necessarily the deserter. It is the husband who is guilty of desertion. The wife has proved cruelty and desertion and is entitled to live separately and claim maintenance from her husband.[303]

Earlier, the high court had directed the husband to appear in person. But on one pretext or the other, he failed to do so. Hence his defense was struck down. The husband was also

restrained by the high court from further proceeding in the divorce case filed by him. This order was challenged by the husband in the Supreme Court,[304] which upheld the order of the high court.

While courts have refused to validate the divorce decrees against women, granted by foreign courts, which contain elements of fraud and misrepresentation, they have also validated decrees which protect women's rights as the following two cases indicate.

In *Deva Reddy* v. *Kamini Reddy*,[305] the parties were Christians. After a few years of marriage, when the wife was pregnant, the husband deserted her, converted to Islam and started living with another woman. When the wife approached the court for a declaration of validity of her marriage, the husband pleaded that the marriage was not valid and challenged the validity of a divorce decree obtained by the wife in respect of her previous marriage by a court in the USA. But the court declined to accept this argument and, while upholding the validity of the decree of divorce granted by American court, held as follows:

The husband contracted marriage, fully conscious of fact that the wife was earlier married and was divorced. He lived with her as husband and they had a child out of the wedlock. It is not permissible for him to argue that the marriage between the two was *non est*[306] for any reason. Before contracting marriage with her, he did not bring action either in a court in the USA or in India that the decree of divorce between his wife and her former husband was invalid for want of jurisdiction.

in accordance with the provisions of the matrimonial law of the parties.

[302] I (2003) DMC 139 Del

[303] See the discussion on Desertion earlier in this Chapter.

[304] *Vikas Aggarwal* v. *Anubha*, I (2002) DMC 633 SC

[305] II (2002) DMC 482 Kar

[306] '*Non est factum*' is a Latin term which permits one of the parties to escape from contractual obligations despite a valid contract which is in existence.

In another case, *Paul Tushar Biswas* v. *Addl. Dist. Judge*,[307] the court upheld a decree of maintenance granted by a court in the USA. The husband and wife were permanent residents of the state of California, USA. When the husband failed to provide maintenance to the wife and child, the wife initiated proceedings in California. The husband submitted to the proceedings by being represented by his lawyer and contested the claim of the wife, but the court upheld the wife's plea and granted her maintenance. Later the husband challenged this by filing proceedings before a court in Gauhati. The Gauhati High Court rejected the plea and held as follows:

The action initiated by the wife in US is neither contrary to international law nor contrary to any law in India. No plea of want of any reasonable opportunity or breach of judicial process was ever raised by the husband. He also did not plead any misrepresentation on jurisdictional facts or otherwise pointed out to indicate any fraud perpetrated by the wife in matter of assumption of jurisdiction by the court in California court. There were no proceedings relating to maintenance pending before any Indian court when interim order was passed by court in California for the maintenance of the child. The proceedings which were filed before the district court at Shillong by the husband were in respect of dissolution of marriage, custody of child and visitation rights. California court passed interim order on merits of case to support child. The order passed by the court in California cannot be defeated on ground of fraud. On date of said order, no other order by any court for maintenance of minor was in existence. No law, policy or convention mandating ouster of California Court's jurisdiction was brought to notice of this court. Section 43 of Divorce Act does not exclude jurisdiction of any other court of competent jurisdiction. Hence the exception under clause (b) and (c) of Section 13, CPC are not applicable to this case.

Where the marriage was performed abroad and thereafter, due to desertion, the wife was constrained to return to India, courts have upheld the woman's right to file proceedings in India, despite the fact that the marriage was performed abroad and for all material time the couple had lived together as husband and wife, abroad.[308]

This issue has been granted statutory recognition through the amendment to the Hindu Marriage Act and the Special Marriage Act. The wife is now entitled to file proceedings at a place of her residence though the marriage was performed and the couple resided together at a different place.[309]

Vulnerability of 'NRI Brides' and Remedial Measures

As we can observe, courts in India have used discretionary powers to redeem women of the archaic notions of domicile. This has become imperative in a globalized world where a large number of people migrate and yet retain the customs, traditions, and practices of their community. This is particularly true for Asian and African communities who strive to retain their cultural identity in foreign countries. At times applying Western standards of the country of residence regarding divorce may violate the principles of equity and natural justice, particularly as far as women are concerned. This is particularly true for dependent wives who are subjected to torture and violence due to exorbitant demands for dowry and are driven out of their residence. Courts have recognized the

[307] II (2006) DMC 59 Gau

[308] *Indira Sonti* v. *Suryanarayana Sonti*, I (2002) DMC 56 Del.

[309] Section.19 (iii-a) and (iv) of Hindu Marriage Act, 1955 and Section 31 (iii-a) and (iv) of Special Marriage Act, 1954 inserted by Act 50 of 2003 with effect from 23 December 2003.

vulnerability of women trapped in such situations and have used innovative legal dicta, discretionary powers, and principles of natural justice to bring some solace by expanding the parameters of women's rights.

Most NRI marriages involve men who are citizens of foreign countries and women who have lived in India and migrate only after their marriage. Usually their residence in a foreign country is a legal incident arising from the fact of marriage. They have a dependent status and do not qualify for an independent status as the citizen of the particular country where the husband has obtained citizenship. Women also become extremely vulnerable as they are uprooted from their native family surroundings and become devoid of all kinship and peer group support networks. They are usually not familiar with the language/culture of the country of migration. Further, their legal status does not allow them to work and they become economically dependent on their husbands. The husband acquires not only emotional and financial control, but also holds the key to the women's legal status of residing in the country of migration. This makes them particularly vulnerable to dowry harassment, physical, verbal, mental, and sexual abuse. In the United States of America, a policy is now being implemented which allows such women to pursue their immigration status based on filing a self petition as a battered spouse of a US citizen or Green Card holder. The required criteria is to establish that they were married to a US citizen or a Green Card holder in good faith, they were subjected to cruelty, they lived with the abuser, and are of good moral character.

Families of the bride often have no way of checking the credentials of the groom and this often leads to problems later on. There have been cases of men contracting bigamous marriages or of misrepresenting their income, family background, etc.

Issues of custody of children and enforcing maintenance orders have also been extremely problematic. This forces the wife to return to India, leaving the children in the custody of the husband. Later, in divorce proceedings, it is easy for the husband to obtain legal custody of the children and the wife has no recourse to fight custody battles. At times even the basic right of visiting her children is denied to her. Maintenance orders granted by Indian courts remain mere paper decrees as it becomes impossible to enforce them in a foreign country.

The Supreme Court, in *Neeraja Saraph* v. *Jayant Saraph*,[310] suggested the need to consider a legislation safeguarding the interests of women trapped in such marriages and had suggested the following remedial measures:

a) No marriage between an NRI and an Indian woman, which has taken place in India, may be annulled by a foreign court.

b) Provision may be made for adequate alimony to the wife in the property of the husband both in India and abroad.

While this judgment expresses a salutary concern for women's rights, the directions are rather sweeping and may even amount to throwing the baby out with the bath water.[311] Confronted with a large number of complaints by women who are married to NRI men, the National Commission for Women had also prepared a report on the problems of NRI

---

[310] (1994) 6 SCC 461

[311] I am using this phrase in the context that all divorces obtained in a foreign country are not fraudulent. Making it mandatory for all couples, who were married in India and have since migrated, to return to India for the purpose of obtaining their divorce is not a realistic or feasible option.

marriages and prepared a draft for a convention on the issue. The report commissioned by them made the following recommendations:

a) Registration of marriages be made compulsory.

b) Bilateral agreements for protection of such marriages to be concluded between India and such other countries where the Indian diaspora is in large numbers.

c) If the NRI husband has not become a citizen of the country in which he resides, concerned Indian laws to apply irrespective of the place of the filing of the petition for dissolution of the marriage.

d) Government monitored conciliation process of settlement of matrimonial disputes be initiated.

e) Suppression of information regarding marital status by NRI grooms to be dealt with under the provisions of the criminal law and steps to be taken through extradition treaties wherever operational.

Other measures suggested in the report include: (i) seeking the help of authorities at the work places of the husband, (ii) attaching property, if any, in India, (iii) initiating legal action against the fraudulent spouse for compensation in India, and (iv) if Overseas Citizenship has been granted to the husband, the same to be withdrawn.

The High Level Committee on People of Indian Origin also dealt with this issue and suggested that a special cell should be created in the relevant ministry to handle diaspora issues, with the mandate to provide free legal counselling for the families of girls contemplating marriage to NRIs/PIOs. Such families should be advised to check the voter or alien registration card of such NRIs/PIOs and their social security number and tax returns for the preceding three years. The bridegroom should be asked to give an affidavit stating his current marital status. That document should be attached to the application for marriage registration. This should be a mandatory pre-requisite to the issuance of a marriage registration certificate.

The issue was again discussed at the *Pravasi Bharatiya Divas*, 2005 and the following conclusions were reached:

1. There should be a comprehensive legislation so that there is a legal remedy available to such girls. Instituting special courts without such legislation would be futile.

2. Registration of marriages should be made compulsory in case of Overseas Indians. This will ensure compliance of conditions of a valid marriage. There will be complete proof of marriage and it would be a very strong deterrent against bigamous marriages.

3. If a person abandons his wife, he should forfeit his property.

4. Such instances may be made criminal offences.

5. Overseas citizenship of such a person should be forfeited.

6. An affidavit to be produced by the overseas Indian intending to marry an Indian citizen stating that he is single, his income, social security, and immigrant status, supported by documentary evidence at the time of registration of marriages. This affidavit should be authenticated by the Indian Embassy of the country he resides.

On the same occasion, the Government also made a commitment to sign the Hague Convention providing for recognition of judicial verdicts among signatory states.

While the concern of various governmental authorities and statutory bodies is genuine, these have not resulted in any concrete and legally enforceable provisions which would protect women placed in this precarious situation. Meanwhile, litigations involving NRI husbands continue in Indian courts, raising newer and more complex problems. The case, discussed below, highlights one of the emerging complexities of the issue. This case is popularly referred to as the 'South African Child Custody Case' and received a great deal of media attention. The husband, a South African citizen of Indian origin, was married in Mumbai. After marriage, when the wife went to South Africa, she was subjected to extreme mental harassment and was made to live in inhuman conditions. She was denied all contact with her family in India and was also not allowed to visit India. Her situation deteriorated after the birth of the child. She was reduced to being a domestic help and was even denied free and unrestrained access to her child. Finally her husband decided to come down to Mumbai along with his wife and child. The husband's scheme was to leave the wife in her parental home and return to South Africa with her passport, along with the minor child. Once this plan was executed, she would have no access to her child, who was a South African citizen. She could conveniently be discarded as she was an Indian passport holder who could enter South Africa only as a dependant of her husband. Due to timely legal intervention she was able to obtain an *ad-interim* order restraining the husband from removing the child from her custody. On receiving summons, the husband fled the country fearing arrest, under the mistaken notion that the proceedings were initiated under Section 498A of the IPC under which he was liable to be arrested. Later, he was awarded the right of access to the child during his visits to Mumbai. The wife was able to use the litigation process to get back the passports of herself and her child as a pre-condition to access.

The important legal issue which surfaced in this case was whether Indian courts have jurisdiction to decide the issue of custody of a South African child. The husband challenged the jurisdiction of the family court at Mumbai and pleaded that the child ordinarily resides in South Africa and is a citizen of that country. The child's visa had expired and the child did not have the legal status to continue to reside in Mumbai. Faced with all these complications, the family court upheld the husband's contention that since the child 'ordinarily' resides in South Africa, the family court in Mumbai has no jurisdiction to entertain the petition for custody.[312] The fact that a petition was filed within ten days of the child entering the country became a factor in favour of the husband. But when the interim order was passed, the child had already been residing in Mumbai for over a year. By the time the appeal filed by the wife against the order of the family court was heard, one more year had gone by. Since efforts at amicable settlement failed, the high court remitted the matter back to the family court to decide the issue on merits and in the meantime, the wife was allowed to retain custody of the child. But the core issue— how a woman would be able to secure custody of her two year old infant son, through litigation in South Africa—remained unresolved.

In this case, through a carefully crafted legal strategy, the woman was able to retain the custody of her minor child. But there are several cases where women could not obtain timely legal help or were unaware of their rights, and thus lost custody. When the wives are abandoned in their native country, they are left without any viable option. It is very easy for husbands to discard them and women are

[312] Order dated 29 September 2007 in Petition No.D-66 of 2006 by 2nd family court, Mumbai.

deprived of every right, including travel documents, citizenship of the foreign country, educational certificates, valuables, and, most importantly, custody of their child/children.

A similar issue was addressed by the Kerala High Court in *Hareendran Pillai* v. *Pushplatha*.[313] The parties were married in Kerala and the child was born in Bahrain. The custody of the child was with the mother, but the father snatched the child and brought her to India. The mother filed a petition in the family court at Kerala, seeking restoration of the custody of the child to her. The father challenged the jurisdiction of the court to decide the issue on the ground that the child was born and was living in Bahrain. But overruling this objection, the High Court of Kerala held that Indian courts have the jurisdiction to adjudicate over this issue. While granting custody to the mother, the court observed that even though the father was the natural guardian of the minor child, he could not, on this ground alone, have any preferential right over the child.

The rules of private international law or appropriate and relevant domestic statutes need to provide certain guidelines to matrimonial courts in defense of women's rights to deal with these complex issues in matrimonial law.

REGISTRATION OF MARRIAGES

Evolution of the Concept

The Special Marriage Act and the Indian Christian Marriage Act, both enacted in 1872, were the first enactments which provided for the registration of marriages. Later, in 1886, to provide for the registration of all births, marriages, and deaths, the Birth, Marriage and Death Registration Act was enacted by the British in order to compile the demographic profile of the territory. This law could not make

[313] AIR 2007 NOC 1064 Ker

much headway with regard to registration of marriages, but it was successful with registration of births and deaths.

Since Muslim, Christian, and Parsi religions are more institutionalized, the rules and procedures for contracting marriage are clear and unambiguous and are complied with. Under laws governing Christians and Parsis, as well as the Special Marriage Act, formalities of solemnizing marriage are strictly prescribed and the officiating priest has to provide a marriage certificate or it is mandated that the marriage be registered with the Registrar of Births, Deaths and Marriages. But Hindu marriages (as well as Hindu law), which are based more on community practices, are relatively less institutionalized and hence their legality is more ambiguous. The situation has deteriorated further due to the breakdown of traditional communities within which these marriages were performed. Lawyers and touts have exploited the situation further by projecting that any sham ceremony can be adopted for solemnizing a Hindu marriage by invoking 'custom'. Marriages run the risk of being declared invalid during litigation. In this context 'Registration of Marriages' has become an important concern under matrimonial law.

Provisions under Personal Laws
The provisions of registering the marriages under various personal laws are discussed below.

Christian Law
It is necessary to emphasize the Indian Christian Marriage Act, 1872 is not a 'religious law' but a civil law of marriage enacted by the colonial rulers, formulated within the then prevailing norms of English law. So though there is a sacramental aspect to a Christian marriage, as far as the state is concerned, it is purely a civil contract and the Act was enacted to prescribe the essential ingredients, conditions, and ceremonies for

Table 1.9   Persons Responsible for Registering the Marriage

Personal Law/Civil Law	Persons Responsible for Registering the Marriage
Hindu law	The parties to the marriage
Muslim law	The qazi performing the nikah
Christian and Parsi law	The priest performing the ceremony
Civil Marriages under the Special Marriage Act	The marriage oath administered by the Registrar of Marriages and the signature of parties in the marriage register maintained by him forms the registration.

the performance of a Christian marriage. It also provided for the registration of these marriages under the state authority, i.e., Registrar of Births, Deaths and Marriages. Hence though a Christian marriage is performed in a church, it cannot be dissolved by a church dictate. It is mandatory for the couple to obtain a civil divorce.

Though the Act was based within the confines of the Protestant (Church of England) based English law, it provided for the registration of marriages of various other Christian denominations as well. The registration of marriages solemnized by the Minister of Religion was regulated by the Clergyman of the Church of England, in accordance with the form laid down in the third schedule of the Act. Section 30 of the Act deals with the registration of marriages solemnized by Clergyman of the Church of Rome, while Section 31 deals with the registration of marriages solemnized by the Clergymen of the Church of Scotland.

The Indian Christian Marriage Act, 1872 also provides for the solemnization of marriages in civil form. This is a purely civil ceremony and the designating civil authority administers the marriage oath to the couple.

On completion of the nuptial ceremony, whether as per the religious norms or the marriage oath under the civil authority, the parties and their respective witnesses sign in a register maintained by the church, in the presence of the officiating priest or in the presence of the civil authority. An extract of this register is issued to the parties as a certificate of Marriage. It is mandatory for the Church to forward the contents of this register to the Registrar of Marriages every three months. This provides for a routine registration of all Christian marriages. Therefore, the certificate of marriage issued by church authorities is a conclusive proof of a valid marriage having been performed.

As an added precaution the Act prescribes a notice period of a minimum of three weeks. Notices of the intended marriage are displayed outside the civil registry or read out during the sunday service in the parish church to which the respective bride and groom belong. This is done to ascertain that there are no impediments or hurdles for the solemnization of the marriage and as a precaution against bigamous marriages. Anyone who knows of any impediment against the performance of the marriage is duty bound to inform the authority. The marriage is performed only after the notice period is over. This is called 'reading of the banns'. Marriage banns, the English equivalent of notice, were primarily addressed to parents and guardians, to alert their vigilance and afford them opportunities of protecting their lawful rights which may be flouted by secrecy. Marriage banns are rooted in centuries of Christian tradition (Diwan and Diwan 1988: 16).

Parsi Law

There are no preliminaries prescribed for a Parsi marriage. The registration of a Parsi marriage is compulsory but non-registration does not affect its validity. The Parsi Marriage and Divorce Act has an in-built mechanism for the registration of the marriages performed by the officiating priest. The marriage certificate issued by the officiating priest is conclusive proof of a valid marriage having been performed.

Muslim Law

A Muslim marriage, since its inception, is a contract. In fact all other civil and religious authorities have borrowed the Islamic concept of a contractual marriage to modernize the institution of marriage and introduce the concept of divorce. The essential ingredients of a valid marriage are offer and acceptance and mandatory mehr, which was deemed as a consideration for marriage. Without these ingredients, there cannot be a valid Muslim marriage.

The contract of marriage, which is referred to as *nikahnama*, bears the name and signatures of the bride and groom, their parents/guardians, their respective pleaders—*vakil-e-nikah*—and the seal of the officiating qazi. Hence, though not conclusive, the nikahanma is valid proof of a Muslim marriage having been performed. In some states, certain enactments provide for voluntary registration of the nikahnama. The earliest statute of this nature is the Bengal Mohammedan Marriages and Divorces Registration Act, 1876. This enactment is now applicable in Bihar and West Bengal. It is relevant to note that even without a law stipulating mandatory registration, it is not easy to deny the solemnization of a Muslim marriage. Also, since Muslim law permits polygamy, the question of the 'real' wife and entitled to maintenance becomes irrelevant during contentious litigation.

Hindu Marriages

Section 8, Hindu Marriage Act, 1955: (1) For the purpose of facilitating the proof of Hindu marriages, the State Government may make rules providing that the parties to any such marriage may have the particulars relating to their marriage entered in such manner and subject to such conditions as may be prescribed in a Hindu Marriage Register kept for the purpose.

(2) Notwithstanding anything contained in sub-Section (1), the State Government may, if it is of opinion that it is necessary or expedient so to do, provide that the entering of the particulars referred to in sub-Section (1) shall be compulsory in the State or in any part thereof, whether in all cases or in such cases as may be specified, and where any such direction has been issued, any person contravening any rule made in this behalf shall be punishable with fine which may extend to twenty-five rupees.

(3) All rules made under this section shall be laid before the State Legislature, as soon as may be, after they are made.

(4) The Hindu Marriage Register shall at all reasonable times be open for inspection, and shall be admissible as evidence of the statements therein contained and certified extracts therefrom shall, on application, be given by the Registrar on payment to him of the prescribed fee.

(5) Notwithstanding anything contained in this section, the validity of any Hindu marriage shall in no way be affected by the omission to make the entry.

Section 8 of the Hindu Marriage Act merely provides for registration of an already solemnized marriage. It does not provide for solemnization of a marriage by a civil authority, i.e., the Registrar of Marriages. Parties to the marriage may apply to the Registrar in whose jurisdiction the marriage is solemnized or to the Registrar in whose jurisdiction either party to the marriage has been residing at least for six months immediately preceding the date of marriage. Both the parties have to appear before the Registrar along with their parents/guardians or other witnesses within one month from the date of marriage. There is provision for condonation of delay up to five years by the Registrar and thereafter by the District Registrar concerned.

Although Section 8 (1) of the Act stipulates registration of marriages, this clause refers to valid marriage performed as per Section 7 of the

Act being registered by the parties. There is no provision for the administration of a marriage oath by the officiating priest. There is no requirement of a notice period or a provision to ascertain whether there are any impediments for the solemnization of the marriage. There is also no requirement of witnesses. Though the Act prescribes a valid consent, the consent does not form part of the marriage ceremony. So what needs to be proved is whether valid ceremonies, as per the custom of the parties, were performed.

In *Kanagavalli* v. *Saroj*[314] it was held that registration of a marriage [Section 8(5)] is a necessity and that it must be made compulsory to avoid bigamous marriage and to prove the status of a woman and the legitimacy of children born out of the alleged marriage. The court held that because of non-registration of marriage, a woman who has given herself physically, emotionally, and otherwise, gains nothing but stands to lose everything if the marriage is denied by the man. The other compelling factor is the trauma that a child may go through in his formative years with his paternity in doubt. This assault on a child's sensibilities can be easily avoided if there is a certificate of registration of marriage between his mother and father which though may not validate the marriage if otherwise void, will at least bear testimony to the identity of his biological parents.

Registration under the Special Marriage Act

The Special Marriage Act, being a secular, civil law, does not prescribe any religious ceremony of marriage. The marriage is performed in the office of the Registrar of Marriages. The designated officer administers the marriage vows to the couple. After this, the couple, along with the three witnesses, has to sign in the register of marriages maintained by the Registrar. The relevant page in the register will also be countersigned by the officiating authority and will bear the seal of the sub-registrar of marriages of the district. The extract from this registrar is issued as a 'Marriage Certificate' which will bear the sign and seal of the designating authority. In matrimonial litigation, the certificate provides proof of a valid marriage and it can not be rebutted.

Ironically, the provisions of the statute and the procedure prescribed for registration is nascent and has not kept up with present day needs, which renders it almost redundant. Several issues concerning these procedures have been raised in recent times in the context of the difficulties which a couple faces in the process of registering their marriage under the Act.

An important component of the Act is that it provides for registering of a marriage solemnized in any other form, under any law, upon the fulfilment of certain conditions. After the registration, all the provisions of the Act will become applicable to such parties.

In the context of re-registering the marriage which has been performed as per the respective personal laws, a question which came up before the Kerala High Court was whether these marriages can be registered before the expiry of the mandatory 30 days notice period. In *Gihy George* v. *Marriage Officer*,[315] it was held that a marriage solemnized between persons who were residing within the jurisdiction of the Special Marriage Officer can be registered even if it was solemnized within 30 days of the filling of an application for registration. In *John Roji* v. *Marriage Officer*,[316] the high court did not accept the plea of the Marriage Officer that a certificate of marriage could be issued only after the statutory period of one month is over and after registering the marriage. Instead, the court directed the Marriage Officer to issue a

---

[314] AIR 2002 Mad 73 : II (2001) DMC 603 Mad

[315] I (2008) DMC 220 Ker
[316] I (2005) DMC 320 Ker

certificate of marriage within a week from the date of production of the copy of the judgment. As a measure of caution, the court ordered that if it is found that the petitioners are not entitled for registration of marriage, it would be open to the Marriage Officer to recall the certificate issued. In *John Lukose v. District Registrar*,[317] while interpreting Section 16 of the Act, it was held that in exceptional cases, the marriage certificate can be issued even before the expiry of 30 days. But a later ruling, in *Deepak Krishna v. District Registrar*,[318] has held that the statutory period of 30 days is mandatory and is not liable to be waived. Discretion to deviate from the statutory provisions is not given to the Registrar of Marriages by the statute.

The mandatory requirement of one month makes it difficult for a couple to register the marriage under the Act. This requirement causes impediments and many times, a couple who needs a certificate expeditiously is in a hurry, prefers to register the marriage under the Hindu Marriage Act where there are no such requirements and registration can be done immediately since registration in the Act implies only the registration of a marriage performed elsewhere.

In order to register the marriage under the Special Marriage Act, the parties are required to be personally present before the registrar. Many a time the registration is done for the sake of securing a spousal visa or travel permit, as per the directions issued by the host country. In such an event, it may not be possible for the spouse who is already residing in a foreign country to be personally present before the Registrar. Regarding this requirement, Ravindra Bhat J. of Delhi High Court, in *Charanjit Kaur Nagi v. Govt. of NCT of Delhi*,[319] held as follows:

Law has to adapt to changing times. The requirements stipulated half a century ago act as impediments to registering a marriage, even though the technology myriad solutions. It is open to evolve suitable mechanisms with the support of technology by incorporating a procedure of video conferencing, authentication of identities by Embassies and attestation of signatures, etc. The inaction or indifference of the State to recognize these developments and provide for a suitable mechanism to facilitate registration of marriages of spouses separated by distances has to be addressed.

In this case, the court directed that the husband's signature on the prescribed form, attested by the Consul General available in the nearest town in the USA along with the description of his passport and affidavit attested by the Consul General and an attested copy of his photograph, should be submitted for the purpose of registration. Based on these documents, the court authorized the Registrar of Marriages to register the marriage. The court clarified that this procedure was prescribed in view of the particular circumstances of the case, since compelling the husband to appear along with the wife for the purpose of registration would entail avoidable delay and expense. In *Nishana Mol v. Alappuzha Municipality*,[320] the Kerala High Court held that the rule of personal appearance before the authority for registration is not a rule but only an exception. Only when there is some reasonable doubt regarding the identity of the parties or credibility of the material produced the presence of parties is required. In other situations the parties need not be present.

In *Firoz Khan v. Union of India*,[321] the Orissa High Court has held that even when one of the parties is not an Indian citizen, the Registrar of

---

[317] I (2008) DMC 271 Ker
[318] I (2008) DMC 34 Ker

[319] I (2008) DMC 45 Del
[320] I (2010) DMC 18
[321] I (2007) DMC 626 Ori

Marriages does not have the authority to refuse registration of the marriage. In this case, a marriage was solemnized between an Indian citizen and a French national as per Islamic law. The French national got married on the strength of the visa and he registered his marriage with the French embassy. Later, the couple sought to register the marriage under the provisions of the Special Marriage Act. But the Registrar of Marriages refused to register the marriage. The parties approached the high court, which held that the refusal to register the marriage by the marriage officer without assigning any reason is not legal and justified. The high court quashed the order of the Marriage Registrar and issued directions to register the said marriage under the Special Marriage Act.

In *Baljit Kaur Boparai* v. *State of Punjab*,[322] the marriage was performed, before the bridegroom attained the minimum age of marriage, as per the Sikh marriage ceremony, *anand karaj*. Subsequently, the Registrar refused to register the marriage on the ground that the parties had not completed the required age of marriage. The high court held that the Registrar does not have the authority to refuse registration of marriages performed when the parties were minors. The court held that the marriage was not void since the boy would complete 21 years within a matter of two months.

Pluralistic Practices and Fraudulent Marriages

In the event that the fact of a Hindu marriage is contested, it becomes the most illusory legal incident which is difficult to prove in a court of law. This is because though the Hindu Marriage Act prescribes certain essential ingredients and ceremonies which are essential for a valid marriage, it also validates customary practices of marriage and divorce.[323]

The problem arises while proving custom, which, according to legal norms, have to be ancient, continuous, and immemorial. But this colonial legal mandate of proving custom has lost its relevance in modern times where communities have altered customary practices to suit the modern day lifestyles. Couples have been declaring themselves as married by exchanging garlands, applying *sindoor* on the bride's forehead, seeking the blessings of a deity, or signing on a judicial stamp paper prepared by a lawyer. The media, particularly Hindi films, have further contributed to the confusion by projecting such practices as legal under the Hindu Marriage Act.

At times the parties declare themselves as married by naming the ceremony as 'Arya Samaj marriage'. Arya Samaj is a reformist sect which revolted against Brahminical rituals and ceremonies and evolved simple, non-ritualistic procedures to solemnize marriages. Unfortunately, this progressive agenda could be exploited to solemnize marriages of couples marrying in haste, against parental dictates. A certificate of marriage can protect the boy against criminal proceedings initiated by the girl's parents.[324] But Arya Samaj norms cannot be applied to anyone who is not an Arya Samaji and does not subscribe to its tenets. Hence, if the validity of such a marriage is contested in matrimonial proceedings, the other spouse would find it difficult to prove the marriage.

The problem has been acute even in an urban city like Mumbai, where fraudulent marriages and sham divorces take place every day. These

---

[322] I (2009) DMC 28 P&H

[323] See Box in Chapter 1 *Personal Laws and Women's Rights* of the first volume for relevant sections under the Hindu Marriage Act which validate customs.

[324] See Section 'Elopement Marriages and Judicial Pronouncements', where the issue of elopement marriages is discussed in detail.

marriage shops, termed as *vivaha karyalayas*, are situated outside the magistrate's courts and have become a very lucrative business for lawyers. Marriages and divorces on stamp paper were routinely conducted with the collusion of lawyers, notaries, touts, and state officials within the office of the Sub-Registrar of Marriages. The mischief was caused by the anomaly between the provisions of the Hindu Marriage Act, 1955 and an earlier Act entitled, Bombay Registration of Marriages Act, 1953. The purpose of the latter was only to inculcate a culture of registration of marriages and it did not prescribe any conditions or ceremonies for a valid marriage. It only provided for the registration of a valid marriage. The Registrar of Marriages did not have the authority to scrutinize the facts submitted and examine whether a valid Hindu marriage had been performed. The parties did not have to present themselves before the Registrar of Marriages; information regarding a marriage having been performed could be sent even by post and memorandum could be obtained. Even a marriage performed in contravention of the provisions of the Hindu Marriage Act could be registered under the Act. The document issued under the seal of the Sub-Registrar of Marriages was only a 'Memorandum of Marriage' and not a 'Certificate of Marriage' as in the case of Christian marriages or marriages solemnised under the Special Marriage Act. Hence it did not provide concrete proof of a valid Hindu marriage having been performed. But the couple believed that it was a valid certificate of marriage.

A writ petition filed by Majlis, a Bombay-based NGO, served to highlight the problem caused by irregular and fraudulent marriages due to which women were deprived of their rights.[325] In response, the Bombay High Court

directed the state government to frame adequate laws to plug the loop holes. Subsequently, a new legislation was enacted, titled the Maharashtra Regulation of Marriage Bureaus and Registration of Marriages Act, 1998. This brought in some regulations in the process of registering Hindu and Muslim marriages. As per the stipulation of this Act, the parties are required to be personally present before the Registrar for registering their marriages and the Registrar has been grounted the power to scrutinize the information and documents produced before the registration authority.[326]

In the same vein, Karnataka Marriages (Registration and Miscellaneous Provisions) Act, 1973, Himachal Pradesh Registration of Marriages Act, 1996, and Andhra Pradesh Compulsory Registration of Marriages Act, 2002, provided for compulsory registration of marriages. In five Indian states, Assam, Bihar, Meghalaya, Orissa, and West Bengal, there are provisions for voluntary registration of Muslim marriages. In Jammu and Kashmir, Section 3 of the Jammu and Kashmir Muslim Marriages Registration Act, 1981 mandates registration of marriages contracted between Muslims after the commencement of the Act, within 30 days from the date of conclusion of nikah ceremony.

In 2005, the National Commission for Women drafted the Compulsory Registration of Marriages Bill, 2005, to provide a legal framework for registration of all marriages, irrespective of the religion of the contracting parties. The Bill does not interfere with the solemnization of marriage and only prescribes the procedure of getting the marriage registered within 30 days of the solemnization. The statement of

---

[325] *Majlis Manch v. State of Maharashtra*, WP 1842 of 1996 (unreported)

[326] Section 6 (1) (b) of the said Act stipulates that the parties to a marriage along with three witnesses should appear in person before the Registrar of Marriages and sign the Memorandum of Marriage.

object and reasons pointed out that registration of marriages was necessary:

i) To prevent child marriages and to ensure minimum age of marriage

ii) As a deterrent to the practice of selling daughters under the garb of marriage

iii) To prevent polygamy, unless the same is permitted under any law or custom

iv) To ensure that prior wives get notice of intended marriage

v) To prevent desertion of women and subsequent denial of marriage

vi) To enable married women, including the women married to NRI/foreigners, to claim their right to shelter and maintenance.

Since it was not presented to Parliament, the Bill lapsed.

Intervention by the Supreme Court

In a transfer petition filed by a woman, Seema, against her husband Ashwin Kumar,[327] Arijit Pasayat and S.H. Kapadia JJ of the Supreme Court issued directions that within three months, all states should frame rules for registration of marriages. They expressed concern that in a large number of cases, unscrupulous persons deny their marriages by taking advantage of the fact that there is no official record of their marriage, since most states do not provide for registration of marriages. In its judgment, the Supreme Court endorsed the view expressed by the National Commission for Women that compulsory registration would be of critical importance to protect the rights of women and children. The court commented that a Central legislation would enable women to claim the inheritance rights and other benefits and privileges which they were entitled to after the death of their husbands and would deter men from deserting women after marriage. It would also

deter parents and guardians from their selling daughters/young girls to any person, including a foreigner, under the garb of marriage. The court endorsed the view that maintenance of official records on registration of marriages would facilitate faster disposal of litigation regarding validity of marriage as a marriage certificate would provide clinching proof of a marriage having been solemnized.

The All India Muslim Personal Law Board expressed its discomfort with this ruling as they felt that the Muslim community has a clear procedure for the registration of marriages and a written document, the contract of marriage (nikahnama), as proof of a valid marriage. They expressed the view that state governments ought to recognize the practice prevailing among Muslims and evolve a system for automatic registration of marriages performed by the officiating cleric, with the government authority. There was an apprehension that compulsory registration of marriage might pave the way for the enactment of a Uniform Civil Code.

Homogenizing the registration of marriages across communities, would cause problems to certain sections if their customary practices are not accepted by the registration officer. For instance, in *Alungaprambil Abdual Khader Suhud* v. *State of Kerala*,[328] a Muslim man who wanted to solemnize his subsequent marriage under the Special Marriages Act was denied registration under the Act as the court decree of dissolution of his previous marriage was not produced. The accepted practice of oral talaq under Muslim law was not recognised by the Registrar. The fact that there was no legal provision for him to approach the court for a decree of divorce as the Dissolution of Muslim Marriages Act, 1939 applies only to Muslim women was not accepted. The high court held

---

[327] *Seema* v. *Ashwani Kumar*, I (2006) DMC 327 SC.

[328] I (2007) DMC 38

that adequate proof of the dissolution of the first marriage as required under Muslim law has been produced, i.e., a certificate issued by the Muslim Jamat. The court directed the Registrar to act on a declaration submitted by petitioner that he is a divorcee and register the marriage under the provisions of the Special Marriage Act.

Though registration of a marriage is intended to provide a clear proof of a valid marriage, there are instances where the marriage has been invalidated when the same is contested in court. For instance in *Gullipilli Sowria Raj* v. *Bandaru Pavani*,[329] the Supreme Court invalidated a marriage registered under Section 8 of the Hindu Marriage Act where a Christian man married a Hindu girl as per Hindu rites by exchanging *thali* in a temple. Later the girl pleaded that the marriage is void as her husband is a Christian. The court upheld this plea. The registration by itself could not come to the rescue and save the situation for the husband.

If the husband has a previous subsisting marriage and gives a false declaration at the time of registering a second marriage under the Special Marriage Act, the mere registration will not come to the rescue of the wife and provide any relief to her and her marriage is likely to be declared void. At best the husband can be prosecuted for fraud but if the marriage is of many years duration and there are children concerned, merely initiating criminal proceedings against the husband will not bring any respite to the wife. The case of Seema who faced similar predicament is discussed in detail in the concluding chapter of this book.

Presumption of Marriage and Legitimacy of Children

These instances bring to the fore the protection awarded to women and children under the Indian Evidence Act regarding certain presumptions regarding validity of marriage and legitimacy of children. The proposed Bills, state enactments, and Supreme Court directions for compulsory registration of marriages need to be viewed in the context of these protective provision. In a country where registration of marriages is not the norm and where the government has failed to provide for adequate and easily accessible facilities for registration of marriages, legal maxims of presumption of marriage and legitimacy have come to the aid of women and children and have helped them to secure their economic rights.

Sections 50, 112, and 114 of the Indian Evidence Act deal with presumption of facts regarding a valid marriage and legitimacy of children. These presumptions are rebuttable but only when there is strong and cogent evidence to the contrary. They cannot be rebutted lightly by a mere balance of probabilities. The evidence repelling the presumption must be strong, distinct, and satisfactory.

When a man and a woman have cohabited continuously for a number of years, law presumes in favour of marriage and against concubinage. The longer the period of cohabitation, the stronger will be the presumption in favour of a valid marriage. If there is some evidence on record that the couple had gone through some form of marriage, the presumption gets further strengthened. Long cohabitation of a person's mother with the father raises the presumption of a lawful wedlock and legitimacy of the child.

While granting maintenance under Section 125 of Cr.PC, which is a beneficial legislation, courts have also held that strict proof of marriage is not necessary as is required under criminal proceedings of bigamy or matrimonial litigation. When the paternity of children is denied, the presumption under Section 112 of the Indian Evidence Act comes to the rescue of children, not just to safeguard their economic rights but also to save them from the social stigma of illegitimacy. Since these challenges

---

[329] I (2009) DMC 164 SC

are posed in the context of maintenance and succession rights, the maxim of presumptions and the manner in which they have been used in litigation are discussed at length in the next chapter, under the law of maintenance.

The proposed move for mandatory registration of marriages needs to be examined within the perspective of women's rights. Though the demand for compulsory registration of marriages is articulated within the framework of protection of women and children, to deter bigamous marriages and child marriages, there is hardly any thought as to the adverse impact it would have upon their rights.

Solemnization of marriage was important at a stage when rights of women and children were located only within formal and monogamous European, Christian marriages. Devolution of rights was confined strictly to children within these 'status' marriages. But this was not the norm under Hindu and Muslim marriages which were polygamous and within this context awarded rights to women and children in plural relationships. Various customary forms of marriages were validated under these systems. The norm of monogamy introduced through the Hindu Marriage Act did not result in curbing polygamous unions but the sum effect has been denial of rights to a large section of women who cannot prove a monogamous marriage. The strict monogamy of the Hindu marriage ushered in through this codification, was not along the lines of medieval Christian marriages which were of a permanent nature and intrinsically linked to land ownership and property devolution.

When divorce, even consent divorce, is firmly entrenched within the legal code, what the law needs to take into consideration is contractual obligations of cohabiting partners, almost along the lines of Muslim law. Even while prescribing the strict norm of monogamy, the law has simultaneously moved in a diagonally opposite direction by awarding rights to those outside the pale of strict monogamy. The first in this realm has been the move to protect illegitimate children, by abolishing the difference between legitimate and illegitimate children in respect of their right to maintenance. The second welfare measure was to award legitimacy to children of void marriages (usually bigamous marriages) in order to bestow upon them the rights of maintenance and succession under matrimonial statutes. More recently, the Protection of Women from Domestic Violence Act, 2005 has granted recognition to informal relationships or 'live in relationships'. Any woman who claims relief under the Act, such as protection against domestic violence, restraining orders, or even maintenance, would not have to prove marriage, as has been held by the Madras High Court in *M. Palani* v. *Meenakshi*.[330]

We cannot afford to be shortsighted and prescribe populist measures which will only provide transient and superficial solutions to deep-rooted social problems. The stipulation of mandatory registration of marriages will lead to enhanced state control over sexuality and sexual choices of its citizens. This will drastically impact women, who are placed in an unequal position within patriarchal power structures and are not well versed in dealing with state institutions. Within an overwhelmingly extremely pluralistic social structure, in order to protect the rights of the weaker and the dependent, we need to widen the scope of validating and legitimizing relationships rather than constrict them.

LEGAL INCIDENTS OF MARRIAGE

Marriage (and its dissolution through death of the husband or divorce) is a legal incidence

---

[330] AIR 2008 Mad 162. For further discussion of this case, see Section titled 'Rights of Women in Informal Relationships' of Chapter 2 *Matrimonial Rights and Obligations*.

which alters a woman's relationship to her family, community and state. Several rights accrue or get altered through this legal incident. So for women, marriage is not just a sexual contract but a social, economic and legal contract which defines their relationship with the state and community, and alters their right to citizenship and nationality.

The oft cited quote from *Manusmriti* which places the dominion over women with various categories of men by stating that a woman must be dependent upon her father in childhood, upon her husband in youth and upon her sons in old age, has a resonance in modern law. Similarly, the Blackstonian principle of English law that after marriage, the husband and wife become one person in law, and that person is the husband, seems to still prevail in certain contexts. These notions have adversely impacted women's claim to citizenship and nationality within modern States and have served to deprive women of their fundamental right to an independent legal identity. Though the constitution of modern States bestowed equal rights of citizenship upon women, women continued to have a dependent nationality, based on the concept of unity of nationality of spouses. The result of the application of this principle was that a woman who married a foreigner automatically acquired the nationality of her husband. Usually this was accompanied by the loss of her own nationality.

The rationale for the principle of dependent nationality derived from two assumptions: first, that all members of a family should have the same nationality and, secondly, that important decisions affecting the family would be made by the husband. It was believed that if a married woman were to have a nationality different from that of her husband, her loyalties would be divided, and she might be placed in a conflicting situation. This assumption was also linked to the idea of

citizenship, which relates to a person's public identity—the relationship between an individual and the State.[331] Loyalty to the State is the counterpart of the State's duty to protect its citizens. In many States, the assumption that a married woman's primary location is in the private sphere, within the home, and under the protection of her husband, prevailed. Hence, her need for a separate public identity and legal relationship with the State was not given due recognition.

By virtue of the application of the principle of dependent nationality, a woman who married a foreigner, despite the fact that she continued to remain in her own country, was deprived of her nationality of origin. This in turn resulted in the loss of her civil, political, economic, social and cultural rights which depend on that nationality. She became an alien in the place where she had always resided, and lost all the privileges of citizenship. Where citizenship is restricted for nationals (for example where foreign nationals are denied the right to hold or inherit property), the position of a woman who had been rendered 'non national' through her marriage was one of total dependence upon her non-national (foreign) husband. Her identity and sense of belonging to her State of origin, and of being important to that State, were compromised and disregarded because of her reduced status within the place she had always called home.

Nationality is the legal basis for the exercise of citizenship. Although frequently used interchangeably with 'nationality', the term 'citizenship' has a wider meaning, and denotes

[331] 'Nationality' has reference to the jural relationship under international law. 'Citizenship' has reference to the jural relationship under municipal (or domestic) law. Nationality determines, the civil rights of a person with reference to international law and citizenship is connected with civil rights under municipal law. See *State Trading Corporation of India Ltd. v. Commercial Tax Officer*, AIR 1963 SC 1811.

a status bestowed on full members of a community (Davis 1997). In many countries, the full exercise of political, social and cultural 'citizenship' rights is predicated on nationality. Nationality frequently determines if individuals are entitled to participate fully in the political processes. Within the notion of dependent citizenship women were denied basic rights such as the right to vote, to obtain an identity card or a travel document such as a passport, to access social welfare schemes and entitlements, the right to secure admissions in educational institutions, the right to own land, and most relevant, the right to pass on citizenship to their children. These rights were mediated through their husbands.

Laws that entrench the principle of dependent nationality disempower married women by depriving them of any choice about their nationality. The problem became more acute after the First World War when many women who had married foreigners in armed forces, became stateless if they became war widows. Hence it was among the first issues that women sought to place on the international legal agenda, alongside issues of social and political inequality and the right to vote. Women held demonstrations and led a deputation to the Hague Codification Conference in Netherlands, in 1930 (Knop and Chinkin (2001).

Later after the Second World War, the Universal Declaration of Human Rights in 1948 proclaimed the notions of non-discrimination and the right to a nationality. Inspired by this, the Convention on the Nationality of Married Women was adopted in 1957, bestowing upon women the right to an independent nationality. However, not all States changed their laws, and some newly independent States maintained the limitations upon the retention of a separate nationality by married women that had existed under colonial laws. While proclaiming in their constitutions that there

shall be no discrimination based on sex, in practice, the legislation on nationality continued with the old practice of denying women their nationality upon marrying men with different nationalities.

This situation is also reflected within Indian laws. While Articles 14 and 15 of the Constitution, which came into effect in 1950, assured equality and non-discrimination, the Citizenship Act of 1955 continued to discriminate against married women. The situation was altered only in 1992 due to the mandate of Article 9 of the CEDAW which declared the right of women to hold independent nationalities.[332]

The relationship between women and the State is mediated not just through their husbands, several other constraints also impinge upon these rights. In Conclusion to the Chapter 2 of the first volume I have discussed the issue which became a national shame after Independence, the abducted women. Though these Hindu women had since then married their Muslim abductors and were quite content to settle down within the new State of Pakistan, they had to be reclaimed to restore the nation's honour. The flip side of this political agenda is that women from Pakistan who marry Indian men are not easily recognized as Indian nationals and have a long wait to gain Indian nationality. This inspite of the prevailing international norm of dependent nationality, where upon marriage, women automatically acquire their

---

[332] Article 9 (1) : States Parties shall grant women equal rights with men to acquire, change or retain their nationality. They shall ensure in particular that neither marriage to an alien nor change of nationality by the husband during marriage shall automatically change the nationality of the wife, render her stateless or force upon her the nationality of the husband. Article 9 (2): States Parties shall grant women equal rights with men with respect to nationality of their children.

husband's nationalities and thereby forsake their own nationality.[333] Even when they are given the status of a dependent national, in the event of a divorce, these women would lose their nationality and would have to be deported despite their long stay in India and despite the fact that they may not have any contact left in Pakistan.

The case of *Sobha Hymavathi Devi* v. *Setti Gangadhara Swamy*[334] unfolds yet another aspect of the contested relationship between women and the state. The woman's election from a seat reserved for backward castes was challenged on the ground that though she had married a person from the backward caste, since she herself belonged to an upper caste prior to her marriage, she could not avail of the reservation meant for the backward castes. So in this case, her identity acquired through her marriage was disregarded. In order to retain her seat, the woman argued that her mother belongs to the backward caste and that she had married her maternal cousin who also belongs to the same caste. Further, though her mother was living with a man from an upper caste, the marriage was not valid since her mother's earlier marriage had not been dissolved and since she is an illegitimate child of that relationship, she inherited her mother's caste. The Supreme Court while rejecting her arguments and setting aside her election, expressed dismay over the extent to which a person could go merely to retain her seat, and even reduce her mother's status to that of a concubine and rendering her other siblings illegitimate. But rather curiously, the Supreme Court paid no attention to the patriarchal scheme where the daughter could not claim her privileges through her mother and had been reduced to advancing an argument of illegitimacy to claim her lineage through her mother.

While mediation with the State is one aspect of married women's disentitlement, there are also several others, which are governed by customary practices and community dictates, which affect women's rights. Even basic issues such as the right to hold a separate surname or the right to continue with the husband's surname after divorce become contested issues for women. In some communities customary practices compel women to change not just their surname but also their first name after marriage. Customs in several regions also mandate a woman to use her husband's first name as her middle name. In this context, a recent ruling of the Bombay High Court which restrained the woman from using her husband's surname after divorce and held that use of such surname after divorce amounts to fraud, raised many eyebrows.[335] Though the ruling was confined to a specific case, the heightened media response projecting the comment as a legal precedent, caused concern among women who were divorced many years ago but had retained their husbands' surname. What did not get highlighted in this entire debate is that the law does not require a woman to use her husband's name or surname after marriage and that she can continue to use her maiden name. Within the patriarchal structure of marriage, all state institutions demand that the woman uses her husband's surname despite the fact that this stipulation has no legal validity. Other conceptions also prevail that after marriage a woman is not permitted to hold bank accounts in her own maiden name and needs her husband's consent to start and operate bank accounts. It is absurd to presume that after going through a name change process at the time of marriage a woman is compelled to reverse this process upon divorce.

---

[333] PTI News report, 'Pak Woman granted Indian Citizenship after 25 Years Wait' in *Times of India* Mumbai: 26 October 2009.

[334] (2005) 2 SCC 244

[335] Deshpande, S. 'Divorced Woman Can't Use Ex's Name: HC' in *Times of India*, Mumbai: 19 February 2010.

Marriage also affects women's rights to hold property. For instance, until the 2005 amendment to the Hindu Succession Act, Section 23 of the Act prevented married women from claiming the right of residence in their natal homes though technically women had the right to inherit their father's property since 1955. Several laws governing rights to the tribal land prohibit women who marry non-tribals from gaining access to common tribal lands as they feel such women betray the cause of the tribal community. There is also the fear that the women will be exploited and the marriage is contracted only to gain access to the tribal land. In March, 2010, a Bill titled, Permanent Resident Disqualification Bill was introduced in the State Assembly of Jammu and Kashmir in order to deprive women, who marry outside of the state, their right to citizenship of the state. The Bill sought to deny women their ancestral rights, property rights and job rights if they marry men outside the state.[336]

There are several other realms even within religious communities, castes and tribes where women lose their affiliations and identity upon marrying 'outsiders'. Under the Parsi law, women who marry non-Parsis lose their right to pass on their Parsi identity to their children.[337] The notion that intermarriage leads to a dilution of faith and weakening of cultural bonds still prevails. The children of such mixed marriages are not recognized as Parsis and are not admitted into the Parsi fold and are not permitted to perform the *Navjot* ceremony (the initiation ceremony).[338] They also

lose all benefits which the Parsi panchayats grant to the community, such as subsidized housing, educational support etc. But this is not the case if a man marries a non-Parsi. Though this amounts to a blatant discrimination against women under Articles 14 and 15 of the Constitution, the same has continued unchallenged.

CONCLUSION

This chapter explored the material basis of the institution of marriage, its historical evolution, forms of dissolving it and the challenges posed to it in contemporary times. Newer issues emerging in the horizon of matrimonial law such as diaspora marriages, or NRI marriages as they are more commonly referred to, as well as newer dimensions of older concerns such as prevention of child marriages, complexities involved in registration of marriages and legal incidents of marriage and its impact upon women also form part of this chapter. By examining contemporary litigation processes through the medium of case law, an exposure to the current trends in matrimonial law is provided.

The prevailing unequal power relationships within marriage and the manner in which rights are assessed through the prism of equality within the matrimonial statutes is the central concern of this chapter. How does one negotiate a super structure of equality which is based on an infrastructure of inequality and how do legal terms such as 'cruelty', 'desertion', 'irretrievable breakdown of marriage'. etc., lend themselves for application within a gendered context—these are some issues which have been contextualised here. When the status, roles, functions, and responsibilities differ so extensively, can the application of a gender-neutral term, 'spouse', be a magic wand which will flatten out inequalities at the ground level? More importantly, can a premise of equality be imposed upon an inherently unequal relationship of superior and subordinate? These become

[336] News report Row Over Bill Denying Rights to Women Marrying Outside J&K in *The Times of India* Mumbai: 14 March 2010.

[337] Dadrawala, Noshir H. "Why Parsis Discourage Mixed Marriages" available at http://tenets.zoroastrianism.com/discour33.html accessed on 26 June 2010.

[338] News report, 'Parsi Woman Approaches Gujarat High Court to Perform Rituals at Agiary' Mumbai: DNA 26 March 2010

crucial questions while we contextualise the rights within marriage and divorce in the Indian setting. Since the norm of equality can only be applied to equals, treating unequals as equals will only widen the gulf of inequality. The contract of marriage and its operational modalities are examined in order to highlight these concerns.

There are several instances where the judiciary has departed from the norm of equality while taking into account the inherent inequality within marriage. In these instances, adhering blindly to the premise of equality, as prescribed by the marriage laws, may have caused further injustice to women, weaker partners within marriage. These important departures need to be flagged for a nuanced understanding of how notions of equality are played out within the family laws.

The hollowness of the promise of equality within marriage confronts us as we examine the trends within criminal law where the domain of the family has emerged as a patriarchal stronghold and a particularly violent terrain for women. The enactment of the Dowry Prohibition Act, special provisions for the offence of dowry death and cruelty to wives within the Indian Penal Code (Sections 304B and 498A) and the more recent enactment, the Domestic Violence Act all of which are applicable only to women serve to highlight the stark and poignant reality of married women in our society.

The humiliation and violence within marriage has been a major concern for Indian women down the ages. Tarabai Shinde, in her famous essay, *Stree Purush Tulna* (a comparison between women and men), published in 1882, provided an incisive analyses of this inequality in the nineteenth century (Tharu and Lalita 1991). The two letters published by Rukhmabai in the *Times of India* in 1885, under the pseudonym, 'A Hindu Lady', around the time of her trial in the case filed against her by her husband for restitution of conjugal rights is another such

example. Addressing the inequalities within marriage, she commented:

> Marriage does not interpose any insuperable obstacle in the course of their (men's) studies. They can marry not only a second wife, on the death of the first, but have the right of marrying any number of wives at one and the same time, or any time they please. If married early they are not called upon to go to the house and to submit to the tender mercies of mother-in-law, nor is any restraint put upon their action because of their marriage. (Chandra 1998: 29)

Early autobiographies by women in nineteenth century Bengal also addressed concerns regarding oppressive marriages and joint family structures, lack of freedom, and the pain of widowhood and the hypocritical stance of sexual morality (Tharu and Lalita 1991). There are several other voices of protest in Indian history and mythology which interrogate these inequities, such as Sita and Draupadi, protesting against the injustice within marriage in the Public domain. Women poets like Akkamahadevi (twelfth century), Lalleshwari or Lal Ded (fourteenth century), Mirabai (sixteenth century), and many others, broke the shackles of oppressive marriages and domesticity and entered the public domain through the medium of *bhakti* (devotion to the divine power).

One of the earliest articulations of protest regarding the status of women in marriage in England was from Mary Wollstonecraft (1792) in her path breaking book, *A Vindication of the Rights of Women*. She criticized the patriarchal claim that woman was created merely to gratify the appetite of man, or to be the upper servant who provides his meals and takes care of his linen. Like the Bhakti poets, she too rebelled against the norm of patriarchy, but her rebellion was expressed through worldly affairs unlike the other-worldliness of the Bhakti poets. She gave birth to a daughter outside marriage. Sadly, she died at the very young age of 38 years.

So women across the world from East and West have been conscious about the inequalities within marriage and have addressed this concern, but these concerns were not adequately addressed in the march towards modernity. While the public domain of civil society was subjected to various political theories, the private domain of the household was excluded from this scrutiny. Carole Pateman (1988) argues that though feminists have persistently pointed to the complex interdependence between the private and pubic domains, 'civil' society is usually treated as a realm that subsists independently, by political theorists.

In the nineteenth century, when Europe and England changed from feudalism to capitalism in the wake of the industrial revolution, land ownership went through a major transformation. In order to make land available for the needs of industrialization, for building factories and mines, the feudal manors and feudal land had to be made alienable. This changed the earlier status based relations into contracts between consenting parties. This emerging concept of contract between individuals affected all other aspects of social life and transformed feudalism into capitalism. It is within this new theory of contracts, that status marriages were transformed into contractual obligations. This enabled women to acquire rights of dissolution of marriage and property ownership. This transformation took place in England around the later half of nineteenth century.

The credit for evolving the new theory of marriage is attributed to the legal scholarship of Sir Henry Sumner Maine. In his monumental work published in 1861, *The Ancient Laws*, he laid down a new prescription for the legal order of marriage. 'Patriarchy' was viewed as synonymous with 'status' and transformation of the old world into a new order was viewed as a movement from 'status to contract'. Contract was synonymous with freedom, in contrast to and in opposition to the order of subjection of status or patriarchy (Pateman 1988: 9).

This was a big leap ahead for women in the Western world. Prior to this, marriages were governed by the legal principles laid down by the English jurist Sir William Blackstone in his *Commentaries on the Laws of England* in 1789. His dictates reduced the position of women to slaves within marriage. After marriage, they had no legal existence. They had no right to enter into contract. Their person and property belonged to their husbands. They had to abandon their own names and take on the name of their husbands. The husband was in control of his wife's chastity and morality and he could chastise her for her lapses with impunity. A notion of 'thumb rule' prevailed where the husband could beat his wife with a stick not thicker than his thumb. He was forbidden to beat her between sunset and sunrise as her wailing would cause disturbance in the neighbourhood. Her 'person' itself became the property of the husband. The husband had the legal right of recovery and restoration of a woman who had escaped from his custody. He could even sell her to clear his debts. If she had committed adultery, the sale would save the adulterer from penal prosecution or from paying a fine, for violating the 'property' of the husband. All these are symptoms of extreme servitude.

After the publication of John Stuart Mill's essay, *Subjection of Women*, in 1869, where he compared the marriage contract to a slave contract, women who were active in the abolitionist movements could quickly draw a parallel between the condition of the slaves and their own condition. The comparisons between wives and slaves reverberated through the women's movement in the nineteenth century in England and the United States (Pateman 1988: 120).

While it did seem for a while, that changing marriages from status to contract would bring an end to matrimonial servitude and transform matrimonial relationships into partnerships of equality, the prevailing situation at the ground level did not meet this expectation. Retrospectively, feminists have questioned whether the marriages were ever transformed into 'pure' contracts between equals, as earlier vestiges of servitude lingered on and cast a deep shadow upon the newer 'contractual' marriages. According to many legal scholars, marriage has continued to be a patriarchal stronghold reinforcing male power and women have continued to be subordinate, their status has continued to be that of glorified slaves (Pateman 1988; Okin 1989; Fineman 1991, 1991a). Since the transition from status to contract was not complete, the notion of a contract between equals works to the detriment of the women's interests.

This change from feudalism to capitalism and from status to contract took place at the height of colonialism and was transported to the colonies through the newly established legal order. This was meant to usher in 'modernity' and pave the way for capitalist economies. But the patriarchal biases framed within unequal partnerships of the colonial legal order served to strengthen local patriarchies. The *Rukhmabai case*, discussed in detail in Chapter 1 of the first volume is a clear indicator of this remoulding of marriage contracts and contractual obligations, in the context of the remedy of restitution of conjugal rights and its impact on women.[339]

Almost all liberal theorists have assumed that the 'individual', who is the basic subject of the theories, is the male head of a patriarchal household. Hence they have not usually considered applying the principles of justice to women or to relations between the sexes. Susan Moller Okin comments:

Theories of justice that apply to only half of us simply won't do; the inclusiveness falsely implied by the current use of gender-neutral terms must become real. The best theorizing about justice is not some abstract "view from nowhere," but results from the carefully attentive consideration of everyone's point of view. (1988: 14–15)

According to Martha Albertson Fineman, understanding the movement of marriage from status to contract is related to two differing ideas of marriage. The first is the more modern view that marriage has been transformed to be more consistent with the 'formalistic notions of equality between the sexes'. The second is the more traditional view that it is an unequal relationship which creates needs and dependencies for women which need to be addressed (Fineman 1991a: 265). While embracing the idea that marriage is a contract, the legal system ignores the existence of these dependencies.[340]

These theoretical formulations which critique the premise of equality need contextualization within the Indian family laws and litigation processes. Since gender roles are clearly defined and since families are patrilocal, the grounds of 'cruelty' and 'desertion', which are clothed in gender-neutral language, become very distinct and gender-specific in divorce contestations because the husband and wife are judged by entirely different set of rules. Their roles, obligations, and expectations are placed in diagonally opposite directions. There is no semblance of equality here. These roles evolved in the context of 'status marriages' and are predefined as per patriarchal norms. Just because the enactment of the Hindu Marriage Act in 1955 transformed the religious and sacrosanct,

---

[339] See section titled 'A Moment of Defiance: The Rukhmabai case' of Chapter 1 *Personal Laws and Women's Rights* of the first volume. The case is also referred to briefly in this chapter.

[340] The doctrine of 'need' and dependencies which Fineman contextualizes is discussed in detail at section titled 'Need Versus Contribution in Division of Property' of Chapter 2 *Matrimonial Rights and Obligations*.

status-based marriages into contractual relationships of equality, it does not mean that the differences between the sexes were flattened out into an equality mould.

The peg on which the notion of cruelty hinges are poles apart for the husband and the wife. Not conceding to the demand for sex, terminating pregnancy without his knowledge and consent, perusing a professional career and 'neglecting marital obligations', refusal to stay in the joint family set up, not serving tea to his friends or refusal to wear the *mangalsutra* (the customary thread or ornament which is worn as a symbol of marital status)—all this could be pleaded as cruelty on the part of the wife, entitling the husband to a decree of divorce. The wife's notion of cruelty rests on a different set of social realities such as physical violence, denial of food, humiliation by the mother-in-law, demands for dowry, and false allegations against her chastity and morality. A gendered pattern is clearly discernible while analysing reported judgments. These grounds cannot be applied in the reverse because they reflect the subordinate status of the wife within the contract of marriage. Even terms like 'neglect of marital obligations' mean different things when applied to the husband and the wife. For the husband, it would be measured in economic terms, such as non-payment of maintenance, whereas for the wife it would be neglect of household duties, not looking after the children, or refusal to have marital intercourse.

The historical ruling in *Dastane* v. *Dastane*,[341] widened the scope of cruelty beyond the physical to the conceptual and the contextual. *V. Bhagat* v. *D. Bhagat*,[342] opened up the boundaries even further by declaring that 'mental cruelty' can be of such a nature that the parties cannot reasonably be expected to live together and it is not necessary to prove that it would be injurious to the health of the petitioner. While these rulings are hailed as progressive because they widened the notion of legal cruelty, it is important to note that both were in the context of a husband's claim to divorce on the ground of cruelty and the rulings were in favour of the husband and against the contentions of the wife. In order to bring an end to the long winding litigation, the Supreme Court, tentatively and cautiously invoked the ground of 'breakdown of marriage' in the *Bhagat case*.

These rulings helped loosen the marital knot and led to a large number of cases being filed by husbands on frivolous grounds. The underlying reason for filing a petition for divorce in most cases was the validation of his subsequent relationship with another woman, defying the dictate of monogamy. The changes brought into the Hindu Marriage Act to protect the rights of wives, could easily be circumvented with the option of an easy divorce invoking the breakdown theory. Though the ground was premised on equality and could be invoked by both men and women, social conditioning, stigma against remarriage, responsibility of motherhood and economic dependency prevented most women from availing of this remedy in a similar manner. So the cases where women have pleaded this ground are few and far between. When the courts were flooded with a large number of cases filed by husbands on flimsy grounds, they were constrained to reign in the scope and impose certain restrictions in order to protect women's rights. Here the courts had to evolve another legal dictum, '*normal wear and tear of marriage*'.

The same holds true when we analyse the reported cases on the ground of desertion. The general norm of traditional marriages is that after marriage, a woman leaves her natal home

---

[341] AIR 1975 SC 1534
[342] (1994) 1 SCC 337 : AIR 1994 SC 710

and enters the matrimonial home. The notion of the two distinct abodes can be applied only to women within the patriarchal structure. Under the Hindu joint family structure, upon birth the man becomes a joint holder of family property. He also has a pious obligation to look after his aged parents and perform their last rites. Conversely, the woman is not even viewed as a member of her own natal family. The ground of desertion needs to be examined within this social reality where the woman leaves her natal home and comes to reside in her 'matrimonial home' where she is an outsider. If she is humiliated, assaulted, or violated, she will return to her natal family if they are willing to accept her back. In most situations, this is not the case.

There are also possibilities of her being thrown out of the matrimonial home. Courts have been confronted with the challenge of having to decide whether such 'leaving' would amount to desertion. The process of 'leaving' and 'returning' is confined to wives. Faced with this problem, courts had to evolve the notion of 'constructive desertion' in the landmark cases, *Bipinchandra* v. *Prabhavati*[343] and *Lachman* v. *Meena*.[344] This legal premise of constructive desertion is invoked in defense of women who are accused of desertion, after being thrown out of the matrimonial home. Courts had to abandon the gender-neutral premise and evolve a gender-specific construct to deal with the problem at hand. Courts have repeatedly reiterated that a husband cannot be allowed to 'take advantage of his own wrong'.

A similar concern emerges as we analyse other matrimonial remedies. For instance, the grounds of annulment of marriage have very different connotations for women and men. As discussed in the following chapter, husbands

can use the ground of not only the wives' bigamy, but also their own, in order to defeat the women's claim of maintenance.[345]

Grounds such as fraud, coercion, concealment of illness, etc., impact men and women very differently. The cases filed against women by their husbands far outnumber the cases filed by wives against their husbands. It is a social reality that natal families, in a desperate urge to marry off their daughters, do conceal severe mental illnesses. For this reason, even when the marriage is annulled on this ground, courts have been compassionate and have advocated a humanitarian approach, as prescribed in *Pramatha Kumar Maity* v. *Ashima Maity*.[346]

Rather curiously, in the midst of gender-neutrality, we also come across a very specific gender-specific ground of pre-marriage pregnancy, which can be used only by the husband against the wife. The notion of a sexually impure bride, carrying in her womb the seed of a stranger, threatens the very basis of a patriarchal marriage. There is no gender-neutrality here and it does not affect the foundation of a patriarchal marriage if another woman is pregnant with the husband's 'seed'. The price for this lapse would have to be paid by that 'other' woman.

Restitution of conjugal rights is yet another contested field. Both historically as well as during the post-Hindu Marriage Act period, this vestige of patriarchal order has been difficult to shed. This is brought out very starkly when we examine the 'Lord and Master' cases, where the courts chastised women for holding on to jobs against the wishes of their husbands, not withstanding the fact that they were the breadwinners of their families. Despite the fact

[343] AIR 1957 SC 176
[344] AIR 1964 SC 40

[345] For a more detailed discussion see section titled 'Maintenance Rights of Women' of Chapter 2 *Matrimonial Rights and Obligations*.
[346] AIR 1991 Cal 123

that Hindu Marriage Act had transformed Hindu marriages into contracts, while awarding orders in favour of husbands, courts relied upon the notion that according to Hindu law, it is the sacred duty of the wife to obey his dictates. This, even when the wife's income was needed to support the family.[347] While examining the constitutionality of this provision, the Delhi High Court validated the sublime nature of sacramental Hindu marriages and held:

In a sensitive sphere which is most intimate and delicate, there is no room for constitutional principles to enter. The 'domestic community' does not rest on contracts sealed with seals and sealing wax, nor on constitutional law. It rests on that kind of moral cement which unites and produces 'two-in-oneship'.[348]

A more recent concern in this discourse on the gender specificity of matrimonial relief is the incorporation of a newer remedy of 'irretrievable breakdown of marriage' through judge-made laws. Usually, when the grounds pleaded for cruelty are flimsy and frivolous and a husband is not able to prove legal cruelty, he invokes the 'breakdown' theory. Courts have been cautious while applying this principle, but there is a pressure to include this remedy within the realm of matrimonial laws. There have also been recommendations of the Law Commission of India to this effect.[349] But the gender-specific context of this remedy has not been sufficiently explored. Women's groups have opposed this move as it would cause untold misery to women and children. Our matrimonial law does not function on the premise of division of property upon divorce. The wife's right to reside in the matrimonial home after divorce has no statutory recognition. A routine use of this ground would seriously hamper the rights of women and children to shelter and economic security. At times courts have offered sums such as Rs 2,00,000 as compensation or economic settlement to the woman for her life time of service to the husbands. Whether such low amounts could indeed provide economic security to women is a question that both the judiciary and the parliamentarians must address. In this context it is interesting to note the recent Supreme Court ruling in *Vishnu Dutt Sharma* v. *Manju Sharma*,[350] where it was held that the courts do not have the power to legislate and add new grounds for dissolution of marriage and that it is the duty of the legislature to do so. Hopefully, in the ensuing wider political debate around this issue, women's concerns will be the primary focus rather than judicial convenience. What is not linked here is the 'need' of the woman, which Fineman refers to in the above cited passage. Unless a clear assessment of the wife's need is made and a policy is in place regarding matrimonial residence and the division of matrimonial assets based on need as well as contribution (in terms of housework, child care, and economic contribution), it would be premature to suggest this ground as it will cause great hardships to women.[351]

In this context, it would be worth our while to learn from the experience of other countries. Lenore Weitman (1985 : xi–xiv), in a detailed study on the non-fault based 'divorce revolution' in California, USA, mentions that a simple

---

[347] See section titled 'Hindu Marriage: A Sanskara and a Contract' of Chapter 1 *Personal Laws and Women's Rights* of the first volume.

[348] *Harvinder Kaur* v. *Harminder Singh*, AIR 1984 Del 66. See Chapter 1 *Personal Laws and Women's Rights* of the first volume where the constitutional validity of the provision of restitution of conjugal rights is discussed.

[349] LC Report No. 217 of March 2009

[350] I (2009) DMC 515 SC

[351] The issue of matrimonial home and property is discussed in detail in section titled Right to 'Matrimonial Home and Property' of Chapter 2 *Matrimonial Rights and Obligations* .

change to gender-neutral divorce rules has had appalling consequences on the condition of women and children. This is because when law views the husband and wife as 'equal', it ignores the inequalities that have been created by the marriage itself and the inequalities between men and women in society. Courts, in this process, violate the norms of the original marriage contract and deprive the wife of a share in the husband's income as they are now equal and equally capable of earning a living. The woman bears great financial burden, given the cost of sole child support, (as women usually get custody) given the fact that they have been outside the labour market for the duration of the marriage, and given that women in general, in society, are offered lower paying jobs than men. Weitman calls the consequence of this law, 'the systematic impoverishment of divorced women and their children'(ibid.: xiv).

While there is a need to contextualize 'gender', a superficial and generalized framework of women's rights may not be adequate to deal with the question of rights and entitlements. This is particularly relevant while we examine the issue of child marriages. In litigation, it is crucial to particularize rights. We cannot impose ideologically determined formulas upon people's lives without understanding the implication of such an imposition on the people whose interest is sought to be served. Here, more than anywhere else, it is essential to bring to the centre stage the concerned individual, woman or child, and her agency in seeking justice. The position advocated by some feminists, that depriving some women/girls of their rights for the greater good of all women, seems to be based on an erroneous presumption. Statutory law, campaigns, and judicial pronouncement weave a complex web of legal claims.

An examination of reported judgments on child marriage serves to further highlight gender-specific rights and entitlements and the contexts in which a legal provision gets activated. There have been cases where girls were married when they were very young and courts had refused to dissolve these marriages at the instance of the girls on the ground that minority is not a ground on which a marriage could be dissolved.[352] These judgments invoked the traditional notion that the Hindu marriage is sacramental and indissoluble. In these cases, the girls were very young, at times even less than 10 years. Upholding this traditional view and not examining the issue from the perspective of women's rights deprived the minor girls of their basic human rights. While adjudicating these cases, judges had to keep in view that at times strict adherence to or mindless application of laws could lead to injustice. This problem was resolved when the option of puberty was included in the Hindu Marriage Act in 1976.

Later cases on this issue came up in the context of imposition of patriarchal norms resulting in denial of rights to women—when husbands challenged the validity of marriage to escape the liability of paying maintenance, when husbands' relatives challenged the validity of marriage of a widow in order to disinherit her, or in defense of parental authority in cases of elopement marriages. Here the judges expressed greater sensitivity towards the rights of minor girls by upholding the validity of such marriages. Mensky brings in a nuanced framework of gender-specificity and comments that judges have to take up the challenge of developing the legislative foundations into a socially meaningful system of regulation within the framework of social responsibility (Mensky 2003: 367). It is this social responsibility of activists and scholars that needs to be contextualized in this debate.

[352] *Premi* v. *Daya Ram*, AIR 1965 HP 15; *Naumi* v. *Narotam*, AIR 1963 HP 15.

When the issue of compulsory registration of marriage is raised through women's rights groups and judicial pronouncements, the adverse effects of this norm needs to be carefully examined. This norm should not be used to deny a large number of vulnerable women of our country their right to maintenance and marital status. I have argued that a framework of 'presumption of marriage' would work better for women than a strict mandate of compulsory registration. Registration can only be a facilitating measure, the responsibility of providing adequate infrastructure, easy procedures, and due publicity regarding the advantages of registering marriages is entirely upon the state. It is one thing to say that all marriages should be registered and another to stipulate that non-registered marriages are invalid and hence women in such marriages will cease to have rights. The price will be paid only by women since their economic rights depend upon the validity of marriage. Children will not suffer economic loss since children of invalid marriages are deemed legitimate. Further, we have observed, through the case law as well as through experiences in court, registration itself will neither obviate the ambiguity within Hindu marriages nor prevent bigamy.

Problems arise when women approach courts for claiming their rights in situations where the community accepts bigamous marriages and the law declares them as void. In this process, women suffer. Men also have the option of entering into 'marriage like' relationships since 'mistresses' and 'concubines' are accepted through community norms. Due to the wide prevalence of these customary practices, such relationships have been awarded judicial recognition through the Domestic Violence Act, in order to avoid hardships to women.

There is a need to bridge the wide gulf between community practices and the legal norms of a modernist, regulating state. Currently they function from two different planes and it becomes the task of the lawyers representing the parties to bring these plural practices within the ambit of law through various means, fair and foul. It is rather unfortunate that the debate around legislative reforms takes place, many a times, without contextualizing the reality of poor, rural, and illiterate women and gets framed in the context of middle class social activists (Singh *et al.* 1994).

Both marriage and its dissolution are determined by community practices, as can be observed from the discussion regarding community-based norms of securing divorce by mutual consent. After the Supreme Court ruling in *Seema* v. *Ashwani Kumar*,[353] the Principle Judge of the family court at Mumbai brought in a rather absurd and ineffective rule, that when a couple approaches courts for a decree of divorce by mutual consent, prior to filing the petition, they ought to register their marriage.[354] This move might augment the figures of registration of marriage, but it seems a futile exercise as the parties would register their marriages only in order to obtain a divorce. The only effect of this stipulation is the delay it would cause in the divorce proceedings.

The issue of diaspora marriages brings out another set of problems for women. Here, the norm, that a woman's domicile follows that of her husband, is followed. Women enter foreign countries as dependent spouses. In a foreign land, they become extremely vulnerable. Further, they have to subject themselves to the law of the land which is contrary to their own culture, values, and traditions. The most difficult cases in this category are the one's where

[353] I (2006) DMC 327 SC

[354] This is based on personal knowledge of the author.

the husband, after marriage, has left the country with the woman's valuables, with the promise of sending the visa and has stopped communicating with her thereafter. At times she receives a decree of divorce based on 'no fault', as applicable in the country of residence of the husband. If by then the woman has become pregnant, one can only imagine her trauma.

Equally traumatizing are the cases where the husband brings the wife and children to India and then leaves the country, deserting her, and takes with him the children as well as valuables and travel documents of the wife. The wife does not even get to see her children who were born abroad and are citizens of the foreign country, while she continues to be an Indian citizen. Her entry into the foreign country depends solely on the whim of the husband as his dependent. At present we lack the legal framework and legal instruments to bring these women within the ambit of rights and entitlements.

In this context, the Law Commission[355] has recommended that amendments must be carried out in the Hindu Marriage Act and the Special Marriage Act to provide for various contingencies that a marriage with an NRI would entail, including issues such as maintenance and alimony, child custody and child support, and settlement of matrimonial property. The Commission has also recommended that the respective state governments must simplify and streamline procedures for succession, transfer of property, reparation of NRI funds, etc. It has also been suggested that the government must accede to the Hague Convention on the Civil Aspects of International Child Abduction.

The legal incidents of being married, widowed or divorced is integrally linked to larger legal and political questions and affects women's fundamental right to citizenship, nationality

and domicile. It also affects women's right to belong to a community, inherit property, use a particular surname and more importantly, to pass on their legal identity to their children in the event that their husband's nationality and domicile varies from theirs. This has caused a great deal of hardship to women, in the context of issues relating to marriage and divorce.

To conclude, we find that traditional personal laws, customary laws as well as statutory law function from a patriarchal base. It was left for the judges to weave-in the notion of gender specificity in order to protect the rights of women. To a certain extent the judiciary has succeeded in achieving this, as we can observe from the volume of case law referred to above. Yet, it is a daunting task, as every case has to be fought with its own facts and merits and in each instance, one must invoke judicial sensitivity, since it is possible for the pendulum to swing either way. It is in this context, that there is a need to evolve a clear perspective or theory of family law, keeping in view the impact legislative reforms will have upon the lives of women.

In 1978, in his thought provoking book titled, *The Death of a Marriage Law: Epitaph for the Rishis*, while commenting on Hindu law, Derrett predicted that the future of Hindu marriage law would be dependent on the balance of power between an individualism in the form of 'contract' and a resistance to it by a 'status' bound family and social relationships. He also predicted that eventually property matters will become more important in the context of matrimonial litigation, than the grounds for divorce. These predictions seem to have come true.

Mensky (2003) contends that modernity propounded on the basis of single linear 'progressive' line of development has not worked well within the complex socio-legal reality of modern India which demands a more sophisticated and nuanced approach. He asserts that within a

---

[355] LC Report No.217 dated March 2009.

manifestly hybrid realm of family law, there is no right answer that fits all situations. Hence the mental energy of judges revolves around solving the real problems of real people, in line with recognition of litigants means and practical needs. Further, it is now impossible to analyse developments in personal laws in isolation from other legal areas. Justice does not respect the subject borders of legal specialisms. Hence in recent times, the Indian higher judiciary has become instrumental in creating a legal regime which is economically sustainable and remarkably justice-focused, but, Mensky laments, ideologically bound to Western-style prescriptions of formal equality and Western interpretations of human rights (Menski 2003 : 259). It is in this context that this chapter has attempted to evolve a theory of marriage and divorce based on Indian realities even while contextualizing Western theories of family law and women's rights.

2

Matrimonial Rights and Obligations

Section A

MAINTENANCE RIGHTS OF WOMEN

This chapter examines three crucial rights which flow from the contract of marriage and assesses their impact upon women when there is a breakdown in matrimonial relationships.

The right of maintenance, which is a right of subsistence and survival, warrants an elaborate discussion. This right is accessed by a wide section of women across class and social strata. Since it is a well established right which is deeply engrained into our matrimonial statutes, a wide range of issues surface during the legal contests. This is the only provision for economic claims within marriage and, hence, is highly contested. The important ingredients are the husband's 'obligation' and the wife's 'need', but, situated within the patriarchal order, it revolves around issues such as 'matrimonial fault' and 'sexual purity'. Rights of children, issues of legitimacy and paternity, inheritance rights of illegitimate children, and the impact of men's bigamy upon women's claims, are contextualized.

Apart from the rights of women, which is the primary concern of this book, incorporated within the provision of maintenance are also claims of minor children, major unmarried daughters, disabled children, educational expenses of major sons, and the rights of parents. More recently, there have also been instances of husbands claiming maintenance from their wives who may be in a more secure financial position. The implications of this provision upon women is also examined. Most challenging among the procedural aspects of the litigation is the process of enforcing a decree, or in other words, execution proceedings. An attempt is made in this section to expose the reader to the various nuances and the ordeal of accessing justice. These issues are addressed in the second section.

The third section deals with yet another important economic right which affects women in conflict marriages, the right to matrimonial property. This right can be further divided into a right to assets and a right to shelter. Though, the right to shelter is implicit in the marriage contract, it was not clearly articulated in matrimonial statutes. Devoid of statutory recognition, this right has evolved through judicial interventions. The right to division of the matrimonial home and joint assets is also being recognized, tentatively and hesitantly, by our courts in a few cases on the basis of contribution.

Since India follows the English common law tradition of separate property regime, marriage does not impact property relations and the courts do not have the power to order division of all matrimonial assets. The notion of community of property or joint matrimonial assets has not yet been awarded statutory recognition. This important aspect of matrimonial litigation requires legislative intervention in order to safeguard women's financial interests upon divorce. Hence, the theoretical framework of this right, the rules which govern the division of property, and the development of this right in England and other common law tradition countries, are briefly sketched out.

Women's right to custody of their children and concern over access rights are discussed in the fourth section. This section traces the transition from the legal maxim 'father as natural guardian' to 'best interest of the child is paramount' and the doctrinal shift from father's 'rights' to parental 'duties and obligations'.

THE RIGHT TO MAINTENANCE

Maintenance: An Overview

Maintenance can be claimed by wives (for themselves as well as their children) under all matrimonial statutes (except under the Dissolution of Muslim Marriages Act) as an ancillary[1] relief in matrimonial proceedings. The right can be claimed only as a subsidiary relief while claiming a primary matrimonial relief such as divorce, judicial separation, annulment of marriage, or restitution of conjugal rights. There are other statutes/legal provisions which grant women, children, parents, and widowed daughters-in-law, an independent right to maintenance according to the Hindu Adoption and Maintenance Act, 1956, the uncodified Muslim Law, Section 125 of the Criminal Procedure Code (Cr.PC), etc. The Protection of Women from Domestic Violence Act, 2005 (PWDVA, also referred to as DVA), provides an additional avenue for women to claim maintenance and compensation from their husbands and live in partners. Under these

[1] This is a legal term indicating that it is a supplementary, subsidiary, or additional relief, but cannot be the main relief in a matrimonial petition.

Table 2.1   Legal Provisions Governing Maintenance Claims

Category	HMA	SMA	DA	ML	PMDA	HAMA	Cr.PC	MWA	DVA
Wives	S. 25	S. 37		Uncodified	S. 40	S. 18	S. 125	S. 3/4	S. 20
Minor Children	S. 26	S. 38	S. 41	Uncodified	S. 49	S. 20	S. 125	S. 3	S. 20
Parents							S. 125		S. 20*
Husbands	S. 24/25				S. 40				
Widowed daughters-in-law						S. 19			S. 20
Adult Daughters									S. 20
Interim Maintenance	S. 24	S. 36	S. 36	Uncodified	S. 39	S. 18	S. 125		S. 23

Notes: HMA – Hindu Marriage Act, SMA – Special Marriage Act, DA – Divorce Act, ML – Muslim Law, PMDA – Parsi Marriage and Divorce Act, HAMA – Hindu Adoption and Maintenance Act, MWA – Muslim Women (Protection of Rights upon Divorce) Act, PWDVA – Protection of Women from Domestic Violence Act.

*Only the mother is entitled to monetary compensation under DVA

provisions, maintenance can be obtained without the necessity of initiating proceedings for a primary matrimonial relief.

Table 2.1 indicates the various statutory provisions under which the right to maintenance can be claimed.

Maintenance as a Measure of Social Justice

The legal provision of maintenance is reflective of a social obligation which the state casts upon the economically stronger members of the family to provide shelter and sustenance to weaker members, that is, women, children, the elderly, and the disabled. The provision for additional safeguards and special privileges for disadvantaged groups is grounded in Article 15 (3) of our Constitution.[2] The Supreme Court, in *Captain Ramesh Chandra Kaushal*[3] v. *Veena Kaushal*, commented that Section 125 of Cr. PC is a measure of social justice which is specially enacted to protect women and children and falls within the constitutional sweep of Article 15(3) reinforced by Article 39.[4] In *Balan Nair* v. *Bhavani Amma Valalamma*,[5] the Kerala High Court commented that though provisions of Section 125 of Cr.PC also benefits the father, the main beneficiary of the provision are women and children in distress, and the provision is consistent with Article 15(3) of the Constitution as a measure of ensuring social justice.

The provision of maintenance needs to be grounded within the constitutional paradigm of ensuring social justice. It is based on the social obligation of preventing destitution and vagrancy. The Supreme Court, in *Bhagwan Dutta* v. *Kamala Devi*,[6] has explained the rationale governing the provision of maintenance under Cr.PC in the following words: 'Section 488,[7] which provides for the maintenance of wives and children is a measure to prevent vagrancy, or at least to prevent its consequences. It is intended to fulfil a social purpose: to compel a man to perform the moral obligation which he owes to society with respect to his wife and children.' In *Vimala* v. *Veeraswamy*,[8] the Supreme Court noted that by providing simple and speedy but limited relief, the provision seeks to ensure that the neglected wife and children are not rendered destitute and, thereby, driven to a life of vagrancy, immorality, and crime, for their subsistence.

More recently, in 2008, the Supreme Court in *Chaturbhuj* v. *Sita Bhai*[9] explained the objective of the provision of maintenance under Section 125 of Cr.PC in the following words: 'The objective of maintenance proceedings is not to punish a person for his past neglect but to prevent vagrancy, by compelling those who can provide support to those who are unable to support themselves, and who have a moral claim to support. It provides a speedy remedy for the supply of food, clothing, and shelter, to the deserted wife. It gives effect to fundamental rights and the natural duties of a man to maintain his wife, children, and parents, when they are unable to maintain themselves.' Similarly, in *Komalam Amma* v. *Kumara Pillai Raghavan Pillai*,[10] which was also reported in 2008, the Supreme Court

---

[2]   See section titled 'Locating Women's Claims within the Constitutional Domain' of Chapter 2 *Constitutional Law and Citizenship Claims* of the first volume for further discussion on special provisions for women and children under Article 15(3) of the Constitution.

[3]   AIR 1978 SC 1807

[4]   Article 39(a) directs the state to provide adequate means of livelihood to men and women.

[5]   AIR 1987 Ker 110

[6]   AIR 1975 SC 83

[7]   This section was re-numbered as Section 125 after the Cr. PC was re-enacted in 1973.

[8]   (1991) 2 SCC 375

[9]   I (2008) DMC 22 SC

[10]   II (2008) DMC 838 SC

explained that 'maintenance', under the Hindu Adoption and Maintenance Act, includes provisions for food, clothing, residence, education, and medical treatment, and emphasized that it must include a provision for residence. The maintenance provided should enable the wife to live in a manner that she is accustomed to in her matrimonial home.

As can be observed from these judicial comments, the provision of maintenance is crucial to women who are in conflict marriages, and to deserted and destitute women. It is obvious that the right of a woman to maintenance needs to be located within citizenship claims enshrined in our Constitution. Within the historical origins of the institution of marriage based on a patriarchal social order, for a vast majority of women, marriage results in economic dependency. The roles and responsibilities assigned to women within marriage compel many to give up their jobs or sacrifice their careers to meet the demands of their marital obligations.

During matrimonial conflict, a trump card often used by the husband is to withdraw financial support to the wife. Further, when either party opts for a divorce to bring an end to a conflict marriage, it is the woman who faces economic hardship and has to engage in a long litigation to enforce her crucial right to economic subsistence. Usually, the issue of maintenance/economic settlement becomes the most contested aspect of any matrimonial/divorce proceedings.

The non-recognition of a woman's contribution to the marriage and home reduces her to a state of destitution when the marriage breaks down. Neither the law nor society recognizes her role as a homemaker in concrete monetary terms. Irrespective of the fact that a woman has looked after the home, nursed and raised her children, and in an invisible manner contributed to the family savings, when the marriage breaks down, the law recognizes only the husband's title to the family assets. The matrimonial home, assets, savings, and securities, are deemed the exclusive property of the man. The women, who, for the duration of their marriage, lived as homemakers, often find themselves without significant personal property or a steady income to sustain themselves during the divorce and in the post-divorce phase of their life. For most women, re-entry into the highly competitive job market is almost impossible. Even when they do enter, due to constraints of age, experience, and qualifications, their earnings will be far lower than their counterparts.

All these factors push women from an affluent class into a lower economic bracket and render women of the lower class, destitute. This is a violation of their constitutional guarantee of a right to life with dignity. The law of maintenance has emerged as a feeble attempt to remedy this malady and provide women with some semblance of economic sustenance and security when the marriage breaks down. Admittedly, the provision is based on the patriarchal premise of a protectionist approach towards women. We need to shift the discourse beyond the protectionist parameter and locate it within the constitutional scheme of citizenship claims of a right to life with dignity and as a measure of social justice.

As this section unfolds, securing an order of adequate maintenance can be an extremely humiliating experience. Since the claim of a woman's economic sustenance within the patriarchal order is pitted against her sexual conduct, allegations of adultery and immorality are constantly hurled against women during litigation. This can extend further to a denial of the marriage itself and, consequentially, the legitimacy and even the paternity of the children. Sexual codes and the morality dictates of a patriarchal marriage often get entangled with the economic claims of women. In the case of Muslim women, their rights get further entwined within communal biases and deliberate misinterpretations of Islamic law.

It is in this context that statutory law and judicial interpretations must lean in favour of destitute women and vulnerable children, by moving away from the rubric of formal equality of Article 14 towards the substantive equality of Article 15(3) within the constitutional scheme, in order to set right a historical wrong.

In view of the high quotient of sexual morality which engulfs the question of maintenance, the categorization of cases under various headings is superficial and is done only for convenience's sake. The issues constantly overlap and lines get blurred as they are intrinsically interwoven to form the complex whole of the fabric of life. The notion of a guilty wife may spill over to a dispute over paternity. Validity of marriage impacts the issue of legitimacy of children and may also adversely affect succession rights. Cases discussed under the section titled 'Prolonged Cohabitation and Presumption of Marriage', concerns the claims of women in bigamous marriages. Hence, the attempt has been to merely expose the reader to trends within an adversarial legal system. What is indeed striking is that every factual and imaginary legal ploy is resorted to during protracted court battles but, increasingly, the courts are able to see through the manipulations and are able to pierce the veneer of false claims while upholding women's rights. But the false and frivolous interventions entangle women in circuitous legal rigmaroles which are time consuming, financially draining, and emotionally charged.

Despite the progressive interpretations and innovative legal maxims, the path to justice has not progressed in a linear trajectory. There is a great deal of judicial latitude which allows contradictory verdicts to emerge on the same issue, not just between various high courts but also within the same court. In addition to the facts and circumstances of each case, the legal strategy adopted by lawyers, the quality of legal representation, and the presiding judge's notion of justice and equity, play a crucial role in the final outcome. The legal precedents have to be contextualised within this litigation reality.

This section traces the challenges and milestones in women's struggle for survival while pursuing their legal claim of maintenance.

Maintenance Under Personal Laws/ Matrimonial Statutes

Under matrimonial law, the term alimony is also used to denote maintenance. This term is derived from English law. In the event of separation, the wife could sue her husband for alimony if the husband refused to make a financial arrangement to enable her to live a life corresponding to her husband's social status. The husband's refusal to maintain his wife was construed as an injury to her, the remedy to which could be sought by compelling the husband to pay for her alimony or maintenance through ecclesiastical censures.[11]

The law of maintenance is based on the ancient English principal of unity of persons within marriage. Upon marriage, the husband became the legal guardian of the wife's person and property. The wife was legally compelled to assign her properties to her husband.[12] Since women could neither work nor own property, in the event of desertion they would be rendered destitute. In order to avert this situation, the husband was legally compelled to provide maintenance to his wife.

Later, when divorce became acceptable, the Matrimonial Causes Act, 1857, and the matrimonial court mandated that the decree of divorce was conditional on the husband setting

---

[11]   Blackstone's Commentaries, Vol III, 94
[12]   Blackstone's Commentaries, Vol I, 430

aside some property for the wife as part of her alimony. The Matrimonial Causes Act, 1886, conferred power on the civil courts to pass orders directing the husband to pay the wife a reasonable weekly or monthly sum as maintenance. The husband was obligated to maintain his wife and pay for her expenses, not only during their marital life but even after the divorce, so long as she did not remarry. The provisions of maintenance under Indian matrimonial statutes and under Section 125 of Cr. PC are based on this principle.

Ancient Hindu law and uncodified Muslim law also cast an obligation on the husband to maintain his wife. The right under the Hindu law was codified in 1946 by enacting the Hindu Married Woman's Right to Separate Residence and Maintenance Act. Subsequently, this was incorporated into the Hindu Adoption and Maintenance Act of 1956 (HAMA). The uncodified Muslim law recognized the wife's right to maintenance during the subsistence of marriage and during the *iddat* period. But, since Muslim marriages were contractual and since the woman was entitled to remarry, Muslim law did not cast an obligation on the husband for post divorce maintenance. But he was required to pay the wife a 'fair and reasonable' settlement at the time of divorce, in addition to settling her mehr dues. This right received legal recognition through the statutory enactment, Muslim Women (Protection of Rights upon Divorce) Act, 1986, (MWA).[13]

A claim for maintenance can be made during the subsistence of marriage, at the time of initiating a divorce, or any other matrimonial relief, or even after obtaining a decree of divorce. An order of permanent alimony and maintenance as ancillary relief in divorce proceedings can be made during the passing of a decree of divorce, or even

subsequently. Permanent alimony is awarded based on the income and property of the parties, other economic liabilities of the spouses, as well as the special circumstances of the case. Parties can also enter into agreements with respect to maintenance through separation agreements or through consent agreements while obtaining a decree of divorce by mutual consent.

Since maintenance is an ancillary relief, the same cannot be claimed if a primary matrimonial relief such as divorce or annulment of marriage has not been prayed for. In such a situation, a Hindu woman can file under HAMA, but for women from the Muslim minority community, the only avenue is to claim maintenance under Section 125 of Cr.PC.

Interim maintenance can be claimed during the litigation process under all legal provisions which entitle a woman to claim maintenance. These proceedings are summary in nature and have to be decided at the earliest, to ensure a level playing ground for the wife, and so that she has the means to survive during the litigation period. Even if divorce proceedings are initiated by the husband on the ground of the wife's misconduct, the court cannot dismiss the wife's application for maintenance. The court has inherent powers to award interim maintenance under Section 18 of HAMA, even though it is not statutorily provided. Interim maintenance can also be awarded under Section 125 of Cr.PC.[14]

Maintenance may be paid as a lump sum settlement or by way of periodic instalments. Lump sum settlements are one time payments which are usually made at the time of the divorce. Periodic payments may be secured with a charge on the property or unsecured. The most common practice of periodic payments is

---

[13] See 'Muslim Women's Right to Maintenance' later.

[14] For further discussion on this issue see section titled 'Interim Maintenance' in Section B of this chapter.

Table 2.2   Relevant Sections of Cr.PC

Relevant Sections	Relevant Provisions
Section 125	Order for maintenance of wives, children, and parents
Section 126	Jurisdiction and Procedure
Section 127	Alterations/Modifications of the Order
Section 128	Enforcement of Order

by way of monthly instalments to cater to the requirements of the salaried class.

Maintenance Under Section 125 of Cr.PC

The provisions relating to maintenance under the Cr.PC are located in Chapter IX (Sections 125–8), but the popular term used while referring to this provision is maintenance under Section 125 of Cr.PC. Hence, this term is used throughout this section. This provision is uniformly applicable to wives, children, and parents.

The purpose of these provisions is to prevent destitution and vagrancy and not to provide economic security to dependents. Since the proceedings are summary, a destitute wife can avail of this remedy without having to file for matrimonial relief. Though, situated within the realm of criminal law, the provision is viewed more as a quasi civil proceeding.[15]

While it provided a speedy remedy for the lower strata, women from the upper strata of society did not avail of any benefit from this provision as the amount awarded was meagre and far below their needs. In 1898, when this remedy was first introduced, the amount which could be claimed was only Rs 100. In 1955, to

change with the times, the ceiling was raised to Rs 500, but, thereafter, it remained unchanged for nearly half a century even though the buying power of Rs 500 dwindled drastically. No efforts were made to raise the ceiling despite recommendations by the Law Commission.[16] The only two states that brought an amendment to this section were West Bengal[17] and Maharashtra,[18] where the amount was enhanced from Rs 500 to Rs 1,500.

With the setting up of the family court, the jurisdiction shifted from the Magistrate's court to the family court, but the amounts awarded continued to be meagre. Finally in 2001, through a Central amendment to Section 125 of Cr.PC, the ceiling was removed.[19] Hence, there is currently no limit on the amount that can be claimed under this section (K.D. Sehgal, Advocate, Chairman, Public Interest Litigation Cell v. Union of India).[20]

The provision of maintenance under Section 125 of Cr.PC offers certain advantages as opposed to personal law. Since it is a provision under the criminal statute, it does not determine the matrimonial status of the parties. Hence, the courts are empowered to award maintenance even when a woman is unable to prove her marriage.[21] Courts also have the power of arrest in execution proceedings, which acts as a deterrent against the non-payment of maintenance.[22]

In contrast, under the civil/matrimonial statutes, though husbands can be arrested for

---

[15]   See the comments of the Jharkhand High Court, in *Ehsan Ansari* v. State of Jharkhand, II (2007) DMC 751 Jha, where the prayer to amend the petition, a relief which is permissible under civil law but prohibited under Criminal law, was allowed. While allowing the prayer, the court commented that proceedings under Section 125 Cr.PC are not strictly criminal they are more in the nature of civil proceedings.

[16]   Law Commission 132nd Report, 19 April 1989.
[17]   Vide W.B. Act 25 of 1992 (w.e.f. 2 August 1993).
[18]   Vide Mah Act 21 of 1999, Section 2 (w.e.f. 20 April 1999).
[19]   Act No.50 of 2001, which came into effect on 24 September 2001.
[20]   I (2003) DMC 440 P&H
[21]   See section titled 'Rights of Women in Informal Relationships' for further discussion on this issue.
[22]   See the discussion on execution proceedings later.

non-payment of maintenance, it is construed as a civil imprisonment and the burden falls on the wife to pay for the cost of civil imprisonment. This is paradoxical, as it defeats the very purpose of awarding maintenance to a destitute woman knocking the doors of the court for a paltry sum of maintenance and casts an additional burden upon her. The advantage of the criminal provision was offset by the ceiling of Rs 500.[23] But after the removal of the ceiling, courts are at liberty to award maintenance commensurate with the economic status of the husband and the needs of the wife. This has proved to be highly advantageous, not just to the woman but also to her children and the elderly as one can discern a gradual upward trend in the amounts awarded as maintenance under Section 125 of Cr.PC.

After the enactment of the Muslim Women (Protection of Rights upon Divorce) Act, 1986, the right of a divorced Muslim woman to maintenance has been placed under this statute. As per the provisions of this enactment, a divorced Muslim woman is entitled to maintenance for the Iddat period and for a fair and reasonable settlement for life. This stipulation entitles a divorced Muslim woman to claim lump sum settlements for her future. On the positive side, this provision relieves the divorced Muslim woman of the liability to execute the order of a recurring monthly maintenance. But on the negative side, a poor Muslim husband may not have the resources to pay an adequate amount as a lump sum settlement, and the divorced wife may be compelled to accept a meagre amount as a lifetime settlement.[24]

Maintenance/Compensation Under the Protection of Women from Domestic Violence Act, 2005

The Protection of Women from Domestic Violence Act (PWDVA or DVA), enacted in 2005, offers yet another economic remedy to women and girls. Wives, sisters, mothers, or any other female relative, living in a shared household in a domestic relationship, including a woman in an informal relationship, can approach the court for a wide range of relief. This includes protection orders, maintenance orders, custody orders, and compensation orders. While the provision of maintenance orders enables the woman to claim maintenance, the provision of compensation orders enables her to claim damages for injuries suffered due to domestic violence.

This provision has proved to be highly beneficial for women seeking an order of injunction against their husbands/partners for protection against domestic violence and for protecting their right to the matrimonial home/shared residence. Women who are not able to prove their marriage, or are in a non-marriage or live-in relationship, have also benefited from this provision.[25]

Matrimonial Misconduct and Right to Maintenance

Historically under English law, only virtuous or good women were entitled to maintenance. If a husband obtained a divorce on the ground of the wife's adultery, cruelty, or desertion, she was denied maintenance and at times even the custody of her children. There is ample evidence of this phenomenon in both English and Indian matrimonial jurisprudence.

---

[23] The amendment does not have a retrospective effect. In *Shail Kumari Devi* v. *Krishan Bhagwan Pathak @ Kishun B. Pathak* II (2008) DMC 363 SC, the Supreme Court has held that maintenance above Rs 500 per month can be awarded only from the date from which the amendment came into effect, and not from an earlier date.

[24] See section titled 'Muslim Women's Right to Maintenance' later for further discussion on this provision.

[25] See section titled 'Rights of Women in Informal Relationships' later where this issue is discussed in detail.

For example, in *Dailey* v. *Dailey*,[26] reflecting the old English position, it was held that a wife who was guilty of adultery, desertion, cruelty, or any other matrimonial misconduct, was not entitled to receive maintenance. At best, she could be awarded a compassionate allowance to save her from utter destitution. Endorsing the view of the ecclesiastical court that wives who had violated their vows 'shall be fed with the bread of affliction and with the water of adversity' (*Manby* v. *Scott*),[27] in *Sardari Lal* v. *Veshano*[28] it was held that 'a woman once divorced on the ground of unchastity should be left to the resources of her immortality.'

The Calcutta High Court in *Sachindra* v. *Bammala*[29] had commented: 'Unchastity on the part of a woman (and sexual intercourse by a man with a woman outside wedlock) is a sin against the ethics of matrimonial morality in this country.' The judge, while conceding that moral law is not the civil law of the country, made the sweeping assumption that the meeting place of law and morality was Section 25 of the Hindu Marriage Act and Section 18 of the Hindu Adoption and Maintenance Act. This apparently justified the denial of maintenance to the wife, letting her survive on the resources of her immortality.

A Compassionate Approach Towards the 'Guilty' Wife

From the 1980s, one can discern a gradual shift to a more compassionate approach towards women who are accused of matrimonial fault in divorce proceedings. It is now an accepted judicial view that merely because the husband has obtained a decree of divorce on grounds of the wife's cruelty or any other matrimonial fault, the same cannot be used to deprive her of the right to maintenance.

In 1985, the Bombay High Court, in *Gulab Jagdusa Kakwane* v. *Kamal Gulab Kakwane*,[30] held that merely because the husband had obtained a decree of divorce on the ground of the wife's adultery does not disentitle her from claiming maintenance. In 1986, the Gujarat High Court, in *Dwarkadas Gurmukhidas* v. *Bhanuben*,[31] while upholding a woman's right to interim maintenance stated: 'Under Section 24 of the Hindu Marriage Act, it is the right of the wife who is unable to support herself to get maintenance. Maintenance should be made available to her without any reference to her conduct.' In 1990, the Andhra Pradesh High Court, in *T. Raja Rao* v. *T. Neelamma*,[32] held that the ground of adultery in divorce proceedings *ipso facto* does not disentitle the wife from claiming maintenance, and the wife is entitled to claim maintenance till she remarries.

In a case reported in 1986, *Shanti Devi* v. *Raghav Prakash*,[33] the wife had burned the husband's thesis. The husband filed a petition for divorce on the ground of the wife's cruelty. The court awarded a decree in the husband's favour but awarded Rs 200 per month as maintenance to the wife. In an appeal, the Rajasthan High Court held that in view of the fact that the divorced wife is a cursed human being, abhorred by society, and illiterate as well, she would not be able to support herself. Remarriage would also be a difficult and far fetched proposition. Therefore, the court decreed that alimony should be a substantial relief for her and raised the amount from Rs 200 to Rs 350. Although

---

26 (1947) All ER 847
27 *Manby* v. *Scott*, (1600) Smith's Leading Cases
28 AIR 1970 J& K 150
29 AIR 1960 Cal 575

30 AIR 1985 Bom. 88
31 AIR 1986 Guj 6
32 1990 Cri.LJ 2430 AP
33 AIR 1986 Raj 13

this can be construed as a positive ruling, it also reflects the contemptuous attitude of the judiciary and society towards divorced women.

In Re: Samsuddin Mohalat,[34] the husband challenged the maintenance of Rs 250 awarded to the wife on the ground that she is living in adultery. Rejecting his plea, the Calcutta High Court commented that the only intention of the husband in making such allegations is to cause death by starvation. The court held that maintenance need not be based on law but on human rights and directed the lower court to enhance the amount. It also decreed that if the husband does not pay, his property should be attached and sold to save the wife from death.

A more recent and significant ruling in the context of the present discussion is Usharani Lenka v. Panigrahi Subhash Chandra Dash.[35] In his petition for divorce, the husband made every possible allegation against his wife. He alleged that the wife was impregnated by another person and had terminated the pregnancy just before the marriage. Hence, the marriage could be annulled on the grounds of Section 12 (1) (d) (pre-marriage pregnancy) of HMA. He also alleged that the wife had a permanent gynaecological problem on account of which she refused to have sexual relations with him and, therefore, claimed that Section 12 (1) (a) (non consummation of marriage owing to impotency of the respondent) could also be invoked to annul the marriage. He also accused her of cruelty and desertion. The court held that the conduct of the wife amounted to mental cruelty and the husband was granted a decree of divorce. But the husband's plea that the wife is not entitled to maintenance, as she is the guilty spouse, was rejected. The court not only upheld her claim for maintenance but

increased the amount of permanent alimony from Rs 40,000 to Rs 1,00,000 on the ground that it would be just, adequate and reasonable.

Distinguishing 'Living in Adultery' from 'Occasional Lapses of Virtue'

Despite this positive shift in judicial approach, the terrain of maintenance litigation continues to be contentious. A notion still prevails that an adulterous woman is not entitled to maintenance. Hence, there is a constant effort to defeat the woman's claim by making baseless allegations and casting aspersion on her character. Two sub-clauses under Section 125 Cr.PC contribute to this confusion:

(4) No woman shall be entitled to receive an allowance if she is living in adultery.

(5) On proof that any wife in whose favour an order has been made under this section is living in adultery, the magistrate shall cancel the order.

These stipulations provide the armour for husbands to entangle women in vicious and dilatory litigation over a pittance of maintenance. But the defence is available to the husband only if he is able to prove that the wife is living in adultery. It is not available if it is proved that the wife was leading an unchaste life prior to her marriage. Only post marriage adulterous conduct is relevant. A wife can only be denied maintenance if she is living in adultery and it can be established that she is being maintained by the adulterer.

In Mahalingam Pillai v. Amsavalli,[36] it was held that a woman who is accused of adultery is entitled to a reasonable amount of maintenance as a matter of right, except in cases where the husband is able to prove that the wife is being supported by the person she is committing

---

[34] II (1997) DMC 212 Cal
[35] AIR 2005 Ori 3

[36] (1956)2 Mad.LJ 289

adultery with. In *Sandha* v. *Narayan*,[37] it was explained that there is an important distinction between a person who is living in adultery and who has merely committed adultery. Living in adultery denotes a continuous course of conduct and not isolated acts of immorality. In *Baishnab Charan Jena* v. *Ritarani Jena*,[38] it was held that a single act of unchastity or a few lapses of virtue will not disentitle a wife from claiming maintenance from her husband under Section 125 Cr.PC.

In *Laxman Naik* v. *Lalita Naik*,[39] the court clarified that while a single act of adultery is sufficient for the purpose of judicial separation under matrimonial law, for the purpose of awarding maintenance under Section 125 Cr.PC, merely proving one or more instances of such lapses is not sufficient to absolve the husband from his liability to pay maintenance.

The above rulings clarify that the denial of maintenance is not intended as a punishment for adultery. Rather, it is in the context of a continued and stable relationship with the person she is alleged to have committed adultery with. The standard of proof required, to prove adultery on the part of the wife, is high in order to prevent this provision from being misused by husbands as a means of escaping from the legal obligation of maintaining their wives (*S.S. Manickam* v. *Arputha Bhavani Rajan*).[40]

Faced with a number of cases involving false allegations of adultery by husbands in proceedings for maintenance, the court in *Baishnab Charan Jena* v. *Ritarani Jena*[41] held that such baseless allegations by the husband and his family members will entitle the wife to live separately and claim maintenance from her husband.

In *Kamal Kishore* v. *State of UP*,[42] the court reprimanded the husband for making reckless charges of immorality against his wife. In *Mahesh Chandra* v. *Addl. Civil Judge*,[43] the Allahabad High Court held that the husband had caused incalculable harm to the wife by terming her a woman of loose morals and awarded Rs 20,000 as exemplary costs. The facts of this case are rather absurd. When the wife, who was hearing impaired, filed for maintenance, in order to create evidence of immoral character, the husband requested a friend to file a false and frivolous case of restitution of conjugal rights against his wife, and later used these as proof of her immorality. In *Mahesh* v. *Madhu*,[44] the wife was driven out of the matrimonial house when she was three months pregnant. Later, the husband made allegations of adultery against her and disputed the paternity of the child. The court directed the husband to pay a compensation of Rs 100,000 along with interest at 6 per cent per annum from the date of filing the suit till its realization. The court commented that the allegations are based on illusion rather than reality.

As we can observe, the courts take a serious view of baseless allegations of immorality which are advanced only as a legal ploy to avoid the payment of maintenance to wives and to humiliate them in court rooms during proceedings.

An interesting comment on this issue is found in *Arun Kumar* v. *Meenu Kumar*.[45] In this ruling, S. Ravindra Bhat J. of the Delhi High Court, warned the lower judiciary to adopt a cautious approach and restrain from making presumptions on the basis of allegations of adultery. His Lordship's comments on this provision are illuminating and contribute substantially

---

[37] II (1999) DMC 411 Ker
[38] 1993 Cri LJ 238
[39] II (2003) DMC 275 Ori
[40] 1980 Cri.LJ 354
[41] 1993 Cri LJ 238

[42] I (2001) DMC 313 All
[43] I (2001) DMC 229 All
[44] I (2007) DMC 779 Del
[45] II (2007) DMC 820 Del

towards ushering a new gender-just legal order, away from conventional patriarchal dictates. Following is an excerpt from this ruling:

Though Section 125 Cr.PC is in the nature of a welfare measure, and perhaps falls within the description of 'special provision' under Article15 (3) of the Constitution, the exception under Section 125 (4) is loaded with gender unequal terms, against the woman. Hence, it must be invoked with due care and circumspection. The enacting part of Section 125, which entitles a woman to maintenance, makes no distinction whether the cause for her approaching the court is adultery or infidelity of the husband. Yet, the possible effect, viz, estrangement and the situation of her living in adultery is sought as a ground to deny that welfare measure. Without examining the logic of this enforcement of morality through the legal process, which has to receive a wider debate, what can be said is that the court should be loath to rush to conclusions or *apriori* assumptions, since Section 125(4) enacts an exception. It should be satisfied about the soundness of such a charge and cannot be content to elevate allegations into findings (Para 13 pp. 824–5).

In cases where the husband is able to prove to the court that the wife has been living in adultery, the courts are bound to deny her maintenance (*Angoori* v. *Phool Kumar*).[46] In *Subal Chandra Saha* v. *Pritikana Saha*,[47] the woman had left her matrimonial home and was found living with another man in rented premises. The court held that their intention to continue living with each other cannot be brushed aside and held that the woman was 'living in adultery' within the scope of Section 125(4) of Cr.PC. More recently, in *Sukro Devi* v. *State of Jharkhand*,[48] it was proved that the wife had voluntarily left her matrimonial home, without reasonable cause or excuse, and was living with another man. Hence, the finding of the trial court and revision court, that it was not

an isolated instance of a lapse in character on the part of wife, was upheld by the high court.

Even after maintenance has been awarded, if the wife is living in adultery, the husband can approach the court for cancellation of the order of maintenance under Section 125(5). If it can be satisfactorily proved that the woman is living in adultery, the magistrate has the power to cancel the order of maintenance. But in such cases, the woman will be entitled to maintenance till the date she commenced living in adultery (*Ram Kishore* v. *Bimla Devi*).[49]

Lump sum amounts awarded to the wife as a divorce settlement cannot be rescinded if a divorced woman subsequently remarries. In *Nanigopal Chakravarty* v. *Renubala Chakravarty*,[50] the Orissa High Court, while dismissing the husband's application for rescinding the lump sum amount awarded to the wife as divorce settlement upon her remarriage, held that such an order would amount to an annulment of a past liability and not a future obligation.

Post Divorce Adultery Not Within the Ambit of Section 125 (4) Cr.PC

If after divorce the woman remarries, the husband is entitled to move the court for a cancellation of the order of maintenance. But this stipulation or the stipulation under Section 125 (4), discussed above, cannot be invoked to deny maintenance to a divorced woman on the ground of her adulterous conduct. The courts have held that the stipulation under Section 125(4) that '*no woman shall be entitled to receive an allowance if she is living in adultery*' refers to her conduct within a prevailing marriage and not to her conduct after she obtains a decree of divorce, or even when she is divorced on an allegation of adultery.

---

[46] II (2003) DMC 688 P&H
[47] II (2003) DMC 640 Gau
[48] I (2008) DMC 425 Jha

[49] AIR1957 All 658
[50] AIR 1965 Ori 154

This clarity on the stipulation was provided by an interesting ruling of the Supreme Court in *Rohtash Singh* v. *Ramendri*.[51] Through this ruling, the court has attempted to contain the mischief caused in this section by holding that it applies only to cases where the marriage between parties is subsisting and not where it has come to an end. The court explained that the relevant provision presupposes the existence of a matrimonial relation since adultery denotes the sexual intercourse of two persons, either of whom is married to a third person.

In *Valsarajan* v. *Saraswathy*,[52] the wife was refused maintenance on the ground that she was living in adultery. Later, the husband obtained a divorce on this ground. After divorce, the wife filed for maintenance under Section 125 of Cr. PC. The high court held that her claim as a divorced wife cannot be defeated on the ground that she was living in adultery, or had lived in adultery, or had suffered an order of divorce on the ground that she was living in adultery (*Gopi* v. *Krishna* and *Dalip Singh* v. *Rajbala*).[53]

In *Sanjeev Kumar* v. *Dhanya*,[54] the husband challenged the order of the family court which awarded the wife Rs 1,500 per month as maintenance on the ground that the woman who has suffered an order of divorce on account of contumacious matrimonial conduct is not entitled to maintenance. The court held: Merely because the woman continues to be the wife for the purpose of claiming maintenance under Section 125 of Cr.PC, no husband can demand cohabitation, loyalty or chastity from his divorced wife as a condition for awarding her maintenance.

> **Box 2.1   The Indian Evidence Act, 1872, Sec. 112: Birth During Marriage, Conclusive Proof of Legitimacy**
>
> The fact that any person was born during the continuance of a valid marriage between his mother and any man, or within 280 days after its dissolution, and the mother remaining unmarried, shall be conclusive proof that he is the legitimate son of that man, unless it can be shown that the parties to marriage had no access to each other at any time when he could have been begotten.

Presumption of Paternity and DNA Testing

Presumption Under Section 112 of the Indian Evidence Act, 1872

The allegation of adultery and immorality sometimes extends to denying the paternity of the child. But if cohabitation is proved, or if the wife is able to prove that there was a likelihood of sexual contact during the time of conception, the courts generally uphold the validity of the marriage and paternity of the child. The law leans in favour of the innocent child and prevents it from being bastardized if there is some indication of the child's parents living together around the time of conception, or even if there was a possibility of sexual access between the two. The well established legal maxim which is invoked in disputes over paternity is *Pater est quem nuptiae demonstrant*: He is the father whom the marriage indicates. The rights of the child to paternity and legitimacy are protected through a presumption contained in Section 112 of the Indian Evidence Act, 1872 (IEA).

In *Dukhtar Jahan* v. *Mohammed Farooq*,[55] the Supreme Court stipulated as follows:

---

[51] I (2000) DMC 338 SC
[52] II (2003) DMC 344 Ker
[53] I (2002) DMC 495 P&H, II (2007) DMC 273 P&H
[54] II (2008) DMC 19 Ker

[55] AIR 1987 SC 1049

...Section112 of IEA lays down that if a person was born during the continuance of a valid marriage between his mother and any man or within two hundred and eighty days after its dissolution and the mother remains unmarried, it shall be taken as conclusive proof that he is the legitimate son of the man, unless it can be shown that the parties to the marriage had no access to each other at any time when he could have been begotten. This rule of law based on the dictates of justice has always made the courts incline towards upholding the legitimacy of a child unless the facts are so compulsive and clinching as to necessarily warrant a finding that the child could not at all have been begotten to the father and as such a legitimization of the child would result in rank injustice to the father. Courts have always desisted from lightly rendering a verdict on the basis of slender evidence, which will have the effect of branding a child a bastard and its mother an unchaste woman.

The child was born after seven months of marriage. Ten months later, the husband divorced the wife. When the wife filed for maintenance the husband denied paternity. The court held that the wife could not have hid her pregnancy from her husband. But the husband continued to cohabit with her until the child was born and for ten months thereafter. Since the parties were close relatives, the husband had access to the wife even prior to marriage.

In *Banarasi Dass v. Teeku Dutta*,[56] the Supreme Court elaborated this concept further:

The law leans in favour of a presumption of marriage and legitimacy of children and against a presumption of vice and immorality. The law presumes both that a marriage ceremony is valid and that every person is legitimate. It is in this context that marriage and filiations (parentage) are presumed. It is a rebuttal presumption of the law that a child born during lawful wedlock is legitimate, and that access occurred between the parents. This presumption can only be displaced by a strong preponderance of evidence and not by a mere balance of probabilities. In matters of this kind, the court must have regard for Section 112 of the *Evidence Act*. This section is based on the well known maxim *pater est*

quem nuptiae demonstrant (he is the father whom the marriage indicates). The presumption of legitimacy is that a child born of a married woman is deemed to be legitimate. The burden of proving that it is not a thrust on the person who is interested in making a case of illegitimacy.

Context in Which the Demand for DNA Test is Raised

Recent innovations in medical technology have contributed towards a more accurate determination of paternity. Blood group testing has been replaced with an advanced process of genetic identification through the use of a DNA (Deoxyribonucleic Acid) test. This sophisticated method of determining the identity of a person was first developed by scientists in 1985 in England, and has been accepted by the legal system (*Anil Kumar v. Turaka Kondala Rao*).[57] Demands for conducting these tests have been made, both in matrimonial and maintenance proceedings, for achieving different objectives.

In instances where the biological father has denied paternity, women have demanded DNA tests of their husbands/partners to conclusively prove paternity and claim their right to maintenance. While the courts have held that no one can be compelled to undergo the test, adverse inference can be drawn if the man refuses to undergo the tests and his contention of denying paternity gets weakened by this denial during the litigation process. There are cases where an illegitimate child has also demanded a DNA test while claiming maintenance from his putative father.

At other times, demands for DNA tests are made frivolously by husbands to delay the judicial process of awarding maintenance to the wife and child, merely as a 'roving' enquiry or a 'fishing' enquiry. In such cases, courts have declined to grant relief to the husband, based

---

[56] (2005) 4 SCC 449

[57] II (1999) DMC 693 AP

on the presumption of legitimacy under Section 112 of the IEA. In cases where a *prima facie* plea of non-access (the possibility of sexual intimacy and consequent conception) has not been made, the presumption under Section 112 of the IEA prevails to save the woman from the humiliation of undergoing a DNA test to determine paternity. The proceedings for maintenance are not criminal and the stringent rule of evidence applicable in criminal proceedings of proof 'beyond reasonable doubt' cannot be applied. But at the same time, the rule of evidence applied in civil proceedings, 'preponderance of possibility' is too lax. Hence, courts have attempted to strike a balance and arrive at a middle ground where the burden of proving 'non-access' is thrust upon the person disputing paternity.

In *Kanti Devi* v. *Poshi Ram*,[58] the Supreme Court explained the concept as follows:

The standard of proof of prosecution to prove guilt beyond any reasonable doubt belongs to criminal jurisprudence whereas the test of preponderance of probabilities belongs to civil cases. The test of preponderance of probability is too light and may expose many children to the peril of being illegitimatised. Hence, by way of caution and as a matter of public policy, the law cannot afford to allow such a consequence to befall an innocent child on the strength of a mere tilting of probability. Its corollary is that the burden on the husband should be higher than the standard of preponderance of probabilities. The standard proof in such cases must at least be of a degree in between the two so as to ensure that there was no possibility of the child being conceived through the plaintiff-husband.

Regarding the relevance of presumption under Section 112 of the IEA in the context of the DNA test, the court explained:

Section 112 of the IEA act was enacted when modern scientific advancements with Deoxyribonucleic Acid (DNA) as well as Ribonucleic Acid (RNA) tests were

not in contemplation by the legislature. The result of a genuine DNA test is said to be scientifically accurate. But even that is not sufficient to escape from the conclusiveness of Section 112 of the Act. For example, if a husband and wife are living together during the time of conception but the DNA test reveals that the child was not born to the husband, the conclusiveness in law would remain unrebuttable. This may seem unfair from the point of view of the husband who would be compelled to bear the fatherhood of the child of which he may be innocent. But even in such a case, the law leans in favour of the innocent child if his mother and her spouse were living together at the time of conception.

As explained by the Supreme Court in the above passage, the courts will exercise abundant caution before a child is subjected to DNA tests, which may cause stigma and humiliation and jeopardise his/her rights as a child. Hence, under the law of maintenance which is a beneficial legislation enacted to prevent destitution and vagrancy, the courts will rarely concede to this demand. Courts have held that since proceedings for maintenance under Section 125 of the Cr.PC are summary and do not finally determine the marital status of the parties concerned, the courts have granted maintenance to the wife and child and directed husbands to initiate civil proceedings by way of declaratory suits to determine legitimacy and paternity. Only in very rare cases when non-access is proved, will the courts entertain the demand for a DNA test during maintenance proceedings.

The third category of cases where the demand for DNA tests is raised is in matrimonial litigation, specifically in proceedings for the annulment of marriage on the ground of pre-marriage pregnancy or in proceedings for divorce on the ground of adultery. Again, courts will not concede to a flippant demand. But if it is necessary to conclusively prove adultery or pre-marital pregnancy, the courts may concede

[58] I (2001) DMC 763 SC

to the husband's demand and subject the woman and child to a DNA test. There are instances where the refusal of the woman to undergo tests has led to an adverse inference being drawn against her.

The following cases illustrate the various strands of this complex legal discourse.

Denial of Paternity and Legitimacy

DNA tests have proven to be extremely useful in determining the rights of illegitimate children. While fathers have tried to wriggle out of the obligation of maintaining children by claiming that there was no valid marriage, the law has pinned the responsibility of maintenance on the father even when there is cohabitation or a presumption of marriage between the mother of the child and the putative father. As per the stipulation under Section 125 of Cr.PC, the obligation to maintain the child extends to both legitimate and illegitimate children. Courts have adopted the principle that while granting maintenance to an illegitimate child, the primary concern is paternity and not the legitimacy of the child.

DNA testing has been a highly disputed matter. The constitutionality of DNA testing in succession, maintenance, and matrimonial cases, has been upheld by the Madras High Court in *Bommi* v. *Munirathinam*,[59] In this case, the husband challenged the order of the trial court directing him to undergo a DNA test to determine paternity, but the Madras High Court declared that such a direction is not in violation of Article 21 of the Constitution. In *Syed Mohd Ghouse* v. *Noounnnisa Begum*,[60] the husband denied both marriage and paternity but challenged the order of the family court to undergo a DNA test. The high court held that

while as per the ruling in *Goutam Kundu* (discussed later) the court cannot compel a person to give a sample of blood; the court can draw inferences as a necessary corollary in sequel thereof. The importance of the DNA test in clarifying a case has been expressed in *Joseph* v. *State of Kerala*,[61] where the Kerala High Court upheld the directions issued by the Kerala State Women's Commission to two men in two different cases to undergo DNA tests. Upon the men disputing marriage and paternity, the women had filed complaints before the State Women's Commission. The latter issued directions which were challenged by both men before the high court. The court upheld the direction of the Women's Commission and held that the test may absolve the women of the slur suffered by them and redeem them of the trauma they were undergoing for several years. On the other hand, if the stand adopted by the two men was correct, they too would be absolved of the false allegations made against them.

Courts exercise the power to direct the person disputing paternity to undergo a DNA test in order to protect the rights and entitlements of the child and, thus, lean towards protecting an innocent child. DNA testing has, therefore, been used in a number of cases.

For example, in *Anil Kumar* v. *Turaka Kondala Rao*,[62] an illegitimate son claiming maintenance from his biological father pleaded that his father, a married man, working as Station Superintendent in the railways, had a sexual relationship with his mother and he was born out of this union. The trial court rejected his application on the ground that it could not be established that the respondent was his putative father. In an appeal, his claim was upheld

---

[59]   2004 MLR 609 Mad
[60]   II (2001) DMC 454 AP

[61]   I (2007) DMC 421 Ker
[62]   II (1999) DMC 693 AP

based on the report of DNA tests and he was awarded Rs 300 as maintenance. Similarly, in *Nani Gopal Kar* v. *State of West of Bengal*,[63] a woman cohabited and conceived under a promise of marriage. When the respondent refused to marry her, the woman filed a criminal complaint of rape and cheating and claimed maintenance for herself and her child. A DNA test proved paternity and the woman and child were awarded maintenance. The court commented that pendency of criminal case (of rape) is not a bar against granting interim maintenance to the child.

If the husband declines to undergo the test, the courts have the power to draw adverse inference. This is seen in the Supreme Court decision of *Dwarika Prasad Satpathy* v. *Bidyut Praya Dixit*,[64] where it was held that if the husband declines to undergo a DNA test he will be disentitled to dispute the paternity. The apex court commented that the provision under Section 125 Cr.PC is not to be utilized for defeating the rights conferred by the legislature upon destitute women, children, or parents, who are victims of the social environment.

In *Kanchan Bedi* v. *Gurpreet Singh Bedi*,[65] when the wife filed for maintenance for her son, the husband denied marriage and paternity. In order to conclusively prove paternity, the wife pleaded for DNA testing. The husband vehemently opposed this on the ground that if the test revealed that he was not the father the child would be defamed and exposed to the risk of being declared a bastard. But, since the husband had already challenged the paternity of the child in his written statement and alleged that the child was illegitimate, the court held that he had no concern for the welfare of the child and

his pleadings on this ground lacked credibility. The court branded the concern as 'crocodilian' and directed the husband to present himself at the hospital for a DNA test.

Maintenance Proceedings and Roving Enquiries

The following cases illustrate the stern response of the higher judiciary to the demands raised by husbands for a DNA test as a delaying tactic, and to avoid the payment of maintenance to their wives/partners and children.

In a leading case, *Goutam Kundu* v. *State of West Bengal*,[66] the Supreme Court laid down the following guidelines for ordering blood tests to determine paternity.

1. Courts in India cannot order a blood test as a matter of course;

2. Whenever applications are made for such prayers in order to have a roving inquiry, the prayer for a blood test cannot be entertained;

3. There must be a strong *prima facie* case that the husband must establish non-access in order to dispel the presumption arising under Section 112 of the IEA;

4. The court must carefully examine the consequence of ordering a blood test—whether it will have the effect of branding a child a bastard, and the mother an unchaste woman;

5. No one can be compelled to give a sample of blood for analysis.

It was held that there is a very strong but rebuttable presumption under Section 112 in favour of legitimacy and the section requires that the party disputing paternity should prove non-access in order to dispel the presumption. The court also explained the term access as the

---

[63] II (2008) DMC 462 Cal
[64] AIR 1999 SC 3348: 2000 Cr.LJ 1 SC
[65] I (2003) DMC 458

[66] II (1993) DMC 162 SC: AIR 1993 SC 2295

existence of opportunities for sexual intercourse and not actual cohabitation.

In conclusion, the court commented that the purpose of the application was nothing more than a ploy to avoid the payment of maintenance, without making any ground whatsoever to have recourse to the test.

The rulings in *Laxmikant v. Premwati, V Yedukondalu v. V. Nageswaramma*[67] and *Nandlal v. Shankari*[68] serve to clarify the point regarding access and cohabitation. In *V. Yedukondalu*, the family court at Vijayawada granted maintenance of Rs 400 per month to the wife and Rs 100 per month for each of the three children. In appeal, the husband denied paternity of the third child and pleaded non access. While upholding the order of the trial court, the high court held that the mere fact that the wife had left the matrimonial home can scarcely constitute evidence of non-access when both husband and wife were living in the same district and the child was born during the continuance of their valid marriage. The court also commented that charges of adultery were not raised in the divorce petition filed by the husband. The wife had left the matrimonial home due to cruelty and harassment for dowry. In *Nandlal* the husband challenged the maintenance awarded to the wife and child on the ground that he was in judicial custody at the time when the child could have been conceived. The high court held that since the wife used to regularly visit him while he was in custody and look after him, sexual contact cannot be ruled out. The court commented: 'Nowadays, nothing is impossible.'

In *Rajesh Chaudhary v. Nirmala Chaudhary*,[69] the Delhi High Court, while admitting that the result of a genuine DNA test is said to be scientifically accurate, ruled that it is not enough to escape the conclusiveness of Section 112 of the IEA. For example, if a husband and a wife are living together during the time of conception but the DNA test reveals that the child was not born to the husband, the conclusiveness in law would still remain irrefutable. In this context, Section 112 assumes primary importance while defending the claim of the paternity of the child. The husband had challenged the paternity of his daughter but in his pleadings, he admitted that he had clear access. Hence, his application for a DNA test was rejected.

In *Md. Mhasin Sk. v. Sayeda Khatun Bibi*,[70] the husband disputed the paternity of the child alleging that the wife had sexual relations with other men. But the wife was able to prove that her husband alone had access to her and, thus, had fathered the child. The Calcutta High Court upheld the wife's contentions and rejected the husband's plea for a DNA test as he had no basis for demanding it. The court commented that DNA tests cannot be ordered without some evidence to substantiate the allegations of non-access or some proof of the wife's adultery.

Similarly, in *Didde Sundara Mani v. Didde Venkata Subbarao*,[71] the Andhra Pradesh High Court quashed the order of the trial court permitting a DNA test. This was done on the ground that the party disputing the paternity of the child has to prove non-access to the mother during the time when the child could have been conceived, to dispel the presumption under Section 112 of the IEA. The presumption would have to be displaced by leading strong preponderance of evidence and not merely by filing a petition for determining the paternity through a DNA test.

---

[67] II (2000) DMC 90 AP, 2004 MLR 231 MP
[68] II (2002) DMC 530 Raj
[69] II (2005) DMC 814 Del
[70] I (2006) DMC 48 Cal
[71] I (2006) DMC 83 AP

In *Partha Majumdar* v. *Sharmishta Majumdar*,[72] the trial court rejected the husband's plea for DNA testing. The Calcutta High Court upheld the order of the magistrate and held that the husband, through this application, wanted to introduce new and inconsistent facts which were totally irrelevant while deciding maintenance. He wanted to project his wife as a prostitute, which cannot be permitted in proceedings under Section 125 of Cr.PC.

It was also held that the Supreme Court ruling in *Sharda* v. *Dharmpal*,[73] which dealt with the issue of annulment of marriage on the ground of a mental disorder, has no relevance to the present case. That ruling was given in proceedings to obtain a matrimonial remedy of annulment of marriage. The same principle cannot be applied to summary proceedings under Section 125 of Cr.PC. This provision is a social device, introduced for the welfare and benefit of poor and neglected wives who are unable to maintain themselves. The court commented that allegations of adultery and accusations that the birth of the child due to the adulterous life of the wife are nothing but wild, vague, and baseless and, hence, the prayer for a DNA test was rightly rejected by the magistrate. The court further commented that if after the decision in proceedings, under Section 125 of Cr.PC on the basis of evidence and materials on record, the husband feels aggrieved, he is at liberty to approach the appropriate civil court for challenging the paternity of the child and for a necessary declaration in this respect.

In *Heera Singh* v. *State of UP*,[74] while dismissing the appeal filed by the husband for a DNA test, the Allahabad High Court held: When the law requires strict and direct proof to rebut the presumption of legitimacy, the DNA test of a minor child cannot be allowed in the absence of evidence and on vague pleadings. The court, in the capacity of *ad litem* guardian of the minor cannot direct such a test in the absence of direct and positive evidence of non-access as required under Section 112 of the Evidence Act.

In *Amarjit Kaur* v. *Harbhajan Singh*,[75] in a petition for divorce filed by the husband on the ground of cruelty and adultery, the wife filed for maintenance. Since the application was rejected, she filed an appeal in the high court which awarded maintenance to her and the minor daughter, but directed the trial court to conduct a DNA test with respect to the son, whose paternity was disputed by the husband. The court held that if the report is negative, the wife and the minor son would not be entitled to maintenance. The Supreme Court set aside the order and held that the court cannot impose conditions for the DNA test to be conducted, and such a condition is unreasonable.

The following two cases are illustrative of the cancellation of maintenance awards upon cogent evidence which rebutted the presumption of paternity under Section 112 of the IEA. In *Noor Alam* v. *State of Bihar*,[76] the trial court awarded Rs 300 per month as maintenance to the daughter. The husband denied paternity, pleading that the daughter was born two years after he had divorced his wife. This explanation was accepted by the high court. In *Abdul Razak Haji Gulambhai Qureshi* v. *Johrabibi Haji*

---

[72]   I (2006) DMC 793 Cal

[73]   I (2003) DMC 627 SC in this case it was held that directing the wife to undergo medical examination to disprove the allegations of mental disorder does not violate Article 21 of the Constitution (Right to Life which includes Right to Life with dignity) and also held that adverse inference can be drawn against her if the wife refuses to comply with the direction.

[74]   I (2006) DMC 19 All

[75]   I (2006) DMC 27 SC

[76]   II (2002) DMC 634 Pat

Kalubhai Qureshi,[77] the trial court awarded Rs 200 per month as maintenance to the minor child despite evidence that the husband had no access to the wife when the child could have been conceived. In an appeal, the high court held that a child who was born while the marriage was subsisting, but without the father having access to wife at the relevant time is not entitled to maintenance. However, the court issued a word of caution and commented: It is necessary to observe that even though the wife herself has not challenged the findings against her, the finding or the inference that she was living in adultery may not be taken as approved or confirmed by this court.

Determination of Pre-Marriage Pregnancy and Adultery

While in maintenance proceedings courts are extremely reluctant to entertain applications for a DNA test to defeat the women's claims, in declaratory suits and matrimonial proceedings, tests are relied upon to prove the husband's allegation of adultery or pre-marriage pregnancy. High courts have upheld the trial courts power to direct the parties to undergo tests while deciding matrimonial disputes. Courts have held that such directions are not in violation of Article 21 of the Constitution. But this power is to be exercised sparingly and only where sufficient material is available with the court that a *prima facie* case has been made out by the applicant.

For instance, in *Jyothi Ammal* v. *K. Anjan*,[78] the court upheld the husband's plea of adultery and granted him a divorce based on the reports of DNA tests which excluded him as the father. Since the husband had no access to the wife during the time she could have conceived the child, the court held that allegations of adultery had been proved.

In *B. Vandana Kumari* v. *P. Praveen Kumar*,[79] the husband had filed for annulment on the ground of pre-marriage pregnancy. The wife delivered the child during the pendency of the petition. The husband sought a DNA test of the wife along with the child which was permitted by the trial court. In appeal, the high court upheld it and stated: To determine the paternity of the child and for an effective adjudication of the controversy between the parties, a DNA test is necessary. The direction is not contrary to conclusive proof enjoined under Section 112 of the IEA.

Maya Ram v. *Kamla Devi*[80] is also a case of pre-marriage pregnancy, where a daughter was born within six months of marriage. The husband was able to prove that he had no access to the wife at the time when the child was begotten. While upholding the direction of the trial court to conduct a DNA test, the court commented that while it has the power to direct the parties to undergo the tests, it cannot compel any party to subject themselves to it. But in case a party does not undergo the test, adverse inference can be drawn.

However, the courts will not entertain any applications by a third party to determine paternity. In *Renubala Moharana* v. *Mina Mohanty*,[81] the court rejected the application filed by the mother of the deceased for a declaration that the child is the illegitimate progeny of her deceased son. The court held that declaratory relief as regards the illegitimacy of the child cannot be granted as it would violate the principles of natural justice.

Similarly, in *Sunil Trambake* v. *Leelavati Trambake*,[82] the wife filed an application for a

---

[77] II (2008) DMC 341 Guj
[78] I (2007) DMC 756 Mad

[79] I (2007) DMC 246 AP
[80] I (2008) DMC 249 HP
[81] AIR 2004 SC 3500
[82] II (2006) DMC 461 Bom

Box 2.2   The Indian Evidence Act, 1872

Section 50–Opinion on Relationship, When Important

When the court has to form an opinion as to the relationship of one person with another, the opinion, expressed by conduct, as to the existence of such a relationship, of any persons who, as a member of the family or otherwise, has special means of knowledge on the subject, is a relevant fact.

Section 114–Court May Presume the Existence of Certain Facts

The court may presume the existence of any fact which it thinks is likely to have happened, regard being had to the common course of natural events, human conduct and public and private business, in their relation to the facts of the particular case.

DNA test of her husband's child through a bigamous marriage in civil proceedings for a divorce filed by the husband. The trial court allowed the application, but in an appeal the high court held that a DNA test cannot be directed as a matter of routine. The tests can be directed only when they become indispensable to resolve the dispute. The court should record a reason as to how and why such a test is necessary to resolve the controversy. This is necessary since these tests will have an adverse impact on the child and mother. The court held that the wife can produce documentary proof such as a birth certificate and school record to prove her case. Since the second wife and her child were not party to divorce proceedings, it would violate the principle of natural justice. Such tests would not be in the interest of the minor child. Further, the court commented that even if the test was positive, it would not help the wife prove her husband's second marriage.

Presumption in Favour of a Valid Marriage

A corollary to the denial of paternity is a denial of the marriage itself. This legal ploy is constantly used in proceedings for maintenance filed by the wife, both under Section 125 of the Cr.PC as well as in civil suits and matrimonial proceedings. If a marriage is not valid, the status of the woman is reduced from that of a wife to a mistress or concubine. The children will also suffer stigma by being branded illegitimate and will have to bear the economic consequences of the denial of their rights. To avoid this eventuality, the law leans in favour of a presumption of the marriage being valid rather than in favour of its being an illegitimate relationship, which the courts would view as a vice.

The plea for invalidity of marriage is often based on technicalities that certain essential ceremonies were not performed or some essential conditions were not fulfilled at the time that the marriage was solemnized. Summarised below are some frequently used grounds for denying women maintenance and the positive approach of the courts while deciding these cases.

Violation of Essential Conditions of a Marriage

Challenges to the validity of marriage are based on the absence of any essential conditions for a valid marriage such as free consent, minimum age, etc. The courts have held that a violation of the stipulation of the minimum age of marriage cannot be used to deprive the minor wife of her right to maintenance.

Regarding the absence of consent, in *Basanti Mohanty* v. *Parikhit Rout*,[83] while upholding the wife's right to maintenance, the Orissa High Court held that even if it can be proved that the

---

[83]   I (2003) DMC 214 Ori

marriage was entered into without the consent of the husband, the mere absence of consent will not render a marriage that has been performed in accordance with the provisions of the Hindu Marriage Act, invalid for the purpose of claiming maintenance.

Similarly, violating the age bar will not render the marriage invalid and the husband cannot escape the liability of paying maintenance to the wife on this ground.[84]

Non-Performance of Essential Ceremonies of Marriage

Another challenge to the validity of marriage is the non-performance of certain essential ceremonies as prescribed by the Hindu Marriage Act. However, various courts have held that if there is other evidence to prove the marriage, evidence of the performance of *saptapadi* (in the context of Hindu marriages) is not necessary, especially since ceremonies vary in different castes and communities.

In *Dwarika Prasad Satpathy* v. *Bidyut Praya Dixit*,[85] the Supreme Court held that once it is admitted that some marriage procedure was followed and if the court is *prima facie* satisfied with regard to the performance of the marriage, it is not necessary to probe further into whether ceremonies were complete as per Hindu rites or if the ceremony is in accordance with the provisions of the Hindu Marriage Act. The marriage would be deemed valid.

Numerous high courts have also held similarly. For instance, in *Subhash Popatlal Shah* v. *Lata Subhash Shah*,[86] the marriage was performed by a priest in a temple who chanted mantras, *tilak* was applied, the bride and groom

garlanded each other, and the marriage was consummated. Later, the husband challenged the validity of the marriage on the ground that saptapadi was not performed. But the court held that saptapadi was not proven to be an essential ceremony as per the customs prevailing among both parties to the marriage. The court further commented that even if it can be proven, it cannot be held that the marriage is invalid on this basis. When some ceremonies of marriage have been performed, there is always a presumption of the validity of the marriage under Section 114 of the IEA. Until this presumption is rebutted by cogent and satisfactory evidence, the marriage will be deemed valid. Based on this presumption, the Bombay High Court upheld the claim of the woman and awarded maintenance of Rs 400 per month to the wife and Rs 500 per month to her son. The court also commented that the Supreme Court ruling requiring strict proof of a valid marriage in the context of prosecution for bigamy under Section 494 of IPC is not relevant in matrimonial proceedings.[87]

The view that saptapadi is not required for a valid Hindu marriage was also upheld by the Rajasthan High Court in *Roop Singh* v. *State of Rajasthan*,[88] where the marriage was performed as per the custom of *nata*,[89] which is permissible amongst many lower caste communities of

---

[84] This issue has been discussed in detail in the previous chapter under 'Rights of Married Minors to Maintenance' in the section titled 'Marriage of Minors'.

[85] AIR 1999 SC 3348: 2000 Cr.LJ 1 SC

[86] I (1994) DMC 115 Bom

[87] The Supreme Court ruling on conviction for bigamy which are referred here are the following: *Bhaurao Shanker Lokhande* v. State of Maharashtra, AIR 1965 SC 1564; *Kanwal Ram* v. *The H.P. Administration*, AIR 1966 SC 614; *Priya Bala Ghosh* v. *Suresh Chandra Ghosh*, AIR 1971 SC 1153; *Lingari Obulamma* v. *L. Venkata Reddy*, AIR 1979 SC 848. In these cases it was held that to prove the second marriage, it is essential to prove that saptapadi was performed.

[88] II (1999) DMC 318 Raj

[89] An acceptable form of informal marriage. The term applies specially to the subsequent marriage of a divorcee woman. The marriage ceremony is informal

Rajasthan. While acknowledging that saptapadi may not be an essential ceremony amongst some communities, the court ruled that the necessary ceremonies had been performed, and that the standard of proof needed to prove a marriage is not as high as that required in connection with proceedings under the IPC for the offence of bigamy.

The Patna High Court commented in *Veena Devi* v. *Ashok Kumar Mandal*,[90] that it is irrelevant for the place of marriage to be mentioned and saptapadi to have taken place in the application in proceedings under Section 125 of Cr.PC. The court also commented that the failure to name the priest and barber who were present at the wedding could hardly serve as a ground to disbelieve the factum of marriage because every bride and bridegroom are not expected to recollect the names of attendees after twenty years of marriage.

In *Laxmikant* v. *Premwati Devi*,[91] the wife had filed for restitution of conjugal rights against her husband in the trial court. Although, the husband pleaded that no marriage existed between him and the woman, the wife pleaded that some marriage ceremonies had been performed. Based on this she was awarded a decree in her favour. When, the husband appealed and produced a voters list as evidence (where the woman was not listed as his wife), the court held that once marriage between the parties is proved, presumption would be drawn that all the required ceremonies of marriage were performed. The court commented that the policy of the law was to lean in favour of the validity of marriage rather than against it.

In *Muthumanicam* v. *Sekaran*,[92] despite the husband's contention that there was no valid

and since the girl is not virgin, saptapadi is not performed during the marriage.

marriage, the Magistrate's court awarded maintenance of Rs 175 to the wife and Rs 125 to the child. The sessions court reversed the order on the ground that the marriage had not been proved as saptapadi was not performed. In an appeal, the Madras High Court upheld the right of the child to maintenance, but did not grant maintenance to the wife. The Supreme Court reversed the orders of the two Appellate courts and upheld the order of the Magistrate's court and commented: 'In Tamil Nadu, marriage by exchange of garlands is permissible. The small discrepancy regarding the time of marriage is not a ground for discarding evidence and denying maintenance to the wife.'

In *Manmohan Vaid* v. *Meena Kumari*,[93] the Delhi High Court commented: As regards the alleged non-performance of saptapadi, firstly, it shall be presumed in the circumstances in the form of *lagan feras* and, secondly, non-performance in itself is not a sufficient condition to declare a marriage invalid/void or voidable. The court declared a marriage solemnized in a Gurudwara Saheb according to rules of the committee as valid. This was a love marriage where the couple were having a relationship for four years and the marriage was performed against the wishes of parents on both sides but the maternal uncles on both sides attended the wedding. Later the husband denied the marriage and alleged that he was drugged. But the court commented that the trial court and the high court had observed the demeanor of the husband and were convinced of the falsity of his contentions. The high court commented that he was a person who could go to any extent (to depose falsity).

The Calcutta High Court, in *Jitendra Nath Das* v. *Minati Das*,[94] upon the husband's denial

90 2000 Cri.LJ 332 Pat
91 2004 MLR 231 MP
92 II (2001) DMC 435 SC
93 II (2003) DMC 723 Del
94 II (2004) DMC 319 Cal

of the marriage, permitted a photograph of the wife with the husband along with its negative, as evidence. In an elaborate and well reasoned order, the Magistrate upheld the wife's claim and awarded Rs 400 per month as maintenance. While dismissing the appeal filed by the husband, the Calcutta High Court held that Section 125 of Cr.PC is a piece of welfare legislation to protect the wife from destitution and vagrancy, and proceedings are summary to facilitate a speedy disposal. Rigours of strict proof of all the formalities of a Hindu Marriage can be dispensed with. The husband could not adduce evidence that was sufficient to question the veracity of the testimony of witnesses for the wife, who were found to be sound, authentic, and dependable.

In *Namita Patnaik* v. *Dillip Patnaik*,[95] the husband alleged that a document titled 'Bibaha Bandhan Agreement' registered before the District Sub-Registrar of Cuttack was fraudulent. He contended that no marriage had taken place between the petitioner and himself. In the registered document, the husband had categorically stated that he had duly married the woman and the District Sub-Registrar stated in court that the document had been presented to him by the husband. It was held that a right accrued by means of a registered document cannot be taken away by a deed of cancellation and, hence, any such deed has no legal basis.

In *Jagdish* v. *Shobha*,[96] the wife pleaded that she was pregnant at the time of marriage, which was performed as per Buddhist rites. Soon after, she gave birth but the child died. The husband denied the marriage but admitted to the pre-marriage pregnancy. The Magistrate court dismissed her application but the sessions court awarded her Rs 400 as maintenance. The high court upheld the order of the sessions court and held: 'Evidence tendered by the wife shows that the husband tied the marriage necklace and applied vermilion on the wife's forehead in the presence of several others. This is in accordance with the customs applicable to Buddhists.'

It is evident that in a pluralistic society, the rigid application of stipulations regarding the essential ceremonies of marriage under the Hindu Marriage Act, only serve to deny the crucial rights of basic survival to women and children. The benefits of such a rigid application of legal provisions only helps husbands validate their manipulations to take advantage of their own wrongdoing. Hence, as can be observed from the above rulings, a strong presumption of the law operates in favour of marriage and legitimacy, which cannot be rebutted by a mere balance of probability. The evidence for rebutting the validity of a marriage should be cogent, satisfactory, and conclusive.

Inter-Religious Marriages

Christian law permits a Christian marriage to be solemnized between a couple, even if one of them is a follower of Christianity. Hence, inter religion marriages are valid under Christian law. Muslim law permits inter-religious marriages under certain specific circumstances. Religion is not a bar under the Special Marriage Act. But Hindu law applies only to Hindus and, hence, an inter-religious marriage performed as per Hindu rites is not valid. The same condition applies to a Parsi marriage wherein, if a Parsi marries a non-Parsi, such a marriage is invalid under the Parsi Marriage and Divorce Act, 1936 (Diwan and Diwan 1997).[97]

---

[95] I (2002) DMC 248 Ori
[96] II (2006) DMC 307 Bom

[97] Paras Diwan and Piyushi Diwan, *Law of Marriage and Divorce*, Delhi: Universal Law Publishing Co.Ltd., 1997 (3rd Edn) p.92.

But, since Hindu society is pluralistic, Hindu law validates diverse ceremonies and no notice period or written document of marriage is required, it is common practice for an inter-religious couple to opt for a Hindu Marriage. Later, when conflicts arise, the husband conveniently advances the plea that since the marriage is inter-religious, it is not legally valid.

Sreedharan v. *Pushpa Bai*[98] is a case of a marriage between a Hindu and Christian belonging to the Nadar community. The validity of the marriage was being contested by the husband. Janaki Amma J. of the Kerala High Court, reiterated that the standard of proof of marriage for awarding maintenance is not as strict as it is for bigamy under the IPC. The court held that a woman cannot be denied the status of a wife after undergoing a ceremony of marriage, merely because the husband and wife follow different religions. It is an insufficient condition to surmise that there was no marriage.

In *K. Selvaraj Surendran* v. *P. Jayakumary*,[99] after the delivery of a child, the husband refused to take the wife back and declined to pay maintenance to her and the child. When the wife filed for maintenance, the husband denied the existence of the marriage and the paternity of the child. He claimed that since he is a Christian and a bachelor, and the wife a Hindu, there cannot be a marriage between them. The wife pleaded that they were both Hindus and married under the HMA. The family court concluded that the woman is legally married and that the child was born within the marriage. It further held that the denial of marriage and paternity was tantamount to cruelty. In an appeal filed by the husband against the order of the family court, the Kerala High Court upheld

it and stated that the wife is entitled to a separate residence and maintenance.

In *Patricia* v. *Purushothaman*,[100] the husband pleaded that he is Hindu and since the wife is Christian, there could be no valid marriage between them. But the court rejected this plea and held that since the parties were accepted by their respective families as husband and wife, it is difficult to infer that their relationship was construed by family members as mere concubinage. Further, it can be justifiably presumed that there was a legal marriage between them due to their long cohabitation for the purpose of awarding maintenance under Section 125 Cr.PC.

In *Madhavi Ramesh Dudani* v. *Ramesh K. Dudani*,[101] the marriage was between a Christian wife and a Hindu husband. When the wife left the matrimonial home due to estrangement and filed for maintenance for herself and her two daughters, the husband denied the validity of the marriage on the ground that certain essential ceremonies like *sudhikaran* were not performed. The trial court upheld this plea. In an appeal filed by the wife, while setting aside the verdict of the trial court, the Bombay High Court held that purification ceremony is not necessary as per Section 4 of the Hindu Marriage Act[102] and hence the absence thereof cannot lead to the conclusion that such a person did not convert to Hinduism prior to the marriage ceremony. Further, it held that Section 114 of the IEA expects the court to presume the

---

[98] (1978) Ker LT 26
[99] II (2001) DMC 13 Ker

[100] II (2006) DMC 273 Ker
[101] I (2006) DMC 386 Bom
[102] Section 4: Overriding effect of the act – save as otherwise expressly provided in this Act, a) Any text, rule or interpretation of Hindu law or any custom or usage as part of that law in force immediately before the commencement of this act shall cease to have effect with respect to any matter for which provision is made in this act.

existence of certain facts which it believes are likely to have happened, regard being shown to the common course of natural events.

Courts usually decline to uphold frivolous pleas such as the invalidity of inter-religious marriages. These claims provide an escape route to husbands from the legal obligation of maintaining the wife with whom they cohabited, in what was perceived by the parties as well as their families, as a valid marriage. If the courts were to accept such frivolous pleas advanced by husbands, the legislative intent of providing maintenance to women in a vulnerable situation would be defeated. Hence, the courts are bound to appreciate the evidence in accordance with the provisions of the statute in order to achieve the goal of social justice.

If the girl herself alleges fraud and misrepresentation regarding religion and social status, the courts are likely to annul an inter-religious marriage performed as per Hindu rites as held by the Supreme Court in *Gullipilli Sowria Raj* v. *Bandaru Pavani*.[103]

Rights of Women in Bigamous Marriages

One of the most commonly used legal strategies to deny a woman maintenance is to claim that the marriage is bigamous. Prior to 1955, Hindu marriages were polygamous. But the codified statute of 1955, the Hindu Marriage Act, rendered Hindu marriages monogamous.[104] But, while it was deemed monogamous in letter, Hindu marriages continue to be polygamous in reality. Within the legal domain, these marriages are void. But historically, most

communities accepted the customary practice of bigamous marriages and treated these unions as valid marriages. Ironically, this situation is prevalent not only in rural areas, but urban centres as well.

The advantage of the mandate of legal monogamy lies with the husband as he can escape from the economic liability of maintaining his wife on the plea that the marriage suffered from a legal defect or lacked legal sanctity. Since ancient Hindu law and customary practices validated the institution of concubinage, even in present times, the plea that the woman concerned is a 'concubine' or 'mistress' and not the 'wife' can be advanced with ease in legal arguments. The fact that husbands have taken undue advantage and grossly misappropriated this mandate is exemplified by the volume of case law on the subject. An oft invoked legal ploy is to term the woman the domestic maid, a mistress or a 'keep', and not the wife with rights, status and entitlements.

Maintenance Rights of Second Wives

On the positive side is the ruling of M.H. Kania J. of the Bombay High Court, in *Govindrao* v. *Anandibai*,[105] delivered in 1976. In this case it was held that since the HMA is a social legislation, it could not have been the intention of the legislature that in a case where a Hindu woman was duped into contracting a bigamous marriage with a Hindu male, she should be deprived of her right to claim maintenance.

Several later decisions followed this legal dictum. In a leading case, *Vimala* v. *Veeraswamy*,[106] the Supreme Court held: Section 125 of Cr.PC is meant to achieve a social purpose. The objective is to prevent vagrancy and destitution. When an attempt is

---

[103] I (2009) DMC 164 SC

[104] Section 5(i) of the Hindu Marriage Act stipulates that neither party should have a spouse living at the time of the marriage. See section titled 'Consequences of Monogamy' in Chapter 1 *Personal Laws and Women's Rights* of the first volume for a detailed discussion on this issue.

[105] AIR 1976 Bom 433

[106] (1991) 2 SCC 375

made by the husband to negate the claim of the neglected wife by depicting her as a kept mistress, on the plea that he was already married, the court insists on strict proof of the earlier marriage. A provision in the law, which disentitles the second wife from receiving maintenance from her husband under Section 125 of Cr.PC for the sole reason that the marriage ceremony, though performed in the customary form, lacks legal sanctity, can be applied only when the husband proves the subsistence of a legal and valid marriage. This is so particularly when Section 125 of Cr.PC is a measure of social justice intended to protect women and children. In the absence of clear proof that the respondent is living with another woman as husband and wife, the court cannot be persuaded to hold that the marriage duly solemnized, between the appellant and respondent, suffers from any legal infirmity.

This view was furthered in a later ruling, *Mallika v. P. Kulandai*,[107] where the woman got married to a man who claimed to be a widower and there was a daughter born out of this union. When she later filed for maintenance, the husband challenged the validity of the marriage on the ground that he had an earlier marriage subsisting. The lower court upheld the husband's plea that the marriage was not legal and denied maintenance to the woman. But in an appeal, the Madras High Court held that though the marriage could not be strictly proven, there was sufficient evidence to establish that the parties lived together continuously for a period of time long enough for a child to be born. The court upheld the woman's claim of Rs 250 maintenance for herself and Rs 50 to the child born of this union. In 2002, the Bombay High Court, in *R. Arora v. B. Arora*,[108] upheld the right of the

second wife to a separate residence and maintenance under Section 18 of the Hindu Adoption and Maintenance Act. In this case, while divorce proceedings were pending against the first wife, the husband entered an informal relationship with another woman, but later, reconciled with his wife. The woman filed for a declaration that her marriage is valid, for an injunction against dispossession, and for maintenance. The family court passed an order restraining the husband from throwing the woman out of the flat in which she was residing along with her daughter, and awarded maintenance of Rs 10,000. In an appeal, the Bombay High Court ruled that since the husband had reconciled with his first wife, the subsequent partner could not be expected to reside in the same house and that she was entitled to a separate residence.

The turning point in this line of arguments came with a contrary view advanced by the full bench verdict in *Bhausaheb Raghuji Magar* v. *Leelabai Bhausaheb Magar*,[109] in 2003 by the Bombay High Court. In this case, it was held that the earlier decision of the Bombay High Court, upholding the right of maintenance to the illegitimate wife (or faithful mistress) by a liberal construction of the word 'wife' as contained in Section 25 of HMA, is not good law. The court commented that though such a liberal construction, which may benefit second wives who are innocently drawn into marriages, it may encourage bigamous marriages with full knowledge, in spite of the existence of a legislation preventing bigamous marriages.

The Supreme Court ruling in 2005, in *Savitaben Somabhai Bhatiya* v. *State of Gujarat*,[110] also endorsed this view. In this case, a woman, claiming to have been married according to customary rites and rituals, pleaded that her

---

[107] I (2001) DMC 354 Mad
[108] I (2002) DMC 136 Bom

[109] AIR 2004 Bom 283: II (2004) DMC 321
[110] AIR 2005 SC 1809: I (2005) DMC 503 SC

husband had an illicit relationship with a woman named Veenaben. The husband denied the marriage and pleaded that Veenaben whom he had married 22 years ago was his lawful wife. The Gujarat High Court upheld the validity of his marriage with Veenaben. Endorsing this verdict, the Supreme Court held that it is inconsequential that the man was treating Savitaben as his wife. However desirable it may be to take note of the plight of the unfortunate woman, it is the intention of the legislature which is relevant and not the attitude of the party. There is no scope for enlarging it by introducing a woman not lawfully married in the expression 'wife'. Following this ruling, the Bombay High Court, in *Atmaram Tukaram Suradkar* v. *Sau Trivenibai Atmaram Suradkar*,[111] held that the position of a woman who is married to a person whose spouse is living at the time of the second marriage is a mistress and not a married wife, and is not entitled to maintenance under Section 125 of Cr.PC. Similarly in *Buddepu Khogayya* v. *Buddepu Kamalu*,[112] the woman admitted that the husband was married at the time of her marriage to him, but that he had promised to divorce her in the course of time, which he did not do. Later, after two children were born, he deserted her. The Magistrate's court awarded her Rs 400 as maintenance, but relying on the Supreme Court ruling in *Savitaben*, the high court reversed the order and held that such a plea under Section 125 of Cr.PC was of no avail to her.

The derogatory attitude towards women who are in such relationships is further reflected in *Malti* v. *State of U.P.*,[113] where the husband developed a sexual relationship with the domestic maid and started cohabiting with her. When

the wife returned, he turned the maid out of the house. When a claim for maintenance was filed by the domestic maid, the judge declared: 'The two may agree to live together to satisfy their animal needs. But such a union is never called a marriage and a woman leading such a life cannot be bestowed with the sacrosanct honour of a wife. No marital obligations accrue to such a woman against her husband.' While comments about the high moral standards may appear salutary, it does seem that the price for immorality is to be paid only by the woman, while the man is left free to exploit both women. This seems to be the outcome of enforcing a strict code of monogamy under the Hindu Marriage Act.

In this context, one needs to elaborate on two recent judgments delivered by the Delhi High Court, reported in 2008. These judicial pronouncements have attempted to cross the stumbling block posed by the stipulation of monogamy under Section 5 of the HMA by invoking innovative legal maxims to protect the rights of women.

In the first case, *Suresh Khullar* v. *Vijay Kumar Khullar*,[114] while contracting the present marriage, the husband's first marriage was dissolved by a court of law. The wife was innocent and oblivious of the fraudulent circumstances under which the husband had obtained an ex parte decree of divorce against his first wife. After a few months of her marriage, the woman was driven out of the matrimonial home. Thereafter, the husband's ex parte decree of divorce was set aside on the ground of fraud and, through this legal incident Suresh Khullar's marriage was rendered bigamous and invalid. The woman filed a suit for damages against the husband and his first wife on the ground of fraud and cheating, which was decreed by a civil judge. While

---

[111] I (2006) DMC 203 Bom
[112] I (2007) DMC 451 AP
[113] I (2001) DMC 204 All

[114] I (2008) DMC 719 Del

upholding the right of the woman, the court with respect to Section 18 of HAMA, the Delhi high court held as follows: 'While interpreting a statute, the courts may not only take into consideration the purpose for which the statute was enacted, but also the mischief it seeks to suppress.' The court invoked the legal maxim *construction ut res magis valeat quam pereat,* that is, where alternative constructions are possible, the court must give effect to that which will be responsible for the smooth working of the system for which the statute has been enacted rather than one which will put a road block in its way. The court commented that if this interpretation is not accepted, it would amount to giving a premium to the husband for defrauding the wife. It was held that for the purpose of claiming maintenance under Section 18 of HAMA, the woman should be treated as the legally wedded wife.

The second ruling was pronounced in *Narinder Pal Kaur Chawla* v. *Manjeet Singh Chawla.*[115] The wife had approached the court for maintenance under Section 18 of HAMA in 1997 and pleaded that her husband had duped her by suppressing his earlier marriage. The couple had lived together for fourteen years and had two daughters. The husband pleaded that since his earlier marriage was valid and subsisting, his marriage with Narinder Pal Kaur was void. After a prolonged and contentious litigation, she was able to secure an order of interim maintenance of Rs 1,500 per month But, when the case was finally decided in 2005, the trial court dismissed her petition on the ground that she could not be treated as a Hindu wife under Section 18 of HAMA as she did not have the status of a legally wedded wife. But in appeal, the Delhi High Court upheld the right of the wife and held that even if the woman

cannot be treated as a Hindu wife, she is entitled to a lump settlement by way of damages.

Customary Divorce and Subsequent Remarriage

Despite the enactment of the Hindu Marriage Act, which provided for a judicial divorce, the practice of customary divorce is prevalent among large sections of society, and more so among the poor in rural areas who find it difficult and expensive to access the formal court structures. The customary divorce and remarriage was an accepted practice among the lower classes and even the codified law validates such practices.[116] But, when women in such marriages claim maintenance, the husbands challenge the customary divorce to invalidate the present marriage and defeat the woman's claim of maintenance. Here, too, the courts have held contradictory views. While some judgments have seen through the falsity of such claims, others have held in favour of husbands, thus, rendering women trapped in such situation extremely vulnerable.

On the positive side is the case of *Pushpabai* v. *Pratap Singh.*[117] When the wife was awarded maintenance of Rs 500 per month by the trial court, the husband filed an appeal and pleaded that there was no valid marriage between the parties since the wife had not obtained a divorce from her first husband and, hence, she is not his legally married wife. The sessions court set aside the order of maintenance. In appeal, the wife pleaded that she had been divorced according to the custom of the caste and the divorce took place before the *Gona* ceremony.[118] On examination of evidence, the Madhya Pradesh High court upheld

---

[115] I (2008) DMC 529 Del

[116] Section 29 (2) of Hindu Marriage Act, 1955.

[117] I (2001) DMC 110 MP

[118] This is a customary practice among certain communities. Gona or Gown is performed after the marriage, before the girl is sent off to her husband's home for consummation of marriage or sexual cohabitation.

the order of the Magistrate's court that the customary divorce and the subsequent marriage is valid, and awarded Rs 1,000 as costs to the wife. While the judgment is positive, it highlights the long and circuitous route to justice which women have to undertake for a paltry sum of maintenance. In 2004, in *Rameshchandra Daga* v. *Rameshwari Daga*,[119] the husband had married Rameshwari, who had obtained a customary divorce (*chor chittee*) through a divorce deed, which was allegedly shown to the husband prior to the marriage. Later, when she claimed maintenance, the husband denied the marriage on the ground that the woman had not been formally divorced. Both the family court at Mumbai as well as the Bombay High Court upheld the wife's and her daughter's right of maintenance. In the final verdict, the Supreme Court upheld the woman's plea that the husband, an advocate, was aware of the customary divorce at the time of his marriage.

The facts of this case tell the tragic tale of an Indian woman, who having gone through two marriages with a child born to her, apprehends destitution as both marriages have broken down', the judges commented with a note of compassion. Further, the Supreme Court accepted that Hindu marriages, like Muslim marriages, were bigamous prior to the 1955 enactment. There is also a tacit acceptance that the ground reality has not changed much since the enactment. So, though such marriages are illegal, as per the statutory provisions of the codified Hindu law, the Supreme Court ruled that they are not immoral and, hence, a financially dependent woman cannot be denied maintenance on this ground.

In *K. Suramma* v. *K. Rammayyamma*,[120] it was held that the parties relying on custom must prove the custom. Since there was no

evidence of the practice of customary divorce being ancient and continuous, and no evidence on record to prove that her divorce with her earlier husband was final, the court declined to uphold the woman's rights to the death benefits of her deceased husband.[121]

In these cases the challenge before the court is to examine whether the marriage contracted by the woman subsequent to her divorce and obtained through customary practices is valid, or whether the subsequent marriage can be declared bigamous and, hence, invalid. The courts also examine the intention of the parties—whether there was an intention to divorce, or whether there was an intention to deceive and fraudulently enter into a second marriage while the earlier one was subsisting.

In *Parikshat* v. *State of UP*, the husband challenged the order of maintenance awarding the wife Rs 500 per month as maintenance on the ground that since she had not obtained divorce from her previous husband, her marriage with him is not valid. The high court upheld the order of the trial court and held that when the factum of marriage is admitted, it should be presumed that the wife is the legally wedded wife. The trial court had held that there had been a customary divorce called *chutta chutti* and, hence, the woman's previous marriage stood terminated. Neither trial court nor the revision court specified that the husband had made a contention that the practice of customary divorce was unacceptable on the basis of the well established principle that custom cannot override written law and, further, that divorce could be acceptable only if it was brought about in accordance with provisions of Hindu law.

After the Supreme Court ruling in *Rameshchandra Daga* v. *Rameshwari Daga*

The section titled 'Marriage of Minors' in the previous chapter has a reference to this custom.

[119] I (2005) DMC 1 SC
[120] II (2002) DMC 54 AP

[121] See section titled 'Validity of Customary Laws' of Chapter 1 *Personal Laws and Women's Rights* of the first volume where this issue has been discussed in detail.

(discussed earlier), it appeared that it will no longer be possible for a Hindu husband to escape from his liability of maintaining his wife on the plea that the wife is not formally divorced from her previous husband, or on the plea that the woman is his concubine since his own previous marriage is still subsisting. But the subsequent ruling in *Savitaben Somabhai Bhatiya* v. *State of Gujarat* (also discussed earlier) has again rendered the situation ambiguous. But subsequent to this ruling, the Protection of Women from Domestic Violence Act was enacted in 2005, which has awarded legal recognition to informal relationships and cohabittee rights. This legal provision which is discussed subsequently, as well as judicial pronouncements of various high courts, have brought in a renewed hope to women whose marriage suffer from legal or technical defect.

Succession Rights of Second Wives

Challenges to the rights of the second wife extend beyond issues of maintenance and spill over into the domain of succession rights. Cases arise because the claims of the second (or subsequent) wife or her heirs are contested either by the first (or former) wife, her children, or the husband's relatives. Here, too, one can find divergent views on the issue.

On the positive side is the ruling in *Shantaram Patil* v. *Dagubai Patil*.[122] In this case, while deciding the right of a widow in an invalid marriage, the Bombay High Court had held as follows: Even if the marriage is void, the woman has a right against the husband. The right can be enforced not only in a proceeding under Section 25 of the HMA, but in any proceeding where validity of marriage and the rights flowing from it are determined. The right can be enforced not only during the lifetime of the husband but also after his death against his property. In this case, the court also ruled that the son from the second marriage is entitled to a share in the father's property along with the first wife and her three children, and the second wife is entitled to maintenance from the property of her deceased husband.

Following is an interesting case where the child of the second wife contested the claim of succession of the third wife and where issues of customary marriage and divorce were also involved. In *Shakuntalabai* v. *Kulkarni*,[123] the husband had remarried as the first wife could not bear children. After the death of the second wife he married for the third time in the customary *Udiki* form. After his death, the daughter of the second wife challenged the succession claim of the third wife. The issue before the court was whether the divorce in customary form and subsequent marriage in customary form was valid under the law. The court observed that in matters of this kind, hearsay evidence, like traditions, may be received as direct evidence since direct evidence of such marriages was not always available, and one of the ways in which the marriage can be proved was from the manner of their living and from the way in which they were treated by their neighbours.

The case of *Resham Bai* v. *Shakuntalabai*[124] involved distribution of assets between the mother and the two wives of the deceased. The trial court had directed that the deposit of Rs 52,248 should be distributed equally between mother and two wives. Both the wives were to get the family pension in equal share. The high court held such distribution of assets to be fair, reasonable, and based on equitable consideration.

---

[122] AIR 1987 Bom 182

[123] (1989) 2 SCC 526
[124] II (2000) DMC 724 MP

In 2008, the Supreme Court, in *Tulsa* v. *Durghatiya*, has laid down that if a couple is living together for a very long period as husband and wife, there would be presumption in favour of wedlock. This presumption is rebuttable, but a heavy burden is cast upon the person who seeks to deprive the relationship of its legal origin to prove that no marriage took place. The Court reiterated that the law leans in favour of legitimacy and frowns upon bastardy. In this case, the couple had lived together for thirty years and had five children. The daughters were given in marriage by the husband. After her husband's death, the woman had legitimate claim over the property as his wife. She had incurred debt at the time of her son's marriage and had sold part of the land for this purpose. The Supreme Court held that she had the right to sell land and there is no question of having any illegal possession. While the trial court upheld her claim, the appellate court without any evidence, had come to an abrupt conclusion that the woman had started living with the man during the lifetime of her husband and, hence, she is not the wife but merely a concubine. Hence, she does not acquire the rights of a widow and cannot inherit his property. But evidence clearly proved that her former husband was not alive when she came and started living with the deceased. The Supreme Court concluded that continuous living as husband and wife had been established.

While the above rulings favour women in invalid marriages, the following judgments are indicative of a contradictory trend.

In *Rajeshbai* v. *Shantabai*,[125] the first wife, Shantabai contested the claim of succession of the second wife, Rajeshbai, who was in possession of the property after the death of her husband. The court commented: The injunctive rule that neither party should have a spouse living at the time of marriage is enacted to prohibit polygamy and to institute measures of monogamy. There may be cases where that status may not be available to a woman because of the injunctive process of law. Though such a woman might have undergone a formal marriage, her status would be that of an illegitimate wife, and such a wife is not conferred with the status which is available to a legitimate wife nor does she have any entitlement, as the lawful wife of her husband, to the property under the provision of the Hindu Succession Act, 1956. Hence, it was held that both by virtue of status and law, Shantabai alone would be considered as a widow and as such would succeed to the properties of the deceased. However, the court ordered payment of Rs 20,000 to Rajeshbai as full and final settlement of her claim.

Similarly, in *Nimbamma* v. *Rathanamma*,[126] the court ruled that the provisions of Section 5(i) and 11 of HMA render the position of a woman married to a person whose wife was living at the time of the second marriage to be that of a *kept mistress* and not that of a legally married wife. Stating that a bigamous marriage is null and void *ab initio*, the court held that such a woman was not entitled to succeed to the properties of that person.

Another interesting case is *Felix* v. *Jemi*.[127] The first wife and her children challenged the succession claims of the second wife and her children. The parties and the deceased husband were Christians. The court held that the divorce obtained in 1971, by the mutual consent, of the first wife and the deceased was not valid under the law applicable to Christians. Hence, as the petitioner was still the lawfully wedded wife of the deceased at the time of the latter's marriage

---

[125] AIR 1982 Bom 231

[126] DMC I (2000) 579 Kar
[127] I (2003) DMC 430 Mad

with the second wife, the court stated that the relationship between him and the second wife was mere concubinage and the children born of that union were illegitimate. Stating that only because they lived under one roof, the woman could not claim the status of the wife of the deceased, the court held that once the marriage between the first wife and deceased was admitted and the marriage was not dissolved in manner known to law, the woman in a subsequent relationship will lose the status of a wife. The case is rather tragic because the Christian law had remained archaic for a very long time and the notion of judicial divorce by mutual consent was introduced only in 2001. There was no legal avenue for the parties concerned to obtain a judicial decree of divorce by consent.[128] So, though the deceased and the first wife had separated with consent, they could not obtain a judicial

---

[128] After the amendment in 2001, this remedy has been incorporated into the Divorce Act under Section 10A of the Act. So, a Christian couple can now avail of the remedy of divorce by mutual consent. See section titled 'Christian Law of Marriage and Succession' of Chapter 1 *Personal Laws and Women's Rights* of the first volume where this issue is discussed in detail.

decree to this effect and the second wife who had in full faith, was denied her succession rights.

Succession Rights of Children of Void Marriages
Rather interestingly, each of the cases discussed earlier concerned the succession rights of children of second wives. In some cases, their rights have been upheld invoking the provision of Section16 of HMA. Prior to the 1976 amendment only children whose parents had obtained a decree of nullity were deemed legitimate and were entitled to rights. But after the 1976 amendment to Section 16, the children of void marriages were awarded the right of maintenance and succession, irrespective of whether the parties had obtained a decree of nullity. This move served to widen the scope of this section and brought within its ambit a large number of children whose parents' marriages were deemed invalid due to the stipulation of monogamy. These children are now deemed legitimate and are awarded rights of maintenance and succession in self acquired property of their parents. While awarding succession rights to an illegitimate child, the courts have also invoked the institution of *dasi putra* (son of a slave) which was prevalent under the ancient Hindu law.

Box 2.3   The Hindu Marriage Act

Section 16: Legitimacy of Children of Void and Voidable Marriages

(1) Notwithstanding that a marriage is null and void under Section 11, any child of such marriage who would have been legitimate if the marriage had been valid, shall be legitimate, whether such child is born before or after the commencement of the Marriage Laws (Amendment) Act, 1976, and whether or not a decree of nullity is granted in respect of that marriage under this Act, and whether or not the marriage is held to be void otherwise than on a petition under this Act.

(3) Nothing contained in Sub-Section (1) or Sub-Section (2) shall be construed as conferring upon any child of a marriage which is null and void or which is annulled by a decree of nullity under Section 12, any rights in or to the property of any person, other than the parents, in any case where, but for the passing of this Act, such child would have been incapable of possessing or acquiring any such rights by reason of his not being the legitimate child of his parents.

These principles are demonstrated in the following cases.

S.P.S. Balasubramanyam v. Suruttayan @ Andali Padayachi[129] concerned the succession rights of Ramaswamy who was the son of a woman Pavayee, who lived with one Chinathambi as his second wife. The couple had been living together since 1920. The fact that Ramaswamy was the son of this couple and was born while they lived together as husband and wife was not disputed. But the trial court had rejected Ramaswamy's suit for declaration and possession of the land which belonged to his father on the ground that there was no valid marriage between his parents. But the first appellate court upheld his claim on the premise that long cohabitation leads to presumption of a valid marriage. But the Madras High Court set aside this order and restored the order of the trial court. In appeal, the Supreme Court rejected the contention that Ramaswamy's mother had left her own husband and was living in an adulterous relationship with the deceased Chinathambi, the father of Ramaswamy, and since she was a mere concubine, her child had no claim over the property of his father. The court held that this contention is irrelevant for deciding the issue of succession rights of the child as children born even of a void marriage are deemed to be legitimate. The Supreme Court set aside the order of the high court and restored the order of the first appellate court and upheld the rights of Ramaswamy over the land which belonged to his father.

In *Lalithamma v. Agricultural Engineer, Karnataka Agro Industries Corporation, Dharwad*,[130] the deceased was entitled to compensation under the Workmen's Sale Compensation Act, 1923. The appellant, a mistress of the deceased, claimed maintenance for her minor son. While the claim was rejected in the lower court, in appeal, the Karnataka High Court held that the illegitimate child of a workman can claim damages for the loss of his father, and he is entitled to a share equal to the other legitimate heirs.

In *Rameshwari Devi v. State of Bihar*,[131] it was held that children born out of an invalid marriage are legitimate and are entitled to family pension and gratuity payments of their father. The court held that it was proved that the second wife and the deceased lived as husband and wife since 1963. This gives rise to a presumption in favour of a valid Hindu marriage. But it is not a legal marriage since it was in contravention of the provision of monogamy under Section 5 of the Hindu Marriage Act and, hence, it is void and the woman cannot be deemed as a widow of the deceased. But the sons of a void marriage being legitimate are entitled to property of the deceased in equal shares along with the first wife and her son.

In *Lakshmamma v. Kamalamma*,[132] the daughter of the second wife, of the deceased, claimed succession rights to the property of her father. The other claimants challenged her claim on the ground that there was no valid marriage between the deceased and her mother. But upholding her claim, the Karnataka High Court ruled that if the parties lived together as husband and wife for several decades and the community accepted them as husband and wife there would be a presumption of a valid marriage between the parties. The oral evidence that the marriage took place several years ago was also accepted as valid evidence.

[129] AIR 1994 SC 133: I (1994) DMC 484 SC
[130] II (1998) DMC 503 Kar
[131] I (2000) DMC 164 SC
[132] II (2001) DMC (DB) 242 Kar

In *Parmanand* v. *Jagrani*,[133] the claim of the children of the second wife was opposed by the children of the first wife on the ground that the children are illegitimate, as neither of their parents were married nor could they have married as the second wife's previous marriage was still subsisting at the time she started living with their father. The second wife was married earlier, but after separating from her earlier husband she had been living for a long time with the deceased and seven children were born out of this union. The high court held that in view of the long cohabitation between the deceased and the mother of the claimants, a marriage could be presumed between them. On the basis of this presumption, the children born would be deemed legitimate and obtain benefits as per Section 16(1) of the HMA and would be entitled to inherit the property of their putative father. The Madhya Pradesh High Court commented that in Khatri community to which the parties belonged, the custom of *natra* marriage prevailed which permitted a wife to contract a second marriage during the lifetime of her first husband. After contracting marriage through natra, if the wife lives with the man as a wife for a number of years and if her former husband takes no action regarding his rights of the marriage then it is presumed that the natra is legal, and children out of this union would be considered legitimate.[134]

The court observed further: The Hindu Marriage Act is a beneficial legislation and, therefore, it has to be interpreted in such a manner as to advance the object of the legislation. The Act intends to bring about social reforms. Conferring the status of legitimacy on innocent children, who are otherwise treated as bastards, is the prime object of Section 16 of the Hindu Marriage Act.

In *Minor Gopi, Rep. by Mother and next Friend Santhi* v. *Rathinam*,[135] it was held that the illegitimate child of a void marriage is entitled to claim a share only in the property of father. While the father is alive, the son cannot claim his share in the property. The right would accrue only after the death of the father.

In *Chinnammal* v. *Elumalai*,[136] it was held that under Section 16 of the HMA, illegitimate children are entitled to an equal share in the individual and self-acquired property of their father, though not in the ancestral property. In *Sarojamma* v. *Neelamma*,[137] the Karnataka High Court pushed the boundaries of the claims of illegitimate children and held that the children born out of wedlock are entitled to a share, not only in the self-acquired properties of the parents, but also in the joint or ancestral properties of parents.

A Supreme Court ruling of 2003, in *Jinia Keotin* v. *Kumar Manjhi*,[138] has contradicted this view and held: 'Though Section 16 was enacted for legitimate children, who would otherwise suffer by becoming illegitimate, in view of an express mandate of the Legislature itself under Sub-Section (3), there is no room for according upon such children who but for Section 16 would have been branded as illegitimate any further rights than envisaged therein by resorting to any presumptive or inferential process of reasoning, having recourse to the mere object or purpose of enacting Section 16 of the Act.

---

[133] AIR 2007 MP 242

[134] Natra is a form of customary remarriage of divorcees or widows which is less formal than the first marriage but carries with it contractual obligations as in a marriage. Customary divorces and natra marriages are accepted customary practices among many lower castes and tribes of North Indian states such as Rajasthan, Madhya Pradesh, Uttar Pradesh, etc.

[135] I (2002) DMC 90 Mad
[136] II (2000) DMC 278 Mad
[137] II (2005) DMC 567 Kar
[138] I (2003) DMC 1 SC

Any attempt to do so would amount not only to voilating the provision specifically engrafted in Sub-section (3) of Section 16 of the Act but also would amount to court re-legislating on the subject under the guise of interpretation, against even the will expressed in the enactment itself.' More recently, the Bombay High Court, in *Maruti Rau Mane v. Shrikant Maruti Mane*,[139] while determining succession rights of the children of the second wife has held that these children are not entitled to inherit ancestral coparcener property. But they are entitled to an equal share in the father's share in coparcener property.

While the amendment to Section 16 of the Hindu Marriage Act, in 1976, has strengthened the succession rights of illegitimate children/ children of void marriages, the Supreme Court in 1961, in *Singhai Ajit Kumar v. Ujayarsingh*,[140] had held that even under the shastric and textual law (or ancient Hindu law), an illegitimate son of a mistress or concubine is entitled to the rights of survivorship as he becomes a coparcener along with the legitimate son and, hence, is entitled to enforce a partition after the father's death.

Some courts have distinguished between a void or voidable marriage, and mere concubinage while determining the rights of illegitimate children in invalid marriages and informal cohabitation. While the maintenance rights of illegitimate children are clearly laid out, when it comes to succession rights, the situation continues to be ambiguous. Relying on technical nuances, bordering on the absurd, and ignoring the legislative intent, some courts have held that children of a second wife are entitled to maintenance being children of a void marriage since some sort of marriage ceremony might have

taken place. But if the woman is merely cohabiting without undergoing any ceremony, the courts have termed her as a concubine who is devoid of rights. Here the courts have adopted a very constrained view of beneficial provision of Section 16 of HMA and have held that an illegitimate child can inherit the property of the father only when it can be proved that the parents have undergone some marriage ceremony. In order to attract this section there should have been a 'marriage' between the parents and that marriage should have been null and void under Section 11. Since bigamous marriage is void under Section 11, the same would be covered under this provision, but benefits cannot be extended to the child of a mistress or concubine.

For instance, in *Singaram Udayar v. Subramaniam*,[141] it was held that children acquire no rights through concubinage. There should be void or voidable marriage between parents of the individual who claims the status of an illegitimate child to get a share from the estate of his father. If there is no proof of any marriage, the children born out of this union cannot be treated as illegitimate children entitled for share. Section16 of HMA does not deal with rights of children through concubinage.

In *Chodan Puthiyoth Shyamalavalli Amma v. Kavalam Jisha*,[142] the Kerala High Court held that if a marriage was solemnized between the parents, the benefit of Section 16 would have been accorded to the children. But if it is established that there was no marriage between the parents, the children born of this relationship cannot acquire the benefits of Section 16. On this ground, the court rejected the claim of the daughter of the deceased to inherit his property.

---

[139] II (2008) DMC 177 Bom
[140] AIR 1961 SC 1334
[141] I (2000) 172 DMC Mad
[142] AIR 2007 Ker 246

In another extremely negative ruling, *Kesari Bai* v. *Parwati*,[143] the Madhya Pradesh High Court held that children born out of a relationship with a mistress are not entitled to a succession certificate, even if nominated by the deceased during his life-time. The lower court had upheld the right of these children. In appeal, the high court set aside this order and held that the status of such a woman is not that of a married wife. The woman had stated that she had gone through a marriage ceremony by exchange of *jaimala*. But the court held that since the parties were Brahmins, saptapadi is an essential ceremony of marriage. Since the woman had not gone through any such ritual, she cannot be held to be the wife/widow of the deceased. The court commented that a woman can claim her rights only when the couple has undergone a marriage ceremony. Otherwise, if she is living together with a person without undergoing a valid legal form of marriage, it will be deemed that she is merely a 'keep' and not a wife and there is a difference between a wife and a mistress.

This judgment is contrary to several rulings discussed earlier in this section and are reflective of the anti-women bias within the judiciary. But perhaps since the children did not have the economic means to challenge it in the Supreme Court, the rulings remained binding on them.

Rights of Women in Informal Relationships

Prolonged Cohabitation and Presumption of Marriage

The law presumes in favour of marriage and against concubinage when a man and woman have cohabited continuously for a number of years.
1929 Privy Council in *Mohabhat Ali* v. *Md. Ibrahim Khann*.[144]

---

[143] I (2000) DMC 392 MP
[144] AIR 1929 PC 135

The discussion on *succession rights of children of void marriages* brings us to our next point—presumption of marriage which arises due to long cohabitation. Even when there is no proof of any ceremonies of marriage having been performed, the courts would lean towards validity of marriage based on the presumption of marriage under Section 114 of the Indian Evidence Act. Section 50 of the Indian Evidence Act provides additional safeguards. These provisions stipulate that the presumption in favour of marriage is not mitigated or weakened merely because there may not be concrete evidence of any marriage having taken place. In such cases, the courts will examine whether a common perception prevailed that the couple are married. If the parties cohabited for long time and if society (for example, the people of the area in which the parties resided) recognized their relationship as a marriage, presumption would arise that they are legally wedded.

In 1952, the Supreme Court, in *Mohammed Amin* v. *Vakil Ahmed*, while deciding the succession rights of a Muslim wife and her children, relied upon the principle of presumption of marriage. The validity of marriage was challenged by other relatives who were claiming the property of the deceased. There were no documents to prove the marriage but the couple had lived together for 23–4 years and four children were born out of their relationship. Based on this fact and on other facts, such as that the husband had purchased property in the name of his sons and had mentioned them as his sons in the sale deed, the court invoked the presumption of a lawful marriage.

The theoretical framework for this presumption was provided by the Privy Council in 1929 in the *Mohabhat Ali case* and was, subsequently, followed by the Supreme Court in the *Mohammed Amin case*. That case concerned a

Muslim marriage where bigamy is permitted and the notion of concubinage is shunned. This was also pronounced at a time when bigamy was permitted even under the Hindu law. But the situation changed after the enactment of the Hindu Marriage Act in 1955. Section 5(i) of the Act read with Section 11 stipulates that bigamous marriages are void. But while monogamy was the statutory dictate, at the ground level there was hardly any change. Customary practices and community norms continued to validate bigamous marriages, though legally they were deemed as void and devoid of any rights.

Confronted with diverse practices, it was left for the courts to find a via media to do justice and protect the rights of women and children within these pluralistic traditions and social realities. It is in the context of safeguarding the rights of innocent children, who were being deprived of their rights and were facing social stigma, that the legislature brought in an amendment to Section 16 HMA (and Section 26 of SMA) and bestowed rights of maintenance and succession on children of marriages which were void, irrespective of whether there was a judicial decree to this effect. This led to a gradual recognition of the rights of illegitimate children or children of void marriages, but women continued to suffer great hardships, particularly after the death of their husbands. Their rights were severely constrained or negated in litigation initiated by the children from their husbands' previous marriage or other relatives.

Technically, the move to award rights to illegitimate children of void marriages would have validated the rights of all children who were born in informal relationships. But the courts went into a further gradation between a wife of a void marriage and a mere mistress. As we have seen in the preceding section, there was some recognition awarded to children whose parents had gone through some ceremony, as opposed to those who had not. The women who could not prove the rituals and ceremonies were relegated to a derogative position of a mistress, concubine, or keep, and had to endure not just judicial contempt but also loss of their economic rights.

The women who were deprived of their status and rights through the mandate of monogamy, introduced by the Hindu Marriage Act of 1955, had to suffer for fifty years before some recognition could be awarded to them. There had been an attempt to voice their concerns through the enactment of the Domestic Violence Act, 2005, and bestow some social status and legal rights on women who were part of a prevailing social system and yet could be branded thus.

The DVA transformed the yesteryear concubines into present day cohabitees and their right to protection from domestic violence and rights of maintenance and residence have been awarded statutory recognition. While some may dismiss the term cohabitee as a western or urban phenomenon, this term can now be invoked to protect the rights of thousands of women, both urban and rural, who were earlier scoffed at as mistresses or keeps in the judicial discourse because of some technical defect in their marriage. The DVA does not clearly prescribe whether the new term cohabitee will safeguard the rights of women who were earlier denigrated as concubines and mistresses. That is left for judicial interpretation. But it helps to bring the debate to a newer plane.

The recent ruling in *Narinder Pal Kaur Chawla* v. *Manjeet Singh Chawla*[145] has an interesting comment regarding the institution of concubinage. It was held that Hindu law recognizes the

---

[145] I (2008) DMC 529 Del

institution of marriage as well as concubinage which is reflected in the provisions of Section 18(e) of HAMA[146] and suggested that this concept needs further dilation and judicial recognition in order to bring in a notion of justice to women. Regarding the protections awarded to women in informal relationships under the ancient Hindu law, the court commented:

One of such recognized obligations inscribed into the property of a Hindu was that of maintenance of dependents. There is no reason to hold that by codification of the laws, this basic concept for providing a sort of social security and having general insurance in favour of dependents has been completely taken away or abrogated by enacting HAMA. The necessity to provide even now may arise out of the premises of that Act and will have to be so worked out.

The call for a wider debate is salutary and also timely. In this context, we need to examine the judicial pronouncements of the preceding years which had attempted to raise this concern, though not as clearly and forthrightly as the *Narender Pal* judgment has attempted to do. But the *Narender Pal* ruling builds on these earlier legal precedents.

In the leading case *Badri Prasad* v. *Dy Director of Consolidation*,[147] in 1978, a distinguished bench of the Supreme Court comprising of V.R. Krishna Iyer J., D.A. Desai J., and O. Chinnappa Reddy J., laid down that if a man and woman have lived as husband and wife for about fifty years, under Section 114 of IEA, a strong presumption arises in favour of wedlock. Although this presumption is rebuttable, a heavy burden lies on him who seeks to deprive the relationship of legal origin. The court reiterated that the

law leans in favour of legitimacy and frowns upon bastardy. It was held that the contention that long after the alleged marriage evidence has not been produced to sustain its ceremonial process, by examining the priest or other witnesses, deserves no consideration. The court commented that if a man and woman who live as husband and wife are compelled to prove half a century later by eye witness evidence that they were validly married, few will succeed.

More recently, in *Radhamma* v. *Union of India*,[148] the fact of marriage was challenged by the mother of the deceased in the context of succession rights. The Karnataka High Court held that long co-habitation between the deceased and concerned woman was proved and the society treated them as a married couple. There had not been any allegation made against the woman that the documents produced by the wife were concocted or forged. Her signatures were also admitted. The woman concerned and the son of the petitioner lived as husband and wife, and this was within the knowledge of the appellant and her family members. Hence, the court commented that a very heavy burden is caste on the person who challenges the validity of such a marriage.

In *Dnyanoba Kamble* v. *Mukta Kamble*,[149] the fact that the respective parents had recognized the parties as a married couple and that the husband himself had accepted the woman as his wife was held to be sufficient to consider the marriage valid. While upholding the order of maintenance awarded by the family court, the high court commented: 'Considering that the wife is not an educated lady and she comes from a backward community, there cannot be any documentary evidence on any of these aspects.

---

[146] Section 18 (2)(e) of HAMA entitled a Hindu wife to live separately from her husband without forfeiting her claim to maintenance, if her husband keeps a concubine in the same house in which his wife is living or habitually resides with a concubine elsewhere.

[147] AIR 1978 SC 1557

[148] I (2000) DMC 51 Kar

[149] II (2002) DMC 791 Bom

These aspects are to be considered from an appropriate angle.'

In *Rajlingu* v. *Sayamabai*,[150] when the wife filed for maintenance the husband alleged that she is his second wife and, hence, the marriage is void. He produced the earlier wife and a daughter born through that marriage as witnesses to prove his case. The present application was filed in 1993. But the wife had earlier filed for maintenance twice in 1971 and in 1973 and on both occasions a compromise was reached, and the parties agreed to live together amicably. At that time, the husband did not raise the plea about his earlier marriage. This contention was raised for the first time in 1993 which the court held was a mere afterthought. While dismissing his appeal, the high court held that the conduct of the parties in such matters plays a very dominant role in determination of the relationship of husband and wife.

Sobha Hymavathi Devi v. *Setti Gangadhara Swamy*[151] raises a slightly different but related question in the context of legitimacy.[152] Contrary to the general trend, here the daughter claimed illegitimacy, which would have awarded her certain advantages. Since according to law, an illegitimate child's identity is attached to her mother, and not to the father as in cases of legitimate children, she claimed illegitimacy so that her election in the reserved category would be held as valid. Ironically, based on presumption that long cohabitation leads to a presumption of valid marriage, the courts conferred on her legitimacy which proved to be disadvantageous to her.

She had married her first maternal cousin, who belonged to a backward caste. But her plea was set aside on the basis that her father was not from a backward caste. So she pleaded that she was the illegitimate child of her parents since her mother's previous marriage with a man from her own caste was subsisting when the mother married her father. The mother belonged to the Bhagatha Community (a scheduled tribe) while her father hailed from a slightly higher caste. Though she denied marriage, she admitted to prolonged cohabitation from which she and five other siblings were born. Since an illegitimate child acquired her mother's caste, she pleaded that her election in the category reserved for schedule tribes was valid. The high court rejected her plea and held that she was the legitimate child of her father and hence it could not be held that she is a member of the Bhagatha Community. On this ground her election, contested in the reserved category, was set aside.

In appeal, the Supreme Court upheld the ruling of the high court on the ground that prolonged cohabitation leads to the presumption of a valid marriage. Hence, it was not possible to hold that it was only a relationship of concubinage. Even assuming that there was an earlier marriage of the mother subsisting, it can be presumed to have been terminated in view of the subsequent long cohabitation of the couple.

Though, personally the woman concerned did not gain, the Supreme Court ruling is important in bridging the gap between a 'void second marriage' and 'mere concubinage' based on the legal presumption prolonged cohabitation leads to a valid marriage. It will bestow certain legitimacy and dignity upon children of such unions and serve to overcome prevailing judicial biases in this realm.

Section 125 of Cr.PC: Beneficial Provision, not Determination of Marital Status

The succession claims are civil suits and the courts are empowered to examine the marital status of the parties. But while awarding

---

[150] I (2007) DMC 396 Bom

[151] (2005) 2 SCC 244

[152] This case has been discussed under section titled 'Legal Incidents of Marriage' in Chapter 1 *Marriage and its Dissolution*.

maintenance to women under Section 125 of Cr.PC, the magistrate does not have the power to examine the validity of marriage as the proceedings are summary in nature and it has been enacted as a measure of social justice.

In *Sunita Kavita More* v. *Vivekanand More*,[153] the Bombay High Court commented that in proceedings under Section 125 of Cr.PC, the magistrate is not competent to decide the validity of marriage. The proper course in such cases is to grant maintenance to the wife. It is up to the husband to establish invalidity of marriage in a competent civil court. In this case, the woman was driven out of the matrimonial home and when she claimed maintenance, the husband denied the marriage and the cohabitation. He also alleged that the wife was in an illicit relationship with another person and had become pregnant, and he denied paternity of the child. The wife pleaded that they were childhood friends and upon a promise of marriage she had cohabited with him and had a child. The trial court upheld the woman's claim and awarded her maintenance of Rs 250 per month. The sessions court reversed the order on the ground that the marriage was not proved. The high court upheld the wife's claim regarding cohabitation and paternity of the child and restored the order of the Magistrate's court.

In *Pradeep Gupta* v. *Kanti Devi*,[154] the Jharkhand High Court reaffirmed that strict proof of marriage is not necessary while awarding maintenance under Section 125 of Cr.PC. The evidence of persons residing in and around the area, who had formed an opinion that the parties were living as husband and wife, was held to be sufficient to prove the wife's case.

In *Krishna Chandra Jerai* v. *State of Jharkhand*,[155] the trial court rejected the application for maintenance by the wife on the ground that she could not prove the marriage, though the fact of long cohabitation was not disputed by the husband. In revision, the sessions court awarded Rs 500 as maintenance to the wife. The high court dismissed the appeal filed by the husband and held that strict proof of marriage is not required in summary proceedings. The court also held that an order under Section 125 of Cr.PC does not finally determine rights and liabilities of parties. The parties are entitled to file a civil suit for determination of their rights.

In *Shyamlal Pathak* v. *State of Bihar*,[156] in a criminal complaint filed by the wife under Section 494 of IPC, the husband was acquitted. But the magistrate granted maintenance of Rs 400 per month to the woman under Section 125 of Cr.PC. In appeal, it was held that the proceedings under Section 125 of Cr.PC are of summary nature and the proof of marriage is not as high as in proceedings under Section 494 or in a proceeding for divorce. All that is required to be shown is that there has been marriage between the woman and the man. If she is able to show that she and the man concerned lived together as husband and wife, the court can presume they are legally married and award maintenance even when the marriage is disputed by the husband, leaving him to establish invalidity of the marriage in a competent civil court.

In *Ramakrishnan* v. *Subadra*,[157] the wife pleaded that she was married in 1979 as per customary rites and they lived together as husband and wife. In 2003, there was an estrangement between them and she filed a

---

[153] II (2001) DMC 693 Bom
[154] I (2003) DMC 265 Jha

[155] I (2005) DMC 437 Jha
[156] I (2008) DMC 461 Pat
[157] I (2008) DMC 421 Ker

petition for maintenance under Section 125 of Cr.PC. The husband admitted cohabitation for a long period, but contended that it was not cohabitation as a legally married couple. He alleged that she was his distant relative and lived in his house as a domestic help. He contended that he was married in 1966 and had a child from this relationship. To prove his case, he also contended that his previous wife was awarded maintenance in 1980. The wife produced the ration card and electoral card to prove that they were cohabiting together as husband and wife. The Court concluded that the subsistence of a valid marriage had been satisfactorily established.

The high court upheld the order of Magistrate's court and held that under Section 125 of Cr.PC, a criminal court is not jurisdictionally competent to make final and authentic pronouncements on the disputed status of the marriage. That jurisdiction vests in civil courts. The husband is entitled to approach a civil court for obtaining an appropriate declaration regarding the validity of the marriage. The husband contended that only because he could not produce the order passed by a Magistrate's court awarding maintenance to his earlier wife in time in the Magistrate's court, the present claimant was awarded maintenance which had resulted in miscarriage of justice. In response, the high court commented: No justifiable reasons have been advanced to explain why the maintenance order granted to the first wife earlier by the court was not produced before the courts below. The scandalous delay in the judicial process is certainly attributable in part to the unrestrained yearning of the courts to do substantive justice. In life, one does not get an opportunity to start the game afresh. What life and divine or nature's justice cannot offer, litigation cannot obviously aspire to. The impression that any and every error or inadequacy committed in the conduct of the case can be rectified later, and courts, in their indulgence and anxiety to do justice, would permit the parties to correct their errors, set the clock back, and proceed afresh, has certainly contributed in no mean measure to the scandalous delay in the judicial process. The law has been well summarized in the statement that the interests of justice may, at times, transcend the interests of mere law.

In *Lakhwinder Kaur* v. *Gurmail Singh*,[158] the magistrate awarded maintenance of Rs 500 per month to the wife and Rs 300 per month to the daughter, respectively, under Section 125 of Cr.PC. The husband had denied the marriage and pleaded that his earlier marriage was subsisting. The sessions court upheld this plea. In appeal, the Punjab and Haryana High Court set aside the order of the sessions court and restored the order of the Magistrate's court and held as follows: The order passed by the magistrate in proceedings under Section 125 of Cr.PC does not finally determine the rights and obligations of the parties. For the purpose of getting his rights determined, the husband had filed a civil suit for declaration that the woman is not his legally wedded wife. The said suit was dismissed by the civil court on the ground that the evidence adduced by the husband was not sufficient to prove that the woman concerned was not his legally wedded wife and the daughter was not his legitimate child. The findings of the civil court were binding not only on the parties but also on the criminal court. Further, the strict proof which is required to prove an offence under Section 494 of IPC is not required in proceedings under Section 125 of Cr.PC. If the wife succeeds in proving that she and the Respondent lived together as husband and wife, the court can presume that they are legally married.

[158] I (2008) DMC 148 P&H

The Supreme Court has also upheld this view in *Dwarika Prasad Satpathy* v. *Bidyut Praya Dixit*[159] and laid down that proof of validity of marriage for the purpose of summary proceeding under Section 125 of Cr.PC is not as strict as is required in a trial of offence under Section 494 of the IPC. Further, the order passed in an application under Section 125 of Cr.PC does not finally determine the rights and obligations of the parties. In *Veena Devi* v. *Ashok Kumar Mandal*,[160] the Patna High Court held that the proceedings under Section 125 of Cr.PC are of a summary nature, and are not intended to determine the status and personal rights of parties and questions of marriage need not be decided like a matrimonial court. Even when the issue is being determined by the family court which has the jurisdiction to determine the matrimonial status of the parties, the court cannot examine this issue in proceedings under Section 125 Cr.PC.

Maintenance to Women in Live-in Relationships under PWDVA

More recently, the Protection of Women from Domestic Violence Act, 2005 has awarded statutory recognition to informal relationships or live-in relationships. Under the provision of this statute, any woman who claims relief such as protection orders, restraining orders, or even maintenance, need not prove the validity of her marriage, as held by the Madras High Court in *M. Palani* v. *Meenakshi*.[161] In this case, the man had filed an application for a declaration that he was not married to the woman concerned and for an order of injunction restraining her from representing and receiving the benefits as his wife. In the said proceedings, the woman filed

an Interim Application for maintenance under the Protection of Women from Domestic Violence Act, 2005. The family court, Chennai, granted her Rs 1,000 per month as interim maintenance.

This was challenged by the appellent, who contended that the woman is not entitled to any maintenance under the provisions of DVA since they have not lived together at any point of time as husband and wife. However, he admitted that they had voluntary sexual contact but alleged that the woman had voluntary submitted to sexual contact despite knowing fully well that he does not believe in the institution of marriage and that the woman herself had not insisted on a formal marriage. Had there been even a slight reference to marriage as a precondition to the sexual contact, he would never have had even the casual sexual contact with her. Further, mere proximity for the sake of mutual pleasure can never be called a domestic relationship, he argued. Rejecting this argument, the Madras High Court held that there is no stipulation under the Act for the parties to live together for a particular period. Since the man had admitted to sexual contact it was evident that the couple enjoyed a close relationship within which sexual contact had taken place.

The constitutional validity of this provision was challenged in the Delhi High Court in *Aruna Parmod Shah* v. *Union of India*,[162] on the ground that it discriminates against the legal wife. While upholding its validity, the high court held that there is no reason why equal treatment should not be accorded to the wife, as well as a woman who has been living with a man as his common-law wife or even as a mistress. The court further commented that like treatment to both does not, in any manner, derogate the sanctity of marriage.

---

[159] AIR 1999 SC 3348: 2000 Cr.LJ 1 SC
[160] 2000 Cri.LJ 332 Pat
[161] AIR 2008 Mad 162

[162] WP-Crl 425/2008 (decided on 7 April 2008) Del.

Since this concept is relatively new to the Indian jurisprudence, it would be useful to draw upon the following guidelines issued by a court in South Africa, for determining the rights of women in relationships in the nature of marriage.

i. The commitments of the parties to the shared household;

ii. The existence of a significant period of cohabitation;

iii. The existence of financial and other dependency between the parties including significant mutual financial arrangements vis-à-vis the household;

iv. The existence of children of the relationship; and,

v. The role of the partners in maintaining the household and in the care of the children.

In *Chanmuniya* v. *Virendra Kumar Singh Kushwaha* the Supreme Court while deciding a case under Section 125 Cr.PC, referred the matter of maintenance to women in informal relationships to a larger bench in view of the conflicting opinions of the Supreme Court in *Savitaben Somabhat Bhatiya* (discussed earlier) and several positive rulings which had granted maintenance to women in informal relationships and bigamous marriages.

The division bench of G.S. Singhvi and A.K. Ganguly JJ recommended that a broad and expansive interpretation should be given to the term 'wife' to include those cases where a man and woman have been living together as husband and wife for a reasonably long period of time, and strict proof of marriage should not be a pre-condition for maintenance so as to fulfill the true spirit and essence of the beneficial provision of maintenance under Section 125, Cr.PC. It was suggested that the benefits awarded to 'live-in relationships' under the PWDVA should be extended to women claiming maintenance

under Section 125 of the Cr.PC as such an interpretation would be a just application of the principles enshrined in our Constitution.

The case concerned a widow with two daughters, who had married her husband's younger brother as per the custom of the community. During such marriages, saptapadi is not performed. As per the custom of the Kushwaha community, the marriage was performed through 'katha' and 'sindur'. When her husband deserted her, the wife filed for maintenance. While the trial court upheld her plea, the high court held that her marriage was not valid since saptapadi was not performed.

While this reference was pending before the larger bench, a later ruling in *D. Velusamy* v. *D. Patchaiammal* delivered by Markandey Katju and T.S. Thakur JJ on 21 October 2010 created a fresh controversy by constraining the scope of PWDVA by holding that 'mistresses', 'keeps' and 'maids' with whom a married man may have had sexual relationships are not entitled to maintenance. This ruling leaves the ground wide open to men to enter into bigamous relationship without any civil or criminal liability. The ruling shifts the burden on women to prove that their relationship is not bigamous, disregarding community practices as well as the fraud men commit by not revealing their prior subsisting marriage. Due to the difficulty women face to prove their marriages, the PWDVA had sought to grant maintenance and compensation to women in 'live-in relationships'. Even prior to this, several rulings of the Supreme Court and various high courts had protected the rights of vulnerable women trapped in such situations, and the reference to a larger bench in *Chanmuniya case* was made to obtain a clear and unambiguous verdict in defense of women, which would overrule the verdict in the *Savitaben case*.

The ruling in *Velusamy case* is devoid of the cautious approach adopted in *Chanmuniya case*. The ruling, which seems to be based on a moral high ground and Western ethos disregards Indian social reality as reflected in the numerous judgements discussed earlier. The larger bench, will hopefully undo the harm caused by this reckless and insensitive ruling which violates the constitutional mandate of protecting the dignity of women, and restore the rights of women in informal and bigamous relationships.

Muslim Women's Right to Maintenance

Notion of 'Fair and Reasonable Settlement' Under the Muslim Women's (Protection of Rights on Divorce) Act

The Muslim Women (Protection of Rights on Divorce) Act was enacted in 1986, after the controversial *Shahbano* judgment. Through this enactment, the right of a divorced Muslim woman was taken out of the purview of the general law of maintenance under Section 125 of Cr.PC and placed under special legislation.[163] After the enactment, several groups filed writ petitions in the Supreme Court challenging the constitutional validity of the Act. While the writ petitions were pending, several high courts began to interpret the Act innovatively. They held that a divorced Muslim woman has the right to a fair and reasonable settlement for her lifetime, in addition to maintenance during the *iddat* period.[164] Further, the courts commented

that a fair and reasonable provision for the woman's future needs (*mataaoon bil ma'aroofe*) is a Quranic injunction.

The leading judgment of the Supreme Court on this issue was pronounced in 2001 in *Daniel Latifi* v. *Union of India*.[165] The Supreme Court confirmed that the MWA has substituted the earlier right of recurrent maintenance under Section 125 of Cr.PC with a new right to a lump sum provision to be made and paid to the woman soon after her divorce. If the husband fails to make the settlement, a divorced Muslim woman has the right to approach the Magistrate's court for enforcement of the right under Section 3 of the MWA.

The court held that a Muslim husband is liable to make a reasonable and fair provision for the future of his divorced wife, which must be made within the iddat period. The court further clarified that the liability of the Muslim husband to the divorced wife, to pay maintenance under the Act, is not confined to the iddat period. A Muslim wife is entitled to a fair and reasonable provision with respect to her future needs.[166]

In cases where the husband is unable to pay the entire amount, the Full Bench of the Bombay High Court, in *Karim Abdul Rehman Shaikh* v. *Shehnaz Karim Shaikh*,[167] held that the amount can be paid in instalments, and until the payment is made, the magistrate can direct monthly payment to the wife even beyond the iddat period.

In *Mustafa* v. *Fathimakutty*,[168] the husband was employed abroad. The court held that the

---

[163] See section titled 'Constitutional Validity of Personal laws' of Chapter 2 *Constitutional Law and citizenship Claims* of the first volume where this issue is discussed in detail.

[164] *Arab A. Abdulla* v. *Arab M. Saiyadbhai*, AIR 1988 Guj 141; *Ahmed* v. *Aysha*, II (1990) DMC 110: 1987 Cri LJ 980; *K. Zunaideen* v. *Ameena Begum*, II (1997) DMC 91; *Karim Abdul Rehman Shaikh* v. *Shehnaz Karim Shaikh*, 2000 Cri.LJ 3560.

[165] 2001 (7) SCC 740: 2001 Cri.LJ 4660 SC: II (2001) DMC 714 SC

[166] See section titled 'Innovative Judicial Interpretation of the Muslim Women's Act' of Chapter 2 *Constitutional Law and Citizenship Claims* of the first volume where this issue is discussed in detail.

[167] 2000 Cri.LJ 3560

[168] I (2007) DMC 820 Ker

husband's contention that after the circumstances which led to divorce he became distracted and was not able to concentrate on work is a fanciful theory with nothing tangible to substantiate the same. The court awarded a lump sum of Rs 1.20 lakh which was computed at Rs 2,000 per month for five years as maintenance of the wife and two children.

In *Haseena* v. *Abdul Jaleel*,[169] it was held that the provision for educational expenses is an important criterion to fix the quantum of reasonable and fair provision. It was held that a divorced woman who has lost the support of her husband can sustain herself and maintain her child only by getting an education. Denying a woman educational support is not justified in such circumstances. Though a former husband cannot be entrusted with the liability to provide for the higher education of his divorced wife, which is expensive, the desire of the wife to continue her studies cannot be said to be unreasonable. It was held that the fact that the woman was studying at the time of her marriage and she wanted to continue after divorce is not an irrelevant factor in fixing the quantum of reasonable and fair provision and maintenance under Section 3(1(a) of the Muslim Woman's Act. In light of this, the amount payable was increased from Rs 2,00,000 to Rs 2,50,000.

In *Nizar* v. *Hyrunneessa*,[170] the Kerala High Court rejected the plea that since the wife had remarried, she is not entitled to a fair and reasonable settlement for the future. The court held that the re-marriage of a divorced woman is not a criterion in determining a fair and reasonable settlement. The only aspect to be considered is the liability of the former husband to make a reasonable and fair provision to the divorced wife and fix the quantum sum as contemplated under Section 3(3) of the Act. The court

awarded Rs 90,000 calculating the amount on the basis of Rs 1,500 per month and commented that the amount awarded as fair and reasonable settlement cannot be set aside on a plea that the divorced wife is leading an adulterous life (see also *M. Alavi* v. *T.V. Safia*, I (1992) DMC 62).

If the husband fails to comply with the order and defaults in payments of the amount ordered, he can be imprisoned. In *Rayinkutty* v. *State of Kerala*,[171] it was held that this, in itself, will not absolve him from the liability of paying the amount which is due to the wife.

Rights Under Section 125 of Cr.PC

When a deserted or destitute Muslim wife files for maintenance under Section 125 of Cr.PC, the usual ploy adopted by the husband is to plead that he has already divorced his wife and hence he is not liable to pay maintenance. This tendency increased after the Muslim Women (Protection of Rights on Divorce) Act was enacted in 1986. The media reports on this enactment led to a popular perception that a Muslim husband is not liable to pay maintenance to a divorced wife.

In the leading case, *Shamim Ara* v. *State of UP*,[172] the Supreme Court held that a mere plea of previous divorce in the written statement cannot be treated as a pronouncement of talaq by the husband on the wife. The liability of the husband to pay maintenance to his wife does not come to an end through such communication. The court commented that for talaq to be valid, it has to be pronounced as per the Quaranic injunction. Several later judgments have reiterated this position. Some of these judgments are summarized later.[173]

---

[169] II (2007) DMC 215 Ker
[170] I (2000) DMC 229 Ker

[171] II (2008) DMC 575 Ker
[172] 2002 (7) SCC 518
[173] These cases have been discussed in detail under section titled 'Islamic Law of Marriage and Succession' in Chapter 1 *Personal Laws and Women's Rights* of the first volume.

When the husband is not able to prove talaq, the trial court is bound to entertain the wife's application for maintenance under Section 125 of Cr.PC and award an adequate amount as the above case discussed in detail illustrates. But there are several other rulings which endorse this view. For instance, in *Musarat Jahan* v. *State of Bihar*,[174] it was held that a divorced Muslim wife is entitled to maintenance under Section 125 of Cr.PC continuously and beyond the iddat period till she remarries, or is able to maintain herself. In response to the wife's claim for maintenance, the husband pleaded that he had divorced his wife. The court commented that the family court judge had erred in holding that the wife is entitled to maintenance only from the date of filing the application till the copy of the written statement was served.

In *Khairunnissa Begum* v. *Aslamkham*,[175] it was held that there cannot be a presumption in favour of talaq. Talaq has to be strictly proven. Since the husband could not prove talaq, the wife was awarded maintenance of Rs 1,000 per month under Section 125 of Cr.PC.

In *Moiden* v. *Ramlath*,[176] the husband pleaded that the woman is his second wife and, hence, is not entitled to maintenance. He also pleaded that he had subsequently remarried. The court, while upholding the woman's right to maintenance, stated that the fact that she is divorced or that her husband has another wife, which is permitted under personal law, is irrelevant in adjudicating the rights of the divorced wife.

In *Muneer Ahmed* v. *Safia Mateen*,[177] while rejecting the husband's plea that he had divorced his wife, the court awarded Rs 1,000 as maintenance. The court described it as the bare

minimum for keeping body and soul together in the context of the present cost of living. The court held that since the woman is suffering from various diseases, she would need money for her medical expenses in addition to her maintenance.

Though, the rights of divorced Muslim women were placed under a specific Act, the Muslim Women's Act, some courts have held that the right under Section 125 of Cr.PC has not been deleted. For instance, in *Abdul Latif Mondal* v. *Anuwara Khatun*,[178] the husband challenged the order of maintenance awarded by the Magistrate's court on the ground that he had divorced his wife two years prior to her filing the application for maintenance. But the Calcutta High Court rejected this contention and held that the Muslim divorced wife is entitled to claim maintenance under Section 125 of Cr.PC and the same are in addition to her claims under the MWA.

But the views of various other high courts as well as that of the Supreme Court in *Noor Saba Khatoon* v. *Mohd. Quasin*,[179] are contrary to this view. Here the Court held that after divorce, the right of a Muslim wife are located within the Muslim Women's Act and not under Section 125 Cr.PC. In *Shaikh Mohamed* v. *Naseembegum*,[180] the Bombay High Court held that a divorced Muslim woman cannot apply for maintenance under Section 125 of Cr.PC. Her remedy is only under the special law enacted for this purpose, that is, the Muslim Women's Act. In *Abdul Salam* v. *Gousiya Bi*, it was held that an order of maintenance that was passed in favour of the divorced wife under Section 125 of Cr.PC was unsustainable.

More recent judgments have reaffirmed that Muslim woman's right to claim maintenance under Section 125 of Cr.PC are not extinguished

---

[174] II (2008) DMC 225 Pat
[175] II (2008) DMC 332 Bom
[176] II (2008) DMC 348 Ker
[177] I (2007) DMC 550 Kar

[178] 2002 Cr.LJ. 2282 Cal
[179] II (1998) DMC 322 SC
[180] I (2007) DMC 226 Bom

upon divorce. The right is extinguished only when she receives a fair and reasonable settlement as stipulated under MWA. In *Iqbal Bano* v. *State of U.P.*,[181] it was held that proceedings under Section 125 are civil in nature. Hence even after the divorce, the woman is entitled to claim maintenance under this Section, considering its beneficial nature. *In Shabana Bano* v. *Iman Khan*,[182] the Supreme Court held that where social legislations enacted to secure the rights of needy women are concerned adherence to rigid rules of procedure and evidence should be avoided. The court held that if a petition filed by the wife under Section 125 of Cr.PC is pending before a family court at the time of her divorce, the same must be disposed of under the provisons of MWA and until such time she should be awarded maintenance under Section 125 of Cr.PC The Kerala High Court in *Kunhimohammed* v. *Ayishakutty*[183] has held that a husband's obligation to pay maintenance is not extinguished upon divorce. The wife will be entitled to receive maintenance under Section 125 of Cr.PC until the husband fulfills his obligation under Section 3 of the Muslim Women's Act or until the wife remains unmarried. These judgments have placed the right of Muslim women to maintenance under a secure footing.

Section B

MAINTENANCE: INCIDENTAL AND PROCEDURAL ASPECTS

Maintenance Rights of Children

Statutory and Pious Obligation of a Father to Maintain his Children

The obligation of the father to maintain his children is both a pious and religious obligation as well as a statutory duty under all personal laws. In *Vinod Babbar* v. *Baby Swati*,[184] the Delhi High Court explained that under Hindu law, a father has not only a moral but even a statutory obligation to maintain his minor children. The scope of his duty is to be regulated directly in relation to the money and status he enjoys. The right of maintenance of a child from his father cannot be restricted to two meals a day, but must be determined on the basis of the benefit, status, and money that the child would have enjoyed if he was living with him as part of his family. Irrespective of the differences and grievances which each spouse may have against the other, the endeavour of the court has to be to provide the best to the child under the facts and circumstances of each case and, more so, keeping the welfare of the child in mind for all such determinations. Liability to maintain one's children is clear from the text of the provisions under HAMA, as well as the various decided cases in this regard. The statutory obligation is paramount to the wish of the father and he cannot be permitted to limit this claim of the child on flimsy and baseless grounds. It is the duty and liability of parents to provide their child the best education and standard of living within their means. The fact that the child is living with the mother, who has sufficient income, will not absolve the father of his obligations towards the child.

In *P.M. Devassia* v. *Ancy*,[185] a Christian father challenged his duty to maintain his daughter who was living with the mother. The Kerala High Court explained that the obligation of a Christian father springs from the fact that he is the guardian of his family. Thus, he has an obligation to maintain his children and carries the duty to give them the best care, and, necessarily, there is a corresponding duty to maintain them.

---

[181] AIR 2007 SC 2215
[182] AIR 2010 SC 305
[183] 2010 (2) KLT 71

[184] II (2007) DMC 73 Del
[185] II (2007) DMC 677 Ker

There was also a corresponding right that the child has the right to be maintained. The husband had not disputed the paternity of the children and the marriage was subsisting, but the parents were living separately and the children were living with the mother. The father had a decent income. The court commented that it cannot be contended that merely because one professes the Christian religion, one does not have the liability to maintain one's children. In view of the law which is laid down, a Christian father has an obligation to maintain his daughters, who are not capable of looking after themselves, notwithstanding the fact that they have attained majority.

The personal obligation of a Muslim father to maintain his children is integrally linked to his property. Explaining this position, in *Ibrahim Fathima* v. *Mohammed Saleem (Minor)*,[186] the Madras High Court, after examining the position under Mohammedan law, held that the children's right to maintenance in a Muslim household always attaches to the father's property in such a way and in such measure that it is not affected by any subsequent alienation of the property by the father. The fact that the Muslim father's obligation to maintain his minor children is personal does not mean that the only sanction which the law imposes, for the performance of the obligation, is to proceed against his person whenever he fails to discharge that obligation. It is quite reasonable and civilized to expect all systems of law to link children's maintenance with property as security and Mohammedan law is not an exception. In the context of the relationship between a father and his minor children, all that the idea of personal obligation imports is that he is under a duty to maintain them even on the mere aspect of his being their parent.

In *K. Masthan Bee* v. *Appalagari Venkataramana*,[187] the Andhra Pradesh High Court reaffirmed this position and held that the a Muslim father is under a legal obligation to maintain his children under the Muslim personal law and if he has alienated any property prejudicial to the interest of the minors, they are entitled to create a charge under Section 39 of the Transfer of Property Act, 1882, over the said property. It is mandatory on the part of the courts to notify under Order 21, Rule 66 of the Civil Procedure Code (CPC) to the intending buyers that the property under sale is subject to such encumbrance or litigation.

Single Mothers and Claims of Children in their Custody

The above discussion makes it amply clear that the legal obligation of maintaining the wife also extends to an obligation to maintain minor children. But in the course of a matrimonial dispute, in order to cause further hardships to deserted women and single mothers, several legal tactics are adopted to deny children in the custody of their mother their legal rights of maintenance. While denying paternity is one ploy used to escape from the liability of maintaining the child, there are several others which have been advanced in the course of litigation. The husbands have gone to the extent of denying that there is a statutory obligation to maintain their children.

In *Praveen Menon* v. *Ajitha Pillai*,[188] the husband contended that Section 24 of the HMA implied maintaining only the wife and not the child. But rejecting this contention the Kerala High Court held that a beneficial provision can not be interpreted so restrictively and that the father's obligation to maintain the child must be

---

[186] AIR 1980 Mad 82

[187] II (2002) DMC 646 AP
[188] I (2002) DMC 288 Ker

read into his obligation to maintain the wife. Since the wife had to maintain the child, it was held that the husband had to pay the wife an amount that was sufficient to maintain the child too. In *Prakash Khot* v. *Chandani Khot*,[189] it was held that awarding maintenance to the wife under HMA will not take away the right of the minor children to claim maintenance from their father, under Section 20 of the Hindu Adoption and Maintenance Act. In *Mandeep Sharma* v. *Kiran Sharma*,[190] it was held that the fact that the wife was being supported by her parents was no ground for the husband to claim discharge of his obligation to pay maintenance to the child. It was also held that the husband could not shirk his liability to provide maintenance merely on the ground that he met with an accident and had to temporarily restrain from working due to his injuries.

The courts have also held that the rights of minor children cannot be defeated through consent agreements between the child's parents or through divorce deeds. In *Happy Anand* v. *Baby Deepali*,[191] the daughter, who was only seven years old at the time of the divorce, filed for maintenance and was awarded maintenance of Rs 2,500 per month. The husband had agreed to pay Rs 50,000 to the wife in proceedings for mutual consent, but had paid only half the amount. In appeal, the high court upheld the order. In *Deepa Devi* v. *Dhiraj Kumar Singh*,[192] the wife contended that her consent for a divorce by mutual consent was fraudulently obtained by her husband and the husband did not make any provision for maintenance for herself and her minor child. The Jharkhand High Court held that that Section 13 B (divorce

by mutual consent) does not empower parties to decide the rights of minor children regarding maintenance and directed the husband to pay Rs 2,00,000 to the wife and the minor son by way of lump sum maintenance.

While a minor child is entitled to maintenance, as soon as the child attains majority the child is denied maintenance. This places an additional burden on single women since most often the child would not be independent at the age of eighteen and would still need support until the child completes the education. Some judges adopt a lenient view and mandate the husband to continue with payment of maintenance/educational expenses for a few more years until the son completes his education and is able to support himself. But usually maintenance will be discontinued as soon as the child turns eighteen. There is some leniency towards dependent major daughters. But if she has an independent source of earning, the maintenance would be discontinued.

In *Avnish Pawar* v. *Sunita Pawar*,[193] the court held that the major son was not entitled to maintenance from the father, and the exception under Section 20(3), HAMA covers unmarried daughters but not major sons. This position was reiterated in *Viswambhran* v. *Dhanya*,[194] where it was held that the liability to maintain the child, whatever be the sex, would continue only till the child attains majority. Then, irrespective of whether child is able to maintain itself out of its earnings or other property, it would not be maintained if it is a male child.

However, the ruling of the Punjab and Haryana High Court, in *Nikhil Kumar Singh* v. *Rakesh Kumar Mahajan*,[195] advances a more humane approach towards maintenance of sons

---

[189] II (2002) DMC 798
[190] AIR 2002 J&K 90
[191] I (2006) DMC 520 Del
[192] I (2006) DMC 55 Jha

[193] II (2000) DMC 283 MP
[194] II (2005) DMC 56 Ker: AIR 2005 Ker 91
[195] II (2008) DMC 111 P&H

who have not yet completed their education. In this case, the son had filed an application for maintenance while he was a minor and was granted interim maintenance of Rs 5,000 per month. When the son attained majority, the father moved the court for cancellation of the maintenance order on the ground that his obligation to maintain his son had come to an end. In an appeal against the order of cancellation of the maintenance amount filed by the son, the high court held that the major son was entitled to claim maintenance from his father for studies and directed the father to pay Rs 8,000 per month towards his educational and other related expenses, and Rs 25,000 lump sum per annum towards additional/ancillary expenses like purchase of books, instruments, etc. The court directed that this arrangement shall remain till the son completed his education up to the post-graduation level.

But so far as the female child is concerned, such right will continue even after she attains majority until she gets married, provided she is unable to maintain herself out of her own earnings or other property. For instance, in *Jitendra Nath Sarkar* v. *Dalia Sarkar*,[196] it was held that a major unmarried daughter is not entitled to maintenance if she has an independent source of income. It is only when she is able to prove that she is unable to maintain herself that her parents are liable to maintain her.

As per the customs prevailing among several communities in India, a father is bound to make provisions for the marriage expenses of his daughters. The courts have awarded judicial recognition to this customary right. In *Kusum Krishnaji Rewatkar* v. *Krishnaji Nathuji Rewatkar*,[197] it was held that a father is bound to make provisions for the marriage expenses of

the daughters as part of maintenance. If the wife has spent for the performance of marriage of daughter, the husband would be liable to reimburse his wife. He cannot escape his liability.

The courts have also upheld the rights of adopted children to maintenance from their father. *Weldone Lyngdoh* v. *Eva Phawa*,[198] is a case concerning a child belonging to the Khasi community. The customary law of the community recognizes the notion of adoption and the child is entitled to claim maintenance from its adoptive father. While upholding the right of the adoptive child for maintenance under Section 125 of Cr.PC, the Gauhati High Court held that the dominant purpose behind the benevolent provisions engrafted in Section 125 clearly is that the wife, child, and parents, should not be left in a state of distress, destitution, and starvation. Having regard to this special purpose, the provisions of Section 125 of Cr.PC shall have to be given a liberal construction to fulfil and achieve the intention of the legislature.

In *Leela Yadav* v. *State of Bihar*,[199] the application filed by the grand mother of the two minor children for maintenance from their father was dismissed by the Magistrate on the ground that she lacks *locus standi* to file for maintenance on behalf of the minor children. The mother of the minor children had died under unnatural circumstances and at the time of her death, had handed over the custody of her two daughters to her mother. In appeal, the high court held that the question of custody is a matter to be decided by a civil and not criminal court. The right which is conferred under Section 125 of Cr.PC for maintenance is not dependent on guardianship. Maintenance to children living with either mother, or even grandmother,

---

[196] II (1999) DMC 127 Ori
[197] II (2008) DMC 113 Bom

[198] II (2007) DMC 550 Gau
[199] I (2006) DMC 444 Jha

cannot be refused on the ground that they are not natural guardians, lawful guardians, or legal guardians. The husband pleaded that he is willing to take their custody but he is not in a position to provide maintenance. The daughters who were interviewed refused to go with the father and they stated that after their mother's death their father had not cared for them, and had no love and affection or attachment towards them. The court commented that the father has not claimed the custody and guardianship of the children and held that the provisions under Section 125 of Cr.PC are not to be utilized for defeating the rights conferred by the legislature on destitute and needy children.

Rights of Children of Divorced Muslim Couple

After the enactment of the Muslim Women's Act, there were several applications filed by husbands to absolve them not just of the obligation of maintaining their wives beyond the iddat period but also of their responsibility of maintaining their children. The confusion was caused by the wordings of Section 3(b) of the Act.

Section 3(b): Where she herself maintains the children born to her before or after her divorce, a reasonable and fair provision and maintenance to be made and paid by her former husband for a period of two years from the respective dates of birth of such children.

While most courts upheld the existing rights of children to claim maintenance under Section 125 of Cr.PC, in some instances, the courts held that the child is entitled to maintenance only up to the age of two. The ambiguity was finally resolved by the ruling of the Supreme Court in *Noor Saba Khatoon* v. *Mohd. Quasin*,[200] in 1997, which upheld the rights of children under Section 125 of Cr.PC in clear and unequivocal terms. The trial court had granted Rs 200 to the wife and Rs 150 to each of the three minor children. Meanwhile,

the husband had divorced the wife and approached the court for modifying the order. The trial court held that the divorced wife is not entitled to maintenance beyond the iddat period and, accordingly, revoked the order of maintenance for the wife, but upheld the maintenance for the children. The revision application was dismissed by the sessions court. But in appeal, the high court cancelled the maintenance order of the elder two children who were above the age of two years. The Supreme Court held that the husband has an obligation to maintain his children till they attain majority or are able to maintain themselves, whichever date is earlier.

This position was reaffirmed in *Mahaboob Ali* v. *Abdul Rasheed*[201] by the Karnataka High Court, which held that the obligation of a father to maintain the minor children is absolute, irrespective of religion. As far as children born of Muslim parents are concerned, there is nothing in Section 125 of Cr.PC which exempts a Muslim father from his obligation to maintain his children. It would indeed be unreasonable, unfair, unequitable, and even preposterous, to deny the benefit of Section 125 of Cr.PC to the children only on the ground that they are born of Muslim parents.

Similarly, in *Riaz Fatima* v. *Mohd. Sharif*,[202] the court reaffirmed that the right of the child to get maintenance is not affected even after the father has divorced the mother of the child. The court set aside the order of the Sessions Judge and restored the order of the Magistrate's court. In *Mufees* v. *State of UP*,[203] the daughter had approached the court for maintenance and the family court had awarded her Rs 1,000 per month as maintenance. In an appeal filed by the

---

[200] II (1998) DMC 322 SC

[201] II (2000) DMC 624 Kar
[202] I (2007) DMC 26 Del
[203] I (2007) DMC 22 All

father, the high court upheld the maintenance awarded to her by the family court.

Maintenance Claims Against Both Parents

Though, traditionally the obligation to maintain the children was always upon the father, if the mother is also employed, both parents are bound to contribute for the maintenance of the child in proportion to their respective incomes.

In *Padmja Sharma* v. *Ratan Lal Sharma*,[204] both parents were gainfully employed. But the husband earned twice as much as the wife. The Supreme Court held that both the parents are bound to contribute towards the maintenance of their children, proportionately. The court awarded a sum of Rs 3,000 per month towards maintenance of each of the children and directed that the same should be borne by both the parents in 2:1 proportion. The court rejected the mother's claim on the ground that she had sufficient earning.

In *Sayali Pathak* v. *Vasant Pathak*,[205] the Delhi High Court clarified that maintenance is not granted as penalty against either of spouses. The purpose is to ensure that parties are able to maintain a standard of living that is in close consonance with that enjoined by them as a family prior to the outbreak of their matrimonial differences. In this particular case, the wife earned approximately Rs 40,000 per month and the husband Rs 1,00,000 per month. The court held that there is no reason to deprive the child of an affluent life style and cultural exposure if the parents can afford it. Since the wife herself had submitted that the expenses of the child should be shared in ratio of 2:1, keeping their respective earnings in perspective, the court directed the husband to contribute

Rs 12,000 per month toward the maintenance of the child.

The Andhra Pradesh High Court, in *N. Sree Ramudu* v. *N. Lahari*,[206] also endorsed this view and held that since both the mother and father of the minor child are gainfully employed and are having equal financial capacity, the responsibility of maintaining the child ought to be shared equally.

Other Substantive Issues

Husband Guilty of Matrimonial Fault

When a deserted wife approaches the courts for maintenance and is on the verge of receiving a favourable order directing the husband to pay maintenance, a ploy, which is often used, is to submit to the court that he is willing to reconcile with his wife and is willing to maintain her. At times, a petition for restitution of conjugal rights is also filed to defeat the woman's claim of maintenance.

If the woman refuses to accept the offer without a reasonable and justifiable cause, her maintenance claim can be defeated. But if the wife is able to prove a matrimonial fault such as bigamy, adultery, and cruelty, the courts are bound to uphold the woman's claim of separate residence and maintenance. The courts have also held that if the husband makes baseless allegations of adultery and unchastity against the wife, she is entitled to live separately and claim maintenance (*Baishnab Charan Jena* v. *Ritarani Jena*).[207]

If the husband is impotent and is unable to fulfil his marital obligations, the wife would be justified in living separately. For instance, in *Ashok Kumar Singh* v. *Addl. Sessions Judge, Varanasi*,[208] the Supreme Court upheld the

---

[204] AIR 2000 SC 1398
[205] I (2004) DMC 632 Del

[206] 2005 MLR 311 AP
[207] 1993 Cri. LJ 238
[208] (1996)1 SCC 554

woman's right of maintenance under Section 125 of Cr.PC on the ground of husband's impotency. In *Poonam Gupta* v. *Ghanshyam Gupta,*[209] the husband, a rich and prosperous businessman, had remarried. Considering the status of the families and the basic requirement for maintenance of wife and child, costs of child's education, upbringing, etc., the high court of Allahabad upheld the lump sum of Rs 8,00,000 awarded to her as just and proper. In *Puliyulla Chalil Narayana Kurup* v. *Thayyulla Parabhath Valsala,*[210] the Kerala High Court held that the wife is fully justified in refusing to live with the husband as the husband was living with another woman and had three children through her. In *Sangeeta Kumari Shaw* v. *State of West Bengal,*[211] the wife was compelled to leave the matrimonial home due to mental and physical cruelty over demands for dowry. The Calcutta High Court upheld the woman's right to live separately and claim maintenance. In *Mohanlal* v. *Lad Kunwar Bai,*[212] the husband contracted a second marriage. The Madhya Pradesh High Court held that on this ground the wife was entitled to live separately and get maintenance from her husband.

In *Vinod Kumar Jolly* v. *Sunita Jolly,*[213] after divorcing his second wife, the husband had married for the third time and had two children. The court commented that if the husband can have the luxury of a third marriage and can bring up the children born of the said marriage, he should own responsibility of the two earlier wives and pay them maintenance. The wife was awarded Rs 1,500 per month and the son was awarded Rs 2,500 per month which the court

commented would hardly ensure their bare existence.

Even under Muslim law, the wife is entitled to reside separately and claim maintenance if the husband has contracted a second marriage, has a mistress, or visits women of ill repute. In *Begum Subanu* v. *A.M. Abdul Gafoor,*[214] the Supreme Court held that irrespective of the husband's right to take a second wife under the personal laws, upon his remarriage, the wife is entitled to claim maintenance and separate residence. The court held that the provision of maintenance must be construed from the point of view of the injury to the matrimonial rights of the wife and not with reference to the husband's right of remarriage.

In *Mumtaz Begum* v. *Yusuf Khan,*[215] when the husband remarried, the wife left her matrimonial residence and claimed maintenance. Her application was rejected on the ground that the husband's remarriage is not a sufficient reason to live separately and claim maintenance. On appeal, the Rajasthan High Court held that the husband cannot deny maintenance to the first wife by taking recourse under the personal laws permitting bigamy.

In *Kadeeja* v. *Aboobacker,*[216] the wife and her four minor children were awarded Rs 200 per month maintenance under the personal law. Since the husband did not pay, the wife filed for recovery. On the husband's plea that he has no means to pay the arrears, the court dismissed her application. The wife challenged the order in the high court which held that under Muslim law husband is bound to maintain his wife, so long as he has the ability to earn. The court cannot examine the husband's earnings while enforcing maintenance orders.

---

[209] I (2003) DMC 467 All
[210] II (2005) DMC 266 Ker
[211] II (2006) DMC 471 Cal
[212] I (2007) DMC 714 MP
[213] I (2008) DMC 371 Del

[214] 1987 Cri.LJ 980
[215] 1999 Cri.LJ 322 Raj
[216] II (1995) DMC 233

In *Sirajmohmedkhan Janmohamadkhan* v. *Hafizunnisa Yasinkhan*,[217] the husband was impotent and was unable to discharge his marital obligations, which the court held was the main objective of marriage, more particularly under Mohammedan law where marriage is treated as a sacrosanct contract and not a purely religious ceremony as in the case of Hindu law. The court commented: 'When a husband is impotent and is unable to discharge his marital obligations, it would amount to both legal and mental cruelty which would undoubtedly be a just ground, as contemplated by Section 125 (3) of Cr.PC, for the wife's refusal to live with her husband and the wife would be entitled to maintenance from her husband according to his means.'

Ashabi v. *Bashasab Takke*[218] is another case where the husband had remarried. Rejecting the wife's application for maintenance, the family court held that the wife was not able to prove that the husband had deserted her. In appeal, the Karnataka High Court held that the wife can not be denied maintenance on the ground of not joining her husband in view of the husband's remarriage and hence, she is entitled to live separately and claim maintenance.

Under Muslim law, failure to provide maintenance is a ground for the wife to dissolve her marriage.[219]

Husband's Obligation to Maintain the Wife

The husband has a legal obligation to maintain his dependent wife. Unless the wife is guilty of a serious matrimonial offence, the courts will uphold the woman's claim of maintenance, often overriding the husband's allegations of adultery,

immorality, denial of marriage, contestation of paternity, etc. Even when the wife is not able to provide proof of her husband's income, the courts will grant maintenance to the wife and children, using the criterion of minimum wages on the premise that an able bodied man, who is capable of earning a livelihood, has a legal obligation to maintain his wife. Only when the husband is old, infirm, or physically or mentally disabled, he will be absolved of his obligation to maintain his wife.

In *Rajesh Kumar* v. *State of Bihar*,[220] it was held that a husband cannot hide behind the plea of his unemployment. The court commented that in any case he must be maintaining himself with whatever means.

In *Meenu Chopra* v. *Deepak Chopra*,[221] it was held that the status of the wife's parents is an irrelevant consideration while deciding the issue of maintenance. The only determining factor for consideration is the status of husband. The husband had pleaded that since the wife comes from a family with modest means, the amount of Rs 20,000 awarded as interim maintenance was excessive. The Delhi High Court held that if the husband is wealthy and is leading an opulent life, his wife also has the right to be a partner in his prosperity and live with the same standard.

Even when the wife is being supported by her parents, the husband is not absolved from his obligation of maintaining his wife (*Radhakumari* v. *M.K. Nair*). The courts will not accept the husband's contention that the woman's own parents are well off and can provide for her, or that she does not need maintenance as she is living with her parents.

In *G.C. Ghosh* v. *Sushmita Ghosh*,[222] the trial court awarded Rs 5,500 to the wife as maintenance and Rs 2,000 for her separate residence

---

[217] (1981) 4 SCC 250

[218] I (2003) DMC 725 Kar

[219] Section 2 (ii) of Dissolution of Muslim Marriages Act, 1939. See also *Raj Mohammed* v. *Saeeda Amina Begam*, AIR. 1976 Kar 201.

[220] II (2002) DMC 546 Pat

[221] AIR 2002 Del 131

[222] I (2001) DMC 469 Del

from the date of filing. The husband pleaded that since the wife was living with her parents, she had not actually spent this amount and hence was not entitled to the same. While upholding the order of the trial court, the Delhi High Court made the following scathing comments:

The husband is living with another wife. The entitlement of the wife to live separately is not in dispute. In the first instance, the husband refuses to maintain his wife and provide her shelter. He marries another woman and walks out of her life. He does not give her maintenance or provide for separate residence to which she is lawfully entitled, forcing her to live separately on her own. She is forced to resort to litigation and husband pleads the wife is not entitled to maintenance for period during pendency of the suit as she had allegedly not spent any such amount on her maintenance or on separate residence. This is wholly unjust. Section 18 of HAMA is a beneficial provision for the purpose of securing a decent living for a Hindu wife and to ameliorate the sufferings of a deserted wife. These provisions must be construed in a manner which better serves the ends of fairness and justice. When such laws are made, it is proper to assume the law makers enact laws which the society considers as honest, fair, and reasonable, and, thus, justice and reason constitute the great general legislative intent in such a piece of legislation. The courts must lean towards an interpretation which is just reasonable, and fair. If the interpretation suggested by the husband is accepted, it would offend the very sense of justice. The husband cannot avoid his obligation under the law by taking shelter of such ingenious pleas.

The fact that the son is maintaining the wife cannot be used as a defence to defeat the woman's right to claim maintenance from her husband. In *Merubhai Mandanbhai Odedara* v. *Raniben Merubhai Odedara*,[223] upholding the woman's right to maintenance, the court commented that the son cannot be made liable for the wife's maintenance unless the husband has died or otherwise has no source of income. In *Rattan Bala* v.

Prahlad Aggarwal,[224] the Delhi High Court commented that the trial court erred in declining interim maintenance to the woman merely on the ground that she is not a destitute as she is supported by her son, who is a qualified Chartered Accountant. The court commented that the husband is legally and morally obliged to maintain his wife.

If the husband is old and infirm, he is absolved of the obligation of maintaining the wife. In *Mugappa* v. *Muniyamma*,[225] where the husband was 75 years old and the wife 65 years, and the six children were all employed and well placed in life, the Karnataka High Court set aside the order of maintenance and held that the petition filed by her was with mala fide motive. The court commented that if her need is genuine, she could have sued her sons for providing maintenance.

A recent judgment delivered by the Delhi High Court brings a curious twist to the legal premise, 'an able bodied man' by extending this notion to women. In this case, *Ritu Raj Kant* v. *Anita*,[226] it was held that maintenance is to be awarded on the basis of actual earnings and not by applying the notion of an able bodied person. The wife failed to provide any proof of her husband's earnings. While quashing the order of the trial court awarding her Rs 1,500 per month as maintenance, the court commented that the wife is equally able bodied.

Maintenance to Working Women
Though, the principle behind the concept of maintenance is to provide economic security for those who are unable to maintain themselves, in certain cases, adopting a pro-women policy, the courts have ruled that a working wife or one

---

[223] AIR 2000 Guj 277

[224] I (2002) DMC 652 Del
[225] II (2003) DMC 188 Kar
[226] II (2008) DMC 827 Del

who is qualified to work is also entitled to maintenance. If the woman is earning a meagre amount, which is not sufficient for her to maintain herself, or if she has secured a temporary job, the courts have held that the woman is entitled to maintenance. Also, in cases where there is great disparity between the income of husband and wife, the courts will strive to bring in some parity by awarding maintenance to the wife. Although, the amounts awarded are far below the expectations of middle and affluent sections of women, the courts attempt to help divorced and separated women to maintain a certain standard of living and not render them destitute and force them to live in penury by virtue of their divorce or separation.

In *Rajathi v C. Ganesan*,[227] the Supreme Court explained that the expression 'unable to maintain herself' would mean the means available to the deserted wife while she was living with her husband and would not take within itself the efforts made by the wife after the desertion to somehow survive. The apex court also pointed that Section 125 of Cr.PC was enacted on the premise that it is the obligation of the husband to maintain his wife and children. This position was reiterated by the Gauhati High Court in *Weldone Lyngdoh v. Eva Phawa*.[228]

In *Chaturbhuj v. Sita Bai*,[229] the Supreme Court held that it is not necessary that the wife must be absolutely destitute before she can apply for maintenance under Section 125 of Cr.PC. Similarly, in *Johnson Joseph v. Anita Johnson*,[230] it was held that the expression 'unable to maintain' does not mean that she should be a destitute before she can apply for

maintenance. The court also commented that a working woman is required to spend more than a housewife as she has to work in office and keep her household. The wife was earning Rs 1,800 per month and the husband's salary was Rs 7,500 per month. It was held that Rs 1,000 per month awarded to her as maintenance was not unjust or unreasonable.

In *Sheela Devi v. Swarup Narain Bijoria*,[231] the trial court declined to grant maintenance to the wife on the ground that she was earning some amount of money by rolling *beedis*. In appeal, the Allahabad High Court awarded her Rs 500 as maintenance and held that the fact that the wife was earning a meagre amount cannot be a ground to refuse her maintenance. The husband, who was a government employee, was drawing a handsome salary.

In *Anita Sharma v. Ramjilal Sharma*,[232] the wife was working as an *Anganwadi* worker and earning Rs 1,000. The court held that this amount was not sufficient to meet the needs of present day life. The husband was earning Rs 8,500, hence, it was held that the wife is entitled to a maintenance of Rs 750 per month.

In *Muraleedharan v. Vijayalakshmi*,[233] the court addressed the issue of maintenance to educated women and held as follows: 'Qualification by itself cannot be held to be synonymous with ability to maintain one's self. The mere fact that wife has qualification is not sufficient *ipso facto* to conclude she was in a position to maintain herself at the time when the claim was made or before the spouses started living separately. The mere fact that after separation on some occasions she worked as a teacher in some school is not sufficient to take her out of the category of persons unable to

---

[227] (1999) 6 SCC 326
[228] II (2007) DMC 550 Gau
[229] I (2008) DMC 22 SC
[230] I (2002) DMC 20 MP

[231] II (2006) DMC 35 All
[232] I (2006) DMC 786 MP
[233] II (2006) DMC 613 Ker

maintain themselves. There is no adamant refusal on her part to engage herself in any income generating activity to maintain herself. It was clearly a case of her inability to secure any such income earning activities and earn an income sufficient to maintain herself.

In *Sudhir Diwan* v. *Tripta Diwan*,[234] the Delhi High Court awarded maintenance to a working woman on the ground that the woman was discharging her moral duty of maintaining her children. This is a welcome shift in judicial approach, as in most cases as soon as the son turned major, the courts discontinue the maintenance awarded to him. In this innovative approach, the fact that the wife who was employed was spending for the needs of the children became an important criterion while awarding maintenance to her. The husband was working as an agent with LIC, but did not disclose his income earned by way of commission. Based on his investments, the trial court arrived at a presumptive figure of Rs Four lakhs per annum. The wife was working as a steno in the district court and her net salary was Rs 19,000 per month. The son was a major but was still a student. Upholding the order of awarding Rs 10,000 as maintenance to her, the Delhi High Court held that the wife was spending around Rs 7,500 on his educational and incidental expenses. She would be left with only Rs 12,500 per month for herself and her minor daughter if the husband was not directed to pay her maintenance. Since the husband's monthly income would be around Rs 30,000, he was directed to contribute at least one third of this amount to the wife towards expenses of maintaining the children. The court commented that the husband would still be left with over Rs 20,000 for his own personal expenses.

In *Ashok Kumar Bhalla* v. *Roopa Bhalla*,[235] the gross monthly salary of the wife was around Rs 19,000. The husband's salary was around Rs 22,000. In addition, he was earning Rs 20,000 by way of rent from his property. The monthly educational and other expenses of the two children were determined at Rs 15,000 p.m. Since, the earnings of the husband and wife were in the ratio of 2:1, it was held that the parents were liable to share the expenses in the same ratio. And the husband was directed to contribute Rs 10,000 per month to his wife for upkeep of the two children.

In *Sushil Kumar Gupta* v. *Reena Gupta*[236] and *Radhika* v. *Vineet Rungta*,[237] two cases which are discussed in *Proof of Income* below, middle class women having moderate incomes were awarded maintenance from their affluent husbands to help them to maintain a standard of life which they were used to in their matrimonial home.

In *Rekha Malhotra* v. *Deepak Malhotra*, AIR 1999 Bom 291 FN, both the husband and wife were professionals. The husband pleaded that his income is only around Rs 40,000 and the wife admitted that she was earning Rs 12,500. There were no children of this marriage. When the wife came to know about the husband's affair with a young girl, she left the matrimonial home and was living with her parents. The wife had alleged that subsequently, the said woman was living in the matrimonial home and also had a child through her husband, which was denied by the husband. He pleaded that the cause for the break of marriage was the wife's refusal to have a child as she was only interested in her own career. He also pleaded that she is able to maintain herself and hence is not entitled to any maintenance. Examining their life style the Bombay

---

[234] I (2008) DMC 481 Del

[235] I (2008) DMC 646 Del
[236] II (2003) DMC 656 Del
[237] AIR 2004 Del 323

High Court commented that the earnings pleaded are on a lower side and the actual income of both would be much higher. Considering all the factors, the court awarded the wife Rs 7500 per month as maintenance to maintain a lifestyle similar to that of the husband.

There have also been instances where the courts have held that if the wife is able to maintain herself, or if the husband's status is not much above that of the wife's, the wife is not entitled to maintenance. In *Rakesh* v. *Smt. Nandu*,[238] the Rajasthan High Court dismissed the maintenance application of the wife who earned Rs 20–5 per day as a daily wage labourer. It was ruled that the status of the husband, who earned Rs 100–150 as a labourer was not much above in comparison to his wife as both were working as daily wage labourers. In *Satvendra Kumar* v. *Mithlesh Kumari*,[239] the wife who was serving as a teacher in a public school and getting a salary of more than Rs 6,000 per month was held as capable of maintaining herself from her own earnings and was not entitled to maintenance. But the court enhanced the maintenance awarded to her daughter. These rulings seem particularly harsh towards women.

Maintenance Claims by Husbands

The notion of maintenance to husbands is relatively new within our family laws. The ancient legal systems did not provide for it. Both Hindu and Muslim legal systems functioned from a protectionist approach towards women. Muslim law went further and provided for the future security of wives by securing their right of mehr within the marriage contract (nikahnama) itself. The ancient Hindu laws also protected the woman's right to separate property (stridhan) and forbade

the male relatives from usurping the property and depriving the woman of her rights.

The colonial legal system, which was introduced in India during the late nineteenth century, also adopted a protectionist approach towards women and granted them the right of maintenance under the personal laws as well as under the secular law, that is, Section 125 of Cr. PC and the Special Marriage Act of 1872 (re-enacted in 1954) as well as the law applicable to Christians, the Indian Divorce Act of 1869 (even after the 2001 amendment) did not bestow upon the husband the right to claim maintenance from the wife. Since the obligation of maintenance was framed within the context of dependents, the right was confined to wives, minor/disabled children, and unmarried daughters, who are deemed to be the weaker members of the family.

This right was first granted to Hindu husbands in the post-Independence period, under the codified enactment, the Hindu Marriage Act, 1955 (HMA). During the codification of the Hindu family law in the 1950s, the constitutional mandate of equality was an overarching presence. So this right was formulated in the context of an illusory notion of equality between the spouses. At this point in history, Hindu women were not granted equal rights to ancestral property and only a male was awarded the right by birth to the joint family property. In 1988, when the Parsi Marriage and Divorce Act, 1936 (PMDA) was amended, this notion of equality was incorporated within it.

Under these two acts (HMA and PMDA), the provision of maintenance is formulated in a gender-neutral term using the word spouse which enables the husband to claim maintenance from his estranged wife. This reflects a new trend in matrimonial laws and, apparently, it appears that the law of maintenance is inching towards gender equality. But such superficial notions of equality and gender neutrality, in a

[238] II (2002) DMC 301 Raj
[239] II (2003) DMC 557 Raj

society which is structured upon patriarchal premises and nurtures deep rooted biases against women, cause more hardships to women by entangling them into vexatious and vindictive litigation.

In *Lalit Mohan* v. *Tripta Devi*,[240] the husband who did not have independent source of income was awarded interim maintenance.

In another unreported judgment, the Allahabad High Court awarded maintenance to a husband in a divorce petition filed by the wife. The husband not only opposed the divorce, but also claimed maintenance and litigation expenses on the ground that he is unemployed. The family court had rejected the claim for interim maintenance on the ground that the husband was an able bodied and healthy man, capable of earning his own livelihood and, therefore, did not deserve any monetary support from his spouse. The husband challenged this order in the high court. On 7 November 2005, a single judge of the Lucknow High Court allowed the appeal and ordered the wife to pay Rs 2,000 per month as maintenance to the husband. The court explained the reasons for awarding the maintenance in the following words: 'Since the petitioner (husband) is residing in his own house and has to incur expenses of his widowed mother, his responsibilities seem to be higher than that of the Respondent wife.' While the wife, 'a hard working and enterprising woman' is employed with the bank, the husband, a 'happy-go-lucky and laid-back' person, pleaded that he is jobless. It appeared to be of little consequence that the wife had filed the petition for divorce in 1997 on the ground of cruelty and dowry harassment by husband and his family.[241]

Though cases such as the one discussed above are few and far between, the stipulation provides an armour to husbands to cause further harassment to wives in divorce proceedings. It appears to be rather unjust that while courts have denied maintenance to a young boy of eighteen, who has not yet completed his education and is dependent upon his divorced mother, on the ground that he is an adult capable of earning his livelihood, the courts entertain applications from adult males who have a primary obligation to maintain their wives and are also able bodied and capable of earning. As we can discern from the discussion in this chapter, women's rights to maintenance are hinged upon their chastity. Remarriage or living in adultery disentitles a woman from claiming maintenance. These are gendered notions which are applied only to women. There is no corresponding premise to disentitle a husband from claiming maintenance. As the above unreported case reveals maintenance can be granted to a husband who has been guilty of causing violence and dowry related harassment to his wife.

Merely by adopting a gender neutral term, these gendered notions will not get diminished or fade away. Notions of equality and gender neutrality can meaningfully be applied only within an egalitarian social structure and not within a patriarchal and gender biased one. Even considering that more and more women are now entering the job market and holding higher positions within the corporate world, it still does not justify the provision of maintenance to husbands unless the gendered role assigned to women as primary care takers of their children and home makers is reversed under such a situation.

Clarifying the concept of maintenance to husbands, in *Govind Singh* v. *Vidya*,[242] the

[240] AIR 1990 J&K 7

[241] *Asian Age*, (Bombay) 10 January 2006 p. 10.

[242] AIR 1999 Raj 304

Rajasthan High Court held that this provision does not entitle the husband who is capable of earning his living to claim maintenance from his wife. The provision does not empower the husband to stop earning and start depending on his wife. The court relied upon the maxim of Anglo Saxon jurisprudence that no person can be allowed to incapacitate himself, and held that the husband had voluntarily incapacitated himself from earning and, hence, he was not entitled to claim maintenance from his wife.

Effect of Consent Agreements Relinquishing the Right of Maintenance

At times, consent agreements drawn up either during the marriage or at the time of divorce, stipulating that the wife would not claim maintenance, are relied upon by husbands to defeat the claims of their wives. But when a wife approaches the courts for maintenance, some courts have declined to rely upon these agreements and have decided the issue of maintenance afresh. The contest arises due to a clause in Section 125(4) of Cr.PC which stipulates that a wife will not be entitled to maintenance if she is living separately as per an agreement to this effect. In *Kaushalyabai Mule* v. *Dinkar Mule*,[243] where the wife relinquished her claims of maintenance under a deed of divorce, it was held that the wife was entitled to maintenance despite this because such a deed of divorce has neither the backing of law or custom.

Similarly in *Manoka Chatterjee* v. *Swapan Chatterjee*,[244] it was held that in proceedings for divorce by mutual consent, terms of consent which include a clause that the wife, upon receiving a lump sum amount perpetually binds herself from any future claim of maintenance,

was not tenable under the law. It was held that since Section 125 of Cr.PC. is a piece of social welfare legislation and its primary purpose is to protect the wife from vagrancy and destitution, even if the wife binds herself consciously or unconsciously to such an agreement, the law has to come to her aid and protect her statutory right to maintenance and also to her right to life, which provision must mean a life with dignity. It was held that future claims cannot be frozen merely because the wife was awarded a lump sum amount at the time of the divorce. The claim is flexible and changes from time to time according to changes in circumstances. In view of this reasoning, the Calcutta High Court set aside the particular clause in the agreement.

In *Biswapriya Bhuiya* v. *Jhumi Banik*,[245] the wife had filed for divorce on the ground of cruelty but, subsequently, the petition was converted into a petition for divorce by mutual consent and the wife agreed for an unconditional divorce. A week later, she filed for maintenance under Section 125 Cr.PC. The family court at Agartala, awarded her Rs 1,500 per month as maintenance. The husband challenged this order on the ground that since the wife had surrendered her right by agreeing for an unconditional divorce, she is barred from claiming maintenance subsequently as per stipulations under Section 125(4) of Cr.PC. But the Gauhati High Court held that there is no bar against the wife from claiming maintenance at a later stage since she has not been awarded any maintenance in the divorce proceedings.

In *P. Archana @ Atchamamba* v. *Varada Siva Rama Krishna*,[246] it was held that there is no bar to claiming maintenance if there is a change in situation even after maintenance had been

---

[243] II (2001) DMC 580 Bom
[244] (2002) 2 Cal.LT 336

[245] II (2007) DMC 631 Gau
[246] II (2008) DMC 217 AP

awarded at the time of divorce by way of compromise between the parties. The court commented that such an interpretation would defeat the very object of Section 25. Further, it was held that an agreement defeating the right of maintenance, provided under the statute, being contrary to public policy is not a valid contract, and cannot operate as a bar to exercise jurisdiction conferred under Section 25(2)[247] of the Act. It was held that the family court of Hyderabad committed an error in holding that the wife's claim is not maintainable and remanded the matter back for retrial.

But the Bombay High Court, in a series of judgments, has held a contrary view. In *Popat Kashinath Bodke* v. *Kamalabai Popat Bodke*,[248] the parties were residing separately by an agreement and some agricultural land was transferred in the wife's name, and the wife had signed a deed of relinquishment. It was held that in view of Section 125(4) of Cr.PC, the wife would cease to have a right to claim maintenance after execution of the agreement and if the agreement has been acted upon.

In *Vitthal Jadhav* v. *Harnabai Jadhav*,[249] the wife was given Rs. 20,000 by the husband in accordance with an agreement by virtue of a customary divorce. The couple had agreed to live separately by mutual consent. Subsequently, the wife filed a petition for maintenance and was awarded Rs 400 as monthly maintenance. The Bombay High Court quashed the order of the Judicial Magistrate which awarded the wife Rs. 400 as monthly maintenance. It further held that the order of the magistrate suffered from legal infirmity as a wife loses her right to claim maintenance from her husband if she

and her husband are residing separately by mutual consent, in light of Section 125 (4) of the Cr.PC.

Similarly, in *Gajanan Solanke* v. *Sheela Solanke*,[250] the woman's claim of maintenance after divorce, for herself and her minor son who was born a few months after the consent deed was signed, was upheld by the sessions court. But in appeal, the high court set aside the order of maintenance on the ground that since the woman had relinquished her claim to maintenance in divorce proceedings, she was barred from claiming further maintenance by provision of Section 127(3)(c) of Cr.PC.[251] The husband also denied paternity of the child. But the court held that at the time of signing the consent deed the woman was pregnant and this fact had not been mentioned in the consent deed. The woman was also not cross examined on this issue, hence, the child was held to be the legitimate and the amount of Rs 400 per month awarded to the minor son was upheld.

At times, the husbands have taken the plea that the parties have gone through a customary divorce where the wife has relinquished her right to maintenance. In *Jairam* v. *Sindhubai*,[252] it was held that custom cannot only be pleaded, but has to be proved that the parties were entitled for the customary divorce. In this context, the deed of divorce could not have the effect to dissolve the marriage between the parties. Once the parties are married, the said marriage cannot be dissolved except by a decree of divorce passed under the provisions of the

---

[247] The section empowers the court to vary, modify or rescind its own order if there is a change in the situation.
[248] II (2003) DMC 193 Bom
[249] I (2004) DMC 572 Bom

[250] II (2005) DMC 134 Bom
[251] Section127(3)(c) of Cr.PC stipulates that if a woman has obtained a divorce from her husband and has voluntarily surrendered her rights to maintenance after her divorce, the Magistrate may cancel the order of maintenance.
[252] I (2001) DMC 407 Bom

Hindu Marriage Act, 1955. The order granting maintenance to the wife cannot be revoked merely on this basis.

In *Rajesh Kumar Madaan* v. *Mamta @ Veena*,[253] after criminal proceedings were initiated by the wife against the husband on the ground of cruelty and dowry harassment, there was a compromise and the husband agreed to pay Rs 4,50,000 as settlement. But after the initial instalment of Rs 50,000 on the date of the compromise, he defaulted and later filed for divorce on the ground of desertion and cruelty stating that the criminal proceedings filed by the wife construed cruelty. The court rejected his plea and dismissed the petition. The husband challenged this order in the high court. Later, he pleaded that there was a customary divorce between them. The high court held that a marriage can only be dissolved by a decree of divorce by a competent court and not in any proceedings before the Panchayat. The wife is not to be bound by a compromise unless she herself consents to the same.

While there are instances where the courts have validated customary divorce, if the plea is advanced to defeat a women's right to maintenance, the courts are bound to reject this plea and award women their statutory rights. Hence, a custom, denying women maintenance, cannot be pleaded as such a custom is against public policy.

Maintenance Claims by Parents

The above provision has imposed a statutory liability on both sons and daughters to maintain their father or mother who is unable to maintain himself or herself. Section 488 of the old code did not contain any such provision aimed at prevention of vagrancy and destitution of parents who do not have means to maintain themselves

(*Vijaya Monohar Arbat* v. *Kashirao Rajaram Sawai*).[254] If there are two or more sons, the parents may seek remedy against any one or more of the sons. The liability to maintain the father is not dependant on failure or otherwise of the father to fulfil his normal obligation of maintaining children during childhood (*Pandurang Dabhade Baburao Dabhade*).[255] The adoptive father is also entitled to maintenance.

Even a married daughter is liable to maintain her parents. But in this context, *Paladugula Vijayalakshmi* v. *Nomula Ramanadham*[256] raises an interesting question. In this case, the parents, aged 60 and 50, had their own property and were running a small grocery store. They had not given any share of the property to their daughter to which she was entitled to. But the son, upon attaining majority was given a share. The parents also did not perform the marriage ceremony of their daughter as she had married against their wishes. The daughter, since then, was living with the husband. The parents claimed maintenance from the daughter and were awarded Rs 400 per month. The high court sent the matter back for retrial as it was held that the procedure as laid down under

> **Box 2.4   Section 125(1)(d) of Cr.PC**
>
> If any person having sufficient means neglects or refuses to maintain, his father or mother, unable to maintain himself or herself, a Magistrate of the first class may, upon proof of such neglect or refusal, order such person to make a monthly allowance for the maintenance of such father or mother, at such monthly rate as such Magistrate thinks fit and to pay the same to such person as the Magistrate may from time to time direct.

[253] II (2005) DMC 101 P&H

[254] AIR 1987 SC 1100
[255] 1979 Mah LJ 729
[256] II (2003) DMC 131 AP

Section 126 was not scrupulously followed by the lower court. The high court directed the trial court to consider all relevant factors before upholding the parents claim for maintenance from the daughter.

In *Akham Ibobi Singh* v. *Akham Biradhwaja Singh*,[257] the father aged 74 years and the mother aged 71 years were claiming maintenance from their son. The family court rejected their claim. In appeal, the Gauhati High Court upheld their claim and held that it is not required to strictly prove their inability to maintain themselves and commented that while rejecting the claim of the parents, the family courts lost sight of Section 14 of the Family Courts Act, where the court has wide powers to receive evidence which is not admissible in other proceedings. The Indian society casts a duty on the children of a person to maintain their parents if they are not in a position to maintain themselves. It is their duty to look after their parents when they become old and infirm. The court lamented over the fact that there was a long drawn legal battle between parents and sons for a matter which is, unfortunately, a moral obligation. They have been fighting from the family court up to the Supreme Court via this high court, and might have spent a lot of money for that purpose. The court commented that there is no law which stipulates that the parents must claim maintenance from all sons and daughters and they should be jointly impleaded in the proceedings. It will suffice, if it is proved that the Respondent has the capacity to maintain and the parents do not have the capacity to maintain themselves.

In *Makiur Rahaman Khan* v. *Mahila Bibi*,[258] it was held that a divorced Muslim woman is entitled to maintenance from her children under Section 125 of Cr.PC. The divorced wife had filed proceedings under the Muslim Women's Act for a fair and reasonable settlement against her husband. While these proceedings were pending, she also filed for maintenance under Section 125 of Cr.PC against her sons. She was awarded Rs 250 from each of her two sons. In an appeal filed by the sons against this order, the high court held that women's rights against their sons under Section 125 of Cr.PC are not substituted by the enactment of Muslim Women's Act. The provisions of MWA are in addition to her rights under Section 125 Cr.PC against her children.

The Supreme Court, in *Kirtikant D. Vadodaria* v. *State of Gujarat*,[259] held that even an adoptive mother and a childless step-mother, is entitled to claim maintenance allowances against her adopted son or her step-son, if she is a widow or her husband, if living, is incapable of maintaining her. The court reiterated that the while dealing with the ambit and scope of Section 125 Cr.PC, it must be borne in mind that the primary object is social justice to those who are unable to maintain themselves, but have a moral claim for support.

The recently enacted *Maintenance of Parents and Senior Citizens Act*, 2007, provides an additional remedy to elderly men and women to claim maintenance from their children. The Act goes a step further and secures the rights of childless senior citizens against their next of kin or persons who would be entitled to inherit their property. The Act also seeks to protect the life and property of senior citizens and parents. In addition to maintenance and provision, the Act also seeks to ensure better medical facilities and mandates the state to set up old age homes and provide institutionalized care to the elderly.

---

[257] II (2006) DMC 523 Gau
[258] II (2002) DMC 549 Cal: 2002 Cr.LJ 1751

[259] II (1997) DMC 164 SC: 1996 (4) SCC 479

In order to provide for an easily accessible avenue of accessing justice and to ensure a speedy remedy, the Act provides for establishment of tribunals and office of Maintenance Officer who will represent the parent or the senior citizen in these proceedings. In order to protect this vulnerable section from the clutches of unscrupulous lawyers, the Act prohibits legal representation. In order to arrive at a settlement, rather than engage in lengthy litigation, the Act also provides for conciliation proceedings. If the dispute is not resolved at this stage, it will proceed before the tribunal and will be decided within a maximum period of ninety days. The maximum amount which can be awarded under this Act is limited to Rs 10,000 per month.

The additional safeguard that the new Act provides is punishment to the children and relatives who abandon their parents or senior citizens in order to avoid vagrancy and destitution. Also, if there is any transfer of property which has been carried out with *mala fide* intention, or by resorting to fraud, or undue influence, it can be set aside.

The Act empowers social organizations to intervene on behalf of the elderly and also empowers them to initiate proceedings, *suo moto*.

While this is a timely measure enacted with the right intentions, the working of this Act at the ground level is yet to be observed. Hopefully, it will not pose more hurdles on the path of the elderly while they seek remedial and protective relief against neglect and destitution.

While it is a positive endeavour, it may take some time till all the infrastructural and institutional support is developed. In the meantime, the parents can still take recourse under the prevailing provision under Section 125 of Cr.PC. Since the procedures are all set in place and the magistrates are well versed with the provisions and the provisions are also summary in nature,

it would provide a viable remedy to a destitute parent. Two additional benefits of filing under Section 125 of Cr.PC would be that no ceiling is stipulated under it and the atmosphere of a criminal court might exert greater pressure on the opposite side to comply with the order due to the fear of imprisonment, which can be availed of in execution proceedings.

Procedural Aspects

As can be observed from the exhaustive list of substantive issues discussed above, the task of claiming maintenance can easily be compared to an ordeal by fire for the women involved. Every legal ploy is invoked in order to humiliate women and defeat their claims to maintenance. Even if these hurdles of substantive law are crossed, women are still left to deal with complex and, at times, absurd procedural aspects, some of which are briefly discussed in this section.

Jurisdiction

Jurisdiction becomes an important issue while initiating matrimonial proceedings or while claiming maintenance. For women, the place of marriage, the matrimonial residence, and her natal home, could be situated at different places. In addition, after separation, she may be constrained to set up residence at yet another place, either to seek employment or to secure school admissions for her children. Keeping in view the displacement which most women are compelled to go through by virtue of marriage patterns which are patrilocal, the law gives women wide jurisdiction while initiating matrimonial and maintenance proceedings.

Initially the jurisdiction under most matrimonial statutes was confined to the place of marriage and the place where the couple last resided together, or the place where the respondent resides. This caused a great deal of hardship to women who usually return to their native place after the marriage breaks up. In view of this, the provision of jurisdiction under the Hindu Marriage Act and the Special Marriage Act was widened in 2003[260] to include the place where the woman resides after the break up of her marriage. So currently, the woman can initiate proceedings at the place of her post-separation residence. Similarly, proceedings under Section 125 of Cr.PC can be filed at the place where the woman last resided with her husband or where she is presently residing (*Syed Khaja Mohiuddin* v. *State of AP*).[261]

At times there are multiple proceedings. The wife may have filed for maintenance under Section 125 of Cr.PC at the place of her residence and, in the meantime, the husband may have filed for divorce at the place of his residence. In such cases, upon a petition for transfer of the proceedings filed by the husband, the courts would be inclined to transfer the husband's petition to a court which would be more convenient for the wife to litigate.

The law is well settled on this aspect. The apex court has repeatedly held that the matrimonial disputes have to be dealt with by courts which are easily accessible to women (*Vinay Pandey* v. *Roshan Kumar* and *Rinku Goel* v. *Rajesh Goel*).[262] The fact that women's lack of exposure to the outside world, the undue hardship caused to them while travelling alone to a distant place to defend the litigation, the concern for their safety, the cost of travel, the fact that there may be young children who need constant care, or the elder children whose studies may be disrupted while the mother

travels to defend the court case, the fact that she is employed at the place of her residence, etc., are factors which the courts have considered while transferring the husband's petition to the place where the woman is residing.

In *Rachana Kanodia* v. *Anuk Kanodia*,[263] the wife was residing in Varanasi, which was the permanent place of residence of her parents. The Supreme Court transferred the petition for divorce filed by her husband in the district court at Thane in Maharashtra to the district court Varanasi on the ground that great hardship will be caused to her to travel all the way to Thane. In *Chayana Das* v. *Tarun Kumar Das*,[264] the wife was residing in Cooch Bihar. The husband had filed a petition for divorce in Tinsukiya. The Supreme Court held that since the distance between Cooch Bihar and Tinsukiya is about 830 km and involves 20 hours of travel and costs Rs 300 to 400, it is not possible for the wife to undertake travel all by herself to defend the petition.

In *Neelam Bhatia* v. *Satbir Singh Bhatia*,[265] the wife filed a petition to transfer proceedings from Korba to the family court at Kolkata on the ground that she lacks financial means to travel, she had no source of income, and she had a minor daughter of five years. The husband resisted the Transfer Petition but assured to cooperate and settle the case without dragging on the proceedings. Hence, the Transfer Petition was dismissed. In *Samita Bhattacharjee* v. *Kulashekar Bhattacharjee*,[266] the wife was residing with her parents at Howrah, West Bengal, along with her minor child. The husband had filed a petition for divorce in the family court at Agartala, West Tripura. The Supreme Court

---

[260] Through Marriage Law (Amendment) Act, 2003 (Act No.50 of 2003) which inserted Section 19(iii-a) in HMA and in Section 31(iii-a) in SMA w.e.f. 23 December 2003.

[261] I (2006) DMC 32 AP

[262] See the rulings in *Vinay Pandey* v. *Roshan Kumar*, II (2000) DMC 571 SC; II (2000) DMC 511 SC.

[263] II (2001) DMC 171 SC

[264] II (2001) DMC (SC) 186

[265] II (2006) DMC 594 SC

[266] I (2008) DMC 354 SC

transferred the case to the court of district judge at Howrah, West Bengal.

When the place of residence of the wife and the place where the husband had initiated proceedings, both are within the direction of a high court, the high court has also issued similar directions for transfer. In *Kirti* v. *Vikas Bhagirat Rao Yeskade*,[267] the Bombay High Court upheld the wife's plea that she was dependent on her aged parents and she had no independent source of income, and that it was not possible for her parents to come to Nagpur to attend the hearing. Her place of residence was about 200 km away from Nagpur. The court upheld her submission that the journey will cause considerable hardship to her. The court also upheld her plea that she apprehends danger to her when she comes to attend proceedings in Nagpur. The court commented that the convenience of the wife is to be preferred over convenience of the husband and it ought to be the husband who should travel from Nagpur to Chandrapur, rather than the wife from Ballarsha (Chandrapur) to Nagpur. In *P. Himabindu* v. *P. Jayasimharaja*,[268] the Andhra Pradesh High Court held that the primary concern for the court should be the convenience of the wife. Since she had no male assistance to travel to Chittoor, the transfer petition filed by her was allowed. In *Shakuntala* v. *Pankaj Chourasiya (Dr)*,[269] the Madhya Pradesh High Court, while transferring the proceedings from a court in Indore to the family court at Panna where the wife was residing, commented that there was nothing on record to show that there was danger to the life of the husband if he travels to Panna to attend the court proceedings. The wife

was employed in Panna and was also looking after her two-year-old child there.

The Orissa High Court in *Sujata Mohanty* v. *Rudra Charan Mohanty*,[270] rather curiously has given a judgment which is contrary to this position. Rejecting the wife's petition, the court held that the fact that the wife feels unsafe to travel alone is not a sufficient ground for transfer of the case.

The high court's power of transfer is limited. It can only transfer cases from a court under its jurisdiction to another court over which it has jurisdiction. In *Jency Elizebath Peter* v. *Biju Thomas*,[271] it was held that the high court of Kerala lacks jurisdiction to transfer the case filed by the husband, which was pending before the family court, Ernakulam, to the family court at Chennai where the wife was residing. But, considering the fact that the wife was residing with her mother in Chennai and had a three-year-old child, the high court directed the family court at Ernakulam to consider the request made by the wife for examining her through a court commissioner at Chennai.

Travelling Expenses

For women, travelling expenses also become an important aspect of litigation. Unless women are provided adequate travelling expenses, they may not be in a position to defend the case filed by their husbands against them.

An important case relating to the issue of travelling expenses is *Anita Laxmi Narayan Singh* v. *Laxmi Narain Singh*.[272] The family court at Bombay had awarded a very low amount towards travel, lodging, and other expenses, for the wife who was staying in Ghaziabad. Since this made it impossible for the wife to travel to defend herself

[267] II (2006) DMC 436 Bom
[268] I (2006) DMC 118 AP
[269] II (2006) DMC 589 MP

[270] I (2008) DMC 708 Ori
[271] I (2006) DMC 189 Ker
[272] (1992) 2 SCC 562

during litigation, the husband was able to secure an ex parte decree of divorce. While setting aside the ex parte decree of divorce, the Supreme Court passed strictures against the family court for its callousness in awarding such a low amount as travel expenses. The Supreme Court also transferred the proceedings from the family court, Bombay, to the district court, Ghaziabad, for disposal in accordance with law. The respondent-husband was asked to pay the cost of the proceedings which was quantified at Rs 5,000.

If the husband is willing to pay the travel costs of the woman, the courts may not pass an order to transfer the proceedings at a place which is convenient to the wife. In *Teena Chhabra* v. *Manish Chhabra*,[273] the Supreme Court accepted the husband's offer to bear the expenses for the travel, boarding, and lodging, of the wife and dismissed her transfer petition which was filed on the ground that she had no source of income to travel. Similarly, in *Kanagalakshmi* v. *A. Venkatesan*,[274] the Supreme Court accepted the plea of the husband that he would bear the expenses not only for the wife but also her companion for their travel, and stay at the place where the case was pending and, accordingly, dismissed her transfer petition. The same principle was also followed in *M. Sivagami* v. *R. Raja*.[275] While disallowing the transfer petition based on monetary grounds, the Supreme Court directed the husband to pay the wife's litigation costs and also her travel costs and expenses along with those of her witnesses.

Delay in Filing Application

While a woman is expected to file for maintenance within a reasonable period after the desertion, the courts will not reject her application merely on the ground that there was delay in filing an application for maintenance. Many times, women who are deserted delay filing for maintenance in the hope that there may be a possibility of reconciliation and approaching the courts for maintenance might enrage their husbands and mar their chances of reconciliation. The legal entitlement for claiming maintenance arises from the date of filing the application and not from the date of desertion. Hence, the woman would lose out if a claim for maintenance is not filed soon after the desertion.

Since the husband is legally obligated to pay maintenance to his wife, non-payment of maintenance is a continuing or an inchoate offence, and every month when the husband fails in his obligation to maintain the wife, a new right is created. It is in this context that in *Mangla Devi* v. *Baluram*,[276] it was held that though the application for maintenance should be filed within a reasonable time, no limitation can be prescribed for the same. The court commented that if there is a satisfactory explanation for the delay, the application cannot be rejected merely on the ground of delay. The woman pleaded that since her father was in service he had maintained her, but after his retirement from service he was not in a position to maintain her and, hence, she had filed an application for maintenance. It was held that the delay was satisfactorily explained.

A similar line of reasoning was also adopted in *Nirmalabai* v. *Dr. Omprakash*.[277] The Applicant No. 1 was a housewife ignorant about the technicalities of the law, and the Applicant No. 2 was a minor child. The court held that sufficient explanation had been given for the delay. Stating that the revision court cannot take a technical view of matter ignoring the fact that Section 125 of Cr.PC is a benevolent

---

[273] (2004) 13 SCC 411
[274] (2004) 13 SCC 405
[275] (2005) 12 SCC 301

[276] II (2006) DMC 565 MP
[277] II (2001) DMC 593 MP

provision. In *Shobha* v. *Krushnakant Pandya*,[278] there was a delay of twenty-five years in filing the application for maintenance. Since her parents were supporting her and since she hoped for reconciliation, the wife had not approached the courts for maintenance. Accepting this explanation, she was awarded Rs 3000 per month as maintenance and set aside the order of the family court, whch had rejected her application. In *Thakur Vyasnarayan Singh* v. *Hemlata*,[279] the wife was living with her maternal uncle after the death of her father. In view of this, it was held that the inordinate delay in filing the petition has been correctly explained. The court also observed that the wife had no source of income and was incapable of maintaining herself.

Even if the application was dismissed on an earlier occasion, a subsequent application on another ground is not barred and the petition will be entitled to maintenance on the fresh ground, if she succeeds in proving this ground (*Puliyulla Chalil Narayana Kurup* v. *Thayyulla Parabhath Valsala*).[280]

Interim Maintenance

The purpose of awarding interim maintenance and litigation expenses is to provide the claimant basic minimum financial support in order to survive and carry on with the litigation process. At times, in contested cases, the litigation may go on for several years and the party claiming maintenance will be subjected to great hardships if interim maintenance is not awarded. The courts are extremely cautious if children are involved, as in the intervening period their education and health may suffer and the damage would be irreparable by the time the courts deliver the final verdict on the issue.

An application for interim maintenance (*maintenance pendente lite*) can be filed along with a petition for a matrimonial relief or after a copy of the petition filed by the husband for matrimonial relief is served on the woman. It can also be filed along with an application under Section18 of HAMA, Section 125 of Cr.PC, or under the Domestic Violence Act. It can also be filed subsequently, but before the trial of the main petition commences. The provision of interim relief is based on an urgency and must be decided expeditiously before taking up other contested issues (*Sushila Viresh Chaddva* v. *Viresh Nagshi Chhadva*).[281]

Even when the statute does not explicitly provide for it, the power to award interim maintenance has been read into the power of the court to do justice.

In *Savitri* v. *Govind Singh*,[282] the Supreme Court upheld the power to award interim maintenance under Section 125 of Cr.PC as follows: 'While interpreting the provision, it had to be done in such a manner so as not to defeat the objective of the legislation. In the absence of any express prohibition, the provision must be interpreted as to pay some reasonable sum by way of maintenance to the applicant pending final disposal of the application. Applications under Section 125 of Cr.PC take several months before final disposal. In order to enjoy the fruits of the proceedings, the applicant has to be alive until the date of the final order. In a large number of cases, the same is possible only if an order for interim payment of maintenance is made. Every court, therefore, must be deemed to possess, by necessary intendment, all

---

[278] II (2008) DMC 639 MP
[279] II (2002) DMC 24 MP
[280] II (2005) DMC 266 Ker

[281] AIR 1996 Bom 94
[282] AIR 1986 SC 984

such powers as are necessary to make its order effective.'

In *P. Srinivasa Rao* v. *P. Indira*,[283] the Andhra Pradesh High Court explained the inherent power to grant interim maintenance under Section 18 of HAMA as follows: 'Independent of the inherent power of the court under Section 151 of CPC, even under the provisions of the Act itself, by necessary implication, power has been conferred on the court to grant interim maintenance to the wife and minor children where circumstances so warrant and justify, to do justice on a *prima facie* satisfaction of the case on merits. In such cases, the court cannot decline to grant interim maintenance *pendente lite* till the final adjudication of the controversy on merits. The inherent powers under Section 151 of CPC and the powers conferred under other provisions of CPC are intended to do complete justice between the parties. A conjoint reading of these provisions clearly discloses that they empower the courts to pass appropriate interim orders as may appear to the courts just and convenient, to prevent justice being defeated. The object of the provisions is to preserve the rights of the parties at the same place till their cause is adjudicated. As a matter of principle, if it is held that no interim maintenance can be awarded in maintenance proceedings, it causes hardship to the parties and in some cases there is the possibility that the main relief may also become infructuous, if the party is not able to maintain herself pending proceedings.'

If the ground for interim maintenance is made out, the court cannot impose any condition on the spouse claiming such maintenance. Even in a petition for divorce filed by the husband on the ground of wife's adultery, the court cannot dismiss the wife's application for interim maintenance. In *Dwarkadas Gurmukhidas* v. *Bhanuben*,[284] it was held that it is the right of the wife, who is unable to support herself for the interim period, to get maintenance and the same should be made available to her without any reference to her conduct. In *Saroj Devi* v. *Ashok Puri*,[285] an order imposing the condition that the wife would undertake to refund the alimony, if the allegations regarding her leading an immoral life were proved, was illegal. In *Bijal Parag Dave* v. *Parag Labhashankar Dave*,[286] it was held that refusal to award interim maintenance to the wife on the ground of misconduct is not proper. In *Neelam Malhotra* v. *Rajinder Malhotra*,[287] it was held that refusal to award interim maintenance based on husband's allegations of gross misbehaviour and infidelity was improper and the trial court could not go into the allegations which would prejudice the main issue. In *Jagir Singh* v. *Jasbir Kaur*,[288] it was held that denial of interim maintenance just on the basis of such an allegation would not be justified until and unless the allegation is substantiated by cogent evidence.

Even when the validity of marriage is disputed, the courts have the power to grant interim maintenance. Similarly, when paternity is disputed, the courts will not go into the lengthy question of deciding paternity while awarding interim maintenance.

The Delhi High Court, in *Rajesh Chaudhary* v. *Nirmala Chaudhary*, (discussed earlier) held that an estranged wife claiming maintenance for herself and her child cannot be denied interim maintenance while awaiting the results of complex DNA tests for determining the issue of alleged illegitimacy. Sustenance of the minor child and its mother, educational, and other

---

[283]   I (2002) DMC 749 AP

[284]   AIR 1986 Guj 6
[285]   AIR 1988 Raj 84
[286]   AIR 1999 Bom 237
[287]   AIR 1994 Del 234
[288]   2005 Cri.LR 572

household expenses do not and cannot await the decision of the court on such a complex issue. The court directed that interim maintenance should be ordered expeditiously, if found payable.

In *Bobby Paulose v. Ronia Mathew*,[289] it was held that while deciding the application for interim maintenance, which is a summary proceeding, the court cannot, in any manner, prejudice the wife's rights. The Kerala High Court commented that since the matter was being indefinitely adjourned due to husband's inconvenience to attend court proceedings, the family court adopted a realistic approach in granting interim maintenance to the wife.

In *Sampa Saha v. Amaresh Saha*,[290] it was held that an order rejecting the prayer of interim maintenance, without assigning any reason and without recording any satisfactory explanation as to why interim maintenance was refused, suffers from serious illegality.

At the stage of awarding interim maintenance the courts will not permit the parties to go into lengthy legal submissions or to cross examine each other. The application for interim maintenance can be decided by affidavits of the parties.

In *Rajesh Burmann v. Mitul Chatterjee (Burman)*,[291] the Supreme Court upheld the grant of medical expenses to the wife by way of interim relief, and held that there was no infirmity in the decision or in the reasoning while awarding interim maintenance to the wife.

While protecting the rights of women, children, and parents for interim maintenance, the courts have also issued a caution that fabulous amounts cannot be awarded at the ad-interim stage in *ex parte* orders without substantive evidence in support of the claim regarding the income of the husband (*Saibal Dey v. Chaitali Dey*).[292]

The courts are empowered to grant interim maintenance under matrimonial proceedings even if the wife and children have been awarded maintenance in proceedings under Section 125 of Cr.PC. In *Ashok Singh Pal v. Manjulata*,[293] while upholding the right of the wife to maintenance under Section 24 of HMA and under Section 125 of Cr.PC, it was held that the remedies under both sections are independent of each other. There is no rule that the amount of maintenance granted under Section 125 of Cr.PC be adjusted towards the amount granted under HMA, or vice versa. But a contrary view has been expressed by the Bombay High Court in *Sanjay v. Swati*[294] which set aside the order of the family court on the ground that it was passed without taking into consideration the husband's existing liability to pay maintenance under Section 125 of Cr.PC.

Considering the urgency of proceedings for interim maintenance, the courts are bound to give short dates to avoid delays. In *Sonia Khurana v. State*,[295] it was held that though Magistrates are burdened with heavy work and normally it is difficult for them to give short dates, it would not justify giving a date after ten months. The courts must keep in view the nature of proceedings and when there is urgency, short dates must be given. In this case, the petitioners are destitute, having no means of livelihood. They had filed an application under Section 125 of Cr.PC for interim maintenance to get immediate support. Such applications must be decided without any delay. The court commented that issuing notice on preliminary

---

[289] I (2007) DMC 514 Ker
[290] I (2006) DMC 465 Cal
[291] II (2008) DMC 830 SC

[292] I (2007) DMC 398 Cal
[293] II (2008) DMC 352 MP
[294] II (2007) DMC 731 Bom
[295] II (2006) DMC 453 Del

hearing for a date after ten months is a travesty of justice.

While awarding interim maintenance, the courts are also empowered to order litigation costs to the claimant to enable her to get adequate legal assistance. While in *Ramesh Babu* v. *Usha*,[296] the husband challenged Rs 2,500, awarded to the wife as litigation cost, on the ground that she can avail of free legal aid. But, the Madras High Court held that the claim of a deserving person for interim maintenance and litigation expenses cannot be rejected on the ground of availability of free legal aid. But at the same time, in *Pritiben Acharya* v. *State of Gujarat*,[297] the Gujarat High Court has held that it is the duty of the judges and advocates to bring to the notice of litigants their right to free legal aid.

In *Jaya Sanjiv Mehta* v. *Sanjiv Baldev Mehta*, the family court, while awarding interim maintenance from the date of the order, assigned no reasons as to why the usual practice of awarding maintenance from the date of application was not followed. The high court set aside this order and awarded maintenance to the wife from the date of filing the application for interim maintenance. The court also commented that the super technical approach adopted by the family court of demanding that the wife should get her train ticket endorsed by the concerned superintendent or station master is not proper. Once the wife satisfies the court that she has travelled from Agra to Mumbai on a valid ticket and the ticket bears name and date of the train, she is entitled to claim travel allowance.

Proof of Income

The entire discussion on maintenance hinges on just one factor—whether the applicant has been able to secure a favourable order of maintenance, and the amount which is awarded. There is no set formula for fixing the amount of maintenance. Within a stratified society, the amount would depend upon the facts and circumstances of each case. The courts cannot be expected to adopt a mechanical approach while interpreting a provision of law which is based on principles of social justice (*Pradeep Kumar Kapoor* v. *Shailja Kapoor*),[298] and much would depend upon humanitarian concerns. The relevant factors for consideration would be:

1. The status of the parties;
2. The needs of the claimants;
3. The income, assets, and lifestyle of the husband;
4. His other financial obligations;
5. The wife's income and assets.

The earlier notion of a dole for bare survival has given way to the notion of physical and emotional well-being of the claimant.[299] The maintenance which is awarded should suffice the woman to take care of her basic needs such as food, clothing, shelter, medical expenses, as well as the expenses of raising her children, including their educational expenses.

From the earlier notion of awarding one-fifth of the income, the thumb rule now is to award one-third of the husband's income as maintenance to the wife (*Dinesh* v. *Usha*).[300] But, while this is the general principle, in each case the

---

[296] I (2004) DMC 581 Mad
[297] II (2002) DMC 557 Guj

[298] AIR 1989 Del 10
[299] The removal of ceiling of Rs 500 for maintenance under Section 125 of Cr.PC has contributed a great deal in achieving this objective.
[300] In actual fact, the sums awarded are much lower, though in recent times one can discern an upward trend in the amounts awarded as maintenance. This is linked to the upward surge in salaries drawn by the middle and upper middle classes in the corporate world (AIR 1979 Bom.173).

court is duty bound to enquire into the actual earnings or income of the respondent. Hence, the claimant is expected to submit proof of income, based on which the court will determine the amount of maintenance.

It is rather ironic that most women are not able to provide the necessary proof as required by a court of law. Women lack basic knowledge regarding their husbands' employment, income, assets, investments, bank accounts, movable and immovable property, agricultural income, or husbands' share in the HUF property. During the subsistence of marriage, most women do not have either access or an interest in the financial arrangements of their husbands or the joint family. They don't have access to the documents such as salary slips, bank passbooks, receipts of fixed deposits, share certificates, property cards, tenancy agreements, income tax returns, etc. In an economic order which thrives on unaccounted money, proving actual income or assets is a daunting task, which is beyond most diligent and prudent women. On the other hand, husbands prefer protracted and expensive litigation rather than conceding the claim of maintenance. At times, it becomes a matter not just of financial liability but also of personal ego. Defeating the claim of maintenance, through adversarial proceedings becomes a retaliatory measure to settle scores with the wife, who has initiated legal proceedings against them. Due to these constraints, even when women do succeed in securing an order of maintenance, the amounts awarded are meagre and far below the expectations of the claimants.

The challenging task before the court is to find a balance between the inflated claims of women and the deflated disclosures of income by husbands. In order to circumvent this lacunae regarding acceptable legal proof, the courts have evolved certain legal maxims for determining the amount of maintenance which would be equitable, just, and fair to the parties concerned. Since, it is not always possible to apply the rule of best evidence in maintenance proceedings, the courts will rely upon probabilities which would enlarge the scope of arriving at reasonable inferences (*Pendiyala Suresh Kumar Ramarao* v. *Sompally Arunbindu*).[301]

One basic criterion is that of an able-bodied man capable of earning a livelihood.[302] The courts will invoke this legal premise if the husband declines to disclose his income. In the absence of evidence, the wife's submissions will be taken into consideration for determining the amount.

In *Ali Hossain* v. *Baby Farida*,[303] the wife was awarded Rs 300 per month as maintenance for herself and Rs 200 per month for each of the two children. The husband worked as a rickshaw puller and casual labourer. He challenged the order on the ground that the amount was excessive and passed without a realistic assessment of his income. The high court held: 'The husband is an able bodied, young, healthy man, and admits that he has a regular job as a rickshaw puller and casual labourer, but he did not care to disclose even his average daily income. This omission to disclose his income is sufficient to warrant an inference that he has the capability of earning sufficient income.'

In *Haseena* v. *Abdul Jaleel*,[304] the Kerala High Court held that the salary drawn by the husband is a fact within his knowledge. The wife cannot be faulted for not proving it. In the absence of evidence from the husband, the evidence adduced by the wife is accepted. The wife was awarded Rs 2,50,000 as reasonable and fair provision, and maintenance.

[301] II (2005) DMC 417 Guj
[302] See 'Husband's Obligation to Maintain the Wife' discussed earlier.
[303] 1998 Cri.LJ 2762
[304] II (2007) DMC 215 Ker

In *Tabassum Shaikh* v. *Sheikh*,[305] the wife pleaded that due to cruelty and accusations of unchastity made against her, she was terrified of returning to her matrimonial home. In her pleadings she provided details of the husband's properties and business. The husband did not give details of his income. While awarding Rs 2,500 per month as maintenance to her it was held that once details of properties and business has specifically been mentioned in the petition, it was for the husband to disclose his income which he failed to do.

In *Javed* v. *State of Uttaranchal*,[306] where there was no documentary evidence to prove the monthly income of the husband, it was held that nowadays, an ordinary labourer who works on a daily wage basis, earns about Rs 150 per day. Hence, the court inferred that the husband's earning would be around Rs 4,000 per month. On this basis Rs 1,500 was awarded as maintenance to the wife.

In *Kishan Dutt Verma* v. *Baby Parul*,[307] the husband, a practicing advocate, had a substantial legal practice. In addition, he also worked as an oath commissioner. His total income was assessed to be around Rs 10,000 per month. The court commented that assuming he requires 50 per cent of this amount for himself, it would be appropriate if he pays the balance 50 per cent towards the maintenance of his wife and children. The conduct of the husband during litigation was deplorable. He did not pay the amount which was ordered by the trial court and his defence was struck down. In this context, the high court made the following observations: 'The appellant is least concerned about the orders passed by any court and thinks that he can get away by flouting them with impunity. This is unfortunate, in view of the fact that the appellant is an advocate.'

Another criterion that is often relied upon is the standard of living. While the criterion of an able bodied man would come to the rescue of women of the poorer sections, the standard of living criterion will aid the women from the middle and affluent classes. The courts have held that a divorced or separated woman is entitled to have the same standard of living after divorce or separation, as she enjoyed in her matrimonial home. In *Meenu Chopra* v. *Deepak Chopra*,[308] while awarding Rs 20,000 per month as interim maintenance, the court held that if the husband is wealthy and is leading an opulent life, his wife also has the right to be a partner in his prosperity. To arrive at this figure, the court, *prima facie*, relied upon the averments made by the wife that the husband's income is around Rs 200,000 per month.

While applying the same standard formula, the courts will take into consideration the immovable property, and income from family business and agricultural property jointly owned by the husband and his family as HUF property, type of residential premises or matrimonial home, memberships to exclusive clubs, number of cars (or other vehicles), and types of cars owned individually by the husband or the entire family, payments made through credit cards, and the electrical and electronic gadgets. These would be fairly good indicators of the lifestyle enjoyed by the husband.

Following are some other rules that have been evolved through judge made laws: Income of the husband from the joint family business should be taken into account to determine the status of the husband and for fixing the quantum of maintenance (*Neelam Malholtra* v. *Rajinder*

---

[305] I (2000) DMC 95 Bom
[306] I (2008) DMC 271 Utt
[307] I (2004) DMC 675 Del

[308] AIR 2002 Del 131

Malhotra).[309] If the husband does not disclose the income earned from joint family business (*Dharamichand v. Sobha Devi*)[310] or attempts to conceal his true income (*Jasbir Kaur Sehgal v. District Judge, Dehradun*)[311] adverse inference about the same may be drawn, based on the wife's pleadings. The husband cannot take advantage of heavy deductions from his salary which is voluntary in nature (*Sawinderjit Singh v. Kuldip Kaur*).[312]

In *Harminder Kaur v. Sukhwinder Singh*,[313] the wife pleaded that her husband owned two businesses and his income was not less than Rs 12,000 per month. Commenting that the wife was entitled to have the same standard of living as her husband, the court awarded Rs 4,800 per month to the wife and Rs 2,400 per month to the child.

In *D. N. Niranjan Kani v. N. Rajee*,[314] the wife was living with her parents and she had no separate income of her own. She was also looking after two minor daughters. The financial and social status of the families was not in dispute and the husband was leading a comfortable life. It was held that to maintain herself in the same standard as her husband, the wife would require Rs 10,000 per month. In addition, the two daughters were awarded Rs 5000 per month each, towards their expenses. In *Sushil Kumar Gupta v. Reena Gupta*,[315] the partnership business in which the husband was involved had a turnover of approximately Rs 2 crore. He also owned an agency of luxury coaches and cars from where he generated an income of around Rs 4 to 5 crore. The wife was earning Rs 6,000

through a temporary job. The high court upheld Rs 20,000 per month awarded to her as maintenance by the trial court.

In *Indira Sonti v. Suryanarayana Sonti*,[316] the husband failed to provide proof of his salary, income, and expenditure. The court awarded US$ 400 per month as reasonable maintenance, and held that in the course of the litigation husband had admitted that his annual savings were around US$ 9000. In *Radhika Rungta v. Vineet Rungta*,[317] the husband was well qualified and gainfully employed in the USA. The court arrived at a presumption that his income would be US$ 70,000 per annum. The court held that even if the income is inferred at a lower level of US$ 50,000 the wife would be entitled to 20 per cent of this amount. Converted into Indian currency it would amount to approximately Rs 5,00,000. The wife was earning a nominal income of Rs 5000. It was held that a person from her social status would require Rs 20,000 per month for meeting routine expenditure. Taking into consideration her own income, she was awarded Rs 15,000 per month as maintenance.

In *Mukesh Mittal v. Seema Mittal*,[318] the court arrived at a presumption that the husband was earning Rs 30,000 by way of rent from eight flats. The husband did not produce his tax returns. The court commented that this factor demonstrates that he was not willing to disclose his true income. But on the contrary, he produced the income tax returns of his wife to prove that she had sufficient income. He also pleaded that the wife is not entitled to maintenance as she is HIV positive, thereby, imputing adultery. It was held that the fact that the wife and the minor daughter are HIV positive cannot be used

---

[309] AIR 1994 Del 234
[310] AIR 1987 Raj 159
[311] AIR 1997 SC 3397: II (1997) DMC 338 SC
[312] AIR 2000 P&H 221
[313] II (2002) DMC 114 Del
[314] II (2002) DMC 742 Mad
[315] II (2003) DMC 656 Del

[316] I (2002) DMC 56 Del
[317] AIR 2004 Del 323
[318] I (2006) DMC 23 Del

to deny them maintenance. The wife pleaded that she had contacted the disease through blood transfusion during her pregnancy. She also submitted that the income tax returns, relied upon by her husband, were filed by the husband himself on her behalf and is not a reflection of her own income. The high court upheld the maintenance of Rs 6000 per month to the wife and Rs 4000 per month to the daughter.

In *Sanjay Kapoor* v. *Meenakshi Kapoor*,[319] the husband approached the high court on the ground that the amount awarded as maintenance was excessive. But upholding the order of Rs 10,000 per month awarded to the wife and child together and litigation expenses of Rs 11,000, the Delhi High Court commented that the district judge was right in disbelieving the husband regarding his averments that his earnings are only around Rs 10,000 per month. The court commented that the husband spends Rs 5,500 per month on house rent, he is the owner of a plot of land, he possesses three FDRs, he is the owner of a Maruti Zen car, and he uses a mobile phone.[320] On this basis, his income was assessed at Rs 25,000.

In *Kiran Sejwal* v. *Yesh Dev Singh Sejwal*,[321] the husband was residing in the Netherlands and he initiated divorce proceedings at his place of residence. The wife initiated criminal proceedings under Sections 406 and 498A of IPC against the husband, his parents, and relatives. She also filed a petition for restitution of conjugal rights and claimed interim maintenance. She pleaded that the husband was employed as a manager in a German firm and was drawing more than Rs 1,50,000 per month, and was also running a hotel. His total income was Rs 2,50,000 per month. The husband denied these allegations and also denied that she was his legally wedded wife. He alleged that the woman and her parents had trapped him and his family for greed and sought annulment of marriage. Considering allegations and counter allegations, the background of the families, the status of the parties, the period they had lived together, etc., a sum of Rs 20,000 per month was awarded as interim maintenance to the wife and Rs 10,000 as litigation expenses.

While suppressing income tax returns adverse inference can be drawn, the courts have also held that these are not true indicators of a person's income and cannot be the sole guide for determining the true income.[322] In *Bharat Hegde* v. *Saroj Hegde*,[323] it was held that in case of self-employed persons or persons employed in the unorganized sector, tax compliance is an exception and tax avoidance is a norm, and, therefore, in each case the court has to carefully verify whether the income disclosed is truthful and accurate. In this respect, the following observations were made:

Unfortunately, nobody pays proper taxes to the Government. Self employed persons seldom disclose their true income. Prudence and worldly wisdom gained by a judge, before whom citizens of all strata of society litigate, can always be used by a judge to ascertain as to what is going on in society. By no means can the said knowledge be used where the law requires a fact to be conclusively proved. But where the law requires a judge to form an opinion based on a host of primary data, a judge can formulate an opinion pertaining to the likely income from the capital asset of the husband.

The wife pleaded that her husband was the son of an ex-Chief Minister, an industrialist,

---

[319] I (2004) DMC 618 Del

[320] The order was passed in the days where mobile phones were considered as a status symbol.

[321] I (2007) DMC 64 Del

[322] *Vinod Dulerai Mehta* v. *Kanak Vinod Mehta.* AIR 1990 Bom 120. See also *Mukesh Mittal* v. *Seema Mittal* where husband's income-tax returns were not produced and adverse inference was drawn.

[323] I (2007) DMC 815 Del

and co-owner in various properties. The court commented that keeping in view the capital assets owned/co-owned by the husband, his social status, and place of residence it is difficult to believe that he does not have the requisite means to provide his wife a monthly maintenance of Rs 25,000. The husband was also directed to pay Rs 25,000 as cost of litigation.

In *Gaurav Nagpal* v. *Sumedha Nagpal*,[324] the court upheld the grant of Rs 25,000, which was awarded to the wife as maintenance, on the ground that the amount was not unrealistic or arbitrary. The court commented that there was substantial material to disapprove the income disclosed by husband in his income tax returns. It was noted that the husband had sustainable means and was living a luxurious life. He was residing in a sprawling house while the wife was residing in modest flat along with her parents. The husband was spending around Rs 10,000 per month on his son's education in a private school. He owned substantial immovable properties, but he did not disclose the details of his assets and income from the HUF property of which he was a coparcener.

In the context of appraising the tax return, it was noted that Sections 56 and 57 of the Indian Evidence Act empowers the courts to take judicial note of all matters of public history, literature, science or arts. Hence, while determining the income, courts can take into account the social and economic ills, and unethical malpractices prevailing in society. The high court commented that recognition of facts without formal proof is a matter of expediency. The need and wisdom to recognize and accept facts in public knowledge is unquestionable. Relying on *Bharat Hegde* (cited earlier), it was held that the courts in India are conscious of the fact that there is a tendency among parties not to disclose truly, fully, and completely, their income. The amount awarded should be sufficient to enable the wife to live in somewhat the same degree of comfort as was available to her in her matrimonial home. But it should not be exorbitant and so high that the husband is unable to pay and is exposed to contempt or other coercive proceedings.

S.S. Bindra v. *Tarvinder*[325] has introduced another principle of awarding maintenance which is based on percentage of income. The court ordered that 60 per cent of pay and allowance as maintenance to the wife and children, and the husband was allowed to retain the balance 40 per cent. The court discarded the formula that the wife should be retained at the same standard of life which she enjoyed at the time of her severance as being unfair. This would restrict the prayer for maintenance in a mindless manner to what has been made years earlier. It was noted that orders should be passed keeping the present in perspective, and bring about justice between parties. Most often, the courts do not grant exactly what is prayed for, but award an amount which is much less. By that very yardstick the court is also not precluded to grant more, if circumstances warrant the same. The husband had stated that he was drawing a salary of Rs 29,000 per month. But this statement did not inspire any confidence since according to his own admission he was spending around Rs 45,000 per month on himself. The trial court concluded that he is earning a sum of Rs 1,30,000 per month. In order to enable the wife and children to live in the same status in which the husband was living, the trial court awarded Rs 75,000 per month as maintenance and Rs 1,00,000 towards litigation expenses.

While upholding a woman's right for adequate maintenance, the courts will decline the

[324] I (2008) DMC 166 Del

[325] II (2004) DMC 297 Del

woman's claim to a life of luxury.[326] Gradually, the courts are moving away from the concept of a perennially dependent wife incapable of earning a living and have started taking note of the fact that a large number of women are holding responsible positions in the corporate sector and are capable of earning and maintaining themselves. Hence, the woman's educational qualifications and earning capacity is also kept in view while awarding maintenance.

Date from which Maintenance is to be Awarded

Whether maintenance is to be paid from the date of filing or from the date of the order is an issue which vastly impacts the actual amount which a woman will receive since applications are heard several years after they are filed. The earlier norm was to award maintenance from the date of the order, except in exceptional situations. In such a case, the court would use its discretion and record reasons for deviating from the norm. If the husband is guilty of causing undue harassment to the wife, the courts will grant maintenance from the date of application.

For instance, in *Kamal Kishore* v. *State of UP*,[327] the husband had levelled charges of adultery against his wife without proving the same in the court. The Allahabad High Court commented that reckless charges of a corrupt life against the wife are levelled without any hesitation by husbands. Such a conduct is incomprehensible and this practice needs to be deprecated. If such charges are levelled and not proved, it cannot be said that the court has fixed maintenance allowance from the date of application without giving appropriate reasons. To discourage such practices, the trial court held that if the charge of adultery could not be proved, then maintenance would be fixed from the date of application. Hence, the wife was awarded maintenance of Rs 350 from the date of application.

In *Ram Nandan Sao* v. *State of Bihar*,[328] the wife was awarded Rs 500 as maintenance from the date of order. In appeal, the sessions court directed that the amount be paid from the date of application. The husband filed an appeal in the high court contending that the wife is not entitled to maintenance as she is living in adultery and, further, that the amount of Rs 500 was excessive, and that the order directing payment of the amount from date of application was unjust and against the stipulated provisions of law. The court rejected the contentions of adultery and upheld the lower court's order. However, it held that the sessions court, in revision, had no power to order maintenance from the date of application. The issue of awarding maintenance from the date of application or date of order is left to the discretion of the magistrate.

A contrary view is held in *Nitha Ranjan Chakraborty* v. *Kalpana Chakraborty*,[329] where there was a delay of seven years in deciding the application. The magistrate awarded maintenance from the date of order, but in appeal, the sessions court reversed it and awarded maintenance from the date of application. But the court did not give a detailed reasoning for the same. While upholding the sessions court order, the Calcutta High Court held that while it was necessary for the court adopting such course to give reasons, the omission to give reason is an act of impropriety and does not render the order illegal.

In *Ameen Khan* v. *State of Rajasthan*,[330] where a divorce case remained pending for a period of

---

[326] *The Times of India,* Bombay, 20 February 2009, P. 11.
[327] I (2001) DMC 313 All

[328] II (2001) DMC 507 Pat
[329] 1 II (2003) DMC 142 Cal
[330] II (1999) DMC 536 Raj

nine years and the minor daughter was suffering as a result of this delay, the court directed maintenance to be granted to the wife from the date of application.

Gradually, taking into account the hardships caused to women and children due to inordinate delays in courts, the judicial approach began to change and, in most cases, the courts started awarding maintenance from the date of application. Over time, this has become a norm, and courts began to hold that if maintenance is awarded from the date of order reasons should be recorded for deviating from the norm.

In *S. Jayanthi* v. *S. Jayaraman*,[331] the court held that alimony should be decided at the earliest keeping in mind the needs of the wife and maintenance should be granted from the date of application and not from date of order, except in exceptional cases.

In *Deepa* v. *Nandkishore*,[332] while awarding maintenance from the date of application in a case under Section 125 of Cr.PC, the high court held that since the provision of maintenance has been enacted for the benefit of the destitute wife and children so as to prevent vagrancy, the circumstances did not warrant a departure from the established norm of awarding maintenance from the date of application. The high court also commented that the trial court had not exercised any discretion and that the discretion of the sessions court in the matter was not sound.

In *Popri Bai* v. *Treeth Singh*,[333] a case under HMA, the Rajasthan High Court reversed the interim order of maintenance under Section 24 of the Act, which awarded maintenance from the date of order, and held that there is no justification for not awarding interim maintenance from the date of application. The court commented

that if the order of the trial court was allowed to stand, it will cause serious prejudice to the wife. In *Fani Bhusan Nanda* v. *Kshiti Sundari Nanda*,[334] a case under Section 18 of HAMA, it was held that the order of maintenance was effective from the date of application, unless there was contrary direction of the court that it was to be awarded from the date of order.

More recently, in 2008, in *Shail Kumari Devi* v. *Krishan Bhagwan Pathak @ Kishun B. Pathak*,[335] it was held that maintenance ought to be granted from the date of application and it is not necessary to record special reasons. Similarly, in *Vinod Kumar Jolly* v. *Sunita Jolly*,[336] it was held that the normal rule while awarding maintenance under Section 18 of HAMA is to grant maintenance from the date of filing. No reasons have been given by the trial court as to why direction is given to pay maintenance from the date of order and not from the date of filing of the petition. The court commented that if the normal rule is to be deviated, there has to be special reasons for adopting such a course.

While several judgments have endorsed this position, there are still instances where the courts consider that as a normal rule, maintenance should be ordered from the date of the order and only in special situations it can be ordered from the date of application after recording reasons. For instance, in *A. Jairam* v. *A. Suman*,[337] it was held that interim maintenance can be granted from the date of application only if the same is specifically pleaded. In another recent case, *Gayatri* v. *Om Prakash*,[338] the Rajasthan High Court held that while granting maintenance from the date of application, the Magistrate ought to record reasons for the same,

---

[331] I (1998) DMC 699 Mad
[332] II (2001) DMC 381 Bom
[333] I (2004) DMC 445 Raj

[334] I (2007) DMC 751 Ori
[335] II (2008) DMC 363 SC
[336] I (2008) DMC 371 Del
[337] II (2005) DMC 345 Raj
[338] I (2006) DMC 709 Raj

thereby implying that such an order can be passed only if the facts of the specific case merit it, and if the wife has no other means of income during the pendency of the case. In *Paramveer Singh* v. *Suresh Kanwar*,[339] it was held that if maintenance is granted from date of application and not from the date of order, reasons are to be recorded by court for the same.

As we can observe from the above discussion, the judicial ambiguity regarding this issue continues. Hence, it is prudent to keep this issue in mind at the time of arguments.

Non-Compliance of the Order: Defence to be Struck Down

In the event that the husband refuses to comply with the order of interim maintenance, the court can strike out the husband's defence, when he is the respondent, or by dismissing his petition, when he is the petitioner (*Ghasiram Das* v. *Arundhati Das*).[340] In *Bani* v. *Prakash Singh*, [341]upholding the trial court order of striking down the defence, it was held that there can be no doubt that the defiant conduct of the husband must be dealt with sternly by dismissing his application, or striking out the defence of the defaulter.

In *S. L. Sehgal* v. *State of Delhi*,[342] while quashing the petition filed by the husband, the court commented that the multiple proceedings initiated by the husband amounted to abuse of the process of law. By filing one petition after another, the husband had successfully circumvented the order of the trial court directing him to pay maintenance of Rs 250 per month to his wife. It was held that the husband was taking undue advantage of the situation. The court

commented that any further indulgence to the petitioner would lead to serious miscarriage of justice, and ordered the husband to deposit the arrears of maintenance.

In *Santosh Sehgal* v. *Murari Lal Sehgal*,[343] while quashing the appeal filed by the husband, it was held that the failure to pay maintenance to the wife, as awarded by the court, will disentitle the husband from claiming any relief in matrimonial proceedings. It was further held that the appeal against the divorce decree, granted to the husband, can be allowed without giving any opportunity to the husband to defend himself, in the event of his failing to pay interim maintenance and litigation expenses granted to the wife during pendency of the appeal.

In *Mahadevanaika* v. *Shivakumar*,[344] in a revision petition filed against the order of maintenance, the court granted stay of recovery of 50 per cent of the arrears of maintenance until the disposal of the revision petition, but ordered the husband to deposit the other 50 per cent which was not covered by the stay. But when the husband failed to deposit the said amount, the petition was dismissed by imposing exemplary costs of Rs 5,000. The court commented that the husband used the judicial process only as a ruse to avoid payment of maintenance. The court further commented that the husband, who was economically in a much better position, was taking advantage of his position to harass and deprive the wife and children even of the meagre sustenance that they had secured through the order.

The provision of striking down the defence is available only in civil proceedings and not for proceedings under criminal statutes. The Bombay High Court, in *Vinod* v. *Chhaya*,[345]

[339] II (2008) DMC 276 Raj
[340] AIR 1994 Ori 15
[341] AIR 1996 P&H
[342] DMC I (2000) 524 Del

[343] II (2006) DMC 179 Del
[344] I (2007) DMC 590 Kar
[345] I (2003) DMC 580 Bom

has held that if the husband defaults in payment of maintenance, the only course open to the court is to issue an arrest warrant under the provisions of Section 125(3) of Cr.PC for levying amount due.

Wife's Claim when Husband's Petition is Dismissed

When the petition for divorce filed by the husband is either dismissed or withdrawn, the Interim Application and Counter Claim filed by the wife for maintenance does not survive. Any order of Interim Maintenance passed by the trial court will also lapse. The option open for a wife is to file under Section 125 of Cr.PC. A Hindu wife is also entitled to file for maintenance under Section 18 of HAMA.

Before the Supreme Court ruling in *Chand Dhawan* v. *Jawaharlal Dhawan* (discussed later), there were conflicting views on this issue between various high courts. The Gujarat, Calcutta, and Allahabad High Courts, had held that the expression 'any decree' under Section 25 (provision for permanent alimony and maintenance) of the Hindu Marriage Act, does not include an order of dismissal (*Harilal* v. *Lilavati*; *Minarani* v. *Dasarath*; *Vinod Chandra Sharma* v. *Rajesh Pathak*).[346] But the Bombay High Court, in *Shantaram* v. *Hirabai*[347] and *Modilal Kalaramji Jain* v. *Lakshmi Modilal Jain*[348] had held that the term 'any decree' used in Section 25 of the Act would include an order refusing to grant a matrimonial relief.

This position was overruled by the apex court in *Chand Dhawan* v. *Jawaharlal Dhawan*.[349] The Supreme Court clarified that the claim to permanent alimony under Section 25 of HMA

is based on the principle that there is a disruption of the marital status. Since the court is seized of the matter of deciding the marital status of the parties, it also acquires the power to invoke its ancillary or incidental power to grant permanent maintenance or alimony. The court also retains this power subsequently, to modify its own order when an application is moved by either of the parties, in view of changed circumstances. Thus, the entire exercise is within the gamut of a marriage that has broken down. But if there is no divorce or any other decree, the wife is entitled to live separately, but her claim for maintenance does not lie within the scope of HMA. The wife's claim of maintenance has to be agitated under the Hindu Adoptions and Maintenance Act, 1956. Subsequently, in *Vishnu Mayekar* v. *Laxmi Mayekar*,[350] the Bombay High Court followed this ruling and held that when a petition for divorce is dismissed, maintenance under Section 25 of HMA cannot be granted. The remedy for the wife lies under Section 125 of Cr.PC or under Section18 of HAMA.

Rather ironically, the position upheld by the Supreme Court causes more hurdles in the path of women claiming maintenance and also leads to multiplicity of proceedings. There are instances where the husbands withdraw the petition for divorce filed by them when an order of interim maintenance is passed in favour of their wives, only to defeat the women's claims. Women are then left with no other choice but to initiate fresh proceedings, either under Section 125 of Cr.PC or under Section 18 of HAMA, which causes considerable hardships, monetary burden and delay.

Execution Proceedings

Execution of an order of maintenance is next in priority only to securing a favourable order.

---

[346] *Harilal* v. *Lilavati*, AIR 1961 Guj 202; *Minarani* v. *Dasarath*, AIR 1963 Cal 428; *Vinod Chandra Sharma* v. *Rajesh Pathak*, AIR 1988 All 150.

[347] AIR 1964 Bom 83

[348] AIR 1991 Bom 440

[349] II (1993) DMC 110 SC

[350] II (2000) DMC 727 Bom

Without stringent and viable enforcement machinery, the order obtained through a strenuous ordeal and prolonged litigation will remain as a paper decree without any relevance or significance to women's lives.

When the person against whom a maintenance order has been obtained defaults in payment or does not comply with the order, the claimant will have to initiate yet another legal proceeding to execute the decree or enforce the order. At this stage, the court battle starts all over again, to the utter dismay of women (or children, or parents, as the case may be). The procedures for enforcing a civil and a criminal order of maintenance are not identical. There is a slight variation between the two. The orders obtained, under the HMA and HAMA, are orders of a civil nature, while the order under Section 125 of Cr.PC is of a criminal nature.

In civil proceedings, the order of maintenance can be executed by attaching the salary, or attachment and sale of moveable or immovable property. The order under Section 125 Cr.PC can be enforced by an arrest warrant and imprisonment. The attachment of salary becomes the most feasible and certain way of ensuring payment of arrears of maintenance for the salaried class. Maintenance can also be a charge on property. But the courts have held that a decree restraining the defendant from alienating the property is not valid (*P.M. Devassia* v. *Ancy*).[351]

In *Rukhsana Kachwala* v. *Saifuddin Kachwala*,[352] the husband agreed to pay a sum of Rs 2,00,000 as divorce settlement, but defaulted in payment. In order to ensure execution of the decree, the court held the plaintiff as decree holders and held that she was entitled for the appointment of a receiver and the sale of the husband's shop. In *Bina Majumder* v. *Ranjit Majumder*,[353] the subsistence of divorce proceedings instituted by the husband, who was a Class IV Government employee, was stayed for non-compliance of the order of interim maintenance and costs of litigation. In execution, the court ordered salary attachment. In *Rajendra Prasad Paul @ Rajendra Pal* v. *State of Jharkhand*,[354] the court issued directions to deduct the arrears of maintenance from the husband's G.P.F. (General Provident Fund) account and deposit the same in the name of the wife and child.

In *Abdus Sovan* v. *Rokia Bibi*,[355] it was held that the mere filing of an application for setting aside an ex parte order of maintenance cannot be used as a ground to grant the stay on execution proceeding.

In *Mani* v. *Jaykumari*,[356] the Madras High Court has held that future salary can be attached. The husband had challenged the order of attachment on the ground that future salary cannot be attached. But the high court held that under both the Civil Procedure Code as well as the Criminal Procedure Code, the courts have the power to attach future salary. The court cryptically commented that the law cannot expect a destitute woman to approach the court each month for execution of the monthly maintenance which is due to her.

The liability of the husband to comply with the maintenance order does not cease upon the death of the husband. It can be executed against the legal heirs. The Supreme Court in a leading case, *Aruna Basu Mullick* v. *Dorothea Mitra*,[357] held that the assets left behind by the husband are liable to be proceeded against in the hands

---

[351] II (2007) DMC 677 Ker
[352] II (2002) DMC 712 Bom
[353] II (2006) DMC 637 Gau
[354] I (2004) DMC 344 Jha
[355] I (2006) DMC 181 Cal
[356] II (1998) DMC 533 Mad
[357] AIR 1983 SC 916

of his legal heirs for satisfaction of the decree for maintenance.

In *Nagamma* v. *Ningamma*,[358] it was held that there is no rationality in the contention that a decree for maintenance or alimony gets extinguished with the death of the husband when any other decree, even though not charged on the husband's property, does not get so extinguished. It is one of the settled principles of interpretation that the court should lean in favour of sustaining a decree and should not permit the benefit under the decree to be lost, unless there are special reasons for it. If the husband has left behind an estate at the time of his death, there can be no justification for the view that the decree is wiped out and the heirs would succeed to the property without the liability of satisfying the decree. The decree indicates that maintenance was payable during the life time of the widow. To make such a decree contingent upon the life of the husband is contrary to the terms and the spirit of the decree.

In *Pavitra* v. *Arun Varma (Decd.) Through L.Rs*,[359] the court commented that the tendency of closing proceedings abruptly, without due application of judicial mind, needs to be abandoned and sincere efforts need to be made for invoking the relevant legal provisions in aid of the poor litigants who are approaching the courts for enforcements of their rights.

In case the order cannot be executed by way of salary or property attachment, it is also possible to obtain an order of imprisonment. The only snag in pressing for civil imprisonment is that the claimant is expected to pay for the cost of this imprisonment. This stipulation renders the remedy, to enforce the maintenance orders passed by the court, out of reach of poor women who are already burdened with complicated litigation to enforce the orders. This is a travesty of justice. In this context, the remedy under Section 125 of Cr.PC appears to be more feasible, especially after the ceiling has been removed since the imprisonment under this provision is governed by criminal law and hence the applicant is not under the burden of bearing the cost of imprisonment. It becomes the responsibility of the state to bear this expense.

But apart from execution proceedings provided for under Section 18 of HAMA the petition can also approach the court in contempt proceedings. In *Amita Devnani* v. *Bhagwan Devnani*,[360] the Bombay High Court held that non-payment of maintenance amounts awarded under Section 18 of HAMA amounts to Contempt of Court and hence the power of the court for exercising the alternate remedy of imprisonment under the Contempts of Court Act to recover the amount is not ousted. The high court commented: 'The conduct of the husband is so reprehensible that the same deserves imposition of maximum punishment provided by law. There was no reason for the husband to drag the proceedings for so long without offering even a single rupee till now. The attitude of the husband was that he shall not pay any amount to the petititioner even if it is in utter disregard of the order of the court.' But while imposing the sentence, the court expressed some leniency and varied the order for 60 days, with directions to the husband to clear the arrears within the stipulated period, failing which the order of civil imprisonment of six months would become operational.

The power of the criminal court to arrest in execution proceedings acts as a deterrent

---

[358] II (1999) DMC 681 Kar
[359] II (2001) DMC 260 MP

[360] II (2007) DMC 119 Bom

against non-payment of maintenance. But the power is curtailed by the stipulation under 125(3) of Cr.PC which lays down that a magistrate can order imprisonment of only one month. In *Shahada Khatoon v. Amjad Ali*,[361] the Supreme Court held that the language of Section 125(3) is quite clear and it circumscribes the power of the magistrate to impose imprisonment for a term which may extend to one month or until the payment, if sooner made. But for a further breach of the order, the claimant can approach the Magistrate again for a similar relief. This ruling was followed by various high courts—the Punjab and Haryana High Court in *Angrej Singh* v. *State of Punjab*,[362] the Andhra Pradesh High Court in *Abdul Gafaoor* v. *Hameema Khatoon*,[363] and the Madras High Court in *Mahboob Basha* v. *Nannima*.[364]

The Kerala High Court, in *Alora Sundaran v. Mammali Sumathi*,[365] has given a different interpretation to the provision as well as to the Supreme Court ruling in *Shahada Khatoon* (discussed above). R. Basant J. of the Kerala High Court commented:

The statutory provisions under Section 125(3) of Cr.PC make it very clear that one month's imprisonment is the maximum imprisonment for each month's default at each time. This must lead to the inevitable and unmistakable conclusion that each month's default would be visited with the maximum sentence of one month's imprisonment. The mere fact that the destitute has not chosen to complain every month and has chosen to complain of the breach in respect of plurality of months in one petition within a period of twelve months, cannot at all deliver to the defaulter any undeserved advantage. On the face of it, the contention appears to me to be illogical, irrational, and unreasonable. It is obviously

unacceptable and unsustainable. The policy of law cannot be to compel such claimants to come to court with separate petitions for each month's default. That would be totally an unreasonable manner of approaching the question.

The Supreme Court was obviously not considering the question whether more than one month's imprisonment can be awarded for breach of the direction to pay maintenance committed in respect of more months than one. I cannot accept the suggestion only because many Family Courts/Magistrate's Courts have chosen to follow this interpretation. It would be myopic and puerile to hold that the Supreme Court said so. This position goes against the policy of law and specific stipulations. Precedents cannot be read or understood ignoring the specific language of the statutory provisions. The interpretations which the Petitioner's (husband's) counsel wants to place on *Shahah Khatoon* is unacceptable for the reason that the same suffers from that specific vice.

The court gave the following formula regarding imprisonment:

If there is no payment of maintenance due for 'n' number of months, the defaulter in one Execution Petition can be sentenced to imprisonment up to a maximum of 'n' months, provided 'n' does not exceed twelve.

If there is a breach of payment of maintenance due for one particular month – not withstanding the fact that such payment was not made for 'n' months from the date on which it became due, the defaulter can be sentenced only to a maximum imprisonment for one month and not 'n' months. Even when the breach in respect of one particular month continues for any length of time, the maximum sentence for breach of the liability to pay one month's maintenance continues to be one month only.

Under Section 125(3) of Cr.PC, if the husband defaults in payment of maintenance, application for issuing warrant for recovery must be filed within one year from the date on which the amount became due. Recovery applications for more than twelve months cannot be filed and the amount would lapse if the applications have not been filed within the prescribed time frame.

---

[361] I (2000) DMC 313 SC
[362] I (2000) DMC 156 P&H
[363] I (2004) DMC 693 AP
[364] I (2006) DMC 106 Mad
[365] I (2007) DMC 136 Ker

However, if the application has been filed within this time frame and was pending in court, then the amount would not lapse. The applicant can also file interim application for mentioning the amounts which have subsequently become due while the original application was pending in court. The Supreme Court in *Shantha @ Ushadevi* v. *Shivnanjappa*,[366] has held that such subsequent applications are only supplementary or incidental to the application already filed within the period of limitation. The Allahabad High Court followed this ruling in *Dilshad Haji Risal* v. *State of UP*,[367] and held that arrears of 41 months, which had become due, are not barred by limitation as the first application was still pending in court.

In *Diksha Rani* v. *Deep Chand*,[368] despite the imprisonment the husband did not comply with the order. The husband tried to evade service and did not appear in court during subsequent proceedings. But when the wife could not be present, the revision court dismissed her application for default. While quashing this order, in an appeal filed by the wife, the high court of Punjab and Haryana commented: The husband, though aware of the present proceedings pending against him, was deliberately not appearing before the court. The husband is violating the orders of the court. If this approach is allowed, it would effect the administration of justice. The revision filed by the wife was dismissed in default for non-prosecution as she could not appear when the case was called out. This has resulted in injustice to the wife and child and cannot be justified. The technicalities cannot be allowed to stand in the way of administration of justice. The revision court was bound to consider that this was a case where a wife and a young child are fighting for their survival. The lower court was directed to secure the presence of the husband, in a manner considered appropriate, including taking him into custody to ensure that he would comply with the directions passed by the high court.

In *Padmo* v. *Surat Ram*,[369] it was held that the power to execute the order of maintenance lies with the judicial magistrate. The gram panchayat does not have the power to issue warrants for default in payment of maintenance dues.

Though, the law provides for imprisonment as a deterrent against default in payment, there are cases where a husband may choose the option of imprisonment rather than paying maintenance to his wife and children. Seeing through such manipulations, the Gujarat High Court in *Bhavanaben Shamhjuvhai* v. *Dinesh Premjibhai Kapadia*,[370] has held that even when the husband has undergone imprisonment, the amount which is due does not become irrecoverable. Warrant for attachment of properties for accumulated arrears of maintenance can be issued. Similarly, in *Rayinkutty* v. *State of Kerala*,[371] it was held that for non compliance of the order for payment of a reasonable and fair settlement to a Muslim wife, the husband can be imprisoned. But this will not absolve him of the liability of paying the amount which is due.

Before concluding this section, I feel constrained to elaborately profile three cases which are briefly mentioned above, to highlight the ordeal that women have to endure while enforcing their legal right of pittance of maintenance amounts. The detailed history provides the timeframe of the winding court battle, but the law reporters do not provide an insight into

---

[366] II (2005) DMC 1 SC
[367] I (2006) DMC 461 All
[368] II (2007) DMC 779 P&H

[369] I (2003) DMC 483 HP
[370] II (2005) DMC 315 Guj
[371] II (2008) DMC 575 Ker

the costs incurred in this winding legal battle. That is left to the imagination of the reader.

In the *Shantha @ Ushadevi v. B.G. Shivananjappa*[372] case, the wife filed for maintenance for herself and her daughter in 1991 and by an order dated 20 January 1993, the trial court awarded Rs 500 per month to her and Rs 300 per month to her daughter. When the husband defaulted, the wife filed execution proceedings under Section 125(3) of Cr.PC for arrears of Rs 5,363 from the date of the order to 31 August 1993. The husband filed criminal revision application before the Sessions Judge, Tumkur, against the order passed by the trial court, which was dismissed on 26 June 1997. The appeal filed by the husband against this order in the Karnataka High Court was also dismissed. Thereafter, the wife filed an Interim Application for arrears of maintenance from 20 January 1993, that is, the date of the trial court's order till the date of filing the Interim Application, that is, 16 June 1998, for the sum of Rs 46,000.

The husband deposited a sum of Rs 5,365 towards the maintenance from 20 January 1993 till 31 August 1993. But he objected to the wife claiming Rs 46,000 on the basis that arrears beyond the period of one year cannot be claimed due to the stipulation under the first proviso to Section125(3) of Cr. PC. Upholding this contention, the trial court dismissed the Interim Application filed by the wife on 13 July 2000 on the ground that it is barred by limitation. The wife challenged this order before the Sessions Judge, Tumkur. The criminal revision petition was allowed by the Sessions Judge by an order dated 23 November 2002, and the matter was remanded back to the trial court.

The Sessions Judge observed that since the first Interim Application was within limitation, there was no need of filing a fresh petition during the pendency of the application under Section 125(3) of Cr.PC for maintenance which had fallen due for the period post this application. It is implicit in the powers of the court to make an order directing the husband to make payment of arrears of maintenance up to the date of the decision while disposing of the first Interim Application for recovery of arrears of maintenance. The Sessions Judge commented that it is not required to file a fresh application which may lead to multiplicity of litigations.

The husband challenged this order in 2003 before the Karnataka High Court. On 11 March 2004, the high court allowed the criminal revision and set aside the order of the Sessions Judge and held that the application for claiming arrears of Rs 46,000 was barred by limitation. Aggrieved by this order, the wife approached the Supreme Court by way of a Special Leave Petition which was decided on 6 May 2005, in her favour. The court held that such subsequent applications are only supplementary or incidental to the application already filed within the period of limitation. By then 14 years had elapsed since the woman concerned had first approached the court for maintenance.

In *Dilshad Haji Risal v. State of UP*[373] the wife Smt Hazara Begum had approached the magistrate's court for maintenance for herself and her two children under Section 125 of Cr.PC on 20 May 1999. Through an *ex parte* order dated 27 July 2000, maintenance of Rs 1,500 per month for three persons was awarded from the date of the application. The husband did not comply with the order and the wife filed execution proceedings on 28 August 2000 for recovery and a warrant was issued against the husband for Rs 22,500 for the period 20 May 1999 to 20 August 2000. Since the husband did not comply with the directions of the court, the

---

husband was imprisoned for one month. Thereafter, the wife filed another application on 13 February 2004 for execution of Rs 61,500, being the amount payable to her for 41 months, for the period between 21 August 2000 to 20 January 2004. The husband filed an objection to this application on 21 July 2004 contending that the claim for Rs 61,500 was time barred as the application was filed after one year of its becoming due. Also, since he was imprisoned for the amount which was due earlier, this matter could not be re-agitated. He also submitted that he was willing to reconcile with his wife and maintain his wife and children. Overriding his objections, the Magistrate directed that a recovery warrant be issued against the husband for the maintenance amount due for the period of fifteen months from 20 May 1999 to 20 August 2000 for Rs 22,500. The husband approached the Allahabad High Court for quashing this order under Section 482 of Cr.PC.

By its order dated 12 September 2005, the high court allowed the appeal and remanded the matter back to the Magistrate's court to consider the offer made by the husband to take back the wife and maintain her and, if necessary, uphold the wife's right to refuse such offer when there is just ground for doing so. If the wife gives adequate reasons for refusing to live with her husband, she would not be deprived of her right to maintenance. The court also commented that awarding a sentence of imprisonment is no substitute for the recovery of the amount of monthly allowance which is due to the wife. The court also held that the application for arrears of 41 months was not barred by limitation when the first application was still pending.

In *Padmo's case*,[374] the wife had approached the Court of Additional Chief Judicial Magistrate, Theog, on 7 May 1996 for maintenance for

herself and her three minor children. On 5 June 1996, the Magistrate referred the matter to the gram panchayat, Basa, Tehsil Theog, District Shimla. The gram panchayat, on 6 June 1997, awarded Rs 300 per month each to the wife and the eldest child, and Rs 200 per month each for the younger two children, a total of Rs 1,000 per month

Since the husband did not comply with this order, the wife filed for execution of the order and for payment of arrears of Rs 3,400 for the period 7 May 1996 to 7 September 1996. The gram panchayat issued notice to the husband to deposit the arrears of maintenance within ten days, failing which the matter would be transferred to the court of the Judicial Magistrate. Since the husband did not appear before the gram panchayat, the application was forwarded to the Judicial Magistrate, Theog, for execution.

The husband did not file his reply. Thereafter, the matter was referred to the Lok Adalat on 18 July 1998, with the hope of some amicable settlement. But since the matter did not get resolved, on 3 March 1999, the Sub-Judge took up the matter. After hearing both the parties on 10 May 1999, he sent the matter back to the gram panchayat for execution. He commented that there was no provision in law for the Gram Panchayat to send the file to his court for execution. The gram panchayat did not take any further action in the matter.

So the wife again filed an application under Section 125 Cr.PC in the court of the Additional Chief Judicial Magistrate, Theog, on 9 April 1999 on the ground that since the earlier order passed by the panchayat could not be executed, a fresh order of maintenance may be passed. The husband opposed this application on the ground that since the earlier order existed, a fresh order could not be passed. After recording evidence of the parties, on 17 July 2001, the Additional Chief Judicial Magistrate upheld the husband's

---

[374] *Padmo* v. *Surat Ram*, I (2003) DMC 483 HP.

contention and held that the fresh application was not maintainable as the previous order passed by the panchayat still existed and the petitioners have not assailed the same. The wife challenged this order in the high court.

On 12 April 2002, the high court passed the following order: If after issuance of notice by the gram panchayat, the defaulter does not come forward to pay the amount, it is difficult for the gram panchayat to execute the order of mainte-nance, and the only course left for it is to forward the order of maintenance for execution to the judicial magistrate in whose jurisdiction it is situated. The gram panchayat had rightly for-warded its order of maintenance for execution to the Additional Chief Judicial Magistrate, Theog. While he took cognizance of it in his capacity as Sub-Judge, he wrongly passed the order that the gram panchayat had no powers to forward the order of maintenance passed by it for execution to his court. Even while passing the second order dated 17 July 2001, dismissing the second petition, the Additional Chief Judicial Magistrate, has not cared to examine the provisions of law, with the result that the petitioners even after obtaining the order of maintenance in their favour, as far back as on 6 June 1997, could not get a penny as mainte-nance from the husband and the very purpose of the provision of Section 125 of Cr.PC is defeated. In this view of the matter, the orders dated 10 May 1999 and 17 July 2001 are set aside, and the Additional Chief Judicial Magistrate, Theog, is directed to execute the order dated 6 June 1997, passed by the gram panchayat in accordance with law and the observations made hereinabove. Since the matter is pending for more than four years, the said court is directed to expedite the matter and provide justice and succour to the hapless wife and children, left in the lurch by the husband to fend for themselves.

The high court also directed that a copy of the judgment should be placed before the Honourable Chief Justice for considering the desirability of circulating a copy of this order to all the Judicial Magistrates in the state to avoid such lapses from occurring in future.

At the end of this ordeal, it is left for our imagination to guess whether any of the three women whose ordeal is recorded here were able to secure the amounts which were ordered as maintenance for their bear survival.

Modification of Orders

Maintenance orders are not orders of a final nature. If subsequent circumstances so warrant, either of the parties can approach the courts for modification of the order. In *Sharda Devi* v. *State of Bihar*,[375] it was held that Section 127 of Cr.PC confers a statutory right to claim enhancement of the original amount awarded under Section 125 Cr.PC subject to the person concerned satisfying the court of the change in circumstances from when the original order was passed.

Increase in expenditure towards the chil-dren's education, woman's own loss of job or inability to earn, the demise of her parents who were providing financial support to her, a sub-stantial increase in the husband's income, etc., are factors which the court will consider while order-ing enhancement of the maintenance amount that has been awarded to the wife. The court will also bear in mind the inflation and the cost of living index and decrease in the value of rupee, so that there may not be such a situation that while the maintenance and litigation expenses remain static, inflation may erode its money value (*Lata* v. *Civil Judge, Bulandshar*).[376]

[375] II (2006) DMC 270 Pat
[376] AIR 1993 All 133

The wife securing permanent employment or increase in her earnings, wife's remarriage or living in adultery, the son attaining majority, the marriage of the daughter, loss of job or significant lowering of his own income, his retirement, illness or old age are circumstances which would entitle a husband to approach the court for a reduction in the amount of maintenance ordered, or even for cancellation of the order. Husband's remarriage is not a condition which would warrant cancellation of the order of maintenance awarded to the earlier wife. But the increase in the number of dependents may be a factor that the courts may consider while hearing the application for modification of the order.

If lump sum amounts are awarded to the wife as divorce settlement, the same cannot be rescinded if the divorced woman subsequently remarries (*Nanigopal Chakravorty* v. *Ranubala Chakravorty*).[377] Similarly, in *Rohtash Singh* v. *Ramendri*,[378] and *Sanjeev Kumar* v. *Dhanya*,[379] the courts have explained that a maintenance order cannot be rescinded on the ground of post-divorce adultery.[380]

In *Rajashree R. Dixit* v. *Rajesh Nagesh Dixit*,[381] alteration of maintenance amount on the basis of change in employment of husband was held to be maintainable. In *Bibhuti Bhushan Pandey* v. *State of Jharkhand*,[382] the family court had enhanced the maintenance awarded to the wife and daughter from Rs 800 per month to Rs 2,000 per month, based on the wife's contention that the husband is earning Rs 12,000 per month as a teacher. The husband's contention

was that the enhanced amount was on the higher side as he is earning only Rs 8,301 and he has to maintain his parents and three children from his first wife. The Jharkhand High Court held that the submission is without substance. On account of inflation in expenditure, the wife and daughter are entitled to the enhanced maintenance as ordered by the family court. In *Narayan Das* v. *Gita Rani Das*,[383] while enhancing the maintenance awarded to the wife, the court held that rise in cost of living, increases in earning of husband, etc., are circumstances which would warrant an increase in the maintenance amount awarded under provisions of Section 127 of Cr.PC.

In *Lalita Rani* v. *Jagdish Lal*,[384] the wife challenged the order which awarded Rs 3,500 per month as maintenance to her and her two children. The daughter, though a major, was still dependent as she was studying in college. The son was in tenth Standard. The wife contended that her husband was working in the public sector and his income had doubled from Rs 10,000 per month to Rs 22,000. She pleaded that the sum awarded is inadequate to meet the needs of maintenance and educational expenses of her children. The high court enhanced the amount to Rs 10,000 and held that reasonable expenses for sustenance and for the care, maintenance, and education of children living with her, constitute important factors which the courts cannot ignore, while the husband's expenditure had decreased and his earnings had increased. On the other hand the wife had to spend more for maintenance and care of her children. Prices of all essential commodities had doubled in the last seven years since filing of her petition. The trial court attached overwhelming importance to what, perhaps, at best could be

[377] AIR 1993 All 133
[378] AIR 1965 Ori 154
[379] II (2008) DMC 19 Ker
[380] See the discussion on post divorce adultery in section titled 'Matrimonial Misconduct and Right of Maintenance' earlier.
[381] AIR 2005 Bom 352
[382] II (2006) DMC 120 Jha

[383] II (2006) DMC 629 Cal
[384] II (2006) DMC 310 Del

one factor, that is, residence of the wife in disputed premises claimed by husband's mother. This factor could not have clouded the court's approach in appreciating facts in the proper perceptive. The court cannot ignore the obligation of husband to maintain his wife and children.

In *Vinod Kumar Rai* v. *Manju Rai*,[385] the daughter was around 16–17 years of age. The court commented that provisions would have to be made for her marriage in addition to the cost of education and living expenses. The high court held that the amount awarded by the trial court that is, Rs 500 for the daughter and Rs 1,500 for the wife was meagre and increased the amount to Rs 2,500 each, for the wife and daughter. The court also directed the husband to bear the expenses of marriage of his daughter when the time came. The court commented that the unjustified and baseless accusations of infidelity hurled at the wife constitute cruelty which would justify the wife's demand to live separately and receive maintenance.

In *Prem Prakash* v. *Nirmal*,[386] the Delhi High Court held that the plea of the husband to modify the maintenance order on the ground of change of circumstances was rightly rejected by the trial court. An order of maintenance of Rs 5,000 was subsisting for fifteen years. The husband had made several unsuccessful attempts to have the order varied, including approaching the Supreme Court. The husband contended that the wife had remarried and the daughter did not bear his name. There was also discrepancy in the date of birth of the daughter. The high court held that the husband's conduct was calumnious, in constantly questioning parentage and legitimacy of child, and such conduct can hardly be appreciated. The High Court commented that the trial court rightly agreed

with the contention of the wife that the child's father was shown as the maternal grandfather since there was a threat of constant harassment by the husband. This possibility cannot be ruled out, having regard to the history of the case. The issue of a wrong date of birth was unnecessarily highlighted by the husband and the trial court had rightly held it to be a mistake. As regards change of appellants' finances, the trial court was rightly sceptical about his claim since he had not disclosed his assets or produced any documentary evidence whatsoever.

In *Sirivella Rao* v. *Sirivella Gnanamani*,[387] the income of the husband, working in a petrol pump, was Rs 2,400 per month. The husband had to look after his aged parents and himself. Maintenance granted by trial court was reduced to Rs 400 per month each, to wife and children from Rs 1,500, as granted by the trial court. In *Satish Kumar Singh* v. *State of Bihar*,[388] the wife and four minor children were living separately and the husband was not maintaining them. The husband submitted that he was ready to accept the wife and the children and maintain them but the wife was not willing to live with the husband. His only source of income was from giving private tuitions. In view of this, the amount of maintenance was reduced from Rs 1,400 per month to Rs 1,000 per month, Rs 300 for the wife and Rs 175 per month for each child.

Remarriage of the divorced wife is a factor to be considered for varying the maintenance order. In *Tapash Kumar Paul* v. *Soma Paul*,[389] it was held that there was no proof that the wife was living in adultery with another person, which disqualified her from getting maintenance. The wife was driven out of the matrimonial house and the husband had neglected to maintain her. But

---

[385] II (2006) DMC 642 All
[386] II (2006) DMC 823 Del

[387] I (2007) DMC 82 AP
[388] I (2007) DMC 791 Pat
[389] II (2007) DMC 541 Cal

based on the husband's earning, the court reduced the amount of maintenance from Rs 1,000 per month to Rs 500 per month. It was held that the wife is entitled to receive this amount as maintenance till the date of her remarriage. The court further commented that Section 127 nowhere lays down that it was the duty of the wife, after her re-marriage, to approach the court to alter or cancel the order of maintenance. The aggrieved person, against whom the order of maintenance is passed, should move the court for alteration, modification, or cancellation of the maintenance order due to change of circumstances. There was no question of refund of Rs 14,000, approximately, obtained by wife as maintenance from petitioner with interest. The wife was expected to live happily with her present husband without any disturbance and the husband ought not to claim the balance amount. In *Gomti v. Ramanand*,[390] the same point was reiterated and the court held that the divorced woman is entitled to maintenance until her remarriage and the burden lies on the husband to prove that the wife has re-married.

Section C

RIGHT TO MATRIMONIAL HOME AND PROPERTY

Two distinct rights which are implicit in the marriage contract are the right to reside in the matrimonial home and the right to a financial settlement at the termination of marriage are examined here. While maintenance is also an economic right, it is a conditional right contingent upon a person's need or ability to sustain oneself. A person capable of supporting oneself is not entitled to maintenance. In this context, the right to reside in the matrimonial home and a right to financial settlement, or division of assets

[390] II (2007) DMC 399 All

at the termination of marriage, are crucial economic rights. While maintenance can be viewed as a sustenance 'dole' for basic survival, which the prevailing social conditions necessitate, matrimonial home and property can be construed as 'rights' which would economically empower a woman and redeem her from the situation of perpetual dependency.

During the later half of the last century when divorce laws became more lax, most countries enacted laws which would economically empower women at the time of divorce. But this issue seems to have escaped the attention of legislators and law reformers in our country during the corresponding period.

The right of residence in the matrimonial home is a crucial right of survival for most married women and is implicit within the contract of marriage. But, since this right was not statutorily protected, a husband could, at his whim, drive the wife out of the domestic residence. Devoid of statutory protection, the right hinged upon astute lawyering, sympathetic and sensitive judges, and stray innovative judicial pronouncements. Women's groups in India had been campaigning for several decades for a specific law which would protect this right. Finally, under the Protection of Women from Domestic Violence Act, 2005 (PWDVA), this right was awarded statutory recognition under the notion of a shared household.

However, the right under the PWDVA is of a limited nature and does not give the woman title or interest in the property. It also does not protect the woman against third parties (for instance, the landlord). It is also difficult to enforce after divorce since divorce severs the marital bond.

Lowe and Douglas (1998: 134) explain that there are two interrelated issues within the notion of the matrimonial home, ownership and occupation. The first is in whom are the legal and beneficial interests in the property vested and, the second, what rights of occupation does each party have in the home, irrespective of ownership. While PWDVA addressed the second concern, the first had remained dormant during the campaign.

In order to expand the scope of economic rights upon divorce, there is a need to evolve the concept of matrimonial property. Since marriage is not viewed as an 'economic partnership', on marriage a woman does not acquire any rights in her husband's property and, hence, she is not entitled to claim division of assets at the time of divorce. The only relevant factors for determining property claims are title and financial contributions. Hence, the property acquired by the husband is treated as his exclusive property. Our matrimonial statutes do not award any recognition to a woman's non-monetary contribution to the domestic household during the subsistence of the marriage. The contribution of the wife in creating family assets, through her unpaid labour by performing her domestic duties, is not considered a relevant factor for determination of her share in these assets.

In this respect, India lags far behind most other countries which award recognition of a woman's contribution to creating family assets and, hence, have evolved detailed guidelines for determining a woman's share in the matrimonial property. Since this is an emerging aspect of family law, it is included here for conceptual clarity and legislative interventions.

RIGHT TO MATRIMONIAL HOME

Concept of Matrimonial Home Under English Law

Since our legal maxims are derived from English common law and Anglo-Saxon jurisprudence, it would be relevant to have an overview of the development of these rights under the English law as it provides some important markers.

The English women had to carry out long and sustained campaigns for their right to own property, for a share in the matrimonial property, and for the right of residence in the matrimonial home. As discussed earlier, until the mid-nineteenth century, married women in England did not have a right to divorce and they had no right to own property. According to the Blackstonian principles then prevailing in England, after marriage, the woman lost her right over her own property. Marriage virtually meant a legal death for the woman. The husband became the custodian of her person and her property, and he could deal with it as per his own whims and fancies.[391]

During the mid-nineteenth century, through the enactment of the Matrimonial Causes Act of 1857, English women were awarded a limited right of divorce under certain stringent conditions.[392] But this enactment did not determine women's right to separate property even after divorce. So during the later decades, along with the suffragette movement which demanded the right to vote for women, they also raised the demand for legal recognition of their right to own property. As a response to this campaign, the first enactment was passed in 1872 which was titled the Married Women's Property Rights Act, which awarded rights over their separate property for women who were divorced or legally separated. This was a limited right over their separate property acquired after divorce/separation and did not alter the situation of women while the marriage was subsisting. This was followed by another

[391] See section titled 'Material Basis for the Notion of Sacramental Indissolubility' of Chapter 1 *Marriage and Its Dissolution.*

[392] See section titled 'The Journey from Sacrament to Compract' of Chapter 1 *Marriage and Its Dissolution.*

legislation with a similar title, the Married Women's Property Rights Act, 1882, which slightly improved the position of married women. But from then onwards, a series of legislations were enacted which further strengthened the married women's right to property. Finally, in 1935, the difference between a married and an unmarried woman was abolished and married women became full owners of their own individual property, even during the subsistence of their marriage. Through this enactment, the Blackstonian principle that women are the property of their husbands and they are not entitled to hold property in their name during the subsistence of their marriage, was finally laid to rest.[393]

Just when one set of problems were resolved, women were confronted with another. These were difficult years of recession and war. A large number of women had to forsake their traditional role as housewives or non-earning members of their households and enter the organized labour force. This enabled them to earn a separate income during their marriage. They were no longer the dependent wives, but were earning members of their families and, in this capacity, contributed to the family income. But, since the matrimonial home was owned by the husband, he could dispossess her. She had no remedy against such dispossession. After the war, the social and economic climate changed. Property ownership increased, with purchases being made with the aid of mortgages. Property prices escalated and divorce rates spiraled. The combination of these factors resulted in a great deal of litigation around the primary asset, the family home. This brought into focus the injustice caused to women through the application of strict rules of property ownership and the

doctrine of separation of ownership, as between the spouses. Traditionally, the claim depended upon which spouse had paid the mortgage bills, since only payment towards the purchase of the property would determine ownership.

But Lord Denning, a legend in his own time and a champion of women's rights, pointed out that it may be purely a matter of convenience as to which spouse pays off the mortgage and which one pays the other household expenses (Lowe and Douglas 1998: 135). The credit for evolving a revolutionary concept of the deserted wife's equity must be attributed to him. He firmly believed that it was his duty to dispense justice rather than merely adhere to legal technicalities. In November 1947, barely three years after he was appointed as a High Court Judge, while he was sitting as Kings Bench judge, he delivered the first historic judgment in a case titled *H* v. *H*.[394] As was the established pattern, the matrimonial home was in the name of the husband. He had lived there with his wife and an invalid son. During the war, the husband left his wife and went to live with another woman. The wife obtained a maintenance order against her husband on the basis that she would go on living in the matrimonial home along with the son. The husband approached the wife for a divorce with the following conditions: 'I'll give you the house, if you will give me my freedom.' The wife declined and the husband initiated proceedings for possession of the house.

The house belonged to the husband and the wife did not even have the status of a tenant. Hence, she had no legal remedy against dispossession by her husband. Invoking Section 17 of the Married Women's Property Act, 1882 (MWPA), which stipulated that 'in case of any dispute between a husband and wife as to the title or possession of property, the judge might

---

[393] Law Reform (Married Women and Tortfeasors) Act, 1935 (c. 30).

[394] (1947) 63 TLR 645 (as cited in Heward 2003: 49)

make such order as he thinks fit,' he protected the woman's right of residence as against the husband's title to the property. This was a historical ruling which turned the tide in favour of women and became a legal precedent (Heward 2003: 49–50).

While the right of residence was getting established, at least against the husband, a newer situation arose which brought in further complexities. Between husband and wife, the 1882 Act worked well, but difficulties arose when the interests of third parties were affected. If the husband went bankrupt, his creditors could dispossess the wife from the matrimonial home. The wife had no protection against the creditors. After the war, it had been established that where the husband owned the matrimonial home and was living there with his wife, he could not turn her out. Lord Denning held that a deserter husband could not be placed in a better position than if they were living together by taking advantage of his own wrong, that is, desertion. The husband's duty was to provide the wife with a roof over her head, and by providing a matrimonial home he gives her the authority to be there. In law, a deserted wife has an irrevocable authority to remain in the matrimonial home. This authority is revocable only by a court.

In *Bendall* v. *McWhirter*, the husband was the owner of the house, where he lived with his wife and children. He deserted the wife but before he left, he assured her that she could have the house and furniture. Later, he went bankrupt and his trustees in bankruptcy proceeded to sell the house and divide the proceeds among the creditors. To get the best price they wanted to sell with vacant possession, but the wife refused to leave the house and the trustees in bankruptcy brought an action for possession against her. When the County Court passed an order in favour of the creditors for possession, the wife

appealed to the Court of Appeals. In 1953, Lord Denning, who heard the appeal as part of a three-Judge Bench, reversed the order and held that a deserted wife in occupation of the matrimonial home had a personal license, revocable only upon the husband obtaining an order under Section 17 of the 1882 Act. Her right of residence does not come to an end automatically on the husband's bankruptcy. The trustee in bankruptcy takes subject to equities. Therefore, he takes subject to the wife's right in equity (ibid.: 50).

From then onwards till 1965, through a series of judgments, he further consolidated the position of the deserted wife. In 1956, the Royal Commission on Marriage and Divorce held: We think it has been right to afford this protection to a deserted wife, to allow her to keep a roof over her head; it would be shocking to contemplate that a husband could put his wife and children into the street, so that he could himself return to live in the house, perhaps with another woman (ibid.: 51).

In a later judgment delivered in 1962, *Hine* v. *Hine*,[395] Lord Denning ruled that family property had to be treated differently from other forms of property. Expanding the scope of the controversial Section 17 of MWPA, he held that this provision was not merely procedural in nature, but in fact conferred a substantive power upon the judge to reallocate property rights between the parties. It was ruled that the discretion transcends all rights, legal and equitable, and enables the court to make such orders as may be fair and just.

However, this principle was overturned by the House of Lords in *Pettitt* v. *Pettitt*,[396] which held that Section 17 of MWPA was merely procedural. This view was reaffirmed again in

[395] (1962) 3 All ER 345
[396] (1969) 2 All ER 385: (1970) AC 777

Gissing v. *Gissing*. These decisions dealt a severe blow to the right of a deserted wife and curtailed the power of the courts to reallocate matrimonial property. In *Pettitt* v. *Pettitt*, it was pointed out that under Section 17 the question for the court was, whose is this and not to whom shall this be given. Following this unanimous ruling, two fundamental rules emerged. First, that English law does not recognize the doctrine of community of property or any separate rules of law applicable to family assets. Consequently, if one spouse buys property intended for common use with the other, whether it is a house, furniture, or a car, this cannot *per se* give the latter any proprietary interest. The second principle which flows from the first, which was stated in *Gissing* v. *Gissing*,[397] that if either of them seeks to establish a beneficial interest in property, the legal title to which is vested in the other, he or she can do so only by establishing that the legal owner holds the property on trust for the claimant (Lowe and Douglas 1998: 136).

Despite these adverse comments, the ruling protected the deserted wife's right to reside in the matrimonial home by invoking a notion called 'constructive trust'. The wife was in occupation of the house through a constructive trust through the contract of marriage, and a husband could not take advantage of his own wrong by dispossessing the wife from the matrimonial home or by deserting her.

In *National Provincial Bank Ltd.* v. *Ainsworth*,[398] Lord Denning delivered yet another historical ruling and held that the bank could not claim possession against the wife, who was in possession of the matrimonial home. He ruled that since the wife has a right to remain in the matrimonial home, it is unlawful for the husband to enter into any agreement designed to turn her out. 'It is a case where I would temper justice with mercy. Justice to the bank with mercy to the wife', he proclaimed. But the House of Lords overruled this decision in 1965, which made the position of a wife precarious against the husband's creditors. Lord Denning responded with a comment that the decision had blown the deserted wife's equity to smithereens.

The public outcry, against this decision of the House of Lords, led to the enactment of the Matrimonial Homes Act in 1967, which specifically empowered the courts to decide the issue of property while dealing with issues of desertion and divorce. But the wife had to register a charge against the husband's property. Subsequent enactments have strengthened women's rights, not only to the matrimonial residence but also to matrimonial property. Important among them is the Matrimonial Proceedings and Property Act, 1970.

The necessity of enacting the 1970 Act arose in the context of reforms in family law which were brought in through an enactment in 1969, the Divorce Reform Act, which introduced the 'breakdown theory' of divorce. Though a gender neutral term spouse was used, there was a fear that many innocent wives, divorced against their will, would be left with inadequate financial provisions and divorce would cause grave economic hardships to them. In 1973, provisions of both these statutes were incorporated into the Matrimonial Causes Act, 1973.[399]

These enactment stipulated that though the courts must give effect to legal rights of parties, they must also honour the wife's right in equity

---

[397] (1971) AC 886: (1970) 2 All ER 780
[398] (1965) 2 All ER 472 HL

[399] The position was further altered through the enactment of the Family Law Act of 1996, which lay emphasis on conciliation and mediation rather than contested litigation.

to reside in the matrimonial home. The courts began to order the quantum of maintenance on the basis of her continued right of residence in the matrimonial home. In several cases, orders of possession were passed against trustees, in cases of bankruptcy of the husband, and in favour of the wife, who had a prior right of residence.

Evolution of the Concept in India

The deserted wife's right in equity was getting formulated around the time when the Hindu Marriage Act was being enacted, but this campaign did not influence the law making process in India. This is obvious when we examine the provisions of the two statutes which were enacted around that time, the Special Marriage Act, 1954, and the Hindu Marriage Act, 1955. These laws were formulated on the basis of the earlier rights under English law and confined only to traditional matrimonial reliefs such as divorce, separation, annulment of marriage, etc., even though the English law had moved on from there.[400]

Section 27 of the Hindu Marriage Act makes a vague reference to property, but contextualizes it within a limited scope of a Hindu woman's rights over the customary gifts, received jointly by the spouses, at the time of marriage. The wording is 'property presented at or about the time of marriage, which may belong jointly to both the husband and the wife.[401] While it is

possible to stretch the scope of this provision to matrimonial property acquired after the marriage, as was done by the Supreme Court in *B. P. Achala Anand* v. *S. Appi Reddy* (discussed later), it is an extrapolation and it does not undermine the need for a separate law regarding distribution of matrimonial property on divorce.

On divorce, women are entitled to only a meagre amount of maintenance which is insufficient to procure separate residential premises for themselves and the children under their custody. Women who have secured a job are not even entitled to maintenance, even though during the subsistence of marriage they may have opted out of paid employment to support the family and to have and raise children. A decree of divorce will disentitle a woman of her right to a shelter or matrimonial residence. This becomes a compelling reason for women not to opt for divorce even in situations of extreme domestic violence. The fear of being rendered shelterless is overwhelming, particularly for women in the urban setting, where housing is expensive and beyond the access of ordinary middle and low income groups.

The only recognition of the right of women to residence is found under the Hindu Adoptions and Maintenance Act, 1956, where maintenance is defined as inclusive of a provision of residence. However, residence does not specifically mean the matrimonial home. But, since residence comes under the ambit of maintenance, the courts seem to think that an enhanced maintenance would compensate the woman for the loss of shelter.

---

[400] Rather surprisingly, the Hindu law did take into account an anti-women premise, which was getting introduced in some Western countries, of equality and gender neutrality within matrimonial statutes, and awarded equal rights of maintenance to both the spouses, though the actual ground level reality of husbands and wives varied drastically in the Indian context.

[401] 'The Act did not even provide for claiming the Hindu woman's customary right of stridhan at the time of divorce. The concept of a woman's claim to stridhan

was evolved in contemporary times through a Supreme Court ruling under the criminal law, under Section 406 of IPC, Criminal Breach of Trust in *Pratibha Rani* v. *Suraj Kumar* AIR 1985 SC 658.

Two legal concepts related to property are relevant in disputes over the matrimonial home, ownership and possession. While ownership implies legal title, the courts are constrained to protect the women's right to shelter by invoking the principle of possession. The courts have the power to protect this right in lieu of the women's contribution to the domestic unit, both economically and through services rendered through performing domestic duties. Though the right is not defined under our prevailing matrimonial statutes, due to escalating property prices, injunction against dispossession is emerging as a highly contested issue in matrimonial litigation.

The earlier accepted notion was that since the title is in the name of the husband or his family members (father-in-law, mother-in-law, brother-in-law, etc.), it is the sole prerogative of the person holding the title to permit residence in these premises. The contract of marriage did not include within itself the woman's right in equity to reside in these premises and it did not protect her against dispossession. Despite the gains made in other areas, here, the notion that a man is the master of his home seemed to prevail until recently. The fact that most women contribute to the matrimonial home either through their own earnings or through their unpaid labour, was overlooked while ascertaining the right of residence and right to property in respect of the matrimonial home. But gradually, this notion gave way to a notion akin to the constructive trust under English law and courts began to recognize the women's right of residence.

For most middle and lower class families, the dwelling house (or matrimonial home) is their only or primary asset. In urban centres, with escalating property prices, the right to the dwelling home becomes a crucial economic issue in matrimonial litigation. Though statutory provision was lacking, the issue of right of residence and settlement of matrimonial assets emerged as a highly contested issue in urban matrimonial disputes. The matrimonial courts are constantly called upon to adjudicate over this issue during matrimonial litigation.

Tentatively and gradually, the courts started awarding recognition to women's right to matrimonial residence. Perhaps it is not surprising, given the highly volatile housing situation in Mumbai, that the concern over right of residence in the matrimonial home was first articulated through decisions of the Bombay High Court in the 1960s, 1970s, and 1980s.

In one of the earliest cases on the issue of matrimonial home, *Banoo Jal Daruwalla* v. *Jal C. Daruwalla*,[402] it was held that the court does not deal with questions of titles to properties and questions arising between a husband and wife as co-owners of properties, except in respect of joint properties presented at or about the time of marriage. In respect of all other properties owned or alleged to be owned as co-owners between husband and wife, the case would be decided as per the general law of property. But a mention was made to the right of a wife to reside in the matrimonial home by relying upon the observations of Lord Denning, in *Bendall* v. *McWhirter*, that it is the duty of the court to ensure that the wife is not thrown out of the matrimonial home. Since it was not possible for the wife to reside in the matrimonial home, the wife was awarded Rs 275 per month as maintenance.

In 1977, in a landmark decision *A.* v. *B*,[403] the Bombay High Court introduced the concept of protective injunctions to safeguard women's rights and held: 'While passing a matrimonial decree, the court has the power to grant an injunction restraining the husband from entering the matrimonial home....' Here the premises

---

[402] (1962) LXV BLR 750
[403] (1977) Mh.LJ 66

belonged to the wife who was separated, and the injunction was granted against the husband, restraining him from entering her premises. After facing extreme physical cruelty and also humiliation, the wife had filed a petition for judicial separation and for an injunction restraining the husband from entering the matrimonial home. While granting her judicial separation, the court held: '…a woman, who wants to be economically independent… would be apprehensive that it would be dangerous to live with a husband who is physically abusive and accuses her of having extra-marital relations with her colleagues….'

The ruling in *Abdul Rahim v. Padma*,[404] is yet another milestone. In this case, the right of the wife in the residential premises owned by the husband's father was awarded recognition. The case concerned a couple in an inter-religious civil marriage. But the husband alleged that later the wife had converted and they had performed nikah. When the relationships between them were strained, the husband pronounced talaq and threw the wife out and restrained her from entering the matrimonial home. Later, he filed a civil suit restraining her entry into the matrimonial home and obtained an ex parte injunction against her on the ground that she is no longer his wife. In appeal, the high court held that since it was a civil marriage, it could not be dissolved through an oral talaq. But, subsequently, on the premise that the marriage had broken down irrevocably, the court granted a judicial divorce.

The wife challenged the injunction on the ground that it was her matrimonial home and she had contributed towards it from her savings. The court ruled: 'The wife has a right to stay in the home since the husband had not provided her any alternate accommodation. It is just and

fair that the flat be partitioned and the wife allocated a specific portion, thereof, for her residence.'

Later, this right was awarded recognition by various other high courts. In the matter of M/s Bharat Heavy Plates and Vessels Ltd., Vishakapatnam,[405] is an interesting case where the employer of the husband was restrained from dispossessing the wife from the company quarters. An employee of a government owned and controlled company and his wife were living together in the company quarters with the apparent consent of the company. The quarter allocated to the couple was their matrimonial home. Soon, differences cropped up between them leading to their estrangement. Finally, the wife went to the court, charging her husband with criminal neglect to maintain her and three minor children and was awarded maintenance. Consequently, the husband left the matrimonial residence and it was occupied solely by the wife and her minor children. As a retaliatory action, the husband terminated the lease of the quarter, exposing the wife and the minor children to eviction, which led the wife to approach the court for protection. Accordingly, an order of injunction restraining the company from evicting the wife and the minor children, pending disposal of the suit, came to be passed. The husband was directed to pay the rent, which was to be adjusted against the maintenance that was payable. Against this order, the company filed a revision petition. However, the same was held to be not maintainable as it neither caused irreparable injury to the company nor occasioned failure of justice. The order of injunction provided for deducting the amount of rent from the salary of the husband and from the amount of maintenance which was due to the wife. Due to this, the court held that neither the company

---

[404] AIR 1982 Bom.341

[405] AIR 1985 AP 207

nor the husband suffered any monetary loss or irreparable injury in the continued possession of the company quarter by the wife.

The court further commented that the quarter was owned by a legal person and not by a natural person and was meant to be used by its employees. The fact that the company was a state instrumentality, under an obligation to act in accordance with Articles 14 and 21, was an additional ground for holding that there was no failure of justice. It was also held that the husband had an obligation to provide shelter to his wife and children. The husband and the company, acting in different ways, had been recognizing all these years the right of occupation of the quarter by the wife as her matrimonial right. It was held that in these circumstances, the interlocutory order could not be said to occasion any failure of justice. By preventing the state instrumentality from rendering the wife and the children homeless, the court only prevented failure of justice.

These early landmark judgments did not receive wide media publicity and, at times, even lawyers and judges in trial courts were not aware of these legal principles. Even women themselves did not believe that they had a right in law to reside in their matrimonial home and that the husband and his relatives could not dispossess them at their whims and fancies. During this period, issues of dowry harassment and dowry deaths were in the news. When a woman complained of domestic violence, social worker interventions were aimed at advising women not to tolerate violence and humiliation and instead of continuing with the marriage, to opt for a divorce. But women themselves were reluctant, as they were aware that entering the realm of litigation would render them shelterless. Most women believed that a compromise through acquiescence to the demands of the husband and his family was their only option.

They did not believe that they had a legal right of residence in their matrimonial home against the husband's wishes. So, they agreed to reconciliations on terms laid down by the husband in order to protect their right to shelter.

However, in later years, divorce petitions increasingly brought into focus issues related to matrimonial home and property and the courts were constrained to examine this right. There were a few positive rulings which recognized the right of women to proceeds from the sale of the matrimonial home.

In *Ajit Bhagwandas Udeshi v. Kumud Ajit Udeshi*,[406] the court upheld the wife's right to occupy a part of the matrimonial home after her divorce since she had no other alternate accommodation. The parties were married for twenty years and had three children. Due to a matrimonial dispute, the husband filed a petition for divorce which was decided, after a long drawn litigation, in favour of husband on the ground of desertion by the wife. The court awarded Rs 1000 as maintenance to the wife and allowed her to reside in one part of the matrimonial home. The husband filed an appeal against the grant of the right of residence to the wife. The Bombay High Court upheld the decision of the family court granting the wife right of residence in part of the matrimonial home. The courts' ruling was based on the premise of financial contribution. It was proved that though both the parties had contributed while acquiring the matrimonial home, a substantial amount of deposit, which is popularly referred to as *pagdi*, was paid by the wife out of the amount received by her from the landlord of the earlier premises that the couple was occupying. The tenancy of the earlier premises was in the name of the wife's grandmother. The husband had also taken away her gold ornaments,

[406] I (2003) DMC 602 Bom

but at that time he did not purchase any premises. This could also be recognized as the financial contribution of the wife.

While upholding the woman's right of residence, the court commented that the husband did not occupy the accommodation though he maintained his possession over one floor of the premises. While he was not in need of the said accommodation, the wife had no alternate accommodation and she had contributed substantially towards acquiring these premises. Hence, the Bombay High Court upheld the order and commented that the order awarding shelter to the wife by the family court could not be held to be perverse or unjustified.

In *Sunita Shankar Salvi* v. *Shankar Laxman Salvi*, the Bombay High Court upheld the woman's right to the matrimonial home which was in the joint names of the parties. In this case, both the husband and the wife had filed for divorce through separate proceedings. The parties settled the issue of divorce and filed consent terms, withdrawing allegations against each other, and a decree of divorce, by mutual consent was awarded. The dispute over the right of residence in the matrimonial home continued. The wife contended that the flat was jointly acquired and, hence, both have an equal right, title, and interest, in the said flat. She relied upon documents admitted by the husband in support of her contention. After hearing the parties, the family court concluded that the wife's name was added at the request of the husband but the wife had not paid any consideration or cost for acquisition of the premises. Hence, she had no right, title, and interest, in the said flat and was not entitled to claim any ownership, or for that matter, any right, title, or interest in the said flat. The family court held that the wife's petition claiming 50 per cent of the share in the flat was devoid of any substance.

Against this decree, the wife approached the high court, which overruled the judgment of the family court and held that though there was no tenancy in the wife's name, the premises were for the benefit of the family. The wife was also occupying the premises along with the husband as a member of the family. The husband had also admitted, unambiguously and unequivocally, that at his request the wife's name was added as co-owner and the admission would operate as an estoppel against him. He was precluded from contending contrary to his admission in the form of admitted documents of title. From the very fact that the name of the wife was joined as one of the owners in the title deed, it would have to be presumed that the wife was entitled to an equal share in the said flat. The court commented that the family court was not justified in refusing to recognize the wife's 50 per cent share in the right, title, and interest, in the flat. In order to execute this decree the court gave an option for either of the parties to purchase 50 per cent share of the opposite party. And if neither of them was in a position to make an offer of purchase, the premises would be sold and the sale proceeds would be divided equally between them.

In *Mala Viswanathan* v. *P. B. Viswanathan*,[407] the wife filed an appeal against the order of the Additional District Judge, Alipore, restraining her entry into the matrimonial home. The Calcutta High Court upheld the right of the wife to reside in the matrimonial home in the following words:

When a question relating to grant of injunction restraining one of the spouses from entering into the matrimonial house comes before the court, the court has to deal with the same with utmost care and caution. Once a person becomes part of the house by reason of marriage, her right to reside in matrimonial house cannot be denied. Marriage confers a right to reside in the

---

[407] II (2003) DMC 809 Cal

matrimonial home on both parties to the marriage as well as their offspring. Such right is a joint and indivisible common right. Such right cannot be taken away from one, by the other. The marriage carries a liability and right to maintenance of one or the other. One half of one cannot deny the other half's right in the matrimonial home. Maintenance includes residence. The court has to be very careful in denying such right by granting injunction restraining the wife from entering into the matrimonial home, of which she is a part of. An injunction can be granted only when an exceptional case is made out. It can be granted sparingly in a case where clear case for it is made out and such a grant will not result in helping one to oust the other from the matrimonial home.

Further, the court commented that the interest of the wife needs to be protected while granting such orders to the husband.

In another important case, *Madhavi Dudani* v. *Ramesh Dudani*,[408] the Bombay High Court recognized the wife's right to shelter upon divorce and directed the husband to purchase a residential premises comprising of a hall, kitchen, and one bedroom, for the exclusive use of the wife and two daughters. The husband had disputed the validity of marriage on the ground that the wife was not a Hindu prior to her marriage and had not converted to Hinduism. Hence, a marriage between a Hindu and a non-Hindu could not be considered as valid under the Hindu Marriage Act. This contention was overruled by the high court.

While these high court rulings brought in some respite to women, there was no clear direction from the Supreme Court regarding the wife's right of residence in the matrimonial home. But finally in 2005, in *B.P. Achala Anand* v. *S. Appi Reddy*,[409] the Supreme Court upheld the wife's right to reside in the matrimonial home, even against the landlord. This ruling pronounced by the Bench comprising

of R.C. Lahoti CJ, G.P. Mathur J. and P.K. Balasubramanyan J. incorporated into the Indian law the age old dictum of the English law, '*deserted wife's right in equity*' discussed earlier.

The husband had deserted the wife and had left the matrimonial home, which was a tenanted apartment and, thereafter, he stopped paying the rent for the apartment. Since he faulted in the payment of rental dues, the landlord initiated proceedings for eviction. Since the wife would be affected by any order of eviction and rendered shelter-less, she approached the court to be impleaded as a party to the proceedings. The Karnataka High Court granted her request and directed her to pay the dues. The case proceeded further and, finally, it was held that the landlord could not evict the tenants from the part of the premises occupied by the wife. Against this decision, the landlord filed an appeal in the high court. The high court ruled in favour of the landlord and held that there was no relationship of landlord and tenant between him and the woman concerned.

The appeal against this order provided the Supreme Court an opportunity to expand the scope of women's rights to their matrimonial home. In its opening comments, the ruling reiterates the power of the judicial law marking in the following words, 'Unusual situations posing issues for resolution is an opportunity for innovation. Law, as administered by courts, transforms into justice. The law does not remain static. It does not operate in a vacuum. As social norms and values changes, laws too have to be re-interpreted, and recast.' It also borrowed the following quote from Lord Denning, 'Law does not stand still; it moves continuously. Once this is recognized, then the task of a judge is put on a higher plain. He must consciously seek to mould the law so as to serve the needs of the time.'

---

[408] I (2006) DMC 386 Bom

[409] I (2005) DMC 345 SC : (2005) 3 SCC 313

Since there were no Indian legal precedents which address the issue directly, the court referred to the legal principles under English law and approvingly quoted Lord Denning: 'A wife is no longer her husband's chattel. She is beginning to be regarded by the law as a partner in all affairs which are their common concerns. Thus, the husband can no longer turn the wife out of the matrimonial home. She has as much right as he, to stay there even though the house does stand in his name ... Moreover, it has been held that the wife's right is effective, not only as against her husband, but also as against the landlord. Thus where a husband who was statutory tenant of the matrimonial home, deserted his wife and left the house, the landlord could not turn the wife out so long as she paid the rent and performed the conditions of the tenancy.'

Expanding the scope of Section 27 of the Hindu Marriage Act, which empowers a matrimonial court to make relevant orders regarding the joint property of the parties,[410] the court ruled that this section can be invoked to pass orders regarding the separate property of the parties or even tenanted premises.

The court empowered the wife to intervene in any proceedings filed by the landlord against her husband and commented that a deserted wife, who has been or is entitled to be in occupation of the matrimonial home, is entitled to contest the suit for eviction filed against her husband in his capacity as tenant, if he is not interested in contesting the same, as it would prejudice the deserted wife, who is residing in the premises. It was ruled that the deserted wife

in occupation of the tenanted premises cannot be placed in a position worse than that of a sub-tenant contesting a claim for eviction on the ground of subletting. Having been deserted by her husband, she cannot be deprived of the roof over her head where the husband has conveniently left her to face the peril of eviction, attributable to default or neglect by him. The court held that the position of the wife is akin to that of an heir of the husband. Since the husband had lost interest in protecting his tenancy rights, the same right would devolve upon the wife so long as she continues in occupation of the premises.

The decision amounted to judicial law making. The Supreme Court clarified that it was using its powers of law making under Article 142 of the Constitution, while responding to the demands of social and gender justice, and in order to do complete justice. The principles proclaimed in this ruling would be binding until a suitable legislation is enacted. The judgment is path breaking and which substantially expanded the scope of women's right to the matrimonial home. But the woman herself did not gain from it as, pending proceedings, she had obtained a decree of divorce by mutual consent and there was no agreement between the parties regarding her right of continued residence in the tenanted premises as part of the husband's obligation to maintain her.

There have also been important judgments in respect of women's right to reside in the matrimonial home, as against the husband, which have protected the wife by an ouster order against the husband. Significant in this realm is an unreported case decided by the Bombay High Court in 1998 (A.F. v. A.F. M.J. Suit No. 3264 of 1994 dated 14 August 1998 (unreported)). The parties belonged to the lower economic background. There were six children of the marriage, five daughters and a son. The one room tenement

---

[410] **Section 27—Disposal of Property:** In any proceedings under this Act, the Court may make such provisions in the decree as it deems just and proper with respect to any property presented at or about the time of marriage, which may belong jointly to both the husband and the wife..

was initially in the name of the husband's mother, was later transferred to the husband's name. The husband who was an alcoholic and drug addict threatened to transfer the tenancy and render the wife and family shelter-less. When he was arrested on account of some petty crime, the wife bailed him out on condition that he transfers the premises to her name. He conceded, and entered into an agreement to this effect. The wife and children were subjected to extreme cruelty and abuse. The girls were living under the constant fear of sexual abuse by a drunken father. When the series of police complaints and NGO interventions did not yield any results, a case was filed for an injunction restraining his entry into the premises along with a prayer for judicial separation under the Indian Divorce Act in the High Court of Bombay. The rights of the wife and children were protected, both through an initial ad-interim and interim order, as well as a final order. The orders were ex parte since the husband refused to attend court proceedings. And the woman faced extreme difficulties in enforcing this order. Violence and abuse continued, but, finally, proceedings under Section 498A (cruelty to wives) resulted in his conviction for three years, and the wife and children could live in peace. This was an extreme case of physical and sexual abuse. In order to do justice and protect the rights of basic survival and dignity, even in the absence of a statutory provision, the courts are empowered to pass protection orders, in the interest of justice, using its own inherent powers.

Protection of Matrimonial Residence Under the Domestic Violence Act, 2005

While there have been no statutory provisions within the matrimonial statutes, the recently enacted Protection of Women from Domestic Violence Act, 2005, provides independent relief to women by providing for protective injunctions against violence, dispossession from the matrimonial home, and alternate residence. Now a victim of domestic violence can seek protection under the provisions of this Act. The Act also provides the scope for claiming economic protection, including maintenance. The wide definition of domestic violence, physical, mental, economical, and sexual, brings under its purview the invisible violence suffered by a large section of women and entitles them to claim protection from the courts.

While the Act does not create any new rights which were not available to women prior to this enactment through statutory or judge made laws, it provides a single window and simple procedures for claiming rights which were scattered under different statutes and legal provisions. The litigation forum is the magistrate's court which is easily accessible by women. In addition, simultaneously, the provisions of this Act can be invoked in any proceedings which are pending in any other civil or criminal court.[411]

The campaigns by women's groups, prior to the enactment and media publicity it received after the enactment, has helped to bring about awareness regarding the woman's right to reside in the matrimonial home. Since the Act gives a statutory recognition to the principle which was advanced through judge made laws, many more women are staking their claims to residence in the matrimonial home and for protection orders restraining the husbands from dispossessing them and causing any harm to them. A judge called upon to provide relief to a woman under the new Act is bound by not just the provisions of the Act, but the ideological framework which underscores the enactment that a husband is bound to provide his wife a roof over her head, and that she has a right to live in that house without the fear of violence.

[411] Section 26 of the Act.

After this enactment, it is no longer possible to hold that the matrimonial home is the exclusive domain of the husband, and the woman has no right to reside in it against her husband's wishes. Even if the woman is not residing in the premises, it is possible for her to obtain an order of re-entry along with a protection order, residence order, and an order of maintenance for herself and her children.

The Act widens the scope of protection against violence beyond the category of wives and extends it not only to mothers, daughters, and sisters, but even to women in informal relationships. Aged women, unmarried girls, and widowed/divorced sisters, can now seek protection from their relatives under this Act. An entire gamut of women, whose marriages are suspect due to some legal defect on the ground that essential ceremonies were not performed or that the man or the woman has an earlier subsisting marriage, are able to seek relief under this Act. The invalidity of a marriage can no longer be used as defence by the man to dispossess the woman, or deny her maintenance.[412]

In *Vandana* v. *T Srikanth*,[413] the Madras High Court provided a broad interpretation to the notions of 'shared household' and 'domestic relationship' under the Act, as defined under Section 2(s) and Section 2(f), respectively. In this case, the husband had contested the right of the aggrieved wife to reside in the shared household under Section 17 of the PWDVA because the parties had not lived together in the shared household for even a single day after their marriage. The husband disputed the very fact of marriage itself. But the court, upholding the right of the aggrieved wife to reside under

Section 17, held that the wife has a *de jure* right to live in the shared household because of her status as a wife in the domestic relationship. This ruling awarded judicial recognition to the concept that the contract of marriage encompasses within it, a right of residence.

In India, most couples, after marriage, live in a joint household, shared with the husband's parents and siblings. The question that has surfaced in judicial discourse is whether such dwellings can be construed as the 'matrimonial home' or 'shared household' of the woman, and whether she is entitled to obtain an order of injunction restraining the husband and his family members from dispossessing her. This has become a highly contested issue while determining the rights of residence of women in such households. While there is some recognition of the right of residence against the husband, especially if the wife is in possession of the premises, there was no recognition of the right of residence against the husband's family members where the couple is living within a joint family unit. It was hoped that the enactment would strengthen this right and broaden its scope.

Rather unfortunately, the first ruling of the Supreme Court pronounced in 2007, in *S.R. Batra* v. *Taruna Batra*,[414] has constrained the scope of this stipulation and has held that the shared household under the Act constitutes only the premises owned by the husband or the premises where he holds an HUF interest in the family property. The Supreme Court, while examining the definition of the shared household under PWDVA, held that a shared household indicates a house belonging to or taken on rent by the husband, or a house which belongs to the joint family of which the husband is a member. Since the house belonged to

---

[412] This issue is discussed at length in sub-section, 'Rights of Women in Informal Relationships', in Section A earlier.

[413] (2007) 6 MLJ 205 Mad

[414] I (2007) DMC 1 SC: 2007 3 SCC 169

the mother-in-law, the daughter-in-law could not claim any rights in the said premises. Further, it was held that the claim for alternative accommodation can only be made against the husband and not against the in-laws, or other relatives. This might prove detrimental to the rights of women living in joint family households owned by the parents-in-law in which the husband himself has no legal right to reside by way of title or interest.

Subsequently, as can be predicted, this plea was taken by several husbands to vacate the initial protection orders passed by lower courts. Various high courts, following the decision of the Supreme Court, struck down the orders granting protection to women in their matrimonial home and women were deprived of their rights of residing in joint family households.

For instance, in *Hemaxi Atul Joshi* v. *Muktaben Karsandas Joshi*,[415] the Bombay High Court, relying upon the above ruling, held that shared household indicates the house belonging to or taken on rent by the husband, or the house which belongs to the joint family of which the husband is a member. The husband had filed a petition for divorce and the wife had filed a corresponding petition to protect her right to reside in the matrimonial home, and sought an injunction against her dispossession. Prior to filing of proceedings for divorce, the parties had shifted out of the joint family household into a separate apartment. The wife staked her claim of residence in the premises owned by her mother-in-law and not against her husband. The court rejected her claim on the ground that merely because the wife stayed in the house of her mother-in-law along with her husband for sometime, she did not accrue a legal right of residence in the said premises. It was not the property in which the husband had a right. The right is available to the wife only against her husband and not against any other member of his family.

Abha Arora v. *Angela Sharma*[416] is another similar case of the wife claiming a right of residence against her mother-in-law, relying upon the notion of a shared household. The mother-in-law had initiated proceedings to restrain the entry of the daughter–in-law into the premises owned by her. The daughter-in-law failed to obtain a counter injunction in her favour for her re-entry. Subsequently, the mother-in-law sold the premises and made an application to the court for permission to withdraw the proceedings filed by her. The daughter-in-law opposed this on the ground that her rights under PWDVA would be defeated if the mother-in-law is allowed to withdraw her suit. But the high court rejected this plea and held that since the property is owned by the mother-in-law, the daughter-in-law cannot claim the right of residence, as the same is not a shared household under the provisions of PWDVA. The high court commented that the daughter-in-law was not residing in the suit property but was residing and working in the UK, and was earning a substantial income. The proceedings filed by her were dismissed for default, as she did not follow up the suit. Hence, there was no reason for preventing the mother-in-law from withdrawing her suit and compelling her to proceed with it.

In *Neetu Mittal* v. *Kanta Mittal*,[417] the wife filed proceedings against her in-laws for an order of permanent injunction under Order 39, Rule 1 and 2 of CPC, and also invoked the relevant provisions for her right to residence

---

[415] SC Suit No 3072 of 2007 (decided on 5 December 2007) Bom.

[416] I (2008) DMC 507 Del
[417] 152 (2008) DLT 691

under PWDVA. While the wife admitted that she had been living separately with her husband, she pleaded that this accommodation is not adequate. Her relationship with the in-laws was not cordial and the couple were living separately due to the settlement arrived at, at the police station, between the parties. Hence, it was held that her staying with the in-laws would be detrimental to their health and interest, and their right to live with dignity. The trial court order was affirmed by the high court. Relying upon the *Batra* case, the court commented that the wife's claim of residence is only against her husband and not against her in-laws.

The facts of *M. Nirmala* v. *Dr. Gandla Balakotaiah*,[418] are slightly different. Here, the wife had filed an application under Order 39 read with Section 151 of CPC seeking an injunction against her husband from dispossessing her. She also invoked Section 19(f) of PWDVA. She contended that the property was purchased in 1997 out of her own and her family's funds, but stood in the name of her husband. While she resided in the premises, the husband had left the home and was now trying to dispossess her. The husband denied this contention and pleaded that the premises were purchased from his own funds and through a bank loan and relied upon relevant documents to prove his case. He also stated that he recognized the right of the wife for shelter and was ready to pay for an alternative accommodation. The trial court dismissed the wife's petition, but directed the husband to pay a sum of Rs 3,500 per month towards rent. The wife challenged this order in the high court on the ground that she was entitled to the possession of the matrimonial house as per Section 19 of the Domestic Violence Act. The high court upheld the order of the family court on the ground that she could not prove

her contribution towards the purchase of the premises.

As can be seen, within a few years of the new enactment a constrained scope of the provision of the shared household is beginning to emerge, which would drastically curtail the rights of women. This has become a routine ploy to deprive women of their right of residence. In some cases, the courts have seen through these strategies and have declined to apply the *ratio* of the *Batra* case, based on facts and circumstances of the particular case.

In *Nidhi Kumar Gandhi* v. *The State*,[419] the wife had filed for re-entry into the matrimonial home from where she and her minor daughter had been dispossessed. The husband resisted her claim by stating that the premises belonged to his father and that he was not residing in the said premises. The wife contended that he shifted his residence only after she had initiated proceedings against him. In view of this, interim orders were passed in her favour. The husband challenged the orders, relying upon the *Batra* case and pleaded that the premises were neither owned nor rented by him, and it was not the joint family property and, thus, could not be construed as a shared household. In view of this, the sessions court varied the residential order passed by the magistrate's court. In appeal, the Delhi High Court restored the orders of the magistrate's court and observed that it was premature on the part of the Sessions Judge to apply the *ratio* of the *Batra* case without any evidence having been led to determine whether, in fact, the husband's father owned the premises and whether the husband had no right to live there. The high court commented that it is inconceivable how at an interlocutory stage, in view of the mandate under the Act to provide urgent relief, a final determination on this

---

[418] 2008 (3) ALD 486

[419] 157 (2009) DLT 472

aspect could be made. Further, it was held that the rights of the husband's family are not affected by the order of restoration and the wife's occupation of the premises.

In *P. Babu Venkatesh, Kandayammal and Padmavathi* v. *Rani*,[420] the wife had been beaten and thrown out of the matrimonial home at midnight. She approached the courts for an urgent residence order against her husband and in-laws. The trial court, taking into consideration the urgency of the case, passed ad-interim reliefs in her favour permitting her to re-enter the matrimonial home. Since the in-laws had locked the house, she was permitted to break open the locks and enter the premises. The husband and in-laws filed an appeal and submitted that the divorce petition filed by him is pending. Further, the house was in the name of his father and referred to the *Batra case* that a wife cannot claim from her in-laws. The wife, however, contended that he had alienated the house in the name of his father during the pendency of the case. The court commented that if the contention of the husband is accepted then every husband will resort to transferring his property in favour of someone else when a matrimonial dispute arises, and then plead that the premises is not the shared household, and, therefore, the wife is not entitled to seek a right of residence. The court further observed that the pendency of the divorce petition has nothing to do with the present application. While upholding the order to break open the locks, the court commented that the wife cannot be made to wait in the street and that husbands will prevent the wives from reaping the benefits of the order by simply locking the premises and walking away.

In *Razzak Khan* v. *Shahnaz Khan*,[421] it was the woman's second marriage and, subsequently, there was a divorce. Thereafter, she filed for residential orders under Section 18 to 20 of PWDVA. The wife contended that she lived with her husband and his two brothers in their ancestral house. The lower court granted her the protection order and maintenance for her and the minor son, the sessions court modified the relief and directed the Protection Officer to provide alternative accommodation to her in the ancestral house of her husband and even granted maintenance to the foster son. It was her husband's contention that she was working as a clerk and comfortably living in her parental house, while he was a mechanic and was not getting regular salary and was a heart patient, and, further, that after divorce it is not proper for her to live in the ancestral house. The high court after perusing the definitions of aggrieved woman, domestic relationship, and shared household, concluded that even a divorced woman is entitled to these reliefs under the Act, hence, the fact that she was a divorced Muslim woman and her staying at her husband's place is *haram* cannot be accepted, and upheld the orders of the lower courts in her favour.

In *Shammi Nagpal* v. *Sudhir Nagpal, Director of Hotel Taj, President, Indian Hotels Company Ltd. and Commissioner of Police*,[422] the wife had filed for an injunction against the husband and his company for restraining them from creating any third party rights in respect of the suit premises and to hand over and restore vacant and peaceful possession to her. She contended that the suit premises were her matrimonial

---

[420] Crl RC No. 48 & 148 of 2008 in MP No. 1 of 2008 (decided on 25 March 2008) Mad.

[421] CRA No.501/07 and 595/07 (decided on on 25 March 2008) MP.

[422] 2008 (5) Bom.CR149: (2008) 110 Bom LR 1797

home which had been allotted to her husband by his company. While she had gone abroad for a short visit, the husband, in collusion with his company, terminated the lease and took away all her belongings. She was informed about it through email after a day. When she returned to Mumbai, she could not enter the suit premises as the locks had been changed.

The court observed that the family members cannot claim exclusive possession or right in the residential premises allotted by the company as a condition of service. However, the husband's act of surrendering the suit premises to his employer, upon termination of the service occupancy agreement in her absence, was not *bona fide* and deserved to be condemned. The company offered to allow her to occupy the premises for a further period of six months until she could make her own alternate arrangements.

The cases discussed above reveal that the right of residence in premises owned by a third party (including the in-laws) is not unconditional, as was initially projected in the media soon after the enactment. The courts will examine the right on a case to case basis. The conduct of the parties concerned is relevant for determining the rights. Also, the orders are summary in nature and therefore temporary. The final determination of the rights will happen in the course of civil proceedings.

NOTION OF MATRIMONIAL PROPERTY AND RULES FOR ITS DIVISION

Historical Origins of the Doctrine of Property Division

As we have observed, the major struggle for women in England had been to acquire the right to own property during the subsistence of their marriage and to fight the legal provision which merged their property with that of their husbands. Hence, under the English common law

tradition, property of the spouses remained separate and marriage did not create any rights in the property of the other spouse. In contrast, the European family laws or the continental legal system adopted the notion of community of property. Under this doctrine, marriage itself alters the rules of property ownership and maintenance, and entitles both the spouses rights and interests in each other's property. All property acquired during the subsistence of marriage by either of the spouses or jointly by them, is pooled into a community of property over which both spouses acquire equal interests and rights of control. Upon divorce, this property becomes divisible between the spouses on an equal basis. Under the legal premise of differed community of property the property remains the separate property of spouses during the subsistence of marriage and is thrown into a common pool only at the time of divorce, when it becomes divisible.

Under the separate property regime, the marriage has no impact upon the title or rights over the property, and the property and assets are governed by the general rules of property laws. Hence, the property does not become divisible at the time of divorce. The woman's financial claim is confined only to maintenance and, more recently, to a right of residence in the dwelling house.

While the Portuguese (and other European powers such as the French, the Dutch, etc.) introduced the continental system in their colonies, the British introduced the common law system. Hence, the family laws of Goa, which are based on the Portuguese family law, adopted the system of community of property, whereas British India adopted the English tradition of separate property. This system continued in the post-Independence period. The notion of community of property has not been introduced into the Indian family law system.

Some states in the United States and most provinces of Canada, commonwealth countries such as Australia, New Zealand, Malaysia, Singapore, etc., followed the English common law traditions of separate property, but in the 1970s, gradually shifted to the system of community of property.

The introduction of various statutory provisions for easy divorces created severe economic hardships to women as they lost the bargaining power for negotiating settlements. Earlier, in fault based divorces, women could defend the frivolous litigation initiated by their husbands as the husbands were mandated to prove the allegations, and if they failed, their petition was likely to be dismissed. In this context the husband was ready to bargain in order to obtain the wife's consent for divorce and, during these negotiation, women could strike some economic bargains as divorce settlements. With the introduction of no-fault divorce, this power was taken out of women's reach as the husbands did not have to prove any matrimonial fault, but could merely plead breakdown of marital relations. This created a great deal of hardship to women in terms of their right of residence and the right to matrimonial assets.

Research studies confirmed that divorce has a major detrimental effect on the standard of living of women. The reason for the differential is primarily that the earning capacity of divorced women is less than that of men––they are more likely to have interrupted their careers to have children and, hence, earn lower amounts than men, and they are less likely to be able to resume (or remain in) full-time employment to make up the shortfall when their marriage breaks down. Even after their children have grown up, they are likely to remain less well off because they are unable to build up sufficient funds for their retirement. Hence, from the 1970s, greater significance is being attached to the financial consequences of divorce upon women and children.

This has led to the introduction of the notion of division of property upon divorce to ensure justice and equity to women at the time of divorce. This concept has been introduced within the family laws of several countries, which have adopted various models of property distribution. While some rely upon the premise of equality, others function from the premise of dependency. The first question which arises while adjudicating over property disputes is what constitutes matrimonial property, and the second and equally important question is the rules which govern the division. This section addresses these two concerns.

The four basic concepts which are invoked while prescribing the rules for division of property at divorce are title, fault, need, and contribution. Title indicates legal ownership and this concept favoured the husband as he usually held the title to the property accrued during the marriage. The notion of matrimonial fault was used to deny women accused of cruelty or adultery their entitlements. The right of maintenance, a lump sum settlement, or the right to reside in the matrimonial home was based on the woman's dependent status within marriage due to which the need for economic support was located. The theory of contribution was the latest, which was evolved to award recognition to the non-monitory contribution of women to the household within the context of a partnership of equality. While title has ceased to be a determinative factor under most matrimonial laws in Western countries, need and to a lesser extent, fault are still relevant in evolving a conceptual framework for the creation and implementation of various distribution factors. The sequencing of the four categories is often used to suggest a progression from the simple common law emphasis on title to the more complex understanding of the function and purpose of the distribution system.

Development of the Doctrine of Distribution of Matrimonial Property in Various Countries

England and Wales

After the introduction of the Divorce Reform Act, 1969, which introduced the breakdown theory, there was a fear that many innocent wives, divorced against their will, would be left with inadequate financial provisions. This led to the passing of the Matrimonial Proceedings and Property Act, 1970, which was re-enacted as Part II of the Matrimonial Causes Act, 1973.

The 1973 Act was amended by the Matrimonial Homes and Property Act, 1981, which gave the divorce courts the express statutory power to order the sale of any of the spouses' property. More importantly, the Matrimonial and Family Proceedings Act, 1984, extended the court's powers by enabling it to impose a clean break (that is, a once-and-for-all settlement between the spouses with no continuing financial ties) upon a spouse, and altered the way the powers to be exercised. Two of the most important changes were:

1) To require the court, when deciding what orders should be made, to give first consideration to the welfare, whilst a minor, of any child of the family under 18; and,

2) To impose a duty upon the court to consider whether it is appropriate to exercise its powers that the financial obligations of each party terminate immediately, or as soon as possible.

The 1984 Act also ended the obligation of the court to attempt to place the parties in the position that they would have been, had the marriage not broken down. Subsequently, the Pensions Act, 1995, extended the court's powers to enable it to make orders directing that all or part of any lump sum or pension arising on a

spouse's retirement be paid to the other spouse (Lowe and Douglas 1998: 778–9).

The Matrimonial Causes Act, 1973, was further amended by the Family Law Act, 1996, principally to reflect the changes to the substantive law of divorce, and the new policy that the parties' financial and other arrangements for the future are to be settled before a marriage is brought to an end, rather than thereafter.

The matrimonial courts now have the statutory power to make an order against either spouse with respect to any one or more of the following matters:

1. Unsecured periodical payments to the other spouse;

2. Secured periodical payments to the other spouse;

3. Lump sum payments to the other spouse;

4. Unsecured periodical payments for any child of the family;

5. Secured periodical payments for any child of the family;

6. A lump sum payment for any child of the family;

7. Transfer of property to the other spouse or for the benefit of any child of the family;

8. Settlement of property for the benefit of the other spouse or any child of the family;

9. Variation of any marriage settlement.

Orders within the scope of points 1–6 are collectively known as financial provision orders and those within the scope of points 7–9, as property adjustment orders (Lowe and Douglas 1998: 779–80).

Where a court makes a secured periodical payments order, a lump sum order, or a property transfer order, it can further order a sale of property belonging to either or both spouses. After 1996, the courts also acquired the power to make financial provision orders (periodical payments and lump sum) directing that a share of a spouse's pension be ear marked and paid to the other on retirement.

The Family Law Act, 1996, emphasizes on mediation as a process by which the parties might reach agreement on financial and other disputes arising on marriage breakdown. An integral part of the new procedures is the holding of an early financial dispute resolution (FDR) appointment where the spouses, in the presence of a district judge, will be encouraged to address the outstanding issues between them with a view to arriving at a settlement. Negotiated settlements may work to reduce hostility and acrimony between the parties. Further, it makes sense for the parties to reach an agreement to save the costs of a full court trial, which can be extremely steep (Lowe and Douglas 1998: 801–2).

While this discussion, in a nutshell, summarizes the position of statutory law, the following landmark cases reflect how the law of division of property has progressed in England.

The notion of division of property was introduced in a very tentative manner during the 1970s in *Wachtel* v. *Wachtel*,[423] when Lord Denning introduced the one third rule of property distribution as a reasonable starting point. He refrained from applying the rule of equal distribution on the basis that it may be appropriate in future, but is not appropriate in the present case. Although he did not state that this rule should be a presumption in subsequent cases, courts routinely applied this principle in claims by wives for division of matrimonial property.

In 1982, in *Preston* v. *Preston*,[424] the concept of need was introduced and it was held that an appropriate approach would be to look at the wife's reasonable requirements and attempt to ascertain what capital sum she would need to achieve a clean break and live comfortably for the rest of her life. This gave rise to the Duxbury calculation, named after a subsequent case *Duxbury* v. *Duxbury*,[425] which was essentially an actuarial calculation made on the basis of the wife's reasonable requirements, normally calculated on her monthly expenses with reference to her age. Based on these factors, a capital sum, which was deemed as appropriate, would be ordered to be paid to the wife by way of a clean break. The Duxbury calculation was such that the capital would slowly diminish until the projected end of the wife's life when she would be left with no capital.

This approach was criticized for being discriminatory against women. But courts continued to apply this principle and it was taken to an extreme in *Thyssen-Bornemisza* v. *Thyssen-Bornemisza*.[426] This case introduced the millionaire's defence, which was essentially that on the basis that the court would adjudicate on the wife's reasonable requirements, there would be no need to make a thorough investigation into the husband's assets as he was so wealthy that he could afford whatever the wife's reasonable needs were assessed at.

In the case of *Gojkovic* v. *Gojkovic*,[427] where there had been a long cohabitation but a relatively short marriage and no children, it was considered relevant to examine whether the wife had made a substantial contribution to the business. It was a hotel business, and it was deemed that the wife's reasonable requirements would include the transfer or purchase of a hotel for her to run. Hence, she was awarded a greater proportion of the total marital assets, in excess

[423] (1973) 1 All ER 829
[424] (1982) 1 All ER 41

[425] (1987) 1 FLR 7
[426] (1985) 1 All ER 328
[427] (1990) 1 FLR 140

of merely her reasonable requirements because she had contributed financially to the marriage.

This approach seemed to discriminate against the wife and mother, who had not directly contributed to the financial well-being of the family. Another problem with this approach was the rather illogical result that if a wife was older her needs would be less, thus, a long marriage would afford her a smaller proportion of the assets. At the same time, as the husband's needs were not assessed, he would be left with the lion's share, even though he was of a comparable age to the wife.

The principle of *Preston* was followed in the UK until the House of Lords decision in 2000 in *White* v. *White*,[428] which established equality as a reasonable starting point in the division of matrimonial assets. It was held that the factors set out under Section 25 of the Matrimonial Causes Act, 1973, should be measured against a yardstick of equality. In this case, the wife received slightly over one-fifth of the total matrimonial assets. On appeal, the Court of Appeal increased the amount to approximately two-fifths of the total assets. The wife was a partner, but it was held that she was entitled to more than her partnership share in recognition of the contribution she had made to the family as wife and mother, over and above her partnership role in the farming business. The House of Lords upheld the decision of the Court of Appeal and gave a detailed analysis in relation to equality, the financial resources, and financial needs of the parties, and the Duxbury paradox discussed earlier. Also considered was the parties' wish to leave money to their children, which was deemed to be a natural parental wish in a case where resources exceed the financial needs. It was held that a judge is entitled to have in mind the wishes of a wife that her award

should not be confined to an accommodation and a diminishing fund of capital, earmarked for living expenses, which would leave nothing for her to pass on to her children. The most important aspect of this decision was the now much-used statement coined by Lord Nicholls, that a judge '… would always be well advised to check his tentative views against the yardstick of equality. As a general guide, equality should be departed from only if, and to the extent that, there is a good reason for doing so. The need to consider and articulate reasons for departing from equality would help the parties and the court to focus on the need to ensure the absence of discrimination.'

Three landmark cases, which came up in subsequent years, are discussed here to ascertain the legal principles which the courts now adopt while deciding the issue of division of property,[429]

In the first case, *Miller* v. *Miller*, it was a short marriage of three years with significant assets which were acquired during the course of the marriage. The husband argued that since the duration of marriage was short, the wife's award should be less. The wife argued that she had given up her employment and adjusted her lifestyle according to the standard of the marriage and, therefore, her award should be substantial. It was held that the wife was entitled to some share of the assets, including the considerable increase in the husband's wealth during the marriage. Had the yardstick of equality been applied to all the assets which accrued during the marriage, the wife would have received substantially more. However, since the

---

[428] (2001) 1 AC 596

[429] I have relied upon an article by Philippa Hewitt, 'Dividing for Equality: The Maturing of Matrimonial Law in Hong Kong' in *Hong Kong Lawyer*, Hong Kong: July, 2008 pp. 26–32. http://www.hwg-law.com/en/news_articles/HWG-Article-Jul08.pdf while discussing these cases and also for tracing the development of case law in England and Wales.

substantial growth was attributed to contacts and capacities the husband brought to the marriage and since the assets were business assets, generated solely by the husband during a short marriage, the norm of equality was sidestepped. A distinction was made between matrimonial and non-matrimonial property in cases of marriages of short duration.

In *MacFarlane* v. *MacFarlane*, the marriage was of sixteen years and there were three children. Both parties were qualified professionals and, until shortly before the birth of their second child, earned similar incomes. Thereafter, the wife remained at home to care for the children while the husband continued a professional career with a salary increasing considerably year after year. In this situation, the family had insufficient capital to achieve a clean break, but the husband's income was substantially more than the parties' budgeted household expenditure. It was held that the wife should be entitled to a share of the future earnings which had been made possible by her past contribution to the husband's career. The court further held that, in exceptional cases, periodical payments should be used by the recipient to accumulate capital, particularly in view of the inability of the parties to satisfy the wife's demand for a clean break. It was held that the wife, having given up her own highly paid career for the family, was not only entitled to a generous income provision, including sums which would enable her to provide for her own old age. She was also entitled to a share in the very large surplus on both the principles of sharing and compensation. This was to continue for her lifetime, and the burden was on the husband to justify a reduction if he wished to make an application to this effect in the future.

The third case, *Charman* v. *Charman*, concerned a long marriage of twenty-eight years and there were two adult children. The matrimonial assets were built up during the course of the marriage, from nothing to over £ 130 million. The husband argued that he had made a special contribution, which was conceded by the wife who sought 45 per cent of the matrimonial assets. The wife was awarded 36.5 per cent of the assets (£ 48 million). The judge based his departure from equality, both on the special contribution by the husband and on the greater risks inherent on the assets retained by him. The House of Lords relied upon the rulings in *Miller* and *MacFarlane*. The three main principles which were relied upon in this case were: need (generously interpreted), compensation, and sharing.

It was held that the yardstick of equality of division, identified by the House of Lords in *White*, had filled the vacuum, which had arisen from abandonment of the criteria of reasonable requirements, but it had now developed into the equal sharing principle. Under this, property should be shared in equal proportions unless there was a good reason to depart from such proportions.

It was further held that each of the three distributive principles identified by the House of Lords in *Miller* could be derived from Section 25 of the MCA:

1. The principle of need required consideration of the financial needs, obligations, and responsibilities of the parties, the standard of living enjoyed by the family, the age of the parties, and any physical or mental disability of either spouse;

2. The principle of compensation related to prospective financial disadvantage which some parties faced upon divorce as a result of decisions taken for the benefit of the family during the marriage; and,

3. The principle of sharing was dictated by reference to the contributions of each party to the welfare of the family, to the length of the

marriage and, in an exceptional case, to the conduct of the party.

Lord Nicholls suggested the possibility of 'an increased recognition that by being at home and having and looking after young children, a wife may lose forever the opportunity to acquire and develop her own money earning qualifications and skills.'

United States and Canada

In the United States and Canada, family laws are state laws or provincial laws, and each state or province enacts its own laws. The states follow the tradition of English common law or the Continental or European law, depending upon the history of their colonization.

The states/provinces following the common law tradition of English law started adopting the continental model of division of property in the 1970s on the basis of equality. With the introduction of the no-fault divorce, it became necessary to move away from the earlier notion of maintenance, which indicates a continued dependency on a theory of clean break, by dividing the assets that accrued during the subsistence of marriage.

The earlier notion of status marriages with the notion of women's dependency, which required the courts to order maintenance, was no longer found to be relevant within the new scheme of equal partners. The language of the statutes became gender neutral and the law functioned from the premise of complete equality between the spouses. Within this framework, obligations ended with divorce and any ongoing economic obligation which is recognized as appropriate, such as child support or payment of existing marital debts, is considered a shared and equal responsibility.

Different states in the United States adopt a variety of specific distribution factors that are typically noted in common law state statutes, or court opinions in states with general statutory directives. These factors include:

1. The length of the marriage;
2. The property brought to the marriage by each party;
3. The contribution of each party to the marriage, often with the explicit admonition that appropriate economic value is to be given to contributions of homemaking and child-care services;
4. The contribution by one party to the education, training, or increased earning power of the other;
5. Whether one of the parties has substantial assets not subject to division by the court;
6. The age and physical and emotional health of the parties;
7. The earning capacity of each party, including educational background, training, employment skills, work experience, and length of absence from the job market;
8. Custodial responsibilities for children;
9. The time and expense necessary to acquire sufficient education or training to enable the party to become self-supporting at a standard of living reasonably comparable to that enjoyed during the marriage.

Increasingly, some consideration is given to the desirability of awarding the family home, or the right to live there for a reasonable period, to the party having custody of any children. In addition, other economic circumstances may be considered. These include, vested or unvested pension benefits, future interests, the tax consequences to each party, and the amount and duration of an order granting maintenance payments.

If a written agreement was made by the parties before or during the marriage concerning any arrangement for property distribution, such agreements are often presumed binding upon the court unless inequitable. Some statutory systems that enumerate various factors explicitly end with a general catch-all for judicial discretion that allows consideration of such other factors, as the court may, in each individual case determine to be relevant.

This tendency to limit the discussion of rights and objectives to those of the spouses reflects an important social dimension and is consistent with the contemporary partnership model of marriage. This individualistic approach, coupled with the undeniable fact that more resources are necessary when an adult has to care for children in addition to herself, means that the allocation of private resources at divorce has a profound economic and social impact because it affects the future ability of a custodial parent to care adequately for her children (Fineman 1991: 42).

The Canadian statutes generally provide for an unequal division, but do so cautiously and under the banner of judicial discretion. Each spouse is generally entitled to half of by whatever name it goes by – all family assets, family property, matrimonial assets, marital assets, or matrimonial property. McLeod and Malimo (2006) comment: 'An equal division of property does not always result in a fair division, for a host of reasons. One party may have taken on all the debts, in another case, a party may have incurred gambling debts and hid them in the mortgage on family loan. A gift or inheritance may bring havoc upon the fairness of an otherwise "equal" division'.

The law is not uniform, the terminology is not uniform, and, also, the criteria is not uniform. Each province uses different terminology in the statute books. For instance, lawyers in British Columbia speak of determining and distributing family assets, while in Ontario the term used is equalizing family property.

Every statute begins with the presumption that each spouse owns half of any matrimonial property, but the first task is to determine what constitutes family assets. Once it can be determined what is within the pool of family assets, a presumption of equal division will apply. From that general theory to which all Canadian provinces subscribe, the court can usually deviate, if equal division is patently unfair.

As eloquently stated in the Marital Property Act, 1980, of New Brunswick, child care, household management, and financial provision, are joint responsibilities of spouses and are recognized to be of equal importance in assessing the contribution of the respective spouses to the matrimonial property as well as to the management, maintenance, and improvement of matrimonial property. The contribution of each spouse to the fulfilment of these responsibilities entitles each to an equal share of the matrimonial property, and imposes on each spouse, in relationship to the other, the burden of an equal share of marital debts.

The Ontario Family Law Act, 1990, stipulates equal division of family property. The first battle is to determine what is and what is not a family asset and, therefore, subject to the cleave of the judicial knife. The Ontario statute uses an esoteric term to describe family assets, any interest, present or future, vested or contingent in real or personal property. The following are the exceptions to this rule:

1. Property, other than a matrimonial home, that was acquired by gift or inheritance from a third person after the date of the marriage;

2. Income from property referred to (above), if the donor or testator has expressly stated that it is to be excluded from the spouse's net family property;

3. Damages or a right to damages for personal injuries, nervous shock, mental distress or loss of

guidance, care and companionship, or the part of a settlement that represents those damages;

4. Proceeds or a right to proceeds of a policy of life insurance, as defined under the (Ontario) Insurance Act, that are payable on the death of the life insured;

5. Property, other than a matrimonial home, into which property referred to (above) can be traced; and,

6. Property that the spouses have agreed by a domestic contract is not to be included in the spouse's net family property.

Section 5(6) of the Ontario Act has a unique clause which excludes the following from equal distribution:

1. A spouse's failure to disclose to the other spouse debts or other liabilities existing at the date of marriage;

2. That debts or other liabilities claimed in reduction of a spouse's net family property were incurred recklessly or in bad faith;

3. The part of a spouse's net family property that consists of gifts made by the other spouse;

4. A spouse's intentional or reckless depletion of his or her net family property;

5. That the amount a spouse would otherwise receive ... is disproportionately large in relation to a period of cohabitation, that is less than five years;

6. That one spouse has incurred a disproportionately larger amount of debts or other liabilities than the other spouse for the support of the family.

The Alberta statute, the Matrimonial Property Act, uses the words, 'the court shall not distribute the property equally between spouses when it appears to the court that it would not be just and equitable to do so, taking into consideration the matter in judicial discretion in Section 8.' Section 8 defines certain circumstances and gives scope for judicial discretion by adding, 'a fact or circumstances that is relevant.' This allows unequal distribution and provides the scope for judicial reapportionment on the basis of fairness.

A similar provision is also found in Section 65 of the Family Relations Act, 1996, of British Columbia which is titled 'Judicial Reapportionment on the Basis of Fairness' and which lists the date when property was acquired or disposed of, as well as the general clause 'any other circumstances relating to the acquisition, preservation, maintenance, improvement or use of property, or the capacity or liabilities of a spouse.'

So, overall, judicial discretion plays an important role while determining the actual distribution of property between the spouses.

Australia and New Zealand

Though, both Australia and New Zealand belong to the common law tradition, the legal provisions of distribution of property vary a great deal between these two countries. New Zealand enacted the Matrimonial Property Act, 1976, which empowered the courts to divide matrimonial property between the spouses at the time of divorce and laid down elaborate guidelines in respect of this. The basic presumption was equality. In 2002, this Act was renamed as the Property Relationships Act, 1976, to award legal recognition to *de facto* couples and partners of same sex relationships. Under the provisions of the revised Act, property is referred to as relational property as opposed to the earlier term matrimonial property and includes the rights of *de facto* couples and same sex relationships. The Act was further amended in 2005 to include civil union couples.

Australia follows the common law approach to family related issues, which is essentially non-interventionist during the subsistence of marriage. Marriage has no legal impact on a spouse's ownership of property. Anything owned before marriage or acquired in any manner during it, remains the property of the owner and is under his or her management and control while the marriage subsists. Detailed provisions defining the nature of family assets or entitlements, and predetermining shares on death or divorce, are quite foreign to the Anglo-Australian legal system. The Family Law Act (FLA) enacted in 1975, contains no definition of what is or is not matrimonial property, other than its unhelpful reference to property to which those parties are, or that party is, as the case may be, entitled, whether in possession or reversion. It also has no presumptions or rules as to distribution (Harrison 1992).

The Act confers wide powers on the court to adjust property after a marriage breakdown in a manner it considers appropriate, provided it is satisfied that, in all the circumstances, the particular order is just and equitable. The discretion is not completely unfettered, as issues of contribution to the property and needs of the parties (both defined in the Act) must be taken into account, although there is no obligation to specify what weightage is to be given to the various criteria when shares are determined.

The Australian system for dividing the matrimonial assets on divorce is a separate property regime. On separation, the starting point when dividing property is that each spouse retains ownership of the property legally theirs. This is, however, only a starting point. Under the financial provisions of FLA, the family courts have the discretionary powers to alter parties' property interests on marriage breakdown if it is just and equitable to make the order. Exercising this power requires the courts to consider the parties' respective contributions to the property and other factors under Section 75(2), including their future financial needs. When dividing the

property, the court is directed to take account of the financial and non-financial contributions made to the property and to the welfare of the family. Non-financial contributions, in particular, include any labour that may have increased the value of the property, as well as contributions made to the welfare of the family through unpaid work at home and care of the children [Section 79(4)].

In theory, the task of dividing property based on the parties' respective contributions appears simple. However, in practice, there are clear difficulties involved in comparing contributions which are fundamentally different. In the case of non-financial contributions, there are difficulties involved in placing a monetary value on the contributions. There is a move to restrict judicial discretion in evaluating contributions by introducing a starting point of equal sharing in the value of the matrimonial property – a starting point that is based on the principle of equal contribution by the parties to the property of the marriage.

Having determined the respective shares of property based on these contributions, the court is directed to make an adjustment which would take account of other factors including the future needs of each of the parties. The estimation of future need is based on factors or circumstances of a broadly financial nature, such as the age and health of the parties, employment prospects, and financial resources, responsibility for the care of children post-separation and divorce, the duration of the marriage, and the extent to which it has affected the future earning capacity of the parties. In all, there are fifteen largely prospective factors for consideration covering what each party is likely to need and what each is able to pay to support the other.[430] In practice, this second stage in

[430] The factors are set out in Section 75(2), FLA

achieving a just and equitable settlement is frequently employed to take into account the future financial needs of women and children. Women with dependent children can be at a considerable disadvantage compared to men in terms of their financial circumstances and their income earning potential following marital dissolution (Sheehan and Hughes 2001).

While simplified here, the detailed financial provisions that govern the allocation of property on divorce are inherently complex, and there is ample scope for disagreement amongst the judiciary and the parties themselves as to the interpretation of these provisions. This is not surprising, given that the law confers such wide discretion in settling property matters. In addition, the law guides the parties' actions at a time in their lives when they are under considerable emotional and financial stress, when mutual consideration for one another's welfare and due recognition of their respective contributions to the marriage may no longer be the norm.

In such an environment, dividing property on divorce is a difficult task, and one which is made even harder for the sizeable minority of women and men who settle their property matters without formal legal representation. There is, therefore, a potential for discordance between the provisions of the law described above, and the application of these provisions by women and men who 'bargain in the shadow of the law' (Mnookin and Kornhauser 1979).

The study conducted by the Australian Institute of Family Studies found that property division failed to show equal or adequate consideration of indirect contributions to the marriage economy by women (McDonald 1986). Mothers had usually withdrawn from the paid workforce to care for young children and, consequently, were often in a parlous financial position when the marriage came to an end. The economic arrangements made during marriage

did not help women after separation, when they lost the benefit of the main income earner but retained responsibility for a large proportion of child-related expenses. Their interrupted job histories and child care responsibilities also did not equip them for regular paid employment.

In New Zealand, married couples were covered by the equal-sharing rules in the Matrimonial Property Act, 1976.[431] The Act classified property under two headings—matrimonial and separate—and provided that matrimonial property would, in general, be divided equally. The Act divided matrimonial property, in turn, into two further categories:

The family home and chattels (including the family car and furniture) would be divided equally unless:

1. The marriage was for less than three years (a marriage of short duration);

2. There were extraordinary circumstances that would have made equal sharing repugnant to justice;

3. In which case, the home and chattels were divided according to the parties' contributions to the marriage partnership.

Other matrimonial property (property such as family businesses, investments, and insurance policies, including superannuation benefits) was divided equally unless the parties' contributions to the marriage partnership were clearly unequal, in which case it was divided according to the parties' contributions to the marriage partnership. This was called balance matrimonial property.

The presumption that the property should be split fifty–fifty was stronger for the family

---

[431] This section is based on the information gathered from the following website: How to: *The division of property when a marriage, civil union or de facto relationship ends* http://www.howtolaw.co.nz/html/ml013.asp (New Zealand)

home and chattels than it was for other matrimonial property.

In the assessment of the different contributions made to the marriage, financial contributions did not rate any more highly than contributions of other kinds, such as caring for children or performing domestic tasks.

The separate property (all property not classed as matrimonial property) remained the property of the person who owned it and was not divided. It included:

1. Property that the parties owned before they married and that they kept separate during the marriage;

2. Any gifts and inheritances that the parties received during the marriage and that they kept separate

Separate property also included all property acquired out of separate property, and the proceeds of selling any separate property.

But if an increase in the value of one party's separate property, or any income or gains derived from the property, was caused wholly or partly by the application of matrimonial property, then the increase, or the income, or gains, was matrimonial property, not separate property.

Similarly, if an increase in the value of one party's separate property, or any income or gains derived from the property, was caused wholly or party by the actions of the other party, the increase, or the income, or gains, was treated as matrimonial property.

In the case of a marriage of less than three years, equal sharing did not apply to:

1. The family home or a particular family chattel, if it was owned wholly or substantially by one spouse at the date of the marriage, or,

2. The family home or a particular family chattel, if it came to one spouse after the marriage began, by succession, by survivorship, as a beneficiary under a trust, or by gift from a third person, or,

3. The family home and all the family chattels, if the contribution of one spouse to the marriage was clearly disproportionately greater than that of the other.

In these cases, each spouse's share in the property in question was determined according to the contribution that each spouse made to the marriage.

In the case of matrimonial property other than the family home and chattels, each spouse was entitled to share equally in the property unless his or her contribution to the marriage had clearly been greater than that of the other spouse, in which case, the shares were determined according to each spouse's contribution to the marriage.

In giving effect to the division of the property, the court could make various orders in relation to the property, generally or to a specific item of property, such as ordering property to be sold or, in the case of the home, ordering that one party has the right to occupy it.

The court considered the interests of any dependent children. In determining the amount and value of the property, the court took into account any outstanding debts. If the spouses had entered into a valid matrimonial property agreement, matrimonial property was divided according to that agreement rather than the Act. This is mandated to as contracting out of the Act. However, in making the agreement the spouses were mandated to follow strict requirements (including each party receiving independent legal advice), or else the agreement was invalid.

In 2002, there were major changes to the division of property laws. The Matrimonial Property Act, 1976, was renamed as the Property (Relationships) Act, 1976, and the property of *de facto* couples (including same-sex couples) was brought within the purview of the Act, and was subjected to the same equal-sharing rules which earlier governed property of married couples. Further, in April 2005, civil unions were established as a legally recognized form of relationship, and civil union couples are now treated the same as married couples under the Property (Relationships) Act.

Just as the old equal-sharing rules were limited in the way they applied to marriages of less than three years (marriages of short duration), the reformed laws also apply only to civil unions and *de facto* couples, who have lived together for at least three years. Prior to these reforms, *de facto* couples were not covered by the equal-sharing rules that applied to married couples, but instead by the ordinary rules of property ownership. It was, therefore, presumed that property owned jointly by the couple would be divided equally, and that property that was owned exclusively by one partner would not be divided.

Singapore and Malaysia

The Republic of Singapore and the Federation of Malaysia were administratively connected and share a common legal tradition inherited from the British. While Malaysia became independent in 1957, Singapore evolved as the State of Singapore in 1959, with the powers of internal self government while the powers of foreign affairs and defence were controlled by Britain. In 1965, Singapore severed its links from Britain and evolved as an independent state. One of the first tasks undertaken was to enact a Women's Charter in 1961 for empowerment of women. The family law reforms in Malaysia were introduced through the Law Reform (Marriage and Divorce) Act, 1976. Due to the common legal traditions, the legal precedents of Singapore can be relied upon in Malaysia. Both Singapore and Malaysia have separate family laws for

Muslims. Family courts were set up in Singapore in 1995.

The laws related to marriage and family relations are located in Section 46 of the Women's Charter which stipulates as follows:

1. Upon the solemnization of marriage, the husband and the wife shall be mutually bound to co-operate with each other in safeguarding the interests of the union and in caring and providing for the children.

2. The husband and the wife shall have the right separately to engage in any trade or profession or in social activities.

3. The wife shall have the right to use her own surname and name separately.

4. The husband and the wife shall have equal rights in the running of the matrimonial household.

This provision was adopted from Section 159 of the Swiss Civil Code and provides a moral framework for regulation of matrimonial relationships in Singapore. The second part of Section 46(4), which was a logical progression, contained the provision of matrimonial property, '... *And in the ownership and management of the property*' had to be deleted as it was vehemently opposed (Leong 2008:25). But in 1996, Section 112 was added to the Women's Charter which empowered the courts to order the just and equitable division of matrimonial assets. This amendment changed the law which was based on the common law tradition of separation of property, with a limited power to make some adjustment to settlements upon divorce, to the concept of differed community of property. Under the differed community of property regime, while the marriage subsists, the common law notion of separation of property prevails and the spouses gain interest in the other's property only by the general rules of property law. But upon termination of marriage, the civil law of community of property gets invoked and the property is divided equitably between the spouses, irrespective of the role each spouse discharged during the course of their marriage. In particular, whether it was a financial or a non-financial role, at the time of divorce, the courts are empowered to divide the property equitably between them.

From the time when this power was first used by courts in *Koo Shirley* v. *Mok Kong Chua Kenneth*[432] in 1989, the body of case laws has grown dramatically. In a study conducted on the divorce settlement, it was highlighted that women were able to secure adequate economic settlements:

No homemaker wife has been given less than 35% of the matrimonial assets, except in two cases involving 'huge money'. Indeed homemaker wives who served their roles for 20 years or more have received 50% … The next most common proportions were where one spouse received 10% more than the other. With these two categories forming the vast majority of decisions given in recent years, it may be suggested that an order of division of matrimonial assets in Singapore is likely to be of equal division or within a narrow range from equal division (Leong 2007: 696–8).

The Malaysian Court of Appeal, in 2003, in *Sivanes Rajaratnam* v. *Usha Rani Subramanium*,[433] relied upon the decision in *Koo Shirley* v. *Mok Kong Chua Kenneth* (mentioned above) while deciding the question of division of matrimonial assets upon divorce under the Malaysian family law. The court commented that while it would be dangerous to rely uncritically on decided cases from other jurisdictions, as far as the decisions of Singapore courts are concerned, this may not necessarily be so as the two share a common tradition.

In Malaysia, Section 76(1) of the Law Reform (Marriage and Divorce) Act, 1976 (LRA), stipulates that the court shall have the power, when granting a decree of divorce or judicial separation, to order the division between the parties of any assets acquired by them during the marriage, either by their joint efforts or the sale of any such assets, and the division between the parties of the proceeds of sale.

Abdullah (2006: 212–4) in her book, *Family Law for Non-Muslims in Malaysia* discusses the following two cases (among others) to elaborate the legal provisions regarding the distribution of matrimonial property upon divorce.

In *Ching Seng Woah* v. *Lim Shook Lin*,[434] it was held that the matrimonial home and everything which is put in it by either spouse, with the intention that their home and chattels should be a continuing resource for the spouses and their children, to be used jointly and severally for the benefit of the family as a whole. It matters not, in this context, whether the assets are acquired solely by the one party or the other, or by their joint efforts. While the marriage subsists, these assets are matrimonial assets. Such assets should be capital assets. The court further ruled that the earning power of each spouse is also an asset.

Koay Cheng Eng v. *Linda Herawati Santoso*[435] concerned a marriage between a Malaysian husband and an Indonesian wife who were married in the United Kingdom in 1980. After six years of marriage, the husband filed for a divorce against the wife. While deciding the issue of division of matrimonial assets, the court held that the wife's entitlement to half the matrimonial assets in Malaysia as is derived under Section 76 (1) and (2) of LRA. The court considered the wife's contribution towards the household, that is, purchase of furniture, kitchen appliances, groceries, etc., as contribution towards acquiring the property and held

---

[432] 1989 SLR 342
[433] (2003) 3 MLJ 273

[434] (1997) 1 MLJ 125
[435] (2004) 4 MLJ 395

that the wife is entitled to half of the assets in Malaysia and in the United Kingdom. In addition, the court considered the Employees Provident Fund (EPF) contributions as matrimonial assets acquired during the marriage. The court commented that the wife had entered into the marriage with the intention of growing old with the husband. On his retirement they would both enjoy the benefit from the money set aside in EPF contributions. Therefore, with the breakdown of the marriage, the husband should not be allowed to solely benefit from the EPF. Hence, it was held that the wife is entitled to half the amount remaining in the husband's EPF account at the time of divorce and such money should be paid to the wife when the same is payable to the husband.

Countries Governed by Islamic Law[436]

In countries governed by Islamic laws, generally, marital assets are divided inequitably, with women receiving the smaller share. Such inequitable distribution results, in part, from the under valuing of women's contributions in at least two distinct ways. First some systems (for instance Iran) link division of marital property with fault rather than comparative contribution of each spouse and if the wife is judged to be responsible for the divorce, she may not be given her share. By treating a woman's right to her share of matrimonial property conditionally, this system fails to recognize a woman's right to her share of matrimonial assets as absolute and presume that only a man's right to such property is absolute. Second, when dividing marital assets the courts and others tend to focus on women's direct financial contributions

[436] This section is based on information provided in *Know Your Rights* by Women Living Under Muslim Laws (2003: 316–19) and a recent news report regarding the situation in Tanzania.

through wages and to undervalue or fail to recognize altogether their contributions through unpaid domestic labour.

In some legal systems, while granting divorce the courts, acting on their own discretion, may determine the division of matrimonial property, for instance, the Central Asian Republics, Fiji, Gambia, Malaysia, Singapore, Tanzania, and Yemen. Under some systems (for instance Cameroon, Iran, Philippines, Senegal), the assets are divided according to the spouses' chosen matrimonial property regimes (communal/joint or separate).

In Fiji, unemployed wives are not recognized as having contributed to the marriage. Senegal's *Code de la Famille* envisages a woman's ownership of assets which she acquired through her paid profession. In such systems, the husbands benefit from a wife's contribution of her labour and time to the family and any family business, yet these benefits are given no value when a marriage ends.

In Malaysia, even assets acquired individually by one party may be divided as long as the party which actually purchased the asset receives a greater share. Though, this may seem just and equitable in theory, it leaves for an insensitive judge to undervalue a woman's contribution and, accordingly, award her with very little. However, a woman's household and familial efforts are sometimes taken into account in countries such as Iran, Malaysia, and Singapore.

Opting for a joint property regime, where all marital assets are considered to belong to the spouses equally, does not necessary solve a woman's problems, especially where polygamy is practiced. Usually the husband remains in the marital home and controls the assets, hence, lack of division results in the wife leaving the marital home with nothing. Also, courts do not always divide joint property equally on divorce and a woman may have problems proving her contribution towards its acquisition (Cameroon, Senegal). Since women return to their natal homes after separation or divorce, they usually lose their share of the matrimonial property as it is controlled by husband or his family members (Central Asian Republics). This tendency for property to remain with the husband and his family can make the enforcement of a court settlement that favours the wife difficult.

Since the South Asia region does not recognize the notion of matrimonial property, Pakistan and Bangladesh do not have any laws regarding property division.

In Nigeria there is no concept of division of property. The suggestion for division is dismissed as Christian and/or Western imposition which, in any case, would be unfair to co-wives.

In Iran, since 1993, a husband wishing to divorce his wife is required to pay wages to her for the housework during the subsistence of marriage, provided she is not found to be at fault in the divorce proceedings. In 1995, it was made compulsory for divorcing husbands to pay the determined wages for housework, along with the wife's other rights, such as *mehr* and *nafaqa*, before the divorce could be registered.

In Singapore, after the 1999 amendments to the Administration of Muslim Law Act, 1966 (ADMLA), the definition of matrimonial assets was clarified and the factors that the courts could take into account, while deciding the division of these assets, was also elaborated. The factors that are to be taken into account are under Section 52(8)(a) of ADMLA:

1. The extent of contribution made by each party in money, property, or work, towards acquiring, improving, or maintaining the property.

2. Any debt owing, or obligation incurred, or undertaken by either party, for their joint benefit or for the benefit of any child of the marriage.

3. The needs of the children, if any.

4. The extent of contribution made by each party to the welfare of the family, including looking after the home, or caring for the family, or any aged or infirm relative, or dependent of either party.

5. Any agreement between the parties with respect to the ownership and division of the property made in contemplation of divorce.

6. Any period of rent free occupation or other benefit enjoyed by one party in the matrimonial home to the exclusion of the other party.

7. The giving of assistance or support by one party to the other party (whether or not of a material kind), including the giving of assistance or support which aids the other party in the carrying on of his or her occupation or business.

8. The income, earning capacity, property, and other financial resources, which each of the parties has, or is likely to have, in the foreseeable future.

9. The financial needs, obligations, and responsibilities, which each of the parties has, or is likely to have, in the foreseeable future.

10. The standard of living enjoyed by the family before the breakdown of the marriage.

11. The age of each party and the duration of the marriage.

12. Any physical or mental disability of either of the parties – the value to either of the parties of any benefit (such as a pension) which, by reason of the dissolution of the marriage, that party will loose the chance of acquiring.

Section 52(14) of the Amendment to ADMLA 1999, defines matrimonial assets as:

1. Any asset acquired before the marriage by one party or both parties to the marriage which had been substantially improved during

the marriage by the other party or by both parties to the marriage.

2. Any asset of any nature acquired during the marriage by one party or both parties to the marriage.

However, this does not include any asset (not being the matrimonial home) that has been acquired by one party at any time by gift or inheritance, and that has not been substantially improved during the marriage by the other party or by both parties to the marriage.

In Tanzania, Section 144(2)(a) of the Law of Marriage Act (LMA) does not define matrimonial property but directs courts to order the division of matrimonial property/asset acquired through joint efforts, when names do not appear in title deed and when a wife cannot prove direct financial contribution, it is left to the discretion of judges. Because LMA does not indicate what should be considered as assets/property acquired through joint efforts, so usually, only financial contribution gets recognized.

In an important case, *Bi Zawadi Abdullah* v. *Ibrahim Iddi* (Dar-es-Salaam Registry, unreported) it was held that the domestic duties of a spouse do not constitute contribution within the meaning of Section 114 of the Act and, thus, do not entitle a spouse to a share of the matrimonial assets. In this case, the court refused to equate housework and child bearing with the husband's paid work in evaluating what constitutes matrimonial property.[437]

But in an earlier case, *Bi Hawa Mohamed* v. *Ally Sefu* (Civil Appeal No. 9 of 1983, Dar es Salaam Registry, unreported), held a more sympathetic view of women regarding their domestic duties of a wife as contribution, entitling the spouse to a share in the matrimonial property. Defining domestic duties, spouses are to be treated as working, not only for their current needs but also for their future needs, both the extent of contribution and such future needs are to be assessed from family assets acquired during the marriage in keeping with extent of contribution.

In this case, the husband argued that he had given money to the wife to start a business which she had squandered away. If she had invested the same in starting a small business, her situation would not be so bad. It was held that she was an irresponsible wife and, hence, she was left with very little money for a financial settlement.[438] It seems that generally courts are more amiable to arguments by the male parties than those by female parties over property entitlements.

Need Versus Contribution in Division of Property[439]

When the concept of a 'no fault divorce' and the partnership model of marriage based on equality was introduced it was felt that the earlier concept of title as well as need and fault would cease to have any relevance while arriving at matrimonial settlements. The earlier status, based model of marriage, was replaced by an egalitarian or equality model under which obligations of spouses ideally end with the marriage and any outgoing economic obligation, such as child support or payment of existing marital debts, are considered shared and equal responsibilities. But, since marriage is not a partnership between equals, these assumptions end up being unjust and inequitable to women who do not fit into this neat formula of a partnership model.

---

[437] Dar-es-Salaam *Daily News*, 1 August 2009

[438] Ibid.

[439] I am relying upon an incisive essay by Martha Fineman (1991a 265–77). While the essay is dated, the arguments are still relevant for our understanding of these concepts.

The movement from the strict common law system, based on title, to the modern notion of a partnership, based on equally valued though different in kind, contributions to a marriage cannot be assumed to have benefited all categories of women. It cannot be assumed that the circumstances that generated arguments for a distribution system focussed on need are no longer in existence. But the material circumstances of divorcing women and children are being detrimentally ignored by supplanting a focus on contribution as the primary distributive concept. According to Fineman (1991a: 270), the ascendancy of contribution may represent a convenient model of conceptual progress to legal academics and law reformers, but for many divorcing spouses, as well as the practising professionals to whom they turn for advice, adverse material circumstances, and the needs they generate, have not been left behind.

She argues that one source of controversy about property distribution rules is the existence of two competing, and perhaps incompatible and unrealistic, political visions of contemporary marriages. The first is the more modern view that marriage as an institution has been transformed so as to be more consistent with the formalistic notions of equality between the sexes. The second is the more traditional policy stance that the family is the appropriate, perhaps solitary, institution to resolve the problems of dependency or need that inevitably arises in the context of families. Highly sceptical of the contribution model, which is based on the assumption that marriage is a partnership between equals, she argues for a "need" based framework (ibid.: 265).

The dominance of equality means that it will also provide the preferred method of valuing contributions and, thus, further avoid the need for anything resembling detailed fact finding or consideration of individualized circumstances on the actual amount of contribution. The equality norm is formally embodied in provisions which establish an initial presumption that all property of the spouses is to be equally divided upon divorce. This equality paradigm is consistent with the organizing concept of marriage as an equal partnership. Equality has significant symbolic importance, and the partnership model is argued as not only reflecting the preferred or correct vision of women, but also as secondarily addressing need. The dependent woman, through an ideological fiat, is considered to be benefitted in being brought up to partnership status and made an equal (ibid.: 272–3).

Marriage is considered a union, a partnership of equals. This view mandates that if a partnership ends, the accumulated assets should be divided in a manner consistent with the model under which they were acquired. If two parties are morally or legally equivalent for one purpose, that they must be morally or legally equivalent for all purposes is an erroneous assumption.

Equality standards, in the distribution of property at a conceptual level, may be linked to broader ideals of placing equal value and promoting freedom of choice in marriage roles. Making equality the ongoing concept of underlying divorce may be considered part of a series of conscious symbolic choices about how to best ensure a more just society. But, when equality rhetoric is translated into specific rules governing distribution, the results must be measured and assessed in more than symbolic terms. Symbolic expression may be important, but Fineman argues that care should be taken so that when translated into legislation having a direct impact on the lives of many people, the results also meet the standards of fairness and justice (ibid.: 276).

Need has no role to play in a true partnership of equals. The dependency image, in contrast, anticipates that a woman has been victimized to a certain extent in a marriage. She is viewed as having sacrificed career goals and ambitions for the marriage. At divorce, she is dependent and that dependency will continue. She, therefore, has needs which should be compensated in addition to her contribution to the marriage. This fact cannot be overlooked while applying the principle of equality while dividing family property.

The need based model and the equality model represent polar ends on the spectrum of transformations that have occurred in the way society views marriage and the position of women within it. The need based factors may warrant a deviation from the equality ideal. Unfortunately, in the statutory schemes and case laws of many countries discussed above, the need factors are neither sufficiently developed nor sufficiently clear to offset the partnership model with its easily grasped contribution factors. The wholesale acceptance of the partnership model means, however, that the burden of production, proof, and persuasion, will be placed upon the one who would argue that the rule of equality concept is inadequate, given her specific circumstances (ibid.: 271).

There are a variety of situations experienced by women at divorce that will not conform to a simplistic application of the contribution conceptualization of the equal partnership model. This failure to adequately accommodate these differences in women's material circumstances has led to a system of rules of property distribution applied to all women, but based on the experiences only of some.

The care of children produces dependency, not only for the children, but for the primary caretaker. It must be recognized that this dependency does not end when the child reaches eighteen or any other magic age (ibid.: 271). Some family relationships tend to last. This is particularly true of the primary caretaking parent who is attached to her children. The obligations that such a parent may feel are not legal, but moral or emotional. A parent who desires to assist a newly adult child may not be dictated to do so by law, but that does not mean that the law should be insensitive to (or unsupportive of) her sensibilities when assessing the most socially useful allocation of property at divorce.

Women who are not mothers but choose to be unemployed during marriage may be considered overcompensated by the imposition of the partnership model. They will be overcompensated to the extent that they do not contribute wages to the accumulation of assets, nor do they contribute by providing a non-monetary service, such as childcare, for the family unit. Mothers who are gainfully employed (and, therefore, are not considered poor), however, may be undercompensated because the need factors will be interpreted too narrowly to remedy the needs generated by their post-divorce situation but may not compensate these women for the double burden they have undertaken during the subsistence of their marriage. The cost to women of deviating from the traditional housewife model is extremely high. When the concept of contribution is simplified and employed solely in an effort to make the housewife an equal partner, other circumstances are ignored. In fact this concept works to the disadvantage of the non-housewife woman. Such a woman not only pays with her time and effort while she is doing two jobs, for example, but also at divorce, she may be viewed as not in need of assistance because she is not a 'traditional' housewife. There is a danger that the contribution concept might, in fact, be used against women who are not in traditional roles.

Commitment to the equality ideal, typified by the partnership metaphor as the appropriate analytical construct to guide divorce policy, does not permit us to face the fact that women's and children's needs in this society have continued to be undervalued and ignored. Fineman argues that the equality rhetoric now associated with the marriage relationship must be challenged as inappropriate for resolving difficult questions in situations such as divorce, where they stand in inherently unequal positions (ibid.: 278).

An equality view of marriage denies reality for many women who assume, during and after the marriage, more than a partner's share in the conduct and burdens associated with household and child care. The partnership metaphor slips easily into equal sharing of property, children, debts, and so on at divorce. The metaphor has symbolic content that is preserved only at significant cost to many women who must suffer equality in this one area while the rest of the society and culture continues to treat them unequally (ibid.).

While women in many Western countries, where the equality model has been adopted and property is divided on the basis of contribution, may suffer due to the equality model, in India, the primary determining factor continues to be need, which gets translated into a traditional remedy of maintenance claims at a basic minimal survival level. As we have observed in the first section on maintenance, guilt continues to overshadow maintenance claims and the amounts awarded range from conservative to meagre and far less than what a divorced woman would require to sustain herself and her children in the same standard of living as her husband. Hence desertion and diovrce renders multitudes of women destitute. To remedy this, property settlements have to be incorporated within matrimonial laws through legislative reforms. The reforms would have to take into account both, need and contribution so that the problem faced by women in Western countries are not replicated. The principles have to also take into account specific Indian realities such as prevalence of joint families as against the nuclear families of the West and the

legal incident of a Hindu joint family property. The principles adopted have to be not just equal but also equitable and just which would remedy the problem of poverty and destitution among divorced women.

Section D

CUSTODY AND GUARDIANSHIP OF MINORS

Historical Evolution of the Notion of Guardianship

The legal terms, guardianship and custody are used in the context of children and imply certain legal responsibilities towards them. Guardianship implies the proprietary rights over the child's person and property. Custody implies the responsibility of raising a child. While the father was favoured in issues of proprietary rights, the mother's role as caretaker of her children had been granted due recognition for well over a century.

Among the ancient systems, both Roman as well as the Muslim law recognized the fact that minor children or children of tender age need care and protection. It is within the context of this social need that a notion of guardianship and custody first evolved. The ancient Hindu society was organized on the basis of the joint family system which was more inclusive. Within this social organization, there was sufficient protection for all minors and dependents. The minors were always deemed to be in the care and protection of the *Karta* as well as the elders in the joint family. Within this social structure, even an orphan child was awarded protection. Hence, the notion of guardianship and custody did not evolve under the Hindu law. Even under tribal customs the minor children were deemed to belong to the clan or tribe.

The Muslim law lays down detailed rules regarding the guardianship of minor's property, but there are very few rules regarding the guardianship of minor's person. This is because the Muslim lawgivers correctly surmised that the guardianship of a minor's person is more a matter of custody. Paras Diwan comments that though Muslim society is essentially patriarchal, a rule was laid down that custody of children of tender age belonged to the mother (Diwan and Diwan 1993: ix). The English law recognized this principle of Islamic law only after a protracted struggle extending over almost two centuries, and that too by legislation. It is rather unfortunate that in the early days of the British rule, some text book writers and judges could not decipher the distinction between guardianship and custody under Muslim law, and either undue prominence was given to paternal rights or the mother was dubbed as the guardian of her children of tender age.

Hizanat (care and control of the child) is a well developed concept under Muslim law. The *Fatwa Alamgiri* declares: Of all persons, the mother is best entitled to the custody of her infant children during marriage and after its dissolution. The term *hazina* is applied to the woman to whom belongs the right of rearing her child. Of all persons, the first and foremost right to have the custody of children belongs to the mother and she cannot be deprived of her right so long as she is not found guilty of misconduct. The mother's right of *hizanat* can be enforced against the father or any other person. But the right of rearing the children is not absolute; it is a right to which obligations are attached. If she is not found suitable to bring up the child, or her custody is not conducive to the physical, moral, and intellectual welfare of the child, she can be deprived of it.

Statutory Provisions

The Guardians and Wards Act (GWA), 1890, is one of the earliest statutes enacted by the British which addresses the issue of guardianship. The Act was of common application, though legal principles under the personal laws could also be invoked. Later, during the post-Independence period, when laws governing family relationships of Hindus were codified, a special Act was enacted, that is, The Hindu Minority and Guardianship Act (HMGA), 1956, and Hindus were taken out of the purview of the general law and were placed under this special law governing the Hindus. Despite this, the principles evolved under the GWA have to be applied while deciding cases under the HMGA as the following cases illustrate:

- The Supreme Court, in *Surinder Kaur Sandhu* v. *Harbax Singh Sandhu*,[440] while awarding custody to the mother ruled that Section 6 of HMGA, 1956, cannot supersede the principles evolved under GWA that the welfare of children is paramount.
- The Patna High Court reaffirmed this principle in *Bimla Devi* v. *Subhas Chandra Yadav Nirala*,[441] and held that from a reading of Section 2 and Section 5(b) of HMGA, 1956, it becomes clear that the 1956 Act is to be treated as a supplement to the 1890 statute.

Hence, principles evolved under the GWA and HMGA can be read interchangeably. So, though HMGA is applied to Hindus and GWA to non-Hindus, custody and guardianship issues of both the Hindus and non-Hindus are decided on the basis of same legal maxims.

Court *Parens Patriae* of all Minors

Some of the earliest statutes enacted by the legislature in British India concerned protection of minors. The provisions, scattered under various British Charters and Regulations, regarding care and custody of children were subsequently consolidated into the GWA in 1890.[442]

---

[440] (1984) 3 SCC 698
[441] AIR 1992 Pat 76
[442] Preamble of the Act

The Indian courts were considered to be the supreme guardians of all minors during colonial rule. As supreme guardians, the courts exercised parental jurisdiction in respect of all children, irrespective of their religion. This notion prevailing under the English law was introduced in India, first through various British Charters and Regulations, and, subsequently, incorporated under the GWA. The courts were entrusted with the same power as the Court of Chancery in England. This power is presently exercised by the district court and the high court under its inherent jurisdiction. The duty of protection and preservation of infants and their property devolves on the guardian judge, the representative of the sovereign state (*Babu Gyan* v. *Sudan*).[443]

When the child is brought before the court, the court assumes charge and endeavours to ensure the well-being of the child in the same manner as a natural parent would have done. This function is discharged by the guardian court by appointing a suitable person as the guardian of the child. When a guardian is appointed under the Act, the control of the person and property is vested in the court, the guardian being its nominee. Following the English doctrine, *parens patriae*, the Act invests its powers in an individual to look after the child. The guardian acts under the superintendence and supervision of the court.

Only a minor is eligible for protection under the Act, but the Act does not define a minor. The Indian Majority Act of 1875, defines a minor in negative terms, that is, a minor is a person who has not attained majority. Since the age of majority is eighteen, it can be construed that a person below this age would be eligible for protection under this Act.[444] Once a guardian is appointed the period of minority extends by a further three years, until the child attains twenty one years. Hence, the courts will restrain from appointing a guardian in respect of a child who is nearing majority (*Apagappa Ayyangar* v. *Mangathai*).[445] The court will appoint a guardian only if it is satisfied that appointment of guardian is necessary for the well-being of the child. The courts have also adopted a view that in the absence of a father, if the mother is fit and competent, there is no need to formally appoint her as a guardian, since she is the natural guardian of the child.

A person should be willing to be appointed as a guardian. A *de facto* guardian (a person who has already assumed guardianship of the child), a testamentary guardian, or a guardian under a deed of instrument, may be declared as a legal guardian by the court in order to avoid any future disputes. Declaring a person as a guardian indicates judicial recognition of his/her status as a guardian. Appointment as a guardian is not a question of private or civil right. Any existing or previous relationship, wishes of the parents, and character and conduct of the person to be appointed as a guardian, are relevant factors. The courts may also consider the wishes of the child. While all these can be contributory factors, the only principle which is mandatory is the welfare of the minor.

Once a guardian is appointed, the minor becomes the ward of the guardian and a fiduciary relationship is established between the guardian and ward, which is of a juridical nature. This is a relationship of utmost trust, akin to the one that subsists between the natural parent and child. The guardian must look after the child's general well-being, health, and education. If appointed as a guardian of the minor's property, the guardian must not profit personally from it.

[443] AIR 1955 Nag 193
[444] Section 4 (1) of the Act
[445] (1917) ILR 40 Mad 672

If the guardian is found unsuitable, the court has the power to deprive the person of the guardianship through a court order.

Custody Disputes and Women's Rights

Challenges to the Notion of Paternal Rights

While a guardian could be appointed for a minor who is an orphan or who has lost his/her father, it was presumed that as a natural guardian the father has a superior right over his children and this right is undisputed. On the other hand, paternal obligations and responsibility towards children were not given due importance. It was more a question of a father's right over his children than his obligations towards them. Even the obligation to maintain the children was not recognized. Under English law, it was a moral (and not a legal) obligation and this was confined only to legitimate children. There was no obligation to maintain the illegitimate children. Though both Muslim and Hindu laws recognized that maintenance of children is a personal obligation, under Hindu law, the obligation was not absolute. But Hindu law recognized the paternal obligation to maintain both legitimate and illegitimate children.

There has been a shift in modern times and today there is an obligation to maintain both legitimate and illegitimate children. The obligation to maintain children is imposed on both parents. Alongside the obligation to maintain and educate children, the modern law of many countries also imposes criminal liability for deliberately neglecting them. A Bombay High Court judgment has gone to the extent of stating that a father who does not maintain his children does not have the welfare of his children at heart and, hence, he is not eligible for (the right of) access to the child.

A statute enacted for the protection of minors who were orphans, came to the rescue of women who were separated from their husbands. Soon after married women were awarded the right of legal separation and divorce, the contentious question of custody started forming a significant aspect of this statute. The GWA was based on the principles of English family law and subscribed to the doctrine that the father is the natural guardian of the child. After the enactment of the Matrimonial Causes Act, 1857, separated and divorced wives started approaching the courts seeking custody of their children and in the process challenged the principle of natural guardianship of their husbands. It is in this context that the principle, the best interest of the child is paramount started gaining recognition as opposed to the paternal rights of the father. By the mid-twentieth century, the principle became one of the primary pillars of the family law in England.

The earliest judicial pronouncements of the English courts acknowledged the undisputed primacy of the father. Even immorality or misconduct could not dislodge the premise that as a natural guardian, he has the primary right to custody of his children. For instance, in 1849, the English courts in *Warde* v. *Warde* held: 'Mere immorality of the father is not sufficient to deprive him of custody.'

The GWA incorporated the tension then prevailing in England. While Section 19 stipulated that father is the natural guardian of the minor, Section 17 prescribed that welfare of the child is paramount. There is an internal inconsistency between these two sections. Hence it was left for the courts to firmly establish the superiority of Section 17 over that of Section 19 and render the doctrine of the welfare of the child is paramount as a non-negotiable mandate in deciding custody of children as against the stipulation under Section 19 that the father is the natural guardian of the minor.

Initially, the courts acknowledged the superior right of the father, as these cases demonstrate:

1. In 1914, in *Annie Besant* v. *Narayaniah,*[446] the Privy Council declared that the father has the paramount right to the custody of the children. He cannot be deprived of this right unless it is clearly shown that he is unfit to be their guardian.

2. In 1924, in *Sukhdeo* v. *Ram Chandra,*[447] the court held: An immoral father has just as good a right to his own children as a moral one, and in many cases, he is just as likely to see that his children are properly brought up even if he himself does not live properly.

3. In 1940, in *Mst Alita Tawaif* v. *Parmatma Prasad,*[448] an errant father was given custody of the child as against the mother who was a *tawaif* (courtesan).

But gradually, courts began to concede that despite being a natural guardian, the father's rights over his children are not absolute (*Captain Rattan Amol Singh* v. *Kamaljit Kaur*).[449] In the 1970s, the courts went further and ruled that if the father is unfit to be the guardian of the minor, or is not in a position to look after the well-being of the child, the court is competent to remove the child from his custody and hand over the child to the mother or anyone else appointed by the court as guardian (*Kamalamma* v. *Laxminarayana Rao* and *Budhulal Shankarlal* v. *An Infant Child*).[450]

While acknowledging the rights of the mother, the courts held that retention of custody with the mother is not unlawful and proceedings cannot be initiated against her for wrongful confinement. The courts also began to chastise the husband for removing the child from the custody of the wife. The courts also

conceded that even an affluent father could be deprived of custody of the child and affluence of the father and his family is not a criterion which could tilt the balance in favour of the father (*Surinder Kaur Sandhu* v. *Harbax Singh Sandhu*).[451] The courts have further held that even if the father is affectionate towards the child and is found to be not unfit, this cannot be a criteria to deny the mother, who might be equally affectionate, caring and competent, the custody of the child. Some recent rulings on this issue are discussed below:

1. In 1987, in *Elizabeth Dinshaw* v. *Arvand M. Dinshaw,*[452] where the father had taken away the child from the custody of the mother who was living in U.S.A., the Supreme Court observed that the conduct of the father in taking the child from the mother, to whom it was entrusted by a competent court, was most reprehensible. The explanation given by him about his father's illness was far from convincing not justifying the gross violation and contempt of the order of the court. The court also observed that the child's presence in India was the result of an illegal act of abduction. The conduct of the father had not been such as to inspire confidence that he is a fit and suitable person to be entrusted with the custody and guardianship of the child. The Court held: 'Whenever a question arises before a court pertaining to the custody of a minor child, the matter is to be decided not on considerations of the legal rights of parties but on the sole and predominant criterion of what would best serve the interest and welfare of the minor.' The court restored the custody to the mother.

In 1993, in *Vinodchandra Gajanan Deokar* v. *Anupama Vinodchandra,*[453] B. N. Srikrishna,

---

[446] AIR 1914 PC 41
[447] AIR 1924 All 622
[448] AIR 1940 All 329
[449] AIR 1961 P&H 51
[450] AIR 1971 Mys 211; AIR 1971 MP 235

[451] (1984) 3 SCC 698
[452] AIR 1987 SC 3
[453] AIR 1993 Bom.232

Justice of the Bombay High Court held that a father can be denied access until he displayed evidence of reform and paid the interim maintenance arrears. The father had refused to comply with the order of interim maintenance to the wife and the child. Observing that fresh air and plenty of love would hardly be sufficient to sustain life, the court held that the necessity of daily sustenance would have to be provided by the father if he loved the child. The court commented that the father had acted with a spirit of vengeance and a vein of sadism. Accordingly, the court denied access to the father unless and until he displayed evidence of contrition, penitence, and reform, and paid the arrears of interim maintenance. This judgment goes a long way in countering the premise of paternal right, not only of custody and guardianship but also of access to the child and turns it into a paternal obligation.

Again, in 1993, in *Om Prakash Bharuka* v. *Shakuntala Modi*,[454] the Gauhati High Court held that the fact that the father loves his children, and is not otherwise unfit, cannot necessarily lead to the conclusion that the welfare of the children would be better promoted by granting their custody to him as against the wife, who may also be equally affectionate towards her children and otherwise equally free from blemish, and who, in addition, because of her profession and financial resources may be in a position to guarantee better health, education, and maintenance for them.

In 1997, in *Anjali Anil Rangari* v. *Anil Kripasagar Rangari*,[455] the Supreme Court held that it cannot be disputed that the mother is also a natural guardian under Section 6 of the HMGA, 1956. Accordingly, the Court held that the custody of the children with the mother

was neither unlawful nor were they wrongfully confined by the mother.

Doctrine of Child of Tender Age or Hizanat

If the principle that in a patriarchal system, the father, as head of the family, is the natural guardian could be used to award custody to the father, a corresponding principle of the patriarchal family system that the mother is the natural care taker of children of tender age, could be used to substantiate the mother's claim to custody. In case of infant children, courts are generally inclined towards the mother. It is generally accepted that mother is the best suited person to look after a child of tender age and that there is no substitute for mother's care and affection. Initially the English law subscribed to the notion of the supremacy of paternal rights and the tender age doctrine did not find a place within battles over child custody. The courts did not hesitate to handover a child at the breast of the mother to the father (*King* v. *De Mannerville*).[456] The Talford Act of 1839 was the first statutory modification recognizing the mother's preferential claim to the custody of children up to the age of seven. The Custody of Infants Act, 1873, raised the age of the tender age child to sixteen. The Guardianship of Infants Act, 1886, popularly known as Mothers' Act gave statutory recognition to the doctrine of child of tender age. Thereafter, the English courts began to give a serious consideration to this principle. In a leading case, *In re A. and B.*, [457]while granting custody of the two minor children to both the parents the court held: 'It is important for children that they should be brought up in their tender age on terms of affection with

---

[454] AIR 1993 Gau.38
[455] (1997) 10 SCC 342

[456] (1804) KB 5 East 221
[457] (1897) 1 Ch 786

each other and that they should know both the parents.'

In 1926, in *W. v. W.*,[458] the court laid down that the child of tender age should ordinarily remain with the mother. In *Allen* v. *Allen*,[459] the trial court awarded custody of an eight-year-old girl to the father as against the mother who was found guilty of adultery. In appeal, it was held: 'It would not be right to snatch the female child from her mother and force her to make a new start with her father and step mother.'

The Indian courts had no difficulty in propounding this principle. Both Muslim law as well as HMGA recognized this principle. The Muslim law, under the notion of *hizanat* lays down that the custody of a son of seven years and a girl of thirteen years should be with the mother. Similarly, HMGA lays down that a child under five years should ordinarily reside with the mother.[460] But the converse does not hold true, and it cannot be construed that the custody of any child above the specified age will ordinarily be with the father. The principle of the welfare of the child has to be applied in all cases.

The Punjab Chief Court,[461] as far back as in 1917, in *Ahmed* v. *Rehmatan*,[462] held that the custody of a child of tender age should be with the mother even if she had remarried. Similarly, in 1926, the Lahore High Court in *Zainab Bibi* v. *Abdul Kareem*[463] awarded custody to a Muslim mother who had remarried. In *Samuel* v. *Stella*,[464] the court awarded the custody of a female child

of thirteen years, who was delicate in health, to the mother.

More recently, the courts have expanded the scope of the notion of *hizanat* and have read principles of Declaration of the Rights of the Child, 1959, adopted unanimously by the United Nations General Assembly, into it as the following case illustrates. The courts also have expanded the notion of best interest of the minor is paramount.

1. In *Mumtaz Begum* v. *Mubarak Hussain*,[465] the husband had retained the custody of a son who was only a few months old after throwing the mother out of her matrimonial home. The court proceedings dragged on for four years and custody was denied to the mother on a technical ground that she had not filed the petition under the GWA. In appeal, while awarding the custody to the mother, the high court relied upon the Declaration of the Rights of the Child, 1959, The court also relied upon a judgment by Rizvi J. of the Lahore High Court in *Bavi* v. *Shah Nawaz Khan*,[466] where the stipulation of hizanat was explained as follows:

The principle of Muhammaden law as regards hizanat is fundamentally based on the principle that it is for the welfare of the minors. ... The child needs motherly love and affection, more than anything else. The environment in which he is being now brought up is unsuited to his mental growth and development. The father hardly finds time even to talk to him, leaving the house in the morning and returning quite late in the evening when the child would be in bed. His stepmother, who has a (tiny infant) of her own, would also, definitely, have little time for him. The child's grandparents, admittedly, being physically handicapped, also cannot do anything for him.

The court explained that in Principle 2 of the Declaration, there is a mandate for enactment of laws for special protection of the child

---

[458] (1926) All ER 111

[459] (1948) 2 All ER 413

[460] *Proviso* to Section 6 (a) of HGMA

[461] The Punjab Chief Court was set up under the Punjab Chief Courts Act of 1866 and was converted into the Lahore High Court later in 1919.

[462] (1917) 40 IC 107

[463] AIR 1926 Lah 117

[464] AIR 1955 Mad 451

[465] AIR 1986 MP 221

[466] PLD (WP) Lah 509

to enable him to 'develop physically, mentally, morally, spiritually and socially in a healthy and normal manner' and stipulated that 'the best interests of the child shall be the paramount consideration'. The court further commented:

When personal laws are divinely sanctioned, a presumption will naturally arise that such laws have a humanistic content because when great seers, saints, and prophets, found any faith, they act as benefactors of the mankind as a whole. No personal law claiming divine sanction can afford to deny paramount consideration to the welfare of the child. It is not difficult, therefore, to see why the Declaration was unanimously adopted by the United Nations General Assembly in 1959.

2. In *Mohd. Ayub Khan* v. *Saira Begum*,[467] the husband vehemently opposed the application for interim maintenance, even for minor children, tooth and nail. Hence, the application for interim maintenance was rejected by the trial court. The wife approached the sessions court which set aside the trial court order and remitted the matter back to the trial court to decide the issue of interim maintenance. Finally, the trial court awarded Rs 300 for each of the minor children as maintenance. The husband pleaded that he has divorced his wife and, hence, she was not awarded any maintenance. The husband did not comply with the order of maintenance and did not pay any money to the wife either at the time of divorce or at any other time, even towards the maintenance of the three children. While these proceedings were pending, the husband realized that the eldest son had turned 7. He took shelter under the Shariat law and filed an application under Section 9 read with Section 25 of the GWA for custody of the eldest son. The husband pleaded that the wife was not looking after the child well and the upkeep, maintenance, and education, of

the child was not possible at the maternal grandfather's place. After interviewing the child, the trial court has remarked that the child was being well brought up by the mother and the grandfather, and was living happily with his two brothers and attending school regularly. Against this trial court order rejecting his petition for custody, the husband approached the high court. The court commented:

The father failed to prove his entitlement to custody of the child. On one side he was contesting the litigation under Section 125 of Cr.PC and on the other was projecting himself to be a caring father, who was interested in the future well-being of his son. A person refusing to pay maintenance to his own child cannot claim he is interested in betterment of very same child. The interest of child is of paramount consideration. While claiming that he is interested in the well-being of his children, he has claimed custody of only one child. If the father was really interested in the betterment of his children, he would have conceded to share his income with his children. But instead, he dragged the wife from court to court while opposing her application for maintenance. After filing this petition, he agreed to deposit some money for the maintenance of the elder son, but not for the other two children. Finally, he deposited Rs 6,000 in court. But this cannot be projected as a ground for awarding custody to the father. The principle of best interest of the child must prevail.

Allegations of Immorality and Women's Right to Custody

While women won the battle against the concept of natural guardianship of the father by using the doctrine of child of tender age and took benefit of the fact that she is the primary care taker of children of tender age, the battle against the notion of immorality was far more difficult. Prostitutes, tawaifs (courtesans), women presumed to be of loose moral character, women found guilty of adultery in matrimonial disputes, and women who had remarried, were routinely denied custody of their children. But the same yardstick of moral character was never

---

[467] I (2002) DMC 234 Chh

applied to husbands, as already discussed earlier. This is because of the differing standards of morality which is applied to men and women in a patriarchal society. Sexual morality is perceived to be the single relevant factor that could be used to deny women custody. At the initial stage, the issue of the women's conduct and character became a crucial ingredient while deciding issues of custody. Hence, allegations of immorality and sexual misconduct were routinely hurled against women in custody battles. A wife who had committed a matrimonial fault like adultery was not awarded custody of her child. In 1862, in *Seddon v. Seddon*,[468] the English courts proclaimed: It will probably have salutary effect on the interests of public morality that it should be known that a woman, if found of guilty of adultery, will forfeit all rights to the custody of, or access to her children (as cited in Diwan and Diwan 1993: 440).

In the Indian context, initially a woman who had committed a matrimonial fault was denied custody of children. In *Skinner v. Orde*,[469] the Privy Council held that upon conversion, the mother loses her right of custody to her child. In *Venkamma v. Savitramma*,[470] the court held that a mother who was leading an immoral life was not entitled to custody of her child. But the same principle was not applied to husbands and the courts did not hesitate to give custody to an errant or immoral father. In *Kaulesra v. Joral*,[471] custody was given to an immoral mother as there was no other suitable person.

But one witnessed a lenient approach towards women who did not have the means to support their children or women who had been accused of adultery. In 1934, the Allahabad

High Court, in *Haidri Begam v. Jawwad Ali*,[472] ruled that the mere fact that the mother does not have adequate means is not sufficient to deny her custody, particularly when there was no allegation of adultery. In *Madhu Bala v. Arun Khanna*,[473] the courts held that in order to deny custody to the mother on the ground of adultery, a very strict standard of proof has to be applied. Later cases have held that even remarriage or accusations of adultery cannot be the governing principles to deprive the mother of her right of custody and guardianship as the following two cases illustrate:

In *Chethana Ramatheertha v. Kumar V. Jahgirdar*,[474] the wife filed an appeal against the order of the family court, Bangalore, directing her to hand over the custody of her minor daughter to her husband on the ground that she had remarried. The Karnataka High Court reversed the order of the family court and allowed the custody of the daughter to be retained with the mother. The Court held:

Even while the parent had not disqualified himself or herself from being the natural guardian of a minor child, it may still be found that the minor's interest is better served if the custody of the child is with the other parent. The remarriage of the mother after divorce does not suffer from any disqualification or drawback. The mother is well educated and can support the child financially. The paramount consideration in appointing any person as guardian of a Hindu minor is the welfare of the minor.

In *Sadhana Randev v. Santosh Kumar*,[475] the father sued for custody of his children, levelling allegations of unchaste behaviour against his former wife. Despite the allegations, the court upheld the right of the mother for custody of her children. The Allahabad High Court held

---

[468] (1862) 2 SW & Tr 640 (as cited by Diwan & Diwan 1993: 476).
[469] 14 MIA 309
[470] ILR 1880 12 Mad 67
[471] ILR 28 All 329

[472] AIR 1934 All 722
[473] AIR 1987 Del 81
[474] 2003 (2) HLR Kar
[475] I (1998) DMC 710 All

that the deciding factor was the welfare and wishes of the minor and ruled as follows: Regardless of whether or not the mother was having relations with anyone (an accusation which was never proved), she should not be disqualified from being the children's guardian and retaining custody on that ground. The children's preference is to stay with their mother, and the emotional value of the motherly instinct are far more important than any allegations of immorality raised by the father. Though the children had passed the age of 13 years, they can not be turned over to their father against their wishes.

Mother as the Natural Guardian:
Gita Hariharan

In the case of *Gita Hariharan* v. *Reserve Bank of India*,[476] the Supreme Court was called upon to decide the constitutional validity of the provision that the father was the natural guardian of a minor.

The issue before the Supreme Court was whether the mother could be the natural guardian of her minor child. As per Anand CJ and M. Srinivasan J., the definition of guardian and natural guardian do not make any discrimination against the mother and she being one of the guardians mentioned in Section 6 would undoubtedly be a natural guardian as defined in Section 4(c). The Supreme Court held that the words 'after him' in Section 6, meant that if the father was absent for any reason whatsoever, such as desertion, the mother would be the natural guardian and that it did not mean after the lifetime of the father. The third judge on the Bench, Banerjee J. held that: 'Be it noted that gender equality is one of the basic principles of our Constitution and in the event the words "after him" is to be read to mean a disqualification

of a mother to act as a natural guardian during the lifetime of the father, the same would definitely run counter to the basic requirement of the Constitution, since the Constitution and the statute would have to be in accordance therewith and not *de hors* the same.'

The court spelt out certain situations—(1) when the father is indifferent towards the child, (2) if the child is in the exclusive custody of the mother, (3) due to physical or mental incapacity the father is incapable of acting as the guardian, (4) when it is decided mutually between the parents that the mother will act as the guardian—the mother could be deemed as the natural guardian, even during the lifetime of the father.

A point to note is that only when the father has abdicated his responsibility or, by consent, agreed to elevate the mother to the status of a natural guardian, would the judgment come into effect. However, in keenly contested custody battles, this judgment will not be relevant.

Custody Rights of Other Relatives

More recently, where the mother has died in unnatural circumstances and the father is facing criminal charges, the courts have been inclined to grant custody or guardianship to maternal relatives. Applying the principle of best interest of the child is paramount, the courts have upheld the right of custody of the relatives as against the right of the father.

In *Kirtikumar Maheshankar Joshi* v. *Pradipkumar Karunashanker Joshi*,[477] the mother had died under tragic circumstances and the father was facing criminal charges under Section 498A of IPC (cruelty to wives). After her death, the children left the father's house and went to live with their maternal

---

[476] AIR 1999 SC 1149

[477] AIR 1992 SC 1447

uncle, Kirtikumar, who filed for guardianship of the minor children on the ground that the father was unfit to be the guardian. The children were presented before the court in chamber proceedings and their wishes were ascertained. The court found the children intelligent and more mature than other children of their age. Both the children were bitter about their father and narrated various episodes showing ill treatment of their mother. They categorically stated that they were not willing to live with their father and were happy with their maternal uncle. Assessing their state of mind, the court was of the view that it would not be in the interests and welfare of the children to hand over their custody to the father. While acknowledging that the father being a natural guardian has a preferential right to the custody of his minor children, the Supreme Court held that keeping in view the facts and circumstances of the case as well as the wishes of the children, the court was not inclined to hand over custody to the father. The custody was retained with the maternal uncle. The father was permitted to meet the children on holidays on prior notice. It was pointed out that the father was at liberty to move the court for modifying the order, if he won over the love and affection of the children

In *Shakuntala Sonawane* v. *Narendra Khaire*,[478] there was marital conflict between the parents of the minor child and the wife had returned to her parents' house when she was pregnant. On the very day of the birth of the child, the husband had filed a divorce petition in the family court at Bandra, Mumbai, on the ground of cruelty and desertion. During the pendency of the proceedings, the custody of the minor child remained with the wife, who was staying with her parents. In February 2000,

[478] 2003 (2) HLR Bom

the wife died under tragic circumstances. The mother, Shakuntala Sonawane, (the maternal grandmother of the minor child and the Petitioner) alleged that the daughter had been set on fire by the husband, the respondent in this petition. The contention of the Respondent was that she had committed suicide. The minor grand-daughter was looked after since her birth by the Petitioner. While awarding custody of the child to the maternal grandmother, the Bombay High Court held: 'Even if a natural guardian is alive and stakes his/her claim, the court can still proceed to appoint some other fit person as the guardian under the provisions of the Act, after ascertaining the welfare of the minor'.

In *Nil Ratan Kundu and Anr.* v. *Abhijit Kundu* (2008) 9 SCC 413, the mother of the child had died due to an unnatural death and the father was charged under Section 498A of IPC for cruelty and was arrested. The minor child was in the custody of maternal grand parents. After his release, he filed for custody and guardianship and was awarded custody by the family court of Calcutta and the Calcutta High Court on the basis that the father is the natural guardian of the child. But in appeal the Supreme Court set aside the orders of the lower court and held that while dealing with custody cases, is neither bound by statutes nor by strict rules of evidence or procedure nor by precedents. In selecting proper guardian of a minor, the paramount consideration should be the welfare and well-being of the child. The court ruled that the welfare of children is controlling consideration governing custody of children and not right of their parents. If the child is old enough to form intelligent decision, wishes of the child should also to be considered in custody cases. Both courts were duty bound to consider allegations against the father under the criminal offence of Section 498A, IPC and have neglected to consider the important factor of 'character' of the proposed guardian.

In *Athar Hussain* v. *Syed Siraj Ahmed*, AIR 2010 SC 1414, the Supreme Court upheld the order of the Karnataka High Court which awarded custody of the minor children to the grandparents. The mother of the minor children had died and the children were being brought up by grand parents and were attached to them. The custody was awarded to the father by the family court, Bangalore, but the high court in appeal reversed the order and the parents were permitted to retain custody until the issue of guardianship was finally decided. The court explained that interim custody and guardianship are two entirely different issues which are independent and distinct from each other. While the father remains a natural guardian under Section 19 unless declared unfit, interim custody is to be guided by the sole factor of welfare of the children. The court commented that welfare of the children demands that their custody which is presently with their maternal relatives should not be disturbed till the final settlement of their guardianship issue by the family court. Irreparable injury would be caused to the children if they, against their will, are uprooted from their present settings.

Issues of Custody in Matrimonial Disputes

In contemporary times, the most bitter and acrimonious battles over custody take place during matrimonial litigation. The old maxim, father is the natural guardian, has given way to the newer maxim, best interest of the child is paramount. This is the primary pillar on which the issue of custody has to be decided. The best interest maxim overrides the stipulations in different personal laws and is applied universally in all custody litigations.

Even a wife, who has committed a matrimonial fault, can be awarded custody of the child if the court comes to a conclusion that it is in the best interest of the child, as the cases already discussed earlier reveal. To deprive a child of tender age of its mother's love and care would not be in the best interest of the child, has been the well-established legal doctrine. The courts have held that the aim of the litigation is not to punish the guilty but only to ensure the welfare of the child. A matrimonial court and counsellors attached to it, as well as lawyers appearing in the matter, must ensure that the child is always the centre of all negotiations over custody and that this principle is never undermined. Since the child remains unrepresented in matrimonial disputes, it is the duty of the court to ensure that the child's interests are not harmed or negated. Courts do not view the child as an object to be tossed around between the warring parents.

But the doctrine, *best interest of the child*, is more complex than it appears on the surface. When the father is wealthy and the mother has no independent source of income, where would the best interest of the child lie? The courts have ruled in several cases that just because a mother does not have the financial resources, it does not mean that she should be denied custody of her children. The superior social status of the father, or even the character and conduct of the mother (including her matrimonial faults), cannot be factors tilting the balance in favour of the father. The only determining factor would be the care and concern shown towards the child as the following case reveals.

In *Ravi Shankar* v. *Uma Tiwari*,[479] the couple was divorced thirteen years prior to the father filing for custody of the child who was all along in the custody of the mother on the ground that his greater wealth would permit him to better provide for the welfare of the child.

---

[479] I (1999) DMC 585 MP

The Madhya Pradesh High Court held that in a case where the father claims custody of a minor child, he must show from his conduct that he is interested in the betterment and upkeep of the minor. The father must demonstrate through action that he would look after the welfare and security of the minor, which would be the paramount consideration of the court. In this case, for thirteen years since his separation, the husband had done nothing to take care of the minor or look after her interest, either by monetary or any other means. The court held that the father could not claim custody of his child purely on the basis of financial status. Financial security can only be one of the components to be considered while providing for the overall welfare of the child. The court dismissed the husband's plea and retained the custody with the mother.

A similar view was also expressed by the Bombay High Court in *Ashok Shamjibhai Dharod* v. *Neeta Ashok Dharode.*[480] It was held that the affluence of the father, or his parents, or relatives, is not a relevant factor for determining the issue of child custody.

While non-working mothers are haunted by the fear of lack of resources, working mothers are faced with another set of anxieties. Would a woman who is employed and spends most of her waking hours outside of the home be in a better position to look after the child? Recent cases have resolved this issue. It has been held that a mother cannot be denied custody merely because she is gainfully employed. This principle has now evolved into an established rule.

In modern day custody battles, neither the father, as the traditional natural guardian, nor the mother, as the biologically equipped parent to care for the child of tender age, are routinely awarded custody. The principle, best interest of the child takes into consideration the existing living arrangements and home environment of the child. The courts are usually hesitant to remove the child from a familiar environment and hand her/him over to the non-custodial parents. Each case will be decided on its own merit, taking into account the overall social, educational, and emotional needs, of the child.

The simple principle followed by the courts once a legal battle commences is usually to award interim custody to the parent who already has the physical custody of the child and award visitation rights to the other parent. This is usually over weekends and school vacations so that the studies are not disrupted. It is important to remember that access to the non-custodial parent or the right of visitation is the right of the child to see the parent, and not that of the parent to impose on the child.

The routine manner in which access is granted to fathers becomes a cause of concern to most women. While they struggle to make ends meet and are raising their children against great odds, the fathers can easily win the children over by showering them with gifts. While the mothers have the responsibility, the fathers are left with the pleasant task of recreation with the child. Hence, courts must ensure that the father's economic responsibility towards maintenance of children forms a part of the terms of custody and access. In this context, the judgment of B.N. Srikrishna, J., in *Vinodchandra Gajanan Deokar* v. *Anupama Vinodchandra,*[481] (discussed earlier) is an important marker, where His Lordship denied access to the father who had not paid interim maintenance and held that until the father displayed evidence of contrition, penitence, and reform, and paid the

[480] II (2001) DMC 48 Bom

[481] AIR 1993 Bom.232

interim maintenance arrears, he will not be entitled to visitation rights.

In another case which has been litigated over a very long period, *Gaurav Nagpal* v. *Sumedha Nagpal*,[482] while upholding the wife's right to custody, the Supreme Court commented that simply because the father loves his children, and has not been proved to be otherwise undesirable, it does not necessarily lead to the conclusion that welfare of children would be better promoted by granting the custody to him. Children are not mere chattel, nor are they toys for their parents. The court does not give emphasis on what parties submit but exercises its jurisdiction for the welfare of minor. The term welfare must be construed literally and must be interpreted in its widest sense. Though, provisions of relevant statutes may be taken into consideration, in matters of custody, the court is entitled to exercise its power of *parens patriae*. The court also commented that the father had played a fraud upon the wife by concealing the fact of his earlier marriage, wherein his wife committed suicide within six months of marriage. The husband's argument that the child was living with him for a long time overlooks the fact that by flouting various orders, leading even to initiation of contempt proceeding, he has managed to retain the custody of child. The court commented that he cannot be a beneficiary of his own wrongs.

In the proceedings under the Hindu Marriage Act, the court could make, from time-to-time, such interim orders as it might deem just and proper with respect to custody, maintenance, and education of minor children, consistently with their wishes, wherever possible.

Custody orders are not permanent orders and can be varied if the changed situation so demands. Even consent orders passed in

petitions for mutual consent divorce can be subsequently varied. In *Vikram Vir Vohra* v. *Shalini Bhalla*, AIR 2010 SC 1675, the Supreme Court upheld the order of the trial court and the Delhi High Court, permitting varying the order of access arrived in the divorce petition filed by the spouses jointly in a petition for divorce by mutual consent and permitted the child to be taken to Australia. The court commented that the mother's autonomy on her personhood cannot be curtailed by a court on the ground of a prior order of custody of the child. Every person has a right to develop his or her potential and the right to development is a basic human right. The mother cannot be asked to choose between her child and her career. Since the mother and the child are attached to each other, separating the child from his mother will be disastrous to both. The mother was required to give an undertaking that she would abide by the order to access the husband.

The courts would view any violation of the undertaking seriously. For instance, in *David Jude* v. *Hannah Grace Jude*, AIR 2003 SC 2925, the mother was allowed to take the minor child to U.S.A. on an unconditional undertaking that she would bring the child back whenever the court required her to do so. But subsequently, she flouted the undertaking and did not produce the child before the trial court and despite several notices, did not herself remain present before the court. She also flouted the several notices issued to her by the Supreme Court in contempt proceedings. The Court held that her attitude in not appearing before the court was defiant and contemptuous and she was held guilty of contempt and was awarded three months of simple imprisonment and a fine of Rs 50,000.

The custody battle takes a harsher toll on women due to their emotional vulnerability and financial dependence. While fathers are left

---

[482] I (2009) DMC 523 SC

free of all responsibilities, the mothers unilaterally bear the emotional, social, and financial obligations, of the children due to their own socialization process. At times, when the economic burden and prolonged litigation become unbearable, women succumb and give up custody, rather than face the daily emotional turmoil for themselves and their children.

The issue of custody becomes even more complicated in situations where the children are citizens of a foreign country and the issue becomes one of conflict of laws.[483] In this context, the Supreme Court ruling in *Sarita Sharma* v. *Sushil Sharma*[484] helps to shed light on the judicial approaches to dealing with the complexity. The children were citizens of USA. The mother was awarded custody but was restrained from removing the children from the jurisdiction of the concerned court in USA. The mother flouted the order and brought the children to India. The husband had an arrest warrant issued against the wife. In a *habeas corpus* writ petition filed by him, the high court granted custody to the father and allowed him to take the children back to USA. In appeal, the Supreme Court set aside the high court order and commented as follows:

The decree passed by the American court, though a relevant factor, cannot override considerations of welfare of minor children. The father resides in USA with his mother aged about 80 years. He appears to be in the habit of taking excessive alcohol. It is doubtful whether the husband will be able to take proper care of the children. Welfare of a female child lies with mother. The mother is not found wanting in taking proper case of children. Considering all aspects, it was not proper for the high court to have allowed the *habeas corpus* writ petition directing the mother to hand over the custody of children to the father and permit him to take them away to USA. Since the husband had an arrest warrant

[483] This issue is discussed in section titled 'Marriages with Expatriate Indians' of Chapter 1 *Marriage and its Dissolution*.

[484] I (2000) DMC 413 SC

issued against the wife in USA the Supreme Court commented that the chances of the mother returning to USA with the children would depend upon the joint efforts of both the parties to get arrest warrant cancelled by explaining the circumstances to the concerned court in USA.

But in two other cases, *Shilpa Aggarwal* v. *Aviral Mittal*, 2010 Cri.LJ 844 and *Dr. V. Ravi Chandran* v. *Union of India*, 2009 (14) SCALE 27, which were decided subsequently, where the children were foreign nationals and the mothers had brought the children to India, the Supreme Court directed that the children should be taken back and subjected to the jurisdiction of their respective countries. The Court further ruled that the best interest of the children lies in sending the children back as the court concerned with the issue of custody would be best suited to decide the principle of welfare of the child. In both these cases the mothers lost out and had to send the children back to the custody of their fathers and it was left for the mothers to agitate the issue of custody in the respective courts in a foreign country.

Traumatised Children and Access Rights

In cases where due to domestic violence the mother is either forced to leave the matrimonial home or is thrown out of the matrimonial home, the children and the mother are most vulnerable due to the sudden separation. If the woman is unable to get physical custody of the children either through the intervention of the police or social work organizations, she is compelled to approach the courts. In these situations, it is important to ask that the children be immediately produced in court and to interview them in a non-threatening and non-intimidating environment in order to ascertain their genuine wishes. When the children are called to court and asked to decide as to which parent they prefer to reside with, the children are not in a position to speak against the parent with whom they may be residing. In these circumstances, the courts must play a proactive role to ensure that the children feel secure and are not threatened by either violence against themselves or their mother.

The principle of best interest of the child gets further complicated in cases of domestic violence where the children have either witnessed incidents of violence against their mother or have themselves been victims of violence. Children remember and relive these moments of abuse and the litigation process contributes to keeping the memory of violence alive. Greater sensitivity in settling issues of access in these situations should be exercised, so that the child is not further traumatized. The courts instead of allowing routine access to the father, must make an attempt to rebuild the child's relationship with the father through short supervised access hours. In this way, the child's wishes can be ascertained and access hours can gradually be increased, depending upon the child's comfort level.

An area that has come to light very recently is the issue of incest or sexual abuse of children by fathers and other male relatives. Many times, this occurs within families where there is already a matrimonial discord. At times the children are abused as a punitive measure against the wife. While a gradual awareness regarding this issue is beginning to surface within the context of criminal law, the relevance of this issue in family litigation and, in particular, while dealing with issues of custody and access, is yet evolve. Some cases which have come up in the context of criminal law are listed here with the view of creating judicial awareness even within the context of family law.

In the case of *Pooran Ram* v. *State of Rajasthan*,[485] when the father looked at the

teenage daughter lustfully, the mother commented and the father became revengeful. A few days later, at night, he gagged the daughter with her *dupatta* and raped her. The next day the daughter informed the mother and when the mother confronted the father, he beat her ruthlessly. Later, a complaint was filed. In his defence the father pleaded that there was a matrimonial dispute between him and his wife and due to this she had filed a false complaint against him. The trial court disbelieved his contentions and convicted the accused for seven years. In appeal, the court commented: The accused is a psychologically sadistic person and needs psychological treatment.

The courts do not always treat these cases as cases of urgency. The prolonged litigation results in causing injustice to the victim girl. In 1992, the Bombay High Court reduced the sentence of a father, who had been convicted of raping his seven-year-old daughter, from life imprisonment to ten years. The high court while reducing the sentence commented sympathetically:

The appellant is a hutment dweller and his poverty has placed him in the difficult position of having to sleep huddled up in a tiny area. Even though his wife had left him, he used to work the whole day and send the children to school, arrange for their meals from the hotel, provide them with toys and pocket money, and cook the night meal for them. The rape was a momentary lapse, due to his pathetic situation (*Abdul Wahid Shaikh* v. *State of Maharashtra*).

This note of sympathy and concern gets even shriller when the parties belong to more affluent strata of society. In the case of *Sudesh Jhaku* v. *K.C.J. & Ors*, a high-ranking government official was charged with indulging in oral sex and finger penetration with his six-year-old daughter. The police refused to charge the father with the offence of rape and instead registered the complaint under Section 377 – unnatural

---

[485] 2001 Cri.LJ 91

offence.[486] The wife filed a writ petition in the Delhi High Court to bring the offence under the scope of Section 376 (rape). The court rejected this argument and held that insertion of objects, etc., amounts only to violation of modesty.

The last, *N.N. v. P.N.* Misc. GP. 37/1999 decided on 4 March 1999 Bom (unreported) is an unreported judgment of the Bombay High Court in a child custody case. The parties belonged to the affluent section of society. The case concerned molestation of a three-year-old by the grand father. The wife opposed the husband's petition for custody. The interim custody was awarded to the mother but access was granted to the father at his residence every week for four hours. The comments by the judge concerned are an eye opener regarding judicial understanding of child sexual abuse:

Prima facie, I am of the view that the allegations which the Respondent (wife) has made against the father of the Petitioner do not appear to be true. I just could not imagine that the grand father, who must be of around sixty years of age, would indulge in such a heinous and pervert act to the children of such tender age. A doubt has lurked in my mind. The Respondent had at the first instance alleged that her minor daughter was molested but later she again added that both the children were molested. The children could not speak even a word with me when I affectionately patted them and asked them their names. Both of them did not even offer to utter a word. I was of course asking them in Hindi thinking that their mother tongue was Hindi. However, both the parents told me to talk with them in English. It was indeed a great surprise that children of three and four years of age were speaking in English. Thereafter,

I spoke to them in English, just putting a question to them asking their names. It is not as though they were looking scared or afraid or anything as even their parents were present. It is, therefore, extremely doubtful to imagine that both of them, the girl of three and the boy of four, would have told their mother about the so called and alleged molestation on them by their grandfather. I wonder what language they would have used to describe a situation of the molestation.

These comments clearly indicate the scepticism and stigma with which sexual abuse cases are met, even in the present day. Without any semblance of an investigation into the mother's claims of abuse, her allegations were brushed aside as an impossibility. Courts must make a concerted effort to identify instances of sexual abuse, especially when perpetrated against children, however heinous or unbelievable they may seem. Turning a blind eye to sexual violence, especially when perpetrated by a family member, can easily place a child within easy access, or even within the custody of his or her abusers.

Issues of custody, guardianship, and access, can no longer be viewed as parental rights. The determining principle is welfare of the child is paramount. The courts must exercise their power with great prudence and caution, so that it does not result in violation of the basic human right of children, the right to life, which includes the right to live without fear and trauma.

CONCLUSION

This chapter examines three distinct rights which flow from the marriage contract. While the laws of marriage and divorce are gender neutral, the issue of rights and obligations is clearly marked with gendered assumptions. Maintenance and matrimonial property concern economic rights of women and deal with entitlements to shelter and sustenance. The third issue also concerns entitlements, but not of economic nature.

---

[486] 'Unnatural offence' is a term which is used in Section 377 of IPC to describe acts of a sexual nature which are outside of the scope of peno-vaginal intercourse. This section was in the news in the context of same sex relationships when the Delhi High Court read down the section to exclude consensual same sex relationships in *Naz Foundation* v. *Government of NCT*, 2010 Cri.LJ 94 Del.

Motherhood is a gendered status not just in its biology but also in its social construction. Within its confines, a woman's role as the primary caretaker of her children creates an economic dependency. But this socially prescribed role has no economic value attached to it. Women's biological status as a mother, the social construction of the gendered role, and the dependency motherhood creates for women, are factors which come into play while determining women's rights to custody and guardianship of the children.

Historically, children were viewed as the property of the father. He was their natural guardian, they carried his name, the sons inherited his property or were deemed joint holders of the property along with him, as in the notion of coparceners or HUF property. Producing children (more specifically sons) was a pious obligation cast upon a Hindu father. The soil and seed doctrine of the ancient Hindu law viewed the mother merely as a carrier of her husband's seed. While motherhood was desired, aspired, and revered, a woman's claim over her children was not recognized by law. This notion prevailed across all personal laws. The section on child custody traces the struggle women had to wage for being recognized as natural guardians of their children, along with the fathers. But while claiming equal rights over children in matters of guardianship, the social construct of the specific notion of 'motherhood' and the constraints it imposes upon women also needs to be recognized in custody battles, beyond the gender neutral term 'parenthood'.

If the notion of equality and gender neutrality creates one set of problems for women, when gender is contextualized, it foregrounds another. Within a framework of clearly defined gendered roles, what gets contextualized is the woman's sexuality, sexual purity, and subordinate status within the marriage. As discussed in Chapter 1 of the first volume, while tracing the history of personal laws, the patriarchal social structure rests upon notions of women's sexual purity and control of women's sexuality. A sure way of ensuring this is to chastise women for their sexual misconduct by denying them their rights. If the entitlements flowed from the husband to the wife, then the wife's capacity to be entitled to these claims rests on her sexual purity. We can clearly see this trend, both in issues of maintenance as well as child custody. It must be conceded that the premise of gender neutrality was evolved to counter these gendered assumptions. But rather ironically, both the premises become inadequate while addressing women's concerns.

The claims of women to custody are located within two statutes, the Guardians and Wards Act (GWA) and the Hindu Minority and Guardianship Act (HMGA). Here, women had to challenge the patriarchal assumption of natural guardianship of fathers while staking their claim. Gradually, the mother was awarded legal recognition as the parent best suited to care for children of tender age. This recognition is based on gendered assumptions and is attributed to their biology and to nature. But women were content, as this assumption helped them to win custody battles against their husbands, as their role as nurturers of their children began to be recognized in court battles. Later this concept was expanded further and was converted into the best interest principle.

Indian courts have also read the United Nations Declaration of the Rights of the Child into domestic statutes in the context of custody and guardianship. By invoking this principle, due weightage is given to the physical, emotional, and moral well-being of the child. Further, since most women are in a lower economic category than their husbands, economic status of the parties is not a determinant. Today, the best interest doctrine applies over the doctrine that the father is the natural guardian of the child. This often overrides marital fault and the economic constraints of the party who has been granted custody. This principle is applied uniformly across all personal laws. This has been a hard earned victory.

However, women find themselves at a disadvantage, as the economic support which is awarded to the child is meagre. Being the primary caretaker of the child creates dependency and hampers job options for women. Motherhood is so intrinsically linked to womanhood that most women are unwilling to give up their claim of child custody. For women, it becomes an issue of emotional bonding beyond mere rights and entitlements. Most women view themselves and their children as a composite family unit and a bond which cannot be severed at the time of divorce. Hence, generally, women will opt to forsake economic advantages during divorce settlements to obtain sole custody of their children. It is not that fathers do not wish to obtain custody of their children, but the reasons for doing so are different from those on which the mother stakes her claims.

While the principle best interest of the child works well for women while determining issues of custody, it poses problems when access to the non-custodial father is awarded on a routine basis. Once the basic framework of awarding custody has been evolved, the courts apply these principles in a mechanical manner without contextualizing the specificity of the situation or the special needs of children. Courts presume that access to the father is in the best interest of the child, even when facts prove otherwise. For instance, even when divorce petitions contain allegations of cruelty, physical abuse, neglect of the child, or child battery, these allegations are not contextualized while determining the right of access. Granting access to the husband in such situations may not be in the best interest of the child.

There is also the lingering discomfort that from his vantage economic position, the father can adversely influence the child against the mother or win over the affection of the child by showering expensive gifts and, thus, communicate a wrong message to the child. In most situations, the father becomes the indulgent parent, while the mother as the primary caretaker of the child is reduced to the role of a strict disciplinarian, which at times children begin to resent. The lowering of the economic standard of the wife, in the post divorce phase, as compared to the more affluent lifestyle of the father, becomes a point of constant tension and worry to single mothers, who are the primary caretakers of their children. For the fathers, the issue of access becomes a lever to settle scores with the divorced wife. But courts are unwilling to examine the issue more minutely while deciding the claims of custody and access.

Worst are the cases where the minor has been subjected to incest or has developed a fear psychosis due to the domestic conflict. Even without providing counselling to deal with the trauma, or monitoring the child during access hours, courts routinely grant access to the father. At times, the access is overnight or may extend to half the school vacations. While these may cause serious harm to the child's emotional and psychological well being, courts remain oblivious to it, even while applying the best interest principle as the unreported cases discussed reveal.

In order to save their children from this emotional stress, there are instances where the mothers have taken drastic steps of absconding and becoming fugitives. For instance in the custody battle, in *Hema Ravishanker v. K. R. Ravishankar*,[487] the mother was awarded custody and the father was awarded access. Since the couple lived in two different cities, the ten-year-old child would have to travel and stay overnight with the father. The child refused. The child also suffered from chronic asthma

---

[487] I (2004) DMC 414 Bom

attacks and the mother was concerned that the tension would induce an asthmatic attack. In appeal against the interim order, the child was interviewed where the child mentioned certain incidents of sexual molestation by the grandfather. The judges disbelieved him and held that the child was tutored and this was a mere afterthought, since this fact was not pleaded earlier. Since she did not comply with the order of access, the wife was held for contempt. In subsequent proceedings the custody was reversed and was granted to the father. At this point the wife absconded with the child. Since then the mother and child have not been heard of.[488]

Non compliance of an order of access is viewed very sternly and the woman runs the risk of being prosecuted for contempt of court and may also lose custody of the child as a measure of reprimanding her, as the above case reveals. These are extreme situations which require more sensitive handling in order to save the children from these drastic measures. The courts cannot abandon their commitment to the principle of welfare of the minor, even in situations which pose challenges to their authority. Right of access is not paramount and cannot override the best interest principle.

There are several instances where the children are taken out of the mother's custody and are either taken out of the country or taken to another state, and women are deprived of both custody and access. Most often, women give up the legal pursuit as it becomes impossible for them to continue the legal battle. There are many ways in which their rights can be frustrated. Unfortunately, most women lack the financial resources to follow up these cases to their logical end and haul up their husbands for contempt of court in the same manner in which

the husbands are able to do when their wives flout the orders of access. So they give up the court battle half way.

In the Indian scenario, when a man claims custody of his children, he need not assure the court that he is capable of being the primary caretaker of the child. All he needs to assure is that there is a female member in the household, for example, a mother or a widowed or unmarried sister, who would play the role of the primary caretaker. It almost appears that the man claims custody of the child to satisfy the urge of mothering of his female relatives. In such cases, in an attempt to deprive the mothers of custody, frequently, allegations of mental instability are made against women to project them as unfit mothers. This is a cause of extreme anxiety for women because they run the risk of losing not just the custody, but even the right of access. Within a set up of a joint family, the custody battles become the battlefield for the entire joint family.

When we examine the economic entitlements of women in the Indian context, we are confronted with a glaring void as Indian matrimonial statutes do not provide for division of property upon divorce. Hence, lowering of economic standard in the post-divorce phase is a major concern for most women during divorce proceedings. Under the legal regime of separate property, the property acquired by either spouse during the period of marriage continues to be the individual property of the spouse that acquired it. While superficially it appears to be a just and equitable premise, when we probe further into the ascribed gender roles within marriage, it is a given premise that the man is the primary breadwinner of the family, and in order to facilitate this process, a woman is expected to sacrifice her career and dedicate herself totally to the task of looking after the well-being of her husband. In addition, she

---

[488] City sees rise in cases of parents kidnapping kids, Bombay: *The Times of India*, 27 April 2009.

must also take on the task of home making and child bearing and child rearing. Even if she is required or permitted to work, it would be only to augment the family income and, hence, her earnings are treated as a supplementary income of the family. The courts would penalize a woman for pursuing her career at the cost of her primary role as the caretaker of the family and this in itself can constitute a ground for divorce (*Suman Kapur* v. *Sudhir Kapur*).[489] At times, the choice for women is either to remain married or hold on to the job. This is a concern confined not only to the private domain of marriage and family, but spills over to the public domain of employment, as we have noticed in the *Air Hostess* case, *Air India* v. *Nergesh Meerza*,[490] in Chapter 2 of the first volume.

Rather ironically, while this is expected of the woman, this role has no economic value attached to it. Women's contribution to the domestic household during the subsistence of their marriage does not get any recognition under the matrimonial statutes. The property acquired by the husband is treated as his exclusive property. Since marriage is not viewed as an economic partnership, a woman is not entitled to claim division of property at the time of divorce. The contribution of the wife in creating these assets by performing domestic chores is not considered as a relevant factor.

Since only non-working women or women who are unable to sustain themselves with their own earnings are entitled to maintenance, most working/professional women lose out on their economic rights. They are perceived to be independent women who are not in need of financial support.

When property is bought by securing bank loans, since the husband is the primary earning

member, he will have the title to the property. In most cases, women are not even aware of these assets. The situation is even more complex as the notion of Hindu Undivided Family (HUF) property still prevails. The husband may have a share in the HUF assets or businesses conducted in the name and title of the HUF, but the wives will not have access to this information. Determining the husband's share in such property and then dividing it between the spouses is a daunting task which most courts do not venture into in the course of a matrimonial litigation. There is no clear mandate for matrimonial courts to order sale of matrimonial property, partition of joint family property or for judicial reapportionment on the basis of fairness in divorce settlements.

Within the separate property regime that is followed in India, there is no acknowledgement for the non-financial contribution of the wife through household labour. She does not acquire any right, title, or interest, in the assets acquired by the husband during the subsistence of the marriage. In the event of dissolution of the marriage by the husband dying intestate, the widow is eligible for a share of her husband's property, according to the rules of the personal law governing them. The personal laws of most communities accord the wife a status no higher than that of the children, thus, completely ignoring her contribution to the household and family in the form of unpaid work. She is treated as a beneficiary, with no claims over the deceased husband's estate, and could be willed out of his estate should he wish to do so (Shankaran 2008: 265).

A woman can claim a share only in property which is purchased in their joint names. This is as per the rules governing general property laws. Even the provisions of Section 27 of HMA that addresses the issue of property is clad in quaint and obscure language as property

[489] II (2008) DMC 774 SC
[490] AIR 1981 SC 1829

presented on or about the time of marriage and, hence, property acquired by their own individual efforts and not given to them at or about the time of marriage to be held jointly, would not be property covered by Section 27 of HMA. In *Kamalakar Ganesh Sambhus* v. *Master Tejas Kamalakar Sambhus*,[491] even though the wife established that she had contributed half the amount towards the construction of the house property, the court held that this could not be the subject matter of an order under Section 27 of the Hindu Marriage Act, and set aside the order of the family court on these grounds.

In recent times, the right of residence in the matrimonial home is protected by the PWDVA. While this is an important development, for a woman who wants to opt out of the marriage this is a very small consolation. Here, too, women have lost out if the matrimonial home stands in the name of the husband's parents or collateral relatives as the cases discussed above reveal. There is no concept of a deserted woman's rights in equity or the notion of constructive trust through which Lord Denning had protected the rights of deserted women, not only against the husband but also against his creditors. Hence, under the Indian statutes, divorced women are not protected from eviction from the landlords. In the path breaking ruling of the Supreme Court, in *B.P. Achala Anand* v. *S. Appi Reddy*,[492] the court awarded legal recognition to the woman's right of residence and placed her in the position of a sub-tenant, awarding her the right to be a party to a litigation which would deprive her right of possession of the matrimonial home. But, while important proclamations were made in this ruling regarding women's right to the matrimonial home, the woman concerned did not benefit from it as she had already been divorced and because the terms of divorce settlement did not include a provision regarding the dwelling home. Hence, the apex court ruled that she had no right to the matrimonial home.

This position was affirmed by the Supreme Court in another ruling, *Ruma Chakraborty* v. *Sudha Rani Banerji*,[493] where a divorced woman and her children were evicted from their home, which was rented in the husband's name, on the pretext that their right of tenancy was terminated with the divorce in which the wife's right to residence in the matrimonial home had not been negotiated. The court stated that although the right to matrimonial home exists for a deserted woman, the same cannot be extended to a divorced woman.

These judgments reflect the societal prejudices against women's right of property ownership. In 1980, the International Labour Organization (ILO) calculated that women do two-thirds of the world's work, for 5–10 per cent of the income, and own one per cent of the assets. Professor Shivaramayya (1999: xiii), in his pioneering work on matrimonial property, has attributed the low ownership of property by women in the world to the social and legal failure to recognize marriage as an economic partnership. According to him, the disproportionate holding of assets occurs primarily for three reasons:

1. Law and policies of the states do not recognize domestic work as productive work – even Marx does not;

2. Nature and nurture burden women with bearing and rearing of children. They are frequently forced to give up their careers to look after their homes;

3. Even when women take up jobs, they are confined to relatively low-paid ones.

[491] AIR 2004 Bom.478
[492] I (2005) DMC 345 SC: (2005) 3 SCC 313
[493] AIR 2005 SC 3557

When the theory of a no-fault divorce was introduced in the 1970s, most countries following the common law tradition, including England, introduced the concept of division of matrimonial assets at the time of divorce. England started off tentatively with the rule of one third allocation, or a need based settlement, but has gradually moved to the principle of equal distribution. In USA, Canada, and New Zealand, the principle governing property distribution is equal division. But judges also have the power to use discretion to ensure fairness. In Australia, in the absence of clear guidance judicial discretion plays a greater role. Other countries such as Malaysia and Singapore have also altered their laws more recently in the 1990s to include the notion of property settlement upon divorce.

The tendency in most countries seems to be to move away from dependency and need, to a theory of clean break, after which the parties are free to move on in life. Maintenance signifies dependency, which has no place in the gender neutral terminology of divorce theories that are prevalent in most countries. So, even when maintenance is awarded, it appears more like a property settlement. But this theory of equality is more a rhetoric than a reality, and several studies have brought out the poverty divorce brings upon women, despite the claim to property distribution.

There are several studies conducted in the United States and Australia in the 1980s, to assess the impact of the no-fault divorce and property settlement on women which are discussed in the section on matrimonial property, which confirm this. In particular, single mothers and older women living alone post-divorce can experience a drastic fall in living standards, with many becoming (and remaining) poor, along with their children. This economic vulnerability of women post-separation can be attributed to a combination of social and economic factors, many of which operate independently of marriage. These factors include women's weaker position in the labour market and their relatively lower earnings compared with similarly situated men. While this comment was made in a study to assess the impact of divorce upon Australian women (Funder 1986; McDonald 1986) the analysis is equally relevant for other countries.

Other factors relate more specifically to the roles that women adopt during and after marriage. For example, during marriage the couple may decide that the husband's income earning capacity will be promoted while the wife assumes greater responsibility for caring for children and home making. Given the needs of children and men's usually higher earning capacity, this arrangement can work well until the marriage ends. Upon divorce or separation, the costs of this division of labour during the marriage, such as loss of immediate earnings and reduced ability to earn in the future, place these women in economically precarious circumstances post-separation and divorce (Funder 1992).

The linkages between a woman's claim of child custody and the dependency it creates while evolving a framework for property division, poses a challenge to the equality model of marriage as partnership and needs further deliberations while evolving a blueprint based on justice and equity. A feminist legal argument in these countires has been that equality model is inadequate and does not take into consideration the needs of women who have the additional responsibility of caring for their children which diminishes their chances of getting back into the job market. Here the more recent arguments has been that in addition to contribution, the need or dependency should also be kept in view while arriving at property settlement terms. In contrast, in India, we still subscribe to the notion of a dependent wife where need and fault play a greater role while awarding maintenance. Within this framework the contribution gets totally excluded from judicial assessment and the courts do not have the power to settle the husband's property in favour of the wife in divorce proceedings. In addition, as Prof Sivarammaya has commented, the existing laws which address issues of property settlement are disparate, chaotic, and scattered (1999 : 20).

What is rather ironic in this entire discussion on property claims is that while maintenance is inherently problematic, as it does not take into account a woman's non-financial contribution to the marriage through housework and child care, taking the need factor totally out of the purview of divorce settlements has not been of great value to women. The English case law discussed in this section also bring out the factor that need alone does not suffice, and for wealthy women the premise can be derogatory.

In the Indian context the discussion is confined to the limited scope within the statutory provisions of maintenance despite its derogatory connotations (reflecting women's subordinate status within marriage) as it remains the only avenue for women to stake their claim of financial entitlement upon divorce. For most women, this entitlement forms the central core of their matrimonial dispute. It is far easier to come to an amicable agreement regarding divorce and custody while maintenance remains a disputed question. The widely contested nature of the maintenance provision makes it a complex terrain of matrimonial litigation, with several substantive and procedural aspects woven into it, and encompasses both civil and criminal procedures.

Curiously, the core of this economic dispute does not revolve around questions of financial arrangements of the family unit, but hinges upon issues of sexual mores. In the context of unequal power relations prevailing within patriarchal normative marriages, women's economic rights are determined in the context of sexual norms and codes. Within this paradigm, it really does not matter whether women are promiscuous, or men bigamous. The end result is the same, denial of economic rights of women. As can be observed, the norm of monogamy can be flouted with impunity by husbands and, to add insult to injury, later during litigation, the fact of a bigamous marriage can be used as an armour to defeat women's claims. This plea is advanced so routinely, that the Supreme Court in *Vimala* v. *Veeraswamy*,[494] was constrained to hold that when a husband pleads that the marriage is bigamous, the previous marriage would have to be strictly proved. In a similar manner, the Bombay High Court dismissed the plea of bigamous marriage, in *Rajlingu* v. *Sayamabai*,[495] as a mere afterthought.

This leaves us perplexed as to how a matrimonial misconduct or guilt can be flagrantly invoked by a husband to defeat the woman's economic claim, without any adverse criminal or civil consequences visiting him during court proceedings. This type of flouting of a legal mandate and its subsequent invocation to gain a financial edge against a vulnerable person can take place only within a blatantly sexist social order.

Despite the progressive interpretations and innovative legal maxims, the path to justice has not progressed in a linear trajectory. For example, the Bombay High Court ruling delivered by M.H. Kania J., way back in 1976. While deciding the rights of a woman in a bigamous marriage, his Lordship had held that since the Hindu Marriage Act is a social legislation, it could not have been the intention of the legislature that even in a case

---

[494] (1991) 2 SCC 375
[495] I (2007) DMC 396 Bom

where a Hindu woman was duped into contracting a bigamous marriage, she should be deprived of her right to claim maintenance (*Govindrao* v. *Anandibai*).[496] In stark contrast is the Supreme Court ruling in 2005, in *Savitaben Somabhai Bhatiya* v. *State of Gujarat*,[497] where the right of maintenance was litigated under Section 125 of Cr.PC, a provision enacted to ensure social justice and prevent vagrancy. Here, Arijit Pasayat J., and S.H. Kapadia J., commented that however desirable it may be to take note of the plight of the unfortunate woman, the legislative intent being clearly reflected in Section 125 of Cr.PC, there is no scope for enlarging it by introducing any artificial definition to include woman not lawfully married in the expression wife. The court further commented that it is inconsequential that the man was treating the woman as his wife. It is the intention of the legislature which is relevant and not the attitude of the party.

Chinnappa Reddy J., a former judge of the Supreme Court commented in this context: The court could probably extend the meaning to be given to the word wife in Section 125(1) to any woman who has gone through a recognized form of marriage, notwithstanding the subsistence of an earlier marriage. A further question may require consideration as to whether a common law wife is also entitled to maintenance under Section 125 of the Cr.PC (Reddy 2008: 122).

Confronted with contradictory viewpoints regarding the criterion for determining the legislative intent of a beneficial provision, what are the crutches that trial court judges have at their disposal while delivering constitutional justice. A.K. Sikri J. and Aruna Suresh J. have attempted to provide an answer: 'Where alternative constructions are possible the court must give effect to that which will be responsible for the smooth working of the system for which the statue has been enacted rather than the one which would put hindrances in its way. If the choice is between two interpretations, the narrower of which would fail to achieve the manifest purpose of the legislation should be avoided. We should avoid a construction which would reduce the legislation to futility and should accept the bolder construction based on the view that Parliament would legislate only for the purpose of bringing about an effective result.'

In this tussle between the old world, feudal value systems reflected in the ancient Hindu law, the law of the Smritis, along side pluralistic traditions validated by customs, at one end, and the newer statutory provisions of the modern codified Hindu law, at the other, what are the avenues for harmonious constructions of legal principles? How do we revisit the provisions of the ancient Hindu law in the context of its modern day distortions, within the statutory framework of contemporary Hindu law, while delivering justice? The same bench, comprising of A.K. Sikri J. and Aruna Suresh J. have provided certain tools of interpretations in this respect: 'The principles of Hindu Personal Law have developed in an evolutionary way out of concern for all those subject to it so as to make fair provision against destitution. There is clear evidence to indicate that the law of maintenance stems out of the secular desire and so as to achieve the social objectives for making bare minimum provision to sustain the members of relatively smaller social groups. Organically and originally the law itself is irreligious. Its fountain spring is humanistic. In its operational field although it lays down the permissible categories under its benefaction, which are so entitled either because of the tenets supported by clear public policy or

---

[496] AIR 1976 Bom.433
[497] AIR 2005 SC 1809: I (2005) DMC 503 SC

because of the need to subserve the social and individual morality measured for maintenance.

Beyond protection of individual rights, the courts also have a mandate to evolve the science of jurisprudence as it was brought to our notice by S.B. Sinha CJ., Ramesh Madhav Bapat J. and N.V. Ramana J. of the Andhra Pradesh High Court, in the following words: 'The interpretation of law is not merely for the determination of a particular case but also in the interest of law as a science. As such, interpretation of law must be in accordance with justice, equity, and good conscience, and more so, in furtherance of justice. If the court prima facie comes to the conclusion that the plaintiff/petitioner is entitled to interim maintenance, it can award interim maintenance in the interest of justice, without being fettered by orthodox prejudices, by showing liberal readiness to move with times.

This call to move with the times and blend the ancient with the modern in pursuit of justice is the call of duty. The judicial oath mandates this. The primary aim of the courts is to do justice as P.N. Bhagwati J. and Ranganath Misra J., had succinctly pointed out: 'The role of the court is not that of silent spectator or of a passive agency. When a dispute is brought before the court where maintenance of a neglected wife or a minor child is in issue, the court must take genuine interest to find out the truth of the matter. If the magistrate had asked proper questions to the witnesses when they were before him and deposing about the marriage, the relevant evidence would have come up before the court. It was the duty of the lawyer appearing for the appellant also to have played his role properly at the right time. Due to this judicial and procedural lapse, a case for a pittance of maintenance, filed in 1971, had to be sent back from the Supreme Court to the magistrate's court for retrial in 1985.[498]

Within this framework of the call of duty and judicial mandate, I am constrained to end this section with the framework provided to us in 1978 by yet another Bench of the Supreme Court comprising of legal luminaries, V.R. Krishna Iyer J. and D.A. Desai J.: 'The brooding presence of the constitutional empathy for the weaker sections like women and children must inform interpretation if it has to have social relevance. So viewed, it is possible to be selective in picking out that interpretation out of two alternatives which advances the cause – the cause of the derelicts.[499]

[498] The magistrate's courts are the lowest in the rung of judicial hierarchies. Between this court and the Supreme Court are two other rungs – the sessions court and the high court.

[499] *Captain Ramesh Chandra Kaushal* v. *Veena Kaushal*, AIR 1978 SC 1807.

3

Family Courts and Gender Justice

This chapter deals with the procedural aspect of matrimonial law in the context of family courts. Family courts, which were set up in most major cities of India during late 1980s and 1990s, served to shift matrimonial litigation from general civil and criminal courts to courts with special expertise in matrimonial law and dispute resolution. These courts were meant to make the litigation process less formal and intimidating, usher in the norm of speedy justice and quick redressal, and facilitate conciliation and settlements. While courts would continue adjudication in family disputes as per matrimonial laws and other legal provisions, it was hoped that the procedural and infrastructural shifts would tilt the balance in favour of disadvantaged sections, that is, women and children, and provide better access to justice to them.

While analysing trends in family law, a striking feature which emerges is that most reported judgments in this branch of law originate from litigation in family courts; the only exception being Delhi, where family courts had not been set up until recently.[1] Family courts have become the trend setters in matrimonial disputes and family law litigation. Hence, the procedural aspect of family courts has become an important component of the study of family law in India.

This chapter is based on a study of family courts conducted by the author, between 2003 and 2005, in four states, namely, Maharashtra, Karnataka, West Bengal and Andhra Pradesh, for the National Law School University of India, Bangalore (Agnes 2006). The study comprised personal visits to various family courts, collection of data from court records, analysis of the data for ascertaining trends in matrimonial litigation, interviews with judges, marriage counselors, and court staff of family courts and interviews with government officials and members of the higher judiciary.

[1] The first family court in Delhi was inaugurated by K.G. Balakrishnan CJ. on 15 May 2009 and started functioning from July 2009. As reported in *Indian Express*, Delhi, 15 May 2009.

The ideological framework of the concept of family courts and its historical evolution, roles and functions of various functionaries, their strengths and challenges, and veracity of their claim to gender justice are some aspects which this chapter attempts to address.

IDEOLOGICAL PREMISE OF THE ACT

Contextualizing the Act

The Family Courts Act, 1984 is a procedural statute which carves out a separate and innovative adjudication fora for family disputes (Gupte 2001: 23). The Act shifts matrimonial litigation from district courts and maintenance litigation (under Chapter IX of the Cr. PC) from magistrate's courts to family courts. These courts are in keeping with the judicial trend of setting up legal institutions which are more accessible to common people. Issues concerning labour, industrial disputes, juvenile delinquents, motor accidents, consumers, etc., have been brought out of the purview of regular courts into specialized courts or tribunals. The setting up of family courts in India needs to be viewed within the same context of de-formalisation of legal structures.

The concern over setting up of special courts for family disputes was first raised in the 1970s. The committee which was set up to evaluate the status of women in India, in its report titled *Towards Equality*, published in 1974, had recommended that all matters concerning the 'family' should be dealt with by courts specifically set up for this purpose. This report was tabled in the Parliament and was presented at the first world conference on the status of women in Mexico City, convened by the United Nations General Assembly to coincide with the 1975 International Women's Year.[2] The Law Commission of India,

in its 59th report published in 1974, while suggesting changes in the Civil Procedure Code had also recommended setting up of family courts. As per these recommendations, the Civil Procedure Code was amended in 1976 and a new section was added, i.e., Order 32A, to provide for setting up of a separate adjudication fora for family matters. But there were no further developments in this area until the women's movement raised the issue in the 1980s.

The 1980s witnessed the emergence of the new women's movement in India. The movement focused attention on the issue of unequal power relationships between men and women. The thrust of the campaign was legislative reforms, particularly in the area of violence against women—rape, dowry related harassment, wife murder, etc. Gender bias within courtrooms and adversarial procedures which prove detrimental to securing women's rights were also a concern expressed by the campaign. In this context, a demand was raised for special courts for family matters.

In response to these demands, a series of enactments and amendments to existing statutes were enacted by the Parliament. The amendment to rape laws (Sections 375 and 376, IPC) enacted in 1983, was the first in this series. In the same year, cruelty to wives was

---

[2]   The conference was called to focus international attention on the need to develop future oriented goals, effective strategies and plans of action for the advancement of women. The General Assembly identified three key objectives that would become the basis for the work of the United Nations on behalf of women:

- full gender equality and the elimination of gender discrimination;
- integration and full participation of women in development;
- an increased contribution by women in the strengthening of world peace.

The conference ushered in a new era for women's rights and women's development globally. Following the conference, the U.N. General Assembly declared the International Women's Decade (1976–85) to carry out the recommendations of the conference.

made an offence by insertion of Section 498A in the IPC. Later, in 1986, dowry death was made an offence by adding Section 304B to the IPC. The Dowry Prohibition Act, enacted in 1961 was amended twice, in 1984 and again in 1986. The Family Courts Act was part of the same trend of legislative reforms concerning women which had been introduced as part of this campaign. This is reflected in the statement of objects and reasons of the Act, which states as follows:

Several associations of women, other organizations and individuals have urged, from time to time, that family courts be set up for the settlement of family disputes, where emphasis should be laid on conciliation and achieving socially desirable results and adherence to rigid rules of procedure and evidence should be eliminated.

The mounting pressure of women's organizations on the Government to render gender justice was the primary reason which was attributed by the Parliament for enacting this legislation. Jagannath Kaushal, the then Minister of Law, Justice, and Company Affairs, while introducing the Bill stated that the objective of the legislation is to provide for a radical new procedure for speedy settlement of family disputes. So it was obvious that gender justice was the underlying compulsion for introducing it. But ironically, the Bill was passed without much discussion in the last few hours of the sixth Lok Sabha.[3]

The ideology underlying the enactment was to create women-friendly adjudication spaces, away from the formal structures of civil and criminal courts. The task ahead was to ensure that crucial rights of survival of women are not subsumed beneath technicalities and legal jargon. Since adversarial procedures adopted by civil courts are dilatory and confrontational,

it was presumed that new litigation fora, less formidable in its appearance, inquisitorial in its approach, and more accessible to women from marginalized sections, would tilt the balance in their favour. In order to achieve this, there was to be a conscious shift away from mainstream lawyers and an increased dependence on counselors to aid the parties to the dispute in arriving at mutually amicable solutions. The presence of conciliators within court premises was intended to enhance the negotiating power of women. The counselors were to deviate from the prevailing framework of 'neutrality' and aid gender justice while working out terms of reconciliation, settlements regarding the quantum of maintenance, issues of custody and access of children, protection against domestic violence, or right of residence in the matrimonial home. In complex legal matters the courts were to be assisted by a panel of lawyers appointed as *amicus curiae*. The articulation of this laudable aspiration is a clear indication that lawyering in family courts was to be defined away from commercial terms. There was a tacit intent of providing assistance to the court in bringing to the fore notions of gender justice embedded in the Constitution and as evolved through case law in defense of women, the disadvantaged and the powerless, within the patriarchal social order.

CHASM BETWEEN THE DEMAND AND THE ENACTMENT

An Act to provide for the establishment of family courts with a view to promote conciliation in, and secure speedy settlement of disputes relating to marriage and family affairs and for matters connected therewith.

Preamble, Family Court Act

Ironically, the principle of 'gender justice', which was the primary motivation for the demand for special courts for family matters, was not clearly spelt out in the enactment.

[3] Lok Sabha Debates (LSD) Vol.LJ No.25 dated 27 August 1984. pp. 182–254.

Instead, the Act emphasized 'preservation of the family' as its primary aim. The primary concern of the campaigners seems to have been lost in the process of transforming the demand from a campaign into an enactment. The tilt in favour of women which is found in various recent legislations and judicial pronouncements was absent in the Family Courts Act.[4] An impression that 'preservation of the family' is synonymous to 'protection of women's rights' seems to have been conveyed to all official functionaries. But legislative history of matrimonial law is contrary to this premise.

It is a historically well established fact that the institution of marriage and family can be preserved only at the cost of women—by denying them property rights and the right of divorce.[5] It is in this context that several legislations were enacted to loosen the sacramental bond of marriage and to give women the right of divorce and the consequential right to property ownership. For instance, the Hindu Marriages Act, 1955, gave Hindu women the statutory right of divorce on certain fault grounds, the Hindu Adoption and Maintenance Act, 1956, recognized the Hindu woman's right to reside separately and yet be maintained by her husband under certain conditions. The amendment to the Hindu Marriage Act in 1976 included the provision of mutual consent divorce which enabled amicable, non-contested divorce. Similarly, the Indian Divorce Act, 1869, the Parsi Marriage and Divorce Act, 1865, and the Dissolution of Muslim Marriages Act, 1939 provided women from minority communities the right to divorce. The Indian Succession Act, 1925 and the Hindu Succession Act, 1956 awarded inheritance rights to women to enable them to lead an independent life, free from familial oppression.

The Family Courts Act was meant to make further progress in this direction by making this right of divorce a practical and feasible reality, rather than a nightmare, by ensuring that matrimonial proceedings were speedy, devoid of anti-women biases, and economically more fair and just to women. So the concern at this stage ought not to have been 'preservation of the family' but 'protection of rights of women and children'. The aim had to be gender justice. The judiciary and court officials had to be carefully selected or, alternatively, oriented towards achieving this end. But unfortunately, the Family Courts Act did not provide for this. Instead, the Preamble laid down that the commitment of the Act is towards preserving the institution of marriage and family.

INSTITUTION AND JURISDICTION

Institution of Family Courts

The Act made it obligatory on state governments to set up family courts in every city or town with a population exceeding one million and gave them discretionary powers regarding areas with a population of less than one million. But though the central statute was enacted on 27 August 1984 and received the President's assent on 14 September 1984, it did not come into effect immediately. The Act could be effected only when individual state governments framed the necessary rules for instituting the family courts.[6]

Despite the mandatory obligation imposed by the statute upon state governments, family courts had not been set up in sixteen states and union territories till 2005. Even Delhi, the

---

[4] Section 125, Cr.PC, Section 498A, 304B, and 376 of the IPC, the Dowry Prohibition Act, the Vishaka guidelines, etc., are reflective of this tilt.

[5] See the sacramental aspects of Hindu and Christian marriage laws which are discussed in Chapter 1 of the first volume and Chapter 1 of this book.

[6] Rajasthan is an exception to this trend.

nation's capital, had failed to institute family courts until recently, despite the fact that rules regarding the same had been framed over a decade ago. Financial and space constraints and opposition from lawyers seem to be the major stumbling blocks for setting up of family courts.

Among the other nineteen states and union territories which had set up family courts before 2005, Rajasthan, Karnataka, and Maharashtra instituted them within five years of the central enactment. The first family court in the country was instituted at Jaipur, Rajasthan, in 1987. Karnataka was the next to follow and the second family court in the country was instituted in Bangalore in 1988. Maharashtra followed soon thereafter and set up family courts in two cities—Pune in January 1989 and Mumbai, in October 1989. Later, family courts were set up in many other states and union territories and by 2005, 91 family courts had been set up in 68 districts in the country.[7]

In *Shanker Khanojia* v. *Mayabai S. Khanojia*,[8] the Madhya Pradesh High Court held that family courts cannot be deemed to be effectively established unless judges are appointed. A similar view was adopted by the Kerala High Court in *Ali Haji* v. *Alima*[9] which held that a family court becomes established when the notification naming the judge as the first Presiding Officer is published. Until then, the jurisdiction is retained by the civil or district courts have the jurisdiction.

In a writ petition challenging the constitutional validity of the Family Courts Act, the Bombay High Court upheld the Act on the ground that it is based on rational categorization and hence does not violate the mandate of equality under Article 14 of the Constitution. The Court commented:

The Act had made it obligatory upon State Governments to establish family courts in a city or town whose population exceeds one million. This is a viable unit which in turn is based upon statistics of pending cases relating to family disputes in various courts situated in such cities or towns. A wide variety of cases relating to matrimonial disputes and other family disputes are required to be filed in different courts. For instance, claim for maintenance under Section 125, Cr.PC is required to be filed in the court of Judicial Magistrate, First Class. A claim for maintenance under the Hindu Adoption and Maintenance Act is required to be filed in a court depending upon the nature and extent of the claim made therein. A petition for divorce under the Hindu Marriage Act is required to be filed in the district court. Accordingly by virtue of S.3 leading to establishment of the family court in a city or town, whose population exceeds one million, all these disputes would come under one roof i.e., the family court. Litigation concerning marriage, divorce, matrimonial property, custody and guardianship and maintenance is consolidated within this court. This is a rational basis of categorization.[10]

Jurisdiction

Territorial Jurisdiction

According to Section 3(2) of the Act, the territorial jurisdiction of family courts is limited to that of a district court or as the state government may by notification stipulate in consultation with the high court. The state government can also reduce or increase its territorial limits from time to time, depending on local factors and circumstances. For instance, locating the jurisdiction for maintenance cases under Section 125, Cr.PC, for the entire district with a large rural population may not be practical or feasible and may cause undue hardship to women who might need to travel long distances with young children. Further, high courts and state governments may constrain the jurisdiction only to a limited area.

---

[7] See Appendix A for a list of states which had instituted family courts before 2005

[8] AIR 1990 MP 246

[9] II (1997) DMC 343

[10] *Lata Pimple* v. *Union of India*, AIR 1993 Bom 225.

The issue of jurisdiction raises considerable legal obstacles during matrimonial litigation. The judgment in *Uma Tiwari* v. *Vikrant Tiwari*[11] reveals a lax attitude on the part of the family court at Gwalior. A petition for a divorce was filed by a couple in January 2004. Six months later, after recording evidence of the parties, the court held that since the marriage was performed at Bhind and the parties lived together at Bhopal, the family court at Gwalior, where the wife was currently residing had no jurisdiction over the matter and returned the plaint to be submitted before the appropriate court. In appeal, while setting aside the order, the high court held that since a petition under Section 13B of HMA is a joint petition, the court under whose jurisdiction the wife resides will have the jurisdiction to entertain it. The high court held that the family court had not considered the scope of the amendment to Section 19 of Hindu Marriage Act[12] and the intention of the legislature in permitting filing of the petition at the place where the wife resides. The lax attitude of the family court resulted in considerable delay and additional costs to the couple for no fault of theirs.

Subject-matter Jurisdiction

The family courts have jurisdiction in respect of suits and proceedings of the nature referred to in the Explanation.

Section 7, Family Courts Act

Section 7(1) of the Act confers on family courts the jurisdiction and powers exercisable by district and subordinate civil courts in respect of civil suits and proceedings enumerated in the explanation clause. All matrimonial disputes enumerated in the explanation and disputes relating to maintenance under Section 125, Cr.PC are to be adjudicated in the family courts after they have been instituted in a particular district.

The suits and proceedings under jurisdiction of family court are:

- Nullity of Marriage
- Restitution of conjugal rights
- Judicial separation
- Validity of marriage
- Matrimonial status of a person
- Disputes regarding property of either of the parties or joint property
- Injunction arising out of marital relations
- Legitimacy of any person
- Maintenance
- Guardianship, custody and access to any minor

The Family Courts Act is only a procedural statute. Hence, the Act does not override personal laws but provides an alternative adjudication forum of dispute resolution. The rights and obligations of the parties to the dispute are to be decided as per their personal or matrimonial laws.

Explanation (a) to Section 7 of the Act does not make any distinctions regarding caste or religion. Hence any dispute arising between parties to a marriage, whatever the caste or creed, can be brought before the family court.[13]

In *R. Durga Prasad* v. *Union of India*,[14] the issue before the Andhra Pradesh High Court was whether the family court has jurisdiction to entertain a dispute where the fact of marriage

---

[11]   I (2005) DMC 690 MP

[12]   Amendment to Section 19 of the HMA w.e.f. from 23 December 2003, by insertion of sub-clause (iiia) which stipulates '*in case the wife is the petitioner, where she is residing on the date of presentation of the petition*'.

[13]   *Reddy Anand Rao* v. *Thota Vani Sujatha*, AIR 2003 NOC 258 AP.

[14]   II (1998) DMC 45 AP

itself is contested. The case concerned a petition filed by a woman in a family court at Visakhapatnam to declare her marriage null and void on the ground that her consent was obtained by force and fraud. The husband challenged the jurisdiction of the family court to adjudicate a dispute concerning the validity of marriage. Rejecting this contention, the Andhra Pradesh High Court held that the phrase 'settlement of disputes relating to marriage' encompasses not only issues regarding an admitted marriage, but also disputes in connection with the very existence of the marriage, as the existence or otherwise of a marriage is also a dispute 'relating to marriage'. The high court commented:

> It has to be borne in mind that while interpreting the statute, the specific provisions are to be read and understood and have to be interpreted in consistence with the language and intention of the legal provisions. If the language and intention of the legal provisions are clear and unambiguous, then, there is no need to take the aid of the Preamble or Statement of Objects and Reasons. In interpreting of a statute, the caption given to the Act is of little significance. It is the express legal provisions which operate and the adjudication has to be made basing only upon the said express provisions of the statute, unguided by the nature of the caption of the Act, or the Statement of Objects and Reasons or even the Preamble thereto.

Here, the reference was to the Preamble of the Act which uses the phrase, '*disputes relating to marriage and family affairs*' and explanation (a) to Section 7 (1), which uses the phrase, '*a suit or proceeding between the parties to a marriage*'.

The term 'family' used in the Act does not include disputes between siblings. In *P. Srihari* v. *P. Sukunda,*[15] a partition suit filed by two sisters against their brother was rejected by a family court at Hyderabad. In appeal, it was argued that since the plaintiffs are women and since the Act

was enacted for the benefit of women, the suit is maintainable before the family court. It was also urged that the word 'family' is not defined under the Act and hence the meaning used in common parlance must be adopted. It was held that since the Act is beneficent in nature, every dispute arising in the family, not necessarily only between wife and husband, must be entertained and the interpretation has to be liberal in this respect. But the Andhra Pradesh High Court rejected this contention and held that family courts have no jurisdiction to entertain disputes between brothers, sisters, and parents regarding property. The court commented that the object and scope of the Family Courts Act is confined to disputes arising out of a matrimonial relationship. It is not for the court to expand its jurisdiction by importing anything which is not stated in the Act.

But a dispute between major daughters and their father would come within the scope of a 'dispute arising out of a matrimonial relationship'. In *Manasi Aniruddha Pusalkar* v. *Aniruddha Ramachandra Pusalkar,*[16] a suit for maintenance filed by major daughters aged 20 and 22 years, under Section 20 of the Hindu Adoption and Maintenance Act was rejected by the family court at Pune on the ground that it was not a dispute between parties to a marriage. But the Bombay High Court held that the same is maintainable under the Family Courts Act. The division bench of H.L. Gokhale J. and V.C. Daga J., commented that as noted in the preamble of the Act, the family court is a court for resolving disputes relating to the family affairs and for matters connected therewith. Hence a suit or proceeding for maintenance by daughters against their father would certainly fall within the purview of Clause (f) of the explanation to Section 7 of the Family Courts Act.

---

[15] II (2001) DMC 135 AP

[16] II (2002) DMC 477

Family courts do not have jurisdiction to appoint a guardian for the property of a minor. This jurisdiction is specifically excluded. Hence, in *Susila Naik* v. *Judge Family Court*,[17] where the family court had appointed the mother as the guardian of the minor and the grand mother as the guardian of the minor's property, the Orissa High Court set aside the order. But the Karnataka High Court, in *In Re: Ashraya, etc.*,[18] has expanded the scope of the Act beyond issues 'arising out a matrimonial relationship'. It was held that the family court has the authority to appoint guardians in respect of destitute minor children under the Guardians and Wards Act. This would come within the purview of Section 7 (1)(g) of the Family Courts Act. It was held that granting permission for removing a child out of the territorial jurisdiction of the concerned court for being taken to a foreign country, an ancillary matter to the appointment of a guardian, is a 'proceeding relating to guardianship of person of minor and the custody of or access to such minor by a guardian'.[19]

Following is a list of relevant statutes which come within the purview of matters listed in explanation to Section 7 (1) of the Family Courts Act.

1. Hindu Marriage Act, 1955
2. Special Marriage Act, 1954
3. Dissolution of Muslim Marriage Act, 1939
4. Foreign Marriages Act, 1969
5. Divorce Act, 1869
6. Parsi Marriage and Divorce Act, 1936
7. Muslim Women (Protection of Rights & Divorce) Act, 1986

8. Muslim Personal Law/Application of Shariat Act, 1937
9. Hindu Adoption and Maintenance Act, 1956
10. Indian Christian Marriage Act, 1872
11. Hindu Minority and Guardianship Act, 1956
12. Guardian and Wards Act, 1890
13. Chapter IX – Criminal Procedure Code, 1973
14. Protection of Women from Domestic Violence Act, 2005

Section 8 of the Family Courts Act excludes the jurisdiction of civil courts in matrimonial matters and of criminal courts in respect of maintenance cases under Section 125 of the Cr.PC. The Act does not award concurrent jurisdiction to district courts. Once a family court is established in a district, the jurisdiction of district and subordinate judges ceases and all suits and proceedings pending before civil courts automatically stands transferred to the family court for settlement. In *Marya Theresa Martin* v. *E. Martin*,[20] the Kerala High Court held that when a family court is set up, the district court has no jurisdiction to entertain matrimonial disputes. In *Sanjay Kumar Sharma* v. *Vidya Sharma*,[21] it was held that once the family court is set up, in respect of matters enumerated in explanation to Section 7 (1), the family court will exercise exclusive jurisdiction. In *M. D. Pansur Ali* v. *Hafia Begum*,[22] the Gauhati High Court held that after the establishment of the family court, no magistrate within the jurisdiction of the family court is competent to exercise any jurisdiction under Chapter IX of the Criminal Procedure Code.

---

[17] II (1997) DMC 235 Ori
[18] AIR 1991 Kar 10
[19] But this is not the situation in all courts. For instance, in Mumbai, matters concerning adoption and appointment of guardian are not within the purview of family courts.

[20] AIR 1994 Ker 264
[21] AIR 2003 Ori 89
[22] II (1993) DMC 329. See also *Anand Govind Bhide* v. *Rohini Bhide*, I (2001) DMC 646 Bom.

However, the position under the recently enacted Protection of Women from Domestic Violence Act, 2005 (PWDVA) is different. Section 26 of the PWDVA awards concurrent jurisdiction to family courts (and other courts) along with magistrate's courts. Hence relief under the Act can be sought in proceedings pending before the family court or along with any other relief in a newly instituted petition. In *Pramodini Fernandes* v. *Vijay Fernandes*[23] the Bombay High Court held that a family court which has passed the initial order of protection has the same powers as the magistrate under Section 31 (2) of the Domestic Violence Act to impose penalty for breach of its order. Breach of protection order is a cognizable an non-bailable offence under Section 31 (1) of the Act which carries a penalty of one year of imprisonment and a fine upto Rs. 20,000. The question before the court was whether family courts being civil courts, have the power to exercise criminal jurisdiction which the high court answered in the affirmative.

Jurisdiction in Issues Related to Property
Explanation to Section 7(1) of the Family Court Act states as under:

(c) a suit or proceeding between the parties to a marriage with respect to the property of the parties or of either of them.

(d) a suit or proceeding for an order or injunction in circumstances arising out of a marital relationship.

By providing these two explanations, the jurisdiction of family courts has been expanded to all issues concerning property between the spouses, even beyond the scope of a matrimonial statute. Contest over the right of residence in the matrimonial home, protective orders and injunctions restraining entry of a spouse,

economic settlements, sale of matrimonial home and other property and distribution of proceeds between the spouses and children, division of property upon divorce, return of valuables and properties given at the time of marriage, etc., are issues which arise during a matrimonial dispute. Family courts have the jurisdiction to entertain these disputes, either in the course of the matrimonial litigation or as separate proceedings.

At times disputes related to property arise after the divorce, when the relationship of the husband and wife is severed through a judicial decree or personal laws. For instance, under Muslim law, if the husband has pronounced talaq, the wife is subsequently entitled, as per the above explanation, to approach family courts to resolve property disputes. It has been clarified that even a demand for sale of the matrimonial home is not in the nature of a partition suit between members of a Hindu joint family. Some judgments on the issue are discussed below.

In *Balkrishna Kadam* v. *Sangeeta Kadam*,[24] the Supreme Court held that the family court has jurisdiction to entertain matters concerning dispute over joint property. The Court explained the scope of Section 27 of the Hindu Marriage Act and held that any property given before marriage, at the time of marriage, or after marriage, but which can be deemed to be given in the context of marriage, is 'joint property' of the spouses. In view of this, it was held that there would not be any need to file a separate civil suit in respect of this property.

In *Mariamma Ninan* v. *K.K. Ninan*,[25] the wife had filed a suit for partition and separate possession of a part of the matrimonial home on the ground that her stridhana money was used

---

[23] I 2010 (DMC) 386 425

[24] II (1997) DMC 495 SC
[25] I (1997) DMC 570 AP

for construction of the house which was in the name of the husband. The family court at Secunderabad returned the plaint for want of jurisdiction. The high court set aside this order and held that since the dispute was between the husband and wife *inter se* and is related to property, it is within the scope of Section 7 (1) (c) of the Act and the family court has jurisdiction over the dispute.

In *Shyni* v. *George*,[26] a suit was filed by the wife against her husband for recovery of cash and valuables given at the time of marriage to the husband and father-in-law. The plaint was rejected by the family court at Ernakulam on the ground that it does not have jurisdiction to entertain an issue against the father-in-law since he is not a 'party to the marriage' as stipulated by explanation (c) to Section 7 (1) of the Family Courts Act. The court directed the wife to amend her suit and delete the claim against the father-in-law or in the alternative, the court would proceed on the basis that the claim was only against the husband. In an appeal against this order filed by the wife, the Kerala High Court held that the dispute is related to marriage and family affairs between the spouses and hence falls clearly within the purview of the family court. The court explained that a suit for partition in which a party to a marriage claims a share in the property of her husband which he holds along with the various other members of the joint family would be totally different from a case where a wife files for recovery of her exclusive property against her husband and someone else who is holding the property on her behalf like the father-in-law in this case.

A later decision of the Kerala High Court in *Devaki Antharjanam* v. *Narayanan Namboodiri*[27] confirmed this position and held that if a property belongs not only to the parties to the marriage but to others as well, a suit for partition of such property cannot be brought within the purview of family courts. This position was also upheld by the Karnataka high court in *Genu @ Ganu* v. *Jalabai*[28]. In this case, the first wife had filed a partition suit against her husband and his second wife in respect of certain ancestral properties held jointly by him with other family members and had obtained a decree in her favour from the family court at Gulberga. In appeal the high court set aside the decree on the ground that the family court has no jurisdiction to decide an issue of division of property in which other members of the family also have a share. Explaining the provisions of clause (c) of Explanation to Section 7 of the Family Courts Act which specifically deals with property disputes, the court held that two conditions must be satisfied for a family court to exercise its jurisdiction: Firstly, the dispute should be between the parties to the marriage; and secondly, the dispute should be in respect of the property of the parties or either of them. Similarly, it was ruled that the suit filed by daughters against their father for partition of joint family property is also not maintainable as they are not 'parties to a marriage'.

In another ruling, *Manita Khurana* v. *Indra Khurana*,[29] the Delhi High Court has held that a dispute between the mother-in-law and daughter-in-law in respect of the property exclusively owned by the mother-in-law is not maintainable in the family court, despite the claim that the same constitutes the matrimonial residence under the Domestic Violence Act. Hence proceedings filed by the mother-in-law were held to be not transferable to the family court. Similarly, the Bombay High Court in *Rakhi* v.

---

[26]   II (1997) DMC 676 Ker
[27]   AIR 2007 Ker 38

[28]   ILR 2009 Kar 612
[29]   AIR 2010 Del 69 : I 2010 (DMC) 386

Jayendra[30], a suit filed by the father-in-law for an injunction restraining the daughter-in-law from entering the house which belongs to him absolutely was held not transferrable to the family court. The court explained that the Family Courts Act is a special legislation which creates a forum and mechanism for beneficial and effective enforcement of existing rights and hence it cannot be construed to bring within its jurisdiction what was not specifically intended and expressed.

Another contentious issue has been regarding the claim of divorced Muslim women in respect of matrimonial home and disputes over such property. In *A. Mannan Khan* v. *Judge of Family Court*,[31] the wife had instituted proceedings in the family court regarding her right and title to the matrimonial home. The husband challenged it on the basis that after divorce, she ceased to be a wife and hence the family court cannot entertain the said suit. In appeal, the Andhra Pradesh High Court held that the expression 'the parties to a marriage' would include divorced spouses and not just parties whose marriage is subsisting.

Later in 2003, in *K. A. Abdul Jaleel* v. *T. A. Shahida*,[32] the Supreme Court confirmed this view and held that the family court has jurisdiction to adjudicate over property disputes between divorced couples. In a suit filed before the family court at Ernakulam, the wife contented that since her money and valuables were used for purchase of properties, the husband had agreed to transfer the properties to her name through an agreement. But when the relationship between the parties became strained, the husband pronounced talaq and dissolved the marriage. Thereafter, he refused to transfer

the properties on the ground that the agreement was signed by him under threat and coercion. When the wife approached the family court for deciding the issue, the husband contented that as per explanation to Section 7(1) of the Family Courts Act, the court only has jurisdiction to settle the property dispute between the 'parties to a marriage', which would mean parties to a subsisting marriage. The family court rejected this contention and held that it has jurisdiction to entertain issues related to property between a divorced Muslim couple. On dismissal of his appeal against the family court order by the high court, the husband approached the Supreme Court. While dismissing the appeal, the Supreme Court held that the family court had the power to decide property matters between spouses even when the marriage is not subsisting. The Apex Court commented:

It is now a well-settled principle of law that the jurisdiction of a court created specially for resolution of disputes of certain kinds should be construed liberally. The restricted meaning if ascribed to Explanation (c) to S.7(1) of the Act would frustrate the object wherefore the family courts were set up.

Nagaraj v. *Ammayamma*[33] concerned the issue of property which was in the name of the husband but was assigned to the exclusive use and occupation of the wife during his lifetime. The wife claimed that she was the second wife and after her, the husband had married again. Since dispute arose between her and the third wife, the husband assigned the property to her for her exclusive use and occupation. She had been residing in the said premises since then and was eking out a living by carrying out a business in the same premises. The husband and his relatives claimed that the woman was only a mistress and a concubine, hence she does not acquire any rights or title to the property by

---

[30] MANU/MH/0799/2008
[31] II (2001) DMC 250 AP
[32] I (2003) DMC 765 SC

[33] I (2002) DMC 439 Kar

virtue of her relationship. It was also argued that since the husband holds the title to the property, his entry to the premises cannot be restrained. The husband expired during the course of the litigation and his legal heirs, i.e., the sons of the first wife, were brought on record. The family court rejected the contention that the woman was a mistress on the ground that prolonged cohabitation leads to presumption of a valid marriage.[34] The court also held that since the husband had taken another wife, under Section 18 of Hindu Adoption and Maintenance Act, she was entitled to a separate residence and maintenance. In appeal, the Karnataka High Court held that under Section 7(1) (c) of the Act, the family court has jurisdiction to decide the matter. The Court commented that neither the husband nor anyone claiming through him could interfere with the possession of the wife. She is entitled to an injunction under Section 18 of HAMA restraining her dispossession from these premises against the husband and his legal heirs.

In *Suprabha* v. *Sivaraman*,[35] the issue was return of gold ornaments, other valuables, and cash given at the time of marriage. Though the spouse was not alive at the time of initiating procedures, it was held that the family court has jurisdiction to adjudicate over this dispute. The Kerala High Court commented that the family court was not right in directing the plaintiff to withdraw the suit and file it in an appropriate court. The high court directed the family court to take back the plaint and proceed with the trial in accordance with law.

Sharada Prabhale v. *Narendra Prabhale*[36] is an extraordinary ruling, which underlines that

the basic mandate of courts is to 'do justice'. H.L. Gokhale J. of the Bombay High Court pronounced this judgment, with the following opening comments:

This case unfolds the story of an unfortunate village woman who was first deceived by her husband by not disclosing his prior relationship with another woman and subsequently leaving her with a daughter and denying a roof over her head. What is worse is that her difficulties are accentuated by a civil judge throwing away her case at the threshold by taking a technical view unsustainable at law.

The woman's husband had married her by projecting that he was a widower. Though she was reluctant, she was pressurized into the marriage. After coming to Bombay and living with him for about a year, she discovered that he was living with another woman and had five children through her. Since she had no other option, she too continued to reside in the one room tenement with her husband, the other woman, and her children. Eventually she had two children of her own, one of whom, a daughter, survived. Meanwhile, the building became dilapidated. When it was repaired by the Repair Board, the husband was given two rooms and Sharada went to reside in this tenement. At this time, the husband started disowning the relationship. Fearing eviction, she filed a suit in February 1980 against her husband, seeking a declaration that she was entitled to use and occupation of the premises. As a proof of her marriage and residence, she relied upon the marriage photographs, the birth certificate of her daughter, and her ration card. After a few months, the husband expired. The son of the other woman was brought on record. When the matter came up for trial in 2000, based on the contention raised by the legal heir, the city civil court held that since it is a matrimonial dispute covered under explanation (c) of Section 7 (1) of Family Courts Act,

---

[34] This issue is discussed at section titled 'The Right to Maintenance' of Chapter 2 *Matrimonial Rights and Obligations*.

[35] II (2006) DMC 404 Ker

[36] I (2001) DMC 524 Bom

it must be filed in the family court and that the city civil court has no jurisdiction to entertain the dispute. Soon thereafter, the woman was thrown out of the premises and was prevented from entering it. In a dire situation, she started living in the verandah of the *chawl*. Through the help of the legal aid, she filed an appeal in the high court. The high court held that the rejection of the plaint after nineteen years was not justified and remanded the matter back to the city civil court for completing the trial. In the interim, the court restored possession to the woman and passed an injunction against her dispossession.

This case is discussed in detail to highlight the plight of migrant, illiterate, and poor women in Mumbai and their desperate struggle to retain possession of their meager dwellings against all odds. A small lapse on the part of the court machinery in not transferring the case from the city civil court to the family court, when the courts were set up in 1989, would have cost the woman her basic right to survival, but for the timely intervention of the high court. But very often, justice becomes a casualty, in the face of technical and procedural snags.

However in the same year, in *Anand Govind Bhide* v. *Rohini Bhide*,[37] the Bombay High Court gave a diagonally opposite ruling. The wife had filed a suit in 1983 against her husband for restraining his entry into the premises owned exclusively by her, which was purchased from her own savings. Due to the matrimonial dispute, the wife had moved out of the matrimonial home but had allowed temporary stay to her husband on occasion of a celebration in the family. But subsequently, when he refused to move out, she was constrained to file a suit in the city civil court.

The husband challenged the jurisdiction of the court, but the matter was decided in favour of the wife in 1988. Subsequently, the parties also obtained a decree of divorce but the property dispute continued. In 1990, the city civil court passed a judgment holding that the wife had proved that she had paid the entire consideration for the premises and passed an order in her favour. The same was upheld by a single judge of the high court. But in a Letters Patent Appeal decided in 2001, Division Bench of the high court held that the judgment delivered by the city civil court in 1990 was without jurisdiction since by then family courts had been instituted and the matter ought to have been transferred to the family court. The high court tried to resolve the matter amicably, but when it failed it was held that there was no other alternative but to follow the rules and transfer the matter for a fresh round of litigation to the family court. The argument on behalf of the wife that the parties had litigated since 1983 and that they should not be made to face a fresh round of litigation and, in the interest of justice, the high court ought to finally decide the matter was rejected. The high court also held that evidence recorded by the city civil court after 9 October 1989, the date on which the family courts in Mumbai started functioning, cannot be taken into consideration unless the parties consent to the same. After nearly two decades, the matter was transferred to the family court for recording evidence afresh.

The lapse on the part of the city civil court in not transferring the matter had an adverse effect on the claims of the woman; as the maxim goes, 'justice delayed is justice denied'. It is rather unfortunate that the high court declined to bring an end to the matter by using its own inherent power and deciding the issue finally

---

[37] I (2001) DMC 646 Bom

and instead stood firm on a technicality rather than the interest of justice.

Exclusive and Concurrent Jurisdiction of High Courts

Section 7 of the Family Courts Act states that, subject to the other provisions of this Act, a family court shall:

(a) have and exercise all the jurisdiction exercisable by any district court or any Subordinate Civil Court under any law for the time being in force in respect of suits and proceedings of the nature referred to in the Explanation.

(b) be deemed for the purpose of exercising such jurisdiction under such law, to be a district court or as the case may be such Subordinate Civil Court for the area to which the jurisdiction of the family courts extends.

While it was relatively easy for high courts to hold that jurisdiction of magistrate's courts and district courts is ousted after the institution of family courts in a particular district, as far as the matrimonial jurisdiction of high courts was concerned, it became a complex question. While it became a contentious legal issue for the Bombay High Court, but was resolved relatively easily by the Madras High Court. Both these high courts, along with the Calcutta High Court, had been awarded matrimonial jurisdiction by Letters Patent under the category 'Ordinary Original Civil Jurisdiction' and in this capacity, for certain stipulated matters, they functioned as district courts. The issue before the courts was whether the term 'district court' in Section 7 (1) of the Family Courts Act would include the high court when it functioned as a civil court while exercising its 'Ordinary Original Civil Jurisdiction'.

Bombay High Court : Exclusive Jurisdiction

While family courts in Bombay have been hailed as a model, the gains of this innovative litigation forum were denied to women from minority communities for well over a decade. Various factors contributed to this process—callous and indifferent legislative drafting, a tendency to overlook the complex system of courts prevailing in the country, and the attitude of the higher judiciary which preferred to resort to the letter rather than the spirit of the Family Courts Act.

As can be observed from the wording of Section 7 (1) of the Family Courts Act, while the jurisdiction exercised by district courts was transferred to family courts, the Act failed to clarify whether it ousted the original jurisdiction exercised by high courts over matrimonial matters. So the question whether a 'high court' is a 'district court' when it functions as a court of original jurisdiction over matrimonial matters was left open to judicial interpretations. At times the interpretations were at variance with the objectives of setting up family courts: to render matrimonial jurisdiction less intimidating and more accessible.

To grasp the confusion, it is necessary to understand the history of these high courts. The high courts of Calcutta, Bombay, and Madras, which were set up in 1862 under the Charter Act of 1853 and the Indian High Courts Act of 1861, were vested with powers of a civil court. As per the Letters Patent issued under the Great Seal of the United Kingdoms, these courts were entrusted with both original and appellate jurisdiction over civil, criminal admiralty and vice admiralty, testamentary, intestate, and matrimonial jurisdiction in the presidency areas of Bombay, Madras, and Calcutta and they functioned as district courts in respect of these matters.[38] But high courts which were established later, including the Allahabad High Court which set up in 1875, were not entrusted with similar

---

[38] See Introduction to Chapter 1 *Personal Laws and Women's Rights* of the first volume.

powers of original jurisdiction. They were mainly courts of appellate jurisdiction.

In 1950, the city civil court was set up in Bombay and this became the court of original jurisdiction. But the matrimonial jurisdiction of the high court was not ousted by the city civil courts Act. The statutes which were enacted subsequent to the setting up of the city civil court granted it jurisdiction over matrimonial matters. Thus Section 2 (e) of the Special Marriage Act clearly stated that 'district court' means, in any area for which there is a city civil court, that Court. A similar provision was also made under Section 2 (b) of the Hindu Marriage Act. But the jurisdiction for the Indian Divorce Act, the Parsi Marriage and the Divorce Act, the Dissolution of Muslim Marriages Act, and matrimonial issues concerning the Jewish community continued to be with the high court under Clauses 12 and 35 of the Letters Patent. The high courts also entertained suits under the Hindu Adoption and Maintenance Act since the jurisdiction depended on the amount claimed. If the maintenance claimed exceeded rupees one lakh per annum, the high court had the jurisdiction to decide the issue.

As per Section 7 (1) (a) and (b) of the Family Courts Act, the jurisdiction of the 'district' court was transferred to the family court. But the legislation did not clearly exclude the original matrimonial jurisdiction exercised by high courts. Thus defective drafting of the Family Courts Act led to a great confusion and ambiguity during the initial phase and became a matter of contradictory judicial interpretations.

The first decision on this issue was delivered by a single judge, M.G Choudhari J. in *Kamal V. M. Allaudin* v. *Raja Shaikh*,[39] which held as follows:

Even assuming that the high court may not be described as the district Court, it can certainly be held that it was exercising the same powers and the same jurisdiction as the district Court if one were to exist in the city of Bombay prior to the establishment of the city civil court. In that sense, the high court was entertaining suits between Muslim, Parsee and Jews and even Hindus when the dispute did not fall within the confines of the *Hindu Marriage Act* and was doing so to the same extent as the district Court would have done. Taking away that jurisdiction and vesting it in the Family court by enacting the *Family Courts Act* the Legislature can not be said to have taken any step which comes in conflict with its inherent jurisdiction under the Letters Patent which is meant to be exercised in the absence of any other law (Para 64) ... Undoubtedly, this Court is the superior Court and its jurisdiction cannot be lightly tinkered with. However, times have changed. New dimensions of public interest and social reform are emerging, taking us in the direction of fulfillment of the obligations arising under Chapter IV of the Constitution of India (the reference was to the mandate of social reform reflected in Part IV - Directive Principles of State Policy). This Court cannot be over-sensitive and feel touchy over loss of its jurisdiction to entertain certain kinds of suits which cannot in any manner come in conflict with its position as the superior court and a Court of Appeal. (para 65)

This view was in conformity with the spirit behind the enactment of the Family Courts Act, i.e., to make matrimonial litigation less formal and more speedy irrespective of persons religious affiliations.

But a subsequent Division Bench ruling in *Kanak Vinod Mehta* v. *Vinod Dulerai Mehta*,[40] relying on the Full Bench ruling of Madras High Court in *Mary Thomas* v. *Dr. K. E. Thomas* (discussed later) reversed the above judgment and upheld the jurisdiction of the high court. Since the Family Courts Act is a central legislation, the principle that, as far as possible, the same construction should be placed by one high court upon a central statute as has found favour with

---

[39]   AIR 1990 Bom 299

[40]   I (1992) DMC 403: AIR 1991 Bom 337

another high court, was adopted. It was further explained that the words 'district court' in Section 7 (1) of the Family Courts Act do not refer to the high court and unless the jurisdiction of the high court is ousted by specific wordings, it continues to exercise jurisdiction. The jurisdiction of a higher court cannot be ousted by mere inference. The court commented:

We must also have regard to the canons of interpretation of statutes. The established rule is that a "statute should not be construed as taking away the jurisdiction of the courts in the absence of clear and unambiguous language to that effect." This is a principle enshrined in the judgments of Indian and English courts. The principle applies with even greater vigour when the statute purports to take away the jurisdiction of a superior court such as the high court. We do not find in the provisions of the said Act words that clearly or unambiguously indicate the intention of Parliament to oust the jurisdiction of the high court in regard to the categories of suits and proceedings mentioned in the Explanation to sub-Section (1) of Section 7. The words that are used apply in clear and unambiguous terms only to the jurisdiction of district courts and subordinate civil courts. (Para 12)

Later, the same view was reconfirmed in *Harinder Kaur* v. *Narendra Singh Retan Singh*,[41] which held that the jurisdiction of the high court on its original side is not ousted by any provisions of the Family Courts Act and that the high court continues to exercise the jurisdiction vested in it, not withstanding Sections 7 and 8 of the Family Courts Act. Hence matters under the Guardians and Wards Act, the Indian Divorce Act, and the Parsi Marriage & Divorce Act rested solely with the high court. Maintenance of higher income groups under Hindu Adoption and Maintenance Act also continued with the high court.

In 1994, in *Vincent Joseph Konath* v. *Jacintha Angela Konath*[42] the Bombay High Court reaffirmed that family courts have no jurisdiction to entertain matters which come under the exclusive jurisdiction of the high court. The Court declared that it has exclusive jurisdiction to entertain suits under the Indian Divorce Act. It was also held that all issues under the Dissolution of Muslim Marriages Act are within the purview of the high court and the family court has no jurisdiction to entertain these disputes.

After these rulings, matters concerning divorce and dissolution of marriage under the Indian Divorce Act and the Dissolution of Muslim Marriages Act were litigated in high courts and hence Christians and Muslims could not avail of the new adjudication as introduced by the Family Courts Act. Poor litigants from minority communities had to bear exorbitant litigation costs in terms of legal fees, as the cost of engaging a lawyer in the high court is much higher as compared to the cost of engaging a lawyer in a lower court. Litigants had to endure enormous delays as matters hardly reached the stage of final hearing and had to be content with interim orders. An overburdened high court did not have the time to record evidence in contested matters. The procedures in the high court were far more formal, technical, and stringent than those adopted by family courts, as the high court was bound strictly by the Code of Civil Procedure and the rules of evidence laid down by the Indian Evidence Act. Earlier, the high court referred matters to the city civil court, which was located in its vicinity, for recording evidence. But since family courts were located in the suburbs, the high court was also burdened with the task of recording evidence. Some high court judges felt that this was an additional burden on an already overburdened senior judiciary, a task which can easily be carried out by the family courts, but they were bound by the rulings of the division bench discussed above.

[41]   II (1992) DMC 623
[42]   AIR 1994 Bom 120

Finally, in 2000, the Full Bench ruling in *Romila Jaidev Shroff* v. *Jaidev Rajnikant Shroff*,[43] overruled the above decision and held that the high court exercising its ordinary original civil jurisdiction relating to matters under the Family Courts Act, would be the district court. The Bench comprising of N.J. Pandya J. Ranjana Desai J. and V.C. Daga J. provided the following explanation for their decision:

Virtually the litigation before the family court is a mixture of inquisitorial trial, participatory form of grievance redressal and adversarial trial. As the court is left to device its own practice, it can have a judicious mixture of all three of them and can as well proceed under any of them exclusively (Para 27) ….. (In the high court,) the procedure is in accordance with the respective rules of the high court on its original side. When legal representation being a certainty with all trappings of a full fledged trial, the Evidence Act, 1872 will apply with force and rigour. (Para 28) … The overriding effect of the Family Court Act is not only confined to the Code of Civil Procedure but also to the Evidence Act. …. (Para 27) The litigants will have the benefit of Family Courts Act which, with reference to the aforesaid changes brought about in the conduct of matters before the family court, is a radical departure from the accepted form of trial in Civil Court. If the Legislature in its wisdom has decided to make this departure, while interpreting any provision of it, in our opinion, the interpretation should be in furtherance of the objective. (Para 30) When thus interpreted, the conclusion would be inescapable that when the high court exercises its Ordinary Original Civil Jurisdiction in relation to the matters under the Family Courts Act, it would be a district court as understood therein. It would, therefore, lose its jurisdiction. (Para 31)[44]

After this ruling, all cases concerning family issues, including those under the Guardians and Wards Act, maintenance under Sections 18 and 20 of the Hindu Adoption and Maintenance Act, the Dissolution of Muslim Marriages Act, and the Indian Divorce Act which were pending in the high court were transferred to family courts. Only matters under the Parsi Marriage and Divorce Act were retained with the high court because Parsi matrimonial jurisdiction rests with the Parsi Bench of the high court which is specially constituted twice a year. The Act provides for a special court consisting of a jury to decide matrimonial matters. The jury is drawn from respectable members of the community. Although the Act was amended in 1988, the jury was not abolished. Because of its special feature, the jurisdiction under this Act was not transferred to family courts and the high court continues to retain the jurisdiction over these matters.[45]

Madras High Court : Concurrent Jurisdiction

The Madras High Court also faced a similar dilemma regarding jurisdiction of the high court after family courts were instituted. But it arrived at a relatively simple solution and concluded that while the jurisdiction of the high court is not ousted, the family courts also have concurrent jurisdiction.

The two rulings of the Madras High Court in this regard in 1989 by a single judge, Abdul Hadi J., in *Patrick Martin, etc.*,[46] and *In the matter of minor Rekha*[47] had held that while exercising original jurisdiction, the high court is a 'district court' as defined by the Family Courts Act. Hence after the institution of family courts, the high court lost its jurisdiction to adjudicate over matrimonial disputes under the Indian Divorce Act and the Guardians and Wards Act.

But this view contradicted with some earlier rulings which had held that the high court is not

---

[45] See Chapter 1 *Personal Laws and Women's Rights* of the first volume, where the issue of Parsi Marriage and Divorce is discussed in detail.

[43] II (2000) DMC 600 FB

[44] At pg. 607

[46] (1989) 1 LW 246

[47] 1 (1989) LW 241

a 'district court'[48], hence a reference was made to the Full Bench in order to conclusively determine the issue in *Mary Thomas* v. *Dr K. E. Thomas*.[49] The Full Bench comprising S. Mohan CJ., S. Ramalingam J., and Bakthavatsalam J. overruled the earlier decision and held as follows:

After the constitution of the family court for the Madras area, the original jurisdiction of the high court in respect of matters that may fall under the Explanation of S.7 of the Family Courts Act is not ousted and the high court can continue to exercise its jurisdiction notwithstanding the coming into force of the Family Courts Act, 1984.

Relying upon the earlier ruling, *S.B.S. Jayam & Co.* v. *Gopi Chemical Industries*,[50] the Full Bench held: N.S. Ramaswami J. has laid down the law correctly that the term 'district court' would not include the high court and the fact that the local limits of the ordinary, original jurisdiction to this Court is a district would not mean that this Court becomes a district court." (para 59)

The Bombay High Court, in *Kanak Vinod Mehta* v. *Vinod Dulerai Mehta* (discussed earlier), had relied on this judgment and had ruled that the jurisdiction of the high court is not ousted. But while the Madras High Court ruling awarded concurrent jurisdiction to the high court and family courts, the Bombay High Court ousted the jurisdiction of family courts and held exclusive jurisdiction over matrimonial disputes concerning Christians, Muslims and Parsis under their personal laws.

A Special Bench of Madras High Court, in *Dr Mary Sheila* v. *Dr Vincent Thamburaj*,[51] reaffirmed

that the family court as well as the high court on its original side will have concurrent jurisdiction in respect of matters falling under Section 7 (1) of the Family Courts Act. In this case, the family court had awarded an *ex parte* decree on a petition filed by the wife for declaring her marriage null and void. The husband challenged the decree on the ground that the family court did not have the jurisdiction to entertain matters under the Indian Divorce Act as the jurisdiction lies with the high court. The Special Bench comprising of Venkataswami Bellie J. and Abdul Hadi J. held that it cannot be disputed that the family court at Madras was established under Section 3 of the Family Courts Act. Consequently, the jurisdiction to adjudicate over matters listed under the explanation to Section 7 (1) of the Act has been awarded to family courts. The ruling reaffirmed the concurrent jurisdiction of high courts and family courts over issues concerning Christian marriages. Hence the *ex parte* decree awarded by the family court was held to be valid and binding.

Family Courts and Muslim Women's Act

In terms of jurisdiction, another dispute arose in the context of the Muslim Women (Protection of Rights on Divorce) Act, 1986. It was held that family courts do not have jurisdiction to adjudicate over these cases. Though Section 7 (2) (b) of the Family Courts Act provides for conferment of jurisdiction by any other enactment upon the family court, the Muslim Women (Protection of Rights on Divorce) Act, which is a later enactment, did not specifically confer jurisdiction upon the family court to adjudicate rights under the said Act. Ironically, issues concerning rights of Muslim women become contested even when they are not framed as a question of 'women versus community' as the controversial *Shah*

---

[48] *Daily Calendar Supply Bureau* v. *The United Concern*, AIR 1967 Mad 381 and *S.B.S. Jayam & Co.* v. *Gopi Chemical Industries*, (1977) 1 MLJ 286.

[49] I (1991) DMC 47

[50] (1977) 1 MLJ 286

[51] AIR 1991 Mad 180

Bano ruling.[52] The ambiguity regarding jurisdiction of family courts over proceedings under the Act has led to multiplicity of litigation leading to unwarranted delays and complexities, in what could have been a simple issue of awarding jurisdiction to family courts.

In 1986, when the Muslim Women's Act was formulated, family courts had not been set up. The jurisdiction over a corresponding right, of maintenance under Section 125, Cr.PC, was vested with the magistrate's courts. Hence it was but logical that jurisdiction under the new Act, which dealt with the claims of a divorced Muslim woman, should also vest with the magistrate's court. But unfortunately, the statute did not stipulate that if family courts were set up, the jurisdiction would shift to them. If one recalls the controversies and polemics around the enactment after the *Shah Bano* ruling, it is understandable that the drafters of the statute did not concern themselves with seemingly innocuous concerns like jurisdiction.[53]

When family courts were set up, all pending cases under Section 125, Cr.PC were transferred to them. But when a Muslim woman approaches the courts for her right of maintenance under Section 125, Cr.PC, if the husband, in his reply, submits that he has already divorced her, and this plea is upheld, the family court ceased to have jurisdiction over the matter and the case had to be litigated afresh in the magistrate's court. This caused immense hardships to women within a system plagued with delays and legal technicalities. The ruling of the Bombay High Court in *Noor Jamaal* v. *Haseena,*[54] pronounced in 1992, provides a glimpse of the ground reality of a divorced Muslim woman. The wife, who was deserted, filed an application for maintenance in 1988 for herself and her minor child under Section 125, Cr.PC. in the magistrate's court. When the family courts were set up in Mumbai in 1989, this case was transferred, along with other pending cases, to the family court. During the proceedings, the husband pleaded that he had divorced the wife. Hence the family court directed the husband to repay the mehr and return her valuables as per the Muslim Women's Act. The husband challenged this order in the high court on the ground that as per the provisions of the said Act, the family court does not have jurisdiction to decide the issue. The high court upheld the husband's contention and set aside the order of the family court and directed the family court to transfer the case back to the magistrate's court to decide the wife's rights under the MWA. Due to judicial ambiguity, the woman lost four crucial years in respect of rights which had to be decided summarily.

Matters were further complicated as women file a single petition for maintenance for themselves and their minor children. If the husband alleges divorce, the petition was transferred to the magistrate's court to be decided under the MWA. But after the family courts had been set up, the magistrate's courts do not have jurisdiction to decide issues under Section 125, Cr.PC. Since it is not possible for two different courts to decide claims filed under one single petition, either the right of the child had to be forsaken or the wife had to forsake her own right. In order to follow up both the rights, the woman would be compelled to engage the services of two different lawyers practicing in two different

---

[52] *Mohd. Ahmad Khan* v. *Shahbano Begum*, AIR 1985 SC 945. This case upheld Muslim women's right to post-divorce maintenance, which led to a major controversy.

[53] Please see section titled 'The Shah Bano Controversy' of Chapter 2 *Constitutional Law and Citizenship Claims* of the first volume for a discussion on this issue.

[54] II (1992) DMC 56

courts and file two different petitions for a claim which could have been decided expeditiously through one application.

Fortunately, women residing outside the jurisdiction of family courts were saved from this misery. This is ironic, as family courts were meant to be an improvement on the existing court system. Since all matters concerning maintenance and divorce settlement, whether under civil or criminal provisions, are now dealt with by the family courts, it is difficult to understand the legal reasoning for sustaining this confused state of affairs.

A Full Bench of the Bombay High Court, in *Karim Abdul Shaikh* v. *Shehnaz Karim Shaikh*,[55] reaffirmed this view and held that the family courts do not have jurisdiction to decide cases under the MWA. The only situation where cases of this nature could be entertained by family courts was when they were filed by mutual agreement under Section 5 of the Muslim Women's Act. (This is rather far fetched because if the husband is amenable, he could provide maintenance through an out of court settlement and the need to litigate would not arise). Similarly, in *Patnam Vahedullah Khan* v. *Ashia Khantoon*,[56] where a petition was filed by the wife in the family court, which directed the husband to pay maintenance for iddat period, the mehr amount, and Rs 2,500 as future provision, the husband challenged the jurisdiction of the family court. The Andhra Pradesh High Court set aside the order of the family court on the ground that the jurisdiction to decide cases under the MWA lies with the magistrate's court.

But this view was not uniformly held by all high courts. While some high courts ruled that family courts did not have jurisdiction to decide cases under the MWA, others upheld their jurisdiction. Rulings of the division benches of the Allahabad and Orissa High Courts, upholding the jurisdiction of family courts to decide issues under the Muslim Women's Act are discussed below.

In *Mohd Sayeed* v. *Rehana Begum*,[57] the court heard two appeals filed against the orders of family courts. In the first case, the divorced wife claimed maintenance for herself and for her minor daughter in the family court at Allahabad. Since the wife was divorced, the court decided the claims of the wife under the Muslim Women's Act and directed the husband to pay Rs 2,500 as mehr dues, Rs 5,000 being the value of ornaments, Rs 400 per month as maintenance for the iddat, and Rs 100 per month as maintenance for the daughter. In the second case the family court directed the husband to pay Rs 30,000 as mehr dues, Rs 1,500 as maintenance for the iddat, Rs 73,720 being the value of the ornaments, and Rs 23,000 being the value of the presents. In both the cases, the husbands filed an appeal challenging the jurisdiction of the family court. The high court decided both the cases through a composite judgment and held that no specific ground was shown to justify that the family court has no jurisdiction to pass orders under the MWA. Sections 7(1) and 20 of the Family Courts Act give jurisdiction to the family court to decide these issues and hence, the decision does not suffer from any error of law or fact. While upholding the orders of the family court, the high court commented:

The entire purpose of the Muslim Women's Act is to provide speedy and expeditious remedy to a destitute woman. This object will be defeated if the appellants are permitted to agitate the issue of jurisdiction in the high court on the ground which was not agitated before the court below.

---

[55] 2000 Cri.LJ 3560
[56] 2000 Cri. LJ 2124

[57] I (1996) DMC 626 All

In *Mustafiran Bibi* v. *Abdul Khan*,[58] the family court rejected the wife's petition for maintenance, return of dowry articles, and mehr, filed under the Muslim Women's Act, on ground of lack of jurisdiction. The Orissa High Court held that the findings of the family court are unsustainable, set aside the order passed by the family court, and remitted the case back for fresh disposal in accordance with guidelines stipulated in the *Daniel Latifi case*.[59]

But finally, in a recent judgment, *Shabana Bano* v. *Imran Khan*,[60] the Supreme Court laid the controversy to rest and confirmed that family courts have the power to decide issues under the Muslim Women's Act. Deepak Verma J. and Sudarshan Reddy J. of the Supreme Court commented that where social legislations enacted to secure the rights of needy women are concerned adherence to rigid rules of procedure and evidence should be avoided. The petitioner, Shabana Bano had approached the family court at Gwalior under Section 125, Cr.PC for maintenance of Rs 3000 per month. Her plea was that when she was pregnant, her husband left her in her natal home with a warning that she would not be allowed to return after her delivery unless his demands for dowry were met. In response, the husband pleaded that he had divorced her and hence he is not liable to pay any maintenance to her. Conceding this plea, the family court awarded Shabana Rs 2000 per month for the four months between the date of filing the petition and the alleged divorce. The Madhya Pradesh High Court had dismissed her appeal against the judgment of the family court. But after the Supreme Court ruling, when a husband pleads that he has divorced his wife, in proceedings under Section 125, Cr.PC the family court has the power to award a lump sum settlement to the divorced wife under the Muslim Women's Act and she is saved from the trouble of approaching the magistrate's court for the same relief.

In a subsequent ruling, the Kerala High Court in *Kunhimohammed* v. *Ayishakutty*[61] has held that a husband's obligation to pay maintenance is not extinguished upon divorce. The wife will be entitled to receive maintenance under Section 125, Cr.PC until the husband fulfills his obligation under Section 3 of the Muslim Women's Act or until the wife remains unmarried.

In view of these two rulings, it is now clear that the family courts will continue to have jurisdiction to adjudicate over the rights of Muslim women even after divorce.

PRESIDING OFFICERS

Appointment and Tenure of Judges

In selecting persons for appointment as Judges, (a) every endeavour shall be made to ensure that persons committed to the need to protect and preserve the institution of marriage and to promote the welfare of children and qualified by reason of their experience and expertise to promote the settlement of disputes by conciliation and counseling are selected; (b) preference shall be given to women

Section 4, Family Courts Act

Since the aim of the Family Courts Act was preservation of the family, it provided that only persons committed to the need to protect and preserve the institution of marriage should be appointed as judges. Ironically, according to this, women's rights activists and lawyers who had campaigned for setting up of the family courts could be disqualified from being appointed as judges (or counselors) in the

---

[58] I (2003) DMC 81 Ori

[59] *Daniel Latifi* v. *Union of India*, 2001 (7) SCC 740: 2001 Cri.LJ 4660 SC: II (2001) DMC 714 SC.

[60] AIR 2010 SC 305

[61] 2010 (2) KLT 71

family courts as their commitment to gender justice could be labeled as 'feminist', which is often equated with being 'anti-men' or 'anti-family'.

Some legal scholars raised their voice against the stipulation of 'preservation of family', as reflected in the following comments of Prof. Lotika Sarkar, a Law professor[62]:

One of the major drawbacks of the Family Courts Act has been the over emphasis on the preservation and protection of the marriage. In appointing judges, S.4 of the Act mentions that every endeavour should be made to appoint persons who are committed to preserve and protect the institute of marriage. It is often forgotten that marriage and family is an area where women are most oppressed – whether it is wife battering, marital rape, or harassment for dowry. Yet, it is this marriage that the judge is asked to preserve and protect. This section read along with the Preamble of the Act conveys the impression that judges should do their best for a settlement between the parties to preserve the marriage. At times this is stretched to an absurd limit. (Sarkar 1994)

There ought to have been a strong resistance within the women's movement to such provisions. But the Act was welcomed as a positive measure and a first step in ensuring procedural justice to women. While conceding that there were some flaws in the Act, it was hoped that these would be ironed out in course of time and in their functioning, the courts would ensure procedural justice women.

The process of appointment of presiding officers for family courts, their background, tenure, and training are crucial for the success family courts. Most appointments to family courts are made through transfer of district and sessions judges. There are several concerns that have been raised about this process. The ideology as well as procedures of regular civil and criminal courts are substantially different from

those of a family court. Well set in adversarial pattern of dispute resolution, judges have to adapt to the needs of high-strung and emotional litigants in family disputes. This transition is not easy. Some legal scholars argue that experienced senior level district judges should be appointed as family court judges as they would have a good grasp over family law and rules of evidence and would also have the confidence to depart from set pattern and experiment with newer forms of dispute resolution. But the senior judges may not accept these transfers as they may view the family courts as tribunals where their skills of 'judging' as per legal principles and rules of evidence cannot be used. At present, most family court judges are mid-career, district judges (Agnes 2006). Some are innovative and dynamic in their approach and are willing to experiment with the new form of adjudication. If they are provided with suitable training and sensitization, they would perform effectively as family court judges. Another suggestion is that judges from all courts should be transferred to family courts at some point of their career. This would contribute to their overall development and provide them a good exposure to the ground level realities of women's lives.

Concerns have also been raised about the general norm of three-year tenure. It was felt that this tenure is too short to be able to function effectively as a family court judge because the process involves learning newer skills. One of the judges who was interviewed for the study, commented:

The duties of a family court judge require a great deal of mental involvement, not just the knowledge of law and legal proceedings. It takes two to three years for a judge to adjust to the family court environment and settle down. By the time he / she gets acclamatized to the tasks involved and is able to change procedural rules it is time for a transfer. A tenure of a minimum of five years would be beneficial to the judge as well as to the

---

[62]   at the Indian Law Institute, Delhi

court. It would give sufficient time to make concrete contributions towards bringing in effective changes.[63]

Whether it is mandatory to appoint only women judges as presiding officers of family courts is another important question that has been raised regarding the Act. This move has been opposed by several senior and middle-level district judges who feel that male judges are equally competent to deal with family matters and are sensitive to issues concerning women. Also, as the number of family courts increase, there may not be sufficient number of women judges available for postings in district towns.

Due to these various constraints, various states have adopted different systems regarding the appointment of family court judges. Maharashtra has evolved a special cadre of family court judges who are appointed through direct recruitments. One significant development in this area has been the elevation of marriage counselors as family court judges. This segment comprises largely of women. The training required for these judges would be different from the training required for judges who are transferred from the district courts. The ideological shift a marriage counselor would have to make to function effectively as a family court judge, faced with complex procedural and statutory legal provisions, ought to be an important factor while conducting such training. It would also be worth examining whether there is a clash of approaches between these appointees and the district judges.

The problems faced by judges who are direct appointees is different from the one faced by those who are transferred from district courts. These judges are seldom transferred and hold the office for a long period of time. Though they are in the same category as a 'district judge', they are not transferred to the districts and have limited options. There is also a perception that competent lawyers are not interested in appointment as judges in family courts, because it is not considered as an appointment in the main stream of the judiciary with future career prospects (Gupte 2001: 4). Sometimes district judges who are at the end of their tenure are posted to family courts which defeats the purpose for which family courts were set up. Here, the convenience and benefit to judicial officers attain priority over the benefit to litigants, and the courts.

In West Bengal, family courts are viewed as a quasi-judicial forum and judges appointed are usually are at the age of retirement. This is because the retirement age for district judges is 60 years, while that of a family court judge is 62 years as per Section 4 (5) of the Family Courts Act.[64] Once appointed as family court judges, they are deemed to be on deputation to the State government. But when they reach the retirement age of 60 years, the high court ceases to have supervisory power over their functioning and the state government ought to assume this role. But government officials feel that they have no role in supervising the functioning of the judiciary. This has resulted in a lack of supervision and accountability.[65]

---

[63] Excerpts from an interview with P. V. Singri, Presiding Judge, Family Court, Raichur, which was conducted as part of the study of family courts in Karnataka in 2003 (Agnes 2006).

[64] Section 4 (5) of the Act stipulates that no person shall be appointed as, or hold the office of a judge of a family court after he has attained the age of sixty-two years.

[65] This information is based on interviews with the two presiding judicial officers conducted in 2004 as part of the Study of family courts in West Bengal (Agnes 2006).

S.10 Procedure generally (3) – Nothing ... ... shall prevent a family court from laying down its own procedure with a view to arrive at a settlement in respect of the subject matter of the suit or proceedings or at the truth of the facts alleged by the one party and denied by the other.

S.14 Application of Indian Evidence Act, 1872 – A family court may receive as evidence any report statement, documents, information or matter that may, in its opinion, assist it to deal effectually with a dispute, whether or not the same would be otherwise relevant or admissible under the Indian Evidence Act, 1872.

S.15 Record of Oral Evidence – In suits or proceedings before a family court, it shall not be necessary to record the evidence of witnesses at length, but the judge, as the examination of each witness proceeds, shall record or cause to be recorded, a memorandum of the substance of what the witness deposes, and such memorandum shall be signed by the witness and the judge and shall form part of the record.

Powers of Judges

Family court judges are placed at the same level as district judge. But family court judges are armed with additional powers to mould and adopt procedures in the interest of justice, a power which the judges of criminal and civil courts do not have. In addition there are two points of departure from the practices adopted in regular courts: (i) judges, as a rule, do not have (or at least ought not to have) the help of lawyers as in regular courts; and (ii) they are to be aided by non-legal support systems, such as of conciliators and experts from other fields, who may not have adequate knowledge of law. The approach of the counselors may at times be in variance with a judge's training and orientation in adjudication. A judge has to negotiate these hurdles while arriving at an amicable resolution of the dispute in a speedy and gender-just manner. This is a challenge most judges of family courts face. Many resolve the conflict by adopting a less legalistic and technical and more humanist approach to dispute resolution.

But there are instances where family court judges seem to forget the purpose behind the additional powers granted to them and their call of duty. While many instances of a callous attitude on the part of family court judges have been discussed in this as well as in earlier chapters, a few of incidents are repeated here to highlight this point.

In *Veena Devi* v. *Ashok Kumar Mandal,*[66] while claiming maintenance under Section 125, Cr.PC, the woman could not state whether the ritual of saptapadi had been performed during the wedding ceremony. Due to this, the presiding judge of the family court disbelieved her evidence regarding the fact of her marriage. In appeal, the Patna High Court commented adversely on the role of the family court in determining this issue and held:

The Principle Judge, Family Court, Dhanbad, while exercising jurisdiction under S.125 Cr.PC was not required to decide the question of marriage like a matrimonial court. The object of such proceeding is only to prevent vagrancy and make a provision for destitute woman or child. The evidence adduced to prove the marriage should not have been viewed with such precision as the learned principal judge has done. If there was any evidence on record to bring out sufficient facts and circumstances to support the case of the petitioner in respect of her marriage, there was no justification for the learned Principal Judge of the family court to take a contrary view by adopting an altogether technical approach to the matter.[67]

---

[66] 2000 Cri.LJ 332 Pat

[67] This case has been discussed earlier in Chapter 2 *Matrimonial Rights and Obligations.*

This is an important ruling which emphasizes the two different roles a family court judge has to perform—a civil judge or district judge while deciding matrimonial petitions and suits for maintenance under the HAMA and a magistrate's court while adjudicating issues of maintenance under Section 125, Cr.PC which are summary proceedings. In these proceedings which are of a summary nature, the court does not have the authority to determine the validity of marriage like a civil or matrimonial court. A family court judge is called upon to keep these different roles in mind so that interest of justice are not hampered in the process.

The Bombay High Court, in *Leela Mahadeo Joshi* v. *Mahadeo Sitaram Joshi*,[68] where the family court judge had declined to grant a decree of divorce on a petition by mutual consent filed by an elderly couple, observed as follows:

It appears to us that the learned trial judge was disinclined to grant divorce to parties who had lived together in matrimony for long years. However, we do not think that personal predilections should be allowed to influence the provisions of a statute. If the necessary ingredients have been proved, there is no other course left open to a trial judge but to comply with the law.

In *Anita Laxmi Narayan Singh* v. *Laxmi Narain Singh*,[69] the husband who was residing in Mumbai filed for divorce in Mumbai. In these proceedings, the wife who was residing in Ghaziabad filed an application for expenses of travel, lodging and other incidentals, for the purpose of defending this litigation. The family court awarded a very low amount to her, due to which she was not able to appear in court and hence the husband was able to secure an *ex parte* decree of divorce. While setting aside this decree and transferring the proceedings to the district court at Ghaziabad, the Supreme Court commented on the callous approach of the family court at Mumbai in awarding such a low amount as travel expenses.

In *Annie Mathews* v. *Rajimon Abraham*,[70] the family court at Bangalore had refused to follow the rulings of three high courts in respect of a Christian woman's right to divorce on the ground of cruelty, stating that it was bound only by the decisions of the Karnataka High Court. The high court pointed out that such reasoning is erroneous and commented that in matrimonial cases where the parties are undergoing intense physical and mental trauma, the first thing that is expected from the court is a helpful attitude.

In several cases discussed earlier in this chapter, the high courts have been critical of family court judgments for adopting a narrow and constrained view of the provisions of the Act which would lead to multiplicity of proceedings. Rulings of the Kerala High Court in *Shyni* v. *George*[71] and *Suprabha* v. *Sivaraman*[72] and the Andhra Pradesh High Court in *Mariamma Ninan* v. *Mr K.K. Ninan*,[73] are examples of this. Similarly, in *Uma Tiwari* v. *Vikrant Tiwari*,[74] the Madhya Pradesh High Court had criticized the family court for not taking note of the amendment to the Hindu Marriage Act, brought about in the preceding year, which had expanded the scope of jurisdiction to enable women to file proceedings at the place of their residence. See also the comments of S. Rajeswaran, J. of the Madras High Court in *Banu* v. *Govindaperumal*,[75] regarding the attitude of the

---

[68] AIR 1991 Bom 105. This case has been discussed at section titled 'Doctrine of No Fault Divorce' of Chapter 1 *Marriage and Its Dissolution*.

[69] (1992) 2 SCC 562. This case has been discussed at section titled 'Travelling Expenses' of Chapter 2 *Matrimonial Rights and Obligations*.

[70] AIR 2002 Kar 385
[71] II (1997) DMC 676 Ker
[72] II (2006) DMC 404 Ker
[73] I (1997) DMC 570 AP
[74] I (2005) DMC 690 MP
[75] AIR 2009 Mad 155

family court judge at Pondichery in dismissing the application of the wife to summon certain witnesses to prove her case of her husband's bigamy, discussed later.[76]

While, in the interest of justice, such lapses ought not occur even in regular trial courts, these become even more glaring and critical when committed by judges presiding over family courts which have a special mandate to alleviate the sufferings of litigants and bring speedy justice to them. The higher judiciary has also repeatedly stressed upon the fact that matrimonial litigation causes extreme emotional trauma and has called upon family court judges and counselors to be sensitive to the needs of litigants. It has been pointed out that the very purpose of establishing family courts was to have a different atmosphere during the settlement of family disputes and family court judges have to take this into account and be lenient with respect to procedural technicalities.

The overarching aim should be to create an atmosphere which is most conducive to an amicable resolution of the dispute, while protecting the rights of the weaker parties.

The concern beneath the wide discretionary powers bestowed upon the presiding officers in the family court is: for whose benefits this procedural latitude and discretionary powers are to be exercised? Since the Act is silent on this issue, individual judges have to grope their way around in the dark and find their own balance relying on constitutional mandate. While this is the norm, today there is also a realization that the discretionary powers are generally used in accordance with the judges own socialization, value system, exposure, and level of gender sensitization. It is in this context that the selection of judges, their training, and sensitization play an important role, lest the powers be used

against women. A guiding principle for judges while using the discretionary power would be Article 15 (3) of the Constitution, which validates special provisions for the benefit of women and children. Principles of neutrality and equality can be sidestepped within this legal premise of constitutional justice. Family court judges need special orientation to evolve this framework.

LAWYERS AND COUNSELORS

Role of Lawyers in Family Courts

Notwithstanding anything contained in any law, no party to a suit or proceeding before a family court shall be entitled, as of right, to be represented by a legal practitioner.

Provided that if the family court considers it necessary in the interest of justice, it may seek the assistance of legal expert as amicus curiae.

Section 13, Family Courts Act

While being strengthened by these powers, judges are also constrained by the Act as they are not (as per the provisions of Section 13 of the Act) aided by lawyers routinely, as a matter of right, like in regular civil and criminal courts. Within the adversarial system of adjudication, which is based on the British common law, the role assigned to a judge is that of a neutral arbiter and is confined to merely 'judging' the merits of a case that is presented before him. The responsibility is placed on lawyers, as officers of the court, to present the court with the latest trends and advance innovative arguments in support of their client's contentions.

Despite these positive aspects, Section 13 restricts the role of lawyers in the family courts. This is reflective of the legislative concern regarding the exploitative role of lawyers. Legal experts, legislators, and women's rights activists pin the blame for the failure of the justice delivery system on lawyers. Exorbitant litigation costs, corrupt court practices, manipulative and

---

[76] See under section titled 'A Call for a Humanitarian Approach to Dispute Resolution' at p. 305.

subversive tactics, prolonged and acrimonious legal battles, refusal to 'compromise' or 'settle', all these are attributed to the presence of lawyers in court rooms. This provision was meant to bring in certain regulatory measures to curb this disturbing trend. But this legislative intent was rather short-sighted and did not address the ground reality of the highly contested terrain of litigation. The presence of lawyers is required to steer litigants through the complex maze of court procedures. Conciliators or counselors would not have the necessary skills and expertise to carry out this task. Also, the phrase 'seeking assistance of legal expert as *amicus curiae*' was not clear. There was ambiguity regarding the difference between 'assisting the court' and 'representing the contesting parties' during litigation. Would 'amicus curiae' be synonymous with 'legal aid' to the poor and the needy? The ambiguity regarding the scope of this section persisted even within the judiciary. Perhaps the demand by women's groups itself was ill conceived. While there is no denying the exploitation by lawyers, it is the illiterate, the marginalized, and the powerless who need support and guidance during litigation.

In this context, Prof. Lotika Sarkar had raised some concerns. According to her the relationship of a husband and wife, in the best of times, is not one of equality. Hence, to expect the woman to put forward her case amounts almost to cruelty. She commented:

Who will strategize for the woman when her rights are violated? Often barely literate, does she know what evidence she should produce? Section 14 of the *Family Courts Act* entitles the court to receive in evidence any report, documents, etc., which will help the court to decide the issue. How does a woman who is not in a position of equality, either because of her lack of exposure, or economic or emotional dependency upon her husband, even know what is relevant and what she should mention to the judge? Will she be able to reply in a coherent manner to cross-examination? Surely the woman, if not both parties, need the help of lawyers.

It is one thing to say that the party cannot, as of right, be represented by a lawyer. But should they not have the assistance of some person?, she had commented (Sarkar 1994).

At another level, this provision has been resented by lawyers who feel that it is in conflict with Section 6 of the Advocates Act, which bestows upon them the right to enter any court. Any curtailment of this right is perceived as an attack on the legal profession. Lawyers seem to reject the concept of a special court for family matters with diminished role for lawyers. Opposition from lawyers' associations is stated as a major hindrance in setting up of family courts in the country.

In 1987, lawyers from the Jaipur Bar Association declared a strike before the setting up of the first family court in the country in Jaipur, Rajasthan, and the agitation resulted in the court being closed down for a few months. There were also writ petitions filed by bar associations challenging the validity of Section 13 of the Family Courts Act. In *Kanpur Bar Association* v. *Union of India*,[77] the Supreme Court upheld the validity of this provision. Subsequently, a Division Bench of the Rajasthan High Court in *Supriya* v. *Naresh Kotwani*[78] and the Bombay High Court in *Vijay Kaur* v. *Radhey Shyam*,[79] also followed the Supreme Court ruling and upheld the validity of the provision.

Some legal experts are also of the opinion that the provision barring entry of lawyers is a drawback as it would keep competent lawyers away from family courts (Gupte 2001: 4). But later events have proved that this fear is unfounded.

Initially, the family courts, as per the stipulation of the Act, restricted the entry of lawyers,

[77] WP 1124/1987, as cited in *Vijay Kaur* v. *Radhey Shyam*, II (1991) DMC 245 Raj.
[78] Civil Misc. Appeal No.401/1989, as cited in *Vijay Kaur* v. *Radhey Shyam*, II (1991) DMC 245 Raj.
[79] II (1991) DMC 245 Raj

but gradually settled down to a familiar pattern of representation by lawyers. Though there is a statutory requirement of seeking permission of the court, many judges feel that this is a 'mere formality'; refusal to grant permission results in further delay, as the parties approach the high courts for the required permission. In Mumbai during the initial years, the entry of lawyers in the court was strictly prohibited. Very few lawyers used to visit family courts. Even these lawyers were not allowed to enter the court rooms. They could only help their clients in the waiting halls outside the court rooms. But a ruling of the Bombay High Court in 1991, in *Leela Mahadeo Joshi v. Mahadeo Sitaram Joshi*,[80] brought in a significant change in the situation. After this ruling, lawyers were permitted to represent the litigants and present arguments on their behalf. M.F. Saldanha J. of the Bombay High Court, in a concurring judgement made the following observations:

Adjudication of a complicated or highly contested matrimonial dispute in the light of law and interpretation of provisions by different courts over a period of time, would require assistance from advocates. The uneducated and poor litigants are being totally handicapped in the conduct of their cases for want of legal assistance. Even the educated and the rich find it difficult to follow court procedures. In the absence of convincing reasons, permission of representation by lawyers ought not to be refused.

Professional legal ethics demand that when lawyers appear before the court on behalf of their clients, they are expected to have a duty not to personally involve themselves in the cause of the clients. They owe a responsibility not just to their clients but also to the court. When the roles are reversed and the lawyer is only expected to act behind the scenes, the litigant willy-nilly may become a proxy and the battle may be fought between the two lawyers using the litigants as puppets or cat's-paw. The result is a fierce no-holds-barred battle between two hapless persons estranged from each other. This defeats the legislative intent of keeping lawyers at bay. The litigants find themselves ill equipped to submit legal arguments and are unable to plead their cases. In any case, they still have to depend on their lawyers for advice and guidance. But the litigants are deprived of the services of a competent and responsible professional in court rooms. The courts have commented that it appears to be a case where the remedy has proved more harmful than the disease itself.

Following this ruling, it became difficult for judges to restrict the entry of lawyers in courts and gradually, the family courts at Mumbai started functioning as regular courts where litigants are represented by their advocates. This was also the case in other family courts of Maharashtra. But at a later point, around 2003, some individual judges started restricting the entry of lawyers during the initial stages of the trial and allowed representation only at the time of arguments.

The issue of representation by lawyers has been raised before several high courts. Some of the opinions expressed by high courts, following the ruling in the *Leela Mahadeo case*, are discussed below.

In *Nandana* v. *Pradeep Bhandari*,[81] the Rajasthan High Court pointed out that the purpose of keeping lawyers away from such litigation was completely defeated in most cases. The parties are required to take upon themselves the task of pleading their respective cases as lawyers have not been allowed. The decorum and dignity with which cases are normally conducted before the civil court, with the aid of professionals steeped in the age old traditions of the Bar, are totally lost and unrestricted and relentless acrimony has taken their place. It cannot be believed that parties to such litigation prosecute it without the aid of lawyers.

In *Prabhat Narain Tickoo* v. *Mamta Tickoo*,[82] the Allahabad High Court clarified the position further and held:

---

[80]   AIR 1991 Bom 105

[81]   I (1996) DMC 285 Raj
[82]   II (1998) DMC 333 All

The words 'as of right' indicates that the intention of Parliament was not to debar Advocates absolutely from appearing in family courts. The judges must use their discretion. The correct approach is not to permit lawyers to appear when the court is trying for a reconciliation between the parties. But where the matter has to be adjudicated, lawyers should allowed to appear. Far from delaying proceedings lawyer will greatly expedite it by using their knowledge of law and procedure.

Similarly, in *R. Durga Prasad* v. *Union of India*,[83] the Andhra Pradesh High Court held that the parties are entitled to engage legal practitioners after conciliatory proceedings are completed and the court is convinced about the impossibility of reconciliation. The court noted that the economically sound party can be directed to bear the legal expenses of the economically weaker party, as provided under Section 24 of the HMA. In addition, the court could also appoint lawyers as *amicus curiae* to assist the court. In *S. Venkataraman* v. *L. Vijayasaratha*,[84] the Madras High Court held that in the interest of justice, taking into consideration the nature of the case and the conditions under which the parties are placed permission for representation ought to be given, even when the request is made orally to the court. When permitted, the counsel could file the *vakalatnama* and do all that is necessary for the client while conducting the case. In *Komal Padukone* v. *Principal Judge, Family Court, Bangalore*,[85] the Karnataka High Court pointed out that a reasonable opportunity to defend oneself is an essential part of the principles of natural justice. Where one side is represented by a legally trained mind, refusing to grant permission to the other side to be similarly represented amounts to violation of the principles of nature justice.

However, the view point of every high court is not uniform. For instance, the Rajasthan High Court clarified in later decisions that representation by advocates is not a matter of right and judicial discretion should be used while granting permission. Some rulings have also attempted to highlight the difference between legal representation and being appointed as *amicus curiae*. In *Sarla Sharma* v. *State of Rajasthan*,[86] it was held that normally a legal practitioner shall not be permitted to appear for a party as a matter of right, but the court has the power to permit engagement of a legal practitioner in exceptional circumstances, in the interest of justice. The discretion to be exercised by a family court is judicial discretion which should be guided by reason. It should not be vague, arbitrary, and fanciful but should be exercised reasonably and in good faith, keeping in view that such permission will be granted only in exceptional circumstances, to meet the ends of justice. While exercising such discretion, the court must keep in mind that the normal rule is that of no intervention of lawyers in the proceedings before the family court and hence the exceptional circumstances must appear from the order of the court.

In *Guru Bachan Kaur* v. *Preetam Singh*,[87] Binod Kumar Roy J. and R.K. Mahajan J. of the Allahabad High Court commented that if it is brought to the notice of the family court that delay or obstacles are caused by lawyers appearing in the case, the family court has the power to immediately cancel the 'vakalatnama' and obey the mandate of the legislature rather than prolong the agony of the litigants.

In *Sadhana Patra* v. *Subrat Pradhan*,[88] the Orissa High Court held that while applying for permission for legal representation, the party

---

[83] II (1998) DMC 45 AP
[84] I (1997) DMC 503 Mad
[85] II (1999) DMC 301 Kar

[86] I (2002) DMC 409 Raj
[87] 1998 (1) AWC 275 All
[88] II (2006) DMC 316 Ori

seeking such relief must state the reasons as to why assistance of legal practitioner is required. Only if the court is satisfied about the reasons, may it allow party to take legal advice while the matter is pending before it. The high court also explained the difference between an amicus curiae and a lawyer representing a litigant. The amicus curiae is a 'friend of the court'. If a lawyer is appointed as amicus curiae, he cannot act in a partisan manner and for personal gain and cannot get involved with the case on behalf of either of the parties. The role of such a person is limited to assisting the court on issues of fact and law, as and when required.

Laxmi Kanwar v. *Laxman Singh*,[89] provides an example of the exceptional circumstances in which such permission may be granted. The wife was staying in Gujarat. It was torturous for her and her parents to travel to Jodhpur in Rajasthan on each date of hearing. But the family court at Jodhpur rejected her application seeking permission to appoint a lawyer. In an appeal filed by her against this order, the Rajasthan High Court commented:

The wife may not have a claim to be represented through a lawyer as of right but if the convenience so requires, it is obligatory on the court to extend such facility. The proviso to Section 13 casts a duty on the court to consider if in the interest of justice, the assistance of a legal expert as *amicus curiae* is necessary. The convenience cannot be compensated in terms of money. There is no reason to deny her the services of a lawyer. The learned judge of the family court, under the facts of the case, has committed an error in refusing the wife to be represented through a legal practitioner.

As we can see from the various high court rulings on this issue, family courts have attempted to adopt a balance between granting permissions in a routine manner and going to absurd lengths to deny permission. Each court has the power to follow its own procedures

regarding this issue. For instance, in Kolkata, the two family courts adopted two different positions, one allowing legal representations in a routine manner and the other following the pattern of blanket denial.[90]

In Bombay, seven different court rooms are situated within the premises that house the family courts, which has attracted a significant number of lawyers who specialize in family disputes. After the ruling in the *Leela Mahadeo Joshi case*, permission for legal representation became a routine matter and a large number of lawyers started regular practice in this court. There is a certain expertise that has developed in the area of family law and rules and procedures of family courts. Since matrimonial disputes are on the rise in the city and there are a large number of contested cases, family law litigation has become a lucrative business. Over the years, the lawyers practicing in this court have been able to form a bar association which has a membership of around 1000 lawyers. In addition, a substantial number of lawyers, who are not members of the Family Court Bar Association, also practice in this court. A large hall is marked as the bar room and is provided for the use of lawyers. The lawyers feel that their presence is essential as the stakes in this court are very high. The court does not have a limit regarding pecuniary jurisdiction in matrimonial matters. Complex property matters with high stakes which, according to the lawyers, are beyond the grasp of marriage counselors. These issues also infringe upon other rights which are located within laws regarding cooperative societies, tenancy, companies, HUF property, negotiable instruments, etc. Within this con-

---

[89]   2005 MLR 388 Raj

[90]   This information is based on interviews with the two presiding judicial officers conducted in 2004 as part of the Study of family courts in West Bengal (Agnes 2006).

text, litigation within family courts becomes as contested and acrimonious as it used to be in the city civil court. These issues are beyond the realm of settlement and involve complex legal principles. While there is a grain of truth in this argument, it must also be stated that the Family Court Bar Association has not concerned itself with curbing corrupt practices or in evolving some code of conduct for lawyers in the context of the underlying principles reflected in the Family Courts Act.

The relationship between the bar and the bench has been contentious. Lawyers have been resenting any attempt by the bench to regulate or restrain legal practice in family courts. In 2004, when the Principle Judge of the family court issued a circular to the bar that that no lawyer would be allowed to enter the court rooms unless their matter is called out, and further, the lockers allotted to lawyers should not encroach the space in court halls, the Family Court Bar Association called an extra-ordinary general body meeting to express their protest against this new procedure.[91] But the judges stood firm on their decision and gradually the lawyers had to comply with the new rule. But attempts to regulate legal practice in family courts inevitably tend to get lax as per the approach of individual judges and the need of the litigants who are generally apprehensive to appear before a judge without the aid of a lawyer.

In Karnataka, lawyers are permitted to appear routinely in all matters, but there have been concerns raised about malpractice by lawyers. Judges presiding over the family courts at Bangalore commented that denying permission only causes further delays as the parties approach the high court and obtain the necessary directions in this respect. Since the aim of the family courts is to deliver speedy justice, this is counter productive. Hence it is more advisable to grant permission as soon as an application is submitted, to avoid delays. One of the judges commented, on a practical note:

If the high court grants permission in a routine manner, we are also bound to follow this practice. Not following this norm may invite adverse comments from the high courts and we would like to avoid it

So overall, it appears the stipulation of restricting entry of lawyers under Section 13 of the Act has not had the desired effect. This is perhaps because it was ill conceived and not logically thought out. Also, the support machinery which was necessary to implement this scheme, such as setting up of a panel of amicus curiae, has not been followed by state governments to support the family courts.

Counselors in Family Courts

The State Government shall, in consultation with the high court, determine the number and categories of counselors ... required to assist a family court in the discharge of its function and provide the family court with such counselors ... as it may think fit.

Section 6, Family Courts Act

Section 6 of the Act is linked to Section 9, which stipulates that it is the duty of the family court to make efforts for settlement. This also has a resonance of Section 23 (2) of the Hindu Marriage Act which stipulates that it shall be the duty of the court to make every endeavour to bring about a reconciliation between the parties. A similar stipulation regarding settlement can also be found in Order 32-A, Rule 3 of the Civil Procedure Code.

The concern of the legislature while enacting the Family Courts Act has been to bring about reconciliation or, in the alternative, an amicable settlement. The purpose of the enactment appears to be to avoid contested litigation and to bring about a speedy resolution of the dispute.

---

[91] Personal knowledge of the author as a member of the Mumbai Family Court Bar Association.

With this in view, the role of lawyers was curtailed and judges were to be aided with non-legal professionals with certain expertise in dispute resolution. This provision also recognized the fact that the presiding officers may not have the time and expertise to get into counseling sessions which require time, skill, and patience.

Within this framework, counselors have been awarded a high position within the Act. The position of a counselor within the court premises was a new concept and both judges and lawyers had to reconcile with it. Within the prevailing legal structure, this was a difficult proposition and the courts had to reorient themselves to accept this proposition. Initially, it was not clear what role a counselor was expected to play. In most states, counseling has remained external to the judicial forum; the mandatory provision of counseling is followed in a cursory manner and their role is confined to the task of ascertaining whether it is possible to reconcile the dispute and save the marriage. Maharashtra is the only exception in this regard, where the counseling process is integrated within the family court structure.

As per the provisions of the Act, state governments, in consultation with their respective high courts, were to provide counselors to assist the judges in the discharge of their functions. There is wide disparity in the procedures adopted for appointment of counselors, their qualifications and remunerations, the role and position awarded to them, and the counseling techniques adopted by individual counselors.

Rules framed by the Andhra Pradesh government, initially did not provide for the appointment of counselors and judges were burdened with the task of counseling, which is time consuming and cumbersome. Judges may not even have the necessary skills to conduct counseling sessions on a regular basis. Since 2005, counseling has been introduced in family

courts under the State Legal Aid Authority and the parties are referred to counselors. Help of NGOs who offer counseling service is also sought, when required.

Under the rules framed by the Tamil Nadu government, counselors are appointed only for a period of three months and have a very limited role. But recently, the situation is improved slightly and trained personnel are appointed as counselors and they are assigned tasks such as ascertaining the wishes of children in child custody issues and negotiating divorce settlements. In April 2006, at the initiative of A.P. Shah CJ, the Madras High Court started a counseling centre along with a psychology centre and a children's complex in the family courts.[92]

In Karnataka, there is no bar against appointing lawyers as counselors. So instead of a diminished role within the family court structure, lawyers' role has been enhanced. Though the counselors are appointed from a list forwarded to the high court by the presiding officer annually, this task is carried out by the clerical staff and it is very easy for any lawyer to get himself/herself appointed as a counselor. There are no mechanisms for monitoring the work of the conciliators, either at the high court level or at the governmental level.

West Bengal adopts yet another pattern regarding the appointment and tenure of counselors. Sections 23 to 27 of the Rules framed by the Calcutta High Court in 1990 deal with the counseling process. Section 26 stipulates that counselors will be appointed by the high court in consultation with one or more professionally qualified experts in family and child welfare. They should preferably be working with a recognized institution of social science or social work. Section 27 prescribes the qualification as

---

[92] As reported in *The Hindu*, Chennai, April 24, 2006.

'a Master's degree in social work with minimum experience of 2 years in family counseling'. However, though untill 2005, there were only two family courts in the entire state, none of the 35 counselors who were appointed in 1995 had the required qualification. Their work had never been evaluated and their names continue on the list of conciliators despite the fact that many of them have full time employment elsewhere. The Calcutta High Court, the West Bengal State Government as well as the Principal Judge of the family court had not evolved any mechanisms for monitoring their functioning. The only way the court had dealt with the complaints received regarding the functioning of the counselors had been to permit representation by lawyers. If legal representation was permitted, the need for counseling was dispensed with.[93]

In Rajasthan, counseling is not given due recognition and many a times the courts do not even allocate space for counselors to conduct sessions with litigants. The policy regarding counseling is not consistent in all the family courts in the State. In some courts, counselors function under the Family Courts Act while in others they function under Lok Adalats under the State Legal Services Authority. Services of the conciliators are used only occasionally and in the limited context of Lok Adalats, which may take place either weekly or periodically. Counselors are used more routinely in the Udaipur family court. In Jaipur family court, counselors come only once a week, on Saturdays. At times voluntary organizations are invited to participate in these proceedings. The counselors offer voluntary services to the court as members of the Lok Adalat. Women litigants complain

that the views of the panel are conservative and women are pressurized to return to their husbands, even against their wishes.[94]

As compared to other states, the counseling process is far more integrated in Maharashtra. This is due to an experiment conducted in the city civil court in 1980. Faced with a huge backlog and stalemates in matrimonial disputes, the judge who was assigned matrimonial matters introduced a process of optional counseling and invited various NGOs in the city to participate in this experiment.[95] The Departmental Head of Family and Child Welfare of the Tata Institute of Social Work was invited to co-ordinate this venture. The success of this experiment has led to these counselors being awarded a high status when the Maharashtra government framed rules under the Family Courts Act in 1988. This experiment served as the basis of formulating further rules to make counseling an integral part of the family courts in the State. Due to the earlier experiment, as well as the elaborate rules framed under the Act, counselors are awarded a respectable position as officers of the court in Maharashtra. The selection interviews are conducted by judges of the high court and they hold a permanent post as Class I gazetted officers.

But even this model has its own drawbacks. The permanency of tenure brings about its own set of problems. This seems to be the only non-transferable position within the family court,

---

[93] This information is based on interviews with presiding officers, two counselors, and the Chairperson of the West Bengal Women's Commission, as part of the study of family courts in West Bengal conducted by the author in 2004.

[94] This information is based on interviews conducted with functionaries of a Jaipur-based NGO, Vishaka, which has a legal aid programme in various family courts of Rajasthan, as part of a para-legal training programme by the author which was held in Jaipur in 2006.

[95] Interview with H. Suresh J., later a judge of the Bombay High Court, who had introduced this programme while he was the judge of the Bombay city civil court in 1980.

where counselor-lawyer or counselor-court nexus can evolve. While it is possible to have a process of internal shuffling of counselors between the seven courts in Mumbai and the five courts in Pune, this is not possible in other districts where the number of courts is limited to just one or two courts. But since there is a strict vigilance at the high court level, some of the malpractices have been investigated and action has been taken. In one case, such investigations have also led to the termination of the concerned counselor.

There is a constant effort to undermine the role of counselors in the highly contested terrain of litigation within the family courts in Mumbai. This has led to allegations about inefficiency and malpractices on the part of counselors. There is a feeling among members of the bar that counselors do their job in a cursory and routine manner. Rather than mediation, they use intimidating measures in order to prevail upon the parties to settle their disputes. They also caution litigants about long drawn and highly contested litigation in order to bring about quick settlements which may not always be in the interest of women. The litigants are caught in this atmosphere of distrust between lawyers and counselors.

But on the positive side, the office of marriage counselors has been a serious effort on the part of the state government to bring in non-commercial support to litigants in family courts. The counselors have been able to effectively carry out various important functions which arise in the course of matrimonial litigation. Converting a contested divorce petition into a petition for divorce by mutual consent, negotiating financial settlements at the time of divorce, acting as court commissioners to conduct on the spot surveys and inventories, home visits and school visits to study the environment of the child while ascertaining custody issues, negotiating a consensus

regarding access to non-custodial parent, etc., have been important functions which the marriage counselors have been able to carry out in Maharashtra. They have also been instrumental in setting up child access rooms within the court, where supervised access to the non-custodial parent is possible. Issues of emotional crises during matrimonial litigation have also been an important concern for the counselors.

Since they are appointed on a permanent basis and are full time employees, judges can refer the matter to them at any stage for further negotiations and settlements and to carry out supervisory functions. While their reports are confidential, presiding officers can assign specific tasks to them, such as interviewing a child to ascertain the wishes and seek a report upon which they can base their decision. Their role in working out minute details of access to a non-custodial parent has been of great value.

If this model is followed in other states, valuable judicial time will be saved and the minute nitty-gritty of matrimonial disputes can be amicably worked out as these require patience and perseverance on the part of the mediator. This can be done only after grievances have been aired out, tempers have cooled down, and bloated egos have been shrunk. It is necessary for sufficient time to be allocated for this healing process to take place. An overburdened court, with its compulsions of clearing back logs and meeting the requirement of a unit-based system, where orders delivered are marked for assessing performances by the higher judiciary, cannot be expected to meet this demand.

There is wide disparity in the remuneration paid to counselors. In Maharashtra, they are appointed on a permanent basis as Class-I officers. This gives dignity to their position. In other States, however, their remuneration ranges from Rs 60 to Rs 300 per day and most function on a part-time basis on selective days and/or selective hours. Within this structure, the counselors have a very limited role. Most of their work is done at the preliminary stage and is confined to ascertaining whether it is possible for the parties to reconcile. This renders the task of counselors as a mere obligatory fulfillment of the statutory provision.

A Gender-Sensitive Framework for Counseling
While the appointment, supervision, and remuneration of counselors are important concerns, the quality of their counseling is another aspect that needs to be examined. As mentioned above, in most courts counseling is only superficial and rights are determined by the judicial process or by interventions of presiding officers. But where the counselors play a substantial role in bringing about negotiations and settlements, there is a need to evolve a pro-woman framework for marriage counseling or for mediated settlements. Since the power balance within the family and society are tilted against women, a neutral stand of the counselor may serve to reflect and endorse internalized patriarchal biases against women. So the apparently neutral position may in fact get translated into an anti-woman posture. Counselors have to be careful to avoid this pitfall. There is a need for periodic training to evolve gender-sensitive, women oriented counseling techniques. Within the mandate of 'speedy settlement', without a clearly defined framework of gender justice, the conciliatory approach adopted by the marriage counselors may further jeopardize the rights of women and the counseling process itself can turn anti-women.

At times the mandate of 'reconciliation' gets transformed into pressurizing women to reconcile and return to the matrimonial home, even at the cost of defeating her human dignity, physical safety, and meager economic rights. When a woman, who was physically abused and thrown out of her matrimonial home, files for

maintenance under Section 125 of the Cr.PC, the common ploy adopted by lawyers defending husbands, is to file for restitution of conjugal rights. The offer of reconciliation forms part of the legal ploy of defeating the woman's claim to maintenance. Without understanding this complexity, the pressure to unconditionally withdraw the allegations and maintenance claim and return at the behest of the husband to save the marriage, results not only in defeating the claim of maintenance, but would also expose the woman to further violence and indignity.

At this point, the counselors need to ensure that a woman's right to maintenance is not defeated by such superficial offers of reconciliation. Even if a woman opts to test the genuineness of the offer by returning to the matrimonial home, the application for maintenance needs to be kept pending. In the event that reconciliation does not work out, the woman would then be in a position to pursue her earlier application for maintenance and will not lose her rights because of the intervening period of reconciliation. But if she has been forced to withdraw the maintenance application at the instance of her husband, it will seriously jeopardize her rights. If due care is not taken and the application for maintenance is withdrawn unconditionally, the woman may not be able to file a fresh application for maintenance using the earlier grounds as it would be deemed as the same are condoned due to her act of reconciliation. Marriage counselors need to be aware of these legal complexities during negotiations.

In this context, the Supreme Court ruling in *Mahua Biswas* v. *Swagata Biswas*[96] is relevant. The Apex Court held that when genuine efforts made by the wife to rehabilitate herself in her matrimonial home did not fructify, the previous order of maintenance could at best be taken to

[96] (1998) 2 SCC 359

have been suspended, but not wiped out altogether. The court restored the position of the wife under the original order of maintenance.

There are instances where the husband may be living with another woman. In such a situation, instead of using investigative powers to ascertain the veracity of the allegations, women are often persuaded to consider the offer made by their husbands. The established legal position is that when a man is in a bigamous relationship or is cohabiting with another woman, the wife is not expected to even consider the husband's offer of reconciliation. Though it may be a desirable goal to save the marriage, the counselors need to understand that marriages cannot be saved at the cost of woman's dignity and self respect. The women need to be explained their legal rights in this respect.

If the man is a government employee this ought to further affect his job.[97] Instead of using persuasive measures to get the husband to pay regular maintenance to the wife, many a times, the counselors merely advise the woman to consider the husband's offer and return to the matrimonial home. When women file criminal cases against the husbands, they are advised by the counselors 'not to harass the husbands' by filing such cases. In this context, the Committee on Empowerment of Women (2001–2002)[98] stated in its recommendations that in cases where there is a history of repeated physical violence or where the husband has committed bigamy or adultery, women should not be compelled to reconcile.[99]

While the guiding principle of family courts is to 'protect and preserve' the family, the efforts of reconciliation are usually carried out only at the instance of the husband, according to his whim and fancy. In the event the husband does not willing to accept the wife back, there is hardly any pressure exerted on him to allow entry to the wife into the matrimonial home and 'save the marriage'. The counselors unquestioningly accept a man's unconditional right to the matrimonial home and any woman who wants to re-enter the home is viewed as encroaching upon the husband's domain. At such a juncture counselors 'advice' the woman that it is undignified for her to return to her matrimonial home since her husband is not willing to accept her back. The woman' right to reside in the matrimonial home is not awarded due recognition. The situation has changed slightly after the enactment of the Protection of Women from Domestic Violence Act, which has awarded statutory recognition to a woman's right to reside in the matrimonial home.

There are several cases where the woman is first thrown out and later, the husband files a divorce petition against her on vague and baseless allegations of adultery or cruelty.[100] Women, who are thus rendered destitute, are opposed to divorce and are keen to return to the matrimonial home and reconcile the marriage. In any case, until the divorce petition is finally decided and a decree of divorce is granted to the woman, she has every right to reside in the matrimonial home. But no reconciliation efforts are conducted at this stage through which a woman can live in her matrimonial home during the pendency of the litigation in the interest of preserving the family. Ironically, in such a situation, where a 'pro-women' position is 'pro-family',

---

[97] Rule 21 of the Central Civil Service (Conduct) Rules, 1964 bars a government employee from entering into a second marriage when his/her spouse is alive.

[98] Constituted by the Thirteenth Lok Sabha

[99] A Report of the Committee on Empowerment of Women (2001–2) on Functioning of Family Courts.

[100] See Chapter 1 *Marriage and its Dissolution* and Chapter 2 *Matrimonial Rights and Obligations.*

marriage counselors turnout to be pro-men and anti-family.

In the context of unequal power relationships that prevail within the family between men and women, the post-litigation counseling need to be nuanced rather than merely 'neutral'.

CHALLENGES CONFRONTING FAMILY COURTS

A Call for a Humanitarian Approach to Dispute Resolution

A concern which has been addressed by several high courts and the Supreme Court is that since the Act mandates a humanitarian approach towards dispute resolution, courts ought not be very technical and rigid in their approach. It has been held that since it is a beneficial legislation aimed at securing the rights of women and children, family courts must adopt a compassionate approach while adjudicating family matters. The higher judiciary has repeatedly stressed that technicalities cannot be allowed to prevail upon substantial interest of justice. Procedures under the Family Courts Act are made to achieve the ultimate objective of dispensing justice.

In *Deepmala Sharma* v. *Mahesh Sharma,*[101] the husband was awarded an ex-parte divorce by the family court at Jhansi, as the wife could not attend the court due to her illness. She also pleaded that subsequently her sister expired and she was grief stricken. Finally, when she could approach the court, she realized that the husband had already obtained an ex-parte order of divorce. She made an application, within the timeframe prescribed by the Limitation Act, for restoration which the family court rejected. In appeal, the high court held that the family court had adopted a pedantic approach in rejecting the explanation furnished by the wife, even though her statement was supported by medical certificate and death certificate.

In *Roopa* v. *Santosh Kumar,*[102] the parties had filed a petition for divorce under mutual consent. But on the date of the hearing, the wife was unable to be present due to her illness and before an order could be passed, she had filed an application to this effect. The husband, who was present, was examined but it was not recorded that he wished to withdraw his consent to the joint petition. The family court at Moradabad dismissed the joint petition. In an appeal filed by the wife, the Allahabad High Court granted the divorce, despite the fact that the husband was not present in court, with directions that he was free to move the court if he was not satisfied with the order. The high court commented that mere technicalities cannot be allowed to prevail upon substantial interest of justice. This is particularly relevant since the Family Courts Act does not allow advocates to appear before them.

In *Sivakami* v. *Shanmugasundaram,*[103] the wife could not remain present on the date of hearing and hence when the husband was examined on oath by his lawyer, the wife lost the opportunity of cross examining him and the case was marked as 'evidence closed'. The woman filed an application for a fresh opportunity to cross-examination, but the family court rejected this on the ground that her affidavit was false. The high court held that though there were some contradictions in her affidavit filed before the family court and the high court, the wife should be given an opportunity to cross-examine her husband. The court commented that the family court is not like an ordinary court where the law has to be applied strictly

---

[101] I (1992) DMC 374 All

[102] AIR 2005 All 172
[103] II (2007) DMC 78 Mad

and vigorously. Some sympathetic consideration should be extended to a woman when she comes and knocks the doors of justice, seeking maintenance to save herself from starvation. The family court was directed to reopen the evidence and proceed with the matter.

In *Banu* v. *Govindaperumal*,[104] S. Rajeswaran J. of the Madras High Court commented:

The family court should see that they are dealing with emotions between the parties and therefore, they should be more considerate and lenient than the Civil Courts in entertaining the family disputes. I am not happy with the way the family court of Pondicherry went out of the way to dismiss the petitions filed by the petitioner/wife to summon certain witnesses to prove the factum of the birth of a male child through her husband and another woman.

An important ruling of the Rajasthan High Court regarding the highly technical approach of the family courts in Rajasthan in numbering the maintenance applications as suits rather than petitions or applications and thereby demanding high court fees is discussed later in this chapter at section titled 'Abolition of Court Fees'. The rigid attitude of family courts has, in many instances, led to considerable delays and increased the cost of litigation, as the aggrieved women were constrained to approach the high courts, against the orders of family courts. This defeats the objective of speedy justice. There are several instances of high-handedness or callousness which take place within family courts on a routine basis that go unreported. The entire experiment of family courts was to bring in procedural measures that would be conducive to a just and equitable resolution of disputes. As the Allahabad High Court observed in *Roopa* v. *Santosh,* the ultimate goal of family courts is to 'dispense justice' and not to pose technical obstacles in the path of justice.

The family courts are also not bound by the strict evidential rules which bind normal courts. Section 14 of the Act invests the courts with discretionary power to accept in evidence, documents, information, or any matter that may, in the opinion of the court, assist it to deal effectually with a dispute. Armed with this provision, family courts can avoid the complicated rules regarding admissibility of documents and the manner of proving them, as stipulated under the Indian Evidence Act. But such power is to be invoked judiciously.

A full bench of the Bombay High Court, in *Romila Jaidev Shroff* v. *Jaidev Rajnikant Shroff,*[105] while transferring the matrimonial jurisdiction of the high court to the family courts, had highlighted this and held that litigation before family courts is a mixture of inquisitorial trial, participatory form of grievance redressal, and adversarial trial. As the court is left to device its own practice, it can have a judicious mixture of all three and can proceed under any of them. The overriding effect of the Family Courts Act is applicable not only to the Code of Civil Procedure but also to the Indian Evidence Act.

However, while some judges are willing to experiment and introduce innovative procedures, most judges prefer to follow the established pattern. There is a constant apprehension that their orders might get struck down at the higher level and strictures may be passed against them. Since this would not auger well for their career graph, most judges prefer to wait for directions from the higher judiciary to introduce changes within the court system. So, it appears that the onus of bringing improvements in the functioning of family court falls on the administrative discretion of high courts.

---

[104]   AIR 2009 Mad 155

[105]   II (2000) DMC 600 FB

Difficulties in Proceedings under Chapter IX of Cr.PC

Some judges presiding over smaller district towns have expressed the view that there are more delays in family courts than there were in magistrate's courts in proceedings for maintenance under Section 125, Cr.PC.[106] According to them, these additional procedural requirements such as mandatory counseling prescribed under the Family Courts Act cause further delays and defeat the very purpose of transferring cases from the magistrate's courts to the family courts. The women litigants had greater proximity to the magistrate's courts which are situated at the block or taluka level than the family courts which are situated in the district headquarters. Poor, deserted wives have to travel greater distances to access these courts with tiny infants in their hands and their plight is pitiable. Some courts do not give permission for legal representation in maintenance cases and insist on personal appearance, which makes litigation more cumbersome. Illiterate women find it difficult to follow up their cases without the help of lawyers and cases are dismissed for default. Without an effective legal aid programme and other support mechanisms, these women find it very difficult to access the family courts and prefer to approach the local or caste panchayat for redressal of their dispute.

At the procedural level, it is mandatory to undergo counseling before the case is heard, even for interim reliefs. The counseling is done on certain specific days and only for a few hours. Without report from counselors, the case does not proceed in court. It is also mandatory to file an application for permission for legal representation. This increases paper work and adds to the cost of litigation and delays the process of obtaining a speedy order of interim maintenance. The magistrate's courts were not bound by these procedural and technical hassles and it was easier to pass an interim order of maintenance. After the enactment of the Domestic Violence Act, where jurisdiction is awarded to magistrate's courts, needy women may revert back to magistrate's courts for maintenance under that Act instead of filing proceedings for maintenance in the family courts, as it provides a speedier option. This would defeat the purpose for which family courts were instituted.

Though, after setting up of family courts in each state, all cases then pending in the magistrate's courts were transferred to the family courts, as per the provisions of the Family Courts Act, the procedure of serving summons through the police, which was followed by the magistrate's courts has not been changed. But since the police is not directly under the family courts, there is a lack of monitoring and seriousness and, at times, even collusion between the police and the opposite party, i.e., the husband.

A presiding officer of the family court at Bijapur, Karnataka commented during an interview that though the institution of family courts was meant to benefit poor and helpless women, much of the beneficial effects have been nullified by the apathy of both the police and the executive. Notices and warrants have to be executed through the police. The police do not execute the process on one pretext or the other and on most occasions they are not returned at all. Since the courts do not have their own police force, there is a scope for collusion between husband and the police, both at the time of serving the notice as well as during the execution proceedings.

This is also the case with revenue officials. Maintenance has to be recovered as sale of properties of defaulting husbands, which has to

---

[106] Excerpts from an interview with N. Subba Rao, J., Presiding Judge, Family Court, Bijapur, which was conducted as part of the study of family courts in Karnataka in 2003 (Agnes 2006).

be done through revenue officials, particularly the *tehsildar*. If they cannot recover the amount, they do not convey to the court the reasons for non-recovery.[107] Hence among the cases filed under Chapter IX, Cr.PC, more cases are filed for recovery of arrears than for claiming maintenance under Section 125, Cr.PC. Many judges feel that it has become more difficult to execute orders in family courts than in the magistrate's courts as the former are not viewed with the same awe and respect as criminal courts.

Further, government departments do not co-operate in effecting the orders for salary attachment. In many cases, when salary warrants are sent to government offices for recovery of maintenance, they are either not given effect to or only small amounts are sent, which cause unnecessary delays and hardships to needy women. Officials need to be adequately oriented to comply with the directions of the courts. Many judges who were interviewed for the study expressed the view that the State Commissions for Women could persuade the government to issue suitable directions to different departments, particularly the police and revenue officials. Enforcing orders through the police or the revenue officials in case of attachment and sale of immovable agricultural lands, defeats the very purpose for which family courts were set up—speedy justice which would include effective enforcement of orders. Hence, it would be appropriate to make provisions in Section 125 of Cr.PC for entrustment of recovery warrants to the process section of the court concerned. Such power vests with the courts under the Code of the Civil Procedure (CPC) and similar powers could be vested with

the family courts as far maintenance under Section 125 of Cr.PC is concerned.

Imprisonment for non-payment of maintenance is meant to act as a deterrent and to exert pressure for compliance with the order. But some judges who were interviewed mentioned that at times the husbands plead inability to comply with the order and welcome a prison stint as they can avail of free government hospitality during this period. This is particularly true in poverty stricken districts of Karnataka, such as Gulbarga and Raichur. After completing the sentence, the husbands return to the department to enquire whether their wives have initiated fresh recovery proceedings with the hope that they will be sent back to prison.[108] In such cases, the order of the court remains a paper decree. Judges feel when such a stage is reached it does not provide any respite to the destitute woman who has been litigating for years to obtain an order for a meager amount of maintenance. In such cases, they suggest that the government should initiate schemes so that at least a minimum amount can be provided to such needy women.

Personal Appearance of Parties

Since family disputes concern rights within personal relationships, it is mandatory for the parties to appear in person. Since representation by lawyers is also not a matter of right, it is the presence of the parties that is of primary concern. There are better chances of negotiations and settlements when it is between the parties concerned rather than their legal representatives or constituted attorneys. There is also the apprehension that the presence of lawyers

---

[107] Excerpts from an interview with N. Subba Rao, J., Presiding Judge, Family Court, Bijapur, which was conducted as part of the study of family courts in Karnataka in 2003 (Agnes 2006).

[108] Excerpts from an interview with P. V. Singri, Presiding Judge, Family Court, Raichur, which was conducted as part of the study of family courts in Karnataka in 2003 (Agnes 2006).

would make litigation far more adversarial and contested, which would hamper the process of settlement.

While there are advantageous for mandatory personal appearances, this stipulation also causes a great deal of hardship to litigants who may not be able to present themselves on each court date. People who live outside the jurisdiction of the court and parties who have a regular job would find it difficult to comply with mandatory personal appearances. Speedy settlement is only an aspiration and not a reality. Contested cases go on for a number of years, without the possibility of settlement. Due to a huge backlog of cases, sometimes the matters that are listed are not even taken up for hearing. The situation is even more difficult for women who attend court with small children. All this adds up to the misery and hardships faced by litigants.

It is in this context, the courts are required to adopt a humanitarian approach. It is the duty of the court to ensure that the parties before it are not put through undue inconvenience. In this context, a ruling on Rajasthan High Court in *Laxmi Kanwar* v. *Laxman Singh*,[109] has already been discussed earlier.

In *Komal Padukone* v. *Principal Judge, Family Court, Bangalore*,[110] the wife was staying in USA. She sought permission to engage a counsel and an exemption from personal appearance till July 1999, which was denied by the family court. In appeal, the Karnataka High Court held that there was nothing unreasonable about either of the requests. Summing up the legal position it was held as follows:

i. A petition to the family court may be presented by a petitioner either in person or through an authorized agent. The petition may be presented even by an advocate as an authorized agent. But if the petitioner wants representation by a legal practitioner he/she should seek and obtain the permission of the family court.

ii. A respondent who is served with notice of the proceedings may either appear in person or enter appearance through an authorized agent (including a legal practitioner). This is different from being represented in the proceedings by a legal practitioner.

iii. Entering appearances in response to a notice/ summons through an authorized agent (including a legal practitioner) is different from being represented in the proceedings by a legal practitioner.

iv. While representation through legal practitioner without permission is barred, entering appearance in a case, in response to a notice/ summons through a legal practitioner is not barred. Having entered appearance, if he/she wants to represent the party during proceedings, permission of the family court should be obtained for such representation.

v. When one party has been permitted to be represented by a legal practitioner, such permission cannot under any circumstances, be denied to the other party.

vi. The authorized agent (or the legal practitioner permitted to represent a party) can prosecute or defend the proceedings and represent the party unless and until the family court makes a specific order for the parties to appear in person, either on a specific date or on further hearing dates, depending on the facts of the case and the stage of the trial. Once an order for personal appearance has been specifically made, a party will have to seek exemption from appearance, if he/she is not able to appear in the matter.

vii. Where a family court has a large backlog of cases, and there is no possibility of taking up

---

109   2005 MLR 388 Raj
110   AIR 1999 Kar 427

all cases listed on a day, it may restrict the requirement of personal appearance of parties to specified stages like conciliation and evidence.

viii. Where it is possible to do so, consistent with the nature and circumstances of the case, the family court, either directly or through counsellors, in the first instance, assist and persuade the parties in arriving at a settlement in respect of the subject-matter of the proceedings.(Para 18)

These guidelines were issued to avert undue hardship to the parties. In this context, the comments of the Kerala High Court in *Moideen Bava* v. *Shahida*,[111] are also relevant. The wife had obtained an ex-parte order of dissolution of marriage. The husband, who was living abroad, sought permission to appoint a lawyer for the limited purpose of collecting a certified copy of the order. When the same was rejected, a writ petition was filed and the high court directed the family court to allow the application for appointing an advocate for this purpose. But the family court rejected the application again. So the high court was constrained to hear the matter again and commented as follows:

On the face of it, the procedure adopted by the learned judge of the family court does not appear to me to be correct, fair and just. The proceedings before the family court are already over. All that the petitioner wants is the issue of a copy of the order. To insist that a party employed abroad must come all the way to India to apply for and receive a copy of the order certainly appeals to me to be not fair, proper or just. The family court which is a special tribunal constituted to render rough and ready justice to the parties to a family dispute should not stand on unnecessary technicality and must invoke the powers that are available under S.13 of the *Family Courts Act*.

In another recent case, *Suma* v. *Rajan Pillai*,[112] the husband filed a suit against the wife for

realization of the value of jewellery. The wife had given the power of attorney to her father as she could not be personally present on every date as she was working as a domestic maid abroad. The family court decreed *ex-parte*. In appeal, it was held that it was a pure money suit and in a money suit, the presence of parties is not mandatory unless under special circumstances like counseling, where presence of the parties is required. Hence if the defendant is not present but is represented by the power of attorney holder, she cannot be declared ex parte.

But the person appointed as power of attorney holder cannot step into the shoes of the litigant and give evidence on his/her behalf. In *Rajiv Dinesh Gadkari* v. *Nilangi Gadkari*,[113] a decree of *ex-parte* divorce granted to the wife was upheld by the high court on the ground that the power of attorney holder appointed by the husband, who was residing abroad, to represent him in these proceedings was not entitled to give evidence on his behalf. The court held that evidence can be given only by the parties to the marriage since certain facts are in the personal knowledge of only the spouses.

Delays and Backlogs

Though the mandate of the family courts was non-adversarial litigation and conciliation resulting in speedy settlements, the matrimonial litigation continues to be extremely contested even within this new adjudicational forum. There has also been a considerable increase in the number of new cases filed in family courts which has resulted in an increasing backlog of cases, in a similar manner as in regular courts. But in the smaller courts in district towns the problem is not as severe as it is in larger urban centres such as Mumbai and Bangalore.

---

[111]   I (2007) DMC 116 Ker
[112]   I (2008) DMC 545 Ker

[113]   2009 (111) Bom.LR 4629

In *Leela Mahdeo Joshi* v. *Mahadeo Sitaram Joshi*,[114] a request for disposing of the appeal expeditiously was made on the ground that the delay would be extremely harsh for the parties. Responding to the expression 'instant justice', it was observed that though ideal, it was not always possible in view of the procedural requirements. However, it was held that it would be useful if family court were to bear in mind the need for utmost expediency while dealing with this branch of litigation. The courts must assist, through a considerate approach, the parties, who have already been through the trauma of a broken marriage, in obtaining the relief they were entitled to.

In *Guru Bachan Kaur* v. *Preetam Singh*,[115] it was brought to the notice of the Allahabad High Court that the case had been adjourned, at times on account of strike by lawyers and at times because the presiding officer was on leave, and on the whole, it took eight years for disposal. The high court commented that the family court ought not to have acted in a causal and indifferent manner with regard to the mandate of the legislature for speedy disposal which is reflected in the aims and objectives of the Act. Referring to Sections 10(3), 13, and 14 of the Act, the court held that these provisions further indicate that matters have to be settled in a simple rather than a complex manner, so as not to prolong the agony and waiting period in matrimonial disputes. The court noted with concern that the prime time of a couple's life should not be wasted, as neither the time spent can be regained nor can the youth be restored. Hence, family courts should avoid protracted trial as is the case in civil courts.

While one of the basic premises of setting up family courts was to avoid delays and backlogs, they still persist, as the following table indicates.

Table 3.1   Backlog of Cases in Some Family Courts as on 1 January 2003[116]

Court	Cases
Mumbai	8000
Pune	4700
Bangalore	4600
Jaipur	2900
Nagpur	2300
Aurangabad	1900
Hyderabad	1500

Despite these statistics, it must be admitted that this new adjudicational forum did bring in some improvement in the situation then prevailing in district courts (or city civil courts, as the case may be). This is particularly true for Bombay, where earlier it would take a decade or two for a case to reach the final hearing stage.[117] This period is now reduced to an average of three years in the family court. In addition, half the cases filed are settled within a year, through the interventions by marriage counselors, and do not reach the stage of acrimonious legal contest. This is a significant achievement which has taken place despite the fact that matrimonial litigation has increased many fold since the family courts were instituted. Earlier there were only two courts within the city civil courts which dealt with matrimonial disputes. Presently, there are seven courts which are dedicated exclusively to these disputes. Thus matrimonial litigation has become a priority concern for the state administration.

---

[114]   AIR 1991 Bom 105

[115]   1998 (1) AWC 275 All

[116]   This data was collected during the study of family courts which was conducted in 2003–4 but it is still relevant as there would not be a significant improvement in the situation from then to now.

[117]   See the time frame in two cases *Sharada Prabhale* v. *Narendra Prabhale* and *Anand Govind Bhide* v. *Rohini Bhide* discussed earlier in this chapter.

A matter which is of grave concern is that a large number of cases filed in many family courts are dismissed for want of completion of preliminary proceedings. It appears that once the case is filed, the lawyer loses interest as the parties have to comply with the mandatory conciliatory proceedings. Since the parties are not able to complete the preliminary procedures on their own, the case is dismissed for default. For instance, in Bangalore, 30 per cent of the cases selected for the study from court filing records were dismissed for default.

Simplified Procedures and Help Desks

This brings us to our next point—simplified procedures and help desks without which the problem of a large number of cases being dismissed for default cannot be solved. A reading of the Family Courts Act makes it clear that the legislative intent was to create an alternate dispute resolution forum. It is in this context that the Act envisaged a diminished role for lawyers. Hence a corresponding increase in support structures and infrastructural facilities ought to have been provided in order to reduce dependency on commercial lawyering and to help poor and illiterate or semi-literate women who approach these courts for accessing their rights. The Committee on Empowerment of Women (2001–2) had recommended several measures to improve the conditions within family courts, including the following:

i. Information centers should be set up at all family courts to explain the procedure and functioning of family courts to all potential litigants.

ii. A standard proforma should be worked out and published in all regional language papers, setting out the list of documents required to be filed in court. The proforma should be simplified, requiring the parties only to state facts, without substantiating each fact with evidence.

iii. The atmosphere in the family courts should be such as to enable a woman to express herself freely.

A transparent and accountable mechanism has not been evolved by any court for simplified drafting on a non-commercial basis and the practice of lengthy and cumbersome legal drafting, a colonial baggage, persists.

However, in some states such as Maharashtra and Karnataka, some efforts have been initiated in this direction. But such efforts are scanty and sporadic and depend upon individual judges and some local NGOs. There is a need to streamline these efforts and incorporate them as best practices in all family courts.

BEST PRACTICES IN FAMILY COURTS

While offering a critique of family courts, it is pertinent to list the best practices and innovative mechanisms prevailing in some of them which could easily be adopted elsewhere to ensure better functioning of family courts in the country.

'In Camera' Proceedings

In every suit or proceedings to which this Act applies, the proceedings may be held in camera if the family court so desires and shall be so held if either party so desires.

Section 11, Family Courts Act

Section 11 of the Family Courts Act is based on Rule 2 of Order XXXII-A, which was incorporated in the Civil Procedure Code by an amendment in 1976.[118] The directions of 'in

---

[118]   Order XXXII-A, Rule 2 of CPC reads as follows: 'Proceedings to be held in camera – In every suit or proceeding to which this order applies, the proceedings may be held in camera if the court so desires and shall be so held if either party so desires'.

camera' or closed door proceedings is contrary to the general norm that proceedings should be held in and orders pronounced or dictated in open court rooms. This provision was meant to bring in transparency. The mandate for the courts was not only that 'justice must be done' but 'justice must seem to be done'. Hence, proceedings in open courts is an integral part of the judicial norm of transparency.

However, for family matters, where the private aspects of people's lives have to be argued and disputes are often plagued with obscene allegations and counter allegations, the general norm is reversed in order to preserve the dignity of the litigants. As we have observed in the preceding chapter on women's rights to maintenance, allegations about the sexual conduct of women are frequently made in order to deny them maintenance and to humiliate women in open court rooms. It is in this context that the norm of 'in camera' proceedings has been statutorily introduced under the Family Courts Act. The Act recognizes the right to privacy of the parties to the dispute against all others. The aim is to prevent personal allegations of a sexual nature from becoming public knowledge. For lawyers, open trials provide the stage for displaying their legal acumen and mastery over cross-examination. Many times this mastery gets translated into humiliating women regarding intimate aspects of their lives.

The Act provides for closed door hearings at the instance of the parties or at the discretion of the court. But this stipulation is observed more as an exception than a rule and women continue to be cross-examined in over crowded court rooms regarding the intimate details about their moral character, sexual behaviour, and norms of motherhood.

The presiding officers who were interviewed for the study stated that if the parties demand, the proceedings would be held 'in camera'. However, in the absence of notice boards in national and regional languages and in the absence of a help desk, it is unlikely that women (even educated women) would be aware of this right. The responsibility therefore rests on the courts to guide the women accordingly and to use its own discretionary powers when necessary.

The family courts at Bombay are an exception. Though proceedings are not held 'in camera', they provide for a restricted entry of litigants and lawyers into court rooms. This is possible because of good infrastructural facilities, where each court is provided with a spacious waiting hall in which the litigants and lawyers can wait for their turns. Most courts do not have this facility.

Abolition of Court Fees

Important among the measures introduced by the Maharashtra government in 1994, as part of its 'Women's Policy', is the abolition of court fee in matters of maintenance and divorce initiated by women.[119] This exemption goes a long way in enabling women to file suits for maintenance under Section 18 of the HAMA. Since these are labelled as civil 'suits' (as opposed to a 'petition' for divorce), the court fees imposed was very high and beyond the reach of most women. At a time when there was a ceiling of Rs 500 on the amount which could be claimed under Section 125, Cr.PC by Hindu women who wanted to claim their right of maintenance without filing a divorce petition, the court fee that had to be paid acted as a great hindrance. It is in this context, upon submissions by various women's organizations, the government abolished the court fees for women for maintenance claims under Section 18 of the HAMA as well as for other proceedings initiated in family courts.

[119] Notification issued by the Government of Maharashtra dated 1 October 1994 under Section 46 of the Bombay Court Fees Act.

While the respite for women in Maharashtra came through legislative interventions, there have also been instances where the courts have stepped in and brought in pro-women changes through judicial pronouncements. *Mamta* v. *Hari Kishan*,[120] is one such instance where the courts have abolished court fees by a positive interpretation of the mandatory provision of payment of court fees.

In this case, when the wife approached the family court for maintenance under Sections 18 and 20 of the HAMA, she was asked to pay court fees of Rs 15,065. The family court at Jodhpur held that unless she complied with the order within the stipulated period, her application would be dismissed. In an appeal filed by the wife, N. N. Mathur J. and O.P. Bishnoi J. while overruling the order of the family court, held as follows:

One of the objectives of the *Family Courts Act* was to bring succor to women and children, who have been abandoned by her husband and others. The framers of the rules (framed by Rajasthan State Government) have casually incorporated all sorts of alternatives i.e. plaint or petition or application. In case, the action instituted before the family court is taken as a 'plaint' and tried as a 'suit', we are of the view that the entire purpose of setting up family courts will be frustrated. With a view to dealing with the action in a matrimonial dispute more quickly different from the procedure adopted in ordinary civil proceedings, the action will have to be taken as instituted on applications. Any other interpretation asking to pay *ad valorem* court-fees will operate harshly and tends to price justice out of reach of many distressed litigants and will destroy the very object of setting-up of the family courts. When women and the children ask for the maintenance, the proceedings are to be initiated by way of an application.

The court relied on a Division Bench judgment of the Kerala High Court in *Saleesh Babu* v. *Deepa*,[121] which had ruled:

It is well established law that in case of fiscal statute, the provision must be strictly interpreted giving every benefit of doubt to the subject and lightening, as far as possible, the burden of court-fees on litigant. Where an adjudication falls within two provisions of Court-fees Act, one of which onerous for the litigant and other more liberal, the court would apply that provision which is beneficial to the litigant.

In another case, *V. Pranav Kumar* v. *V. Sulekha @ Payal*,[122] the Andhra Pradesh High Court commented that despite the circular issued by the high court in June 2004 which stated that all proceedings should be numbered as 'petitions' and a standard court fee of Rs 10 should be imposed, family courts have continued to number the proceedings as 'suits', charging exorbitant court fees. In this case, the wife had claimed maintenance of Rs 12,000 per month and had proceeded on the assumption that she would have to pay a huge sum as court fees. Hence she filed an application to be declared as an indigent person and be dispensed from payment of court fees under Order XXXIII of the CPC. The husband, a practicing advocate, was issued notice several times, which was also published in newspapers as per the requirement under the CPC. But in order to cause harassment to the wife and delay litigation, he deliberately did not appear before the court, though he personally kept a tab on the proceedings. When the court passed an *ex-parte* order of maintenance, he challenged the same on the ground that it was passed without first hearing the application filed by the wife for declaring herself as an indigent person and he was not issued notice in respect of the same. The high court held that in view of its earlier circular, the application filed by the wife was superfluous and the appeal filed by the husband is redundant.

Such directions from high courts and state governments are extremely relevant for proceedings in family courts as they take away

---

[120] I (2004) DMC 558 Raj: AIR 2004 Raj 47
[121] (1996) 2 HLR 441

[122] I (2006) DMC 528 AP

the burden of paying court fees from a large number of women who approach these courts. Taking the issue even further, in *C. Govindraj* v. *Padmini*[123] it was held that the court fee for appeals against the orders of family courts would be only Rs 15/- and not Rs 100/- as stipulated for an appeal under HMA. Since FCA is a special statute it will prevail over the general provisions applicable for filing of appeals.

Adequate Infrastructural Facilities

When setting up the alternate dispute resolution forum, it was expected that state governments would take due care and provide adequate infrastructure and set up support mechanisms to help litigants. Merely designating a court room as a 'family court' which is presided over by the district judge and where the proceedings are carried out in the same old manner would not amount to complying with the legislative mandate. But unfortunately, this is precisely what happened in most states when the courts were set up. It is the lawyers who had a say as to where the courts should be located. Their concerns became the priority and they could also lobby for their demands. The Supreme Court, while rejecting one such demand by a bar council opposing the shifting of the family court to a new and more specious location, in *M.P. Gangadharan* v. *State of Kerala*,[124] held:

> The procedures which are required to be followed in a family court are different from regular courts. Hence the court must have sufficient space and must house a room for family counselors.

The court commented that the present building is not suitable to meet requirements of litigants. Lack of space has made it very inconvenient to house the family court in the said building.

123   AIR 2009 Kar 108
124   I (2006) DMC 803 SC

In terms of infrastructural support, the family court at Mumbai offers the best model with seven courts located in one building and one floor assigned to each court. Each court has large waiting halls and spacious court rooms. The two counselors attached to each court have their own cabins which ensures privacy. The court also has a children's complex with facilities for supervised access within its premises. Stress management and child counseling services are also provided within the court complex. Marriage counselors have played an important role in initiating these services.

Following this model, the family courts in Chennai have also introduced special rooms for counselors, a children's complex, and a stress management centre. Some courts have attempted to involve local NGOs, as envisaged by the Act, in providing certain facilities like managing information desks, supervising access, etc.

While infrastructurally, the family courts in Mumbai offer a good model, the fact that all the courts are located within one building poses problems. While the City, Civil and sessions courts as well as the Small Causes Court have two separate locations to cater to the needs of the island city and the suburbs, the family courts continue to be located within one building. This causes a problem for litigants.

Though 16 family courts were set up in Maharashtra prior to 2005, they were located only in four districts – Mumbai, Pune, Nagpur and Aurangabad.[125] Hence most districts of the state did not benefit by this model. Even the densely populated industrial district of Thane, which is adjacent to Bombay, did not have a family court until 2010.[126] As compared to this,

125   See Appendix A
126   Family courts were sanctioned for four districts Thane, Amravati, Nasik and Akola but of these only Thane and Akola have started functioning while the other two are awaiting availability of adequate space and infrastructure.

a small state like Kerala with 14 districts can boast of 16 family courts with at least one family court in each district.[127]

The infrastructure provided at Pune, Nagpur, and Aurangabad are far below the facilities provided in Mumbai.[128] But there have been efforts to set up a children's complex for supervised access even within the constrained space. Faced with lack of space and infrastructural facilities, the family court at Nagpur has involved various local NGOs in providing space for supervised access in contested custody matters.

Unfortunately, some courts function without even basic necessities like a waiting hall or a ladies toilet. Judges complain that women travel long distances with infants and then wait in open spaces outside the court for their cases to be called out. Many a time, courts are even housed in dilapidated structures with leaking roofs, which makes it difficult to carry out even the basic task of dispensation of justice, let alone introduce additional support measures.

It is the duty of the State administration to allocate adequate funds and provide basic infrastructure so that the convenience of litigants is not unduly hampered. This is more so, when half the people who approach these courts are women needing additional facilities. There would also be a larger number of children visiting these courts than any other types of courts. The State administration must, therefore, take due care and allocate sufficient funds and necessary infrastructure to make the experience of litigants less harrowing while they pursue the task of seeking justice which is a fundamental right. The atmosphere within family courts has to move away from a predominantly male oriented and masculinist setup to a less daunting and more litigant-friendly structure where disadvantaged sections and people with disabilities, do not feel intimidated by the atmosphere and the ethos.

The family court at Mumbai has also introduced certain innovative and simplified measures for depositing and withdrawing maintenance amounts which could be introduced in other courts. The cash section works like a bank, with ledger folio number allocated to individual women. The application for withdrawal has to be made only once, at the initial stage. The woman's photograph is attested by the marriage counselor and is affixed on the ledger folio. The need to approach a lawyer each time the husband deposits the maintenance amounts is dispensed with and the withdrawal of cash deposited is immediate.

CONCLUSION

The reason for the enactment of the *Family Courts Act* was to set up a court that would deal with the disputes concerning the family by adopting an approach radically different from that adopted in ordinary civil proceedings.[129]

It is evident from the above quote that the judiciary envisages a radically different role for the family courts. This view is endorsed by various rulings discussed in this chapter. Of particular relevance is the Full Bench ruling of the Bombay High Court in *Romila Shroff* v. *Jaidev Shroff*,[130] which also held that litigation before family courts is a radical departure from the accepted

---

[127] http://highcourtofkerla.nic.in/sj/html accessed on 2nd June, 2010

[128] Recently, while hearing a public interest litigation filed for setting up more family courts in the district, the division bench of the Bombay High Court admonished the state government for the poor infrastructure facilities in the newly set up Nasik family court as well as the cramped situation in the Pune family court. News report in the daily, *DNA* dated 10 April 2010.

[129] V.N. Khare CJ, S.B. Sinha J., and Dr. A.R. Lakshmanan J. in *K. A. Abdul Jaleel* v. *T. A. Shahida I*, (2003) DMC 765 SC.

[130] II (2000) DMC 600 FB

form of trial in a civil court. It is a mixture of inquisitorial trial, participatory form of grievance redressal, and adversarial trial and the court is left to device its own practice which can be a judicious mixture of all three.

Ironically, at the ground level, when we examine the functioning of family courts, this aspiration of 'radical departure' expressed by the higher judiciary has not yet been achieved. Taking stock of the situation quarter of a century since the enactment of the Act, one must conclude with a sense of remorse that the expectations with which the demand for the institution of family courts was made in early 1980s by the women's movement have not yet been realized. The goals for which family courts were conceptualized have remained illusive and out of the reach of most women litigants. Family courts have failed to usher in a new and dynamic approach to family litigation and to ensure gender justice. The project of introducing a less formal and technical and more women-friendly environment has been abandoned. Courts have remained formidable and technical and the difficulties of accessing justice persists.

As it has been demonstrated in the preceding chapters, anti-women assumptions underpin much of our family law. The mandate of family courts was to work towards overcoming this lacuna through procedural interventions. But rather curiously, the wordings of the statute do not compel a family court judge to contextualize gender. Since the premise of 'gender justice' finds no mention in the Family Courts Act, judges and other functionaries who work within the framework of this statute do not get exposed to the concerns of women's rights within family law. A family court judge is armed with special powers which would help him/her to shift the power balance in favour of women through procedural shifts. This shift empowers a family court judge to move away from the legal technicalities and

rigid evidentiary norms. But without a clear mandate of gender justice, these powers cannot be effectively utilized to aid women. Though the higher judiciary has underlined this concern in a series of judgments discussed in this chapter, a framework of gender justice cannot be evolved on a case to case basis. Family court judges themselves feel that they are not competent to bring in a conceptual shift. It is much easier for them to follow certain guidelines in this respect rather than innovate. There is always the fear that such procedural departures may be struck down by the higher judiciary in appeals and their efforts would be wasted. Additionally, there could also be strictures passed against the concerned judges. The training and exposure which trial court judges receive do not equip them to bring in radical shifts in procedures within family laws to aid women. Many trial court judges expressed these concerns during interviews and in training workshops.

As the field of law that most overtly concerns women and deals extensively with relationships between women and men, family law has a high visibility of women. The ratio of women litigants to total litigants would be far higher in these courts as compared to other courts. Hence it is possible for statutory bodies such as the state women's commissions or for the Ministry of Women and Child Welfare to conduct a gender specific analysis of the functioning of family courts and make appropriate recommendations to the respective State governments and the high courts to improve their functioning and ensure gender justice. However, any such analysis must take place against the background of family law enactments which are drafted in a gender-neutral manner but operate in the context of a highly gendered society.[131] In this

---

[131] See conclusions to Chapter 1 *Marriage and Its Dissolution*.

context it might be relevant to draw parallels between a gender specific legal provision, the Domestic Violence Act, located in a gender neutral space of the criminal courts, but awards remedies of a civil nature by way of protective injunctions, and provides for certain procedural departures from the general norms of a criminal court to ensure gender justice.

In the absence of a built-in monitoring mechanism, either at the state level or at the central level of judicial administration, family courts are firmly set in their own specific style and pattern of functioning, which varies from court to court and from state to state. Efforts of bringing in uniformity which have been initiated by national bodies such as the National Commission for Women have also not made much progress. Most judges follow established procedures of civil courts with which they are familiar. Few attempts to depart from these norms have been chaotic and have caused more problems to the litigants.

The functioning of family courts is a concern as around 100 new courts have been set up / sanctioned between 2005 and 2010.[132] This is a fall out of the recommendations of the Parliamentary Committee on Empowerment of Women (2001–2002) which stipulated that family courts must be set up in each district. A scheme for financial assistance was started in 2002–03 which allocated Rs 10 lakhs per every new court from the Department of Justice (Central Government) with recommendations of equal matching funds from the state budgets. Further, under Non-Plan funds, Rs 5 lakh is provided for the annual recurring expenditure of these family courts.[133] This gave a boost to the

family court project. But the core issue still persists both at the ideological as well as the infrastructural level, whether these newly set up courts are functioning as per the legislative intent as well as the conceptual framework under which a family court is mandated to function.

While there have been some attempts at the National Judicial Academy, Bhopal to frame guidelines and evolve a manual which can be used for evolving a constitutional framework of gender justice, this effort is still at a preliminary stage. Meanwhile, the judges have to grope in the dark and explore innovative solutions at their own initiative. Overburdened with caseload and emotionally drained with dealing with highly charged personal cases, family court judges are left with very little time for reflection or for pursuing academic interests. It becomes the duty of the higher judiciary and the state administration to provide these guiding principles to family court judges and update them on the developments in law and the legal and constitutional frameworks on a periodic basis. There is a need for clear guidelines from the higher judiciary to judges presiding over family courts.

No institution, however lofty and laudable its objectives, will yield results unless it is constantly monitored and is subjected to periodic social audit in order to find the lacunae and plug the loopholes. The time is now ripe to examine the extent to which the ideological framework of gender justice has been integrated within the family court project. There is a need to assess the impact family courts have had in protecting the rights of women and children in the arena of family disputes. This innovative experiment in dispute resolution is of immense value for women who are burdened under the stress of lengthy, technical, and costly legal battles for crucial rights of survival and human dignity. Rather than writing off this institution, there is a great need to strengthen it in defense of women's rights.

---

[132]   See Appendix 'A' and 'B'

[133]   See the official website of the Ministry of Women and Child Development available at http://wcd.nic.in/empwomen.htm, accessed on 25th May, 2010.

In this context, Prof (Dr) N. R. Madhava Menon, former Director of the National Judicial Academy, Bhopal has commented as follows:

Judiciary has to explain as to why the family courts instituted expressly to deliver gender justice have not been performing as per the expectations. Though they were supposed to be managed by women who were specially trained[134] and supported by a variety of professional services most family courts function like any other civil courts, defeating the gender justice goals of the legislation. The judiciary seems to not to have given the attention this institution deserved for whatever reasons (2005).

He further comments that there are enough empirical studies available now to show where it is not performing and why. A well conceived and co-ordinated effort to make family courts around the country to perform its tasks in a woman-friendly manner may be initiated. The rules may be appropriately revised and experienced judges, specially selected may be put on the job to make a difference in the state of affairs. In order to enhance the confidence of women in the judicial system and to restore the image of the judiciary as a women-friendly institution, he suggests an organized programme of judicial education on gender justice which should be imparted to judges at all levels through the National and State Judicial Academies.

The courts have to move with the times and understand the changing economic and social dynamics within which the institution of the family is located. The justice delivery system has to respond to the changes that are taking place within the family and in society at large. In the last few decades, dramatic changes have taken place in the structure of the family—breakdown of large joint family households

into nuclear family units, entry of a large number of women into the labour force, two income families which have brought about the need for a newer definition of gender roles within the family and redistribution of family responsibilities such as housework and child-care, etc. These emerging trends have necessitated a new framework for determining inter-family relationships.

Though the Family Courts Act was conceptualized within a simplistic premise of 'speedy settlement' or 'reconciliation', currently in metropolitan cities, the litigation has become extremely contested and involves high economic stakes. Matrimonial litigation in metropolitan cities is becoming extremely complex and extends far beyond the premise of 'speedy settlement' or 'reconciliation'. Economic concerns, such as right of residence in the matrimonial home, determination of property held jointly by spouses, ascertaining 'matrimonial property' and devising rules for its division, collateral concerns such as share in HUF property, partnership firms and private limited companies, etc., are emerging as contested claims which pose a challenge to the traditional notion of matrimonial litigation. In respect of NRI marriages, issues regarding recognition of foreign decrees, implementation of decrees across domestic borders, issues of custody and access in cases where the child is a citizen of a foreign country, etc., are also looming large on the horizon of matrimonial courts.

At a broader societal level, globalization and opening up of our markets has impacted families in varied ways—economic boom and salary hikes and job related international migrations, sky rocketing real estate prices, newer investment patterns of stocks, mutual funds and foreign banks and newer spending patterns through credit cards at one level and job insecurities, short term contract-based employment

---

[134] While I agree with the suggestion for special training, I personally do not endorse the view that women judges would be more sensitive to women's concerns. One has come across very sensitive male judges as well as extremely insensitive women judges.

and recessions and collapse of the economic boom at another, and the closures of mills and factories, job losses, home-based or low paid jobs in unorganized sector, extreme poverty and farmer's suicides at the third. The nature of the 'matrimonial home' itself has gone through radical changes, from the earlier well-established dwelling houses or flats owned within a co-operative society to more transient types of lease agreements and property acquired through long-term 'home loans' and mortgaged to financial institutions, etc., where it is difficult to stake a 'residential' claim. A family court judge would have to assess the situation keeping these changes in context, while also recognizing that women still take on the major share of housework and childcare and bear the brunt of economic upheavals in the family. What would be the newer yardsticks to measure women's contributions while deciding their entitlements? Judges are faced with this challenge when they have to apply legal principles which were evolved in a very different socio-economic reality to the needs and expectations of the parties within the current scenario, more specifically, to the needs of women and children.

There are also significant differences between the situation at the urban and rural levels. Interviews with judges presiding over family courts located in rural areas have helped highlight these differences and specific concerns. For instance, many judges have expressed the view that the removal of ceiling of Rs 500 under Section 125 of Cr.PC has had no impact over family courts in poverty stricken rural areas and maintenance orders, even for paltry amounts, are reduced to paper decrees which cannot be enforced.

While addressing the concern regarding delays, there is also an apprehension that the emphasis on 'conciliation' and 'speedy settlements' reduces family courts into 'courts doling out maintenance orders', which cannot even be enforced, or merely pronouncing consent decrees of 'settlements' and 'reconciliations' which harm women's interests.

Within this complexity, what would be the role of a family court judge in ensuring gender justice? This question can best be answered by reproducing the comments of R.C. Lahoti J. former Chief Justice of India:

The laws cannot change society overnight, but they can certainly ensure that the disadvantaged are not given a raw deal. The courts certainly go beyond mere legality, insulating women against injustice suffered due to biological and sociological factors. But all law is not justice nor is all justice law alone. At times it could be more justice without law and likewise there could be times where strict adherence to or mindless application of laws could lead to injustice. Justice is a combination of various factors; enactment of laws responsive to the changing needs of time, their effective enforcement, progressive and proactive interpretations and application so as to fill up any void that is left and not taken care of by statutory enactments.

It is the law in action and not just the law which is important. If we were to ask to name a significant single factor which could make the delivery of justice, just and meaningful, the answer would be – a sensitive judiciary – a judiciary which views circumstances and situation in a holistic manner. Judges too have their own philosophy and their own convictions, depending on the background wherefrom they come, but then there is a collective qualitative philosophy of justice dispensation in which personal inhibitions and predilections have no place.

It is the judiciary which interprets and implements the laws. A judge is an eye witness to a real-life drama–how the script written by the legislature is played by real-life characters. The parties while critically evaluating the laws may tend to have a partisan look; a judge can make a correct and realistic evaluation of the laws and find out authoritatively the difficulties in implementation of or lacunas in legislation.

Landmark decisions delivered by the Indian judiciary, in particular during the last two decades, bear testimony to the fact that judges cannot be accused of gender injustice. They have shown the requisite sensitivity expected of them. However, all that can be said is that such sensitivity is individual and needs to be institutionalized (2005 : 2 SCC (J) 49–54).

The Chief Justice also endorsed the views of Michael Kirby J. of Austraila, who said:

In a pluralist society judges are the essential equalizers. In upholding law and justice, judges have a vital function in a pluralist society to make sure that diversity is respected and the rights of all are protected.

Lahoti J. laid down the following guidelines which he urged the judges to keep in mind to ensure basic gender sensitivity:

1. be informed of the historical and cultural background in which women have lived over the ages, understand their feelings, and have regard to their needs as a class;

2. because women are weaker sections of the society, strike a balance in your approach in dealing with any issue related to gender, or where a woman is victim, in such a way, that the weaker are not only treated as equals but also feel confident that they are equals;

3. treat women with dignity and honour and inculcate confidence in them by your conduct, behaviour, and ideology whenever they come to you as victims or seekers of justice;

4. do not allow them to be harassed and certainly do not do anything which may amount to harassment of a woman; and

5. make efforts to render a woman victim quick, speedy, cheaper and effective justice – true to its meaning. (Ibid at p. 53)

Justice Lahoti's comments that while some judges are sensitive, it is at an individual level and that such sensitivity needs to be institutionalized, is of great significance to our discussion here. Several legal scholars have argued that the best of laws will fail if, at the implementation level, judges lack sensitivity. Even when changes are successfully made at the doctrinal level through legislative reforms, they will fail to have impact upon the outcome of the litigation if judges revert to interpretations that merely replicate old results. In this context, Martha Fineman argues that some reformers forget the extent to which 'context' controls the ultimate practical content of a purist ideal and distorts worthy goals beyond recognition. As a result, reforms not only fail to have the desired impact, but even make things worse for those they were designed to help (Fineman 1995: 17). In the Indian context, we have seen this happen with the reforms in rape laws brought about through criminal law amendments in 1983. In the ultimate analysis, it is judicial sensitivity that will ensure gender justice.

While highlighting instances of insensitivity and callousness towards women on the part of presiding officers of the family courts, to set the balance right, it is also imperative to examine the role of the higher judiciary in this context. There is an apprehension among the lower judiciary that their pro-women rulings and procedural laxity may be struck down in appeal. Appeals are filed in the high court by husbands against orders of even extremely conservative amounts of maintenance and at times, the order is vacated or stayed at the admission stage itself which causes great hardship to women who would have to wait for many years till the appeal is finally decided. Family court judges point out that it ought to be mandatory for the husbands to clear at least a part of the maintenance dues before their appeal is admitted, in order to protect women's rights.

Several instances where the higher courts have over ruled pro-women rulings under the Muslim Women's Act are discussed in this chapter. The ruling of the Bombay High Court in *Noor Jamaal* v. *Haseena*,[135] pronounced in

[135] II (1992) DMC 56. This is discussed earlier under the Section titled 'Family Courts and Muslim Women's Rights'.

1992 is particularly stark. The ruling seems to be devoid of the legal maxim that beneficial statutes must be interpreted liberally in favour of the vulnerable and disadvantaged sections, which is so often cited in judicial pronouncements. Since most often poor women lack the resources to file appeals in Supreme Court, there was a gap of 20 years before the Supreme Court could shed some clarity on this issue.[136] Meanwhile several other high courts also denied divorced Muslim women reliefs in family courts.[137] In this context, the rulings of Allahabad, Orissa and Kerala High Courts seem to be far more progressive and pro-women.[138]

The approach of the Madhya Pradesh High Court in the *Shabano case* (cited earlier) also needs comments. Shabana Bano was married in 2001, the year of the *Daniel Latifi* ruling which had upheld the Muslim woman's post divorce economic rights. She had been divorced in 2004. This right had been in existence for several years before her case reached the high court, yet the high court declined to intervene and set aside the order of the family court which had denied her the rights.

Another glaring example of procedural injustice is the ruling in *Kanak Vinod Mehta* v. *Vinod Dulerai Mehta,*[139] which overturned the ruling of a single judge in *Kamal V. M. Allaudin* v. *Raja Shaikh,*[140] which had upheld the rights of Muslims to litigate their disputes in the family courts. The ruling denied needy, vulnerable and disadvantaged litigants the right to avail of a beneficial statute, for whose sake the Act was enacted in the first place. The litigants from Muslim and Christian minority communities had to wait for almost a decade till the full bench ruling in *Romila Shroff case*[141] set right this procedural injustice caused to them. Curiously, both *Vinod Mehta* and *Romila Shroff* concerned rights of Hindu women from affluent sections to litigate for high amounts of maintenance in the high court. But the core issue that was decided was the rights of Muslims and Christians to approach family courts regarding their matrimonial disputes. These sections who would be affected by these rulings were not represented before the court while their rights were being contested. Ironically, the judgments did not affect the rights of Hindu women, the segment whose rights were being contested, under the Hindu Adoption and Maintenance Act, as the *Vinod Mehta* ruling did not oust the concurrent jurisdiction of the family courts to decide this issue. It appears that women from minority communities suffer not only due to patriarchal biases within their own communities but also due to a callous and insensitive attitude of the judiciary and the legislature.

I am constrained to end here, with a comment by one of the greatest jurists of our times, which though made way back in 1980 before the Family Courts Act was enacted, is as relevant today as it was at the time when it was made.

A socially sensitized judge is a better statutory armour against gender outrage than long clauses of a complex section with all the protections writ into it.

—Justice Krishna Iyer in *Krishnalal* v. *State of Haryana,* AIR 1980 SC 926

---

[136]   *Shabana Bano* v. *Iman Khan,* AIR 2010 SC 305.

[137]   See for instance the ruling of Andhra Pradesh High Court in *Patnam Vahedullah Khan* v. *Ashia Khantoon,* 2000 Cri. LJ 2124.

[138]   See the rulings in *Mohd Sayeed* v. *Rehana Begum,* I (1996) DMC 626 All *Mustafiran Bibi* v. *Abdul Khan,* I (2003) DMC 81 *Ori Kunhimohammed* v. *Ayishakutty* 2010 (2) KLT 71 discussed earlier under the section titled 'Family Courts and Muslim Women's Rights'.

[139]   I (1992) DMC 403: AIR 1991 Bom 337.

[140]   AIR 1990 Bom 299.

[141]   See *Romila Jaidev Shroff* v. *Jaidev Rajnikant Shroff,* II (2000) DMC 600 FB discussed earlier.

Appendix A

Family Courts in India in 2005

No.	STATES	Total No. of FCs	Districts with FCs	District/City	No. of FCs
1	Uttar Pradesh	14	12	Kanpur	2
				Lucknow	2
				Gorakhpur	1
				Jhansi	1
				Bareily	1
				Allahabad	1
				Meerut	1
				Agra	1
				Varanasi	1
				Moradabad	1
				Faizabad	1
				Azamgarh	1
2	Andhra Pradesh	7	7	Hyderabad	1
				Secunderabad	1
				Vijayawada	1
				Vishakhapatnam	1
				Tirupathi	1
				Warangal	1
				Kurnool	1
3	Kerala	7	7	Thiruvananthapuram	1
				Kovallam	1
				Ernakulam	1

Continued

No.	STATES	Total No. of FCs	Districts with FCs	District/City	No. of FCs
				Thrissur	1
				Kozhikode	1
				Kottayam	1
				Manjeri	1
4	Karnataka	9	7	Bangalore	3
				Belgaum	1
				Bijapur	1
				Gulbarga	1
				Mysore	1
				Raichur	1
				Davangere	1
5	Madhya Pradesh	6	6	Bhopal	1
				Indore	1
				Gwalior	1
				Jabalpur	1
				Ujjain	1
				Rewa	1
6	Rajasthan	6	5	Jaipur	2
				Jodhpur	1
				Udaipur	1
				Kota	1
				Ajmer	1
7	Jharkhand	4	4	Dhanbad	1
				Ranchi	1
				Hazaribagh	1
				East Singhbhum	1
8	Maharashtra	16	4	Mumbai	7
				Pune	5
				Nagpur	2
				Aurangabad	2
9	Tamilnadu	6	4	Chennai	3
				Madurai	1
				Coimbatore	1
				Salem	1
10	Uttaranchal	2	2	Nainital	1
				Pauri Garhwal	1
11	Orissa	2	2	Cuttack	1
				Rourkela	1

Continued

No.	STATES	Total No. of FCs	Districts with FCs	District/City	No. of FCs
12	West Bengal	2	1	Kolkata	2
13	Gujarat	4	1	Ahmedabad	4
14	Sikkim	1	1	Gangtok	1
15	Jammu and Kashmir	1	1	Jammu	1
16	Manipur	1	1	Imphal (West Dist)	1
17	Pondicherry	1	1	Pondicherry	1
18	Bihar	1	1	Patna	1
19	Assam	1	1	Guwahati	1
	TOTAL		**68**		**91**

Source: Information gathered by the author during the study of family courts in 2005 (Agnes 2006).

Appendix B

Family Courts in India in 2010

Sr. No.	Name of the State	Total Districts	No. of FCs
1	Andhra Pradesh	23	8
2	Assam	27	5
3	Bihar	37	31
4	Chhattisgarh	16	11
5	Delhi	9	15
6	Gujarat	26	7
7	Jammu & Kashmir	22	1
8	Jharkhand	22	6
9	Karnataka	27	12
10	Kerala	14	16
11	Madhya Pradesh	50	7
12	Maharashtra	35	22
13	Manipur	9	2
14	Nagaland	8	2
15	Orissa	30	2
16	Pondicherry	4	1
17	Punjab	20	2
18	Rajasthan	33	6
19	Sikkim	4	1
20	Tamil Nadu	31	6
21	Tripura	4	3
22	Uttar Pradesh	71	14

Continued

Sr. No.	Name of the State	Total Districts	No. of FCs
23	Uttaranchal	13	7
24	West Bengal	19	7
	TOTAL	**554**	**194**

Source: http://mha.nic.in/pdfs/Familycourts.pdf accessed on 25th May, 2010 with additional information collected from the Bombay High Court by the author.

The figure for Maharashtra is misleading as it does not reflect the districts in which family courts are situated.

This is because 16 of the 22 courts are situated in three cities - Mumbai, Pune and Nagpur.

The total number of districts with family courts is only 8.

4

The Interface between Life and Law

LEGAL CONSCIOUSNESS IN LEGAL NARRATIVES
In the preceding chapters of both the volumes, I have embarked upon a journey to evolve a framework for feminist legal theory by weaving in legal dictates, reported judgments and legal and social campaigns. But this journey will remain incomplete unless an attempt is made to explore the interface between life and law, between meta-narratives of justice and the isolated experiences of individual women who venture out to claim their rights. In this interface, the mundane and the ordinariness of life gets intermingled with lofty jurisprudential concepts and gets transformed into a legal narrative. The manner in which women negotiate their claims and entitlements within the realm of law and the manner in which the fluidity of women's life experiences are fitted into the rigid structures of courts, statutes, and sections is an indicator for testing our notions of law and justice.

The process, through which a novice learns the ropes of litigation and evolves strategies that tilt the scales of justice in favour of one's clients, is an important facet of law and lawyering. But this process is seldom reflected in law books.

As Marc Galanter (1989) has pointed out, a study of law must extend beyond law libraries. Law is more than the statutes and in order to find it, we must look beyond the lawyers' law—the records of legislatures and the rulings of higher courts. The pursuit of law must extend to the workings of the lawyers' chambers and proceedings in local courts, to the operations of informal tribunals, the mediations within the level of family and community, and to popular notions of legality.

While legal theory relies upon reported judgments of higher courts, these judgments do not give us a complete picture of all that transpires in a particular case. These are cases where the ruling of a lower court is challenged by the losing party and is reviewed by the superior court, sometimes two or three times removed from the trial court. The recorded opinion is not a narrative record of the appellate proceedings but is only the last stage of it. It reveals how the subordinate courts acted under given circumstances and records the decision of the superior court, either approving such action or ordering some modification to it. Hence, a single reported judgment is only an indicator and its importance cannot be assessed by examining it in isolation. Although lofty claims may be made in a judgment, each case decides only a few specific points as they arise in a specific factual situation. It is only by comparison with cases involving other similar situations that we can determine the thrust of the legal reasoning. By collecting a set of related cases, we may form a mosaic lens through which we may view the pattern of regulation (Galanter 1989: 4).

Further, reported cases are only a small and unrepresentative fraction of all appellate cases. They are selected to be reported because they represent some modification or new application of existing law. While all the decisions of the higher courts, whether reported or not, are theoretically binding on subordinate courts, in practice, only those which are reported become effectively part of the body of binding and authoritative precedents (Galanter 1989: 5).

In the context of a later study conducted in the United States, Ewick and Silbey (1998: 19) address this phenomenon even more elaborately. According to them, very few of all the contests and disputes actually reach the courts. Less than 3 per cent of cases filed in courts in the United States go for trial. Less than 5 per cent of these are appealed. Fewer than 100–200 cases are decided annually by the Supreme Court of the United States, representing a miniscule top of a giant pyramid of legal engagements. Even those pushed to the top, by way of trials and appeals, are produced of informal as well as official considerations.

Hence, a case law centred methodology, though popular among legal scholars, essentially suffers from a glaring lacuna. To get a more rounded perspective, a legal scholar must extend the exploration beyond legal texts to everyday functioning of courts and the negotiations that are carried out in court corridors.

Ewick and Silbey (1998) suggest that the everyday experience of law is the computation of multiple sites of accommodation and resistance and that law itself is constituted out of an accretion of these experiences, not through grand narratives of justice. This approach seeks to incorporate the relationship between structure and agency, where state authority and local action encounter, and where law, self, and social practice are mutually constituted. It is within the framework of what Silbey (2001) refers to as legal consciousness that I wish to provide a thumbnail sketch of some legal cases and interrogate notions of truth and fact, legality and morality, and law and justice.

These narratives reveal how lived experiences have to be constantly flattened out to fit within the confines of law as laid down in statute books or have to be dressed up and inflated to meet its requirements. I analyse them from the vantage point of a legal practitioner. They reflect a diverse range of complexities and provide a glimpse of trial court litigations and the bargainings that take place in court corridors and lawyers' chambers, and even within formal courts, under the shadow of law.[1]

FARZANA: RECONSTITUTING THE SELF THROUGH THE LEGAL PROCESS

Farzana, a frail woman in her mid-thirties, approached a women's organization in 2007, with a sense of urgency. Her husband was plotting to divorce her. He had approached the *mohalla* (a lower class neighbourhood) committee for mediation and the committee had decided in the husband's favour. The neighbours

---

[1] I am using this phrase first popularised by Robert Mnookin and Lewis Kornhauser in their essay, 'Bargaining in the Shadow of Law: The Case of Divorce' (*Yale Law Journal* 88, 1979 : 980 – 97) while discussing divorce settlements and that has subsequently been used by several scholars within a similar context.

were tired of the daily quarrels that disturbed the calm of the neighbourhood and felt that if the husband pronounces *talaq*, it would resolve matters and restore peace. The husband was extremely abusive towards her. He also suspected her character and labelled her as a prostitute. Though the allegation was baseless, the neighbours were in agreement with the husband and wanted her out of the mohalla. Despite the violence, Farzana was opposed to the divorce as it would render her and her four children destitute. She had no other support and had nowhere to go. All she wanted was that the violence should stop and her husband should provide her regular maintenance. A well wisher in the area had told her about a Muslim women's support group.

Farzana spent almost a week trying to locate this group. Finally, when she managed to reach the place, the counsellor felt that she needed legal intervention and referred her to a legal advocacy centre for women. After initial consultation, it became evident that she needed a restraining order preventing the husband from dispossessing her of the matrimonial home, which could be obtained under the then newly enacted, Domestic Violence Act, 2005 (DVA). Though the right of residence of a divorced woman is protected under the DVA, Farzana believed that, according to the tenets of Islam, it would not be appropriate for a divorced woman to live under the same roof as her ex-husband. Hence, obtaining an urgent order was crucial. If the husband pronounced talaq after the initial order of injunction, the validity of the talaq could be challenged. Farzana could not easily be evicted from her home if she had a pre-existing order in her favour due to the sanctity attached to a formal court order. The lawyers explained to her that her husband and her neighbours would not easily flout a court order and throw her out. It would also give

her a better bargaining power at the time of negotiations.

The next evening, Farzana was back along with her four children. When she removed her *burqa*, the blue patches on her face, the black eye, and the bruises on her arms were clearly visible. The children had not eaten since the previous evening. Farzana herself was on the verge of fainting. Her situation had become precarious. The lawyers decided to move the magistrate's court the very next day for an urgent injunction restraining the husband from assaulting her and worked overnight on her case. But the magistrate was not swayed by the plea of urgency and declined to grant an urgent, ad-interim, *ex-parte* order[2] and adjourned the matter for seven days so that the husband could be served with a notice. Farzana was scared, but there was nothing more to be done except wait for the seven days to pass off peacefully without any major violent eruptions.

On the next date, the concerned magistrate was absent. The court had not yet received the police report regarding service of summons. But the magistrate who was in charge turned out to be more sympathetic and passed an ad-interim injunction restraining the husband from dispossessing her of the matrimonial home. This was an initial victory which was followed by another, a week later, when she was granted interim maintenance of Rs 3,000 per month and compensation of Rs 1,000 for her medical expenses. Since the husband was earning only Rs 7,000 per month, it was a reasonably good order.

It seemed that Farzana had won. But as the case progressed, this turned out to be only a minor victory and the major battle was still

---

[2]   An order passed without giving notice to the opposite side. This is done only when the judge is convinced of the urgency.

ahead of her. Since they were both living under the same roof, a fortnight later the violence erupted again. The husband had flouted the order and had brutally beaten her up. Armed with a medical report from a public hospital, an application under Section 31 of DVA[3] was filed by her lawyer for violation of the protection order.

The magistrate ordered an inquiry to ascertain the veracity of her allegations. The police report was favourable and it seemed that she had won yet again. But this did not lead to any concrete response from the magistrate and the application lay dormant in the court for several months. Meanwhile, Farzana continued to be beaten up, but there was a change in her. She had learnt one lesson. She knew that every time she was beaten she had to rush to a public hospital and get a medical report. She had learnt the law of evidence. On the next occasion when she was beaten, as per her lawyer's advice, she approached the court directly. This brought in a slight change in the attitude of the magistrate. At least, he heard her and issued directions to the police to arrest the husband for assault under the relevant sections of the IPC. But the magistrate was still not prepared to pass an order of imprisonment under the provisions of the DVA for flouting the order as it carries a far more stringent punishment of imprisonment for one year, in addition to a fine.

When the husband appeared before the court, he submitted that Farzana should move out since she had another dwelling in a slum which had been leased out on rent. When Farzana's lawyer heard this, she was thrown

off the track and lost her cool. She was annoyed with Farzana for not disclosing this information earlier. But Farzana was composed. She explained that the dilapidated room was located in a far off area and was too small for her to live along with her four children. In any case, it belonged to her father and was used in her name only for convenience. The father had remarried after the death of her mother. He and her stepmother were not supportive of her.

Farzana continued to be severely assaulted while the case kept dragging in court. The husband and his lawyer were using delaying tactics to defeat her rights. The hard reality was that while it was relatively easy to obtain orders under DVA, it was extremely difficult to enforce them. In the meanwhile, both Farzana and her husband had developed a familiarity with the court and the local police station. These places no longer held their awe or terror. They approached them as they would approach the local community centre or the market place. Every week one of them would lodge a complaint against the other. The police officials were wary of them and were exhausted with the daily nuisance the complaints caused them. They advised Farzana and her husband to either patch up and live peacefully or separate amicably. But this was easier said than done. The situation had become volatile as by now Farzana had become bold and would not take the beatings lying down.

One day, when the husband assaulted her she retaliated and both received minor injuries. The husband complained against her and got himself admitted in a public hospital. When Farzana approached the police station to file her complaint, she was arrested. To teach them a lesson, the police filed cross cases against both of them under Section 324, IPC (grievous assault). While Farzana and her husband spent a night in jail, the children were left at the mercy

---

[3] Section 31 (1): A breach of protection order, or of an interim protection order, by the respondent shall be an offence under this Act and shall be punishable with imprisonment of either description for a term which may extend to one year, or with fine which may extend to twenty thousand rupees, or with both.

of the neighbours. With the help of the women's group, she managed to get bail and was released the next day, while her husband remained in police custody for fifteen days as there was no one to bail him out.

Thereafter, Farzana had to appear in court as an accused in these proceedings and needed a criminal lawyer to follow up her case. She had no money. The legal cases were weighing her down. The magistrate suggested that it was best to settle the matter. Through efforts of mediation, it was agreed that the residential premises would be sold and the proceedings would be divided equally between them. The residential premises in question was a small 10×12 feet room in a chawl,[4] but given the exorbitant price of real estate in Mumbai, Farzana and her husband estimated that it would fetch around Rs 6,00,000. Following this, certain consent terms were drawn up.

At this point, Farzana stopped attending court and her lawyer had to make excuses for her on each court date. This caused loss of face to the lawyer who had pressed for an urgent ad-interim order at the initial stage. The magistrate was curious but did not comment. He just adjourned matter on each court date. After about eight months, Farzana approached her lawyer again with bruises all over her body. The husband had stopped paying her maintenance. The case was back to square one. This time, when the lawyer moved the court for orders, the husband appeared without a lawyer and pleaded that he had no money to engage a lawyer. Thereafter, he started appearing in person, which gained him the sympathy of the magistrate.

On one occasion when she was violently assaulted, she retaliated by hitting her husband with a bamboo stick. The husband suffered

injuries. She rushed to the police station and filed a complaint and also went to a public hospital and got herself admitted. In her own way, Farzana was learning to defend herself against her husband and was also learning to manipulate the system. The husband also admitted himself into the same hospital and they both spent the night in adjacent wards. The magistrate issued an arrest warrant, and the husband was given a short prison sentence. He came out and made allegations that the women's group was harassing him and instigating his wife to assault him.

Through the course of the litigation, gradually Farzana changed. The burqa was gone. She was well groomed and wore light make up. Her salwar-kurta was of the latest fashion, with short sleeves and a wide open neck. The frail and hesitant woman had been transformed into a confident and assertive one. She had secured a temporary job and was managing the house with her earnings. She wanted to settle the legal case and mentioned that her boss, who was sympathetic towards her, was willing to pay the husband for his share of the house so she could retain the place for herself. On her next visit, she coyly mentioned that her boss was willing to marry her and that she was now agreeable to talaq. The young Muslim lawyer from a conservative background, who was dealing with her case, was taken aback at the ease with which Farzana was narrating her involvement with her boss. In a quiet and unobtrusive manner, Farzana was challenging the lawyer's value system and it took a while for the lawyer to come to terms with the developments in Farzana's life and also to convince herself that Farzana had a right to live her life and mould her destiny.

By the next court date, Farzana had slid back. She had quit her job. She said that her boss had evil intentions (*uski nazar kharab thi*). Perhaps

---

[4]   A lower class housing tenement.

he didn't want to marry her but only sexually exploit her. She didn't explain further. She and her husband were back together, entangled in the same confrontational relationship. But in the process of interacting with courts and lawyers, Farzana had learnt to live life. She had become an active member of the Muslim women's support group. She went to movies, picnics and out of town excursions with the group members. She attended literacy classes and a course in English speaking conducted by the group. This exposure transformed her into a new person. She continued to be beaten on and off but she had learnt to deal with it. The violence no longer had the capacity to consume her or destroy her entire life. It was reduced to a small part of her life, while she lived the rest of her life on her own terms.

Farzana was constantly challenging the popular stereotype of the dependent Muslim woman, shunted between the father and the husband. She wanted to negotiate her claims and entitlements outside of the purview of patriarchal controls. She also challenged the notions of law and justice. Her facts always came out in bits and pieces, and it was a daunting task to fit them into a composite frame and dress them up for legal scrutiny. She could not fathom the relevancy and irrelevancy of facts in legal terms. Her relationship with her lawyer was turbulent because the fluidity of her life did not fit in neatly with the requirements of the formal legal structure. This created several awkward moments for the lawyer, who felt used, but through it all, a special bond developed between the lawyer and Farzana. Farzana's case exposed the lawyer, trained in family law, to the workings of a criminal court and the efficacy of the Domestic Violence Act.

Having been accused of immorality and constantly humiliated on this score within her own neighbourhood, Farzana had become defiant.

The husband continued to label her as a prostitute, but this did not have the same impact upon her as it did earlier. She didn't even feel guilty about her brief involvement with her boss. She was convinced that she had a right to a better life but also realized that her boss would not be the person who could offer this to her. One could see the hurt in her eyes as she replied to the queries regarding this incident. But she didn't want to elaborate. Her poised comments during the interview were, 'men are like that, they are interested only in sex.' She had learnt to venture out, negotiate newer relationships, and judge them on the basis of what would be good for her. When probed about her sex life with her husband, she replied in a matter of fact tone, 'that goes on, every husband will demand it and a wife has to give in.'

Did the new law against domestic violence come to her rescue? To a certain extent, it did, but not in the manner in which the legislators and campaigners had envisaged. It was not a magic wand that transformed a violent marriage into a harmonious or even cordial one. In fact, Farzana states that the violence increased and became even more brutal after she had initiated the court proceedings. But it provided her a lever to rework the power balance in her marriage. While the gains in court were limited and far below her expectations, Farzana had used the process to rebuild her own life. She had learnt to deal with formal institutions and meet their requirements. The law, the courts, the lawyer, the support group, all had a role to play in this process. Her struggle becomes emblematic of what Ewick and Silbey (1998) refer to as the interaction between structure and agency, where State authority and local action encounter, and where law, self, and social practice are mutually constituted.

Farzana's will never be a reported case, because it will never reach the high court. It may not even reach the state of a final order in the magistrate's court and may just hover around the realm of the 'interim'. The magistrate also understands the limits of the law and has the wisdom to know that stringency of a statute needs to be tempered and softened to suit the practicality of the situation. Most women's lives proceed in this manner, occupying a space between the formal and the informal, where the formal influences the informal and at times the formal itself reflects the informal, and both become avenues of constant negotiations. In most cases, it is the process that becomes far more relevant than a final legal solution, in shifting the power balance within intimate relationships.

SEEMA AND REKHA: COPING WITH TREACHERY AND DECEIT

In contrast to Farzana's case, we are able to follow Seema's case from the lawyer's chamber to its final order, through its journey back and forth from the trial court to the appeal court, until it transcends into the realm of reported cases.[5] The contest here was between two women, who were locked together in a tug of war, through a cruel stroke of fate. The case impacted three minor children, though they remained in the shadows, at the periphery of the litigation, two sons of Seema and the daughter of Rekha. But within the legal discourse their claim of legitimacy was the central concern. It took seven years for the case to reach the level of finality. This case is traced through interactions with Seema.

In an unusual occurrence, Rekha, an illiterate woman from a small village, in rural Maharashtra, had filed a suit in the family court at Mumbai for a declaration regarding the validity of her marriage. The man in question was not alive. He was afflicted with AIDS and had

succumbed to the disease a few months earlier. The court had to determine who the real widow was, and who would be entitled to his end-of-service benefits.

Seema was a teacher in a primary school and belonged to the middle income group. She was a Christian and had converted to marry. The marriage was not performed as per the Hindu rites, but was a civil marriage, registered under the Special Marriage Act. Life posed several challenges to Seema. Within a few years of marriage she discovered that he was afflicted with this incurable disease. She supported him throughout and paid for all his medical expenses. In order to make him more comfortable, she moved from a one room tenement, into a one-bedroom apartment. To secure a higher loan amount, she bought it jointly in both their names. But she alone was repaying the instalments as the husband's earnings were not sufficient to even meet his basic needs of food and medication. After a time, he became extremely weak and couldn't even perform basic tasks and was on constant medication. The boys were growing up and there were several additional expenses. But Seema faced the challenge bravely. At the time of her husband's death she had a debt of around Rs 8,00,000. But she was confident that she would be able to pay a part of it from her husband's end-of-service benefits and she would also be eligible for a pension. Though the amount was meagre, it would help in coping with the daily expenses.

She forwarded her application to the concerned authorities. It was then that a bolt out of the blue hit her. The authorities told her that they could not disburse the amount since another woman had filed a claim as his wife. Since Seema was the nominee, the authorities had told this woman to file a petition in the family court for a declaration that her marriage was valid. Hence, the declaratory suit in the family court.

---

5   *S. v. R.* 2010 (1) Mh.LJ 253.

Seema was totally unprepared for the litigation. On the first date, when she pleaded with the judge that she had no lawyer and no money to engage one, she was referred to a women's rights programme of a local NGO. The NGO was hesitant to enter the domain of a contest between two women. But Seema convinced her lawyers that Rekha's claim was false. During her past several visits to the village, no one had ever mentioned a previous marriage. A fraud was being committed upon her by her husband's relatives in order to grab her husband's property in the village.

The petition on behalf of Rekha was filed rather haphazardly, without documentary proof. A colour photograph of the couple was annexed. Since the negative was not submitted, the court doubted its veracity and discarded it as tampered evidence. The court concluded that it was impossible to have a coloured photograph of a marriage which had taken place in a remote village thirty years ago. There were eye witnesses who were present at the time of the customary marriage, but the court declined to give time to produce these witnesses as it felt this was only a delaying tactic. This worked in Seema's favour.

As opposed to this, Seema had ample documentary evidence. As her marriage was registered under the Special Marriage Act, she had a marriage certificate issued under the seal of the Registrar of Marriages. This would lead to a strong presumption in her favour. In addition, she had the birth certificates of her two children, the house document, the loan agreement, the joint bank accounts, nomination in the Provident Fund. In the face of such clinching evidence, the plea of a prior customary marriage could not withstand the legal test. Without much hesitation, the judge ruled in her favour and dismissed the declaratory suit.

A month later, Seema received a notice to appear in the high court in an appeal filed by Rekha. The senior judge presiding over the division bench hailed from a small town, as against the urban upbringing of the trial court judge. He was well versed with the customary marriages performed in villages which are not registered and which hardly have any documentary proof. The only way such marriages can be proved is through evidence of eye witnesses. He felt that sufficient time had not been granted to the woman to prove her case and great injustice had been caused to her through the hasty ruling. He asked the woman concerned to produce the birth certificate of her daughter and also the extracts of land records under Sections 7 and 12 of the Maharashtra Land Revenue Code (popularly referred to by the relevant sections as *saat baara utara*). This document includes the names of members of a joint family household who are part of a rural agricultural landholding.

The organization providing legal aid to Seema, advised her to go to the village and personally examine the records to rule out possibilities of tampering. She returned within a week with copies of the required documents. The birth certificate revealed that her husband was mentioned as the father of the girl child, who was now 11 years old. The land documents also included Rekha's name. Seema was devastated. The matter was not as simple as it had initially seemed. If the case was ruled against her, her two children would be deemed illegitimate. Her entire life was at stake. In addition to the financial loss, it would also cause social stigma to her and her children.

The case had to be argued against this evidence. On her behalf it was urged that justice was beyond law, the court must act in equity and not just by statute and sections. Seema had spent her entire life time looking after a man afflicted with AIDS, spent all her savings in making his life comfortable, and could not be divested of her status as a wife at this juncture. The husband's relatives and the alleged wife had not been in the picture and she had borne the burden single handed. It would be against the principle of equity if she was now deprived of all her rights. The judges grasped the dilemma but the case had to be decided as per the legal provisions and not by humanitarian considerations. However, the court could not ignore the fact that there were two women and three innocent children, hapless victims of a fraud committed by a man who was not even present before the court to be reprimanded or punished for his acts. It was a difficult situation.

Placed in an awkward position, the judges suggested a via media, a settlement! The court held that since Seema had paid for the matrimonial home from her own savings, Rekha could not claim any share in the 50 per cent of the property belonging to the husband. Regarding the end-of-service benefits, the court suggested that Seema be awarded the Provident Fund benefits, amounting to Rs 300,000, since she had incurred a loan to meet the medical expenses of her husband. Rekha would be awarded the monthly pension and an additional sum of Rs 60,000 to meet the marriage expenses of the daughter. Rekha's lawyers agreed but Seema was not ready to compromise. In her despair, she could not see reason. She accused her lawyer and the judges of colluding with Rekha's lawyers. She even threatened to commit suicide if the case was ruled against her and implicate her lawyers. 'How can a marriage certificate issued by the Registrar of Marriages be false?' she asked in anguish. She felt that the whole system, the state machinery, the high court, and the lawyers, were party to the fraud being committed upon her. In view of the allegations made against them in a letter submitted to the Chief Justice, the lawyers appearing for Seema withdrew their appearances. Since

their client had lost trust in them, they felt that they had no right to represent her. The two judges on the bench were taken by surprise. They called Seema to their chamber and tried to reason with her, but to no avail. They explained to her that if an order was passed declaring the other woman's marriage as valid, she would lose all her rights. It was advisable to settle the matter at this stage. But Seema was not prepared to budge from her position. The case was reverted back to the family court for a fresh trial with directions to consider the evidence that had now been produced before the high court.

The scene of the contest shifted from the high court to the family court, Mumbai. Seema was struggling without a lawyer. Since she could not afford the fees of a regular mainstream lawyer, she sought help from a well wisher, who had helped her with legal technicalities at the initial stage. At the end of a prolonged trial where fresh evidence was adduced, the family court held against her and declared Rekha's marriage as valid. Since she was declared as the legal wife, she was permitted to withdraw the entire amount which had accumulated in the Provident Fund and she also became eligible for the monthly pension. This verdict rendered Seema's children illegitimate.

Now Seema went all out to reclaim legitimacy of her children. Borrowing some money, she engaged the services of a well reputed lawyer in the high court and filed an appeal against the order of the family court. She had to win this case at any cost. After seven years of court battle, she was rewarded with an order in her favour. There was a spelling mistake in the birth certificate produced by Rekha. The husband's name was mentioned as Krishnat while his name in the marriage certificate and other documents produced by Seema was Krishna. It is this additional letter 't' that clinched the case in her favour! The fact that Rekha could not produce a marriage certificate or a marriage photograph also went against Rekha.

Further, the appeal court held that the relevant documents, the birth certificate, and the land revenue records were not produced at the initial stage of the trial in the family court, but were produced later when the case was remanded back for retrial. The high court also held that the documents were issued at the instance of Rekha without revealing that they were to be produced in court proceedings. This was another factor that was held against her. Ironically, the documents were produced as per the directions issued by the high court in the first instance and it is on the basis of these documents the case was reverted back to the family court. After perusing these documents, the family court in the second instance had ruled in favour of Rekha.

How does a rural woman, discarded by a husband who comes to the city to make a new life for himself, meet the technical formalities of a court in order to prove her marriage? And more importantly, based on the same evidence, how, in one set of proceedings the family court and the high court rule in favour of one woman and the same courts hold in favour of another woman in another set of proceedings, both of which form part of the same case? What are the other factors that come into play which cause this shift? These are mind boggling questions. But they also form an intricate part of the litigation process.

By any conservative estimate, both women would easily have spent an amount almost equal to their claim. As Rekha could not afford the onward journey to the Supreme Court, the case ended there. Or else, in the hands of yet another set of astute lawyers and a bench with different sensibilities, it might have led to a different ending. There was every likelihood that the pendulum could swing to the other end. In the preceding chapter, several cases where the judicial pendulum had swung from one end to the other, from the appellate court to the Supreme Court, have been discussed. The women entrapped in those litigations might have gone through similar emotional upheavals. When a case reaches its finality, there can only be one winner and in this gamble, the dice could be cast either way because rights hinge upon a slender thread.

JULIET: THE INTERPLAY BETWEEN THE CIVIL AND THE CRIMINAL

Juliet's case brings out further dilemmas as notions of rights and justice get challenged and, in the process, reconstituted. Juliet, in her late twenties, needed help to file a case of custody of her child. This was in 1996. For the next six years, Juliet had to be steered through the labyrinthine system of courts, rules, and procedures as the case journeyed through different stages and various courts. It was a complex case which required careful manoeuvring and astute skills of lawyering at each stage.

Her husband had snatched away her five-year-old daughter and she was denied all access to the child. The child was not being sent to school. Her concern was that unless the child was able to attend school she would not be promoted to the next grade. Juliet was a teacher in the pre-primary section of the same school. For about a month, she had gone from pillar to post—church authorities, family service centres, the local police station, social worker agencies, the state women's commission—she had approached anyone and everyone who could be of help, but in vain. She was being shunted from one agency to another, and finally had been referred to a legal advocacy centre for women. In their referral letter, the social workers had alerted that the case was complicated and needed a cautious approach.

It turned out that all of Juliet's earlier efforts had been thwarted by her husband who appeared with his lawyer and produced documents of a murder case pending against her in the sessions court. The allegation was that she had murdered her older child, a daughter, who was two years old at that time. Now, to seek vengeance upon her husband, she was threatening to kill the younger daughter and it would be dangerous to hand over the custody of the child to such a woman. Faced with such serious allegations, each agency had backtracked from the assurances given to her of restoring to her the custody of her daughter.

The lawyers at the legal centre were bogged down with moral and ethical questions. Was it appropriate and in the best interest of the child to file proceedings in the court for custody in such a situation? Would a move aimed at securing the rights of the woman cause irreparable harm to a child of tender age? The questions of right and wrong and rights and justice were getting blurred. While these ethical issues were being sorted out, critical time was slipping. Finally the agency decided to plunge into the case and threw in its lot with that of Juliet's. By the time the case was filed, the child had been away from her custody for about two months. In the process of collating the facts, the grim reality of Juliet's life was pieced together.

Juliet was in her first year of college when she was married at the age of eighteen. She belonged to a large, lower middle class family. Though both the families hailed from the same native village, the husband's family had progressed rapidly. The small chemical factory which her father-in-law, a chemical engineer, had set up had paid rich dividends. They were now living in a large apartment in an affluent part of the city, while Juliet's parents still lived in the dilapidated two-room tenement.

Soon after marriage, she realized that her husband, the eldest sibling in his family, had no voice. He lacked confidence. Though he worked with his father, he was not paid any salary, only a small stipend. The father was the patriarch. Juliet was subjected to taunts and humiliation, both because of the modest means of her parents and her husband's position in the family. The conventional issue of dowry worked in the reverse in her case. There were no demands on her family. Her mother-in-law did not want her to bring anything from her parent's home as what her parents could afford was far below their own social status. Juliet felt extremely humiliated by the constant taunts that her parents are from a lower class, but she suffered in silence as she did not want to disturb her parents. She had half a dozen sisters of marriageable age and if her marriage did not work out, it would cause social stigma and mar their chances of marriage.

She was treated as a beast of burden in her matrimonial home. Since her husband did not have any money, she had to plead with her mother-in-law even for personal clothing and undergarments. It was not that she did not have silk saris or expensive diamond jewellery. She even learnt to drive expensive foreign cars to run errands and do the grocery shopping. But she lacked freedom and autonomy as all decisions were taken by her father-in-law. Outwardly, all seemed well with her life, with all its upper class trappings. But gradually, she slipped into depression.

After the birth of her daughter, the family business suffered a setback. Juliet was blamed for this and was constantly told that her daughter had brought bad luck to the family. She slid further into depression. When the baby was around two years, Juliet challenged her father-in-law when he prevented her from attending the marriage function of her sister. She could not contain her anger at the scathing comments he made about her parents and retaliated for the first time. This led to a major showdown. She was told that from then onwards, she would be treated worse than a maid in the house. She would have no status. She would be forbidden to use the family cars and, henceforth, she and her daughter would have to travel only by bus. The father-in-law even refused to eat the meals cooked by her.

In her depressed state, she could not cope with this humiliation. This was the last straw. She didn't want to live any more. So she attempted suicide by consuming pesticide. She left a suicide note implicating her father-in-law. All she remembers before she blanked out was the sight of the baby crying on the bed and reaching out to her. When the husband returned home and found the door locked, he broke it open with the help of the building security guard. The mother and the child were found in an unconscious state and were rushed to the hospital. The child was declared dead on admission. Juliet was admitted in a critical condition.

Based on the suicide note, the father-in-law was arrested and charged with cruelty (Section 498A, IPC). But through the intervention of the police, a compromise was worked out. The father-in-law agreed to purchase a flat in her husband's name, for their separate matrimonial residence and also agreed to deposit a substantial amount as corpus fund in a bank so she and her husband could live from the interest. Her parents were informed that all criminal cases had been settled by bribing the police. Her parents were happy that their daughter had got a new lease of life and that she and her husband were making a new beginning in a new home, away from the influence of the over bearing father-in-law.

Life continued to be a struggle, but it was better than what it had been in her in-laws' place. To augment the family income, she started taking private tuitions and also started training as a teacher. Meanwhile she had another daughter and her life revolved around her new baby. She shouldered the entire burden of running the household and looking after the child. The daughter was a vivacious and outgoing child and Juliet encouraged her to participate in various activities during social events in her church and neighbourhood. When the child was admitted into a prestigious school, Juliet was fortunate to secure temporary employment in the same school.

The husband suffered bouts of mental illness and had to undergo treatment. During these times, he would turn violent and abusive and would accuse her of sexual promiscuity, even with the principal of the school and the priest in the church. The relationship between her husband and his father also deteriorated and he was not allowed to enter the factory. But his mother was indulgent towards him and occasionally he would leave home and go to live with his mother. It was during one of his bouts of mental illness that he had snatched the child and run away to his parents' place.

During this entire period, a murder case was pending against Juliet. She had to visit the court every six months to mark her attendance. The same lawyer who had defended the father-in-law against charges of cruelty and harassment (levied by her against him) was now defending her in the murder trial. This is against legal ethics. But Juliet was oblivious to all this and was unperturbed about these occasional visits to the court. She lived in the faith that all matters connected with the incident had been taken care of. It was only when her daughter was snatched away that these unresolved issues came back to haunt her. Ironically, the general framework of murder did not fit her case, but criminal law makes no exceptions for extraordinary situations such as Juliet's and deals with all crimes even-handedly.

Within a week of filing the case for custody, she was able to obtain an initial order of access in the court premises. But when the child was produced, she refused to meet the mother. When interviewed in chamber, she narrated to the judge that her mother locked her up in the toilet, beat her, and threatened to kill her. The daughter had been given a graphic account of the previous incident to strengthen the husband's case in court. The mother bore the humiliation with grit, as she had the confidence that it was a temporary phase which would pass. During access, the five-year-old refused to eat the snacks brought by the mother as she had been told that her mother was planning to poison her. She wouldn't even drink the water from the bottle that the mother was carrying and clung to the male lawyer representing the husband, a total stranger, rather than go to her mother.

This shattered Juliet. She was on the verge of a nervous breakdown. Her whole life was dedicated to the daughter who meant everything to her. Perhaps it was best to let go of the daughter and give up her custody claims to save herself from further trauma. However, Juliet persisted with tenacity. She had a positive approach to life and tremendous faith in the power of prayers. Her lawyers had no choice but to go along with her. They advised her not to carry any food items but only toys and an old family photo album so that past memories could be revived and the child would long for the home environment, and for her mother's love and care. The strategy worked. Gradually, over the weeks, the child's rigid attitude towards the mother thawed and she started showing some signs of affection towards her during the regular twice-a-week access in the court complex. On her birthday, Juliet sought permission to take the child out to a nearby restaurant for a treat. The child was excited. While the permission

was granted, the father insisted that he too would come along, and Juliet did not resist. At this time the only aim was to rebuild the child's confidence in her mother.

Juliet was ready to compromise if she could get regular overnight access and the child could continue in the same school till the end of the school term. This would give the mother sufficient time to gain the child's love and trust. But the husband and his lawyer refused even minimum access. The case had to be argued for interim custody. The odds were stacked steeply against Juliet. But the fact that the child was not being sent to school and would be required to repeat the class were factors in her favour. The main plea in her defence was that the child could not be deprived of her mother's love on an allegation that she was a murderess, an offence committed prior to the child's birth. The allegations of murder had yet to be proved. And, as per the legal maxim, a person is innocent till proven guilty. If the husband was convinced of her guilt, he would not have let such a woman become the mother of his next child. The arguments had the desired impact. Despite the odds, Juliet won, and the child was handed over to her. This was a great victory.

The husband filed an appeal against the order of interim custody armed with a new set of lawyers. The lawyer, in the open court, read out the forensic reports of the child's death, with graphic and gruesome details of cotton balls dipped in poison which were taken out from the child's throat and marks of throttling around the child's neck. There was pin drop silence in the court room. A statement allegedly made by Juliet was read out in which it was recorded that her father-in-law treated her like his own daughter and that she was a hypersensitive woman and had attempted suicide because of depression. These documents came as a shock to Juliet's lawyers who were not aware that they exist. All eyes in the packed courtroom were riveted on Juliet but she managed to maintain her composure with immense stoicism. The judge could not believe that the family court had awarded custody to a woman charged with murder of her child when there was such clinching evidence against her. He enquired whether the woman was a psychotic or schizophrenic. Then he glanced at Juliet, and met her soulful eyes pleading for mercy with a quiet prayer on her lips. At this, the judge appeared to be perplexed and a bit unnerved. By the time this case came up for hearing, the child had been living peacefully with the mother for six months. So her lawyer pleaded that custody could not be disturbed at this stage without the child being interviewed in chamber. The judge did not reverse the order of custody, but reverted the case to the family court for finally determining the issue of custody in a time bound manner, within three months. She had crossed yet another hurdle.

When confronted about the documents, Juliet mentioned that she too was unaware of them. Everything was handled by her father-in-law. Her signature had been obtained while she was in a semi delirious state, to save the father-in-law from charges of abetment to suicide in the event that she succumbed.

At this point there were attempts at settlement. The husband was willing to give up his claim of custody provided she vacated the matrimonial home. But the lump sum alimony offered by him was not sufficient for Juliet to buy another place in the same locality. So the talks failed and the matter was listed for hearing. In the witness box, she was cross examined regarding the events surrounding the death of her first child, for which she was facing criminal trial. She went blank and could not comprehend the question. The objection that she could not examine oath regarding an offence pending

trial in a criminal court, as it is unconstitutional to do so, was overruled.[6]

A slight faltering on her part would cause serious damage to her impending murder trial. The judge refused to adjourn the matter and give time to approach the high court for clarification on this issue on the grounds that the matter was time bound. Caught between the devil and the deep sea, her lawyer took an unconventional stance and informed the court that Juliet would withdraw her case. Everyone was taken aback. Her lawyer submitted that no one could force Juliet to litigate against her wishes. The husband had not filed any application for custody. The opposing lawyer warned Juliet that the protective injunction restraining the husband from taking away the child would also be vacated. But, by then it didn't matter. The child was in her custody and this fact had been recorded. If the father snatched the child away, Juliet knew her way around and could approach the police or the courts to restore custody to her. She would no longer have to run helter-skelter and be lost in a maze as on the previous occasion. The daughter was two years older now and could be trained to be more alert and not be easily swayed or lured. The unconventional approach worked in Juliet's favour.

The child had been emotionally harmed and had become withdrawn. She had to be sent for trauma counselling. Juliet herself needed a lot of support which her family, the school, and the church provided her. Just when she had settled back into her normal routine, the trial for the murder case started in the sessions court. She had everything to lose if she were convicted, her child, her home, her job as a teacher.

---

[6] Article 22 (3) of the Constitution: *No person accused of any offence shall be compelled to be a witness against himself.*

Through the intervention of some agency, she was able to get a reputed senior criminal lawyer to appear on her behalf, *pro boxo*. The team of lawyers worked relentlessly to gather the necessary evidence and expert opinion regarding poisonous chemical components, upon which the case hinged.

The trial went on for two years under extremely stressful conditions. The entire family of the husband rallied to secure her conviction. Even the building watchman, who had helped to break open the door, was summoned to the witness box from Dubai. But through efficient legal strategies and through the intervention of a sensitive judge, she was acquitted of the charge of murder. The police had messed up the investigations! The chemical component of the poison found in the child belonged to a different category from the chemical components of the poison found in her body. This was a sheer stroke of good luck. It was a slender and almost miraculous escape.

MEENAKSHI: SEXUALITY, MORALITY, AND THE BURDEN OF GUILT

Meenakshi was recovering in a public hospital from a suicide attempt. She was referred, for legal advice, through a hospital based programme for battered women. Her dishevelled hair and blank look revealed her state of acute depression. She kept staring at her feet. The only thing one could gather was that her husband had filed a case against her on grounds of adultery and had brought the co-respondent (her ex-lover) to the court. But she had denied the affair. She kept clinging to a bunch of papers she was holding in her hand and which appeared to be a legal petition. Her forthrightness was striking. Usually, it takes a while for a woman to confide in her lawyer about such incriminating details. She was not able to speak beyond a few sentences and her voice would trail off. She kept repeating that it would be better to die as her life was in shambles.

A few days later, when she approached the legal advocacy centre with her sister, she still carried the same blank expression and continued to be incoherent. This time she was crying incessantly. She had a son through this adulterous relationship and she had abandoned the child. She carried this guilt and also remorse over the affair. Again she kept repeating that her ex-lover had appeared in court and had given a statement against her at her husband's insistence. It appeared that she felt extremely let down by this. She continued with the refrain that it was better to die as there was no hope for her.

Even during subsequent sessions, the lines between facts, fiction, imagination, and apprehensions continued to be blurred. At times, she would imagine that there was a group of men waiting outside to kill her. Sometimes, she would state that her son had been poisoned and would soon die. At other times she would insist that Madhav (her former lover) still loved her but that she had broken the relationship and given up the child only to save her marriage. In the midst of all this, she would break down and lose track.

Meenakshi was living with her sister who could not keep her any longer. Her parents and her brother were not ready to accept Meenakshi. Her six-year-old younger son was with her, while the older twelve-year-old was with her husband's brother. It took several sessions to piece together the facts of her life. Meenakshi is from a backward caste and was married at a very young age, soon after completing schooling. Her husband was doing some odd jobs. Unable to afford a rented place of their own, they lived with her husband's brother and his family in a slum. As a young bride, she faced a great deal of violence and humiliation. Since her sister-in-law worked as a domestic-help, Meenakshi had to do all the work in the house including looking after her young twins. Instigated by the sister-in-law, Meenakshi's husband would often thrash her. He always sided with his brother's wife against her. At times, they punished her by depriving her of food and locking her up for hours together. Within a year of her marriage, her elder son was born. Since it was impossible to continue at her brother-in-law's place, she asked her parents to help her rent a small room and they moved out. She borrowed some more money from them, sold her *mangalsutra* and other valuables, and bought a small room in a slum. Though she had organized most of the money, the tenement was purchased in her husband's name as was the accepted convention. The tenement turned out to just a small open square enclosed with plastic sheets on top of a hillock, adjacent to a small forest from where the animals came out at night. Despite this, she struggled hard to turn it into home. She collected stones from the hill top and made a makeshift kitchen platform, brought a few utensils from her mother's house and began her life. Her husband continued to be extremely abusive towards her. One day when the food was not ready in time, he dragged her out. While she was trying to balance herself at the threshold, he kicked her and she came rolling down the stone steps to the bottom of the hill. She suffered a miscarriage and an injury to her spine. Her parents had to come to admit her into a hospital. They also paid for her medical expenses.

Some time later, the husband lost his job. He would while away his time gambling, unconcerned that at times there was not even a morsel of food at home. Meenakshi's health deteriorated and as she could not survive in these circumstances, she returned to her parents' home with her child. Again her family helped her.

Later, her brother found a job for her husband as a cook in a hotel in South Africa. Before leaving, the husband rented out the place. He assured her that on his return he would buy a decent apartment and the quality of their life would improve. She lived with this hope. Her husband did not return for two years and would send money only occasionally. She felt that she was a burden on her family. Disturbed about this, she sank into depression and had to be medically treated. When her parents informed her husband and asked him to return, he told them to send her to South Africa. Even though she was unfit to travel, her family thought it is best that she join her husband.

Her condition improved in South Africa, and she had her second child. But the husband continued to be abusive and when the child was a few months old, he sent her back to her parents. He continued to come only once in two years and periodically sent her money, but did not bother to set up a separate house for her.

Around this time, she met Madhav, her brother's friend, who showed an interest in her. In her state of loneliness, she responded. Gradually the friendship grew into a relationship and she eloped with him. Her brother tracked them down and thrashed both of them. So they left the city and went to Madhav's village. His family members accepted her but were not aware that Meenakshi was married and had two children. On her part, she missed her children and felt guilty about leaving them behind. This led to another bout of depression and again she had to be medically treated. It was around this time that Madhav's family came to know about her marriage. It was no longer possible to live in the village, so they returned to Mumbai along with Madhav's mother. Meenakshi found out that she was pregnant. She continued to suffer from bouts of depression.

Meenakshi's brother informed her husband about her affair and her pregnancy. Enraged, the husband threatened to file a criminal case of adultery against her and Madhav. He also came down and took away the children from her parents' house, kept them with his brother and sister-in-law, and returned to South Africa. Around this time, Madhav left the city for employment. Meenakshi continued to live with his mother till her child was born. When the child was about a year old she left the child with Madhav's mother and came back to live with her parents.

Thereafter, she tried to meet her older children, but the husband's sister-in-law had instigated them against her. Her elder son had turned hostile and talked to her in an extremely derogatory manner. She was subjected to humiliation and social stigma, not only by her husband's family but also by her own. Her brother was extremely contemptuous of her and the neighbours looked down upon her. Unable to cope with the disgrace, she attempted suicide. Her sister remained her only support. She nurtured her back to health, and with time Meenakshi recovered.

There were other developments around this time. The slum in which their tenement was located was facing demolition. There were agitations and appeals to the government to provide alternate housing. Meenakshi got involved in this struggle and was part of several delegations which met concerned government officials and housing board authorities. In this process, she developed a small support network of women from the slum community. When an inventory of all houses was taken to produce in court, Meenakshi truthfully gave her husband's name along with hers, though technically she was not required to do so. She had paid all the installments for the new apartment with the help of her sister.

She was keen to get her children back, but she realized that there was no point in fighting for custody of her older child who was hostile towards her. So she tried to gain custody of her younger son, who was being neglected by her husband's sister-in-law. But every time she approached them and pleaded with them to hand over the child, they flatly refused. So, one day, with the support of some women from the local *Mahila Mandal* (women's group), she picked up the child from school and brought him to her sister's place. The husband's relatives did not bother to retrieve the child. Meenakshi was happy. She admitted him into a school. The child was constantly ill. After several tests it was found that he was suffering from tuberculosis. This put an additional strain on her, but she tried her best to cope.

On the advice of some friends, she approached the state run Free Legal Aid Board for guidance regarding her marital problem. When her husband visited Mumbai next, he was called for a joint meeting to settle the dispute. He made several allegations against her, abused her and called her a prostitute. He stated that he was not interested in saving the marriage. He then returned to South Africa.

A few months later, she received summons from the family court. Her husband had filed for divorce on grounds of adultery and cruelty, and had named Madhav as the co-respondent. When she went to court, she was shocked to find the same lady lawyer from the Free Legal Aid Board, before whom she had filed the complaint and who had presided over the joint meeting, now appearing for her husband. This was against legal ethics. Though Meenakshi was unaware of these legal technicalities, she felt let down by this woman in whom she had confided and whose intervention she had sought. On the advice of this lady lawyer, he had also procured an affidavit from Madhav regarding the adultery so as to make his case foolproof. Madhav was present in court and when asked by the presiding judge, he admitted to adultery. When Meenakshi was asked the same question, through some stroke of luck, she denied it. If she had admitted it, the case would have been over on the first date and a decree on admission would have been awarded to the husband.

The case proceeded apace. During the mandatory counselling session, the husband offered to take her back. Meenakshi was overjoyed at his change of heart, but this turned out to be a ploy. The next day he took her along with him to the housing board authorities. The alternate housing which the government had provided for the slum dwellers after the agitations was ready for occupation. Since a direction was issued by the government that the apartments would be handed over jointly to the husband and wife (though ownership was in the sole name of the husband), the allocation letter could be issued only after obtaining both their signatures. Meenakshi and her husband were handed over the allotment letter and were given possession of the premises. The next morning, in a typical manner, the husband thrashed her and sent her back. He locked up the house, made his brother the custodian of the premises and returned to South Africa. Meenakshi was back with her sister. The situation appeared totally bleak to her. She attempted suicide once again and was admitted to the hospital in a critical condition. The legal intervention on her behalf commenced at this juncture.

Since shelter was the pressing concern, the first challenge was to take possession of the apartment through an extra-legal strategy. Meenakshi had participated in all the demonstrations and was also part of various delegations. The housing board authorities knew her well and recognized her when she approached them. Her sister brought along all the necessary documents, the initial survey report, receipts of various payments to the authorities, etc. Based on these, the supervisor provided her with a duplicate set of keys. After Meenakshi occupied the premises, an order securing her rights could be obtained. Obtaining an order of injunction is much easier if one is in possession as opposed to an order of re-entry into the premises. Meenakshi was hesitant. She had a history of attempted suicide and, hence, this seemed like a risky move. She finally decided that it was worth taking the risk. As soon as she entered the house along with her younger son, an order of ad-interim injunction was secured restraining the husband and his relatives from dispossessing her.

The husband's brother and sister-in-law used intimidating tactics to drive her out of the premises, but she refused to be cowed down. She knew she was protected by a court order. After some time the husband was ready for a settlement. He wanted the house to be sold and the proceeds to be divided equally. Meenakshi was not interested in any settlement. She needed a place to stay and a regular monthly maintenance and was willing to proceed with the matter. But through the settlement meeting, she could get some access to the elder son who was now studying in a boarding school and an assurance that her younger son would not be snatched from her custody. After a certain period, the divorce case filed by the husband was dismissed as he did not attend the court proceedings.

Even while the case was pending, Meenakshi was well on her way to recovery. She found a job as an *anganwadi sevika* (crèche teacher) in a semi-governmental programme. Her initially meagre salary of Rs 1,500 gradually increased to Rs 3,000. She just managed to stay afloat with this amount. At least she had a roof over her head.

Over the years, she has progressed. There is a significant change in her. She dresses well, talks coherently, and actively engages with various stages of the intricate court proceedings. She is now waiting for a maintenance order in her favour, though this might turn out to be only a paper decree, as the chances of enforcing the decree against a husband who lives in South Africa are remote. However, her rights of residence are secure and she cannot easily be dispossessed. She has even managed to obtain a new ration card for herself and her minor son. This was a major hurdle as her husband did not cooperate in the process, and without his signature the authorities would not budge. Finally, she paid a bribe to the officials and managed to obtain the ration card on the basis of her sole signature. This is an important document which will further secure her right of residence. By now she had grasped the functioning of the bureaucracy and had also learnt how to manipulate the system.

Though there is a possibility that Meenakshi could lapse into depression again, the legal process itself turned out to be therapeutic in her case. When she entered the legal arena she had lost everything and was in an abject state. From this point on, things could only get better.

Meenakshi's life brings to the fore the realities of poor women from backward castes. Judged by the yardstick of middle class morality, her choices seem deviant and immoral. Meenakshi too is ridden with guilt for transgressing the norm of sexual morality as she too has imbibed the same values. This manifests as severe mental depression. Despite the turbulent trajectory of her life, her dream continues to be that of a middle class housewife, to have a caring husband and a 'normal' family life.

LAW'S LOCATIONS

The profiles sketched here reveal a complex range of experiences and read like fiction or a film script, but for the fact that they concern real women. The narratives are not linear and cannot be compartmentalized into neatly defined categories. They portray life as it is lived, with all its murkiness, and defy the notion purity and sanctity of law. The lofty legal principles are ground in the mill of life and are reconstituted as legal consciousness, and re-enter the domain of the courts for determination of rights. The role of the lawyer is critical in this reconstitution.

The lawyer forms the link between the law and the litigant. It is left to the lawyer to translate these diverse experiences into a linear language of rights. The challenge before a lawyer is to make legal sense out of these experiences and streamline the facts to fit into a legal mould. For a women's rights lawyer, the task is even more challenging since a woman must enter the legal precincts in a victim mould to be viewed as deserving of rights. This demands a level of subversion. This, in turn, results in a contentious interaction between the lawyer, bound by the norms of a formal court, and the client, the fluidity of whose life defies all norms and conventions. Innovative legal strategies have to be evolved to meet the demands of unconventional situations. I tend to use the term, feminist lawyering, to label this process. Most often, the legal strategies evolved in the lawyers' chambers and the settlement meetings held in bar rooms determine the fate of a case.

Within the emotionally charged arena of family law litigation, balancing the claims of contesting parties is a tight rope walk. Often, the litigation extends beyond the scope of the statute and rights spills over into the domain of intimate human relationships. The negotiations and settlements, and the fine tuning of rights and claims, become as important as the legal arguments based on legal precedents and statutory provisions. This may be true for other realms of law as well, but within family law and matrimonial litigation, this becomes an over-arching concern.

There are several strands in these legal narratives that can be flagged for further analyses. The agency of women, their perceptions and articulations, the incidents that are foregrounded in the context of the claims and held up for legal scrutiny, the dynamics of client–lawyer relationships, the manner in which women interact with the state machinery and legal institutions, to list a few.

The narratives challenge popular notions of victimhood and our ideas of legality and morality. Facts and truth acquire a different hue as we enter the complex terrain of litigation. The game has its own sets of rules. The manipulation of facts, admission of guilt, and flouting of orders can be done only within its confines. One cannot stray too far from its narrow path or one may run into rough weather, or, in other words, invoke the wrath of the court.

Sexuality and morality form the base upon which the entire edifice of matrimonial litigation is mounted. Within the patriarchal framework, this game too has its own sets of rules and its own grammar. Women cannot easily win this game, even when they choose to play it. The cost of playing the game on masculine terms is too high as Meenakshi's case reveals. The hypocrisy of a blatantly patriarchal social order is striking. Different sets of rules apply to men and women. In this realm, the diverse sets of personal laws are rendered insignificant and invisible, and contemporary social norms, perceptions, and values become governing principles. Contestations over legality of marriage and legitimacy of children become highly volatile. For most women, their children are their weakest links. It is here that the game is toppled. Beyond this, there is no game left to play. There is only an emptiness.

The local socio-economic realities constantly infringe upon the matrimonial claims. In a city like Mumbai, with sky rocketing real estate prices, shelter becomes the primary concern. The legal strategies revolve around notions of ownership, possession, and occupation, the general concerns under property laws. Other urban realities also get contextualised—the slum rehabilitation projects, government directives of joint occupation, division and sale of matrimonial home which may comprise just a small room in a slum, joint ownership of premises to secure a higher bank loan, and so on. Land records of rural agricultural land and several other collateral concerns crowd the domain of the matrimonial litigation.

The legal narratives reaffirm the popular perception of law which Ewick and Sylbey (1998: 20) have enlisted:

1. Law as magisterial and remote
2. a game of rules that can be manipulated to one's own advantage
3. an arbitrary and capricious product of power that can be actively resisted.

When mundane and ordinary lives are transposed to the legal domain, they are subjected to a mighty power that can render the familiar strange, the intimate public, the violent passive, the mundane extraordinary and the awesome banal (ibid.: 16). The terrain is also full of contradictions. It can be deadly serious and, at the same time, a source of humour and entertainment. It can also transform into a game of treachery, bribery, and deceit and suck into its web all the players.

The life experiences do not neatly correspond to formal institutional locations. There is a constant shift from the formal to the informal, from the civil to the criminal, from contests to negotiations, from the legal to the extra legal. At times, the water becomes murky and the doctrine opaque. It is through these lived experiences that the law gets constituted in a bottom up manner, as opposed to the top down process of law making by legislators and judges.

While dealing elaborately with law, I am acutely conscious of its limits and exclusions. Access to justice is a luxury which only a few can afford. Most women tumble into it accidentally, through a sheer stroke of fate. Even those who enter cannot afford to follow their case to its logical end. Their claims hover within the realm of the interim. The formalistic structure, the alien settings, the prolonged process, dependency upon lawyers, the cost factor, the fear of manipulations, the uncertainty of verdicts—these factors render courts beyond the reach of ordinary people. They prefer to mediate their disputes through other informal structures of family and community, and seek softer and more pliable options. Realizing this predicament, the formal structures have now began to move towards the realm of the informal, with *nyaya panchayats*, and *lok adalats* and family counselling centres in police stations (Nagaraj, unpublished paper). Increasingly, there is a feeling that the finality of the law, where one person is declared the winner and the other becomes the loser, may not adequately address the concerns of the litigants. It is for this reason the emphasis on family courts is for mediated settlements. However, the significance of settlements can also be discerned within strictly formal spaces such as the high court in its magisterial function of an appeal court.

The legal narratives are mediated stories, constructed in a legal chamber, with a definite focus of litigation, constantly keeping in view the law's mandates and locations. This results in a yawning gap within the narratives. These gaps point towards women's culpability and bring us back, yet again, to the claims of facts and truth, and legality and morality. Uncomfortable questions loom large on the horizon and continue to haunt us: Was Farzana justified in assaulting her husband and then filing a false complaint against him? Had not Juliet committed a heinous crime of killing her infant and deserved to be hanged? Did she deserve to win the custody battle? Should Meenakshi have denied the affair before the judge in the hallowed precinct of the court room, and wasn't her husband justified in bringing her former lover to court to establish her juiet? Didn't Shubangi know that her husband had abandoned his earlier wife? Was the court justified in denying the daughter of the earlier union the right to legitimacy and economic support?

The moot question persists. Through their culpability, did the women become undeserving of their rights and entitlements, enshrined in the Constitution and legislations, as citizens? Here, the perception of law as a set of rules that can be manipulated to one's own advantage becomes the supreme concern. If the rules are already set, then the players must play within their confines as consumers of law. As Martha Fineman (1995: 17) argues, law is a crude and limited device and is circumscribed by the dominant ideologies of the society in which it is produced. When the rules are starkly laid out, there is no scope to advance a feminist argument that Juliet's heinous crime was committed within the larger patriarchal domain of gender oppression, which not only drives women to suicide but also compels them, even on their death bed, to think of the fate of their daughters. Juliet's case is not unique. Many women chose to take their daughters along with them to an afterlife, rather than leave them behind in this world of pain and humiliation. Law has not awakened to these realities. As a lawyer playing the game of litigation, there is no scope for experimentation upon a life entrusted to your care. When I probed with the criminal lawyer defending Juliet whether one could push the boundaries of law to encompass this reality, there was a look of dismay and shock in his eyes. He felt that I had not grasped the starkness and the magisterial power of a criminal trial which rules over life and death. Here, the perception of law as an arbitrary and capricious product of power confronts you.

A similar concern also reflects in Meenakshi's case, as we understand law as reflective of dominant cultural and social ideologies. Martha Fineman (1998: 19) makes a succinct argument:

If law is understood to be enmeshed in society, also problematic are some of the prevalent notions about the neutrality and objectivity of law with which policy makers and politicians, judges and attorneys drape their processes. Once the ideas of neutrality and objectivity are exposed as myths rather than as attainable and maintainable goals, the law is put into perpetual contest.

The space for claiming rights is limited and a lawyer must perform within its narrow confines. The legal acumen lies in tailoring the experiences of the subaltern woman within an acceptable legal discourse, so that the voice of the violated woman reaches the higher echelons of the legal edifice and the law gets constituted within the realm of her realities, and not as a distant and sublime domain far beyond her reach.[7] The preceding chapters contain elaborate discussions on personal laws, constitutional rights, marriage and divorce, matrimonial rights and obligations, and procedural aspects of family courts. The claims made in the preceding chapters come alive only when they are tested against the experiences of women whose lives are profiled here. These legal narratives provide us with a link between social processes and legal domains and compel us to examine the interface. It is to the women whose lives are profiled here, and to several others like them, that I must pay my tribute, because it is through them that I have learnt the interface between life and law.

[7] Here I am borrowing the analytical framework of Gayatri Spivak (2001), in her seminal essay titled 'Can the Subaltern Speak?'

List of Cases

B.P. Achala Anand v. *S. Appi Reddy,* I (2005) DMC 345 SC: (2005) 3 SCC 313.

Babu Gyan v. *Sudan,* AIR 1955 Nag 193.

Badri Prasad v. *Dy Director of Consolidation,* AIR 1978 SC 1557.

Baishnab Charan Jena v. *Ritarani Jena,* 1993 Cri. LJ 238.

Balan Nair v. *Bhavani Amma Valalamma,* AIR 1987 Ker 110.

Baljit Kaur Boparai v. *State of Punjab,* I (2009) DMC 28 P&H.

Balkrishna Kadam v. *Sangeeta Kadam,* II (1997) DMC 495 SC.

Balwinder Kaur v. *Gurumukh Singh,* AIR 2007 P&H 74.

Banarasi Dass v. *Teeku Dutta,* (2005) 4 SCC 449.

Bani v. *Prakash Singh,* AIR 1996 P&H.

Banoo Jal Daruwalla v. *Jal C. Daruwalla,* (1962) LXV BLR 750.

Banu v. *Govindaperumal,* AIR 2009 Mad 155.

Basanta Samal v. *State of Orissa,* II (2005) DMC 105 Ori.

Basanti Mohanti v. *Parikhit Rout,* I (2003) DMC 214 Ori.

Bavi v. *Shah Nawaz Khan,* PLD (WP) Lah 509.

Beena v. *Varghese,* I (2000) DMC 704 Ker FB.

Begum Subanu v. *A.M. Abdul Gafoor,* 1987 Cri. LJ 980.

Bendall v. *McWhirter,* (1952) 2 QB 466.

Bhagwan Dutta v. *Kamala Devi,* AIR 1975 SC 83.

Bharat Hegde v. *Saroj Hegde,* I (2007) DMC 815 Del.

Bhaurao Shanker Lokhande v. *State of Maharashtra,* AIR 1965 SC 1564.

Bhausaheb Raghuji Magar v. *Leelabai Bhausaheb Magar,* AIR 2004 Bom 283: II (2004) DMC 321.

Bhavanaben Shamhjuvhai v. *Dinesh Premjibhai Kapadia,* II (2005) DMC 315 Guj.

Bhupinder Kaur v. *Budh Singh,* I (2002) DMC 735 P&H.

Bi Hawa Mohamed v. *Ally Sefu,* Civil Appeal No. 9 of 1983, Dar-es-Salaam Registry (unreported).

Bi Zawadi Abdullah v. *Ibrahim Iddi,* Dar es Salaam Registry (unreported).

Bibhuti Bhushan Pandey v. *State of Jharkhand,* II (2006) DMC 120 Jha.

Bijal Parag Dave v. *Parag Labhashankar Dave,* AIR 1999 Bom 237.

Bimla Devi v. *Subhas Chandra Yadav Nirala,* AIR 1992 Pat 76.

Bina Majumder v. *Ranjit Majumder,* II (2006) DMC 637 Gau.

Binapani Bhattacharjee v. *Pratap Bhattacharjee,* I (2007) DMC 460 Gau.

Binod Biswal v. *Tikli @ Padmini Biswal,* II (2002) DMC 446 Ori.

Bipinchandra v. *Prabhavati,* AIR 1957 SC 176.

Biswapriya Bhuiya v. *Jhumi Banik,* II (2007) DMC 631 Gau.

Bobby Paulose v. *Ronia Mathew,* I (2007) DMC 514 Ker.

Bommi v. *Munirathinam,* 2004 MLR 609 Mad.

Brajesh Kumar v. *Anjali,* I (2009) DMC 579 All.

Buddepu Khogayya v. *Buddepu Kamalu,* I (2007) DMC 451 AP.

Budhulal Shankarlal v. *An Infant - Child,* AIR 1971 MP 235.

Butti v. *Gulab Chand Pandey,* AIR 2002 MP 123.

C. Govindraj v. *Padmini,* AIR 2009 Ker 108.

C.R. Chenthilkumar v. *K. Sutha,* II (2008) DMC 278 Mad.

Captain Ramesh Chandra Kaushal v. *Veena Kaushal,* AIR 1978 SC 1807.

Captain Rattan Amol Singh v. *Kamaljit Kaur,* AIR 1961 P&H 51.

Chand Dhawan v. *Jawaharlal Dhawan,* II (1993) DMC 110 SC .

Chandra Mohan Khurana v. *Neeta Khurana,* I (2006) DMC 780 Utt..

Chandralekha Trivedi v. *S. P. Trivedi,* (1993) 4 SCC 232.

Chanmuniya v. *Virendra Kumar Singh Kushwaha,* (SLP-Civil No.15071) judgment delivered by G.S. Singhvi and A. K. Ganguly on 7 October 2010 SC.

Dukhtar Jahan v. *Mohammed Farooq*, AIR 1987 SC 1049.

Duxbury v. *Duxbury*, (1987) 1 FLR 7.

Dwarakabai v. *Prof. Mainam Mathews*, AIR 1953 Mad 792.

Dwarika Prasad Satpathy v. *Bidyut Praya Dixit*, AIR 1999 SC 3348: 2000 Cr.LJ 1 SC.

Dwarkadas Gurmukhidas v. *Bhanuben*, AIR 1986 Guj 6.

E.G. Ravi v. *Jayshree*, I (2007) DMC 878 Mad.

Ehsan Ansari v. *State of Jharkhand*, II (2007) DMC 751 Jha.

Elizabeth Dinshaw v. *Arvand M. Dinshaw*, AIR 1987 SC 3.

Ethel Robinson Women's Legal Centre Trust v. *Richard Gordon Volkas etc.*, Case No 7178/03, in the High Court of South Africa, Cape Province Division (as cited in Jaising 2009: 28).

Fani Bhusan Nanda v. *Kshiti Sundari Nanda*, I (2007) DMC 751 Ori.

Farida Bano v. *Kamruddin*, II (2006) DMC 698 MP.

Felix v. *Jemi*, I (2003) DMC 430 Mad.

Firoz Khan v. *Union of India*, I (2007) DMC 626 Ori.

G. C. Ghosh v. *Sushmita Ghosh*, I (2001) DMC 469 Del.

Gajanan Solanke v. *Sheela Solanke*, II (2005) DMC 134 Bom.

Gajara Naran Bhura v. *Kanbi Kunverbai Parbat*, AIR 1997 Guj 185.

Gama Nisha v. *Chottu Mian*, II (2008) DMC 472 Jha.

Gaurav Nagpal v. *Sumedha Nagpal*, I (2008) DMC 166 Del.

Gaurav Nagpal v. *Sumedha Nagpal*, I (2009) DMC 523 SC.

Gayatri v. *Om Prakash*, I (2006) DMC 709 Raj.

Genu @ Ganu v. *Jalabai*, ILR 2009 Kar 612.

Ghasiram Das v. *Arundhati Das*, AIR 1994 Ori 15.

Giby George v. *Marriage Officer*, I (2008) DMC 220 Ker.

Gissing v. *Gissing*, 1971 AC 886: 1970 2 All ER 780.

Githa Hariharan v. *Reserve Bank of India*, (1999) 2 SCC 228: AIR 1999 SC 1149.

Gojkovic v. *Gojkovic*, (1990) 1 FLR 140.

Gomti v. *Ramanand*, II (2007) DMC 399 All.

Gopi v. *Krishna*, I (2002) DMC 495 P&H.

Goutam Kundu v. *State of West Bengal*, II (1993) DMC 162 SC: AIR 1993 SC 2295.

Govind Singh v. *Vidya*, AIR 1999 Raj 304.

Govindrao v. *Anandibai*, AIR 1976 Bom 433.

Gracy v. *Cleetus*, I (2002) DMC 401 Ker.

Gulab Jagdusa Kakwane v. *Kamal Gulab Kakwane*, AIR 1985 Bom. 88.

Gullipilli Sowria Raj v. *Bandaru Pavani*, I (2009) DMC 164 SC.

Gurbalwinder Singh v. *Baljit Kaur*, I (2005) DMC 595 P&H.

Guru Bachan Kaur v. *Preetam Singh*, 1998 (1) AWC 275 All.

H. v. *H.*, 1947 63 TLR 645 (as cited in Heward 2003: 49).

Haidri Begam v. *Jawwad Ali*, AIR 1934 All 722.

Happy Anand v. *Baby Deepali*, I (2006) DMC 520 Del.

Hareendran Pillai v. *Pushplatha*, AIR 2007 NOC 1064 Ker.

Harilal v. *Lilavati*, AIR 1961 Guj 202.

Harinder Kaur v. *Narendra Singh Retan Singh*, II (1992) DMC 623.

Harish Chandra Singh Chilwal v. *Pushpa*, II (2008) DMC 454 Utt.

Harminder Kaur v. *Sukhwinder Singh*, II (2002) DMC 114 Del.

Harpit Singh Anand v. *State of West Bengal*, II (2003) DMC 741 SC.

Haseena v. *Abdul Jaleel*, II (2007) DMC 215 Ker.

Heera Singh v. *State of U.P*, I (2006) DMC 19 All.

Hema Ravishankar v. *K.R. Ravishankar*, I (2004) DMC 414 Bom.

Parshotam Lal v. *Surjeet,* II (2008) DMC 253 Del.

Partha Majumdar v. *Sharmishta Majumdar,* I (2006) DMC 793 Cal.

Patnam Vahedullah Khan v. *Ashia Khantoon,* 2000 Cri. LJ 2124.

Patricia v. *Purushothaman,* II (2006) DMC 273 Ker.

Patrick Martin, etc., (1989) 1 LW 246.

Paul Tushar Biswas v. *Addl. Dist. Judge,* II (2006) DMC 59 Gau.

Pavitra v. *Arun Varma (Decd.) Through L.Rs.,* II (2001) DMC 260 MP.

Payal Sharma alias Kamla Sharma v. *Superintendent, Nari Niketan, Agra,* AIR 2001 All 254.

Pendiyala Suresh Kumar Ramarao v. *Sompally Arunbindu,* II (2005) DMC 417 Guj.

Perminder Charan Singh v. *Harjit Kaur,* I (2003) DMC 742 SC.

Pettitt v. *Pettitt,* (1969) 2 All ER 385: (1970) AC 777.

Poonam Gupta v. *Ghanshyam Gupta,* I (2003) DMC 467 All.

Pooran Ram v. *State of Rajasthan,* 2001 Cri.LJ 91.

Popat Kashinath Bodke v. *Kamalabai Popat Bodke,* II (2003) DMC 193 Bom.

Popri Bai v. *Treeth Singh,* I (2004) DMC 445 Raj.

Prabhat Kumar Chakraborty v. *Papiya Chakraborty,* 2004 MLR 576 Cal.

Prabhat Narain Tickoo v. *Mamta Tickoo,* II (1998) DMC 333 All.

Pradeep Gupta v. *Kanti Devi,* I (2003) DMC 265 Jha.

Pradeep Kumar Kapoor v. *Shailja Kapoor,* AIR 1989 Del 10.

Pradip Kumar Kalita v. *Hiran Kalita,* II (2003) DMC 316 Gau.

Prakash Khot v. *Chandani Khot,* II (2002) DMC 798.

Prakash Kumar Bachlaus v. *Chanchal,* AIR 2007 NOC 1032 Raj.

Prakash Singh Thakur v. *Bharati,* II (2000) DMC 368 MP.

Prakash v. *Kavita,* II (2008) DMC 390 Raj.

Pralay Kumar Bose v. *Shyama Bose,* II (1998) DMC 19 Cal.

Pramatha Kumar Maity v. *Ashima Maity,* AIR 1991 Cal 123.

Pramodini Fernandes v. *Vijay Fernandes,* I 2010 (DMC) 386 425.

Pran Nath v. *Pushpa Devi,* I (2007) DMC 211 Del.

Praveen Menon v. *Ajitha Pillai,* I (2002) DMC 288 Ker.

Prem Prakash v. *Nirmal,* II (2006) DMC 823 Del.

Premi v. *Daya Ram,* AIR 1965 HP 15.

Preston v. *Preston,* (1982) 1 All ER 41.

Principal Judge, Family Court Civil Lines, Nagpur v. *Nil,* II (2008) DMC 402 Bom.

Pritiben Acharya v. *State of Gujrat,* II (2002) DMC 557 Guj.

Priya Bala Ghosh v. *Suresh Chandra Ghosh,* AIR 1971 SC 1153.

Priyamvada Limaye v. *Sharad Limaye,* I (2000) DMC 134 Bom.

Puliyulla Chalil Narayana Kurup v. *Thayyulla Parabhath Valsala,* II (2005) DMC 266 Ker.

Puran Singh v. *Shanty Devi,* II (2002) DMC 270 Raj.

Pushpabai v. *Pratap Singh,* I (2001) DMC 110 MP.

Puspa Kumari v. *Parichhit Pandey,* 2005 MLR 551.

Queens Empress v. *Huree Mohan Mythee,* (1891) ILR (Cal) 49.

R. Arora v. *B. Arora,* I (2002) DMC 136 Bom.

R. Durga Prasad v. *Union of India,* II (1998) DMC 45 AP.

Rabindra Prasad v. *Sita Dass,* AIR 1986 Pat 128.

Rachana Kanodia v. *Anuk Kanodia,* II (2001) DMC 171 SC.

Rachna Jain v. *Neeraj Jain,* II (2006) DMC 410 Del.

Radhakumari v. *M.K. Nair,* AIR 1983 Ker 139.

Renubala Moharana v. *Mina Mohanty*, AIR 2004 SC 3500.

Resham Bai v. *Shakuntalabai*, II (2000) DMC 724 MP.

Riaz Fatima v. *Mohd. Sharif*, I (2007) DMC 26 Del.

Rinku Goel v. *Rajesh Goel*, II (2000) DMC 511 SC.

Ritu Raj Kant v. *Anita*, II (2008) DMC 827 Del.

Rohtash Singh v. *Ramendri*, I (2000) DMC 338 SC.

Romila Jaide Shroff v. *Jaidev Rajnikant Shroff*, II (2000) DMC 600 FB.

Roop Narayan Verma v. *Union of India*, AIR 2007 Chh 64.

Roop Singh v. *State of Rajasthan*, II (1999) DMC 318 Raj.

Roopa v. *Santosh Kumar*, AIR 2005 All 172.

Rukhsana Kachwala v. *Saifuddin Kachwala*, II (2002) DMC 712 Bom.

Ruma Chakraborty v. *Sudha Rani Banerji*, AIR 2005 SC 3557.

S. B.S. Jayam & Co. v. *Gopi Chemical Industries*, (1977) 1 MLJ 286.

S. Jayanthi v. *S. Jayaraman*, I (1998) DMC 699 Mad.

S. L. Sehgal v. *State of Del*, DMC I (2000) 524 Del.

S. v. R., 2010 (1) Mh.LJ 253.

S. Venkataraman v. *L. Vijayasaratha*, I (1997) DMC 503 Mad.

S.K. Karg v. *Chanchal Kumari*, I (2005) DMC 96 P&H.

S.P.S. Balasubramanyam v. *Suruttayan @ Andali Padayachi*, AIR 1994 SC 133: I (1994) DMC 484 SC.

S.R Batra v. *Taruna Batra*, I (2007) DMC 1 SC: 2007 3 SCC 169.

S.S. Bindra v. *Tarvinder*, II (2004) DMC 297 Del.

S.S. Manickam v. *Arputha Bhavani Rajan*, (1980) Cri.LJ 354.

Sachindra v. *Bammala*, AIR 1960 Cal. 575.

Sadana Kolvankar v. *Sachidanand Kolvankar*, II (2004) DMC 738 Bom.

Sadhana Patra v. *Subrat Pradhan*, II (2006) DMC 316 Ori.

Sadhana Randev v. *Santosh Kumar*, I (1998) DMC 710 All.

Saibal Dey v. *Chaitali Dey*, I (2007) DMC 398 Cal.

Saleesh Babu v. *Deepa*, (1996) 2 HLR 441.

Samar Ghosh v. *Jaya Ghosh*, (2007) 4 SCC 511: I (2007) DMC 597 SC.

Samita Bhattacharjee v. *Kulashekar Bhattacharjee*, I (2008) DMC 354 SC.

Sampa Saha v. *Amaresh Saha*, I (2006) DMC 465 Cal.

Samuel v. *Stella*, AIR 1955 Mad 451.

Sandha v. *Narayan*, II (1999) DMC 411 Ker.

Sangeeta Kumari Show v. *State of West Bengal*, II (2006) DMC 471 Cal.

Sanghamitra Singh v. *Kailash Singh*, AIR 2001 Ori151.

Sanjay Kapoor v. *Meenakshi Kapoor*, I (2004) DMC 618 Del.

Sanjay Kumar Sharma v. *Vidya Sharma*, AIR 2003 Ori 89.

Sanjay v. *Swati*, II (2007) DMC 731 Bom.

Sanjeev Kumar v. *Dhanya*, II (2008) DMC 19 Ker.

Santosh Kumari v. *Harish Kumar*, I (2005) DMC 453 P&H.

Santosh Kumari v. *Surjit Singh*, AIR 1990 HP 70.

Santosh Sehgal v. *Murari Lal Sehgal*,.

Santoshi Devi @ Madhuri Devi v. *Sadanand Das Goswami*, II (2004) DMC 301 Jha.

Sardari Lal v. *Veshano*, AIR 1970 J& K 150.

Sarita Sharma v. *Sushil Sharma*, I (2000) DMC 413 SC.

Sarla Sharma v. *State of Rajasthan*, I (2002) DMC 409 Raj.

Saroj Devi v. *Ashok Puri*, AIR 1988 Raj 84.

Skinner v. *Orde*, 14 MIA 309.

Smruti Pahariya v. *Sanjay Pahariya*, AIR 2009 SC 2840.

Sobha Hymavathi Devi v. *Setti Gangadhara Swamy*, (2005) 2 SCC 244.

Sobha Hymavathi Devi v. *Setti Gangadhara Swamy*, (2005) 2 SCC 244.

Sonia Khurana v. *State*, II (2006) DMC 453 Del.

Soya v. *A.K. Mohanan*, II (2006) DMC 298 Ker.

Sreedharan v. *Pushpa Bai*, (1978) Ker LT 26.

State Trading Corporation of India Ltd. v. *Commercial Tax Officer*, AIR 1963 SC 1811.

Subal Chandra Saha v. *Pritikana Saha*, II (2003) DMC 640 Gau.

Subhash Popatlal Shah v. *Lata Subhash Shah*, I (1994) DMC 115 Bom.

Subhasree Datta v. *Nil*, II (2008) DMC 582 Del.

Sudesh Jhaku v. *K.C.J. & Ors*, 1998 Cri.LJ 2428 Del.

Sudhir Diwan v. *Tripta Diwan*, I (2008) DMC 481 Del.

Sujata Mohanty v. *Rudra Charan Mohanty*, I (2008) DMC 708 Ori.

Sukhdeo v. *Ram Chandra*, AIR 1924 All 622.

Sukhwinder Kaur v. *Jatinderbir Singh*, I (2007) DMC 492 P & H.

Sukro Devi v. *State of Jharkhand*, I (2008) DMC 425 Jha.

Suma v. *Rajan Pillai*, I (2008) DMC 545 Ker.

Suman Kapur v. *Sudhir Kapur*, II (2008) DMC 774 SC.

Suman v. *Surendra Kumar*, I (2003) DMC 805 Raj.

Sumitra Devi v. *Bhikan Choudhary*, AIR 1985 SC 765.

Sunil Mirchandani v. *Reena Mirchandani*, I (2000) DMC 79 Bom.

Sunil Kumar v. *State (NCT Delhi)*, I (2007) DMC 786 Del.

Sunil Trambake v. *Leelavati Trambake*, II (2006) DMC 461 Bom

Sunita Kavita More v. *Vivekanand More*, II (2001) DMC 693 Bom.

Sunita Shankar Salvi v. *Shankar Laxman Salvi*, I (2003) DMC 700 Bom.

Suprabha v. *Sivaraman*, II (2006) DMC 404 Ker.

Supriya v. *Naresh Kotwani* (Civil Misc. Appeal No.401/1989) cited in *Vijay Kaur* v. *Radhey Shyam*, II (1991) DMC 245 Raj.

Suram Pal Singh v. *Savita*, I (2007) DMC 833 Del.

Suresh Babu v. *V. P. Leela*, AIR 2007 NOC 285 Ker.

Suresh Khullar v. *Vijay Kumar Khullar*, I (2008) DMC 719 Del.

Sureshata Devi v. *Omprakash*, AIR 1992 SC 1904: I (1991) DMC 313 SC.

Surinder Kaur Sandhu v. *Harbax Singh Sandhu*, (1984) 3 SCC 698.

Surjeet v. *Raj Kumari*, AIR 1967 Pun 172.

Susarla Subrahmanya Sastry v. *S. Padmakshi*, II (2005) DMC 707 AP.

Sushil Kumar Gupta v. *Reena Gupta*, II (2003) DMC 656 Del.

Sushila Gothala v. *State of Rajasthan*, AIR 1995 SC 90.

Sushila Naik v. *Judge, Family Court*, II (1997) DMC 235 Ori.

Sushila Viresh Chaddva v. *Viresh Nagshi Chhadva*, AIR 1996 Bom 94.

Susmita Acharya v. *Dr. Rabindra Mishra*, I (2003) DMC 421 Ori.

Swapan Kumar Ganguly v. *Smritikana Ganguly*, AIR 2002 Cal 6.

Swapna Ghosh v. *Sadananda Ghosh*, AIR 1989 Cal 1 SB.

Swati Verma v. *Rajan Verma*, II (2003) DMC 795 SC.

Syed Khaja Mohiuddin v. *State of AP*, I (2006) DMC 32 AP.

Syed Mohd Ghouse v. *Noounnnisa Begum*, II (2001) DMC 454 AP.

T. Raja Rao v. *T. Neelamma*, 1990 Cri.LJ 2430 AP.

Tabassum Shaikh v. *Sheikh*, I (2000) DMC 95 Bom.

Tapash Kumar Paul v. *Soma Paul*, II (2007) DMC 541 Cal.

Teena Chhabra v. *Manish Chhabra*, (2004) 13 SCC 411.

Teerth Ram v. *Parvati Devi*, AIR 1995 Raj 86.

Thakur Vyasnarayan Singh v. *Hemlata*, II (2002) DMC 24 MP.

Thyssen-Bornemisza v. *Thyssen-Bornemisza*, (1985) 1 All ER 328.

Tiveni Singh v. *State of UP*, I (2008) DMC 731 All.

Tulsa v. *Durghatiya*, I (2008) DMC 161 SC.

Uma Tiwari v. *Vikrant Tiwari*, I (2005) DMC 690 MP.

Uppu Lakshmi v. *Uppu Narayan*, I (2006) DMC 622 AP.

Usha Rani v. *Sham Lal*, II (2008) DMC 202 Pun & Har.

Usha v. *Abraham*, AIR 1988 Ker 96.

Usharani Lenka v. *Panigrahi Subhash Chandra Dash*, AIR 2005 Ori 3.

V. Bhagat v. *D. Bhagat*, (1994) 1 SCC 337: AIR 1994 SC 710.

V. Mallikarjunaiah v. *H.C. Goowaramma*, AIR 1997 Kar 77.

V. Pranav Kumar v. *V. Sulekha @ Payal*, I (2006) DMC 528 AP.

V. Yedukondalu v. *V. Nageswaramma*, II (2000) DMC 90 AP.

Valsarajan v. *Saraswathy*, II (2003) DMC 344 Ker.

Vandana v. *T Srikanth*, (2007) 6 MLJ 205 Mad.

Varalaxmi Charka @ Renuka v. *Satyanarayana Charka*, II (2008) DMC 43 AP.

Veena Devi v. *Ashok Kumar Mandal*, 2000 Cri.LJ 332 Pat.

Venkamma v. *Savitramma*, ILR 1880 12 Mad 67.

Vidyadhar Chodankar v. *Malini Chodankar*, II (2006) DMC 609 Bom.

Vijay Kaur v. *Radhey Shyam*, II (1991) DMC 245 Raj.

Vijay Kumar v. *Surinder Kaur @ Sunita*, I (2008) DMC 605 P&H.

Vijaya Manohar Arbat v. *Kashirao Rajaram Sawai*, AIR 1987 SC 1100.

Vijaykumar Bhate v. *Neela Bhate*, I (2003) DMC 685 SC: AIR 2003 SC 2462.

Vikas Aggarwal v. *Anubha*, I (2002) DMC 633 SC.

Vikram Vir Vohra v. *Shalini Bhalla*, AIR 2010 SC 1675.

Vimala (K) v. *Veeraswamy (K)*, (1991) 2 SCC 375.

Vinay Pandey v. *Roshan Kumar*, II (2000) DMC 571 SC.

Vincent Joseph Konath v. *Jacintha Angela Konath*, AIR 1994 Bom 120.

Vinita Saxena v. *Pankaj Pandit*, AIR 2006 SC 1662.

Vinod v. *Chhaya*, I (2003) DMC 580 Bom.

Vinod Babbar v. *Baby Swati*, II (2007) DMC 73 Del.

Vinod Chandra Sharma v. *Rajesh Pathak*, AIR 1988 All 150.

Vinod Dulerai Mehta v. *Kanak Vinod Mehta*, AIR 1990 Bom.120.

Vinod Kumar Gupta v. *Santosh Gupta*, I (2007) DMC 871 Del.

Vinod Kumar Jolly v. *Sunita Jolly*, I (2008) DMC 371 Del.

Vinod Kumar Rai v. *Manju Rai*, II (2006) DMC 642 All.

Vinodchandra Gajanan Deokar v. *Anupama Vinodchandra*, AIR 1993 Bom.232.

Vishnu Mayekar v. *Laxmi Mayekar*, II (2000) DMC 727 Bom.

Vishnu Dutt Sharma v. *Manju Sharma*, I (2009) DMC 515 SC.

Vishwanath v. *Abdul Wajid*, AIR 1963 SC 1.

Viswambhran v. *Dhanya*, II (2005) DMC 56 Ker: AIR 2005 Ker 91.

Vitthal Jadhav v. *Harnabai Jadhav*, I (2004) DMC 572 Bom.

W. v. *W.*, (1926) All ER 111.

Wachtel v. *Wachtel*, (1973) 1 All ER 829.

Warde v. *Warde*, (1849) Ph.786.

Weldone Lyngdoh v. *Eva Phawa*, II (2007) DMC 550 Gau.

White v. *White*, (2001) 1 AC 596.

William Rebello v. *Jose Angelo Vaz*, II (1996) DMC 339: AIR 1996 Bom 204.

Y. Narasimha Rao v. *Y. Venkata Lakshmi*, II (1991) DMC 366 SC: 1991 3 SCC 451.

Yousuf v. *Sowramma*, AIR 1971 Ker 261.

Zahida Begum v. *Mushtaque Ahmed*, I (2006) DMC 110 Kar.

Zainab Bibi v. *Abdul Kareem*, AIR 1926 Lah 117.

Bibliography

Books

Abdullah, Nuraisyah Chua, *Family Law for Non-Muslims in Malaysia*, Darul Ehsan (Malaysia): International Law Book Services, (2006).

Basu, M., *Hindu Women and Marriage Law*, New Delhi: Oxford University Press, (2001).

Black's Law, St. Paul, Minnesota: West Publishing Co., (1990) (6th ed.).

Blackstone, William (Sir), *Commentaries on the Law of England*, (1769) (4th ed.), J. Dewitt Andrews, Chicago: Callaghan and Company, (1899).

Bromley, P.M., *Family Law*, London: Butterworths, (1976) (5th ed.).

Burn E.H., *Cheshire's Modern Law of Property*, London: Butterworths, (1972) (11th ed.).

Chakraborty, Gangotri, *Law of Maintenance*, Allahabad: Sodhi Publications, (2007) (2nd ed.).

Davis, U., *Citizenship and the State: A Comparative Study of Citizenship Legislation in Israel, Jordan, Palestine, Syria and Lebanon*, London: Ithaca Press, (1997).

Derrett, J.D.M., *The Death of a Marriage Law: Epitaph for the Rishis*, New Delhi: Vikas, (1978).

Diwan, Paras. and Peeyushi Diwan, *Law of Marriage and Divorce*, New Delhi: Universal Law Publishing Co.Ltd., 1997 (3rd ed.).

Diwan, Paras and Peeyushi Diwan, *Law of Adoption, Minority, Guardianship and Custody*, Allahabad: Wadhwa & Co., (1993).

Diwan, Paras and Peeyushi Diwan, *Law of Marriage and Divorce*, Delhi: Universal Law Publishing Co. Ltd., (1988) (2nd ed.).

Diwan, Paras and Peeyushi Diwan, *Law of Marriage and Divorce*, New Delhi: Universal Law Publishing Co. Ltd., (1997) (3rd ed.).

Engels, F., *The Origins of Family, Private Property and the State*, (1884), Reprinted, New York: Pathfinder Press, (1972).

Ewick, P. and S. Silbey, *The Commonplace of Law: Stories From Everyday Life*, Chicago: University of Chicago Press, (1998).

Fineman, Martha Albertson., *The Neutered Mother, The Sexual Family and Other Twentieth Century Tragedies*, New York: Routledge, (1995).

Fineman, Martha, Albertson, *Illusion of Equality: The Rhetoric and Reality of Divorce Reform*, Chicago: The University of Chicago, (1991).

Fyzee, A.A.A., *Outlines of Muslim Law*, New Delhi: Oxford University Press, (1974) (4th ed.).

Galanter, M., *Law and Society in Modern India*, New Delhi: Oxford University Press, (1989).

Gough, K. E., *Rural Changes in Southeast India: 1950s to 1960s*, Oxford: Oxford University Press, (1989).

Gough, K. E., *Rural Society in Southeast India*, Cambridge: Cambridge University Press, (1981).

Gupte, N. Y., *Law Relating to Family Courts Act, 1984*, Mumbai: Ravindra Publications, (2001).

Heward, Edmund, *Lord Denning A Biography*, Delhi: Universal Law Publishing Co. Pvt. Ltd., (2003).

Iyer, K. J., *Islamic Law in Modern India* as cited by Diwan & Diwan, (p.22 fn. 8).

Jaising, I. (ed), *Handbook on Law of Domestic Violence*, Nagpur: LexisNexis-Butterworths, Wadhwa, (2009).

Karve, I., *Kinship Organisation in India: A study of Various Social Institutions in India*, vol. XI, Poona: Deccan College Monograph Series, (1953).

Kishwar, M. P., *Zealous Reformers, Deadly Laws: Battling Stereotypes*, New Delhi: Sage Publications, (2008).

Kuppuswami, A., *Mayne's Treatise on Hindu Law & Usage*, New Delhi: Bharat Law House, (1993) (13th ed.).

Leong, Wai Kum, *Elements of Family Law in Singapore*, Singapore: LexisNexis, (2007).

Leong, Wai Kum, *Fifty Years and More of the Women's Charter of Singapore*, Singapore: LexisNexis, (2008).

Lowe, Nigel and Gillian Douglas, *Bromley's Family Law*, London: Butterworths, (1998) (9th ed.).

Maine, Henry Sumner, *Ancient Law: Its Connection the Early History of Society and Its Relation to Modern Ideas*, London: John Murray, (1861).

McDonald, P. (ed.), *Settling Up: Property and Income Distribution on Divorce in Australia*, Sydney: Australian Institute of Family Studies and Prentice Hall of Australia, (1986).

McLeod, J and Malimo A, *Matrimonial Property Law in Canada*, Toronto: Thomson Carswell, (2006).

Menon, N., *Recovering Subversion*, New Delhi: Permanent Black, (2004).

Mensky, Werner F., *Hindu Law Beyond Tradition and Modernity*, New Delhi: Oxford University Press, (2003).

Mody, P., *The Intimate State: Love-Marriage and the Law in Delhi*, Routledge: Delhi, (2008).

Okin, Susan Moller, *Justice Gender And The Family*, New York: Basic Books, (1989).

Pateman, C, *The Sexual Contract*, Stanford: Stanford University Press, (1988).

Reddy, Chinnappa, O., *The Court and the Constitution of India*, New Delhi: Oxford University Press, (2008).

Sachs, A., and J.H. Wilson, *Sexism and the Law: a Study of Male Beliefs and Judicial Bias*, Law in Society Series: Oxford Free Press, (1978).

Sagade, J., *Child Marriage in India*, New Delhi: Oxford University Press, (2005).

Sarkar S. K. and Ejaz Ahmed, *Law of Evidence*, vols I & II, New Delhi: Ashoka law House, (2006), (6th ed.).

Shah, P., *Legal Pluralism in Conflict*, London: Glass House Press, (2005).

Sivaramayya, B., *Matrimonal Property in India*, New Delhi: Oxford University Press, (1999).

Srinivas M.N., *Village, Caste, Gender and Method: Essays in Indian Social Anthropology*, Delhi: Oxford University Press, (1998).

Srinivas, M.N., *Caste in Modern India and Other Essays*, Bombay: Media Promoters & Publishers, (1962) (Reprinted 1986).

Tharu, Susie and K. Lalita (eds), *Women Writing in India 600 BC. To the Present*, vol. I, New Delhi: Oxford University Press, (1991).

Uberoi, P., *Family, Kinship and Marriage in India*, New Delhi: Oxford University Press, (1993).

Weitman, Lenore J., *The Divorce Revolution: The Unexpected Social and Economic Consequences for Women and Children in America*, New York: The Free Press, (1985).

Welchman, L., and Sara Hossain, *'Honour' Crimes, Paradigms, and Violence Against Women*, London and New York: Zed Press, (2005).

Wollstonecraft, Mary, *A Vindication of the Rights of Women: With Strictures on Political and Moral Subjects*, London: J. Johnson, (1796) (3rd ed.).

Articles in Books and Journals

'Tarabai Shinde's Stri Purush Talana' in O'Hanlon Rosalind (ed.), *A Comparison Between Women and Men: Tarabi Shinde and the Critique of Gender Relations in Colonial India*, New Delhi: Oxford University Press, (1994).

'Women Living Under Muslim Laws', *Knowing Our Rights*, New Delhi: Zuban, (2003).

Agnes, Flavia, 'Women, Marriage, and the Subordination of Rights' in Chatterjee, P and P. Jeganathan (eds), *Community, Gender and Violence*, Subaltern Studies, vol. XI, Delhi: Permanent Black, (2000).

Chakravarthy, U., 'From fathers to husbands: of love, death and marriage in North India' in Welchman, Lynn and Sara Hossain, *Honour Crimes, Paradigms, and Violence Against Women*, London: Zed Press, (2005), pp. 308–31.

Chowdhry, P., 'Private Lives, State Intervention: Cases of Runaway Marriage in Rural North India', 38 *Modern Asian Studies* 55, (2004).

Fineman, M. A, 'Societal Factors Affecting The creation of Legal Rules for Distribution of Property at Divorce' in M. A. Fineman and N. S. Thomadsen (eds), *At the Boundaries of Law: Feminism and Legal Theory*, New York: Routledge, (1991a), pp.265–79.

Funder, K., 'Australia: a Proposal for Reform', in L.J. Weitzman and M. Maclean (eds), *Economic Consequences of Divorce*, Oxford: Clarendon Press, (1992).

Funder, K., 'His and Her Divorce', in McDonald, P. (ed.), *Settling Up: Property and Income Distribution on Divorce in Australia*, Australian Institute of Family Studies and Prentice Hall of Australia, Sydney, (1986), pp.224–40.

Haksar, Nandita, 'Human Rights Layering: A Feminist Perspective', in Amita Dhanda and Archana Parasher (eds), *Essays in Honour of Lotika Sarkar*, Lucknow: Eastern Book Company, (1999), pp.71–88.

Knop, Karen and Christine Chinkin, (2001), 'Remembering Chrystal MacMillan: Women's Equality and Nationality in International Law' in *Michigan Journal of International Law*, No. 22, p. 525.

Lahoti, R.C. (Former Chief Justice), 'Women's Empowerment: Role of Judiciary and Legislature', (2005) 2 SCC (J), pp.49–54.

Menon, Madhava, N.R. (Dr) (Former Director National Judicial Academy, Bhopal), 'Gender Justice and Judiciary: An Assessment' in Background Reading for Judicial Seminar on Securing Constitution Justice in the Family: Key Challenges, 12–14 December 2008, National Judicial Academy Bhopal, pp.382-6.

Mnookin R. and L. Kornhauser, 'Bargaining in the Shadow of the Law' 88 *Yale Law Journal*, (1979), 950.

Nagaraj, Vasudha, 'Local and Customary Forums: Adapting and Innovating Rules of Formal Law', Negotiating Spaces, in

Flavia Agnes (ed.), New Delhi: Oxford University Press (forthcoming).

Parejko, Judy 'No Fault Divorce: America's Divorce Mill' in *Catholic Exchange*, New York, 18 May 2009.

Sampath, B.N., 'Marriageable Age, Consent and Soundness of Mind in Indian Matrimonial Law: A Plea for Rationalisation', *Benares Law Journal*, vol. V, (1969).

Sankaran, Kamala, 'Family, Work and Matrimonial Property: Implications for Women and Children' in A. Parashar and A. Dhandha (eds), *Redefining Family Law in India*, New Delhi: Routledge, (2008).

Sheehan, Grania and Jody Hughes, *Division of Matrimonial Property in Australia*, Melbourne: Australian Institute of Family Studies, (2001), Research Paper No.25.

Silbey S., 'Legal Culture and Legal Consciousness', in *International Encyclopedia of Social and Behavioral Sciences*, New York: Elsevier, Pergamon Press, (2001).

Singh, S., Nikhil Dey and Aruna Roy, 'Child Marriage, Government and NGOs' In *Economic and Political Weekly*, vol. XXIX/23, (1994) ,pp. 1377–9.

Spivak, Gayatri Chakravorty, 'Can the Subaltern Speak?' in Peter J. Cain and Mark Harrison (eds), *Imperialsim: Critical Concepts in Historical Studies*, vol. III, London: Routledge, (2001), pp. 171–219.

Uberoi, P., 'When is a Marriage Not a Marriage? Sex, Sacrament and Contract in Hindu Marriage' in Uberoi, P., (ed.), *Social Reform, Sexuality and the State*, New Delhi: Sage Publications India Pvt. Ltd., (1996), pp. 319–46.

Official Documents

A Report of the Committee on Empowerment of Women on Functioning of Family Courts, (2001–2).

Law Commission 132nd Report, 19 April 1989.

Law Commission Report No. 219, March 2009.

Legislative Assembly Debates

Lok Sabha Debates (LSD), vol.LJ No.25, 27 August 1984, pp. 182-254.

Report of the National Commission for Women on the Functioning of Family Courts (2002).

Report of the Status of Committee, *Towards Equality*, New Delhi: Government of India, (1974).

Informal Publications

'Choosing a Life…Crimes of Honor in India: The Right to, If, When and Whom to Marry', Lucknow: AALI (2004).

Agnes, Flavia, 'A Study of Family Courts', Bangalore: National Law School of India University, (2006) Unpublished.

Baxi, Pratiksha, *Habeas Corpus Juridical Narraitves of Sexual Governance*, New Delhi: Centre for the Study of Law and Governance, Jawaharlal Nehru University, (2009).

Sarkar Lotika, 'Functioning of Family Courts' Paper presented at the Conference on Family Courts organized by ILS Law College, Pune, (1994)

Newspaper Articles

'Chief Justice Underscores Need for a Family Court, Inaugurates Capital's First', *Indian Express*, (Delhi), 16 May 2009.

'City Sees Rise in Cases of Parents Kidnapping Kids', *Times of India*, (Bombay), 27 April, 2009.

'One in Five Slum Dwellers Practice Child Marriage', *Midday*, (Mumbai), 14 March 2009.

'Counseling Centre Opened at Family Court', in *The Hindu*, (Chennai), 24 April 2006.

'Parsi Woman Approaches Gujarat High Court to Perform Rituals at Agiary', in the *DNA*, (Mumbai), 26 March 2010.

'Row Over Bill Denying Rights to Women Marrying Outside J&K' in *The Times of India*, (Mumbai), 14 March 2010.

Asian Age, (Bombay), January 10 2006, p. 10.

Daily News, (Dar-es-Salaam), 01 August 2009.

Dandavate, Madhu, 'Rape of Justice in Bhanwari Case' in *Times of India*, (Mumbai), 7 February 1996.

Deshpande, S., 'Divorced Woman Can't Use Ex's Name: HC' in *Times of India*, (Mumbai), 19 February 2010.

Indian Express, (Bombay), 12 Feb 2009.

The Times of India, (Bombay), 20 February 2009, p. 11.

Times of India, (Bombay), 14 Feb 1996.

Times of India, (Bombay), 20 Feb 2009.

Internet Sources

'The Division of Property When a Marriage, Civil Union or De Facto Relationship Ends', New Zealand, available at (http://www.howto-law.co.nz/html/ml013.asp).

Dadrawala, Noshir H. 'Why Parsis Discourage Mixed Marriages', available at (http://tenets.zoroastrianism.com/discour33.html) accessed on 26 June 2010.

Harrison, Margaret 'Matrimonial Property Reform' in *Family Matters*, No.31(April 1992), pp.18–21, availbale at (http://www.aifs.org.au/institute/pubs/fm1/fm31/fm31mh.html).

Hewitt, Philippa, 'Dividing for Equality: The Maturing of Matrimonial Law in Hong Kong' in *Hong Kong Lawyer*, Hong Kong: July 2008, pp. 26–32, available at (http://www.hwg-law.com/en/news_articles/HWG-Article-Jul08.pdf).

Index